Lecture Notes in Computer Sci

Commenced Publication in 1973
Founding and Former Series Editors:
Gerhard Goos, Juris Hartmanis, and Jan van Leeuwen

Roland Backhouse Jeremy Gibbons
Ralf Hinze Johan Jeuring (Eds.)

Datatype-Generic Programming

International Spring School, SSDGP 2006
Nottingham, UK, April 24-27, 2006
Revised Lectures

 Springer

Volume Editors

Roland Backhouse
University of Nottingham
School of Computer Science
Jubilee Campus, Wollaton Road, Nottingham NG8 1BB, UK
E-mail: rcb@cs.nott.ac.uk

Jeremy Gibbons
Oxford University, Computing Laboratory
Wolfson Building, Parks Road, Oxford, OX1, 3QD, UK
E-mail: Jeremy.Gibbons@comlab.ox.ac.uk

Ralf Hinze
Universität Bonn
Institut für Informatik III
Römerstraße 164, 53117 Bonn, Germany
E-mail: ralf@informatik.uni-bonn.de

Johan Jeuring
Utrecht University
Institute of Information and Computing Science
3508 TB Utrecht, The Netherlands
E-mail: johanj@cs.uu.nl

Library of Congress Control Number: Applied for

CR Subject Classification (1998): D.3, D.1, D.2, F.3, E.1

LNCS Sublibrary: SL 1 – Theoretical Computer Science and General Issues

ISSN   0302-9743
ISBN-10   3-540-76785-1 Springer Berlin Heidelberg New York
ISBN-13   978-3-540-76785-5 Springer Berlin Heidelberg New York

Springer is a part of Springer Science+Business Media

springer.com

© Springer-Verlag Berlin Heidelberg 2007
Printed in Germany

Typesetting: Camera-ready by author, data conversion by Scientific Publishing Services, Chennai, India
Printed on acid-free paper   SPIN: 12191963   06/3180   5 4 3 2 1 0

Preface

A leitmotif in the evolution of programming paradigms has been the level and extent of parametrisation that is facilitated — the so-called *genericity* of the paradigm. The sorts of parameters that can be envisaged in a programming language range from simple values, like integers and floating-point numbers, through structured values, types and classes, to kinds (the type of types and/or classes). *Datatype-generic programming* is about parametrising programs by the structure of the data that they manipulate.

To appreciate the importance of datatype genericity, one need look no further than the internet. The internet is a massive repository of structured data, but the structure is rarely exploited. For example, compression of data can be much more effective if its structure is known, but most compression algorithms regard the input data as simply a string of bits, and take no account of its internal organisation.

Datatype-generic programming is about exploiting the structure of data when it is relevant and ignoring it when it is not. Programming languages most commonly used at the present time do not provide effective mechanisms for documenting and implementing datatype genericity. This volume is a contribution towards improving the state of the art.

The emergence of datatype genericity can be traced back to the late 1980s. A particularly influential contribution was made by the Dutch STOP (Specification and Transformation of Programs) project, led by Lambert Meertens and Doaitse Swierstra. The idea that was "in the air" at the time was the commonality in ways of reasoning about different datatypes. Reynolds' parametricity theorem, popularised by Wadler [17] as "theorems for free," and so-called "deforestation" techniques came together in the datatype-generic notions of "catamorphism," "anamorphism" and "hylomorphism," and the theorem that every hylomorphism can be expressed as the composition of a catamorphism after an anamorphism. The "theory of lists" [5] became a "theory of Fs," where F is an arbitrary datatype, and the "zip" operation on a *pair* of equal-length *lists* became a generic transformation from an F structure of same-shape G structures to a G structure of same-shape F structures [1, 11].

In response to these largely theoretical results, efforts got underway in the mid-to-late 1990s to properly reflect the developments in programming language design. The extension of functional programming to "polytypic" programming [14, 12] was begun, and, in 1998, the "generic programming" workshop was organized by Roland Backhouse and Tim Sheard at Marstrand in Sweden [4], shortly after a Dagstuhl Seminar on the same topic [13]. The advances that had been made played a prominent part in the Advanced Functional Programming summer school [16, 3, 15, 6], which was held in 1998.

Since the year 2000, the emphasis has shifted yet more towards making datatype-generic programming more practical. Research projects with this goal have been the Generic Haskell project led by Johan Jeuring at Utrecht University (see, for example, [10, 9]), the DFG-funded Generic Programming project led by Ralf Hinze at the Universtiy of Bonn, and the EPSRC-supported Datatype-Generic Programming project at the universities of Nottingham and Oxford, which sponsored the Spring School reported in this volume. (Note that although the summer school held in Oxford in August 2002 [2] was entitled "Generic Programming," the need to distinguish "datatype" generic programming from other notions of "generic" programming had become evident; the paper "Patterns in Datatype-Generic Programming" [8] is the first published occurrence of the term "datatype-generic programming.")

This volume comprises revisions of the lectures presented at the Spring School on Datatype-Generic Programming held at the University of Nottingham in April 2006. All the lectures have been subjected to thorough internal review by the editors and contributors, supported by independent external reviews.

Gibbons ("Datatype-Generic Programming") opens the volume with a comprehensive review of different sorts of parametrisation mechanisms in programmming languages, including how they are implemented, leading up to the notion of datatype genericity. In common with the majority of the contributors, Gibbons chooses the functional programming language Haskell to make the notions concrete. This is because functional programming languages provide the best test-bed for experimental ideas, free from the administrative noise and clutter inherent in large-scale programming in mainstream languages. In this way, Gibbons relates the so-called design patterns introduced by Gamma, Helm, Johnson and Vlissides [7] to datatype-generic programming constructs (the different types of morphism mentioned earlier). The advantage is that the patterns are made concrete, rather than being expressed in prose by example as in a recent Publication [7].

Hinze, Jeuring and Löh ("Comparing Approaches to Generic Programming in Haskell") compare a variety of ways that datatype-generic programming techniques have been incorporated into functional programming languages, in particular (but not exclusively) Haskell. They base their comparison on a collection of standard examples: encoding and decoding values of a given datatype, comparing values for equality, and mapping a function over, "showing," and performing incremental updates on the values stored in a datatype. The comparison is based on a number of criteria, including elements like integration into a programming language and tool support.

The goal of Hinze and Löh's paper ("Generic Programming Now") is to show how datatype-generic programming can be enabled in present-day Haskell. They identify three key ingredients essential to the task: a *type reflection* mechanism, a *type representation* and a generic *view* on data. Their contribution is to show how these ingredients can be furnished using generalised algebraic datatypes.

The theme of type reflection and type representation is central to Altenkirch, McBride and Morris's contribution ("Generic Programming with Dependent

Types") . Their paper is about defining different universes of types in the *Epigram* system, an experimental programming system based on dependent types. They argue that the level of genericity is dictated by the universe that is chosen. Simpler universes allow greater levels of genericity, whilst more complex universes cause the genericity to be more restricted.

Dependent types, and the Curry-Howard isomorphism between proofs and programs, also play a central role in the $\Omega mega$ language introduced by Sheard ("Generic Programming in $\Omega mega$"). Sheard argues for a type system that is more general than Haskell's, allowing a richer set of programming patterns, whilst still maintaining a sound balance between computations that are performed at run-time and computations performed at compile-time.

Finally, Lämmel and Meijer ("Revealing the X/O Impedance Mismatch") explore the actual problem of datatype-generic programming in the context of present-day implementations of object-oriented languages and XML data models. The X/O impedance mismatch refers to the incompatibilities between XML and object-oriented models of data. They provide a very comprehensive and up-to-date account of the issues faced by programmers, and how these issues can be resolved.

It remains for us to express our thanks to those who have contributed to the success of the School. First and foremost, we thank Fermín Reig, who was responsible for much of the preparations for the School and its day-to-day organization. Thanks also to Avril Rathbone and Pablo Nogueira for their organizational support, and to the EPSRC (under grant numbers GR/S27085/01 and GR/D502632/1) and the School of Computer Science and IT of the University of Nottingham for financial support. Finally, we would like to thank the (anonymous) external referees for their efforts towards ensuring the quality of these lecture notes.

June 2007

Roland Backhouse
Jeremy Gibbons
Ralf Hinze
Johan Jeuring

References

1. Backhouse, R.C., Doornbos, H., Hoogendijk, P.: A class of commuting relators (September 1992), Available via World-Wide Web at
   http://www.cs.nott.ac.uk/~rcb/MPC/papers
2. Backhouse, R., Gibbons, J. (eds.): Generic Programming. LNCS, vol. 2793. Springer, Heidelberg (2003)
3. Backhouse, R., Jansson, P., Jeuring, J., Meertens, L.: Generic programming. An introduction. In: Swierstra, et al., pp. 28–115, Braga98
4. Backhouse, R., Sheard, T. (eds.): Workshop on Generic Programming, Informal proceedings (1998), available at http://www.win.tue.nl/cs/wp/papers.html
5. Bird, R.S.: An introduction to the theory of lists. In: Broy, M. (ed.) Logic of Programming and Calculi of Discrete Design. NATO ASI Series, vol. F36, Springer, Heidelberg (1987)
6. de Moor, O., Sittampalam, G.: Generic program transformation. In: Swierstra, et al., pp. 116–149, Braga98
7. Gamma, E., Helm, R., Johnson, R., Vlissides, J.: Design Patterns – Elements of Reusable Object-Oriented Software. Addison-Wesley, Reading (1995)
8. Gibbons, J.: Patterns in datatype-generic programming. In: Striegnitz, J., Davis, K. (eds.) Multiparadigm Programming, John von Neumann Institute for Computing (NIC), First International Workshop on Declarative Programming in the Context of Object-Oriented Languages (DPCOOL), vol. 27 (2003)
9. Hinze, R., Jeuring, J.: Generic Haskell: Applications. In: Backhouse and Gibbons, pp. 57–96, gp03
10. Hinze, R., Jeuring, J.: Generic Haskell: Practice and theory. In: Backhouse and Gibbons, pp. 1–56, gp03
11. Hoogendijk, P., Backhouse, R.: When do datatypes commute? In: Moggi, E., Rosolini, G. (eds.) CTCS 1997. LNCS, vol. 1290, pp. 242–260. Springer, Heidelberg (1997)
12. Jansson, P., Jeuring, J.: PolyP - a polytypic programming language extension. In: POPL '97: The 24th ACM SIGPLAN-SIGACT Symposium on Principles of Programming Languages, pp. 470–482. ACM Press, New York (1997)
13. Jazayeri, M., Musser, D.R., Loos, R.G.K. (eds.): Generic Programming. LNCS, vol. 1766. Springer, Heidelberg (2000), at
    http://www.cs.rpi.edu/~musser/gp/dagstuhl/
14. Jeuring, J., Jansson, P.: Polytypic programming. In: Launchbury, J., Sheard, T., Meijer, E. (eds.) Advanced Functional Programming. LNCS, vol. 1129, pp. 68–114. Springer, Heidelberg (1996)
15. Sheard, T.: Using MetaML: a staged programming language. In: Swierstra, et al., pp. 207–239, Braga98
16. Swierstra, S.D., Oliveira, J.N. (eds.): AFP 1998. LNCS, vol. 1608. Springer, Heidelberg (1999)
17. Wadler, P.: Theorems for free. In: 4'th Symposium on Functional Programming Languages and Computer Architecture, pp. 347–359. ACM, London (1989)

Contributors

Thorsten Altenkirch
School of Computer Science and Information Technology,
University of Nottingham, Nottingham, NG8 1BB, UK
txa@cs.nott.ac.uk
http://www.cs.nott.ac.uk/~txa/.

Roland Backhouse
School of Computer Science and Information Technology,
University of Nottingham, Nottingham, NG8 1BB, UK
rcb@cs.nott.ac.uk
http://www.cs.nott.ac.uk/~rcb/.

Jeremy Gibbons
Computing Laboratory, University of Oxford, Oxford, OX1 3QD, UK
jeremy.gibbons@comlab.ox.ac.uk
http://www.comlab.ox.ac.uk/jeremy.gibbons/.

Ralf Hinze
Institut für Informatik III, Universität Bonn, Römerstraße 164,
53117 Bonn, Germany
ralf@informatik.uni-bonn.de
http://www.informatik.uni-bonn.de/~ralf/.

Johan Jeuring
Institute of Information and Computing Sciences, Utrecht University,
P.O.Box 80.089, 3508 TB Utrecht, The Netherlands
and
Open University, Heerlen, The Netherlands
johanj@cs.uu.nl
http://www.cs.uu.nl/~johanj/

Ralf Lämmel
Data Programmability Team, Microsoft Corporation, Redmond WA, USA
ralf.lammel@microsoft.com
http://homepages.cwi.nl/~ralf/.

Andres Löh
Institut für Informatik III, Universität Bonn, Römerstraße 164,
53117 Bonn, Germany.
loeh@informatik.uni-bonn.de
http://www.informatik.uni-bonn.de/~loeh/.

Conor McBride
School of Computer Science and Information Technology,
University of Nottingham, Nottingham, NG8 1BB, UK
ctm@cs.nott.ac.uk
http://www.cs.nott.ac.uk/~ctm/.

Erik Meijer
SQL Server, Microsoft Corporation, Redmond WA, USA
emeijer@microsoft.com
http://research.microsoft.com/~emeijer/.

Peter Morris
School of Computer Science and Information Technology,
University of Nottingham, Nottingham, NG8 1BB, UK
pwm@cs.nott.ac.uk
http://www.cs.nott.ac.uk/~pwm/.

Tim Sheard
Computer Science Department, Maseeh College of Engineering and
Computer Science, Portland State University, Portland OR, USA
sheard@cs.pdx.edu
http://web.cecs.pdx.edu/~sheard/

Table of Contents

Datatype-Generic Programming

Jeremy Gibbons

Oxford University Computing Laboratory
Wolfson Building, Parks Road
Oxford OX1 3QD, United Kingdom
http://www.comlab.ox.ac.uk/jeremy.gibbons/

Abstract. *Generic programming* aims to increase the flexibility of programming languages, by expanding the possibilities for parametrization — ideally, without also expanding the possibilities for uncaught errors. The term means different things to different people: *parametric polymorphism, data abstraction, meta-programming*, and so on. We use it to mean polytypism, that is, parametrization by the *shape* of data structures rather than their contents. To avoid confusion with other uses, we have coined the qualified term *datatype-generic programming* for this purpose. In these lecture notes, we expand on the definition of datatype-generic programming, and present some examples of datatype-generic programs. We also explore the connection with *design patterns* in object-oriented programming; in particular, we argue that certain design patterns are just higher-order datatype-generic programs.

1 Introduction

Generic programming is about making programming languages more flexible without compromising safety. Both sides of this equation are important, and becoming more so as we seek to do more and more with computer systems, while becoming ever more dependent on their reliability.

The term 'generic programming' means different things to different people, because they have different ideas about how to achieve the common goal of combining flexibility and safety. To some people, it means *parametric polymorphism*; to others, it means libraries of *algorithms and data structures*; to another group, it means *reflection and meta-programming*; to us, it means *polytypism*, that is, type-safe parametrization by a datatype. Rather than trying to impose our meaning on the other users of the term, or risk confusion by ignoring the other uses, we have chosen to coin the more specific term *datatype-generic programming*. We look in more detail at what we mean by 'datatype-generic programming', and how it relates to what others mean by 'generic programming', in Section 2.

Among the various approaches to datatype-generic programming, one is what we have called elsewhere *origami programming* [38], and what others have variously called *constructive algorithmics* [12,123], *Squiggol* [93], *bananas and lenses* [101], the *Bird-Meertens Formalism* [122,52], and the *algebra of programming* [9], among other names. This is a style of functional (or relational) programming

R. Backhouse et al. (Eds.): Datatype-Generic Programming 2006, LNCS 4719, pp. 1–71, 2007.

based on maps, folds, unfolds and other such higher-order structured recursion operators. Malcolm [92], building on earlier theoretical work by Hagino [56], showed how the existing ad-hoc datatype-specific recursion operators (maps and folds on lists, on binary trees, and so on) could be unified datatype-generically. We explain this school of programming in Section 3.

The origami approach to datatype-generic programming offers a number of benefits, not least of which is the support it provides for reasoning about recursive programs. But one of the reasons for our interest in the approach is that it seems to offer a good way of capturing precisely the essence of a number of the so-called Gang of Four *design patterns*, or reusable abstractions in object-oriented software [35]. This is appealing, because without some kind of datatype-generic constructs, these patterns can only be expressed extra-linguistically, 'as prose, pictures, and prototypes', rather than captured in a library, analysed and reused. We argue this case in Section 4, by presenting higher-order datatype-generic programs capturing ORIGAMI, a small suite of patterns for recursive data structures.

A declarative style of origami programming seems to capture well the computational structure of at least some of these patterns. But because they are usually applied in an imperative setting, they generally involve impure aspects too; a declarative approach does not capture those aspects well. The standard approach the functional programming community now takes to incorporating impure features in a pure setting is by way of *monads* [105,135], which elegantly model all sorts of impure effects such as state, I/O, exceptions and non-determinism. More recently, McBride and Paterson have introduced the notion of *idiom* or *applicative functor* [95], a slight generalization of monads with better compositional properties. One consequence of their definitions is a datatype-generic means of *traversing* collections 'idiomatically', incorporating both pure accumulations and impure effects. In Section 5, we explore the extent to which this construction offers a more faithful higher-order datatype-generic model of the ITERATOR design pattern specifically.

These lecture notes synthesize ideas and results from earlier publications, rather than presenting much that is new. In particular, Section 3 is a summary of two earlier sets of lectures [37,38]; Section 4 recaps the content of a tutorial presented at ECOOP [39] and OOPSLA [40], and subsequently published in a short paper [41]; Section 5 reports on some more recent joint work with Bruno Oliveira [44]. Much of this work took place within the EPSRC-funded *Datatype-Generic Programming* project at Oxford and Nottingham, of which this Spring School marks the final milestone.

2   Generic Programming

Generic programming usually manifests itself as a kind of parametrization. By abstracting from the differences in what would otherwise be separate but similar specific programs, one can make a single unified generic program. Instantiating the parameter in various ways retrieves the various specific programs one started with. Ideally, the abstraction increases expressivity, when some instantiations of the parameter yield new programs in addition to the original ones; otherwise, all one has gained is some elimination of duplication and a warm fuzzy feeling. The different interpretations of the term 'generic programming' arise from different notions of what constitutes a 'parameter'.

Moreover, a parametrization is usually only called 'generic' programming if it is of a 'non-traditional' kind; by definition, traditional kinds of parametrization give rise only to traditional programming, not generic programming. (This is analogous to the so-called *AI effect*: Rodney Brooks, director of MIT's Artificial Intelligence Laboratory, quoted in [79], observes that 'Every time we figure out a piece of [AI], it stops being magical; we say, "Oh, that's just a computation" '.) Therefore, 'genericity' is in the eye of the beholder, with beholders from different programming traditions having different interpretations of the term. No doubt by-value and by-reference parameter-passing mechanisms for arguments to procedures, as found in Pascal [74], look like 'generic programming' to an assembly-language programmer with no such tools at their disposal.

In this section, we review a number of interpretations of 'genericity' in terms of the kind of parametrization they support. Parametrization by *value* is the kind of parameter-passing mechanism familiar from most programming languages, and while (as argued above) this would not normally be considered 'generic programming', we include it for completeness; parametrization by *type* is what is normally known as polymorphism; parametrization by *function* is sometimes called 'higher-order programming', and is really just parametrization by value where the values are functions; parametrization by *structure* involves passing 'modules' with a varying private implementation of a fixed public signature or interface; parametrization by *property* is a refinement of parametrization by structure, whereby operations of the signature are required to satisfy some laws; parametrization by *stage* allows programs to be partitioned, with meta-programs that generate object programs; and parametrization by *shape* is to parametrization by type as 'by function' is to 'by value'.

2.1   Genericity by Value

One of the first and most fundamental techniques that any programmer learns is how to parametrize computations by values. Those old enough to have been brought up on structured programming are likely to have been given exercises to write programs to draw simple ASCII art: Whatever the scenario, students soon realise the futility of hard-wiring fixed behaviour into programs:

```
procedure Triangle4;
begin
    WriteString ("*"); WriteLn;
    WriteString ("**"); WriteLn;
    WriteString ("***"); WriteLn;
    WriteString ("****"); WriteLn
end;
```

and the benefits of abstracting that behaviour into parameters:

```
procedure Triangle (Side : cardinal);
begin
  var Row, Col : cardinal;
  for Row := 1 to Side do begin
    for Col := 1 to Row do WriteChar ('*');
    WriteLn
  end
end
```

Instead of a parameterless program that always performs the same computation, one ends up with a program with formal parameters, performing different but related computations depending on the actual parameters passed: a *function*.

2.2 Genericity by Type

Suppose that one wants a datatype of lists of integers, and a function to append two such lists. These are written in Haskell [112] as follows:

```
data ListI = NilI | ConsI Integer ListI
appendI :: ListI → ListI → ListI
appendI NilI          ys = ys
appendI (ConsI x xs) ys = ConsI x (appendI xs ys)
```

Suppose in addition that one wanted a datatype and an append function for lists of characters:

```
data ListC = NilC | ConsC Char ListC
appendC :: ListC → ListC → ListC
appendC NilC          ys = ys
appendC (ConsC x xs) ys = ConsC x (appendC xs ys)
```

It is tedious to repeat similar definitions in this way, and it doesn't take much vision to realise that the repetition is unnecessary: the definitions of the datatypes *ListI* and *ListC* are essentially identical, as are the definitions of the functions *appendI* and *appendC*. Apart from the necessity in Haskell to choose distinct names, the only difference in the two datatype definitions is the type of list elements, *Integer* or *Char*. Abstracting from this hard-wired constant leads to a single *polymorphic* datatype parametrized by another type, the type of list elements:

```
data List a = Nil | Cons a (List a)
```

(The term 'parametric datatype' would probably be more precise, but 'polymorphic datatype' is well established.) Unifying the two list datatypes in this way unifies the two programs too, into a single polymorphic program:

```
append :: List a → List a → List a
append Nil          ys = ys
append (Cons x xs) ys = Cons x (append xs ys)
```

There is a precise technical sense in which the process of abstraction by which one extracts type parameters reflects that by which one extracts value parameters. In Haskell, our definition of the polymorphic datatype *List* introduces a polymorphic value *Nil* of type *List a* for any type *a*; in the polymorphic lambda calculus [51,116], the polymorphism is made manifest in a type parameter: *Nil* would have type $\Lambda a. List\ a$ abstracted on the list element type *a*, and *Nil* τ would have type *List* τ for some specific element type τ.

This kind of type abstraction is called *parametric polymorphism*. It entails that the instantiated behaviour is *uniform* in the type parameter, and cannot depend on what actual parameter it is instantiated to. Informally, this means that a polymorphic function cannot examine elements of polymorphic types, but can merely rearrange them. Formally, this intuition was captured by Reynolds in his *abstraction theorem* [117], generalized by Wadler to the *parametricity theorem* and popularized under the slogan 'Theorems for Free' [132]. In the case of *append*, (a corollary of) the free theorem states that, for any function *a* of the same type as *append*,

$$a\ (mapL\ f\ xs)\ (mapL\ f\ ys) = mapL\ f\ (a\ xs\ ys)$$

where the function *mapL* (explained in Section 2.3 below) applies its first argument, a function, to every element of its second argument, a list.

Related to but not quite the same as parametric polymorphism is what Cardelli and Wegner [16] call *inclusion polymorphism*. This is the kind of polymorphism arising in object-oriented languages. Consider, for example, the following Java method:

```
public void addObserver (Observer obs){
    observers.addElement (obs);
}
```

This method takes a parameter *obs* of varying type, as does the Haskell function *append*; moreover, it behaves uniformly in the type of the actual parameter passed. However, it doesn't accept parameters of an arbitrary type, like *append* does, but only parameters whose type is included in the type *Observer*. (Alternatively, one could say that the method takes a parameter exactly of type *Observer*, but that subtypes of *Observer* are subsumed within this type.) We discuss the relationship between inclusion polymorphism and parametric polymorphism, and between these two and so-called ad-hoc forms of polymorphism, in Section 2.8 below.

One well-established interpretation of the term 'generic programming' is exactly as embodied by parametric polymorphism and inclusion polymorphism. Cardelli and Wegner [16, p. 475] state that 'the functions that exhibit parametric polymorphism are [...] called generic functions', and give *length* :: *List a* → *Integer* as an example. Paradigmatic languages exhibiting parametric polymorphism are ML [104] and Haskell [112], which provide (variations on) Hindley–Milner–Damas typing [103,23]. These have influenced the 'generics' in recent versions of Java [13] and C# [80]. (On the other hand, CLOS [81] also uses the term 'generic function', but in a sense related to inclusion polymorphism.)

Ada 83 [1] had a notion of generics, by which procedures and 'packages' (modules) can be parametrized by values, types, procedures (which gives a kind of higher-order parametrization, as discussed in Section 2.3) and packages (which gives what we call parametrization by structure, and discuss in Section 2.4). For example, the code below shows: (1) the declaration of a generic subprogram *Swap*, parametrized by a type *Element*; (2) the generic body of the subprogram, which makes use of the formal parameter *Element*; and (3) the instantiation of the generic unit to make a non-generic subprogram that may be used in the same way as any other subprogram.

```
generic
   type Element is private;
procedure Swap (X, Y : in out Element);        -- (1)

procedure Swap (X, Y : in out Element) is      -- (2)
   Z : constant Element := X;
begin
   X := Y;
   Y := Z;
end Swap;

procedure SwapInteger is new Swap (Integer);   -- (3)
```

However, Ada generic units are templates for their non-generic counterparts, as are the C++ templates they inspired, and cannot be used until they are instantiated; Cardelli and Wegner observe that this gives the advantage that instantiation-specific compiler optimizations may be performed, but aver that 'in true polymorphic systems, code is generated only once for every generic procedure' [16, p. 479].

2.3   Genericity by Function

Higher-order programs are programs parametrized by other programs. We mentioned above that Ada 83 generics allow parametrization by procedure; so do languages in the Algol family [111,108,138,128]. However, the usefulness of higher-order parametrization is greatly reduced in these languages by the inability to express actual procedure parameters anonymously in place. Higher-order parametrization comes into its own in functional programming, which promotes exactly this feature: naturally enough, making functions first-class citizens.

Suppose one had strings, represented as lists of characters, that one wanted to convert to uppercase, perhaps for the purpose of normalization:

```
stringToUpper :: List Char → List Char
stringToUpper Nil           = Nil
stringToUpper (Cons x xs) = Cons (toUpper x) (stringToUpper xs)
```

where *toUpper* converts characters to uppercase. Suppose also that one had a list of integers for people's ages, which one wanted to classify into young and old, represented as booleans:

$$classifyAges :: List\ Integer \rightarrow List\ Bool$$
$$classifyAges\ Nil \qquad\qquad = Nil$$
$$classifyAges\ (Cons\ x\ xs) = Cons\ (x < 30)\ (classifyAges\ xs)$$

These two functions, and many others, follow a common pattern. What differs is in fact a value, but one that is higher-order rather than first-order: the function to apply to each list element, which in the first case is the function *toUpper*, and in the second is the predicate (<30). What is common between the two is the function *mapL*, mentioned in Section 2.2 above:

$$mapL :: (a \rightarrow b) \rightarrow (List\ a \rightarrow List\ b)$$
$$mapL\ f\ Nil \qquad\qquad = Nil$$
$$mapL\ f\ (Cons\ x\ xs) = Cons\ (f\ x)\ (mapL\ f\ xs)$$

We treat this kind of parametrization separately from parametrization by first-order value, because it has far-reaching consequences. Among other things, it lets programmers express control structures within the language, rather than having to extend the language. For example, one might already consider *mapL* to be a programmer-defined control construct. For another example, recall the parametrically polymorphic *append* function from Section 2.2:

$$append :: List\ a \rightarrow List\ a \rightarrow List\ a$$
$$append\ Nil \qquad\quad ys = ys$$
$$append\ (Cons\ x\ xs)\ ys = Cons\ x\ (append\ xs\ ys)$$

A second function, *concat*, concatenates a list of lists into one long list:

$$concat :: List\ (List\ a) \rightarrow List\ a$$
$$concat\ Nil \qquad\qquad = Nil$$
$$concat\ (Cons\ xs\ xss) = append\ xs\ (concat\ xss)$$

A third sums a list of integers:

$$sum :: List\ Integer \rightarrow Integer$$
$$sum\ Nil \qquad\qquad = 0$$
$$sum\ (Cons\ x\ xs) = x + sum\ xs$$

Each of the three programs above traverses its list argument in exactly the same way. Abstracting from their differences allows us to capture that control structure as a pattern of recursion. The common pattern is called a 'fold':

$$foldL :: b \rightarrow (a \rightarrow b \rightarrow b) \rightarrow List\ a \rightarrow b$$
$$foldL\ n\ c\ Nil \qquad\qquad = n$$
$$foldL\ n\ c\ (Cons\ x\ xs) = c\ x\ (foldL\ n\ c\ xs)$$

(We write the suffix 'L' to denote an operation over lists; Sections 2.7 and 3 discuss generalizations to other datatypes. It so happens that this function is equivalent to the function *foldr* — 'fold from the right' — in the Haskell standard library [112].) Instances of *foldL* replace the list constructors *Nil* and *Cons* with supplied arguments:

$$append\ xs\ ys = foldL\ ys\ Cons\ xs$$
$$concat\qquad = foldL\ Nil\ append$$
$$sum\qquad = foldL\ 0\ (+)$$

In fact, *mapL* turns out to be another instance of *foldL*:

$$mapL\ f = foldL\ Nil\ (Cons \circ f)$$

where $\circ$ is function composition (itself another higher-order operator).

2.4 Genericity by Structure

Perhaps the most popular interpretation of the term 'generic programming' is as embodied in the C++ Standard Template Library, an object-oriented class library providing *containers*, *iterators* and *algorithms* for many datatypes [4]. Indeed, some writers have taken the STL style as the definition of generic programming; for example, Siek et al. [120] define generic programming as 'a methodology for program design and implementation that separates data structures and algorithms through the use of abstract requirement specifications'.

As the name suggests, the STL is implemented using the C++ template mechanism, which offers similar facilities to Ada generics: class- and function templates are parametrized by type- and value parameters. (Indeed, a predecessor to the STL was an Ada library for list processing [107].) Within the STL community more than any other, it is considered essential that genericity imposes no performance penalty [25,129].

The *containers* that are provided in the STL are parametrically polymorphic datatypes, parametrized by the element type; these are further classified into *sequence containers* (such as *Vector*, *String* and *Deque*) and *associative containers* (such as *Set*, *Multiset* and *Map*).

Bulk access to the elements of a container type is provided by *iterators*. These are abstractions of C++ pointers to elements, and so support pointer arithmetic. They are further classified according to what pointer operations they support: *input iterators* (which can be incremented, copied, assigned, compared for equality, and read from — that is, used as r-values), *output iterators* (which are similar, but can only be written to — that is, used as l-values), *forwards iterators* (which refine both input and output iterators), *bidirectional iterators* (which can also retreat, that is, supporting decrement), and *random-access iterators* (which can move any number of steps in one operation, that is, supporting addition).

Iterators form the interface between container types and *algorithms* over data structures. The algorithms provided in the STL include many general-purpose operations such as searching, sorting, filtering, and so on. Rather than operating directly on containers, an algorithm takes one or more iterators as parameters; the algorithm is *generic*, in the sense that it applies to any container that supports the appropriate kind of iterator.

For example, here is a code fragment (taken from [4, §1.1]) implementing a simplified version of the Unix **sort** utility.

```
int main () {
    vector⟨string⟩ v;
    string tmp;
    while (getline (cin, tmp))
        v.push_back (tmp);
    sort (v.begin (), v.end ());
    copy (v.begin (), v.end (), ostream_iterator⟨string⟩(cout, "\n"));
}
```

It shows a container v (a vector of strings); applications of generic algorithms (*sort* and *copy*); and a pair of iterators ('pointers' $v.begin$ () and $v.end$ () to the beginning and just past-the-end of the vector v) mediating between them.

In the C++ approach, the exact set of requirements on parameters (such as the iterator passed to a generic algorithm, or the element type passed to a generic container) is called a *concept*. A concept encapsulates the operations required of a formal type parameter and provided by an actual type parameter. Algorithms and containers are parametrized by the concept, and instantiated by passing a *structure* that implements the concept. For example, the STL's 'input iterator' concept encompasses pointer-like types which support comparison for equality, copying, assignment, reading, and incrementing. The success of the STL lies pretty much in the careful choice of such concepts as an organizing principle for a large library; as Siek and Lumsdaine [121] explain, the same principle has worked for many other C++ class libraries too.

The C++ template mechanism provides no means to define a concept explicitly; it is merely an informal artifact rather than a formal construct. (However, work is proceeding to formalize concepts as language constructs; see for example [54,121,53].) In that sense, it is a retrograde step from earlier languages supporting data abstraction. For instance, Liskov's CLU language [89] from the mid-1970s had a **where** clause, for specifying the requirements (names and signatures) on a type parameter to a *cluster*; the following declaration [89, p13] for a cluster *set* parametrized by a type t states that t must support a binary predicate *equal*.

> $set = $ **cluster** $[t : $ **type**$]$ **is** *create, member, size, insert, delete, elements*
> **where** t **has** *equal* : **proctype** (t, t) **returns** (*bool*)

This retrograde step is somewhat ironic, since CLU's clusters were, via Ada generics, the inspiration for the C++ template mechanism in the first place.

The notion in Haskell analogous to C++'s concepts, and the basis for current proposals to to provide linguistic support for concepts in C++ [53], is the *type class*, which also captures the requirements required of and provided by types, but which is formally part of the language. For example, a function *sort* in Haskell might have the following type:

> $sort :: Ord\ a \Rightarrow List\ a \rightarrow List\ a$

The constraint 'Ord a ⇒' is a *type class context*; the function *sort* is not para-metrically polymorphic, because it is not applicable to all types of list element, only those in the type class *Ord*. The type class *Ord* includes exactly those types that support the operation ≤, and might be defined in Haskell as follows:

> **class** *Ord a* **where**
>   (≤) :: *a* → *a* → *Bool*

(The actual definition is more complex than this [112]; but this simpler version serves for illustration.) Various types are instance of the type class, by virtue of supporting a comparison operation:

> **instance** *Ord Integer* **where**
>   (*m* ≤ *n*) = *isNonNegative* (*n* − *m*)

Attempting to apply ≤ to two values of some type that is not in the type class *Ord*, or *sort* to a list of such values, is a type error, and is caught statically. In contrast, while the equivalent error using the C++ STL 'less-than comparable' concept is still a statically caught type error, it is caught at template instan-tiation time, since there is no way of declaring the uninstantiated template's dependence on the concept.

As we stated above, the kind of polymorphism provided by C++ STL concepts and Haskell type classes is not parametric, because it is not universal. For the same reason, neither is it inclusion polymorphism, even though C++ concepts and Haskell type classes both form hierarchies. In fact, the member functions of the Haskell type class, such as the operation (≤) :: *Ord a* ⇒ *a* → *a* → *Bool*, are *ad-hoc polymorphic*, which is to say non-uniform: there is no requirement, and indeed it is generally not the case, that definitions of ≤ on different types will be implemented using the same code.

2.5   Genericity by Property

We have seen that generic programming in the C++ sense revolves around con-cepts, which are abstractions of the requirements on and provisions of a type parameter, specifically in terms of the operations available. In fact, in typical usage, concepts are more elaborate than this; as well as signatures of operations, the concept might specify the laws these operations satisfy, and non-functional characteristics such as the asymptotic complexities of the operations in terms of time and space. For example, the 'less-than comparable' concept in the STL stipulates that the ordering should be a partial ordering, and the 'random-access iterator' concept stipulates that addition to and subtraction from the pointer should take constant time. Correctness of operation signatures can be *verified* at instantiation time, and this information is useful to a compiler, for example in providing efficient dispatching. The laws satisfied by operations and non-functional characteristics such as complexity cannot be verified in general, although testing frameworks such as QuickCheck [18] and JUnit [34] can go some way towards *validation*; this information nevertheless might still be useful to a sophisticated optimizing compiler.

In the Haskell setting, the formal part of a type class declaration states the names and signatures of the operations provided, and the equally important but informal accompanying documentation may stipulate additional properties, typically in the form of axioms. For example, the *Ord* type class might stipulate that $\leqslant$ forms a total order or a total preorder; we make use later of a type class *Monoid*:

> **class** *Monoid m* **where**
> $\emptyset \quad :: m$
> $(\oplus) :: m \to m \to m$

with the usual monoid laws:

> $$x \oplus (y \oplus z) = (x \oplus y) \oplus z$$
> $$x \oplus \emptyset \quad\quad = x$$
> $$\emptyset \oplus x \quad\quad = x$$

In Section 3, we make use of a two-parameter version of the following one-parameter *Functor* type class:

> **class** *Functor f* **where**
> $\mathit{fmap} :: (a \to b) \to (f\ a \to f\ b)$

(Strictly speaking, *Functor* is a *constructor class* rather than a type class, since its members are type constructors rather than base types: in Haskell terminology, 'types of kind $* \to *$' rather than 'types of kind $*$', where kinds classify types in the same way that types classify values. But in these lecture notes, we use the term 'type class' even for classes of type constructors.) The intention is that this class contains types supporting functions like *mapL*:

> **instance** *Functor List* **where**
> $\mathit{fmap} = mapL$

The informal intention 'functions like *mapL*' can be captured more formally in terms of the functor laws:

> $$\mathit{fmap}\ (f \circ g) = \mathit{fmap}\ f \circ \mathit{fmap}\ g$$
> $$\mathit{fmap}\ id \quad\quad = id$$

In Section 5, we generalize the *Monad* type class, a subclass of *Functor*:

> **class** *Functor m* $\Rightarrow$ *Monad m* **where**
> $return :: a \to m\ a$
> $(\ggeq) \quad :: m\ a \to (a \to m\ b) \to m\ b$

(The Haskell 98 standard library [112] omits the *Functor* context, but without any increase in generality, since the operation *fmap* can be reconstructed from *return* and $\ggeq$.) Instances of *Monad* correspond to types of 'computations with

impure effects'. The exception monad is a simple instance; a 'computation yielding an a' might fail.

> **data** $Maybe\ a = Nothing \mid Just\ a$
>
> $foldM :: b \to (a \to b) \to Maybe\ a \to b$
> $foldM\ y\ f\ Nothing = y$
> $foldM\ y\ f\ (Just\ x) = f\ x$
>
> **instance** $Functor\ Maybe$ **where**
> $fmap\ f\ Nothing = Nothing$
> $fmap\ f\ (Just\ x) = Just\ (f\ x)$
>
> **instance** $Monad\ Maybe$ **where**
> $return\ a\ = Just\ a$
> $mx \ggg k = foldM\ Nothing\ k\ mx$
>
> $raise :: Maybe\ a$ -- raise an exception
> $raise = Nothing$
>
> $trycatch :: (a \to b) \to b \to Maybe\ a \to b$ -- handle an exception
> $trycatch\ f\ y = foldM\ y\ f$

Another instance is the state monad, in which a 'computation yielding an a' also
affects a state of type s, amounting to a function of type $s \to (a, s)$:

> **newtype** $State\ s\ a = St\ (s \to (a, s))$
>
> $runSt :: State\ s\ a \to s \to (a, s)$
> $runSt\ (St\ f) = f$
>
> **instance** $Functor\ (State\ s)$ **where**
> $fmap\ f\ mx = St\ (\lambda s \to \mathbf{let}\ (a, s') = runSt\ mx\ s\ \mathbf{in}\ (f\ a, s'))$
>
> **instance** $Monad\ (State\ s)$ **where**
> $return\ a\ = St\ (\lambda s \to (a, s))$
> $mx \ggg k = St\ (\lambda s \to \mathbf{let}\ (a, s') = runSt\ mx\ s\ \mathbf{in}\ runSt\ (k\ a)\ s')$
>
> $put :: s \to State\ s\ ()$ -- write to the state
> $put\ s = St\ (\lambda\_ \to ((), s))$
>
> $get :: State\ s\ s$ -- read from the state
> $get = St\ (\lambda s \to (s, s))$

Haskell provides a convenient piece of syntactic sugar called '**do** notation' [134],
allowing an imperative style of programming for monadic computations. This
is defined by translation into expressions involving $return$ and $\ggg$; a simplified
version of the full translation [112, §3.14] is as follows:

> $\mathbf{do}\ \{\ mx\ \}$ $= mx$
> $\mathbf{do}\ \{\ x \leftarrow mx;\ stmts\ \} = mx \ggg \lambda x \to \mathbf{do}\ \{\ stmts\ \}$
> $\mathbf{do}\ \{\quad mx;\ stmts\ \} = mx \ggg \lambda() \to \mathbf{do}\ \{\ stmts\ \}$

In addition to the laws inherited from the $Functor$ type class, a $Monad$ instance
must satisfy the following three laws:

$$return\ a \ggg k = k\ a$$
$$m \ggg return = m$$
$$m \ggg (\lambda x \rightarrow k\ x \ggg h) = (m \ggg k) \ggg h$$

The first two are kinds of unit law, and the last one a kind of associative law. Their importance is in justifying the use of the imperative style of syntax; for example, they justify flattening of nested blocks:

$$\mathbf{do}\ \{\ p;\mathbf{do}\ \{\ q;r\};s\ \} = \mathbf{do}\ \{\ p;q;r;s\ \}$$

We leave it to the reader to verify that the *Maybe* and *State* instances of the *Monad* class do indeed satisfy these laws.

More elaborate examples of genericity by property arise from more sophisticated mathematical structures. For example, Horner's rule for polynomial evaluation [21] can be parametrized by a semiring, an extremal path finder by a regular algebra [5,7], and a greedy algorithm by a matroid or greedoid structure [27,85]. Mathematical structures are fertile grounds for finding more such examples; the Axiom programming language for computer algebra [73,14] now has a library of over 10,000 'domains' (types).

Whereas genericity by structure is an outcome of the work on abstract datatypes [90], genericity by property follows from the enrichment of that work to include equational constraints, leading to *algebraic specifications* [28,29], as realised in languages such as Larch [55] and Casl [20,8].

2.6   Genericity by Stage

Another interpretation of the term 'generic programming' covers various flavours of *metaprogramming*, that is, the development of programs that construct or manipulate other programs. This field encompasses *program generators* such as `lex` [75, §A.2] and `yacc` [75, §A.3], *reflection techniques* allowing a program (typically in a dynamically typed language) to observe and possibly modify its structure and behaviour [33], *generative programming* for the automated customization, configuration and assembly of components [22], and *multi-stage programming* for partitioning computations into phases [125].

For example, an *active library* [129] might perform domain-specific optimizations such as unrolling inner loops: rather than implementing numerous slightly different components for different loop bounds, the library could provide a single *generic metaprogram* that specializes to them all. A compiler could even be considered a generative metaprogram: rather than writing machine code directly, the programmer writes meta-machine code in a high-level language, and leaves the generation of the machine code itself to the compiler.

In fact, the C++ template mechanism is surprisingly expressive, and already provides some kind of metaprogramming facility. Template instantiation takes place at compile time, so one can think of a C++ program with templates as a two-stage computation; as noted above, several high-performance numerical libraries rely on templates' generative properties [129]. The template instantiation mechanism turns out to be Turing complete; Unruh [126] gives the unsettling example of a program whose compilation yields the prime numbers as error messages, Czarnecki and Eisenecker [22] show the Turing-completeness of the template mechanism by implementing a rudimentary Lisp interpreter as a template meta-program, and Alexandrescu [3] presents a *tour de force* of unexpected applications of templates.

2.7   Genericity by Shape

Recall the polymorphic datatype *List* introduced in Section 2.2, and the corresponding polymorphic higher-order function *foldL* in Section 2.3; recall also the polymorphic datatype *Maybe* and higher-order function *foldM* from Section 2.5. One might also have a polymorphic datatype of binary trees:

data *Btree a* = *Tip a* | *Bin* (*Btree a*) (*Btree a*)

The familiar process of abstraction from a collection of similar programs would lead one to identify the natural pattern of recursion on these trees as another higher-order function:

$$foldB :: (a \to b) \to (b \to b \to b) \to Btree\ a \to b$$
$$foldB\ t\ b\ (Tip\ x)\quad = t\ x$$
$$foldB\ t\ b\ (Bin\ xs\ ys) = b\ (foldB\ t\ b\ xs)\ (foldB\ t\ b\ ys)$$

For example, instances of *foldB* reflect a tree, and flatten it to a list, in both cases replacing the tree constructors *Tip* and *Bin* with supplied constructors:

$$reflect :: Btree\ a \to Btree\ a$$
$$reflect = foldB\ Tip\ nib\qquad \textbf{where}\ nib\ xs\ ys = Bin\ ys\ xs$$

$$flatten :: Btree\ a \to List\ a$$
$$flatten = foldB\ wrap\ append\ \textbf{where}\ wrap\ x = Cons\ x\ Nil$$

We have seen that each kind of parametrization allows some recurring patterns to be captured. For example, parametric polymorphism unifies commonality of computation, abstracting from variability in irrelevant typing information, and higher-order functions unify commonality of program shape, abstracting from variability in some of the details.

But what about the two higher-order polymorphic programs *foldL* and *foldB*? We can see that they have something in common: both replace constructors by supplied arguments; both have patterns of recursion that follow the datatype definition, with one clause per datatype variant and one recursive call per substructure. But neither parametric polymorphism, nor higher-order functions, nor module signatures suffice to capture this kind of commonality.

In fact, what differs between the two fold operators is the *shape* of the data on which they operate, and hence the shape of the programs themselves. The kind of parametrization required is by this shape; that is, by the datatype or type constructor (such as *List* or *Tree*) concerned. We call this *datatype genericity*; it allows the capture of recurring patterns in *programs of different shapes*. In

Section 3 below, we explain the definition of a datatype-generic operation *fold* with the following type:

$$fold :: Bifunctor\ s \Rightarrow (s\ a\ b \rightarrow b) \rightarrow Fix\ s\ a \rightarrow b$$

Here, in addition to the type a of collection elements and the fold body (a function of type $s\ a\ b \rightarrow b$), the shape parameter s varies; the type class *Bifunctor* expresses the constraints we place on its choice. The shape parameter determines the shape of the input data; for one instantiation of s, the type *Fix s a* is isomorphic to *List a*, and for another instantiation it is isomorphic to *Tree a*. (So the parametrization is strictly speaking not by the recursive datatype *List* itself, but by the bifunctor s that yields the shape of *Lists*.) The same shape parameter also determines the type of the fold body, supplied as an argument with which to replace the constructors.

The *Datatype-Generic Programming* project at Oxford and Nottingham [43] has been investigating programs parametrized by datatypes, that is, by type constructors such as 'list of' and 'tree of'. Such programs might be *parametrically datatype-generic*, as with *fold* above, when the behaviour is uniform in the shape parameter. Since the shape parameter is of higher kind, this is a higher-order parametricity property, but it is of the same flavour as first-order parametricity [117,132], stating a form of coherence between instances of *fold* for different shapes. A similar class of programs is captured by Jay's theory of *shapely polymorphism* [72].

Alternatively, such programs might be *ad-hoc datatype-generic*, when the behaviour exploits that shape in some essential manner. Typical examples of the latter are pretty printers and marshallers; these can be defined once and for all for lists, trees, and so on, in a typesafe way, but not in a way that guarantees any kind of uniformity in behaviour at the instances for different shapes. This approach to datatype genericity has been variously called *polytypism* [68], *structural polymorphism* [118] or *typecase* [131,26], and is the meaning given to 'generic programming' by the Generic Haskell [60,91] team. Whatever the name, functions are defined inductively by case analysis on the structure of datatypes; the different approaches differ slightly in the class of datatypes covered. For example, here is a Generic Haskell definition of datatype-generic encoding to a list of bits.

```
type Encode{[*]}        t = t → [Bool]
type Encode{[k → l]} t = ∀a.   Encode{[k]} a → Encode{[l]} (t a)

encode{[t :: k]}              :: Encode{[k]} t
encode{[Char]} c              = encodeChar c
encode{[Int]} n               = encodeInt n
encode{[Unit]} unit           = []
encode{[:+:]} ena enb (Inl a) = False : ena a
encode{[:+:]} ena enb (Inr b) = True : enb b
encode{[:×:]} ena enb (a :×: b) = ena a ++ enb b
```

The generic function *encode* works for any type constructed from characters and integers using sums and products; these cases are defined explicitly, and the cases for type abstraction, application and recursion are generated automatically. Note that instances of *encode* are very different for different type parameters, not even taking the same number of arguments. In fact, the instances have different *kinds* (as mentioned in Section 2.5, and discussed further in Hinze and others' two chapters [61, §3.1] and [63, §2.1] in this volume), and *type-indexed values have kind-indexed types* [57].

As we have seen, ad-hoc datatype-generic definitions are typically given by case analysis over the structure of types. One has the flexibility to define different behaviour in different branches, and maybe even to customize the behaviour for specific types; consequently, there is no guarantee or check that the behaviours in different branches conform, except by type. This is in contrast to the parametrically datatype-generic definition of *fold* cited above; there, one has less flexibility, but instances at different types necessarily behave uniformly. Ad-hoc datatype genericity is more general than parametric; for example, it is difficult to see how to define datatype-generic encoding parametrically, and conversely, any parametric definition can be expanded into an ad-hoc one. However, parametric datatype genericity offers better prospects for reasoning, and is to be preferred when it is applicable.

We consider parametric datatype genericity to be the 'gold standard', and in the remainder of these lecture notes, we concentrate on parametric datatype-generic definitions where possible. In fact, it is usually the case that one must provide an ad-hoc datatype-generic hook initially, but then one can derive a number of parametrically datatype-generic definitions from this. In Sections 3 and 4, we suppose an (ad-hoc) datatype-generic operator *bimap*, and from this derive various (parametrically) datatype-generic recursion operators. In Section 5.2 we suppose a different (ad-hoc) datatype-generic operator *traverse*, and from this derive various (parametrically) datatype-generic traversal operators. Clarke and Löh [19] use the name *generic abstractions* for parametrically datatype-generic functions defined in terms of ad-hoc datatype-generic functions.

Datatype genericity is different from various other interpretations of generic programming outlined above. It is not just a matter of parametric polymorphism, at least not in a straightforward way; for example, parametric polymorphism abstracts from the occurrence of 'integer' in 'lists of integers', whereas datatype genericity abstracts from the occurrence of 'list'. It is not just interface conformance, as with concept satisfaction in the STL; although the latter allows *abstraction from* the shape of data, it does not allow *exploitation of* the shape of data, as required for the data compression and marshalling examples above. Finally, it is not metaprogramming: although some flavours of metaprogramming (such as reflection) can simulate datatype-generic computations, they typically do so at the cost of static checking.

2.8   Universal vs Ad-Hoc Genericity

Strachey's seminal notes on programming languages [124] make the fundamental distinction between *parametric* polymorphism, in which a function works uniformly on a range of types, usually with a common structure, and *ad-hoc* polymorphism, in which a function works (or appears to work) on several different types, but these need not have a common structure, and the behaviour might be different at different types.

Cardelli and Wegner [16] refine this distinction. They rename the former to *universal* polymorphism, and divide this into *parametric* polymorphism again and *inclusion* polymorphism. The difference between the two arises from the different ways in which a value may have multiple types: with parametric polymorphism, values and functions implicitly or explicitly take a type parameter, as discussed in Section 2.2; with inclusion polymorphism, types are arranged into a hierarchy, and a value of one type is simultaneously a value of all its supertypes. Cardelli and Wegner also refine ad-hoc polymorphism into *overloading*, a syntactic mechanism in which the same function name has different meanings in different contexts, and *coercion*, in which a function name has just one meaning, but semantic conversions are applied to arguments where necessary.

The uppermost of these distinctions can be applied to other kinds of parameter than types, at least informally. For example, one can distinguish between *universal parametrization* by a number, as in the structured program in Section 2.1 to draw a triangle of a given size, and *ad-hoc parametrization* by a number, as in 'press 1 to listen to the message again, press 2 to return the call, press 3 to delete the message. . . '-style interfaces. In the former, there is some coherence between the instances for different numbers, but in the latter there is not. For another example, sorting algorithms that use only comparisons obey what is known as the *zero-one principle* [21]: if they work correctly on sequences of numbers drawn from the set $\{0, 1\}$, then they work correctly on arbitrary number sequences (and more generally, where the element type is linearly ordered). Therefore, sorting algorithms defined using only comparisons are universally parametric in the list elements [24], whereas sorting algorithms using other operations (such as radix sort, which depends on the 'digits' or fields of the list elements) are ad-hoc parametric, and proving their correctness requires more effort. *Data independence* techniques in model checking [87,88] are a third illustration. All of these seem to have some relation to the notion of naturality in category theory, and (perhaps not surprisingly) Reynolds' notion of parametricity. For Cardelli and Wegner, 'universal polymorphism is considered true polymorphism, whereas ad-hoc polymorphism is some kind of apparent polymorphism whose polymorphic character disappears at close range'; by the same token, we might say that *universal parametrization is truly generic, whereas ad-hoc parametrization is only apparently generic.*

2.9   Another Dimension of Classification

Backhouse et al. [7] suggest a second dimension of classification of parametrization: not only in terms of the varieties of entity that can be abstracted, but also in terms of what support is provided for this abstraction — the varieties of construct from which these entities may be abstracted, and whether instances of those entities can be expressed anonymously in place, or must be defined out of line and referred to by name.

For an example of the second kind of distinction, consider values and types in Haskell 98: values can be parametrized by values (for example, a function *preds* taking an integer n to the list $[n, n-1, ..., 1]$ can be considered as a list parametrized by an integer), types can be parametrized by types (for example, the polymorphic list type $[a]$ is parametrized by the element type a), values can be parametrized by types (for example, the empty list $[]$ is polymorphic, and really stands for a value of type $[a]$ for any type a), but types cannot easily be parametrized by values (to capture a type of 'lists of length n', one requires dependent types [96], or some lightweight variant such as generalized algebraic datatypes [113,119]). We referred in Section 2.3 to an example of the third kind of distinction: although procedures in languages in the Algol family can be parametrized by other procedures, actual procedure parameters must be declared out of line and passed by name, rather than being defined on the fly as lambda expressions.

3   Origami Programming

There is a branch of the mathematics of program construction devoted to the relationship between the structure of programs and the structure of the data they manipulate [92,101,6,9,37]. We saw a glimpse of this field in Sections 2.3, 2.5 and 2.7, with the definitions of *foldL*, *foldM* and *foldB* respectively: the structure of each program reflects that of the datatype it traverses, for example in the number of clauses and the number and position of any recursive references. In this section, we explore a little further. Folds are not the only program structure that reflects data structure, although they are often given unfair emphasis [48]; we outline *unfolds* and *builds* too, which are two kinds of dual (producing structured data rather than consuming it), and *maps*, which are special cases of these operators, and some simple combinations of all of these. There are many other datatype-generic patterns of computation that we might also have considered: paramorphisms [98], apomorphisms [130], histomorphisms and futumorphisms [127], metamorphisms [42], dynamorphisms [78], destroy [36], and so on.

The beauty of all of these patterns of computation is the direct relationship between their shape and that of the data they manipulate; we go on to explain how both can be parametrized by that shape, yielding *datatype-generic* patterns of computation. We recently coined the term *origami programming* [38] for this approach to datatype-generic programming, because of its dependence on folds and unfolds.

3.1   Maps and Folds on Lists

Here is the datatype of lists again.

data $List\ a = Nil \mid Cons\ a\ (List\ a)$

The 'map' operator for a datatype applies a given function to every element of a data structure. In Section 2.3, we saw the (higher-order, polymorphic, but list-specific) map operator for lists:

$$mapL :: (a \rightarrow b) \rightarrow (List\ a \rightarrow List\ b)$$
$$mapL\ f\ Nil \qquad = Nil$$
$$mapL\ f\ (Cons\ x\ xs) = Cons\ (f\ x)\ (mapL\ f\ xs)$$

The 'fold' operator for a datatype collapses a data structure down to a value. Here is the (again higher-order, polymorphic, but list-specific) fold operator for lists from Section 2.3:

$$foldL :: b \rightarrow (a \rightarrow b \rightarrow b) \rightarrow List\ a \rightarrow b$$
$$foldL\ e\ f\ Nil \qquad = e$$
$$foldL\ e\ f\ (Cons\ x\ xs) = f\ x\ (foldL\ e\ f\ xs)$$

As a simple application of *foldL*, the function *filterL* (itself higher-order, polymorphic, but list-specific) takes a predicate p and a list xs, and returns the sublist of xs consisting of those elements that satisfy p.

$$filterL :: (a \rightarrow Bool) \rightarrow List\ a \rightarrow List\ a$$
$$filterL\ p = foldL\ Nil\ (add\ p)$$
$$\textbf{where}\ add\ p\ x\ xs = \textbf{if}\ p\ x\ \textbf{then}\ Cons\ x\ xs\ \textbf{else}\ xs$$

As we saw in Section 2.3, the functions *sum*, *append* and *concat* are also instances of *foldL*.

3.2   Unfolds on Lists

The 'unfold' operator for a datatype grows a data structure from a value. In a precise technical sense, it is the dual of the 'fold' operator. That duality isn't so obvious in the implementation for lists below, but it becomes clearer with the datatype-generic version we present in Section 3.8.

$$unfoldL :: (b \rightarrow Bool) \rightarrow (b \rightarrow a) \rightarrow (b \rightarrow b) \rightarrow b \rightarrow List\ a$$
$$unfoldL\ p\ f\ g\ x$$
$$= \textbf{if}\ p\ x\ \textbf{then}\ Nil$$
$$\textbf{else}\quad Cons\ (f\ x)\ (unfoldL\ p\ f\ g\ (g\ x))$$

For example, here are two instances. The function *preds* returns the list of predecessors of an integer (which will be an infinite list if that integer is negative); the function *takeWhile* takes a predicate p and a list xs, and returns the longest initial segment of xs all of whose elements satisfy p.

$$preds :: Integer \rightarrow List\ Integer$$
$$preds = unfoldL\ (0 ==)\ id\ pred\ \textbf{where}\ pred\ n = n - 1$$
$$takeWhile :: (a \rightarrow Bool) \rightarrow List\ a \rightarrow List\ a$$
$$takeWhile\ p = unfoldL\ (firstNot\ p)\ head\ tail$$
$$\textbf{where}\ firstNot\ p\ Nil \qquad = True$$
$$firstNot\ p\ (Cons\ x\ xs) = not\ (p\ x)$$

3.3 Origami for Binary Trees

We might go through a similar exercise for a datatype of internally labelled binary trees.

> **data** *Tree a = Empty | Node a (Tree a) (Tree a)*

The 'map' operator applies a given function to every element of a tree.

> *mapT :: (a → b) → (Tree a → Tree b)*
> *mapT f Empty   = Empty*
> *mapT f (Node x xs ys) = Node (f x) (mapT f xs) (mapT f ys)*

The 'fold' operator collapses a tree down to a value.

> *foldT :: b → (a → b → b → b) → Tree a → b*
> *foldT e n Empty   = e*
> *foldT e n (Node x xs ys) = n x (foldT e n xs) (foldT e n ys)*

For example, the function *inorder* collapses a tree down to a list.

> *inorder :: Tree a → List a*
> *inorder = foldT Nil glue*
>
> *glue x xs ys = append xs (Cons x ys)*

The 'unfold' operator grows a tree from a value.

> *unfoldT :: (b → Bool) → (b → a) → (b → b) → (b → b) → b → Tree a*
> *unfoldT p f g h x*
>   = **if** *p x* **then** *Empty*
>   **else** *Node (f x) (unfoldT p f g h (g x))*
>   *(unfoldT p f g h (h x))*

For example, the Calkin–Wilf tree, illustrated in Figure 1, contains each of the positive rationals exactly once:

> *cwTree :: Tree Rational*
> *cwTree = unfoldT (const False) frac left right (1, 1)*
>   **where** *frac (m, n) = m % n*
>   *left (m, n)   = (m, m + n)*
>   *right (m, n) = (n + m, n)*

Here, *const a* is the function that always returns *a*, and the operator % constructs a rational from its numerator and denominator. For a full derivation of this algorithm, see [2,49]; briefly, the paths in the tree correspond to traces of Euclid's algorithm computing the greatest common divisor of the numerator and denominator.

Another example of an unfold is given by the function *grow* that generates a binary search tree from a list of elements.

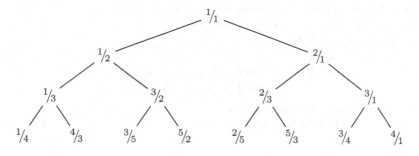

Fig. 1. The first few levels of the Calkin–Wilf tree

> $grow :: Ord\ a \Rightarrow List\ a \rightarrow Tree\ a$
> $grow = unfoldT\ isNil\ head\ littles\ bigs$
> $littles\ (Cons\ x\ xs) = filterL\ (\leqslant x)\ xs$
> $bigs\ (Cons\ x\ xs)\ \ = filterL\ (>x)\ xs$

(where *isNil* is the predicate that holds precisely of empty lists). As with the function *sort* mentioned in Section 2.4, *grow* has a type qualified by the context *Ord a*: the element type must be ordered.

3.4 Hylomorphisms

An unfold followed by a fold is a common pattern of computation [101]; the unfold generates a data structure, and the fold immediately consumes it. For example, here is a (higher-order, polymorphic, but list-specific) hylomorphism operator for lists, and an instance for computing factorials: first generate the predecessors of the input using an unfold, then compute the product of these predecessors using a fold.

> $hyloL :: (b \rightarrow Bool) \rightarrow (b \rightarrow a) \rightarrow (b \rightarrow b) \rightarrow c \rightarrow (a \rightarrow c \rightarrow c) \rightarrow b \rightarrow c$
> $hyloL\ p\ f\ g\ e\ h = foldL\ e\ h \circ unfoldL\ p\ f\ g$
>
> $fact :: Integer \rightarrow Integer$
> $fact = hyloL\ (0 ==)\ id\ pred\ 1\ (*)$

With lazy evaluation, the intermediate data structure is not computed all at once. It is produced on demand, and each demanded cell consumed immediately. In fact, the intermediary can be *deforested* altogether.

> $hyloL :: (b \rightarrow Bool) \rightarrow (b \rightarrow a) \rightarrow (b \rightarrow b) \rightarrow c \rightarrow (a \rightarrow c \rightarrow c) \rightarrow b \rightarrow c$
> $hyloL\ p\ f\ g\ e\ h\ x$
> $\quad = \mathbf{if}\ p\ x\ \mathbf{then}\ e\ \mathbf{else}\ h\ (f\ x)\ (hyloL\ p\ f\ g\ e\ h\ (g\ x))$

A similar definition can be given for binary trees, as shown below, together with an instance giving a kind of quicksort (albeit not a very quick one: it is not in-place, it has a bad space leak, and it takes quadratic time).

$$hyloT :: (b \rightarrow Bool) \rightarrow (b \rightarrow a) \rightarrow (b \rightarrow b) \rightarrow$$
$$c \rightarrow (a \rightarrow c \rightarrow c \rightarrow c) \rightarrow b \rightarrow c$$
$$hyloT\ p\ f\ g_1\ g_2\ e\ h\ x$$
$$= \textbf{if}\ p\ x\ \textbf{then}\ e$$
$$\quad \textbf{else}\ \ h\ (f\ x)\ (hyloT\ p\ f\ g_1\ g_2\ e\ h\ (g_1\ x))$$
$$\quad\quad\quad\quad\quad (hyloT\ p\ f\ g_1\ g_2\ e\ h\ (g_2\ x))$$

$$qsort :: Ord\ a \Rightarrow List\ a \rightarrow List\ a$$
$$qsort = hyloT\ isNil\ head\ littles\ bigs\ Nil\ glue$$

3.5   Short-Cut Fusion

Unfolds capture a highly structured pattern of computation for generating recursive data structures. There exist slight generalizations of unfolds, such as
monadic unfolds [109,110], *apomorphisms* [130] and *futumorphisms* [127], but
these still all conform to the same structural scheme, and not all programs that
generate data structures fit this scheme [46]. Gill et al. [50] introduced an operator they called *build* for unstructured generation of data, in order to simplify
the implementation and broaden the applicability of deforestation optimizations
as discussed in the previous section. During the Spring School, Malcolm Wallace
proposed the alternative term 'tectomorphism' for *build*, maintaining the Greek
naming theme.

The idea behind *build* is to allow the identification of precisely where in a
program the nodes of a data structure are being generated; then it is straightforward for a compiler to fuse a following fold, inlining functions to replace those
constructors and deforesting the data structure altogether. The operator takes
as argument a program with 'holes' for constructors, and plugs those holes with
actual constructors.

$$buildL :: (\forall b.\ \ b \rightarrow (a \rightarrow b \rightarrow b) \rightarrow b) \rightarrow List\ a$$
$$buildL\ g = g\ Nil\ Cons$$

The function *buildL* has a rank-two type; the argument g must be parametrically
polymorphic in the constructor arguments, in order to ensure that all uses of
the constructors are abstracted. (In fact, the argument g is the Church encoding
of a list as a polymorphic lambda term, and *buildL* converts that encoding to a
list as a familiar data structure [59].) We argued above that *unfoldL* is a dual
to *foldL* in one sense; we make that sense clear in Section 3.8. In another sense,
buildL is *foldL*'s dual: whereas the fold deletes constructors and replaces them
with something else, the build inserts those constructors.

The beauty of the idea is that fusion with a following fold is simple to state:

$$foldL\ e\ f\ (buildL\ g) = g\ e\ f$$

Perhaps more importantly, it is also easy for a compiler to exploit.

Build operators are strictly more expressive than unfolds. For instance, it is
possible to define *unfoldL* in terms of *buildL*:

$unfoldL :: (b \rightarrow Bool) \rightarrow (b \rightarrow a) \rightarrow (b \rightarrow b) \rightarrow b \rightarrow List\ a$
$unfoldL\ p\ f\ g\ b = buildL\ (h\ b)$
   where $h\ b\ n\ c =$ **if** $p\ b$ **then** n **else** $c\ (f\ b)\ (h\ (g\ b)\ n\ c)$

However, some functions that generate lists can be expressed as an instance of *buildL* and not of *unfoldL* [46]; the well-known fast *reverse* is an example:

$$reverse\ xs = buildL\ (\lambda n\ c \rightarrow foldL\ id\ (\lambda x\ g \rightarrow g \circ c\ x)\ xs\ n)$$

The disadvantage of *buildL* compared to *unfoldL* is a consequence of its unstructured approach: the former does not support the powerful *universal properties* that greatly simplify program calculation with the latter [37].

Of course, there is nothing special about lists in this regard. One can define build operators for any datatype:

$buildT :: (\forall b.\ b \rightarrow (a \rightarrow b \rightarrow b \rightarrow b) \rightarrow b) \rightarrow Tree\ a$
$buildT\ g = g\ Empty\ Node$

3.6 Datatype Genericity

As we have already argued, data structure determines program structure [64]. It therefore makes sense to abstract from the determining shape, leaving only what programs of different shape have in common. What datatypes such as *List* and *Tree* have in common is the fact that they are recursive — which is to say, a datatype *Fix*, parametrized both by an element type a of basic kind (a plain type, such as integers or strings), and by a shape type s of higher kind (a type constructor, such as 'pairs of' or 'lists of', but in this case with two arguments rather than one).

   data $Fix\ s\ a = In\ (s\ a\ (Fix\ s\ a))$
   $out :: Fix\ s\ a \rightarrow s\ a\ (Fix\ s\ a)$
   $out\ (In\ x) = x$

Equivalently, we could use a record type with a single named field, and define both the constructor *In* and the destructor *out* at once.

   data $Fix\ s\ a = In\{\ out :: s\ a\ (Fix\ s\ a)\}$

The generic datatype *Fix* is what the specific datatypes *List* and *Tree* have in common; the shape parameter s is what varies. Here are three instances of *Fix* using different shapes: lists and internally labelled binary trees as seen before, and also a datatype of externally labelled binary trees.

   data $ListF\ a\ b = NilF\ |\ ConsF\ a\ b$
   type $List\ a = Fix\ ListF\ a$
   data $TreeF\ a\ b = EmptyF\ |\ NodeF\ a\ b\ b$
   type $Tree\ a = Fix\ TreeF\ a$

data *BtreeF a b* = *TipF a* | *BinF b b*
type *Btree a* = *Fix BtreeF a*

Note that the types *List* and *Tree* here are equivalent to but different from the types *List* in Section 3.1 and *Tree* in Section 3.3.

The datatype *Fix s a* is a recursive type; the type constructor *Fix* ties the recursive knot around the shape *s*. Typically, as in the three instances above, the shape *s* has several variants, including a 'base case' independent of the second argument. But with lazy evaluation, infinite structures are possible, and so the definition makes sense even with no base case. For example, the datatype *Fix ITreeF a* with shape parameter **data** *ITreeF a b* = *INodeF a b b* is a type of infinite internally labelled binary trees, which would suffice for the *cwTree* example above.

3.7   Bifunctors

Not all valid binary type constructors *s* are suitable for *Fix*ing; for example, function types with the parameter appearing in *contravariant* (source) positions cause problems. It turns out that we should restrict attention to (covariant) *bifunctors*, which support a *bimap* operation 'locating' all the elements. We capture this constraint as a type class.

class *Bifunctor s* **where**
    bimap :: $(a \to c) \to (b \to d) \to (s \, a \, b \to s \, c \, d)$

Technically speaking, *bimap* should satisfy some properties:

$$bimap \; id \; id \qquad\qquad = id$$
$$bimap \; f \; g \circ bimap \; h \; j = bimap \; (f \circ h) \; (g \circ j)$$

These properties cannot be expressed formally in most languages today, as we noted in Section 2.5, but we might expect to be able to express them in the languages of tomorrow [18,115], and they are important for reasoning about programs using *bimap*.

All sum-of-product datatypes — that is, consisting of a number of variants, each with a number of arguments — induce bifunctors. Here are instances for our three example shapes.

instance *Bifunctor ListF* **where**
    bimap f g NilF   = *NilF*
    bimap f g (*ConsF x y*) = *ConsF* (*f x*) (*g y*)
instance *Bifunctor TreeF* **where**
    bimap f g EmptyF   = *EmptyF*
    bimap f g (*NodeF x y z*) = *NodeF* (*f x*) (*g y*) (*g z*)
instance *Bifunctor BtreeF* **where**
    bimap f g (*TipF x*)   = *TipF* (*f x*)
    bimap f g (*BinF y z*) = *BinF* (*g y*) (*g z*)

The operator *bimap* is datatype-generic, since it is parametrized by the shape s of the data:

$$bimap :: Bifunctor\ s \Rightarrow (a \rightarrow c) \rightarrow (b \rightarrow d) \rightarrow (s\ a\ b \rightarrow s\ c\ d)$$

However, because *bimap* is encoded as a member function of a type class, the definitions for particular shapes are examples of ad-hoc rather than parametric datatype genericity; each instance entails a proof obligation that the appropriate laws are satisfied. It is a bit tedious to have to provide a new instance of *Bifunctor* for each new datatype shape; one would of course prefer a single datatype-generic definition. This is the kind of feature for which Generic Haskell [60] is designed, and one can almost achieve the same effect in Haskell [17,58,26]. One might hope that these instance definitions would in fact be inferred, in the languages of tomorrow [97,62]. But whatever the implementation mechanism, the result will still be ad-hoc datatype-generic: it is necessarily the case that different code is used to locate the elements within data of different shapes.

3.8   Datatype-Generic Recursion Patterns

It turns out that the class *Bifunctor* provides sufficient flexibility to capture a wide variety of recursion patterns as datatype-generic programs. The datatype-specific recursion patterns introduced above can all be made generic in a bifunctorial shape s; a little bit of ad-hockery goes a long way. (These definitions are very similar to those in the PolyP approach [68], discussed in more detail in [61, §4.2] in this volume.)

$$map :: Bifunctor\ s \Rightarrow (a \rightarrow b) \rightarrow (Fix\ s\ a \rightarrow Fix\ s\ b)$$
$$map\ f = In \circ bimap\ f\ (map\ f) \circ out$$
$$fold :: \quad Bifunctor\ s \Rightarrow (s\ a\ b \rightarrow b) \rightarrow Fix\ s\ a \rightarrow b$$
$$fold\ f = f \circ bimap\ id\ (fold\ f) \circ out$$
$$unfold :: Bifunctor\ s \Rightarrow (b \rightarrow s\ a\ b) \rightarrow b \rightarrow Fix\ s\ a$$
$$unfold\ f = In \circ bimap\ id\ (unfold\ f) \circ f$$
$$hylo :: \quad Bifunctor\ s \Rightarrow (b \rightarrow s\ a\ b) \rightarrow (s\ a\ c \rightarrow c) \rightarrow b \rightarrow c$$
$$hylo\ f\ g = g \circ bimap\ id\ (hylo\ f\ g) \circ f$$
$$build :: \quad Bifunctor\ s \Rightarrow (\forall b.\ (s\ a\ b \rightarrow b) \rightarrow b) \rightarrow Fix\ s\ a$$
$$build\ f = f\ In$$

The datatype-generic definitions are surprisingly short — shorter even than the datatype-specific ones. The structure becomes much clearer with the higher level of abstraction. In particular, the promised duality between *fold* and *unfold* is readily apparent. (But note that these datatype-generic definitions are applicable only to instantiations of *Fix*, as in Section 3.6, and not to the datatypes of the same name in Section 2.)

4 The Origami Patterns

Design patterns, as the subtitle of the seminal book [35] has it, are 'elements of reusable object-oriented software'. However, within the confines of existing mainstream programming languages, these supposedly reusable elements can only be expressed extra-linguistically: as prose, pictures, and prototypes. We believe that this is not inherent in the patterns themselves, but evidence of a lack of expressivity in those mainstream programming languages. Specifically, we argue that what those languages lack are higher-order and datatype-generic features; given such features, the code parts of some design patterns at least are expressible as directly reusable library components. The benefits of expressing patterns in this way are considerable: patterns may then be reasoned about, type-checked, applied and reused, just as any other abstraction can.

We argue our case by capturing as higher-order datatype-generic programs a small subset ORIGAMI of the Gang of Four (GOF) patterns. (Within these notes, for simplicity, we equate GOF patterns with design patterns; we use SMALL CAP-ITALS for the names of patterns.) These programs are parametrized along three dimensions: by the *shape* of the computation, which is determined by the shape of the underlying data, and represented by a type constructor (an operation on types); by the *element type* (a type); and by the *body* of the computation, which is a higher-order argument (a value, typically a function).

Although our presentation is in a functional programming style, we do not intend to argue that functional programming is the paradigm of the future (whatever we might feel personally!). Rather, we believe that functional programming languages are a suitable test-bed for experimental language features — as evidenced by parametric polymorphism and list comprehensions, for example, which are both now finding their way into mainstream programming languages such as Java and C#. We expect that the evolution of programming languages will continue to follow the same trend: experimental language features will be developed and explored in small, nimble laboratory languages, and the successful experiments will eventually make their way into the outside world. Specifically, we expect that the mainstream languages of tomorrow will be broadly similar to the mainstream languages of today — strongly and statically typed, object-oriented, with an underlying imperative approach — but incorporating additional features from the functional world — specifically, higher-order operators and datatype genericity.

4.1 The Origami Family of Patterns

In this section we describe ORIGAMI, a little suite of patterns for recursive data structures, consisting of four of the Gang of Four design patterns [35]:

- COMPOSITE, for modelling recursive structures;
- ITERATOR, for linear access to the elements of a composite;
- VISITOR, for structured traversal of a composite;
- BUILDER, to generate a composite structure.

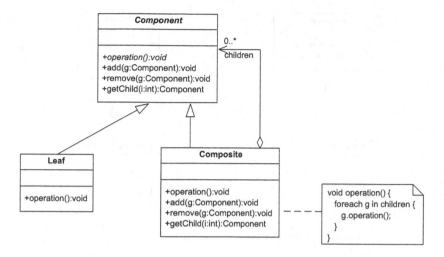

Fig. 2. The class structure of the COMPOSITE pattern

These four patterns belong together. They all revolve around the notion of a hierarchical structure, represented as a COMPOSITE. One way of constructing such hierarchies is captured by the BUILDER pattern: a client application knows what kinds of part to add and in what order, but it delegates to a separate object knowledge of their implementation and responsibility for creating and holding them. Having constructed a hierarchy, there are two kinds of traversal we might perform over it: either considering it as a container of elements, in which case we use an ITERATOR for a linear traversal; or considering its shape as significant, in which case we use a VISITOR for a structured traversal.

Composite. The COMPOSITE pattern 'lets clients treat individual objects and compositions of objects uniformly', by 'composing objects into tree structures'. The essence of the pattern is a common supertype (*Component*), of which both atomic (*Leaf*) and aggregate (*Composite*) objects are subtypes, as shown in Figure 2.

Iterator. The ITERATOR pattern 'provides a way to access the elements of an aggregate object sequentially without exposing its underlying representation'. It does this by separating the responsibilities of containment (*Aggregate*) and iteration (*Iterator*). The standard implementation is as an *external* or client-driven iterator, illustrated in Figure 3 and as embodied for example in the Java standard library.

In addition to the standard implementation, GOF also discuss *internal* or iterator-driven ITERATORs, illustrated in Figure 4. These might be modelled by the following pair of Java interfaces:

> **public interface** *Action*{ *Object apply* (*Object o*); }
> **public interface** *Iterator*{ **void** *iterate* (*Action a*); }

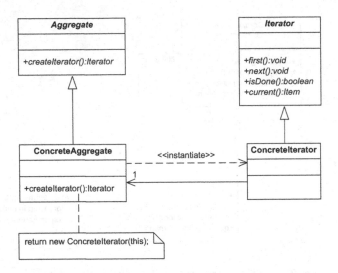

Fig. 3. The class structure of the EXTERNAL ITERATOR pattern

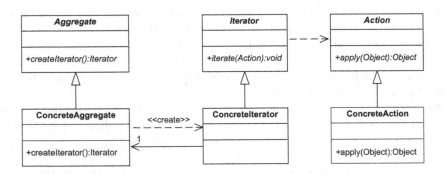

Fig. 4. The class structure of the INTERNAL ITERATOR pattern

An object implementing the *Action* interface provides a single method *apply*, which takes in a collection element and returns (either a new, or the same but modified) element. The C++ STL calls such objects 'functors', but we avoid that term here to prevent a name clash with type functors. A collection (implements a FACTORY METHOD [35] to return a separate subobject that) implements the *Iterator* interface to accept an *Action*, apply it to each element in turn, and replace the original elements with the possibly new ones returned. Internal IT-ERATORs are less flexible than external — for example, it is more difficult to have two linked iterations over the same collection, and to terminate an iteration early — but they are correspondingly simpler to use.

Visitor. In the normal object-oriented paradigm, the definition of each traversal operation is spread across the whole class hierarchy of the structure being traversed — typically but not necessarily a COMPOSITE. This makes it easy to

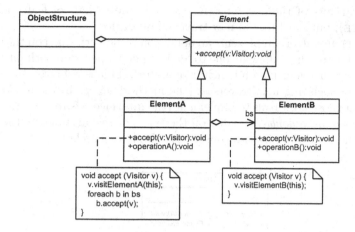

Fig. 5. The class structure of the elements in the INTERNAL VISITOR pattern

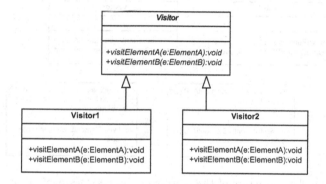

Fig. 6. The class structure of the visitors in the INTERNAL VISITOR pattern

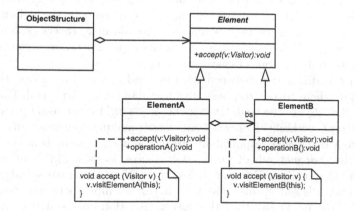

Fig. 7. The class structure of the elements in the EXTERNAL VISITOR pattern

add new variants of the datatype (for example, new kinds of leaf node in the COMPOSITE), but hard to add new traversal operations.

The VISITOR pattern 'represents an operation to be performed on the elements of an object structure', allowing one to 'define a new operation without changing the classes of the elements on which it operates'. This is achieved by providing a hook for associating new traversals (the method *accept* in Figure 5), and an interface for those traversals to implement (the interface *Visitor* in Figure 6); the effect is to simulate *double dispatch* on the types of two arguments, the element type and the operation, by two consecutive single dispatches.

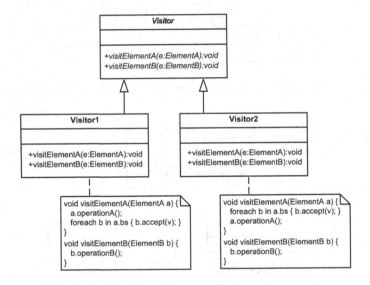

Fig. 8. The class structure of the visitors in the EXTERNAL VISITOR pattern

The pattern provides a kind of *aspect-oriented programming* [82], modularizing what would otherwise be a cross-cutting concern, namely the definition of a traversal. It reverses the costs: it is now easy to add new traversals, but hard to add new variants. (Wadler [137] has coined the term *expression problem* for this tension between dimensions of easy extension.)

As with the distinction between internal and external iterators, there is a choice about where to put responsibility for managing a traversal. Buchlovsky and Thielecke [15] use the term 'INTERNAL VISITOR' for the usual presentation, with the *accept* methods of *Element* subclasses making recursive calls as shown in Figure 5. Moving that responsibility from the *accept* methods of the *Element* classes to the *visit* methods of the *Visitor* classes, as shown in Figures 7 and 8, yields what they call an EXTERNAL VISITOR. Now the traversal algorithm is not fixed, and different visitors may vary it (for example, between preorder and postorder). One might say that this latter variation encapsulates simple case analysis or pattern matching, rather than traversals per se.

Builder. Finally, the BUILDER pattern 'separates the construction of a complex object from its representation, so that the same construction process can create different representations'. As Figure 9 shows, this is done by delegating responsibility for the construction to a separate *Builder* object — in fact, an instance of the STRATEGY pattern [35], encapsulating a strategy for performing the construction.

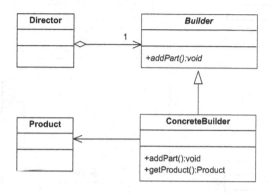

Fig. 9. The class structure of the BUILDER pattern

The GOF motivating example of the BUILDER pattern involves assembling a product that is basically a simple collection; that is necessarily the case, because the operations supported by a builder object take just a part and return no result. However, they also suggest the possibility of building a more structured product, in which the parts are linked together. For example, to construct a tree, each operation to add a part could return a unique identifier for the part added, and take an optional identifier for the parent to which to add it; a directed acyclic graph requires a set of parents for each node, and construction in topological order; a cyclic graph requires the possibility of 'forward references', adding parts as children of yet-to-be-added parents.

GOF also suggest the possibility of COMPUTING BUILDERs. Instead of constructing a large *Product* and eventually collapsing it, one can provide a separate implementation of the *Builder* interface that makes the *Product* itself the collapsed result, computing it on the fly while building.

4.2 An Application of Origami

As an example of applying the ORIGAMI patterns, consider the little document system illustrated in Figure 10. (The code for this example is presented as an appendix in Section 7.)

- The focus of the application is the COMPOSITE structure of documents: *Sections* have a *title* and a collection of sub-*Components*, and *Paragraphs* have a *body*.

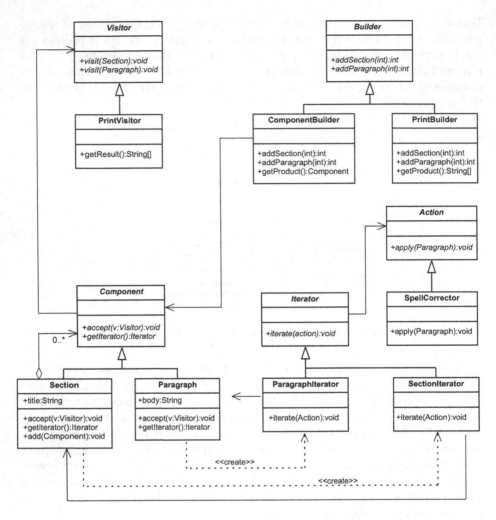

Fig. 10. An application of the ORIGAMI patterns

- One can iterate over such a structure using an INTERNAL ITERATOR, which acts on every *Paragraph*. For instance, iterating with a *SpellCorrector* might correct the spelling of every paragraph body. (For brevity, we have omitted the possibility of acting on the *Section* titles of a document, but it would be easy to extend the *Action* interface to allow this. We have also made the *apply* method return *void*, so providing no way to change the identity of the document elements; more generally, *apply* could optionally return new elements, as described under the ITERATOR pattern above.)
- One can also traverse the document structure with a VISITOR, for example to compute some summary of the document. For instance, a *PrintVisitor* might yield a string array with the section titles and paragraph bodies in order.

- Finally, one can construct such a document using a BUILDER. We have used the structured variant of the pattern, adding *Sections* and *Paragraphs* as children of existing *Components* via unique *int* identifiers (only non-negative *int*s are returned as identifiers, so a parentless node can be indicated by passing a negative *int*). A *ComponentBuilder* constructs a *Component* as expected, whereas a *PrintBuilder* is a COMPUTING BUILDER, incorporating the printing behaviour of the *PrintVisitor* incrementally and actually constructing a string array instead.

This one application is a paradigmatic example of each of the four ORIGAMI patterns. We therefore claim that any alternative representation of the patterns cleanly capturing this structure is a faithful rendition of those patterns. In Section 4.3 below, we provide just such a representation, in terms of the higher-order datatype-generic programs from Section 3.8. Section 4.4 justifies our claim of a faithful rendition by capturing the structure of the document application in this alternative representation.

4.3   Patterns as HODGPs

We now revisit the ORIGAMI patterns, showing that each of the four patterns can be captured using higher-order datatype-generic program (HODGP) constructs. However, we consider them in a slightly different order; it turns out that the datatype-generic representation of the ITERATOR pattern builds on that of VISITOR.

Composite in HODGP. COMPOSITEs are just recursive data structures. So actually, these correspond not to programs, but to types. Recursive data structures come essentially for free in functional programming languages.

$$\textbf{data } Fix\ s\ a = In\{\ out :: s\ a\ (Fix\ s\ a)\}$$

What is datatype-generic about this definition is that it is parametrized by the shape s of the data structure; thus, one recursive datatype serves to capture *all* (technically *regular*, that is, first-order fixed points of type functors admitting a *map* operation) recursive data structures, whatever their shape.

Visitor in HODGP. The VISITOR pattern collects fragments of each traversal into one place, and provides a hook for performing such traversals. The resulting style matches the normal functional-programming paradigm, in which traversals are entirely separate from the data structures traversed. No explicit hook is needed; the connection between traversal and data is made within the traversal by dispatching on the data, either by pattern matching or (equivalently) by applying a destructor. What was a double dispatch in the OO setting becomes in HODGP the choice of a function to apply, followed by a case analysis on the variant of the data structure. A common case of such traversals, albeit not the most general, is the fold operator introduced above.

$$fold \quad :: Bifunctor\ s \Rightarrow (s\ a\ b \rightarrow b) \rightarrow Fix\ s\ a \rightarrow b$$
$$fold\ f = f \circ bimap\ id\ (fold\ f) \circ out$$

This too is datatype-generic, parametrized by the shape s: the same function $fold$ suffices to traverse any shape of COMPOSITE structure.

Iterator in HODGP. EXTERNAL ITERATORs give sequential access to the elements of a collection. The functional approach would be to provide a view of the collection as a list of elements, at least for read-only access. Seen this way, the ITERATOR pattern can be implemented using the VISITOR pattern, traversing using a body *combiner* that combines the element lists from substructures into one overall element list.

$$elements :: Bifunctor\ s \Rightarrow (s\ a\ (List\ a) \rightarrow List\ a) \rightarrow Fix\ s\ a \rightarrow List\ a$$
$$elements\ combiner = fold\ combiner$$

With lazy evaluation, the list of elements can be generated incrementally on demand, rather than eagerly in advance: 'lazy evaluation means that lists and iterators over lists are identified' [136].

In the formulation above, the *combiner* argument has to be provided to the *elements* operation. Passing different *combiner*s allows the same COMPOSITE to yield its elements in different orders; for example, a tree-shaped container could support both preorder and postorder traversal. On the other hand, it is clumsy always to have to specify the *combiner*. One could specify it once and for all, in the class *Bifunctor*, in effect making it another datatype-generic operation parametrized by the shape s. In the languages of tomorrow, one might expect that at least one, obvious implementation of *combiner* could be inferred automatically.

Of course, some aspects of external ITERATORs can already be expressed linguistically; the interface *java.util.Iterator* has been available for years in the Java API, the iterator concept has been explicit in the C++ Standard Template Library for even longer, and recent versions of Java and C# even provide language support ('**foreach**') for iterating over the elements yielded by such an operator. Thus, element consumers can already be written datatype-generically today. But still, one has to implement the *Iterator* anew for each datatype defined; element producers are still datatype-specific.

An INTERNAL ITERATOR is basically a map operation, iterating over a collection and yielding one of the same shape but with different or modified elements; it therefore supports write access to the collection as well as read access. In HODGP, we can give a *single generic* definition of this.

$$map \quad :: Bifunctor\ s \Rightarrow (a \rightarrow b) \rightarrow (Fix\ s\ a \rightarrow Fix\ s\ b)$$
$$map\ f = In \circ bimap\ f\ (map\ f) \circ out$$

This is in contrast with the object-oriented approach, in which internal *Iterator* implementations are ad-hoc datatype-generic. Note also that the HODGP version is more general than the OO version, because it can safely return a collection of elements of a different type.

On the other hand, the object-oriented ITERATOR can have side-effects, which the purely functional *map* cannot; for example, it can perform I/O, accumulate a measure of the collection, and so on. However, it is possible to generalize the *map* operation considerably, capturing all those effects in a datatype-generic way. This is the subject of Section 5.

Builder in HODGP. The standard protocol for the BUILDER pattern involves a *Director* sending *Parts* one by one to a *Builder* for it to assemble, and then retrieving from the *Builder* a *Product*. Thus, the product is assembled in a step-by-step fashion, but is unavailable until assembly is complete. With lazy evaluation, we can in some circumstances construct the *Product* incrementally: we can yield access to the root of the product structure while continuing to assemble its substructures. In the case that the data structure is assembled in a regular fashion, this corresponds in the HODGP style to an unfold operation.

$$unfold \quad :: Bifunctor\ s \Rightarrow (b \rightarrow s\ a\ b) \rightarrow b \rightarrow Fix\ s\ a$$
$$unfold\ f = In \circ bimap\ id\ (unfold\ f) \circ f$$

When the data structure is assembled irregularly, a build operator has to be used instead.

$$build \quad :: Bifunctor\ s \Rightarrow (\forall b.\ (s\ a\ b \rightarrow b) \rightarrow b) \rightarrow Fix\ s\ a$$
$$build\ f = f\ In$$

These are both datatype-generic programs, parametrized by the shape of product to be built. In contrast, the GOF BUILDER pattern states the general scheme, but requires code specific for each *Builder* interface and each *ConcreteBuilder* implementation.

Turning to GOF's computing builders, with lazy evaluation there is not so pressing a need to fuse building with postprocessing. If the structure of the consumer computation matches that of the producer — in particular, if the consumer is a fold and the producer a build or an unfold — then consumption can be interleaved with production, and the whole product never need be in existence at once.

Nevertheless, naive interleaving of production and consumption of parts of the product still involves the creation and immediate disposal of those parts. Even the individual parts need never be constructed; often, they can be deforested [133], with the attributes of a part being fed straight into the consumption process. When the producer is an unfold, the composition of producer and consumer is (under certain mild strictness conditions) a hylomorphism.

$$hylo \quad :: Bifunctor\ s \Rightarrow (b \rightarrow s\ a\ b) \rightarrow (s\ a\ c \rightarrow c) \rightarrow b \rightarrow c$$
$$hylo\ f\ g = g \circ bimap\ id\ (hylo\ f\ g) \circ f$$

More generally, but harder to reason with, the producer is a build, and the composition replaces the constructors in the builder by the body of the fold.

$$\begin{aligned}
&foldBuild \quad :: Bifunctor\ s \Rightarrow (\forall b.\ (s\ a\ b \to b) \to b) \to (s\ a\ c \to c) \to c \\
&foldBuild\ f\ g = f\ g
\end{aligned}$$

(that is, $foldBuild\ f\ g = fold\ g\ (build\ f)$.) Once again, both of these definitions are datatype-generic; both take as arguments a producer f and a consumer g, both with types parametrized by the shape s of the product to be built. Note especially that in both cases, the fusion requires no creativity; in contrast, GOF's computing builders can take considerable insight and ingenuity to program — see the code for *PrintBuilder* in Section 7.14.

4.4   The Example, Revisited

To justify our claim that the higher-order datatype-generic representation of the ORIGAMI patterns is a faithful rendition, we use it to re-express the document application discussed in Section 4.2 and illustrated in Figure 10. It is instructive to compare these 40 lines of Haskell code with the equivalent Java code in Section 7.

- The COMPOSITE structure has the following shape.

  ```
  data DocF a b = Para a | Sec String [b]
  type Doc = Fix DocF String

  instance Bifunctor DocF where
      bimap f g (Para s)   = Para (f s)
      bimap f g (Sec s xs) = Sec s (map g xs)
  ```

  We have chosen to consider paragraph bodies as the 'contents' of the data structure, but section titles as part of the 'shape'; then mapping over the contents will affect the paragraph bodies but not the section titles. That decision could easily be varied.
- We used an INTERNAL ITERATOR to implement the *SpellCorrector*; this would be modelled now as an instance of *map*.

  ```
  correct :: String → String   -- definition omitted
  corrector :: Doc → Doc
  corrector = map correct
  ```

- The use of VISITOR to print the contents of a document is a paradigmatic instance of a *fold*.

  ```
  printDoc :: Doc → [String]
  printDoc = fold combine

  combine :: DocF String [String] → [String]
  combine (Para s)   = [s]
  combine (Sec s xs) = s : concat xs
  ```

- Finally, in place of the BUILDER pattern, we can use *unfold* for constructing documents, at least when doing so in a structured fashion. For example, consider the following simple representation of XML trees.

$$\textbf{data } XML = Text\ String \mid Entity\ Tag\ Attrs\ [XML]$$
$$\textbf{type } Tag\ \ = String$$
$$\textbf{type } Attrs = [(String, String)]$$

From such an XML tree we can construct a document.

$$fromXML :: XML \rightarrow Doc$$
$$fromXML = unfold\ element$$

Text elements are represented as paragraphs, and *Entity*s as sections having appropriate titles.

$$element :: XML \rightarrow DocF\ String\ XML$$
$$element\ (Text\ s)\qquad\quad = Para\ s$$
$$element\ (Entity\ t\ kvs\ xs) = Sec\ (title\ t\ kvs)\ xs$$

$$title :: Tag \rightarrow Attrs \rightarrow String$$
$$title\ t\ [\,] = t$$
$$title\ t\ kvs = t + paren\ (join\ (map\ attr\ kvs))\ \textbf{where}$$
$$\quad paren\ s\quad\ \ = "\ ("\ +\ s\ +\ ")"$$
$$\quad join\ [s]\quad\ \ = s$$
$$\quad join\ (s:ss) = s + ",\ "\ +\ join\ ss$$
$$\quad attr\ (k,v)\ \ = k + "='"\ +\ v\ +\ "'"$$

- Printing of a document constructed from an XML file is the composition of a fold with an unfold.

$$printXML :: XML \rightarrow [String]$$
$$printXML = printDoc \circ fromXML$$

It is therefore also a hylomorphism:

$$printXML = hylo\ element\ combine$$

- For constructing documents in a less structured fashion, we have to resort to the more general and more complicated *build* operator. For example, here is a builder for a simple document of one section with two sub-paragraphs.

$$docBuilder :: (DocF\ String\ b \rightarrow b) \rightarrow b$$
$$docBuilder\ f = f\ (Sec\ "\texttt{Heading}"\ [f\ (Para\ "\texttt{p1}"), f\ (Para\ "\texttt{p2}")])$$

We can actually construct the document from this builder, simply by passing it to the operator *build*, which plugs the holes with document constructors.

$$myDoc :: Doc$$
$$myDoc = build\ docBuilder$$

If we want to traverse the resulting document, for example to print it, we can do so directly without having to construct the document in the first place; we do so by plugging the holes instead with the body of the *printDoc* fold.

$$printMyDoc :: [\,String\,]$$
$$printMyDoc = docBuilder\ combine$$

5   The Essence of the Iterator Pattern

In Section 4, we argued that the ITERATOR pattern amounts to nothing more than the higher-order datatype-generic *map* operation. However, as we mentioned, there are aspects of an ITERATOR that are not adequately explained by a *map*; in particular, the possibility of effects such as I/O, and dependencies between the actions executed at each element.

For example, consider the code below, showing a C# method *loop* that iterates over a collection, counting the elements and simultaneously interacting with each of them.

```
public static int loop⟨MyObj⟩ (IEnumerable⟨MyObj⟩ coll){
    int n = 0;
    foreach (MyObj obj in coll){
        n = n + 1;
        obj.touch ();
    }
    return n;
}
```

The method is parametrized by the type *MyObj* of collection elements; this parameter is used twice: to constrain the collection *coll* passed as a parameter, and as a type for the local variable *obj*. The collection itself is rather unconstrained; it only has to implement the *IEnumerable⟨MyObj⟩* interface.

In this section, we investigate the structure of such iterations. We emphasize that we want to capture both aspects of the method *loop* and iterations like it: *mapping* over the elements, and simultaneously *accumulating* some measure of those elements. This takes us beyond the more simplistic *map* model from Section 4. We still aim to construct a *holistic* model, treating the iteration as an abstraction in its own right; this leads us naturally to a higher-order presentation. We also want to develop an *algebra* of such iterations, with combinators for composing them and laws for reasoning about them; this strengthens the case for a declarative approach. We argue that McBride and Paterson's recently introduced notion of *idioms* [95], and in particular the corresponding *traverse* operator, have exactly the right properties. (The material in this section is based on [44]; the reader is warned that this work, and especially the results in Section 5.7, is more advanced and less mature than in the earlier parts of these notes.)

5.1 Functional Iteration

In this section, we review a number of simpler approaches to capturing the essence of iteration. In particular, we look at a variety of datatype-generic recursion operators: maps, folds, unfolds, crushes, and monadic maps. The traversals we discuss in Section 5.3 generalize all of these.

Origami. We have already considered the *origami* style of programming [37,38], in which the structure of programs is captured by higher-order datatype-generic recursion operators such as *map*, *fold* and *unfold*. And we have already observed that the recursion pattern *map* captures iterations that modify each element of a collection independently; thus, *map touch* captures the mapping aspect of the C# loop above, but not the accumulating aspect.

At first glance, it might seem that the datatype-generic *fold* captures the accumulating aspect; but the analogy is rather less clear for a non-linear collection. In contrast to the C# program above, which is sufficiently generic to apply to non-linear collections, a datatype-generic counting operation defined using *fold* would need a datatype-generic numeric algebra as the fold body. Such a thing could be defined polytypically [68,60], but the fact remains that *fold* in isolation does not encapsulate the datatype genericity.

Essential to iteration in the sense we are using the term is linear access to collection elements; this was the problem with *fold*. One might consider a datatype-generic operation to yield a linear sequence of collection elements from possibly non-linear structures, for example by *fold*ing with a content combiner, or *unfold*ing to a list. This could be done (though as with the *fold* problem, it requires a datatype-generic sequence algebra or coalgebra as the body of the *fold* or *unfold*); but even then, this would address only the accumulating aspect of the C# iteration, and not the mapping aspect — it loses the shape of the original structure. Moreover, although the sequence of elements is always definable as an instance of *fold*, it is not always definable as an instance of *unfold* [46].

We might also explore the possibility of combining some of these approaches. For example, it is clear from the definitions above that *map* is an instance of *fold*. Moreover, the *banana split theorem* [31] states that two folds in parallel on the same data structure can be fused into one. Therefore, a map and a fold in parallel fuse to a single fold, yielding both a new collection and an accumulated measure, and might therefore be considered to capture both aspects of the C# iteration. However, we feel that this is an unsatisfactory solution: it may indeed simulate or implement the same behaviour, but it is no longer manifest that the shape of the resulting collection is related to that of the original.

Crush. Meertens [99] generalized APL's 'reduce' [67] to a *crush* operation, $\langle\!\langle \oplus \rangle\!\rangle :: t\, a \to a$ for binary operator $(\oplus) :: a \to a \to a$ with a unit, polytypically over the structure of a regular functor t. For example, $\langle\!\langle + \rangle\!\rangle$ polytypically sums a collection of numbers. For projections, composition, sum and fixpoint, there is an obvious thing to do, so the only ingredients that need to be provided are the binary operator (for products) and a constant (for units). Crush captures the accumulating aspect of the C# iteration above, accumulating elements independently of the shape of the data structure, but not the mapping aspect.

Monadic Map. Haskell's standard library [112] defines a *monadic map* for lists, which lifts the standard map on lists (taking a function on elements to a function on lists) to the Kleisli category (taking a monadic function on elements to a monadic function on lists):

$$mapM :: Monad\ m \Rightarrow (a \rightarrow m\ b) \rightarrow ([a] \rightarrow m\ [b])$$

(For notational brevity, we resort throughout Section 5 to the built-in type $[a]$ of lists rather than the datatype-generic type *List a*.) Fokkinga [30] showed how to generalize this from lists to an arbitrary regular functor, datatype-generically. Several authors [102,106,70,110,84] have observed that monadic map is a promising model of iteration. Monadic maps are very close to the *idiomatic traversals* that we propose as the essence of imperative iterations; indeed, for certain idioms — specifically, those that arise from monads — traversal reduces exactly to monadic map. However, we argue that monadic maps do not capture accumulating iterations as nicely as they might. Moreover, it is well-known [77,83] that monads do not compose in general, whereas it turns out that idioms do; this gives us a richer algebra of traversals. Finally, monadic maps stumble over products, for which there are two reasonable but symmetric definitions, coinciding when the monad is commutative. This stumbling block forces either a bias to left or right, or a restricted focus on commutative monads, or an additional complicating parametrization; in contrast, idioms generally have no such problem, and in fact turn it into a virtue.

Closely related to monadic maps are operations like Haskell's *sequence* function:

$$sequence :: Monad\ m \Rightarrow [m\ a] \rightarrow m\ [a]$$

and its datatype-generic generalization to arbitrary datatypes. Indeed, *sequence* and *mapM* are interdefinable:

$$mapM\ f = sequence \circ map\ f$$

and so

$$sequence = mapM\ id$$

Most writers on monadic maps have investigated such an operation; Moggi *et al.* [106] call it *passive traversal*, Meertens [100] calls it *functor pulling*, and Pardo [110] and others have called it a *distributive law*. It is related to Hoogendijk and Backhouse's *commuting relators* [65], but with the addition of the monadic structure on one of the functors. McBride and Paterson introduce the function *dist* playing the same role, but as we shall see, more generally.

5.2   Idioms

McBride and Paterson [95] recently introduced the notion of an *idiom* or *applicative functor* as a generalization of monads. ('Idiom' was the name McBride originally chose, but he and Paterson now favour the less evocative term 'applicative functor'. We prefer the original term, not least because it lends itself nicely to adjectival uses, as in 'idiomatic traversal'.) Monads [105,135] allow the expression of effectful computations within a purely functional language, but they do so by encouraging an *imperative* [114] programming style; in fact, Haskell's monadic **do** notation is explicitly designed to give an imperative feel. Since idioms generalize monads, they provide the same access to effectful computations; but they encourage a more *applicative* programming style, and so fit better within the functional programming milieu. Moreover, as we shall see, idioms strictly generalize monads; they provide features beyond those of monads. This will be important to us in capturing a wider variety of iterations, and in providing a richer algebra of those iterations.

Idioms are captured in Haskell by the following type class. (In contrast to McBride and Paterson, we insist that every *Idiom* is also a *Functor*. This entails no loss of generality, since the laws below ensure that defining *fmap f x = pure f* ⊛ *x* suffices.)

> **class** *Functor m* ⇒ *Idiom m* **where**
> $pure :: a \rightarrow m\ a$
> $(\circledast) :: m\ (a \rightarrow b) \rightarrow (m\ a \rightarrow m\ b)$

Informally, *pure* lifts ordinary values into the idiomatic world, and ⊛ provides an idiomatic flavour of function application. We make the convention that ⊛ associates to the left, just like ordinary function application.

In addition to those inherited from the *Functor* class, idioms are expected to satisfy the following laws.

$$
\begin{aligned}
pure\ id \circledast u &= u \\
pure\ (\circ) \circledast u \circledast v \circledast w &= u \circledast (v \circledast w) \\
pure\ f \circledast pure\ x &= pure\ (f\ x) \\
u \circledast pure\ x &= pure\ (\lambda f \rightarrow f\ x) \circledast u
\end{aligned}
$$

(recall that (∘) denotes function composition). These two collections of laws are together sufficient to allow any expression built from the idiom operators to be rewritten into a canonical form, consisting of a pure function applied to a series of idiomatic arguments:

$$pure\ f \circledast u_1 \circledast ... \circledast u_n$$

(In case the reader feels the need for some intuition for these laws, we refer them forwards to the stream Naperian idiom discussed below.)

Monadic Idioms. Idioms generalize monads; every monad induces an idiom, with the following operations. (Taken literally as a Haskell declaration, this code provokes complaints about overlapping instances; it is therefore perhaps better to take it as a statement of intent instead.)

> **instance** $Monad\ m \Rightarrow Idiom\ m$ **where**
> $pure\ a\quad = \mathbf{do}\ \{\, return\ a\,\}$
> $mf \circledast mx = \mathbf{do}\ \{\, f \leftarrow mf;\, x \leftarrow mx;\, return\ (f\ x)\,\}$

The *pure* operator for a monadic idiom is just the *return* of the monad; idiomatic application $\circledast$ is monadic application, here with the effects of the function preceding those of the argument. There is another, completely symmetric, definition, with the effects of the argument before those of the function. We leave it to the reader to verify that the monad laws entail the idiom laws (with either definition of monadic application).

Naperian Idioms. One of McBride and Paterson's motivating examples of an idiom arises from the environment monad:

> **newtype** $Env\ e\ a = Env\{\, unEnv :: e \to a\,\}$

The *pure* and $\circledast$ of this type turn out to be the K and S combinators, respectively.

> **instance** $Idiom\ (Env\ e)$ **where**
> $pure\ a\qquad\qquad = Env\ (\lambda e \to a)$
> $Env\ ef \circledast Env\ ex = Env\ (\lambda e \to (ef\ e)\ (ex\ e))$

One can think of instances of $Env\ e$ as datatypes with *fixed shape*, which gives rise to an interesting subclass of monadic idioms. For example, the functor *Stream* is equivalent to $Env\ Nat$; under the equivalence, the K and S combinators turn out to be the familiar 'repeat' and 'zip with apply' operators.

> **data** $Stream\ a = ConsS\ a\ (Stream\ a)$
>
> **instance** $Idiom\ Stream$ **where**
> $pure\ a\quad = repeatS\ a$
> $mf \circledast mx = zipApS\ mf\ mx$
> $repeatS\quad :: a \to Stream\ a$
> $repeatS\ x = xs\ \textbf{where}\ xs = ConsS\ x\ xs$
> $zipApS :: (a \to b \to c) \to Stream\ a \to Stream\ b \to Stream\ c$
> $zipApS\ (ConsS\ f\ fs)\ (ConsS\ x\ xs) = ConsS\ (f\ x)\ (zipApS\ fs\ xs)$

The *pure* operator lifts a value to a stream, replicating it for each element; idiomatic application is pointwise, taking a stream of functions and a stream of arguments to a stream of results. We find that this idiom is the most accessible one for understanding the idiom laws.

A similar construction works for any fixed-shape datatype: pairs, vectors of length n, two-dimensional matrices of a given size, infinite binary trees, and so on. Peter Hancock [94] calls such a datatype *Naperian*, because the environment or position type acts as a notion of logarithm. That is, datatype t is Naperian if $t \, a \simeq a^p \simeq p \to a$ for some type p of positions, called the logarithm $\log t$ of t. Then $t \, 1 \simeq 1^p \simeq 1$, so the shape is fixed, and familiar properties of logarithms arise — for example, $\log (t \circ u) \simeq \log t \times \log u$.

> **class** *Functor* $t \Rightarrow$ *Naperian* $t \, p \mid p \to t, \; t \to p$ **where**
>   *fill* $:: (p \to a) \to t \, a$ -- *index* $\circ$ *fill* $=$ *id*
>   *index* $:: t \, a \to (p \to a)$ -- *fill* $\circ$ *index* $=$ *id*
>   *indices* $:: t \, p$
>
>   *indices* $=$ *fill id*
>   *fill f* $=$ *fmap f indices*

(Here, $p \to t, t \to p$ are *functional dependencies*, indicating that each of the two parameters of the type class *Naperian* determines the other.) We leave as an exercise for the reader to show that the definitions

> *pure a* $=$ *fill* $(\lambda p \to a)$
> *mf* $\circledast$ *mx* $=$ *fill* $(\lambda p \to (index \, mf \, p) \, (index \, mx \, p))$

satisfy the idiom laws.

Naperian idioms impose a fixed and hence statically known shape on data. We therefore expect some connection with data-parallel and numerically intensive computation, in the style of Jay's language FISh [71] and its *shapely operations* [72], which separate statically analysable shape from dynamically determined contents. Computations within Naperian idioms tend to perform a transposition of results; there appears also to be some connection with what Kühne [86] calls the *transfold* operator.

The 'bind' operation of a monad allows the result of one computation to affect the choice and ordering of effects of subsequent operations. Idioms in general provide no such possibility; indeed, as we have seen, every expression built just from the idiom combinators is equivalent to a pure function applied to a series of idiomatic arguments, and so the sequencing of any effects is fixed. Focusing on the idiomatic view of a Naperian datatype, rather than the monadic view in terms of an environment, enforces that restriction. The interesting thing is that many useful computations involving monads do not require the full flexibility of dynamically chosen ordering of effects; for these, the idiomatic interface suffices.

Monoidal Idioms. Idioms strictly generalize monads; there are idioms that do not arise from monads. A third family of idioms, this time non-monadic, arises from constant functors with monoidal targets. McBride and Paterson call these *phantom idioms*, because the resulting type is a phantom type (as opposed to a container type of some kind). Any monoid $(\emptyset, \oplus)$ induces an idiom, where the *pure* operator yields the unit of the monoid and application uses the binary operator.

newtype $K\ b\ a = K\{unK :: b\}$

instance $Monoid\ b \Rightarrow Idiom\ (K\ b)$ **where**
$\quad pure\ \_ = K\ \emptyset$
$\quad x \circledast y\ = K\ (unK\ x \oplus unK\ y)$

Computations within this idiom accumulate some measure: for the monoid of integers with addition, they count or sum; for the monoid of lists with concatenation, they collect some trace of values; for the monoid of booleans with disjunction, they encapsulate linear searches; and so on. Note that sequences of one kind or another therefore form idioms in three different ways: monadic with cartesian product, modelling non-determinism; Naperian with zip, modelling data-parallelism; and monoidal with concatenation, modelling tracing.

Combining Idioms. Like monads, idioms are closed under products; so two independent idiomatic effects can generally be fused into one, their product.

data $Prod\ m\ n\ a = Prod\{pfst :: m\ a, psnd :: n\ a\}$

$fork :: (a \rightarrow m\ b) \rightarrow (a \rightarrow n\ b) \rightarrow a \rightarrow Prod\ m\ n\ b$
$fork\ f\ g\ a = Prod\ (f\ a)\ (g\ a)$

instance $(Idiom\ m, Idiom\ n) \Rightarrow Idiom\ (Prod\ m\ n)$ **where**
$\quad pure\ x\quad = Prod\ (pure\ x)\ (pure\ x)$
$\quad mf \circledast mx = Prod\ (pfst\ mf \circledast pfst\ mx)\ (psnd\ mf \circledast psnd\ mx)$

Unlike monads in general, idioms are also closed under composition; so two sequentially dependent idiomatic effects can generally be fused into one, their composition.

data $Comp\ m\ n\ a = Comp\{unComp :: m\ (n\ a)\}$

instance $(Idiom\ m, Idiom\ n) \Rightarrow Idiom\ (Comp\ m\ n)$ **where**
$\quad pure\ x\quad = Comp\ (pure\ (pure\ x))$
$\quad mf \circledast mx = Comp\ (pure\ (\circledast) \circledast unComp\ mf \circledast unComp\ mx)$

We see examples of both of these combinations in Section 5.4.

5.3   Idiomatic Traversal

Two of the three motivating examples McBride and Paterson provide for idiomatic computations, sequencing a list of monadic effects and transposing a matrix, are instances of a general scheme they call *traversal*. This involves iterating over the elements of a data structure, in the style of a 'map', but interpreting certain function applications within the idiom.

In the case of lists, traversal may be defined as follows.

$traverseL :: Idiom\ m \Rightarrow (a \rightarrow m\ b) \rightarrow ([a] \rightarrow m\ [b])$
$traverseL\ f\ []\quad\quad = pure\ []$
$traverseL\ f\ (x : xs) = pure\ (:) \circledast f\ x \circledast traverseL\ f\ xs$

A special case is for the identity function, when traversal distributes the data structure over the idiomatic structure:

$$distL :: Idiom \; m \Rightarrow [m \; a] \rightarrow m \; [a]$$
$$distL = traverseL \; id$$

The 'map within the idiom' pattern of traversal for lists generalizes to any (finite) functorial data structure. We capture this via a type class of *Traversable* data structures (again, unlike McBride and Paterson, but without loss of generality, we insist on functoriality):

> **class** *Functor t* $\Rightarrow$ *Traversable t* **where**
>   *traverse*   :: *Idiom* $m \Rightarrow (a \rightarrow m \; b) \rightarrow (t \; a \rightarrow m \; (t \; b))$
>   *dist*   :: *Idiom* $m \Rightarrow t \; (m \; a) \rightarrow m \; (t \; a)$
>   *traverse f* = *dist* $\circ$ *fmap f*
>   *dist*   = *traverse id*

As intended, this class generalizes *traverseL*:

> **instance** *Traversable* [] **where** *traverse* = *traverseL*

Although *traverse* and *dist* are interdefinable (intuitively, *dist* is to *traverse* as monadic join μ is to bind $\ggg$), so only one needs to be given, defining *traverse* and inheriting *dist* is usually simpler and more efficient than vice versa.

> **data** *Btree a* = *Tip a* | *Bin* (*Btree a*) (*Btree a*)
> **instance** *Traversable Btree* **where**
>   *traverse f* (*Tip a*)   = *pure Tip* $\circledast$ *f a*
>   *traverse f* (*Bin t u*) = *pure Bin* $\circledast$ *traverse f t* $\circledast$ *traverse f u*

McBride and Paterson propose a special syntax involving 'idiomatic brackets', which would have the effect of inserting the occurrences of *pure* and $\circledast$ implicitly; apart from these brackets, the definition of *traverse* then looks exactly like a definition of *fmap*. This definition could be derived automatically [62], or given polytypically once and for all, assuming some universal representation of datatypes such as sums and products [60] or regular functors [38]:

> **class** *Bifunctor s* $\Rightarrow$ *Bitraversable s* **where**
>   *bidist* :: *Idiom* $m \Rightarrow s \; (m \; a) \; (m \; b) \rightarrow m \; (s \; a \; b)$
> **instance** *Bitraversable s* $\Rightarrow$ *Traversable* (*Fix s*) **where**
>   *traverse f* = *fold* (*fmap In* $\circ$ *bidist* $\circ$ *bimap f id*)
> **instance** *Bitraversable BtreeF* **where**
>   *bidist* (*TipF a*)   = *pure TipF* $\circledast$ *a*
>   *bidist* (*BinF t u*) = *pure BinF* $\circledast$ *t* $\circledast$ *u*

When *m* is specialized to the identity idiom, traversal reduces to the functorial map over lists.

newtype $Id\ a = Id\{\,unId :: a\,\}$

instance $Idiom\ Id$ **where**

$\qquad pure\ a \quad = Id\ a$

$\qquad mf \circledast mx = Id\ ((unId\ mf)\ (unId\ mx))$

In the case of a monadic idiom, traversal specializes to monadic map, and has the same uses. In fact, traversal is really just a slight generalization of monadic map: generalizing in the sense that it applies also to non-monadic idioms. We consider this an interesting insight, because it reveals that monadic-map-like traversal in some sense does not require the full power of a monad; in particular, it does not require the bind or join operators, which are unavailable in idioms in general.

For a Naperian idiom, traversal transposes results. For example, interpreted in the pair Naperian idiom, *traverseL id* unzips a list of pairs into a pair of lists.

For a monoidal idiom, traversal accumulates values. For example, interpreted in the integer monoidal idiom, traversal accumulates a sum of integer measures of the elements.

$\qquad tsum :: Traversable\ t \Rightarrow (a \to Int) \to t\ a \to Int$

$\qquad tsum\ f = unK \circ traverse\ (K \circ f)$

5.4   Examples of Traversal: Shape and Contents

As well as being parametrically polymorphic in the collection elements, the generic traversal introduced above is parametrized along two further dimensions: it is ad-hoc datatype-generic in the datatype being traversed, and parametrically datatype-generic in the idiom in which the traversal is interpreted. Specializing the latter to the lists-as-monoid idiom yields a generic *contents* operation, which is in turn the basis for many other generic operations, including non-monoidal ones such as indexing:

$\qquad contents :: Traversable\ t \Rightarrow t\ a \to [\,a\,]$

$\qquad contents = unK \circ traverse\ (K \circ single)$

$\qquad single \quad :: a \to [\,a\,]$

$\qquad single\ x = [\,x\,]$

This *contents* operation yields one half of Jay's decomposition of datatypes into shape and contents [72]. The other half is obtained simply by a map, which is to say, a traversal interpreted in the identity idiom:

$\qquad shape :: Traversable\ t \Rightarrow t\ a \to t\ ()$

$\qquad shape = unId \circ traverse\ (Id \circ bang)$

$\qquad bang :: a \to ()$

$\qquad bang = const\ ()$

Of course, it is trivial to combine these two traversals to obtain both halves of the decomposition as a single function, but doing this by tupling in the obvious way entails two traversals over the data structure. Is it possible to fuse the two traversals into one? The product of idioms allows exactly this, yielding the decomposition of a data structure into shape and contents in a single pass:

$decompose' :: Traversable\ t \Rightarrow t\ a \rightarrow Prod\ Id\ (K\ [a])\ (t\ ())$
$decompose' = traverse\ (fork\ (Id \circ bang)\ (K \circ single))$

It is then a simple matter of removing the tags for the idiom product and the idioms themselves:

$decompose :: Traversable\ t \Rightarrow t\ a \rightarrow (t\ (), [a])$
$decompose = getPair \circ decompose'$

$getPair :: Prod\ Id\ (K\ b)\ a \rightarrow (a, b)$
$getPair\ xy = (unId\ (pfst\ xy), unK\ (psnd\ xy))$

Moggi et al. [106] give a similar decomposition, but using a customized combination of monads; the above approach is arguably simpler.

A similar benefit can be found in the reassembly of a full data structure from separate shape and contents. This is a stateful operation, where the state consists of the contents to be inserted; but it is also a partial operation, because the number of elements provided may not agree with the number of positions in the shape. We therefore make use of both the *State* monad and the *Maybe* monad; but this time, we form their composition rather than their product. (As it happens, the composition of the *State* and *Maybe* monads in this way forms another monad, but that is not the case in general.)

The crux of the traversal is the partial stateful function that strips the first element off the list of contents, if this list is non-empty:

$takeHead :: State\ [a]\ (Maybe\ a)$
$takeHead = \mathbf{do}\ \{ xs \leftarrow get;$
$\qquad\qquad\qquad \mathbf{case}\ xs\ \mathbf{of}$
$\qquad\qquad\qquad\quad []\qquad \rightarrow return\ Nothing$
$\qquad\qquad\qquad\quad (y : ys) \rightarrow \mathbf{do}\ \{ put\ ys; return\ (Just\ y)\} \}$

This is a composite idiomatic value, using the composition of the two monadic idioms *State* [a] and *Maybe*; traversal in the composite idiom using this operation returns a stateful function for the whole data structure.

$reassemble' :: Traversable\ t \Rightarrow t\ () \rightarrow State\ [a]\ (Maybe\ (t\ a))$
$reassemble' = unComp \circ traverse\ (\lambda() \rightarrow Comp\ takeHead)$

Now it is simply a matter of running this stateful function, and checking that the contents are entirely consumed.

$reassemble :: Traversable\ t \Rightarrow (t\ (), [a]) \rightarrow Maybe\ (t\ a)$
$reassemble\ (x, ys) = allGone\ (runState\ (reassemble'\ x)\ ys)$

$allGone :: (Maybe\ (t\ a), [a]) \rightarrow Maybe\ (t\ a)$
$allGone\ (mt, [])\qquad = mt$
$allGone\ (mt, (\_ : \_)) = Nothing$

5.5   Collection and Dispersal

We have found it convenient to consider special cases of effectful traversals in which the mapping aspect is independent of the accumulation, and vice versa.

$$
\begin{aligned}
&collect \quad :: (Traversable\ t, Idiom\ m) \Rightarrow \\
&\qquad\qquad (a \to m\ ()) \to (a \to b) \to t\ a \to m\ (t\ b) \\
&collect\ f\ g = traverse\ (\lambda a \to pure\ (\lambda() \to g\ a) \circledast f\ a) \\
&disperse :: (Traversable\ t, Idiom\ m) \Rightarrow \\
&\qquad\qquad m\ b \to (a \to b \to c) \to t\ a \to m\ (t\ c) \\
&disperse\ mb\ g = traverse\ (\lambda a \to pure\ (g\ a) \circledast mb)
\end{aligned}
$$

The first of these traversals accumulates elements effectfully, but modifies those elements purely and independently of this accumulation. The C# iteration at the start of Section 5 is an example, using the idiom of the *State* monad to capture the counting:

$$
\begin{aligned}
&loop :: Traversable\ t \Rightarrow (a \to b) \to t\ a \to State\ Int\ (t\ b) \\
&loop\ touch = collect\ (\lambda a \to \mathbf{do}\ \{n \leftarrow get; put\ (n+1)\})\ touch
\end{aligned}
$$

The second kind of traversal modifies elements effectfully but dependent on the state, evolving the state independently of the elements. An example of this is a kind of converse of counting, labelling every element with its position in order of traversal.

$$
\begin{aligned}
&label :: Traversable\ t \Rightarrow t\ a \to State\ Int\ (t\ (a, Int)) \\
&label = disperse\ step\ (,) \\
&step :: State\ Int\ Int \\
&step = \mathbf{do}\ \{n \leftarrow get; put\ (n+1); return\ n\}
\end{aligned}
$$

5.6   Backwards Traversal

Unlike the case with pure maps, the order in which elements are visited in an effectful traversal is significant; in particular, iterating through the elements backwards is observably different from iterating forwards. We can capture this reversal quite elegantly as an *idiom adapter*, via the 'marker type' *Backwards*.

$$
\begin{aligned}
&\mathbf{newtype}\ Backwards\ m\ a = B\{runB :: m\ a\} \\
&\mathbf{instance}\ Idiom\ m \Rightarrow Idiom\ (Backwards\ m)\ \mathbf{where} \\
&\quad pure\ = B \circ pure \\
&\quad f \circledast x = B\ (pure\ (\lambda x\ f \to f\ x) \circledast runB\ x \circledast runB\ f)
\end{aligned}
$$

Informally, *Backwards m* is an idiom if *m* is, but any effects happen in reverse; in this way, the symmetric 'backwards' embedding of monads into idioms referred to in Section 5.2 can be expressed in terms of the forwards embedding given there. (Such marker types are generally a useful technique for selecting a particular ad-hoc datatype-generic implementation.)

An adapter can be parcelled up existentially:

> **data** *IAdapter m* = ∀*g. Idiom* (*g m*) ⇒
> *IAdapter* (∀*a. m a* → *g m a*) (∀*a. g m a* → *m a*)
> *backwards* :: *Idiom m* ⇒ *IAdapter m*
> *backwards* = *IAdapter B runB*

and used in a parametrized traversal, for example to label backwards:

> *ptraverse* :: (*Idiom m, Traversable t*) ⇒
> *IAdapter m* → (*a* → *m b*) → *t a* → *m* (*t b*)
> *ptraverse* (*IAdapter wrap unwrap*) *f* = *unwrap* ∘ *traverse* (*wrap* ∘ *f*)
> *lebal* = *ptraverse backwards* (λ*a* → *step*)

Of course, there is a trivial *forwards* adapter too, which can be used as a default.

> **newtype** *Forwards m a* = *F*{ *runF* :: *m a*}
> **instance** *Idiom m* ⇒ *Idiom* (*Forwards m*) **where**
>   *pure* = *F* ∘ *pure*
>   *f* ⊛ *x* = *F* (*runF f* ⊛ *runF x*)
> *forwards* :: *Idiom m* ⇒ *IAdapter m*
> *forwards* = *IAdapter F runF*

5.7 Laws of Traverse

The *traverse* operator is ad-hoc datatype-generic; one must define it independently for each *Traversable* datatype (although, as noted above, its definition
is in principle derivable). The type class *Traversable* determines its signature,
but in line with other instances of genericity by signature such as *Functor* and
Monad, we should consider 'healthiness conditions' on the definition.

Free Theorems. The free theorem [117,132] arising from the type of *dist* is

> *dist* ∘ *fmap* (*fmap k*) = *fmap* (*fmap k*) ∘ *dist*

As corollaries, we get the following two free theorems of *traverse*:

> *traverse* (*g* ∘ *h*)   = *traverse g* ∘ *fmap h*
> *traverse* (*fmap k* ∘ *f*) = *fmap* (*fmap k*) ∘ *traverse f*

These laws are not constraints on the implementation of *dist* and *traverse*; they
follow automatically from their types.

Composition. We have seen that idioms compose: there is an identity idiom *Id*
and, for any two idioms *m* and *n*, a composite idiom *Comp m n*. We impose on
implementations of *dist* the constraint of respecting this compositional structure.
Specifically, the distributor *dist* respects the identity idiom:

$$dist \circ fmap\ Id = Id$$

and the composition of idioms:

$$dist \circ fmap\ Comp = Comp \circ fmap\ dist \circ dist$$

As corollaries, we get analogous properties of *traverse*.

$$\begin{aligned}
traverse\ (Id \circ f) &= Id \circ fmap\ f \\
traverse\ (Comp \circ fmap\ f \circ g) &= Comp \circ fmap\ (traverse\ f) \circ traverse\ g
\end{aligned}$$

Both of these corollaries have interesting interpretations. The first says that *traverse* interpreted in the identity idiom is essentially just *fmap*, as mentioned in Section 5.3. The second provides a fusion rule for traversals, whereby two consecutive traversals can be fused into one. We use this fusion rule in Section 5.8.

Naturality. We also impose the constraint that the distributor *dist* is *natural in the idiom*, as follows. An *idiom transformation* $\phi :: m\ a \to n\ a$ from idiom m to idiom n is a polymorphic function (natural transformation) that respects the idiom structure:

$$\begin{aligned}
\phi\ pure_m\ a &= pure_n\ a \\
\phi\ (mf \circledast_m mx) &= \phi\ mf \circledast_n \phi\ mx
\end{aligned}$$

(Here, the idiom operators are subscripted by the idiom, for clarity.) Then *dist* must satisfy the following naturality property: for idiom transformation ϕ,

$$dist_n \circ fmap\ \phi = \phi \circ dist_m$$

For example, $pure_m \circ unId$ is an idiom transformation from idiom Id to idiom m, because

$$\begin{aligned}
&pure_m \circ unId \circ pure_{Id} \\
={}& \{\ pure_{Id} = Id\ \} \\
&pure_m
\end{aligned}$$

and

$$\begin{aligned}
&pure_m\ (unId\ (mf \circledast_{Id} mx)) \\
={}& \{\ mf \circledast_{Id} mx = Id\ ((unId\ mf)\ (unId\ mx))\ \} \\
&pure_m\ ((unId\ mf)\ (unId\ mx)) \\
={}& \{\ \text{pure homomorphism}\ \} \\
&pure_m\ (unId\ mf) \circledast_m pure_m\ (unId\ mx)
\end{aligned}$$

Therefore $pure_m \circ unId$ must commute with *dist*, in the following sense:

$$dist_m \circ fmap\ (pure_m \circ unId) = pure_m \circ unId \circ dist_{Id}$$

As a consequence, we get a 'purity law':

$$traverse\ pure = pure$$

because

$$
\begin{aligned}
&traverse_m\ pure_m \\
&= \quad \{\ traverse\ \} \\
&dist_m \circ fmap\ pure_m \\
&= \quad \{\ unId \circ Id = id\ \} \\
&dist_m \circ fmap\ pure_m \circ fmap\ unId \circ fmap\ Id \\
&= \quad \{\ assumption\ \} \\
&pure_m \circ unId \circ dist_{Id} \circ fmap\ Id \\
&= \quad \{\ compositionality:\ dist_{Id} \circ fmap\ Id = Id\ \} \\
&pure_m
\end{aligned}
$$

This is an entirely reasonable property of traversal; one might say that it imposes a constraint of shape preservation. (But there is more to it than shape preservation: a traversal that twists pairs necessarily 'preserves shape', because pairs are Naperian, but still breaks this law.) For example, consider the following definition of *traverse* on binary trees, in which the two children are swapped on traversal:

> **instance** *Traversable Btree* **where**
> $traverse\ f\ (Tip\ a)\quad = pure\ Tip \circledast f\ a$
> $traverse\ f\ (Bin\ t\ u) = pure\ Bin \circledast traverse\ f\ u \circledast traverse\ f\ t$

With this definition, $traverse\ pure = pure \circ reflect$, where *reflect* (defined in Section 2.7) reverses a tree, and so the purity law does not hold; this is because the corresponding definition of *dist* is not natural in the idiom. Similarly, a definition with two copies of *traverse f t* and none of *traverse f u* makes *traverse pure* purely return a tree in which every right child has been overwritten with its left sibling. Both definitions are perfectly well-typed, but (according to our constraints) invalid.

On the other hand, the following definition, in which the traversals of the two children are swapped, but the *Bin* operator is flipped to compensate, is blameless.

> **instance** *Traversable Btree* **where**
> $traverse\ f\ (Tip\ a)\quad = pure\ Tip \circledast f\ a$
> $traverse\ f\ (Bin\ t\ u) = pure\ (flip\ Bin) \circledast traverse\ f\ u \circledast traverse\ f\ t$

(Here, $flip\ f\ x\ y = f\ y\ x$.) The effect of the reversal is that elements of the tree are traversed 'from right to left', which we consider to be a reasonable, if rather odd, definition of *traverse*. The corresponding distributor is

> $distB\ (Tip\ a)\quad = pure\ Tip \circledast a$
> $distB\ (Bin\ t\ u) = pure\ (flip\ Bin) \circledast distB\ u \circledast distB\ t$

or equivalently

$$distB = foldB\ f\ g\ \textbf{where}$$
$$f\ ma\quad = pure\ Tip \circledast ma$$
$$g\ mt\ mu = pure\ (flip\ Bin) \circledast mu \circledast mt$$

where $foldB$ is the fold for $Btree$ defined in Section 2.7, for which the free theorem turns out to be the following fusion law:

$$h \circ foldB\ f\ g = foldB\ f'\ g' \circ fmap\ h$$
$$\Leftarrow$$
$$h\ (f\ a) = f'\ (h\ a) \wedge h\ (g\ a\ b) = g'\ (h\ a)\ (h\ b)$$

We leave as a straightforward task for the reader the proof using this fusion law that

$$distB \circ fmap\ \phi = \phi \circ distB$$

Hence $distB$ is natural in the idiom, and as a consequence the purity law applies to this right-to-left traversal.

Composition of Monadic Traversals. Another consequence of naturality is a fusion law specific to monadic traversals. The natural form of composition for monadic computations is called *Kleisli composition*:

$$(\bullet) :: Monad\ m \Rightarrow (b \to m\ c) \to (a \to m\ b) \to (a \to m\ c)$$
$$(f \bullet g)\ x = \textbf{do}\ \{y \leftarrow g\ x; z \leftarrow f\ y; return\ z\}$$

The monad m is *commutative* if, for all mx and my,

$$\textbf{do}\ \{x \leftarrow mx; y \leftarrow my; return\ (x, y)\}$$
$$= \textbf{do}\ \{y \leftarrow my; x \leftarrow mx; return\ (x, y)\}$$

When interpreted in the idiom of a commutative monad m, traversals with $f :: b \to m\ c$ and $g :: a \to m\ b$ fuse:

$$traverse\ f \bullet traverse\ g = traverse\ (f \bullet g)$$

This follows from the fact that $\mu \circ unComp$ forms an idiom transformation from $Comp\ m\ m$ to m, for a commutative monad m with join operator μ. (The proof is straightforward, albeit a little messy.)

This fusion law for the Kleisli composition of monadic traversals shows the benefits of the more general idiomatic traversals quite nicely. Note that the corresponding more general fusion law for idioms in Section 5.7 allows two different idioms rather than just one; moreover, there are no side conditions concerning commutativity. The only advantage of the monadic law is that there is just one level of monad on both sides of the equation; in contrast, the idiomatic law has two levels of idiom, because there is no analogue of the μ operator of a monad for collapsing two levels to one (and besides, those two levels may be for different idioms).

We conjecture (but have not proved) that the monadic traversal fusion law also holds even if m is not commutative, provided that f and g themselves commute ($f \bullet g = g \bullet f$); but this no longer follows from naturality of the distributor in any simple way, and it imposes the alternative constraint that the three types a, b, c are equal.

No Duplication. Another constraint we impose upon a definition of *traverse* is that it should visit each element precisely once. For example, we consider this definition of *traverse* on lists to be bogus, because it visits each element twice.

> **instance** *Traversable* [] **where**
> *traverse f* [ ]　　　 = *pure* [ ]
> *traverse f* (*x* : *xs*) = *pure* (*const* (:)) ⊛ *f x* ⊛ *f x* ⊛ *traverse f xs*

Note that this definition satisfies the purity law above; but we would still like to rule it out.

This axiom is harder to formalize, and we do not yet have a nice theoretical treatment of it. One way of proceeding is in terms of indexing. We require that the function *labels* returns an initial segment of the natural numbers, where

> *labels* :: *Traversable t* $\Rightarrow$ *t a* $\rightarrow$ [*Int*]
> *labels t* = *contents* \$ *fmap snd* \$ *fst* \$ *runState* (*label t*) 0

Here, \$ denotes function application, and *label* is as defined in Section 5.5. The bogus definition of *traverse* on lists given above is betrayed by the fact that we get *labels* "abc" = [1, 1, 3, 3, 5, 5], which is not an initial segment of the naturals.

5.8　Example

As a small example of fusion of traversals, we consider the familiar *repmin* problem [11]. The task here is to take a binary tree of integers, compute the minimum element, then replace every element of the tree by that minimum — but to do so in a single traversal rather than the obvious two. Our point here is not the circularity for which the problem was originally invented, but simply an illustration of the two kinds of traversal (mapping and accumulating) and their fusion.

Flushed with our success at capturing different kinds of traversal idiomatically, we might try computing the minimum in a monoidal idiom,

> **newtype** *Min a* = *Min*{ *unMin* :: *a* }
> **instance** (*Ord a*, *Bounded a*) $\Rightarrow$ *Monoid* (*Min a*) **where**
> $\emptyset$　　　 = *Min maxBound*
> $x \oplus y$ = *Min* (*unMin x* '*min*' *unMin y*)
> *tmin*$_1$ :: (*Ord a*, *Bounded a*) $\Rightarrow$ *a* $\rightarrow$ *K* (*Min a*) *a*
> *tmin*$_1$ = *K* ∘ *Min*

and replacing in the idiom of the environment monad.

$$trep_1 :: a \rightarrow Env\ b\ b$$
$$trep_1 = \lambda a \rightarrow Env\ id$$

These two compose elegantly (modulo the type isomorphisms):

$$trepmin_1 :: (Ord\ a, Bounded\ a) \Rightarrow Btree\ a \rightarrow Btree\ a$$
$$trepmin_1\ t = unEnv\ (traverse\ trep_1\ t)\ (unMin\ \$\ unK\ \$\ traverse\ tmin_1\ t)$$

However, the two traversals do not fuse: the first traversal computes the minimum and discards the tree, which then needs to be reintroduced for the second traversal.

Notice that $trepmin_1$ could be datatype-generic in the data structure traversed; the only constraint is that it should be *Traversable*.

$$grepmin_1 :: (Ord\ a, Bounded\ a, Traversable\ t) \Rightarrow t\ a \rightarrow t\ a$$
$$grepmin_1\ t = unEnv\ (traverse\ trep_1\ t)\ (unMin\ \$\ unK\ \$\ traverse\ tmin_1\ t)$$

The same observation applies to all versions of *trepmin* in this section; but to avoid carrying the *Traversable t* context around, we specialize to *Btree* throughout.

The problem with $trepmin_1$ is that the traversal that computes the minimum discards the tree. Apparently this first phase ought to retain and return the tree as well; this suggests using the idiom of the state monad. The state records the minimum element; the first traversal updates this state, and the second traversal reads from it.

$$tmin_2 :: Ord\ a \Rightarrow a \rightarrow State\ a\ a$$
$$tmin_2\ a = \mathbf{do}\ \{\ b \leftarrow get;\ put\ (min\ a\ b);\ return\ a\ \}$$

$$trep_2\ :: a \rightarrow State\ a\ a$$
$$trep_2\ a\ = get$$

Again, traversals with $tmin_2$ and $trep_2$ compose.

$$trepmin_2 :: (Ord\ a, Bounded\ a) \Rightarrow Btree\ a \rightarrow Btree\ a$$
$$trepmin_2\ t = fst\ (runState\ iteration\ maxBound)$$
$$\mathbf{where}\ iteration = (traverse\ trep_2 \bullet traverse\ tmin_2)\ t$$

But when we try to apply the fusion law for monadic traversals, we are forced to admit that the *State* monad is the epitome of a non-commutative monad, and in particular that the two stateful operations $tmin_2$ and $trep_2$ do not commute; therefore, the two traversals do not fuse.

There is a simple way to make the two stateful operations commute, and that is by giving them separate parts of the state on which to act. The following implementation uses a pair as the state; the first component is where the minimum element is accumulated, and the second component holds what is copied across the tree.

$tmin_3 :: Ord\ a \Rightarrow a \rightarrow State\ (a, b)\ a$
$tmin_3\ a = \textbf{do}\ \{(a', b) \leftarrow get; put\ (min\ a\ a', b); return\ a\}$
$trep_3 :: a \rightarrow State\ (a, b)\ b$
$trep_3\ a = \textbf{do}\ \{(a', b) \leftarrow get; return\ b\}$

Of course, the whole point of the exercise is that the two parts of the state *should* interact; but with lazy evaluation we can use the standard circular programming trick that originally motivated the repmin problem [11] to tie the two together, outside the traversal.

$trepmin_3 :: (Ord\ a, Bounded\ a) \Rightarrow Btree\ a \rightarrow Btree\ a$
$trepmin_3\ t = \textbf{let}\ (u, (m, \_)) = runState\ iteration\ (maxBound, m)\ \textbf{in}\ u$
  where $iteration = (traverse\ trep_3 \bullet traverse\ tmin_3)\ t$

Now, although the *State* monad is not commutative, the two stateful operations $tmin_3$ and $trep_3$ commute (because they do not interfere), and the two traversals may be fused into one.

$trepmin'_3 :: (Ord\ a, Bounded\ a) \Rightarrow Btree\ a \rightarrow Btree\ a$
$trepmin'_3\ t = \textbf{let}\ (u, (m, \_)) = runState\ iteration\ (maxBound, m)\ \textbf{in}\ u$
  where $iteration = traverse\ (trep_3 \bullet tmin_3)\ t$

Modifying the stateful operations in this way to keep them from interfering is not scalable, and it is not clear whether this trick is possible in general anyway. Fortunately, idioms provide a much simpler means of fusion. Using the same single-component stateful operations $tmin_2$ and $trep_2$ as above, but dispensing with Kleisli composition, we get the following composition of traversals.

$trepmin_4 :: (Ord\ a, Bounded\ a) \Rightarrow Btree\ a \rightarrow Btree\ a$
$trepmin_4\ t = \textbf{let}\ (sf, m) = runState\ iteration\ maxBound$
        in $fst\ (runState\ sf\ m)$
  where $iteration = fmap\ (traverse\ trep_2)\ (traverse\ tmin_2\ t)$

Kleisli composition has the effect of flattening two levels into one; here we have to deal with both levels separately, hence the two occurrences of *runState*. The payback is that fusion of idiomatic traversals applies without side conditions!

$trepmin'_4 :: (Ord\ a, Bounded\ a) \Rightarrow Btree\ a \rightarrow Btree\ a$
$trepmin'_4\ t = \textbf{let}\ (sf, m) = runState\ iteration\ maxBound$
        in $fst\ (runState\ sf\ m)$
  where $iteration = unComp\ \$\ traverse\ (Comp \circ fmap\ trep_2 \circ tmin_2)\ t$

Note that the Kleisli composition of two monadic computations imposes the constraint that both computations are in the same monad; in our example above, both computing the minimum and distributing the result use the *State* monad. However, these two monadic computations are actually rather different in structure, and use different aspects of the *State* monad: the first writes, whereas the second reads. We could capture this observation directly by using two different monads, each tailored for its particular use.

$$tmin_5 :: (Ord\ a, Bounded\ a) \Rightarrow a \rightarrow Writer\ (Min\ a)\ a$$
$$tmin_5\ a = \mathbf{do}\ \{\ tell\ (Min\ a);\ return\ a\ \}$$
$$trep_5 :: a \rightarrow Reader\ a\ a$$
$$trep_5\ a = ask$$

Here, *tell* adds a value to a monoidal state, returning unit, and *ask* retrieves the state.

$$\mathbf{newtype}\ Writer\ s\ a = Writer\{\ runWriter :: (a, s)\ \}$$
$$tell :: Monoid\ s \Rightarrow s \rightarrow Writer\ s\ ()$$
$$\mathbf{newtype}\ Reader\ s\ a = Reader\{\ runReader :: s \rightarrow a\ \}$$
$$ask :: Reader\ s\ s$$

The use of two different monads like this rules out Kleisli composition. However, idiomatic composition handles two different idioms (and hence two different monads) with aplomb.

$$trepmin_5 :: (Ord\ a, Bounded\ a) \Rightarrow Btree\ a \rightarrow Btree\ a$$
$$trepmin_5\ t = \mathbf{let}\ (r, m) = runWriter\ iteration\ \mathbf{in}\ runReader\ r\ (unMin\ m)$$
$$\mathbf{where}\ iteration = fmap\ (traverse\ trep_5)\ (traverse\ tmin_5\ t)$$

These two traversals fuse in exactly the same way as before.

$$trepmin'_5 :: (Ord\ a, Bounded\ a) \Rightarrow Btree\ a \rightarrow Btree\ a$$
$$trepmin'_5\ t = \mathbf{let}\ (r, m) = runWriter\ iteration\ \mathbf{in}\ runReader\ r\ (unMin\ m)$$
$$\mathbf{where}\ iteration = unComp\ \$\ traverse\ (Comp \circ fmap\ trep_5 \circ tmin_5)\ t$$

6   Conclusions

The material in these lecture notes owes much to the work of a number of colleagues. Section 2 builds on many discussions with colleagues in and around the *Datatype-Generic Programming* project at Oxford and Nottingham. My views on origami programming in Section 3 are based on ideas from the Algebra of Programming ('Squiggol') community, and especially the work of: Roland Backhouse and Grant Malcolm [92,7,6]; Richard Bird and Oege de Moor [9,10]; Maarten Fokkinga, Erik Meijer and Ross Paterson [32,101]; Johan Jeuring, Patrik Jansson, Ralf Hinze and Andres Löh [68,69,57,60,91]; and John Hughes [66]. The analogy between design patterns and higher-order datatype-generic programs discussed in Section 4 elaborates on arguments developed in a course presented while on sabbatical at the University of Canterbury in New Zealand in early 2005, and explored further at tutorials at ECOOP [39] and OOPSLA [40] later that year; the contribution of participants at those venues and at less formal presentations of the same ideas is gratefully acknowledged. The results reported in Section 5 are the outcome of joint work with Bruno Oliveira, and have benefited greatly from discussions with Conor McBride and Ross Paterson, whose work provided most of the technical results. To all of these people, and to the unnamed others who have also contributed, I am very grateful for encouragement, inspiration and insight. I would like to add final thanks to Andres Löh and Ralf Hinze for their extremely useful lhs2TEX translator.

References

1. Reference manual for the Ada programming language. American National Standards Institute, Inc., ANSI/MIL-STD-1815A-1983 (1983)
2. Aigner, M., Ziegler, G.M.: Proofs from The Book, 3rd edn. Springer, Heidelberg (2004)
3. Alexandrescu, A.: Modern C++ Design. Addison-Wesley, Reading (2001)
4. Austern, M.: Generic Programming and the STL: Using and Extending the C++ Standard Template Library. Addison-Wesley, Reading (1998)
5. Backhouse, R.C., Carré, B.A.: Regular algebra applied to path-finding problems. Journal of the Institute of Mathematics and Applications 15, 161–186 (1975)
6. Backhouse, R., Hoogendijk, P.: FIP TC2/WG2.1 State-of-the-Art Report on Formal Program Development. In: Möller, B., Schuman, S., Partsch, H. (eds.) Formal Program Development. LNCS, vol. 755, pp. 7–42. Springer, Heidelberg (1993)
7. Backhouse, R.C., Jansson, P., Jeuring, J., Meertens, L.G.L.T.: Generic programming: An introduction. In: Swierstra, S.D., Oliveira, J.N. (eds.) AFP 1998. LNCS, vol. 1608, pp. 28–115. Springer, Heidelberg (1999)
8. Bidoit, M., Mosses, P.: User Manual. In: Bidoit, M., Mosses, P.D. (eds.) CASL User Manual. LNCS, vol. 2900, Springer, Heidelberg (2004)
9. Bird, R., de Moor, O.: The Algebra of Programming. Prentice-Hall, Englewood Cliffs (1996)
10. Bird, R., de Moor, O., Hoogendijk, P.: Generic functional programming with types and relations. Journal of Functional Programming 6(1), 1–28 (1996)
11. Bird, R.S.: Using circular programs to eliminate multiple traversals of data. Acta Informatica 21, 239–250 (1984)
12. Bird, R.S.: Lectures on constructive functional programming. In: Broy, M. (ed.) Constructive Methods in Computer Science, pp. 151–218. Springer, Heidelberg Also available as Technical Monograph PRG-69, from the Programming Research Group, Oxford University (1988)
13. Bracha, G., Cohen, N., Kemper, C., Marx, S., Odersky, M., Panitz, S.-E., Stoutamire, D., Thorup, K., Wadler, P.: Add generic types to the Java programming language (April 2001), JSR 14 http://www.jcp.org/en/jsr/detail?id=014
14. Bronstein, M., Burge, W., Daly, T., Davenport, J., Dewar, M., Dunstan, M., Fortenbacher, A., Gianni, P., Grabmeier, J., Guidry, J., Jenks, R., Lambe, L., Monagan, M., Morrison, S., Sit, W., Steinbach, J., Sutor, R., Trager, B., Watt, S., Wen, J., Williamson, C.: The Thirty-Year Horizon (2003), http://wiki.axiom-developer.org/Mirrors?go=/public/book2.pdf
15. Buchlovsky, P., Thielecke, H.: A type-theoretic reconstruction of the Visitor pattern. In: 21st Conference on Mathematical Foundations of Programming Semantics. Electronic Notes in Theoretical Computer Science, vol. 155 (2005)

16. Cardelli, L., Wegner, P.: On understanding types, data abstraction and polymorphism. ACM Computing Surveys 17(4), 471–522 (1985)
17. Cheney, J., Hinze, R.: A lightweight implementation of generics and dynamics. In: Haskell Workshop, pp. 90–104 (2002)
18. Claessen, K., Hughes, J.: Specification based testing with QuickCheck. In: Gibbons, de Moor[45], pp. 17–40
19. Clarke, D., Löh, A., Haskell, G.: specifically. In: Gibbons, Jeuring [47], pp. 21–47
20. Mosses, P.D. (ed.): CASL Reference Manual. LNCS, vol. 2960. Springer, Heidelberg (2004)
21. Cormen, T.H., Leiserson, C.E., Rivest, R.L.: Introduction to Algorithms. MIT Press, Cambridge (1990)
22. Czarnecki, K., Eisenecker, U.: Generative Programming: Methods, Tools and Applications. Addison-Wesley, Reading (2000)
23. Damas, L., Milner, R.: Principal type schemes for functional programs. In: Principles of Programming Languages, pp. 207–212 (1982)
24. Day, N., Launchbury, J., Lewis, J.: Logical abstractions in haskell. In: Haskell Workshop. Utrecht University Department of Computer Science, Technical Report UU-CS-1999-28 (October 1999)
25. Dehnert, J., Stepanov, A.: Fundamentals of generic programming. In: Jazayeri, M., Musser, D.R., Loos, R.G.K. (eds.) Generic Programming. LNCS, vol. 1766, pp. 1–11. Springer, Heidelberg (2000)
26. dos Santos Oliveira, B.C., Gibbons, J.: TypeCase: A design pattern for type-indexed functions. In: Leijen, D. (ed.) Haskell Workshop (2005)
27. Edmonds, J.: Matroids and the Greedy Algorithm. Mathematical Programming 1, 125–136 (1971)
28. Ehrig, H., Mahr, B.: Fundamentals of Algebraic Specification 1: Equations and Initial Semantics. Springer, Heidelberg (1985)
29. Ehrig, H., Mahr, B.: Fundamentals of Algebraic Specification 2: Module Specifications and Constraints. Springer, Heidelberg (1990)
30. Fokkinga, M.: Monadic maps and folds for arbitrary datatypes. Department INF, Universiteit Twente (June 1994)
31. Fokkinga, M.M.: Tupling and mutumorphisms. The Squiggolist 1(4), 81–82 (1990)
32. Fokkinga, M.M., Meijer, E.: Program calculation properties of continuous algebras. Technical Report CS-R9104, CWI, Amsterdam (January 1991)
33. Forman, I.R., Danforth, S.: Putting Metaclasses to Work. Addison-Wesley, Reading (1999)
34. Gamma, E., Beck, K.: JUnit: Testing resources for extreme programming (2000) http://www.junit.org/
35. Gamma, E., Helm, R., Johnson, R., Vlissides, J.: Design Patterns: Elements of Reusable Object-Oriented Software. Addison-Wesley, Reading (1995)
36. Ghani, N., Uustalu, T., Vene, V.: Build, augment and destroy, universally. In: Chin, W.-N. (ed.) APLAS 2004. LNCS, vol. 3302, Springer, Heidelberg (2004)
37. Gibbons, J.: Calculating functional programs. In: Blackhouse, R., Crole, R.L., Gibbons, J. (eds.) Algebraic and Coalgebraic Methods in the Mathematics of Program Construction. LNCS, vol. 2297, pp. 148–203. Springer, Heidelberg (2002)
38. Gibbons, J.: Origami programming. In Gibbons, de Moor [45], pp. 41–60
39. Gibbons, J.: Design patterns as higher-order datatype-generic programs (June 2005), Tutorial presented at ECOOP http://2005.ecoop.org/8.html
40. Gibbons, J.: Design patterns as higher-order datatype-generic programs (October 2005) Tutorial presented at OOPSLA http://www.oopsla.org/2005/ShowEvent.do?id=121

41. Gibbons, J.: Design patterns as higher-order datatype-generic programs. In: Hinze, R. (ed.) Workshop on Generic Programming (September 2006)
42. Gibbons, J.: Metamorphisms: Streaming representation-changers. Science of Computer Programming 65, 108–139 (2007)
43. Gibbons, J., Backhouse, R., Oliveira, B., Reig, F.: Datatype-generic programming project (2003), http://web.comlab.ox.ac.uk/oucl/research/pdt/ap/dgp/
44. Gibbons, J., Oliveira, B.C.d.S.: The essence of the Iterator pattern. In: Uustalu, T., McBride, C. (eds.) Mathematically-Structured Functional Programming (2006)
45. Gibbons, J., de Moor, O. (eds.).: The Fun of Programming. Cornerstones in Computing, Palgrave (2003) ISBN 1-4039-0772-2
46. Gibbons, J., Hutton, G., Altenkirch, T.: When is a function a fold or an unfold? Electronic Notes in Theoretical Computer Science. In: Proceedings of Coalgebraic Methods in Computer Science, vol. 44(1) (2001)
47. Gibbons, J., Jeuring, J.: Generic Programming. Kluwer Academic Publishers, Dordrecht (2003)
48. Gibbons, J., Jones, G.: The under-appreciated unfold. In: Proceedings of the Third ACM SIGPLAN International Conference on Functional Programming, pp. 273–279, Baltimore, Maryland (September 1998)
49. Gibbons, J., Lester, D., Bird, R.: Enumerating the rationals. Journal of Functional Programming 16, 281–291 (2006)
50. Gill, A., Launchbury, J., Peyton Jones, S.: A short cut to deforestation. In: Functional Programming Languages and Computer Architecture (1993)
51. Girard, J.-Y.: Interprétation Fonctionnelle et Élimination des Coupures de l'Arithmétique d'Ordre Supérieur. PhD thesis, Université de Paris VII (1972)
52. Gorlatch, S., Lengauer, C.: Parallelization of divide-and-conquer in the Bird-Meertens Formalism. Formal Aspects of Computing 3 (1995)
53. Gregor, D., Järvi, J., Siek, J.G., Reis, G.D., Stroustrup, B., Lumsdaine, A.: Concepts: Linguistic support for generic programming in C++. In: Object-Oriented Programming, Systems, Languages, and Applications (2006)
54. Gregor, D., Schupp, S.: Making the usage of STL safe. In: Gibbons, Jeuring [47], pp. 127–140
55. Guttag, J.V., Horning, J.J., Garland, S.J., Jones, K.D., Modet, A., Wing, J.M.: Larch: Languages and Tools for Formal Specification. Texts and Monographs in Computer Science. Springer, New York (1993)
56. Hagino, T.: A Categorical Programming Language. PhD thesis, Department of Computer Science, University of Edinburgh (September 1987)
57. Hinze, R.: Polytypic values possess polykinded types. In: Backhouse, R.C., Oliveira, J.N. (eds.) MPC 2000. LNCS, vol. 1837, pp. 2–27. Springer, Heidelberg (2000)
58. Hinze, R.: Generics for the masses. In: International Conference on Functional Programming, pp. 236–243. ACM Press, New York (2004)
59. Hinze, R.: Church numerals, twice! Journal of Functional Programming 15(1), 1–13 (2005)
60. Hinze, R., Jeuring, J.: Generic Haskell: Practice and theory. In: Backhouse, R., Gibbons, J. (eds.) Generic Programming. LNCS, vol. 2793, pp. 1–56. Springer, Heidelberg (2003)
61. Hinze, R., Jeuring, J., Löh, A.: Comparing approaches to generic programming in Haskell. In this volume (2006)
62. Hinze, R., Peyton Jones, S.: Derivable type classes. In: Haskell Workshop (2000)

63. Hinze, R., Löh, A.: Generic programming, now! In this volume (2006)
64. Hoare, C.A.R.: Notes on data structuring. In: Dahl, O.-J., Dijkstra, E.W., Hoare, C.A.R. (eds.) Structured Programming, APIC studies in data processing, pp. 83–174. Academic Press, London (1972)
65. Hoogendijk, P., Backhouse, R.: When do datatypes commute? In: Moggi, E., Rosolini, G. (eds.) CTCS 1997. LNCS, vol. 1290, pp. 242–260. Springer, Heidelberg (1997)
66. Hughes, J.: Why functional programming matters. Computer Journal 32(2), 98–107 (1989)
67. Iverson, K.E.: A Programming Language. Wiley, Chichester (1962)
68. Jansson, P., Jeuring, J.: PolyP - a polytypic programming language extension. In: Principles of Programming Languages, pp. 470–482 (1997)
69. Jansson, P.: Functional Polytypic Programming. PhD thesis, Computing Science, Chalmers University of Technology and Göteborg University, Sweden (May 2000)
70. Jansson, P., Jeuring, J.: Polytypic data conversion programs. Science of Computer Programming 43(1), 35–75 (2002)
71. Jay, B., Steckler, P.: The functional imperative: Shape! In: Hankin, C. (ed.) ESOP 1998 and ETAPS 1998. LNCS, vol. 1381, pp. 139–153. Springer, Heidelberg (1998)
72. Jay, C.B.: A semantics for shape. Science of Computer Programming 25(2-3), 251–283 (1995)
73. Jenks, R.D., Sutor, R.S.: Axiom: The Scientific Computing System. Springer, Heidelberg (1992)
74. Jensen, K., Wirth, N.: Pascal User Manual and Report. Springer, Heidelberg (1975)
75. Jesperson, H.: POSIX shell and utilities (p1003.2) (September 1991), Draft 11.2 http://www.nic.funet.fi/pub/doc/posix/p1003.2/
76. Jeuring, J., Meijer, E.: In: Jeuring, J., Meijer, E. (eds.) Advanced Functional Programming. LNCS, vol. 925, Springer, Heidelberg (1995)
77. Jones, M.P., Duponcheel, L.: Composing monads. Technical Report RR-1004, Department of Computer Science, Yale (December 1993)
78. Kabanov, J., Vene, V.: Recursion schemes for dynamic programming. In: Uustalu, T. (ed.) MPC 2006. LNCS, vol. 4014, Springer, Heidelberg (2006)
79. Kahn, J.: It's alive! Wired, 10.03:72-77 (March 2002)
80. Kennedy, A., Syme, D.: Design and implementation of generics for the.NET Common Language Runtime. In: Programming Language Design and Implementation, Snowbird, Utah, pp. 1–12 (2001)
81. Kiczales, G., des Riviéres, J., Bobrow, D.G.: The Art of the Metaobject Protocol. MIT Press, Cambridge (1991)
82. Kiczales, G., Lamping, J., Menhdhekar, A., Maeda, C., Lopes, C., Loingtier, J.-M., Irwin, J.: Aspect-oriented programming. In: Aksit, M., Matsuoka, S. (eds.) ECOOP 1997. LNCS, vol. 1241, pp. 220–242. Springer, Heidelberg (1997)
83. King, D.J., Wadler, P.: Combining monads. In: Launchbury, J., Sansom, P.M. (eds.) Functional Programming, Glasgow 1992, Springer, Heidelberg (1993)
84. Kiselyov, O., Lämmel, R.: Haskell's Overlooked Object System. Technical Report cs/0509027, arXiv.org (September 2005)
85. Korte, B., Lovász, L., Schrader, R.: Greedoids. Springer, Heidelberg (1991)
86. Kühne, T.: Internal iteration externalized. In: Guerraoui, R. (ed.) ECOOP 1999. LNCS, vol. 1628, pp. 329–350. Springer, Heidelberg (1999)
87. Lazic, R.: A Semantic Study of Data Independence with Applications to Model Checking. D.Phil. thesis, Oxford University Computing Laboratory (1999)

88. Lazic, R., Nowak, D.: On a semantic definition of data independence. In: Hofmann, M.O. (ed.) TLCA 2003. LNCS, vol. 2701, pp. 226–240. Springer, Heidelberg Technical Report CS-RR-392, Department of Computer Science, University of Warwick (2003)

89. Liskov, B.: A history of CLU. ACM SIGPLAN Notices 28(3), 133–147 (1993)

90. Liskov, B., Guttag, J.: Abstraction and Specification in Program Development. MIT Electrical Engineering and Computer Science Series. MIT Press, Cambridge (1986)

91. Löh, A.:Exploring Generic Haskell. PhD thesis, Utrecht University (2004)

92. Malcolm, G.: Data structures and program transformation. Science of Computer Programming 14, 255–279 (1990)

93. Martin, U., Nipkow, T.: Automating Squiggol. In: Broy, M., Jones, C.B. (eds.) IFIP TC2 Working Conference on Programming Concepts and Methods, Sea of Galilee, Israel, pp. 233–246. North-Holland, Amsterdam (1990)

94. McBride, C.: Naperian functors. Personal communication by email (5th April 2006)

95. McBride, C., Paterson, R.: Applicative programming with effects. Journal of Functional Programming (to appear)

96. McKinna, J.: Why dependent types matter. In: Principles of Programming Languages (2006)

97. Meacham, J.: DrIFT homepage (2004), http://repetae.net/ john/computer/ haskell/DrIFT/

98. Meertens, L.: Paramorphisms. Formal Aspects of Computing 4(5), 413–424 (1992)

99. Meertens, L.: Calculate polytypically! In: Kuchen, H., Swierstra, S.D. (eds.) PLILP 1996. LNCS, vol. 1140, pp. 1–16. Springer, Heidelberg (1996)

100. Meertens, L.: Functor pulling. In: Backhouse, R., Sheard, T. (eds.) Workshop on Generic Programming, Marstrand, Sweden (1998)

101. Meijer, E., Fokkinga, M., Paterson, R.: Functional programming with bananas, lenses, envelopes and barbed wire. In: Hughes, J. (ed.) Functional Programming Languages and Computer Architecture. LNCS, vol. 523, pp. 124–144. Springer, Heidelberg (1991)

102. Meijer, E., Jeuring, J.: Merging monads and folds for functional programming. In: Jeuring and Meijer [76]

103. Milner, R.: A theory of type polymorphism in programming. Journal of Computer and System Sciences 17, 348–375 (1978)

104. Milner, R., Tofte, M., Harper, R., MacQueen, D.: Definition of Standard ML. revised edn., MIT Press, Cambridge (1997)

105. Moggi, E.: Notions of computation and monads. Information and Computation 93(1) (1991)

106. Moggi, E., Bellé, G., Barry Jay, C.: shapely functors and traversals. In: Hoffman, M., Pavlovic, D., Rosolini, P. (eds.) Category Theory in Computer Science (1999)

107. Musser, D.R., Stepanov, A.A.: The Ada Generic Library linear list processing packages. Springer, New York (1989)

108. Naur, P., Backus, J.W., Bauer, F.L., Green, J., Katz, C., McCarthy, J., Perlis, A.J., Rutishauser, H., Samelson, K., Vauquois, B., Wegstein, J.H., van Wijngaarden, A., Woodger, M.: Revised report on the algorithmic language ALGOL 60. Communications of the ACM 6(1), 1–17 (1963)

109. Pardo, A.: Fusion of recursive programs with computation effects. Theoretical Computer Science 260, 165–207 (2001)

110. Pardo, A.: Combining datatypes and effects. In: Vene, V., Uustalu, T. (eds.) AFP 2004. LNCS, vol. 3622, pp. 171–209. Springer, Heidelberg (2005)

111. Perlis, A.J., Samelson, K.: Preliminary report: International Algebraic Language. Communications of the ACM 1(12), 8–22 (1958)
112. Peyton Jones, S.: The Haskell 98 Language and Libraries: The Revised Report. Cambridge University Press, Cambridge (2003)
113. Peyton Jones, S., Vytiniotis, D., Weirich, S., Washburn, G.: Simple unification-based type inference for generalized algebraic data types. In: International Conference on Functional Programming (2006)
114. Peyton Jones, S., Wadler, P.: Imperative functional programming. In: Principles of Programming Languages, pp. 71–84 (1993)
115. Programatica Team. Programatica tools for certifiable, auditable development of high-assurance systems in Haskell. In: High Confidence Software and Systems Conference. National Security Agency (April 2003)
116. Reynolds, J.C.: Towards a theory of type structure. In: Robinet, B. (ed.) Programming Symposium. LNCS, vol. 19, pp. 408–425. Springer, Heidelberg (1974)
117. Reynolds, J.C.: Types, abstraction and parametric polymorphism. In: Information Processing 83, pp. 513–523. Elsevier, Amsterdam (1983)
118. Ruehr, F.: Analytical and Structural Polymorphism Expressed Using Patterns over Types. PhD thesis, University of Michigan (1992)
119. Sheard, T.: Generic programming in Ωmega In this volume (2006)
120. Siek, J., Lee, L.-Q., Lumsdaine, A.: The Boost Graph Library. Addison-Wesley, Reading (2002)
121. Siek, J., Lumsdaine, A.: Essential language support for generic programming. In: Programming Language Design and Implementation, pp. 73–84 (2005)
122. Skillicorn, D.B.: The Bird-Meertens Formalism as a parallel model. In: Kowalik, J.S., Grandinetti, L. (eds.) Software for Parallel Computation. NATO ASI Series F, vol. 106, Springer, Heidelberg (1993)
123. STOP project. International Summer School on Constructive Algorithmics, Hollum, Ameland (1989)
124. Strachey, C.: Fundamental concepts in programming languages. Higher-Order and Symbolic Computation. Lecture notes from Summer School in Computer Programming 13(1/2), 1–49 (2000)
125. Taha, W.: A gentle introduction to multi-stage programming. In: Lengauer, C., Batory, D., Consel, C., Odersky, M. (eds.) Domain-Specific Program Generation. LNCS, vol. 3016, pp. 30–50. Springer, Heidelberg (2004)
126. Unruh, E.: Prime number computation. ANSI X3J16-94-0075/ISO WG21-462 (1994)
127. Uustalu, T., Vene, V.: Primitive (co)recursion and course-of-value (co)iteration. Informatica 10(1), 5–26 (1999)
128. van Wijngaarden, A., Mailloux, B.J., Peck, J.E.L., Koster, C.H.A., Sintzoff, M., Lindsey, C.H., Meertens, L.G.L.T., Fisker, R.G.: Revised report on the algorithmic language ALGOL 68. Acta Informatica 5(1-3) (1975)
129. Veldhuizen, T.: Active Libraries and Universal Languages. PhD thesis, Computer Science, Indiana University (2004)
130. Vene, V., Uustalu, T.: Functional programming with apomorphisms (corecursion). Proceedings of the Estonian Academy of Sciences: Physics, Mathematics. In: 9th Nordic Workshop on Programming Theory 47(3), 147–161 (1998)
131. Vytiniotis, D., Washburn, G., Weirich, S.: An open and shut typecase. In: International Conference on Functional Programming (2004)
132. Wadler, P.: Theorems for free! In Functional Programming Languages and Computer Architecture, pp. 347–359. ACM, New York (1989)

133. Wadler, P.: Deforestation: Transforming programs to eliminate trees. Theoretical Computer Science 73, 231–248 (1990)
134. Wadler, P.: Comprehending monads. Mathematical Structures in Computer Science 2(4), 461–493 (1992)
135. Wadler, P.: Monads for functional programming. In: Broy, M. (ed.) Program Design Calculi: Proceedings of the Marktoberdorf Summer School. Also in [76] (1992)
136. Wadler, P.: How to solve the reuse problem? Functional programming. In: International Conference on Software Reuse, pp. 371–372. IEEE, Los Alamitos (1998), http://doi.ieeecomputersociety.org/10.1109/ICSR.1998.685772
137. Wadler, P.L.: The expression problem. Posting to java-genericity mailing list (November 12, 1998)
138. Wirth, N., Hoare, C.A.R.: A contribution to the development of ALGOL. Communications of the ACM 9(6), 413–432 (1966)

7 Appendix: Java Programs

Section 4.4 provides a nearly complete implementation of the document application in a higher-order datatype-generic style; all that is missing is a definition for the spelling corrector *correct*. In contrast, Section 4.2 presents only the outline of a Java implementation of the same application. For completeness, this appendix presents the Java code.

7.1 Component

```
public interface Component{
    void accept (Visitor v);
    Iterator getIterator ();
}
```

7.2 Section

```
import java.util.Vector;
import java.util.Enumeration;
public class Section implements Component{
    protected Vector children;
    protected String title;
    public Section (String title){
        children = new Vector ();
        this.title = title;
    }
    public String getTitle (){
        return title;
    }
    public void addComponent (Component c){
        children.addElement (c);
```

```
  }
  public Enumeration getChildren (){
    return children.elements ();
  }
  public Iterator getIterator (){
    return new SectionIterator (this);
  }
  public void accept (Visitor v){
    v.visitSection (this);
  }
}
```

7.3   Paragraph

```
public class Paragraph implements Component{
  protected String body;
  public Paragraph (String body){
    setBody (body);
  }
  public void setBody (String s){
    body = s;
  }
  public String getBody (){
    return body;
  }
  public Iterator getIterator (){
    return new ParagraphIterator (this);
  }
  public void accept (Visitor v){
    v.visitParagraph (this);
  }
}
```

7.4   Iterator

```
public interface Iterator{
  void iterate (Action a);
}
```

7.5   SectionIterator

import *java.util.Enumeration*;

```
public class SectionIterator implements Iterator{
  protected Section s;
  public SectionIterator (Section s){
    this.s = s;
  }
  public void iterate (Action a){
    for (Enumeration e = s.getChildren ();
        e.hasMoreElements (); ){
      ((Component) (e.nextElement ())).
        getIterator ().iterate (a);
    }
  }
}
```

7.6   ParagraphIterator

```
public class ParagraphIterator implements Iterator{
  protected Paragraph p;
  public ParagraphIterator (Paragraph p){
    this.p = p;
  }
  public void iterate (Action a){
    a.apply (p);
  }
}
```

7.7   Action

```
public interface Action{
  void apply (Paragraph p);
}
```

7.8   SpellCorrector

```
public class SpellCorrector implements Action{
  public void apply (Paragraph p){
    p.setBody (correct (p.getBody ()));
  }
  public String correct (String s){
    return s.toLowerCase ();
  }
}
```

7.9   Visitor

```
public interface Visitor{
  void visitParagraph (Paragraph p);
  void visitSection (Section s);
}
```

7.10   PrintVisitor

```
import java.util.Enumeration;
import java.util.Vector;
public class PrintVisitor implements Visitor{
  protected String indent = "";
  protected Vector lines = new Vector ();
  public String [] getResult (){
    String [] ss = new String [0];
    ss = (String []) lines.toArray (ss);
    return ss;
  }
  public void visitParagraph (Paragraph p){
    lines.addElement (indent + p.getBody ());
  }
  public void visitSection (Section s){
    String currentIndent = indent;
    lines.addElement (indent + s.getTitle ());
    for (Enumeration e = s.getChildren ();
         e.hasMoreElements (); ){
      indent = currentIndent + "   ";
      ((Component) e.nextElement ()).accept (this);
    }
    indent = currentIndent;
  }
}
```

7.11   Builder

```
public interface Builder{
  int addParagraph (String body, int parent)
    throws InvalidBuilderId;
  int addSection (String title, int parent)
    throws InvalidBuilderId;
}
```

7.12   InvalidBuilderId

```
public class InvalidBuilderId extends Exception{
  public InvalidBuilderId (String reason){
    super (reason);
  }
}
```

7.13   ComponentBuilder

```
import java.util.AbstractMap;
import java.util.HashMap;

public class ComponentBuilder implements Builder{
  protected int nextId = 0;
  protected AbstractMap comps = new HashMap ();
  public int addParagraph (String body, int pId)
        throws InvalidBuilderId{
    return addComponent (new Paragraph (body), pId);
  }
  public int addSection (String title, int pId)
        throws InvalidBuilderId{
    return addComponent (new Section (title), pId);
  }
  public Component getProduct (){
    return (Component) comps.get (new Integer (0));
  }
  protected int addComponent (Component c, int pId)
        throws InvalidBuilderId{
    if (pId < 0){    // root component
      if (comps.isEmpty ()){
        comps.put (new Integer (nextId), c);
        return nextId++;
      }
      else
        throw new InvalidBuilderId
          ("Duplicate root");
    } else {    // non-root
      Component parent = (Component) comps.
        get (new Integer (pId));
      if (parent == null){
        throw new InvalidBuilderId
          ("Non-existent parent");
      } else {
        if (parent instanceof Paragraph){
          throw new InvalidBuilderId
```

```
          ("Adding child to paragraph");
       } else {
          Section s = (Section) parent;
          s.addComponent (c);
          comps.put (new Integer (nextId), c);
          return nextId++;
       }
     }
   }
 }
}
```

7.14   PrintBuilder

This is the only class with a non-obvious implementation. It constructs the
printed representation (a *String* []) of a *Component* on the fly. In order to do so,
it needs to retain some of the tree structure. This is done by maintaining, for
each *Component* stored, the unique identifier of its right-most child (or its own
identifier, if it has no children). This is stored in the *last* field of the corresponding
Record in the vector *records*. This vector itself is stored in the order the lines will
be returned, that is, a preorder traversal. When adding a new *Component*, it
should be placed after the rightmost descendent of its immediate parent, and this
is located by following the path of *last* references. (The code would be cleaner
if we were to use Java generics to declare *records* as a *Vector⟨Record⟩* rather
than a plain *Vector* of *Objects*, but we wish to emphasize that the datatype-
genericity discussed in this paper is a different kind of genericity to that provided
in Java 1.5.)

```
import java.util.Vector;
public class PrintBuilder implements Builder{
   protected class Record{
      public int id;
      public int last;
      public String line;
      public String indent;
      public Record (int id, int last,
                       String line, String indent){
         this.id = id;
         this.last = last;
         this.line = line;
         this.indent = indent;
      }
   }
   protected Vector records = new Vector ();
```

```
protected Record recordAt (int i){
  return (Record) records.elementAt (i);
}
protected int find (int id, int start){
  while (start < records.size () &&
         recordAt (start).id ! = id)
    start++;
  if (start < records.size ())
    return start;
  else
    return − 1;
}
protected int nextId = 0;
protected SpellCorrector c = new SpellCorrector ();
public int addParagraph (String body, int pid)
      throws InvalidBuilderId{
  return addComponent (c.correct (body), pid);
}
public int addSection (String title, int pid)
      throws InvalidBuilderId{
  return addComponent (title, pid);
}
public String [] getProduct (){
  String [] ss = new String [records.size ()];
  for (int i = 0; i < ss.length; i++)
    ss [i] = recordAt (i).indent + recordAt (i).line;
  return ss;
}
protected int addComponent (String s, int pId)
      throws InvalidBuilderId{
  if (pId < 0){
    if (records.isEmpty ()){
      records.addElement (new Record
        (nextId, nextId, s, ""));
      return nextId++;
    }
    else
      throw new InvalidBuilderId
        ("Duplicate root");
  } else {
    int x = find (pId, 0);
    Record r = recordAt (x);
    String indent = r.indent;
    if (x == − 1){
```

```
        throw new InvalidBuilderId
          ("Non-existent parent");
      } else {
        int y = x;
        while (r.id ! = r.last){
          y = x;
          x = find (r.last, x);
          r = recordAt (x);
        }
        records.insertElementAt (new Record
          (nextId, nextId, s, indent + "   "), x + 1);
        recordAt (y).last = nextId;
        return nextId++;
      }
    }
  }
}
```

7.15   Main

```
public abstract class Main{
  public static void build (Builder b){
    try{
      int rootId = b.addSection ("Doc", −1);
      int sectId = b.addSection ("Sec 1", rootId);
      int subsId = b.addSection ("Subsec 1.1", sectId);
      int id = b.addParagraph ("Para 1.1.1", subsId);
      id = b.addParagraph ("Para 1.1.2", subsId);
      subsId = b.addSection ("Subsec 1.2", sectId);
      id = b.addParagraph ("Para 1.2.1", subsId);
      id = b.addParagraph ("Para 1.2.2", subsId);
      sectId = b.addSection ("Sec 2", rootId);
      subsId = b.addSection ("Subsec 2.1", sectId);
      id = b.addParagraph ("Para 2.1.1", subsId);
      id = b.addParagraph ("Para 2.1.2", subsId);
      subsId = b.addSection ("Subsec 2.2", sectId);
      id = b.addParagraph ("Para 2.2.1", subsId);
      id = b.addParagraph ("Para 2.2.2", subsId);
    }catch (InvalidBuilderId e){
      System.out.println ("Exception: " + e);
    }
  }
  public static void main (String [] args){
    String [] lines;
```

```
    if (false){
        ComponentBuilder b = new ComponentBuilder ();
        build (b);
        Component root = b.getProduct ();
        root.getIterator ().iterate (new SpellCorrector ());
        PrintVisitor pv = new PrintVisitor ();
        root.accept (pv);
        lines = pv.getResult ();
    } else {
        PrintBuilder b = new PrintBuilder ();
        build (b);
        lines = b.getProduct ();
    }
    for (int i = 0; i < lines.length; i++)
        System.out.println (lines [i]);
    }
}
```

Comparing Approaches to Generic Programming in Haskell

Ralf Hinze[1], Johan Jeuring[2], and Andres Löh[1]

[1] Institut für Informatik III, Universität Bonn
Römerstraße 164, 53117 Bonn, Germany
{ralf,loeh}@informatik.uni-bonn.de
[2] Department of Information and Computing Sciences, Utrecht University
P.O.Box 80.089, 3508 TB Utrecht, The Netherlands
johanj@cs.uu.nl

Abstract. The last decade has seen a number of approaches to data-type-generic programming: PolyP, Functorial ML, 'Scrap Your Boiler-plate', Generic Haskell, 'Generics for the Masses', and so on. The approaches vary in sophistication and target audience: some propose full-blown programming languages, some suggest libraries, some can be seen as categorical programming methods. In these lecture notes we compare the various approaches to datatype-generic programming in Haskell. We introduce each approach by means of example, and we evaluate it along different dimensions (expressivity, ease of use, and so on).

1 Introduction

You just started implementing your third web shop in Haskell, and realize that a lot of the code you have to write is similar to the code for the previous web shops. Only the data types have changed. Unfortunately, this implies that all reporting, editing, storing and loading in the database functionality, and probably a lot more, has to be changed. You've heard about generic programming, a technique which can be used to automatically generate programs depending on types. But searching on the web gives you at least eight approaches to solve your problem: DrIFT, PolyP, Generic Haskell, Derivable Type Classes, Template Haskell, Scrap Your Boilerplate, Generics for the Masses, Strafunski, and so on. How do you choose?

In these lecture notes we give arguments as to why you would choose a par-ticular approach to generic programming in Haskell to solve your generic pro-gramming problem. We compare different approaches to generic programming along different lines, such as for example:

- Can you use generic programs on all types definable in the programming language?
- Are generic programs compiled or interpreted?
- Can you extend a generic program in a special way for a particular data type?

R. Backhouse et al. (Eds.): Datatype-Generic Programming 2006, LNCS 4719, pp. 72–149, 2007.

Before we compare the various approaches to generic programming we first discuss in detail the criteria on which the comparison is based.

'Generic' is an over-used adjective in computing science in general, and in programming languages in particular. Ada has generic packages, Java has generics, Eiffel has generic classes, and so on. Usually, the adjective 'generic' is used to indicate that a concept allows abstractions over a larger class of entities than was previously possible. However, broadly speaking most uses of 'generic' refer to some form of parametric polymorphism, ad-hoc polymorphism, and/or inheritance. For a nice comparison of the different incarnations of generic concepts in different programming languages, see Garcia et al. [23]. Already in the 1970s this was an active area of research [89,66,20].

In the context of these lecture notes, 'generic programming' means a form of programming in which a function takes a type as argument, and its behavior depends upon the *structure* of this type. The type argument is the type of values to which the function is applied, or the type of the values returned by the function, or the type of values that are used internally in the function. Backhouse and Gibbons [24,10,25] call this kind of generic programming *datatype-generic* programming. A typical example is the equality function, where a type argument t dictates the form of the code that performs the equality test on two values of type t. In the past we have used the term *polytypic* [48] instead of 'generic', which is less confusing and describes the concept a bit more accurately. However, the term hasn't been picked up by other people working on conceptually the same topic, and maybe it sounds a bit off-putting.

The first programming languages with facilities for datatype-generic programming, beyond generating the definition of equality on user-defined data types, were Charity [18], and the lazy, higher-order, functional programming language Haskell [86]. Since then Haskell has been the most popular testbed for generic programming language extensions or libraries. Here is an incomplete list of approaches to generic programming in Haskell or based upon Haskell:

- Generic Haskell [31,34,71,73].
- DrIFT [99].
- PolyP [48,81].
- Derivable Type Classes [41].
- Lightweight Generics and Dynamics [15].
- Scrap Your Boilerplate [61,64,62,44,43].
- Generics for the Masses [35,84].
- Clean [3,2]. (Clean is not Haskell, but it is sufficiently close to be listed here.)
- Using Template Haskell for generic programming [82].
- Strafunski [65].
- Generic Programming, Now! [42]

Although Haskell has been the most popular testbed for generic programming extensions, many non-Haskell approaches to generic programming have been designed:

- Charity [18].
- ML [14,22].
- Intensional type analysis [30,19,96].
- Extensional type analysis [21].
- Functorial ML [56,78], the Constructor Calculus [53], the Pattern Calculus [54,55], FISh [52].
- Dependently-typed generic programming [6,11].
- Type-directed programming in Java [98].
- Adaptive Object-Oriented Programming [69].
- Maude [17].

We have tried to be as complete as possible, but certainly this list is not exhaustive.

In these lecture notes we compare most of the approaches to generic programming in Haskell or based upon Haskell. We do not include Strafunski and Generic Programming, Now! in our comparison. Strafunski is rather similar to Scrap Your Boilerplate, and Generic Programming, Now! is an advanced variant of the lightweight approaches we will discuss. Besides that, a paper [42] about the Generic Programming, Now! approach is included in these lecture notes, and itself contains a comparison to other approaches to generic programming. In future work we hope to also compare approaches to generic programming in other programming languages.

Types play a fundamental rôle in generic programming. In an untyped or dynamically typed language, it is possible to define functions that adapt to many data structures, and one could therefore argue that it is much easier to do generic programming in these languages. We strongly disagree: since generic programming is fundamentally about programming with types, simulating generic programming in an untyped language is difficult, since the concept of types and the accompanying checks and guidance are missing. Generic programs are often complex, and feedback from the type system is invaluable in their construction. This difficulty can also be observed in our treatment of DrIFT and Template Haskell, both approaches with only limited support from the type system.

We introduce each approach to generic programming by means of a number of, more or less, canonical examples. This set of examples has been obtained by collecting the generic functions defined in almost twenty papers introducing the various approaches to generic programming. Almost all of these papers contain at least one function from the following list:

- *encode*, a function that encodes a value of any type as a list of bits. The function *encode* is a simple recursive function which 'destructs' a value of a data type into a list of bits.
- *decode*, the inverse of *encode*, is a function which *builds* a value of a data type from a list of bits.
- *eq*, a function that takes *two* values, and compares them for equality.
- *map*, a generalization of the standard *map* function on lists. On a parametrized data type, such as lists, function *map* takes a function argument and a value of the data type, and applies the function argument to all parametric

values inside the value argument. The function *map* is only useful when applied to type constructors, i.e., parametrized data types such as lists or trees. In particular, on types of kind $\star$ it is the identity function.

- *show*, a function that shows or pretty-prints a value of a data type.
- *update*, a function that takes a value of a data type representing the structure of a company, and updates the salaries that appear in this value. The characteristic feature of this example is that *update* is only interested in values of a very small part of a possibly very large type. It is generic in the sense that it can be applied to a value of any data type, but it only updates salaries, and ignores all other information in a value of a data type.

The above functions all exhibit different characteristics, which we use to show differences between approaches to generic programming. We do not define all of these functions for each approach, in particular not for approaches that are very similar, but we use these examples to highlight salient points. We then investigate a number of properties for each approach. Examples of these properties are: whether it is possible to define a generic function on any data type that can be defined in the programming language (full reflexivity), whether the programming language is type safe, whether generic functions satisfy desirable properties, and so on. Sometimes we use examples beyond the above functions to better highlight specifics and peculiarities of a certain approach.

These notes are organized as follows. In Section 2 we discuss why generic programming matters by means of a couple of representative examples. We use these examples in Section 4 to compare the various approaches to generic programming by means of the criteria introduced and discussed in Section 3. Section 5 concludes.

2   Why Generic Programming Matters

Software development often consists of designing a data type, to which functionality is added. Some functionality is data type specific, other functionality is defined on almost all data types, and only depends on the type structure of the data type. Examples of generic functionality defined on almost all data types are storing a value in a database, editing a value, comparing two values for equality, and pretty-printing a value. A function that works on many data types is called a generic function. Applications of generic programming can be found not just in the rather small programming examples mentioned, but also in:

- XML tools such as XML compressors [37], and type-safe XML data binding tools [7,63];
- automatic testing [60];
- constructing 'boilerplate' code that traverses a value of a rich set of mutually-recursive data types, applying real functionality at a small portion of the data type [61,71,62];

- structure editors such as XML editors [29], and generic graphical user interfaces [1];
- typed middleware for distributed systems, such as CORBA [85];
- data-conversion tools [50] which for example store a data type value in a database [29], or output it as XML, or in a binary format [94].

Change is endemic to any large software system. Business, technology, and organization frequently change during the life cycle of a software system. However, changing a large software system is difficult: localizing the code that is responsible for a particular part of the functionality of a system, changing it, and ensuring that the change does not lead to inconsistencies in other parts of the system or in the architecture or documentation is usually a challenging task. *Software evolution* is a fact of life in the software-development industry [67,68,87].

If a data type changes, or a new data type is added to a piece of software, a generic program automatically adapts to the changed or new data type. An example is a generic program for calculating the total amount of salaries paid by an organization. If the structure of the organization changes, for example by removing or adding an organizational layer, the generic program still calculates the total amount of salaries paid. Since a generic program automatically adapts to changes of data types, a programmer only has to program 'the exception'. Generic programming has the potential to solve at least an important part of the software-evolution problem [58].

In the rest of this section we show a number of examples of generic programs. We write the generic programs in Generic Haskell [31,38,70]. Generic Haskell is an extension of Haskell that supports generic programming. Any of the other approaches to generic programming could have been chosen for the following exposition. We choose Generic Haskell simply because we have to start somewhere, and because we are responsible for the development of Generic Haskell. We use the most recent version of Generic Haskell, known as *Dependency-style Generic Haskell* [71,70]. Dependencies both simplify and increase the expressiveness of generic programming. In Section 4 we show how these programs are written in other approaches to generic programming.

2.1 Data Types in Haskell

The functional programming language Haskell 98 provides an elegant and compact notation for declaring data types. In general, a data type introduces a number of constructors, where each constructor takes a number of arguments. Here are two example data types:

```
data CharList = Nil | Cons Char CharList
data Tree     = Empty | Leaf Int | Bin Tree Char Tree.
```

A character list, a value of type CharList, is often called a *string*. It is either empty, denoted by the constructor *Nil*, or it is a character c followed by the remainder of the character list cs, denoted *Cons c cs*, where *Cons* is the constructor. A tree, a value of type Tree, is empty, a leaf containing an integer, or a binary node containing two subtrees and a character.

These example types are of kind $\star$, meaning that they do not take any type arguments. We will say a bit more about kinds in Section 3.1. A kind can be seen as the 'type of a type'. The following type takes an argument; it is obtained by abstracting Char out of the CharList data type above:

> **data** List a $= Nil \mid Cons$ a (List a).

Here List is a type constructor, which, when given a type a, constructs the type List a. The type constructor List has the functional kind $\star \rightarrow \star$. The list data type is predefined in Haskell: the type List a is written $[a]$, the expressions Nil and $Cons\ x\ xs$ are written $[\,]$ and $x:xs$, respectively. A type can take more than one argument. If we abstract from the types Char and Int in the type Tree, we obtain the type GTree defined by:

> **data** GTree a b $= GEmpty \mid GLeaf$ a $\mid GBin$ (GTree a b) b (GTree a b).

The type constructor GTree takes two type arguments, both of kind $\star$, and hence has kind $\star \rightarrow \star \rightarrow \star$.

Arguments of type constructors need not be of kind $\star$. Consider the data type of Rose trees, defined by:

> **data** Rose a $= Node$ a [Rose a].

A Rose tree is a $Node$ containing an element of type a, and a list of child trees. Just like List, Rose has kind $\star \rightarrow \star$. If we abstract from the list type in Rose, we obtain the data type GRose defined by:

> **data** GRose f a $= GNode$ a (f (GRose f a)).

Here the type argument f has kind $\star \rightarrow \star$, just like the List type constructor, and it follows that GRose has kind $(\star \rightarrow \star) \rightarrow \star \rightarrow \star$. We call such a kind that takes a kind constructor as argument a *higher-order* kind. The other kinds are called *first-order* kinds.

All the examples of data types we have given until now are examples of so-called *regular* data types: a recursive, parametrized type whose recursive definition does not involve a change of the type parameter(s). Non-regular or *nested* types [12] are practically important since they can capture data-structural invariants in a way that regular data types cannot. For instance, the following data-type declaration defines a nested data type: the type of perfectly-balanced, binary leaf trees [32] – perfect trees for short.

> **data** Perfect a $= ZeroP$ a $\mid SuccP$ (Perfect (Fork a))
> **data** Fork a $= Fork$ a a

This equation can be seen as a bottom-up definition of perfect trees: a perfect tree is either a singleton tree or a perfect tree that contains pairs of elements. Here is a perfect tree of type Perfect Int:

$$SuccP\ (SuccP\ (SuccP\ (ZeroP\ (Fork\ (Fork\ (Fork\ 2\ 3)$$
$$(Fork\ 5\ 7))$$
$$(Fork\ (Fork\ 11\ 13)$$
$$(Fork\ (Fork\ 17\ 19)))))).$$

Note that the height of the perfect tree is encoded in the prefix of *SuccP* and *ZeroP* constructors.

2.2 Structure-Representation Types

To apply functions generically to all data types, we view data types in a uniform manner: except for basic predefined types such as Float, IO, and →, every Haskell data type can be viewed as a labeled sum of possibly labeled products. This encoding is based on the following data types:

```
data a :+: b  = Inl a | Inr b
data a :*: b  = a :*: b
data Unit     = Unit
data Con a    = Con a
data Label a  = Label a.
```

The choice between *Nil* and *Cons*, for example, is encoded as a sum using the type :+: (nested to the right if there are more than two constructors). The constructors of a data type are encoded as sum labels, marked by the type Con. While the representation types are generated, the compiler tags each occurrence of Con with an abstract value of type ConDescr describing the original constructor. The exact details of how constructors are represented are omitted [38,70]. Record names are encoded as product labels, represented by a value of the type Label, which contains a value of type LabelDescr. Arguments such as the a and List a of the *Cons* are encoded as products using the type :*: (nested to the right if there are more than two arguments). In the case of *Nil*, an empty product, denoted by Unit, is used. The arguments of the constructors are not translated. Finally, abstract types and primitive types such as Char are not encoded, but left as they are.

Now we can encode CharList, Tree, and List as

```
type CharList° = Con Unit :+: Con (Char :*: CharList)
type Tree°     = Con Unit :+: Con Int :+: Con (Tree :*: (Char :*: Tree))
type List° a   = Con Unit :+: Con (a :*: (List a)).
```

These representations are called *structure-representation types*. A structure-representation type represents the top-level structure of a data type. A type t and its structure-representation type t° are isomorphic. (Strictly speaking this is not true, because the two types may be distinguished using (partially) undefined values.) Here and in the rest of the paper 'isomorphism' should be read as isomorphic modulo undefined values. The isomorphism between a type and its structure-representation type is witnessed by a so-called *embedding-projection pair*: a value $conv_t :: t \leftrightarrow t°$ of the data type

$$\textbf{data } a \leftrightarrow b = EP\{\textit{from} :: a \rightarrow b, \textit{to} :: b \rightarrow a\}.$$

For example, for the List data type we have that $conv_{\mathsf{List}} = EP \; \textit{from}_{\mathsf{List}} \; \textit{to}_{\mathsf{List}}$, where $\textit{from}_{\mathsf{List}}$ and $\textit{to}_{\mathsf{List}}$ are defined by

$$
\begin{array}{ll}
\textit{from}_{\mathsf{List}} & :: \mathsf{List}\; a \rightarrow \mathsf{List}°\; a \\
\textit{from}_{\mathsf{List}} \; \textit{Nil} & = \textit{Inl}\,(\textit{Con}\; \textit{Unit}) \\
\textit{from}_{\mathsf{List}} \; (\textit{Cons}\; a\; as) & = \textit{Inr}\,(\textit{Con}\;(a :\!*\!: as)) \\
\textit{to}_{\mathsf{List}} & :: \mathsf{List}°\; a \rightarrow \mathsf{List}\; a \\
\textit{to}_{\mathsf{List}} \; (\textit{Inl}\,(\textit{Con}\;\; \textit{Unit})) & = \textit{Nil} \\
\textit{to}_{\mathsf{List}} \; (\textit{Inr}\,(\textit{Con}\;(a :\!*\!: as))) & = \textit{Cons}\; a\; as.
\end{array}
$$

The Generic Haskell compiler generates the translation of a type to its structure-representation type, together with the corresponding embedding-projection pair. More details about the correspondence between these and Haskell types can be found elsewhere [34].

A generic program is defined by induction on the structure of structure-representation types. Whenever a generic program is applied to a user-defined data type, the Generic Haskell compiler takes care of the mapping between the user-defined data type and its corresponding structure-representation type. Furthermore, a generic program may also be defined directly on a user-defined data type, in which case this definition takes precedence over the automatically generated definitions. A definition of a generic function on a user-defined data type is called a *default case*. To develop a generic function, it is best to consider first a number of its instances for specific data types.

2.3   Encoding and Decoding

A classic application area of generic programming is parsing and unparsing, i.e., reading values of different types from some universal representation, or writing values to that universal representation. The universal representation can be aimed at being human-readable (such as the result of Haskell's *show* function); or it can be intended for data exchange, such as XML. Other applications include encryption, transformation, or storage.

In this section we treat a very simple case of compression, by defining functions that can write to and read from a sequence of bits. A bit is defined by the following data-type declaration:

$$\textbf{data } \mathsf{Bit} = O \mid I.$$

Here, the names O and I are used as constructors.

Function encode on CharList. To define *encode* on the data type CharList, we assume that there exists a function $encodeChar :: \mathsf{Char} \rightarrow [\mathsf{Bit}]$, which takes a character and returns a list of bits representing that character. We assume that *encodeChar* returns a list of 8 bits, corresponding to the ASCII code of the character. A value of type CharList is now encoded as follows:

$$
\begin{aligned}
&encodeCharList && :: \textsf{CharList} \rightarrow [\textsf{Bit}] \\
&encodeCharList\ Nil && = [O] \\
&encodeCharList\ (Cons\ c\ cs) && = I : encodeChar\ c \mathbin{+\!\!+} encodeCharList\ cs.
\end{aligned}
$$

For example, applying *encodeCharList* to the string "Bonn" defined as a CharList by $bonn = Cons$ 'B' $(Cons$ 'o' $(Cons$ 'n' $(Cons$ 'n' $Nil)))$ gives

$$
\begin{aligned}
ComparingGP\rangle\ &encodeCharList\ bonn \\
[I,O,&I,O,O,O,O,I,O,I,O,I,I,O,I,I,I,I,I \\
,O,&I,I,O,I,I,I,O,I,O,I,I,O,I,I,I,O,O].
\end{aligned}
$$

Note that the type of the value that is encoded is not stored. This implies that when decoding, we have to know the type of the value being decoded.

Function encode on Tree. To define *encode* on the data type Tree, we assume there exists, besides a function *encodeChar*, a function $encodeInt :: \textsf{Int} \rightarrow [\textsf{Bit}]$, which takes an integer and returns a list of bits representing that integer. Function *encodeInt* should be defined such that the resulting list of bits can be unambiguously decoded back to an integer again. A value of type Tree can then be encoded as follows:

$$
\begin{aligned}
&encodeTree && :: \textsf{Tree} \rightarrow [\textsf{Bit}] \\
&encodeTree\ Empty && = [O] \\
&encodeTree\ (Leaf\ i) && = [I,O] \mathbin{+\!\!+} encodeInt\ i \\
&encodeTree\ (Bin\ l\ c\ r) && = [I,I\ ] \\
& && \quad \mathbin{+\!\!+} encodeTree\ l \\
& && \quad \mathbin{+\!\!+} encodeChar\ c \\
& && \quad \mathbin{+\!\!+} encodeTree\ r.
\end{aligned}
$$

The *Empty* constructor of the Tree data type is encoded with a single bit, and the other two constructors are encoded using a sequence of two bits.

Function encode on List a. The data type CharList is an instance of the data type List a, where a is Char. How do we define an encoding function on the data type List a? For character lists, we assumed the existence of an encoding function for characters. Here we take the same approach: to encode a value of type List a, we assume that we have a function for encoding values of type a. Abstracting from *encodeChar* in the definition of *encodeCharList* we obtain:

$$
\begin{aligned}
&encodeList && :: (\textsf{a} \rightarrow [\textsf{Bit}]) \rightarrow \textsf{List\ a} \rightarrow [\textsf{Bit}] \\
&encodeList\ encodeA\ Nil && = [O] \\
&encodeList\ encodeA\ (Cons\ x\ xs) && = I : encodeA\ x \\
& && \quad \mathbin{+\!\!+} encodeList\ encodeA\ xs.
\end{aligned}
$$

Generic encode. The encoding functions on CharList, Tree and List a follow the same pattern: encode the choice made for the top level constructors, and concatenate the encoding of the children of the constructor. We can capture this common pattern in a single generic definition by defining the encoding function by induction on the structure of data types. This means that we define *encode* on sums (:+:), on products (:*:), and on base types such as Unit, Int and Char, as well as on the sum labels (Con) and the product labels (Label).

The only place where there is a choice between different constructors is in the :+: type. Here, the value can be either an *Inl* or an *Inr*. If we have to encode a value of type Unit, it can only be *Unit*, so we need no bits to encode that knowledge. Similarly, for a product we know that the value is the first component followed by the second – we need no extra bits except the encodings of the components.

In Generic Haskell, the generic *encode* function is rendered as follows:

$$
\begin{aligned}
encode\{|a :: \star|\} &&& :: (encode\{|a|\}) \Rightarrow a \to [\mathsf{Bit}] \\
encode\{|\mathsf{Unit}|\} && Unit &= [\,] \\
encode\{|\mathsf{Int}|\} && i &= encodeInt\ i \\
encode\{|\mathsf{Char}|\} && c &= encodeChar\ c \\
encode\{|\alpha :+: \beta|\} && (Inl\ x) &= O : encode\{|\alpha|\}\ x \\
encode\{|\alpha :+: \beta|\} && (Inr\ y) &= I\ : encode\{|\beta|\}\ y \\
encode\{|\alpha :*: \beta|\} && (x_1 :*: x_2) &= encode\{|\alpha|\}\ x_1 \mathbin{+\mkern-8mu+} encode\{|\beta|\}\ x_2 \\
encode\{|\mathsf{Label}\ l\ \alpha|\} && (Label\ a) &= encode\{|\alpha|\}\ a \\
encode\{|\mathsf{Con}\ c\ \alpha|\} && (Con\ a) &= encode\{|\alpha|\}\ a.
\end{aligned}
$$

There are a couple of things to note about generic function definitions:

- The function *encode*$\{|a|\}$ is a type-indexed function. The type argument appears in between special parentheses $\{|$, $|\}$. An instance of *encode* is obtained by applying *encode* to a type. For example, *encode*$\{|\mathsf{CharList}|\}$ is the instance of the generic function *encode* on the data type CharList. This instance is semantically the same as the definition of *encodeCharList*.
- The constraint *encode*$\{|a|\}$ that appears in the type of *encode* says that *encode* *depends on* itself. A generic function f depends on a generic function g if there is an 'arm' (or branch) in the definition of f, for example the arm for $f\{|\alpha :+: \beta|\}$ that uses g on a variable in the type argument, for example $g\{|\alpha|\}$. If a generic function depends on itself it is defined by induction over the type structure.
- The type of *encode* is given for a type a of kind $\star$. This does not mean that *encode* can only be applied to types of kind $\star$; it only gives the type information for types of kind $\star$. The type of function *encode* on types with kinds other than $\star$ is derived automatically from this base type. In particular, *encode*$\{|\mathsf{List}|\}$ is translated to a value that has the type (a $\to$ [Bit]) $\to$ (List a $\to$ [Bit]).
- The Generic Haskell code as given above is a bit prettier than the actual Generic Haskell code. In the actual Generic Haskell code we use the prefix

type constructor Sum instead of the infix type constructor · :+: ·, and similarly Prod instead of · :*: ·.

– The constructor case Con has an extra argument c, which contains the constructor description of the current constructor. Similarly, the label case Label has an extra argument l that contains a description of the current label. This is a special type pattern also containing a value, namely a constructor (label) description. The constructor (label) description can only be accessed in the Con (Label) case.

The Con and the Label case are useful for generic functions that use the names of constructors and labels in some way, such as a generic *show* function. Most generic functions, however, essentially ignore these arms. In this case, Generic Haskell allows to omit these arms from the generic function definition.

Generic decode. The inverse of *encode* recovers a value from a list of bits. This inverse function is called *decode*, and is defined in terms of a function *decodes*, which takes a list of bits, and returns a list of values that are recovered from an initial segment of the list of bits. We introduce a type Parser that is used as the type of function *decodes*. Furthermore, we assume we have a map function on this type. The reason we define this example as well, is that we want to show how to generically build or construct a value of a data type.

$$
\begin{aligned}
&\textbf{type } \textsf{Parser } a = [\textsf{Bit}] \rightarrow [(a, [\textsf{Bit}])] \\
&mapP \qquad\qquad :: (a \rightarrow b) \rightarrow \textsf{Parser } a \rightarrow \textsf{Parser } b \\
&decodes\{\!|a :: \star|\!\} \qquad :: (decodes\{\!|a|\!\}) \Rightarrow \textsf{Parser } a \\
&decodes\{\!|\textsf{Unit}|\!\} \quad xs = [(\mathit{Unit}, xs)] \\
&decodes\{\!|\textsf{Int}|\!\} \qquad xs = decodesInt\ xs \\
&decodes\{\!|\textsf{Char}|\!\} \quad xs = decodesChar\ xs \\
&decodes\{\!|\alpha :\!+\!: \beta|\!\}\ xs = bitCase\ (mapP\ Inl\ (decodes\{\!|\alpha|\!\})) \\
&\qquad\qquad\qquad\qquad\qquad\quad (mapP\ Inr\ (decodes\{\!|\beta|\!\})) \\
&\qquad\qquad\qquad\qquad\qquad\ xs \\
&decodes\{\!|\alpha :\!*\!: \beta|\!\}\ xs = [(y_1 :\!*\!: y_2, r_2) \mid (y_1, r_1) \leftarrow decodes\{\!|\alpha|\!\}\ xs \\
&\qquad\qquad\qquad\qquad\qquad\qquad\quad , (y_2, r_2) \leftarrow decodes\{\!|\beta|\!\}\ r_1] \\[4pt]
&bitCase \qquad :: \textsf{Parser } a \rightarrow \textsf{Parser } a \rightarrow \textsf{Parser } a \\
&bitCase\ p\ q = \lambda bits \rightarrow \textbf{case } bits \textbf{ of} \\
&\qquad\qquad\qquad\qquad\quad O : bs \rightarrow p\ bs \\
&\qquad\qquad\qquad\qquad\quad I : bs\ \rightarrow q\ bs \\
&\qquad\qquad\qquad\qquad\quad [] \qquad \rightarrow []
\end{aligned}
$$

The function is a bit more involved than *encode*, because it has to deal with incorrect input, and it has to return the unconsumed part of the input. We therefore use the standard list-of-successes technique [93], where the input list is transformed into a list of pairs, containing all possible parses with the associated unconsumed part of the input. Assuming that the decoding of primitive types such as Int and Char is unambiguous, the decoding process is not ambiguous, so only lists of zero (indicating failure) and one (indicating success) elements occur. As with *encodeChar*, we assume a function *decodesChar* is obtained from somewhere.

A value of type Unit is represented using no bits at all, hence it is decoded without consuming any input. Except for the primitive types such as Char and Int, the case for :+: is the only place where input is consumed (as it is the only case where output is produced in *encode*), and depending on the first bit of the input, we produce an *Inl* or an *Inr*. Decoding fails if we run out of input while decoding a sum. The product case first decodes the left component, and then runs *decodes* for the right component on the rest of the input.

The inverse of *encode* is now defined by:

$$decode\{|a :: \star|\} \ :: \ (decodes\{|a|\}) \Rightarrow [\mathsf{Bit}] \rightarrow a$$
$$decode\{|a|\} \ bits = \mathbf{case} \ decodes\{|a|\} \ bits \ \mathbf{of}$$
$$[(y, [])] \rightarrow y$$
$$\_ \qquad \rightarrow error \ \texttt{"decode: no parse"}.$$

Note that although this is a generic function, it is not defined by induction on the structure of types. Instead, it is defined in terms of another generic function, *decodes*. A generic function f that is defined in terms of another generic function g is called a *generic abstraction*. Such a generic function does not depend on itself, but on g instead. Using a generic abstraction, we can thus define a function that depends on a type argument, but is not defined using cases on types. A generic abstraction only works on types that have the specified kind ($\star$ in the case of function *decode*).

For each type t in the domain of both *decode* and *encode*, we have that for any finite and total value x of type t,

$$(decode\{|t|\} \ . \ encode\{|t|\}) \ x \ \texttt{==} \ x.$$

2.4   Equality

The generic equality function takes two arguments instead of a single argument as *encode* does. We define the equality function on two of the example data types given in Section 2.1. Two character lists are equal if both are empty, or if both are non-empty, the first elements are equal, and the tails of the lists are equal.

$$
\begin{aligned}
&eqCharList :: \mathsf{CharList} \rightarrow \mathsf{CharList} \rightarrow \mathsf{Bool} \\
&eqCharList \quad Nil \qquad\qquad Nil \qquad\quad = True \\
&eqCharList \quad (Cons \ x \ xs) \ (Cons \ y \ ys) = eqChar \ x \ y \wedge eqCharList \ xs \ ys \\
&eqCharList \quad \_ \qquad\qquad\quad \_ \qquad\quad = False,
\end{aligned}
$$

where *eqChar* is the equality function on characters.

Two trees are equal if both are empty, both are a leaf containing the same integer, determined by means of function *eqInt*, or if both are nodes containing the same subtrees, in the same order, and the same characters.

$$eqTree :: \mathsf{Tree} \rightarrow \mathsf{Tree} \rightarrow \mathsf{Bool}$$
$$eqTree \quad Empty \qquad Empty \qquad = True$$
$$eqTree \quad (Leaf\ i) \quad (Leaf\ j) \quad = eqInt\ i\ j$$
$$eqTree \quad (Bin\ l\ c\ r)\ (Bin\ v\ d\ w) = eqTree\ l\ v \wedge eqChar\ c\ d \wedge eqTree\ r\ w$$
$$eqTree \quad \_ \qquad\qquad \_ \qquad\qquad = False$$

The equality functions on CharList and Tree follow the same pattern: compare the top level constructors, and, if they are equal, pairwise compare their arguments. We can capture this common pattern in a single generic definition by defining the equality function by induction on the structure of data types.

$$eq\{|a :: \star|\} \qquad\qquad\qquad :: (eq\{|a|\}) \Rightarrow a \rightarrow a \rightarrow \mathsf{Bool}$$
$$eq\{|\mathsf{Unit}|\} \quad \_ \qquad\quad \_ \qquad\quad = True$$
$$eq\{|\mathsf{Int}|\} \quad\ \ i \qquad\quad j \qquad\quad = eqInt\ i\ j$$
$$eq\{|\mathsf{Char}|\} \quad c \qquad\quad d \qquad\quad = eqChar\ c\ d$$
$$eq\{|\alpha :+: \beta|\}\ (Inl\ x)\ \ (Inl\ y)\ \ = eq\{|\alpha|\}\ x\ y$$
$$eq\{|\alpha :+: \beta|\}\ (Inl\ x)\ \ (Inr\ y)\ = False$$
$$eq\{|\alpha :+: \beta|\}\ (Inr\ x)\ (Inl\ y)\ \ = False$$
$$eq\{|\alpha :+: \beta|\}\ (Inr\ x)\ (Inr\ y)\ = eq\{|\beta|\}\ x\ y$$
$$eq\{|\alpha :*: \beta|\}\ (x :*: y)\ (v :*: w) = eq\{|\alpha|\}\ x\ v \wedge eq\{|\beta|\}\ y\ w$$

2.5   Map

In category theory, the functorial map is defined as the action of a functor on an arrow. There is no way to describe functors in Generic Haskell, and neither is it possible to distinguish argument types in structure-representation types. The approach we take to defining *map* in Generic Haskell illustrates the importance of kinds in generic programming. To understand the definition of the generic *map* function, it helps to first study the generic copy function:

$$copy\{|a :: \star|\} \qquad\qquad :: (copy\{|a|\}) \Rightarrow a \rightarrow a$$
$$copy\{|\mathsf{Unit}|\} \quad x \qquad = x$$
$$copy\{|\mathsf{Int}|\} \quad\ \ x \qquad = x$$
$$copy\{|\mathsf{Char}|\} \quad x \qquad = x$$
$$copy\{|\alpha :+: \beta|\}\ (Inl\ x)\ = Inl\ (copy\{|\alpha|\}\ x)$$
$$copy\{|\alpha :+: \beta|\}\ (Inr\ x)\ = Inr\ (copy\{|\beta|\}\ x)$$
$$copy\{|\alpha :*: \beta|\}\ (x :*: y) = copy\{|\alpha|\}\ x :*: copy\{|\beta|\}\ y.$$

Given a value, the *copy* function produces a copy of that value and is thus a generic version of the identity function. Note that we have made a choice in the code above: the definition is written recursively, applying the generic copy deeply to all parts of a value. We could have simplified the last three lines, removing the dependency of *copy* on itself:

$$copy\{|\alpha :+: \beta|\}\ x = x$$
$$copy\{|\alpha :*: \beta|\}\ x = x.$$

But retaining the dependency and applying the function recursively has an advantage: using a so-called *local redefinition* we can change the behavior of the function. Function *copy* has a dependency on itself. This implies that whenever *copy* is used on a type of a kind different from $\star$, extra components are needed. For example, applying *copy* to the type [a], where the type list has kind $\star \to \star$, requires a component of *copy* on the type a. The copy function on [a] takes a copy function on the type a as argument, and applies this copy function whenever it encounters an a-value. The standard behavior of generic functions with dependencies is that argument functions are constructed in exactly the same way as the instance of the generic function itself. So the copy function on [Char] would be the instance of the generic copy function on lists, taking the instance of the generic copy function on Char as argument. Local redefinition allows us to adapt the standard behavior. As an example, we can increase all elements of a list by one, using the function

$$incBy1 \ x = \textbf{let } copy\{\!|\alpha|\!\} = (+1) \textbf{ in } copy\{\!|[\alpha]|\!\} \ x.$$

Here we locally redefine *copy* to behave as the function $(+1)$ on values of type α that appear in a list of type $[\alpha]$. Obviously, this is only type correct if α equals Int (or, more generally, is an instance of the *Num* class). Note that *incBy1* is something that would normally be written as an application of *map*:

$$incBy1 \ x = map \ (+1) \ x.$$

If we compare *map* with the locally redefined version of *copy*, then two differences spring to mind. First, the function *map* can only be used on lists, whereas *copy* can be used on other data types as well. Second, *map* has a more liberal type. If we define

$$map' \ f = \textbf{let } copy\{\!|\alpha|\!\} = f \textbf{ in } copy\{\!|[\alpha]|\!\},$$

then we can observe that *map'*, compared to *map* has a more restricted type:

$$map' :: (a \to a) \to [a] \to [a]$$
$$map \ :: (a \to b) \to [a] \to [b].$$

The function passed to *map* may change the type of its argument; the function passed to *map'* preserves the argument type.

Inspired by this deficiency, we can ask ourselves if it is possible to also pass a function of type a $\to$ b while locally redefining *copy*. The function $copy\{\!|[a]|\!\}$ has the qualified type

$$copy\{\!|[a]|\!\} :: (copy\{\!|a|\!\} :: a \to a) \Rightarrow [a] \to [a],$$

but we are now going to generalize this type to something like

$$map\{\!|[a]|\!\} :: (map\{\!|a|\!\} :: a \to b) \Rightarrow [a] \to [b],$$

thereby renaming function *copy* to *map* (but using exactly the same definition). For this to work, *map* needs a different type signature, in which the b is also bound:

$$map\{|a :: \star, b :: \star|\} :: (map\{|a, b|\}) \Rightarrow a \rightarrow b.$$

The type of the *map* function is now parametrized over *two* type variables, and so is the dependency. The arms in the definition of *map* are still parametrized by a single type (Generic Haskell does not allow more than one type argument in definitions of generic functions). Function *map* is always called with a single type argument, which is the type argument that is used to induct over. When *map* is used at a constant type, both variables a and b are instantiated to the same constant type. Only when locally redefining the function for a dependency variable, the additional flexibility is available. Figure 1 shows some types (with explicit kind annotations for the type variables) for applications of *map* to specific type arguments.

$map\{|Tree :: \star|\} :: Tree \rightarrow Tree$
$map\{|List (a :: \star) :: \star|\} ::$
    $\forall(a_1 :: \star) (a_2 :: \star) . (map\{|a|\} :: a_1 \rightarrow a_2) \Rightarrow List\ a_1 \rightarrow List\ a_2$
$map\{|GTree (a :: \star) (b :: \star) :: \star|\} ::$
    $\forall(a_1 :: \star) (a_2 :: \star) (b_1 :: \star) (b_2 :: \star) . (map\{|a|\} :: a_1 \rightarrow a_2, map\{|b|\} :: b_1 \rightarrow b_2) \Rightarrow$
                                            $GTree\ a_1\ a_2 \rightarrow GTree\ b_1\ b_2$
$map\{|GRose (f :: \star \rightarrow \star) (a :: \star) :: \star|\} ::$
    $\forall(f_1 :: \star \rightarrow \star) (f_2 :: \star \rightarrow \star) (a_1 :: \star) (a_2 :: \star) .$
        $(map\{|f (c :: \star)|\} :: \forall(c_1 :: \star) (c_2 :: \star) . (map\{|c|\} :: c_1 \rightarrow c_2) \Rightarrow f_1\ c_1 \rightarrow f_2\ c_2$
        $, map\{|a|\} :: a_1 \rightarrow a_2$
        $) \Rightarrow GRose\ f_1 \cdot a_1 \rightarrow GRose\ f_2\ a_2.$

Fig. 1. Example types for generic applications of *map* to type arguments of different forms

For example, assume the (data) types Pair and Either are defined by:

type Pair a b $= (a, b)$
data Either a b $= Left\ a \mid Right\ b.$

Then the expressions

$map\{|[]|\}$ $(+1)$ $[1, 2, 3, 4, 5]$
$map\{|Pair|\}$ $(*2)$ $("y"+)$ $(21, "es")$
$map\{|Either|\}$ $not\ id$ $(Left\ True)$

evaluate to $[2, 3, 4, 5, 6]$, $(42, "yes")$, and $Left\ False$, respectively.

2.6 Show

The function *show* shows a value of an arbitrary data type. In Haskell, the definition of *show* can be derived for most data types. In this subsection we explain how to define *show* as a generic function in Generic Haskell. We do not treat field labels, so our implementation is a simplification of Haskell's *show*; the complete definition of *show* can be found in Generic Haskell's library. The function *show* is an example of a function that uses the constructor descriptor in the Con case. We define *show* in terms of the function *showP*, a slightly generalized variant of Haskell's *show* that takes an additional argument of type String → String. This parameter is used internally to place parentheses around a fragment of the result when needed.

$$showP\{|a :: \star|\} :: (showP\{|a|\}) \Rightarrow (\text{String} \to \text{String}) \to a \to \text{String}$$

$$
\begin{aligned}
&showP\{|\text{Unit}|\} && p\ Unit && = \text{""} \\
&showP\{|\alpha :\!+\!: \beta|\} && p\ (Inl\ x) && = showP\{|\alpha|\}\ p\ x \\
&showP\{|\alpha :\!+\!: \beta|\} && p\ (Inr\ x) && = showP\{|\beta|\}\ p\ x \\
&showP\{|\alpha :\!*\!: \beta|\} && p\ (x_1 :\!*\!: x_2) && = showP\{|\alpha|\}\ p\ x_1 +\!\!+\ \text{" "} +\!\!+\ showP\{|\beta|\}\ p\ x_2 \\
&showP\{|\text{Con}\ c\ \alpha|\} && p\ (Con\ x) && = \textbf{let}\ parens\ x = \text{"("} +\!\!+ x +\!\!+ \text{")"} \\
&&&&& \qquad\quad body\ \ = showP\{|\alpha|\}\ parens\ x \\
&&&&& \textbf{in if}\ null\ body \\
&&&&& \quad \textbf{then}\ conName\ c \\
&&&&& \quad \textbf{else}\ \ p\ (conName\ c +\!\!+ \text{" "} +\!\!+ body) \\
&showP\{|[\alpha]|\} && p\ xs && = \textbf{let}\ body = (concat \\
&&&&& \qquad\qquad\quad .\ intersperse\ \text{", "} \\
&&&&& \qquad\qquad\quad .\ map\ (showP\{|\alpha|\}\ id) \\
&&&&& \qquad\qquad\quad)\ xs \\
&&&&& \textbf{in}\ \ \text{"["} +\!\!+ body +\!\!+ \text{"]"}
\end{aligned}
$$

The type Unit represents a constructor with no fields. In such a situation, the constructor name alone is the representation, and it is generated from the Con case, so we do not need to produce any output here. We just descend through the sum structure; again, no output is produced because the constructor names are produced in the Con case. A product concatenates fields of a single constructor; we therefore show both components, and separate them from each other by a space.

Most of the work is done in the arm for Con. We show the body of the constructor, using parentheses where necessary. The body is empty if and only if there are no fields for this constructor. In this case, we only return the name of the constructor. Here we make use of the function *conName* on the constructor descriptor *c* to obtain that name. Otherwise, we connect the constructor name and the output of the body with a space, and possibly surround the result with parentheses.

The last case is for lists and implements Haskell's list syntax, with brackets and commas, using the function *intersperse* from Haskell's List module.

In addition to the cases above, we need cases for abstract primitive types such as Char, Int, or Float that implement the operation in some primitive way.

The function *show* is defined in terms of *showP* via generic abstraction, instantiating the first parameter to the identity function, because outer parentheses are not required.

$$show\{a :: \star\} :: (showP\{a\}) \Rightarrow a \rightarrow \text{String}$$
$$show\{a\} \quad = showP\{a\}\ id$$

The definition of a generic *read* function that parses the generic string representation of a value is also possible using the Con case, and only slightly more involved because we have to consider partial consumption of the input string and possible failure.

2.7   Update Salaries

Adapting from Lämmel and Peyton Jones [61], we use the following data types to represent the organizational structure of a company.

$$
\begin{aligned}
&\textbf{data } \text{Company} = C\ [\text{Dept}] \\
&\textbf{data } \text{Dept} \quad = D\ \text{Name Manager } [\text{SubUnit}] \\
&\textbf{data } \text{SubUnit} = PU\ \text{Employee} \mid DU\ \text{Dept} \\
&\textbf{data } \text{Employee} = E\ \text{Person Salary} \\
&\textbf{data } \text{Person} \quad = P\ \text{Name Address} \\
&\textbf{data } \text{Salary} \quad = S\ \text{Float} \\
&\textbf{type } \text{Manager} = \text{Employee} \\
&\textbf{type } \text{Name} \quad = \text{String} \\
&\textbf{type } \text{Address} \quad = \text{String}
\end{aligned}
$$

We wish to update a Company value, which involves giving every Person a 15% pay rise. To do so requires visiting the entire tree and modifying every occurrence of Salary. The implementation requires pretty standard "boilerplate" code which traverses the data type, until it finds Salary, where it performs the appropriate update – itself one line of code – before reconstructing the result.

In Generic Haskell writing this function requires but a few lines. The code is based on the generic *map* function. The code to perform the updating is given by the following three lines, the first of which is the mandatory type signature, the second states that the function is based on *map*, and the third performs the update of the salary. The **extends** construct denotes that the cases of *map* are copied into *update*. These are the *default cases* described by Clarke and Löh [16].

$$
\begin{aligned}
&update\{a :: \star\} :: (update\{a\}) \Rightarrow a \rightarrow a \\
&update \textbf{ extends } map \\
&update\{\text{Salary}\}\ (S\ s) = S\ (s * (1 + 0.15))
\end{aligned}
$$

Semantically, this is the same function as

$$
\begin{aligned}
&update\{\text{Unit}\} \quad x \quad\quad = x \\
&update\{\text{Int}\} \quad\ x \quad\quad = x \\
&update\{\text{Char}\} \quad x \quad\quad = x
\end{aligned}
$$

$$update\{\!|\alpha :+: \beta|\!\} \ (Inl \ x) \ \ = Inl \ (update\{\!|\alpha|\!\} \ x)$$
$$update\{\!|\alpha :+: \beta|\!\} \ (Inr \ x) \ \ = Inr \ (update\{\!|\beta|\!\} \ x)$$
$$update\{\!|\alpha :*: \beta|\!\} \ (x :*: y) = update\{\!|\alpha|\!\} \ x :*: update\{\!|\beta|\!\} \ y$$
$$update\{\!|\mathsf{Salary}|\!\} \ \ (S \ s) \ \ \ \ = S \ (s * (1 + 0.15)).$$

The **extends** construct allows us to abbreviate such small variations of generic functions.

3   Criteria for Comparison

This section discusses the criteria we use for comparing approaches to generic programming in Haskell. This is a subset of the criteria we would use for comparing approaches to generic programming in any programming language. Together, these criteria can be viewed as a characterization of generic programming. Adding generic programming capabilities to a programming language is a programming-language design problem. Many of the criteria we give are related to or derived from programming-language design concepts. We don't think that all criteria are equally important: some criteria discuss whether or not some functions can be defined or used on particular data types, whereas other criteria discuss more cosmetic aspects. We illustrate the criteria with an evaluation of Generic Haskell.

3.1   Structure in Programming Languages

Ignoring modules, many modern programming languages have a two-level structure. The bottom level, where the computations take place, consists of values. The top level imposes structure on the value level, and is inhabited by types. On top of this, Haskell adds a level that imposes structure on the type level, namely kinds. Finally, in some dependently-typed programming languages there is a possibly infinite hierarchy of levels, where level $n + 1$ imposes structure on elements of level n [90].

In ordinary programming we routinely define values that depend on values, that is, functions, and types that depend on types, that is, type constructors. However, we can also imagine having dependencies between adjacent levels. For instance, a type might depend on a value or a type might depend on a kind. The following table lists the possible combinations:

kinds depending on kinds	parametric and kind-indexed kinds
kinds depending on types	dependent kinds
types depending on kinds	polymorphic and kind-indexed types
types depending on types	parametric and type-indexed types
types depending on values	dependent types
values depending on types	polymorphic and type-indexed functions
values depending on values	ordinary functions

There even exist dependencies between non-adjacent levels: properties of generic functions are values that depend on kinds [33,51]. However, we will not further discuss these non-adjacent dependencies in these notes.

If a higher level depends on a lower level we have so-called dependent types or dependent kinds. Programming languages with dependent types are the subject of current research [76,9,90,100]. Generic programming is concerned with the opposite direction, where a lower level depends on the same or a higher level. For instance, if a value depends on a type we either have a polymorphic or a type-indexed function. In both cases the function takes a type as an argument. What is the difference between the two? A polymorphic function is a function that happens to be insensitive to what type the values in a data type are. Take, for example, the length function that calculates the length of a list. Since it does not have to inspect the elements of an argument list, it has type $\forall a . \text{List } a \rightarrow \text{Int}$. By contrast, in a type-indexed function the type argument guides the computation which is performed on the value arguments.

Not only values may depend on types, but also types. For example, the type constructor List depends on a type argument. We can make a similar distinction as on the value level. A parametric type, such as List, does not inspect its type argument. A *type-indexed type* [39], on the other hand, is defined by induction on the structure of its type argument. An example of a type-indexed data type is the zipper data type introduced by Huet [46]. Given a data type t, the zipper data type corresponding to t can be defined by induction on the data type t. Finally, we can play the same game on the level of kinds. The following table summarizes the interesting cases.

kinds defined by induction on the structure of kinds	kind-indexed kinds
kinds defined by induction on the structure of types	−
types defined by induction on the structure of kinds	kind-indexed types
types defined by induction on the structure of types	type-indexed types
types defined by induction on the structure of values	−
values defined by induction on the structure of types	type-indexed values
values defined by induction on the structure of values	−

For each of the approaches to generic programming we discuss what can depend on what.

Structural dependencies. Which concepts may depend on which concepts?

Generic Haskell supports the definition of type-indexed values, as all the examples in the previous section show. Type arguments appear between special parentheses ⦇, ⦈. A type-indexed value has a kind-indexed type, of which the base case, the case for kind $\star$, has to be supplied by the programmer. The inductive case, the case for kind $\kappa \rightarrow \kappa'$, cannot be specified, but is automatically generated by the compiler (as it is determined by the way Generic Haskell specializes generic functions). Generic abstractions only generate code for functions on types of the kind specified in the type of the generic abstraction.

Generic Haskell also supports the definition of type-indexed types. A type-indexed type is defined in the same way as a type-indexed function, apart from the facts that every line in its definition starts with **type**, and its name starts with a capital. A type-indexed type has a kind-indexed kind [39].

3.2 The Type Completeness Principle

The Type Completeness Principle [95] says that no programming-language operation should be arbitrarily restricted in the types of its operands, or, equivalently, all programming-language operations should be applicable to all operands for which they make sense. For example, in Haskell, a function can take an argument of any type, including a function type, and a tuple may contain a function. To a large extent, Haskell satisfies the type completeness principle on the value level. There are exceptions, however. For example, it is not possible to pass a polymorphic function as argument (some Haskell compilers, such as GHC, do allow passing polymorphic arguments). Pascal does not satisfy the type completeness principle, since, for example, procedures cannot be part of composite values.

The type completeness principle leads to the following criteria.

Full reflexivity. A generic programming language is fully reflexive if a generic function can be used on *any* type that is definable in the language.

Generic Haskell is fully reflexive with respect to the types that are definable in Haskell 98, except for constraints in data-type definitions. So a data type of the form

data *Eq* a ⇒ Set a = *NilSet* | *ConsSet* a (Set a)

is not dealt with correctly. However, constrained data types are a corner case in Haskell and can easily be simulated using other means. Furthermore, Nogueira [80] shows how to make Generic Haskell work for data types with constraints.

Generic functions cannot be used on existential data types, such as for example

data Foo = ∀a . *MkFoo* a (a → Bool).

Although such types are not part of Haskell 98, they are supported by most compilers and interpreters for Haskell. Furthermore, generic functions cannot be applied to *generalized algebraic data types* (GADTs), a recent extension in the Glasgow Haskell Compiler (GHC), of which the following type Term, representing typed terms, is an example:

```
data Term :: * → * where
   Lit    :: Int → Term Int
   Succ   :: Term Int → Term Int
   IsZero :: Term Int → Term Bool
   If     :: Term Bool → Term a → Term a → Term a
   Pair   :: Term a → Term b → Term (a, b).
```

Note that the result types of the constructors are restricted for Terms, so that if we pattern match on a Term Bool, for example, we already know that it cannot be constructed by means of *Lit*, *Succ* or *Pair*. The structural representation using sums of products that Generic Haskell uses to process data types uniformly is not directly applicable to data types containing existential components or to GADTs. Generic Haskell is thus not fully reflexive with respect to modern extensions of Haskell.

Type universes. Some generic functions only make sense on a particular set of data types, or on a subset of all data types. For example, Malcolm [75] defines the *catamorphism* only for regular data types of kind $\star \to \star$. Bird and Paterson [13] have shown how to define catamorphisms on nested data types, and using tupling it is possible to define catamorphisms on mutually recursive types, but we are not aware of a single definition of a catamorphism that combines these definitions. Many generic functions, such as *show* and equality, cannot sensibly be defined on the type of functions. Is it possible to define generic functions on a particular set of data types, or on a subset of data types? Can we describe *type universes* [11]?

Generic Haskell has some facilities to support defining generic functions on a particular set of data types. If we only want to use a generic function on a particular set of data types, we can define it for just those data types. This is roughly equivalent to defining a class and providing instances of the class for the given data types.

Furthermore, by not giving a case for the function space (or other basic types for which we do not want to define the generic function), a generic function is not defined for data types containing function spaces, and it is a static error for a generic function to be used on a data type containing function spaces.

Finally, Generic Haskell supports so-called *generic views* [45] on data types, by means of which we can view the structure of data types in different ways. Using generic views, we can for example view (a subset of) data types as fixed points of regular functors, which enables the definition of the catamorphism.

First-class generic functions. Can a generic function take a generic function as argument? We will also use the term higher-order generic functions for first-class generic functions. An example where a higher-order generic function might be useful is in a generic *show* function that only prints part of its input, depending on whether or not some property holds of the input.

Generic Haskell does not have first-class generic functions. To a certain extent first-class generic functions can be mimicked by means of dependencies and extending existing generic functions, but it is impossible to pass a generic function as an argument to another (generic) function. The reason for this is that generic functions in Generic Haskell are translated by means of specialization. Specialization eliminates the type arguments from the code, and specialized instances are used on the different types. Specialization has the advantage that types do not appear in the generated code, but the disadvantage that specializing higher-order generic programs becomes difficult: it is hard to determine which translated components are used where.

Multiple type arguments. Can a function be generic in more than one type argument? Induction over multiple types is for example useful when generically transforming values from one type structure into another type structure [8].

Generic functions in Generic Haskell can be defined by induction on a single type. It is impossible to induct over multiple types. Note that the *type* of a generic function may take multiple type arguments (such as the type of *map*).

Transforming values from one type structure into another type structure is the only example we have encountered for which multiple type arguments would be useful. Usually, transforming one type structure into another can be achieved by combining two generic functions – one that maps a value into a universal structure, and another that recovers a value from the universal structure. Instances of these functions on for example the data type lists can be implemented by means of a *fold* (mapping into a universal structure) and an *unfold* (parsing from a universal structure). Compositions of unfolds with folds are so-called *metamorphisms* [26]. Since we are not aware of generic metamorphisms, we do not weigh this aspect heavily in our comparison.

3.3   Well-Typed Expressions do not go Wrong

Well-typed expressions in the Hindley-Milner type system [77] do not go wrong. Does the same hold for generic functions?

Type system. Do generic functions have types?

In Generic Haskell, generic functions have explicit types. Type-correctness is only partially checked by the Generic Haskell compiler. Haskell type-checks the generated code. A type system for Generic Haskell has been given by Hinze [33] and Löh [70] (an extension of Hinze's system with several extra features).

Type safety. Is the generic programming language type safe? By this we mean: is a type-correct generic function translated to a type-correct instance? And is a compiled program prevented from crashing because a non-existing instance of a generic function is called?

Generic Haskell is type safe in both aspects.

3.4   Information in Types

What does the type of a generic function reveal about the function? Can we infer a property of a generic function from its type? Since generic programming is about programming with types, questions about the type language are particularly interesting.

The type of a generic function. Do types of generic functions in some way correspond to intuition? A generic function $f\{|a|\}$ that has type a $\rightarrow$ a $\rightarrow$ Bool is probably a comparison function. But what does a function of type $(\forall b . Data$ a $\Rightarrow$ f (a $\rightarrow$ b) $\rightarrow$ a $\rightarrow$ f b) $\rightarrow$ ($\forall$a . a $\rightarrow$ f a) $\rightarrow$ a $\rightarrow$ f a do (this is a rather powerful combinator, which we will encounter again in one of the approaches)? This question is related to the possibility to infer useful properties, like free theorems [92], for a generic function from its type [57,28].

Generic Haskell's types of generic functions are relatively straightforward: a type like

$$eq\{\!|a :: \star|\!\} :: (eq\{\!|a|\!\}) \Rightarrow a \to a \to \mathsf{Bool}$$

is close to the type you would expect for the equality function, maybe apart from the dependency. The type for *map*:

$$map\{\!|a :: \star, b :: \star|\!\} :: (map\{\!|a, b|\!\}) \Rightarrow a \to b$$

is perhaps a little bit harder to understand, but playing with instances of the type of *map* for particular types, in particular for type constructors, probably helps understanding why this type is the one required by *map*.

Properties of generic functions. Is the approach based on a theory for generic functions? Do generic functions satisfy algebraic properties? How easy is it to reason about generic functions?

In his habilitation thesis [33], Hinze discusses generic programming and generic proofs in the context of (a 'core' version of) Generic Haskell. He shows a number of properties satisfied by generic functions, and he shows how to reason about generic functions.

3.5   Integration with the Underlying Programming Language

How well does the generic programming language extension integrate with the underlying programming language, in our case Haskell?

A type system can be *nominal* (based on the names of the types), *structural* (based on the structure of the types), or a mixture of the two. If a type system is nominal, it can distinguish types with exactly the same structure, but with different names. Generic functions are usually defined on a structural representation of types. Can such a generic function be extended in a non-generic way, for example for a particular, named, data type? Or even for a particular constructor? The general question here is: how does generic programming interact with the typing system?

A generic program can be used on many data types. But how much work needs to be done to use a generic function on a new data type? Is it simply a matter of writing **deriving** ... in a data-type declaration, or do we also have to implement the embedding-projection pair for the data type, for example?

Using default cases, a generic function can be extended in a non-generic way in Generic Haskell. The *update* function defined in Section 2.7 provides an example. Generic functions can even be specialized for particular constructors. Generic functions can be used on data types with no extra work. Generic Haskell generates the necessary machinery such as structure-representation types and embedding-projection pairs behind the scenes.

3.6   Tools

Of course, a generic programming language extension is only useful if there exists an interpreter or compiler that understands the extension. Some 'lightweight' approaches to generic programming require no additional language support: the compiler for the underlying programming language is sufficient. However, most approaches require tools to be able to use them, and we can ask the following questions.

Specialization versus interpretation. Is a generic function interpreted at run-time on data types to which it is applied, or is it specialized at compile-time? The latter approach allows the optimization of generated code.

Generic Haskell specializes applications of generic functions at compile-time.

Code optimization. How efficient is the code generated for instances of generic functions? What is the speed of the generated code? Ideally generic programming does not lead to a performance penalty. For example, in the STL community, this is a requirement for a generic function [79] (not to be confused with a datatype-generic function).

Generic Haskell does not optimize away the extra marshaling that is introduced by the compiler for instances of generic functions. This might be an impediment for some applications. There exists a prototype implementation of Generic Haskell in which the extra marshaling is fused away [91], but the techniques have not been added to the Generic Haskell compiler releases. The fusion optimization techniques in the underlying programming language Haskell are not strong enough to optimize generated Generic Haskell code.

Separate compilation. Can a generic function that is defined in one module be used on a data type defined in another module without having to recompile the module in which the generic function is defined?

Generic Haskell provides separate compilation.

Practical aspects. Does there exist an implementation? Is it maintained? On multiple platforms? Is it documented? What is the quality of the error messages given by the tool?

Generic Haskell is available on several platforms: Windows, Linux and Mac-OSX, and it should be possible to build Generic Haskell anywhere where GHC is installed. The latest release is from October, 2006. The distribution comes with a User Guide, which explains how to install Generic Haskell, how to use it, and introduces the functions that are in the library of Generic Haskell. The Generic Haskell compiler reports syntax errors. Type errors, however, are only reported when the file generated by Generic Haskell is compiled by a Haskell compiler. Type systems for Generic Haskell have been published [33,71,70], but only partially implemented.

3.7 Other Criteria

This section lists some of the criteria that do not fall in the categories discussed in the previous subsections, or that are irrelevant for comparing the generic programming approaches in Haskell, but might be relevant for comparing approaches to generic programming in different programming languages.

Type-language expressiveness of the underlying programming language. If all values in a programming language have the same type, it is impossible to define a function the behavior of which depends on a type, and hence it is impossible to define generic functions. But then, of course, there is no need for defining generic functions either.

The type languages of programming languages with type systems vary widely. Flexible and powerful type languages are desirable, but the more expressive a type language, the harder it becomes to write generic programs. What kind of data types can be expressed in the type language?

Haskell has a very powerful, flexible, and expressive type language. This make generic programming in Haskell particularly challenging.

Size matters. The size of a program matters – some people are even paid per line of code –, and the same holds for a generic program. It is usually easier to read and maintain a single page of code than many pages of code, although sometimes extra information, such as type information, properties satisfied by a program, or test cases for a program, are useful to have. So code size matters, but not always. Except for some obvious cases, we will not say much about code size in our comparisons.

Ease of learning. Some programming approaches are easier to learn than others. Since there are so many factors to the question how easy it is to learn a programming language, and since it is hard to quantify, we refrain from making statements about this question, other than whether or not the approach to generic programming is documented. However, it is an important question.

4   Comparing Approaches to Generic Programming

In this section we describe eight different approaches to generic programming in Haskell. We give a brief introduction to each approach, and evaluate it using the criteria introduced in the previous section.

We can distinguish three groups of approaches with similar characteristics among the approaches to generic programming in Haskell.

- Generic Haskell and Clean are programming-language extensions based on Hinze's theory of type-indexed functions with kind-indexed types [34].
- DrIFT and implementations of generic programming using Template Haskell are based on a kind of reflection mechanism.

– Derivable Type Classes, Lightweight Generics and Dynamics, Generics for the Masses, and PolyP2 ([81], the latest version of PolyP [48]) are lightweight approaches that do not require reflection or programming-language extensions.

PolyP (in its original version) and Scrap Your Boilerplate are sufficiently different to not be placed in one of these groups. We evaluate the approaches in the groups together, since most aspects of the evaluation are the same. Of course, we already evaluated Generic Haskell in the previous section, so Clean is evaluated separately.

4.1 Clean

Clean's generic programming extension [3,2] is based on Hinze's work on type-indexed functions with kind-indexed types [34], just like Generic Haskell.

The language of data types in Clean is very similar to that of Haskell, and the description from Section 2.1 on how to convert between data types and their structure-representation types in terms of binary sums of binary products applies to Clean as well, only that the unit type is called UNIT, the sum type EITHER, and the product type PAIR. There are special structural markers for constructors and record field names called CONS and FIELD, and one for objects called OBJECT.

Clean's generic functions are integrated with its type-class system. Each generic function defines a kind-indexed family of type classes, the generic function itself being the sole method of these classes. Let us look at an example.

Function encode. Here is the code for the generic function *encode*.

$$
\begin{aligned}
&\textbf{generic } encode \text{ a} :: \text{a} \rightarrow [\text{Bit}] \\
&encode\{\!|\text{UNIT}|\!\} && UNIT && = [\,] \\
&encode\{\!|\text{Int}|\!\} && i && = encodeInt\ i \\
&encode\{\!|\text{Char}|\!\} && c && = encodeChar\ c \\
&encode\{\!|\text{EITHER}|\!\}\ enc_a\ enc_b\ (LEFT\ x) && && = [\,O : enc_a\ x\,] \\
&encode\{\!|\text{EITHER}|\!\}\ enc_a\ enc_b\ (RIGHT\ y) && && = [\,I : enc_b\ y\,] \\
&encode\{\!|\text{PAIR}|\!\}\ enc_a\ enc_b\ (PAIR\ x\ y) && && = enc_a\ x \mathbin{+\!\!+} enc_b\ y \\
&encode\{\!|\text{CONS}|\!\}\ enc_a\ (CONS\ x) && && = enc_a\ x \\
&encode\{\!|\text{FIELD}|\!\}\ enc_a\ (FIELD\ x) && && = enc_a\ x \\
&encode\{\!|\text{OBJECT}|\!\}\ enc_a\ (OBJECT\ x) && && = enc_a\ x \\
&\textbf{derive } encode \text{ Tree}
\end{aligned}
$$

The keyword **generic** introduces the type signature of a generic function, which takes the same form as a type signature in Generic Haskell, but without dependencies. Each generic function automatically depends on itself in Clean, and in the cases for types of higher kinds such as EITHER$:: \star \rightarrow \star \rightarrow \star$ or CONS$:: \star \rightarrow \star$, additional arguments are passed to the generic function representing the recursive calls. This is very close to Hinze's theory [34] which states that the type of *encode* is based on the kind of the type argument as follows:

$encode\{|a :: \kappa|\} :: Encode\{|\kappa|\}$ a

$Encode\{|\star|\}$ $a = a \rightarrow [Bit]$

$Encode\{|\kappa \rightarrow \kappa'|\}$ f $= \forall a :: \kappa . Encode\{|\kappa|\}$ a $\rightarrow Encode\{|\kappa'|\}$ (f a).

In particular, if we instantiate this type to the kinds $\star$, $\star \rightarrow \star$, and $\star \rightarrow \star \rightarrow \star$, we get the types of the UNIT, EITHER, CONS cases of the definition of $encode$, respectively:

$encode\{|a :: \star|\}$ $:: a \rightarrow [Bit]$

$encode\{|f :: \star \rightarrow \star|\}$ $:: (a \rightarrow [Bit]) \rightarrow (f\ a \rightarrow [Bit])$

$encode\{|f :: \star \rightarrow \star \rightarrow \star|\} :: (a \rightarrow [Bit]) \rightarrow (b \rightarrow [Bit]) \rightarrow (f\ a\ b \rightarrow [Bit])$.

The **derive** statement is an example of how generic behavior must be explicitly derived for additional data types. If Tree is a type that we want to encode, we have to request this using a **derive** statement.

Because generic functions automatically define type classes in Clean, the type arguments (but not the kind arguments) can usually be inferred automatically. The function $encode$ can thus be invoked on a tree $t ::$ Tree by calling $encode\{|\star|\}$ t.

If $encode\{|\star|\}$ x is used in another function on a value $x :: a$, then a class constraint of the form $encode\{|\star|\}$ a arises and is propagated as usual. Other first-order kinds can be passed to $encode$, but Clean does not currently support generic functions on higher-order kinds, maybe because uniqueness annotations for higher-order kinded (higher-kinded) types are not supported.

Functions decode, eq, map and show. Apart from the already mentioned differences and a few syntactic differences between Clean and Haskell, many of the other example functions can be implemented exactly as in Generic Haskell. We therefore present only map as another example.

generic map a b $:: a \rightarrow b$

$map\{|\text{UNIT}|\}$	x	$= x$
$map\{|\text{Int}|\}$	i	$= i$
$map\{|\text{Char}|\}$	c	$= c$
$map\{|\text{EITHER}|\}$ map_a map_b	$(LEFT\ x)$	$= LEFT\ (map_a\ x)$
$map\{|\text{EITHER}|\}$ map_a map_b	$(RIGHT\ y)$	$= RIGHT\ (map_b\ y)$
$map\{|\text{PAIR}|\}$ map_a map_b	$(PAIR\ x_1\ x_2)$	$= PAIR\ (map_a\ x_1)\ (map_b\ x_2)$
$map\{|\text{CONS}|\}$ map_a	$(CONS\ x)$	$= CONS\ (map_a\ x)$
$map\{|\text{FIELD}|\}$ map_a	$(FIELD\ x)$	$= FIELD\ (map_a\ x)$
$map\{|\text{OBJECT}|\}$ map_a	$(OBJECT\ x)$	$= OBJECT\ (map_a\ x)$

The type of map makes use of two type variables and is equivalent to the Generic Haskell type $(map\{|a, b|\}) \Rightarrow a \rightarrow b$ or the kind-indexed type signature

$map\{|a :: \kappa|\} :: Map\{|\kappa|\}$ a a

$Map\{|\star|\}$ $a\ b = a \rightarrow b$

$Map\{|\kappa \rightarrow \kappa'|\}$ f g $= \forall a :: \kappa\ (b :: \kappa) . Map\{|\kappa|\}$ a b $\rightarrow Map\{|\kappa'|\}$ (f a) (g b).

As before, Clean leaves the dependency of map on itself implicit, but otherwise uses type signatures similar to Generic Haskell.

Function update. Reusing the definition of *map* to define *update* is not possible in Clean, as it supports neither default cases nor higher-order generic functions. To define *update*, we have to reimplement the *map* function plus the special case for Salary.

Evaluation

Structural dependencies. Clean supports the definition of generic functions in the style of Generic Haskell. It does not support type-indexed data types.

Full reflexivity. Generic functions in Clean do not work for types with higher-order kinds, so the generic programming extension of Clean is not fully reflexive.

Type universes. Clean can define generic functions on subsets of data types in the same way as Generic Haskell, but it does not support default cases or generic views.

First-class generic functions. Generic functions are treated as kind-indexed families of type classes. Type classes are not first-class, so generic functions are not first-class either.

Multiple type arguments. Clean allows the definition of classes with multiple type arguments. All type arguments, however, must be instantiated to the same type at the call site. Therefore, true multi-argument generic functions are not supported.

Type system. Generic functions are fully integrated into Clean's type system, by mapping each generic function to a family of type classes. The compiler ensures type-correctness.

Type safety. Clean's generic programming extension is fully type safe.

The type of a generic function. The type of a generic function is declared using the **generic** construct. The types are very similar in nature to those of Generic Haskell. They lack dependencies, which makes them a bit less expressive, but in turn a bit easier to understand.

Properties of generic functions. Again, Hinze's theory is the basis of Clean's generic programming extension. Therefore it is possible to state and prove theorems following his formalism.

Integration with the underlying programming language. Generic programming is fully integrated with the Clean language. Only the module StdGeneric must be imported in order to define new generic functions. To use a generic function *g* on a data type t we write **derive** *g* t; no type-specific code is needed.

Specialization versus interpretation. Clean uses specialization to compile generic functions. Specialization is explicit, using the **derive** construct.

Code optimization. Because Clean uses essentially the same implementation technique as Generic Haskell, there is a risk that specialized code is inefficient. There is extensive work on optimizing specialized code for generic functions generated by Clean [4,5], and the resulting code is almost as efficient as hand-written specialized code. Not all optimization algorithms have been included in the compiler yet.

Separate compilation. Generic programming is integrated into Clean, and Clean supports separate compilation.

Practical aspects. Clean is maintained and runs on several platforms. However, the documentation of generic programming in Clean is lacking. The chapter in the Clean documentation is missing, and there's a gap between the syntax used in papers and the implementation. Furthermore, the error messages of the Clean compiler with respect to generic functions are not very good. Nevertheless, generic programming in Clean seems very usable and has been used, for example, to implement a library for generating test data [60] as well as a GUI library [1].

4.2   PolyP

PolyP [48] is an extension of Haskell with a construct for defining so-called polytypic programs. There are two versions of PolyP: the original version [48], called PolyP1 from now on, is an extension of Haskell that requires a compiler to compile the special constructs for generic programming. The second version, PolyP2 [81], is a lightweight approach, with an optional compiler for generating the necessary code for a data type. In this section we will mainly describe PolyP1, but we will sometimes use PolyP2 to explain special constructs. If the distinction is not important, we will use PolyP.

PolyP allows the definition of generic functions on *regular* data types of kind $\star \rightarrow \star$. A data type is regular if it does not contain function spaces, and if the arguments of the data type constructor on the left- and right-hand sides in its definition are the same. Examples of regular data types are List a, Rose a, and Fork a. The data types CharList, Tree, and GRose are regular, but have kind $\star$, $\star$, and $(\star \rightarrow \star) \rightarrow \star \rightarrow \star$, respectively. The data type Perfect a is not regular: in the right-hand side Perfect is applied to Fork a instead of a. Another example of a data type that is not regular is the data type Flip defined by **data** Flip a b = *MkFlip* a (Flip b a).

PolyP1 is rather similar to Generic Haskell in that it translates data types to structure-representation types. The structure-representation types are then used together with polytypic definitions to generate Haskell code for (applications of) generic functions. The structure-representation type of a data type d a is given by

Mu (FunctorOf d) a,

where FunctorOf d is a type constructor of kind $\star \rightarrow \star \rightarrow \star$ representing the recursive structure of the data type d, and the data type Mu takes a type constructor and a type variable of kind $\star$, and returns the fixed point of the type constructor:

> **data** Mu f a $= Inn$ (f a (Mu f a)).

FunctorOf d is sometimes also called the *bifunctor* of d. The isomorphism between a data type and its structure-representation type is witnessed by the functions *inn* and *out*.

> inn :: FunctorOf d a (d a) $\rightarrow$ d a
> inn $= Inn$
>
> out :: d a $\rightarrow$ FunctorOf d a (d a)
> $out\ (Inn\ x) = x$

The restriction to regular data types imposed by PolyP is caused by the way the structure-representation types are built up.

Structure-representation types are expressed in terms of bifunctors. In PolyP2, bifunctors are defined by:

> **data** $(g + h)$ a b $= InL$ (g a b) $|\ InR$ (h a b)
> **data** $(g * h)$ a b $=$ g a b :*: h a b
> **newtype** Par a b $= ParF$ $\{unParF$ :: a $\}$
> **newtype** Rec a b $= RecF$ $\{unRecF$ :: b $\}$
> **newtype** (d@g) a b $= CompF\{unCompF$ :: d (g a b) $\}$
> **newtype** Const t $= ConstF\{unConstF$ :: t $\}$
> **data** Empty $= EmptyF$.

Binary functors are sums (+, with constructors InL and InR) of products (*, with constructor :*:) of either the parameter type of kind $\star$ (represented by Par, with constructor $ParF$ and destructor $unParF$), the data type itself (represented by Rec, with constructor $RecF$ and destructor $unRecF$), compositions of data types and bifunctors (represented by @, with constructor $CompF$ and destructor $unCompF$), or constant types (represented by Const t where t may be any of Float, Int, and so on, with constructor $ConstF$ and destructor $unConstF$). An empty product is represented by the unit type (represented by Empty). For example, for the data types List a, Rose a, and Fork a, PolyP uses the following internal representations:

> FunctorOf List == Empty + Par * Rec
> FunctorOf Rose == Par * List@Rec
> FunctorOf Fork == Par * Par.

There is an important difference between this encoding of data types and the encoding of data types in Generic Haskell. In Generic Haskell the structure types only represent the top-level structure of a value, whereas in PolyP the encoding of values is *deep*: the original data type has disappeared in the encoded structure.

In PolyP1, bifunctors are only used internally to construct structure-representation types. Furthermore, Empty is called (), and Const is called Con. Bifunctors can only appear in the type cases of a generic (called polytypic in PolyP) function. Furthermore, the constructors and destructors are added automatically.

An important recursion combinator in PolyP is the *catamorphism* [75], which is defined in PolyLib, the library of PolyP [49]. The catamorphism is a generalization of Haskell's *foldr* to an arbitrary data type. It takes an algebra as argument, and is defined in terms of a polytypic function *fmap2*, representing the action of the bifunctor of the data type on functions. The catamorphism is intimately tied to the representation of data types as fixed points of bifunctors; it is impossible to define the catamorphism if this fixed point is not explicitly available (as in Generic Haskell).

$$cata \quad :: Regular\ \mathsf{d} \Rightarrow (\mathsf{FunctorOf}\ \mathsf{d}\ \mathsf{a}\ \mathsf{b} \to \mathsf{b}) \to (\mathsf{d}\ \mathsf{a} \to \mathsf{b})$$
$$cata\ alg = alg\ .\ fmap2\ id\ (cata\ alg)\ .\ out$$

Function *fmap2* is a polytypic function, the two-argument variant of *map*. It is defined by induction over the structure of bifunctors. It takes two functions p and r as arguments, and applies p to occurrences of the parameter, and r to occurrences of the recursive data type.

$$\textbf{polytypic}\ fmap2 :: (\mathsf{a} \to \mathsf{c}) \to (\mathsf{b} \to \mathsf{d}) \to \mathsf{f}\ \mathsf{a}\ \mathsf{b} \to \mathsf{f}\ \mathsf{c}\ \mathsf{d}$$
$$= \lambda p\ r \to$$
$$\quad \textbf{case}\ \mathsf{f}\ \textbf{of}$$

$\mathsf{g} + \mathsf{h}$	$\to (fmap2\ p\ r)\ \text{-+-}\ (fmap2\ p\ r)$
$\mathsf{g} * \mathsf{h}$	$\to (fmap2\ p\ r)\ \text{-*-}\ (fmap2\ p\ r)$
Empty	$\to id$
Par	$\to p$
Rec	$\to r$
d@g	$\to pmap\ (fmap2\ p\ r)$
Const t	$\to id$

Here -+- and -*- have the following types:

$$(\text{-+-}) :: (\mathsf{g}\ \mathsf{a}\ \mathsf{b} \to \mathsf{g}\ \mathsf{c}\ \mathsf{d}) \to (\mathsf{h}\ \mathsf{a}\ \mathsf{b} \to \mathsf{h}\ \mathsf{c}\ \mathsf{d}) \to ((\mathsf{g} + \mathsf{h})\ \mathsf{a}\ \mathsf{b} \to (\mathsf{g} + \mathsf{h})\ \mathsf{c}\ \mathsf{d})$$
$$(\text{-*-}) :: (\mathsf{g}\ \mathsf{a}\ \mathsf{b} \to \mathsf{g}\ \mathsf{c}\ \mathsf{d}) \to (\mathsf{h}\ \mathsf{a}\ \mathsf{b} \to \mathsf{h}\ \mathsf{c}\ \mathsf{d}) \to ((\mathsf{g} * \mathsf{h})\ \mathsf{a}\ \mathsf{b} \to (\mathsf{g} * \mathsf{h})\ \mathsf{c}\ \mathsf{d}),$$

where + and * are the internal sum and product types used by PolyP.

Function encode. Function *encode* takes an encoder for parameter values as argument, and recurses over its argument by means of a catamorphism. The algebra of the catamorphism is given by the polytypic function *fencode*. The choice between an O and an I is made, again, in the sum case. The encoder for parameter values is applied in the Par case. The other cases are standard.

$$encode \quad :: Regular\ \mathsf{d} \Rightarrow (\mathsf{a} \to [\mathsf{Bit}]) \to \mathsf{d}\ \mathsf{a} \to [\mathsf{Bit}]$$
$$encode\ enca = cata\ (fencode\ enca)$$

polytypic *fencode* :: (a → [Bit]) → f a [Bit] → [Bit] =
  λ*enca* →
    case f **of**
      g + h   → (λ*x* → *O* : *fencode enca x*) '*foldSum*'
                        (λ*y* → *I* : *fencode enca y*)
      g * h   → λ(*x*, *y*) → *fencode enca x* ++ *fencode enca y*
      Empty   → *const* []
      Par   → *enca*
      Rec   → *id*
      d@g   → *encode* (*fencode enca*)
      Const Int   → *encodeInt*
      Const Char → *encodeChar*
  foldSum :: (g a b → c) → (h a b → c) → ((g + h) a b → c)

Function decode. Function *decode* is the inverse of function *encode*. It is defined in terms of function *decodes*:

  decodes   :: *Regular* d ⇒ Parser a → Parser (d a)
  decodes deca = *mapP inn* (*fdecodes deca* (*decodes deca*))
  polytypic *fdecodes* :: Parser a → Parser b → Parser (f a b) =
    λ*deca decb* →
      case f **of**
        g + h   → *bitCase* (*mapP Left* (*fdecodes deca decb*))
                          (*mapP Right* (*fdecodes deca decb*))
        g * h   → λ*bits* → [((*x*, *y*), *r₂*)
                          | (*x*, *r₁*) ← *fdecodes deca decb bits*
                          , (*y*, *r₂*) ← *fdecodes deca decb r₁*]
        Empty   → λ*bits* → [((), *bits*)]
        Par   → *deca*
        Rec   → *decb*
        d@g   → *decodes* (*fdecodes deca decb*)
        Const Int   → *decodesInt*
        Const Char → *decodesChar*.

Given the definition of function *encode*, the definition of functions *decode* (omitted) and *decodes* is rather standard. We have used a list comprehension in the product case of function *fdecodes* to stay as close as possible to the implementation of *decodes* in Generic Haskell. List comprehensions are not supported by PolyP, so to compile the program, this piece of code should be replaced by its equivalent not using list comprehensions.

The definition of the polytypic functions *eq* and *map* contain no surprises: both are similar to the definitions of function *fmap2* and *encode*, and can be found in PolyLib [49].

Function update. It is impossible to define a generic function in PolyP that can be used to update the salaries in a Company value. First, the data type Company does not have kind $\star \to \star$. But even if we add a superfluous type variable to the data type Company, PolyP does not 'look into' the constituent Dept values, and hence never changes a Salary. The only way to update a salary in a company structure is by defining Company as one big recursive data type, 'inlining' the definitions of most of the constituent data types, and by adding a superfluous type variable.

Evaluation

Structural dependencies. PolyP adds polytypic functions, which depend on types, to Haskell.

Full reflexivity. PolyP is not fully reflexive: polytypic functions can only be used on regular data types of kind $\star \to \star$. Important classes of data types for which polytypic functions do not work are mutually-recursive data types and data types of kind $\star$.

Type universes. PolyP only works on regular data types of kind $\star \to \star$. Besides the obvious disadvantages, this has an advantage as well: since the structure of regular data types of kind $\star \to \star$ can be described by a bifunctor, we can define functions like the catamorphism on arbitrary data types in PolyP. The catamorphism cannot be defined in Generic Haskell without the concept of generic views [45]. PolyP supports defining generic functions on particular data types using the Const case.

First-class generic functions. Polytypic functions are not first class in PolyP1. In the lightweight approach PolyP2 polytypic functions are first class.

Multiple type arguments. Polytypic functions are defined by induction over a single bifunctor.

Type system. Polytypic functions are explicitly typed. The compiler checks type-correctness of polytypic functions.

Type safety. Type-correct polytypic functions are translated to type-correct Haskell functions. Forgetting an arm in the case expression of a polytypic function leads to an error when the generated Haskell is compiled or interpreted.

The type of a generic function. Types of polytypic functions are direct abstractions of types on normal data types, and closely correspond to intuition.

Properties of generic functions. Jansson and Jeuring [57,50] show how to reason about polytypic functions, and how to derive a property of a polytypic function from its type.

Integration with the underlying programming language. The integration of polytypic programming and Haskell is not completely seamless. PolyP1 and the optional compiler of PolyP2 do not know about classes, or types of kind other than $\star \rightarrow \star$, and lack several syntactic constructions that are common in Haskell, such as **where** clauses and operator sections. It is wise to separate the polytypic functions from other functions in a separate file, and only compile this file with PolyP1 or PolyP2. The Haskell library part of PolyP2 integrates seamlessly with Haskell.

Polytypic functions can be used on values of data types without any extra work. It is not necessary to specify a type argument: PolyP1 infers the data types on which a polytypic function is called, and uses this information to specialize a polytypic function for a particular data type.

Specialization versus interpretation. PolyP1 and the optional PolyP2 compiler specialize applications of polytypic functions at compile-time. The PolyP2 Haskell library interprets bifunctors at run time.

Code optimization. Like Generic Haskell, PolyP1 does not optimize away the extra marshaling that is introduced by the compiler for instances of polytypic functions. This might be an impediment for some applications.

Separate compilation. PolyP provides separate compilation.

Practical aspects. A compiler for PolyP can be downloaded. It is usable on the platforms on which GHC is available. It is not very actively maintained anymore: the latest release is from 2004. It is reasonably well documented, although not all limitations are mentioned in the documentation. PolyP's error messages could be improved.

4.3   Scrap Your Boilerplate

Scrap Your Boilerplate (SYB) [61,64] is a library that provides combinators to build traversals and queries in Haskell. A traversal processes and selectively modifies a possibly complex data structure, whereas a query collects specific information from a data structure. Using SYB one can extend basic traversals and queries with type-specific information, thereby writing generic functions.

Generic functions in SYB are applicable to all data types of the type class *Data*. This class provides fundamental operations to consume or build values of a data type, as well as general information about the structure of a data type. All other functions are built on top of methods of the class *Data*.

A partial definition of the class *Data* is shown in Figure 2.

The function *toConstr* yields information about the data constructor that has constructed the given value. The data type Constr is abstract and can be queried for information such as the name of the constructor, or the data type it belongs to.

Similarly, *dataTypeOf* returns information about the data type of a value, again encapsulated in an abstract data type DataType.

```
class (Typeable a) ⇒ Data a where
   toConstr    :: a → Constr
   dataTypeOf  :: a → DataType
   gfoldl      :: ∀f.
                  (∀a b. Data a ⇒ f (a → b) → a → f b)
                → (∀a. a → f a)
                → a → f a
```

Fig. 2. Partial definition of the type class *Data*

The function *gfoldl* is a very general function that allows the destruction of a single input value – the third argument – of type a into a result of type f a. Almost any Haskell value is an application of a data constructor to other values. This is the structure that *gfoldl* works on. If a value v is of the form

$$C\ v_1\ v_2 \ldots v_n$$

then *gfoldl* $(\diamond)$ c v is

$$(\cdots ((c\ C \diamond v_1) \diamond v_2) \diamond \cdots \diamond v_n).$$

The second argument c is applied to the data constructor C, and each application is replaced by the first argument $(\diamond)$. In particular,

$$unId\ .\ gfoldl\ (\lambda x\ y \to Id\ (unId\ x\ y))\ Id$$

is the identity on types of class *Data*. Here, the auxiliary type

newtype Id a $= Id\{unId :: a\}$

is used, because the result type of f a of *gfoldl* can be instantiated to Id a, but not directly to a in Haskell. If we could, then

$$gfoldl\ (\$)\ id$$

would be the identity, making the role of *gfoldl* more obvious.

With the help of *gfoldl*, a basic query combinator can be defined, which also forms part of the SYB library:

$$gmapQ :: \forall a.\ Data\ a \Rightarrow (\forall b.\ Data\ b \Rightarrow b \to c) \to a \to [c].$$

A call *gmapQ* q x takes a query q (of type $\forall b.\ Data\ b \Rightarrow b \to c$) and applies it to the immediate subterms of x, collecting the results in a list.

Function encode. A good example of a function using *gmapQ* is the function *encode*, which can be written using the SYB library as follows:

$$encode :: Data\ a \Rightarrow a \rightarrow [\text{Bit}]$$
$$encode\ x = concat\ (encodeConstr\ (toConstr\ x) : gmapQ\ encode\ x).$$

The function $encodeConstr$ takes the current constructor and encodes it as a list of bits:

$$encodeConstr :: \text{Constr} \rightarrow [\text{Bit}]$$
$$encodeConstr\ c = intinrange2bits\ (maxConstrIndex\ (constrType\ c))$$
$$(constrIndex\ c - 1).$$

The function $intinrange2bits$, which encodes a natural number in a given range as a list of bits, comes from a separate Haskell module for manipulating bits. In $encode$, the constructor for the current value x is encoded, and we use $gmapQ$ to recursively encode the subterms of x.

With $encode$, we can for instance encode booleans, lists, and trees: we have a generic function. However, the default behavior is unsuitable for handling base types such as Int and Char. If we want to use type-specific behavior such as $encodeInt$ and $encodeChar$, the SYB library allows us to extend a query with a type-specific case, using $extQ$:

$$extQ :: \forall a\ b\ c\,.\,(Typeable\ a,\ Typeable\ b) \Rightarrow (a \rightarrow c) \rightarrow (b \rightarrow c) \rightarrow (a \rightarrow c).$$

This function makes use of run-time type information which is encapsulated in the type class $Typeable$ and available for all types in $Data$, as $Typeable$ is a superclass of $Data$. It is essentially a one-arm $type\text{-}case$ [83]. Using $extQ$, we can write $encode$ with type-specific behavior for Ints and Chars:

$$encode :: Data\ a \Rightarrow a \rightarrow [\text{Bit}]$$
$$encode = (\lambda x \rightarrow concat\ (encodeConstr\ (toConstr\ x) : gmapQ\ encode\ x))$$
$$`extQ`\ encodeInt$$
$$`extQ`\ encodeChar.$$

Note that we cannot reuse the previously defined version of $encode$ in this new definition, because the recursive call to $encode$ that appears as an argument to $gmapQ$ must point to the extended function (this is solved by the modified approach discussed in the section on "SYB with Class").

Function decode. The $gfoldl$ combinator is only suitable for *processing* values. In order to write a generic *producer* such as $decode$, a different combinator is required. The $Data$ class provides one, called $gunfold$:

$$gunfold :: \forall a\ f\,.$$
$$(\forall a\ b\,.\,Data\ a \Rightarrow f\ (a \rightarrow b) \rightarrow f\ b)$$
$$\rightarrow (\forall a\,.\,a \rightarrow f\ a)$$
$$\rightarrow \text{Constr} \rightarrow f\ a.$$

If $d ::$ Constr is the constructor information for the data constructor C, which takes n arguments, then *gunfold app c d* is

$$app \; (\cdots \; (app \; (c \; C)) \; \cdots),$$

thus *app* applied n times to $c \; C$. As with *gfoldl*, SYB provides several combinators built on top of *gunfold*, the most useful being *fromConstrM*, which monadically constructs a value of a certain constructor:

$$fromConstrM :: \forall a \; f . (Data \; a, Monad \; f) \Rightarrow (\forall b . Data \; b \Rightarrow f \; b) \rightarrow$$
$$Constr \rightarrow f \; a$$

fromConstrM p = gunfold ('ap'p) *return.*

Here, $ap :: \forall b \; f . Monad \; f \Rightarrow f \; (a \rightarrow b) \rightarrow f \; a \rightarrow f \; b$ is lifted function application.

Using *fromConstrM*, we can define *decodes*, but since *fromConstrM* requires a monad, we have to turn our parser type into a monad. Recall that

type Parser a $= [\mathsf{Bit}] \rightarrow [(\mathsf{a}, [\mathsf{Bit}])]$.

We turn Parser into a state monad by wrapping it into a **newtype** construct and defining appropriate class instances:

newtype *ParserM* a $= M \{ \; runM :: $ Parser a $\}$

instance *Monad ParserM* **where**
$\quad return \; x = M \; (\lambda s \rightarrow [(x, s)])$
$\quad f \ggg g \;\; = M \; (\lambda s \rightarrow [r \mid (x, s') \leftarrow runM \; f \; s, r \leftarrow runM \; (g \; x) \; s'])$

instance *MonadState* $[\mathsf{Bit}]$ *ParserM* **where**
$\quad get \;\; = M \; (\lambda s \rightarrow [(s, s)])$
$\quad put \; s = M \; (\lambda\_ \rightarrow [((), s)])$.

The code for *decodes* is then defined as follows:

$decodes :: Data \; a \Rightarrow$ Parser a
$decodes \quad\;\; = decodes' \perp$
$\qquad\qquad\quad$ '$extR$' *decodesInt*
$\qquad\qquad\quad$ '$extR$' *decodesChar*
$\quad$**where**
$\qquad decodes' \qquad\quad :: Data \; a \Rightarrow a \rightarrow$ Parser a
$\qquad decodes' \; dummy = runM \; \$$
$\qquad\quad$**do let** $d \;\; = dataTypeOf \; dummy$
$\qquad\qquad\quad\;\; l \;\;\; = length \; (int2bits \; (length \; (dataTypeConstrs \; d) - 1))$
$\qquad\qquad c \leftarrow consume \; l$
$\qquad\qquad$**let** $con = decodeConstr \; c \; d$
$\qquad\qquad fromConstrM \; (M \; decodes) \; con.$

A few remarks are in order. The function *decodes* calls *decodes'* with $\perp$. This is a convenient way to obtain a value of the result type a, so that we can apply *dataTypeOf* to it. The function *decodes'* reads in l bits from the input via *consume*, interprets these bits as a constructor *con* using *decodeConstr*, and finally employs *fromConstrM* to decode the children of the constructor recursively. In addition, *decodes'* performs the necessary conversions between Parser and *ParserM*.

The functions *consume* and *decodeConstr* are both easy to define. Type-specific behavior for integers and characters is added to *decodes* using the SYB extension operator *extR*, which plays a role analogous to *extQ*, in the context of monadic generic producers:

$$extR :: \forall a\ b\ f\ .\ (Monad\ f,\ Typeable\ a,\ Typeable\ b) \Rightarrow f\ a \rightarrow f\ b \rightarrow f\ a.$$

From *decodes*, we get *decode* in the obvious way:

$$decode :: Data\ a \Rightarrow [\text{Bit}] \rightarrow a$$
$$decode\ bs = \textbf{case}\ decodes\ bs\ \textbf{of}$$
$$(r, [\,]) \rightarrow r$$
$$\_ \qquad \rightarrow error\ \texttt{"decode: no parse"}.$$

Function eq. The definition of generic equality in SYB is simple, but requires yet another combinator:

$$eq :: Data\ a \Rightarrow a \rightarrow a \rightarrow \text{Bool}$$
$$eq = eq'$$
$$eq' :: (Data\ a,\ Data\ b) \Rightarrow a \rightarrow b \rightarrow \text{Bool}$$
$$eq'\ x\ y = toConstr\ x \mathrel{\texttt{==}} toConstr\ y \wedge and\ (gzipWithQ\ eq'\ x\ y).$$

The function *eq* is a type-restricted variant of *eq'*, which accepts two arguments of potentially different types. The constructors of the two values are compared, and *gzipWithQ* is used to pairwise compare the subterms of the two values recursively.

The combinator *gzipWithQ* is a two-argument variant of *mapQ*. It is a bit tricky to define, but it can be defined in terms of *gfoldl*.

Note that *eq'* requires the relaxed type, because the subterms of *x* and *y* only have compatible types if they really are of the same data constructor. If we compare unequal values, we are likely to get incompatible types sooner or later.

The trick to relax the type of a generic function is not always applicable. For example, if we also want to extend equality on an abstract type for which we only have a normal equality function (one that expects two arguments of the same type), we have to make sure that both arguments are indeed of the same type. In this case, we can use the dynamically available type information from class *Typeable* to define a unification function

$$unify :: (Typeable\ a,\ Typeable\ b) \Rightarrow \text{Maybe}\ (a \rightarrow b)$$

and then call *unify* to coerce the types where necessary.

Function map. A generic function such as *map* that abstracts over a type constructor cannot be defined using SYB, because the *Data* class contains only types of kind ⋆. It is possible to define variants of *map*, such as traversals that increase all integers in a complex data structure, but it isn't possible to define a function of type

$$\forall \mathsf{a}\ \mathsf{b}\ \mathsf{f}\ .\ (\mathsf{a} \rightarrow \mathsf{b}) \rightarrow \mathsf{f}\ \mathsf{a} \rightarrow \mathsf{f}\ \mathsf{b},$$

where the arguments of the container type f are modified, and the function is parametrically polymorphic in a and b (see also the section on "SYB Revolutions" below).

Function show. We define *show* in two steps, as we have done in the Generic Haskell case. The function *showP* takes an additional string transformer that encodes whether to place surrounding parentheses on non-atomic expressions or not.

We have already seen how constructor information can be accessed in the definition of *encode*. Therefore, the definition of *showP* does not come as a surprise:

$$
\begin{aligned}
&showP :: Data\ \mathsf{a} \Rightarrow (\mathsf{String} \rightarrow \mathsf{String}) \rightarrow \mathsf{a} \rightarrow \mathsf{String} \\
&showP\ p = (\lambda x \rightarrow showApp\ (showConstr\ (toConstr\ x)) \\
&\qquad\qquad\qquad\qquad\qquad (gmapQ\ ((\mathbin{+\!\!+})\ "\ "\ .\ showP\ parens)\ x)) \\
&\qquad\qquad\ \text{`}ext1Q\text{`}\ showList \\
&\qquad\qquad\ \text{`}extQ\text{`}\ (Prelude.show :: \mathsf{String} \rightarrow \mathsf{String})
\end{aligned}
$$

where

$$parens\ x = "("\mathbin{+\!\!+} x \mathbin{+\!\!+}")"$$

$$showApp :: \mathsf{String} \rightarrow [\mathsf{String}] \rightarrow \mathsf{String}$$
$$showApp\ x\ [] = x$$
$$showApp\ x\ xs = p\ (concat\ (x : xs))$$

$$showList :: Data\ \mathsf{a} \Rightarrow [\mathsf{a}] \rightarrow \mathsf{String}$$
$$showList\ xs = $$
$$"["\mathbin{+\!\!+} concat\ (intersperse\ ","\ (map\ (showP\ id)\ xs)) \mathbin{+\!\!+}"]".$$

We feed each constructor application to *showApp*. On atomic subexpressions, *showApp* never produces parentheses, otherwise it consults *p*.

The most interesting part is how to define type-specific behavior for lists and strings. Placing strings between double quotes is achieved by the standard Haskell *show* function using the *extQ* extension operator. However, the more general syntactic sugar for lists (placed between square brackets, elements separated by commas) is not achieved so easily, because *showList* is a polymorphic function, and *extQ* only works if the second argument is of monomorphic type. SYB therefore provides a special, polymorphic, extension operator

$$
\begin{aligned}
&ext1Q :: \forall \mathsf{a}\ \mathsf{c}\ .\ (Typeable1\ \mathsf{f}, Data\ \mathsf{a}) \Rightarrow \\
&\qquad (\mathsf{a} \rightarrow \mathsf{c}) \rightarrow (\forall \mathsf{b}\ .\ Data\ \mathsf{b} \Rightarrow \mathsf{f}\ \mathsf{b} \rightarrow \mathsf{c}) \rightarrow (\mathsf{a} \rightarrow \mathsf{c}).
\end{aligned}
$$

Note that polymorphic extension requires a separate operator for each kind, and also a separate variant of the cast operation: the run-time type information of the type constructor f of kind $\star \to \star$ is made available using the type class *Typeable1* rather than *Typeable*.

Function update. Traversals that update a large heterogeneous data structure in selective places were one of the main motivations for designing SYB. Therefore, it isn't surprising that defining such a traversal is extremely simple:

$$update :: Data\ a \Rightarrow a \to a$$
$$update = everywhere\ (id\ `extT`\ (\lambda(S\ s) \to S\ (s * (1 + 0.15)))).$$

The argument to *everywhere* is the identity function, extended with a type-specific case for the type Salary. The function *everywhere* is a SYB combinator that applies a function at any point (constructor) in a data structure. It is defined in terms of

$$gmapT :: \forall a\ .\ Data\ a \Rightarrow (\forall b\ .\ Data\ b \Rightarrow b \to b) \to (a \to a),$$

a variant of *gmapQ* that applies a given generic function to the immediate subterms of a value. The *gmapT* can again be defined using *gfoldl*. Note that all these functions similar to, but different from the generic *map* function, which applies an argument function to all occurrences of values of a parameter type in a data type of a higher kind.

Derived work: SYB with Class. Lämmel and Peyton Jones have shown [62] that using type classes rather than run-time type casts can make generic programming using SYB more flexible. Their work aims at replacing SYB extension operators such as *extQ* and *extR*: each generic function is then defined as a class with a default behavior, and type-specific behavior can be added by defining specific instances of the class.

To achieve this added flexibility, some alterations to the class *Data* are required. The class must be parametrized over a *context* parameter:

```
class (Typeable a, Sat c a) ⇒ Data c a where
    toConstr    :: Proxy c → a → Constr
    dataTypeOf :: a → DataType
    gfoldl      :: ∀f . Proxy c
                → (∀a b . Data c a ⇒ f (a → b) → a → f b)
                → (∀a . a → f a)
                → a → f a.
```

The context parameter c together with the class constraint on *Sat* c a simulates abstracting over a superclass: recursive generic functions are defined as a class. Because the class methods make use of the generic combinators such as *gfoldl* or derived combinators such as *gmapQ*, *Data* must be a superclass of the class of the function. But because the *Data* constraint occurs inside the type of the generic combinators such as *gfoldl*, the class of the function must also be a superclass of *Data*. This is not directly possible, hence the encoding via the context parameter.

The presence of this encoding leads to a number of encumbrances and subtleties in the "SYB with Class" approach. Sometimes, Haskell is not clever enough to figure out the correct instantiation of the context parameter itself. Therefore, the class methods of *Data* all take an additional parameter of type Proxy c, with the sole purpose to make the instantiation of c explicit. Furthermore, the possible instantiations of c are dictionary types that have to be defined for each generic function (or group of mutually recursive generic functions).

As an example, let us look at *encode* again. In the class-based approach, we define *encode* simply as follows:

> **class** *Encode* a **where**
> $\quad$ *encode* :: a $\rightarrow$ [Bit].

However, to turn it into a generic definition, we must now define a suitable context to use in the argument of *Data*. This requires the following definitions:

> **data** Encode a $=$ *Encode*{ *encodeD* :: a $\rightarrow$ [Bit]}
>
> *encodeProxy* :: Proxy Encode
> *encodeProxy* $= \perp$
>
> **instance** *Encode* a $\Rightarrow$ *Sat* Encode a **where**
> $\quad$ *dict* $=$ *Encode*{ *encodeD* $=$ *encode* }.

The class *Sat* need only be defined once and is given simply as

> **class** *Sat* c a **where**
> $\quad$ *dict* :: c a.

We are now in a position to give the generic definition of *encode*:

> **instance** (*Data* Encode a) $\Rightarrow$ *Encode* a **where**
> $\quad$ *encode* x $=$ *concat* (*encodeConstr* (*toConstr* *encodeProxy* x) :
> $\qquad\qquad\qquad\qquad$ *gmapQ* *encodeProxy* (*encodeD* *dict*) x).

If we compare this definition with the definition of *encode* in original SYB style on page 106, then there are only few differences: first, the type-specific cases are missing (they can be added later using specific class instances); second, the proxy arguments are passed (also *gmapQ* takes a proxy argument now) to help the type checker along; third, the recursive call of *encode* is replaced by *encodeD* *dict*. The latter is because the argument to *gmapQ* must actually have type $\forall$a. *Data* Encode a $\Rightarrow$ a $\rightarrow$ [Bit] in this case, and the direct use of *encode* would introduce an illegal constraint on *Encode* a.

Type-specific cases can now be defined separately (and later) as additional instances of *Encode*:

```
instance Encode Int where
    encode = encodeInt
instance Encode Char where
    encode = encodeChar.
```

As we can see from this example, there is a significant advantage to using SYB with classes, but there are disadvantages as well: the user has additional work, because for each generic function, an additional context type, a proxy, and an embedding instance for *Sat* must be defined. The use of *dict* rather than direct recursive calls, and the passing of proxy arguments is quite subtle. Furthermore, the class structure used here requires the GHC extensions of overlapping and undecidable instances.

Derived work: SYB Reloaded and Revolutions. In their SYB Reloaded and Revolutions papers, Hinze, Löh and Oliveira [44,43] demonstrate that SYB's *gfoldl* function is in essence a catamorphism on the Spine data type, which can be defined as follows:

```
data Spine a where
    Constr :: Constr → a → Spine a
    (◇)    :: Data a ⇒ Spine (a → b) → a → Spine b.
```

Furthermore, a "type spine" type is given as a replacement for *gunfold*, and a "lifted spine" type for generic functions that are parametrized over type constructors. For example, using the lifted spine type, *map* can be defined.

Evaluation

Structural dependencies. SYB allows the definition of generic functions. There is no support for defining type-indexed data types.

Full reflexivity. The SYB approach is not fully reflexive. Generic functions are only applicable to data types for which a *Typeable* instance can be specified. This implies, amongst others, that higher-kinded data types such as GRose cannot be turned into instance declarations as this requires so-called *higher-order contexts*. The original proposal for Derivable Type Classes (discussed in Section 4.5) recognizes this shortcoming and proposes a solution in the form of higher-order contexts, but this extension has never been implemented.
    Type-specific behavior is only possible for types of kind ⋆.

Type universes. There is no support for type universes in SYB. All generic functions are supposed to work on all types in the *Typeable* class.

First-class generic functions. In SYB, generic functions are normal polymorphic Haskell functions, and as such are first-class. However, so-called *rank-n types* are required (a function has rank 2 if it takes a *polymorphic function* as an argument). Most Haskell implementations support rank-n types.

Multiple type arguments. There is no restriction on the number of type arguments that a generic function can have in SYB, although the basic combinators are tailored for functions of the form

$$Data\; \mathsf{a} \Rightarrow \mathsf{a} \rightarrow \ldots$$

that consume a single value.

Type system. SYB is completely integrated in Haskell's type system.

Type safety. SYB is type-safe, but type-specific extensions of generic functions rely on run-time type casting via the *Typeable* class. It is possible for a user to break type safety by defining bogus instances for the *Typeable* class. The implementation could be made more robust if user-defined instances of class *Typeable* would not be allowed, and all *Typeable* instances would be derived automatically by the compiler.

The type of a generic function. Types of generic functions have one or more constraints for the *Data* class. The types are intuitive, maybe except for the generic combinators such as *ext1Q* and *gunfold*.

Properties of generic functions. The use of type classes *Data* and *Typeable* at the basis of SYB makes proving properties relatively difficult. Instances for these classes can be generated automatically, but automatic generation is only described informally. User-defined instances of these classes can cause unintended behavior. There is no small set of fundamental data types (such as Generic Haskell's unit, binary sum, and binary pair types) to which Haskell data types are reduced. Lämmel and Peyton Jones state a few properties of basic SYB combinators in the original paper, but provide no proof. The only work we are aware of trying to prove properties about SYB is of Reig [88], but he translates SYB combinators into Generic Haskell to do so.

Integration with the underlying programming language. SYB is fully integrated into GHC. Making SYB available for Hugs or another Haskell compiler would be a major effort. The module `Data.Generics` contains all SYB combinators. The options `-fglasgow-exts` is required for GHC to support the higher-ranked types of some of the SYB combinators. No extra work is needed to use a generic function on a data type other than writing **deriving** (*Data*, *Typeable*) after the data-type declaration.

Specialization versus interpretation. The SYB approach makes use of run-time type information. Generic functions have *Data* class constraints. Most Haskell compilers implement type classes using *dictionary passing*: for each *Data* constraint, a record containing the appropriate class methods is passed along at run-time. The *Data* is a subclass of *Typeable*, which provides the actual structure of the type at run-time. This information is used to provide run-time type casts to enable type-specific behavior.

Code optimization. As SYB is a Haskell library, the code is not optimized in any special way. The implementation of generic functions is relatively direct. The passing of class dictionaries, the type casts, and the use of many higher-order functions might sometimes lead to a considerable overhead.

Separate compilation. Generic functions are normal Haskell functions, and can be placed in different modules and compiled separately. Generic functions themselves are not extensible, however. If new specific cases must be added to a generic function, the whole definition has to be repeated. This restriction is lifted by "SYB with Class".

Practical aspects. SYB is shipped as a library with current releases of GHC and supported. It is planned to provide the functionality of "SYB with Class" in future releases of GHC. The Spine data type from "SYB Reloaded" is not yet used in the official release, but might be integrated in the future.

4.4   Approaches Based on Reflection

Both DrIFT [99] and generic programming approaches using Template Haskell [82] use a kind of reflection mechanism to generate instances of generic functions for a data type. Generic functions are defined on an abstract syntax for data types. This section introduces and evaluates these two approaches.

DrIFT

DrIFT is a type sensitive preprocessor for Haskell. It extracts type declarations and directives from Haskell modules. The directives cause rules to be fired on the parsed type declarations, generating new code which is then appended to the bottom of the input file. An example of a directive is:

  {- ! **for** Foo **derive** : *update, Show* -} .

Given such a directive in a module that defines the data type Foo, and rules for generating instances of the function *update* and the class *Show*, DrIFT generates a definition of the function *update* on the data type Foo, and an instance of *Show* for Foo. The rules are expressed as Haskell code, and a user can add new rules as required.

DrIFT comes with a number of predefined rules, for example for the classes derivable in Haskell and for several marshaling functions between Haskell data and, for example, XML, ATerm, and a binary data format.

A type is represented within DrIFT using the following data definition.

```
data Statement = DataStmt | NewTypeStmt
data Data = D{ name        :: Name          -- type name
            , constraints :: [(Class, Var)]  -- constraints on type vars
            , vars        :: [Var]           -- parameters
            , body        :: [Body]          -- the constructors
```

```
                    , derives    :: [Class]       -- derived classes
                    , statement  :: Statement     -- data or newtype
                    }
    type Name      = String
    type Var       = String
    type Class     = String
```

A value of type Data represents one parsed data or newtype statement. These are held in a D constructor record. The body of a data type is represented by a value of type Body. It holds information about a single constructor.

```
    data Body = Body{ constructor :: Constructor    -- constructor name
                    , labels      :: [Name]         -- label names
                    , types       :: [Type]         -- type representations
                    }
    type Constructor = String
```

The definition of Type is as follows.

```
    data Type = Arrow Type Type    -- function type
              | Apply Type Type    -- application
              | Var String         -- variable
              | Con String         -- constant
              | Tuple [Type]       -- tuple
              | List Type          -- list
                    deriving (Eq, Show)
```

For example, the data type CharList is represented internally by:

```
    reprCharList = D{ name        = "CharList"
                    , constraints = []
                    , vars        = []
                    , body        = [bodyNil, bodyCons]
                    , derives     = []
                    , statement   = DataStmt
                    }
    bodyNil      = Body{ constructor = "Nil"
                       , labels      = []
                       , types       = []
                       }
    bodyCons     = Body{ constructor = "Cons"
                       , labels      = []
                       , types       = [Con "Char"
                                       , Con "CharList"]
                       }.
```

A rule consists of a name and a function that takes a Data and returns a document, a value of type Doc, containing the textual code of the rule for the Data value. The type Doc is defined in a module for pretty printing, and has several operators defined on it, for example for putting two documents beside each other (<+>) (list version *hsep*), above each other $$ (list version *vcat*), and for printing texts (*text* and *texts*) [47]. Constructing output using pretty-printing combinators is easier and more structured than manipulating strings.

Function encode. We now explain the rules necessary for obtaining a definition of function *encode* on an arbitrary data type. For that purpose, we define the following class in our test file.

> **class** *Encode* a **where**
>   *encode* :: a → [Bit]

and ask DrIFT to generate instances of this class for all data types by means of the directive {- ! **global** : *encode* -} . For example, for the type CharList it generates:

> **instance** *Encode* CharList **where**
>   *encode Nil*   = [*O*]
>   *encode* (*Cons aa ab*) = [*I*] ++ *encode aa* ++ *encode ab*.

Rules for generating such instances have to be added to the file UserRules.hs.

> *encodefn*   :: Data → Doc
> *encodefn d* =
>   *instanceSkeleton* "Encode"
>   [(*makeEncodefn* (*mkBits* (*body d*)), *empty*)]
>   *d*
> *mkBits*   :: [Body] → Constructor → String
> *mkBits bodies c* = (*show*
>   . *intinrange2bits* (*length bodies*)
>   . *fromJust*
>   . *elemIndex c*
>   . *map constructor*
>   ) *bodies*

The function *encodefn* generates an instance of the class *Encode* using the utility function *instanceSkeleton*. It applies *makeEncodefn* to each *Body* of a data type, and adds the *empty* document at the end of the definition. The function *mkBits* takes a list of bodies, and returns a function that when given a constructor returns the list of bits for the constructor in its data type. For example, the list of bits for a data type with three constructors are [[*O*, *O*], [*O*, *I*], [*I*, *O*]]. As before, we use the utility function *intinrange2bits* to encode a natural number in a given range.

   The function *makeEncodefn* takes an encoding function and a body, and returns a document containing the definition of function *encode* on the constructor represented by the body. If the constructor has no arguments, *encode* returns the list of bits for the constructor, obtained by means of the encoding function that is passed as an argument. If the constructor does have arguments, *encode* returns the list of bits for the constructor, followed by the encodings of the arguments of the constructor. For the argument of *encode* on the left-hand side of the definition we have to generate as many variables as there are arguments to the constructor. These variables are returned by the utility function *varNames*. Function *varNames* takes a list, and returns a list of variable names, the length of which is equal to the length of the argument list. The constructor pattern is now obtained by prefixing the list generated by *varNames* with the constructor. This is *conPat* in the definition below. The encodings of the arguments of the constructor are obtained by prefixing the generated variables with the function *encode*, and separating the elements in the list with the list-concatenation operator ++. Finally, *equals* is a utility function that returns the document containing an equality sign, '='.

```
makeEncodefn :: (Constructor → String) → (Body → Doc)
makeEncodefn enc (Body{ constructor = constructor, types = types }) =
    let bits       = text (enc constructor)
        encodeText = text "encode"
        constrText = text constructor
    in let newVars = varNames types
        conPat     = parens . hsep $ constrText : newVars
        lhs        = encodeText <+> conPat
        rhs        = ( fsep
                     . sepWith (text "++")
                     . (bits:)
                     . map (λn → encodeText <+> n)
                     ) newVars
    in lhs <+> equals <+> rhs
```

Function decode. Decoding is a bit more complicated. First, we define the following class in our test file.

```
class Decode a where
    decodes    :: Parser a

    decode     :: [Bit] → a
    decode bits = case decodes bits of
                    [(y, [])] → y
                    _         → error "decode: no parse"
```

Then we ask DrIFT to generate instances of this class for all data types by means of the directive {- ! **global** : *decode* -} . For example, for the type CharList it should generate:

```
instance Decode CharList where
    decodes (O : xs) = [(Nil, xs)]
```

$$decodes\ (I : xs) = [(Cons\ res_1\ res_2, xs_2) \mid (res_1, xs_1) \leftarrow decodes\ xs$$
$$, (res_2, xs_2) \leftarrow decodes\ xs_1]$$
$$decodes\ [] \qquad = error\ \texttt{"decodes"}.$$

The decode function generates an instance of the class *Decode*. It adds the declaration of *decodes* on the empty list as the last line in each class instance.

```
decodefn   :: Data → Doc
decodefn d =
  instanceSkeleton "Decode"
               [(mkDecodefn (mkBitsPattern (body d))
               , text "decodes [] = error \"decodes\"")
               ]
               d
```

Here, function *mkBitsPattern* is almost the same as function *mkBits*, except for the way in which the list of bits is shown. We omit its definition.

The function *mkDecodefn* produces the cases for the different constructors. The left-hand side of these cases are obtained by constructing the appropriate bits pattern. The right-hand side is obtained by means of the function *decodechildren*, and returns a constructor (applied to its arguments). If a constructor has no arguments this is easy: return the constructor. If a constructor does have arguments, we first *decode* the arguments, and use the results of these decodings as arguments to the constructor. The implementation of function *mkDecodefn* is almost a page of Haskell code, and can be found in the accompanying technical report [40].

Instances of class Eq. The rules necessary for generating an instance of the class *Eq* for a data type are very similar to the rules for generating an instance of the class *Encode*. These rules are omitted, and can be found in the file `StandardRules.hs` in the distribution of DrIFT.

Function map. The rules for generating instances of the *map* function on different data types differ from the rules given until now. The biggest difference is that we do not generate instances of a class. Any class definition is of the form **class** *C* **t where** ..., in which the kind of the type t is fixed. So suppose we define the following class for *map*:

class *Map*{|t|} **where**
    map :: (a → b) → t a → t b.

Then we can only instantiate this class with types of kind $\star \to \star$. Since the data type of generalized trees GTree has kind $\star \to \star \to \star$, we cannot represent the 'standard' *map* function on GTree by means of an instance of this class. Instead, we generate a separate *map* function on each data type. For example, on the type GTree we obtain:

$$mapGTree\ fa\ fb\ GEmpty\quad = GEmpty$$
$$mapGTree\ fa\ fb\ (GLeaf\ a)\quad = GLeaf\ (fa\ a)$$
$$mapGTree\ fa\ fb\ (GBin\ l\ v\ r) = GBin\ (mapGTree\ fa\ fb\ l)$$
$$(fb\ v)$$
$$(mapGTRee\ fa\ fb\ r).$$

It is impossible to define a generic map that works on types of different kinds for many of the other approaches to generic programming. DrIFT allows us to do anything we want, which we illustrate by defining map in an alternative fashion.

The function *mapfn* generates a definition of *map* for each constructor using *mkMapfn*. The function *mkMapfn* takes as arguments the name of the data type (for generating the name of the *map* function on the data type) and the variables of the data type (for generating the names of the function arguments of *map*).

$$mapfn :: \mathsf{Data} \to \mathsf{Doc}$$
$$mapfn\ (D\{\,name = name, vars = vars, body = body\,\}) =$$
$$vcat\ (map\ (mkMapfn\ name\ vars)\ body)$$

Function *mkMapfn* creates the individual arms of the *map* function. For generating the right-hand side, it recurses over the type of the constructor in the declaration *rhsfn*.

$$mkMapfn\ name\ vars\ (Body\{\,constr = constructor, types = types\,\}) =$$
$$\mathbf{let}\ mt\ name = text\ (\texttt{"map"} \mathbin{+\!\!+} name)$$
$$mapArgs\quad = hsep\ (texts\ (map\ (\lambda v \to \texttt{'f'} : v)\ vars))$$
$$newVars\quad = varNames\ types$$
$$conPat\quad = parens\,.\,hsep\ \$\ text\ constr : newVars$$
$$lhs\quad\quad = mt\ name <\!+\!> mapArgs <\!+\!> conPat$$
$$rhs\quad\quad = hsep\ (text\ constr$$
$$: map\ (parens\,.\,rhsfn)\ (zip\ newVars\ types)$$
$$)$$
$$rhsfn\quad\quad = \lambda(newVar, rhstype) \to$$
$$\mathbf{case}\ rhstype\ \mathbf{of}$$
$$LApply\ t\ ts \to hsep$$
$$(mt\ (getName\ t)$$
$$: hsep\ (map\ mkMapName\ ts)$$
$$\mathbin{+\!\!+} [newVar]$$
$$)$$
$$Var\ v\quad\quad \to text\ (\texttt{'f'} : v) <\!+\!> newVar$$
$$Con\ s\quad\quad \to mt\ s <\!+\!> newVar$$
$$List\ t\quad\quad \to text\ \texttt{"map"}$$
$$<\!+\!> parens\ (mt\ (getName\ t)$$
$$<\!+\!> mapArgs$$
$$)$$
$$<\!+\!> newVar$$
$$x\quad\quad \to newVar$$
$$\mathbf{in}\ lhs <\!+\!> equals <\!+\!> rhs$$

The utility functions *mkMapName* and *getName* return the name of the function to be applied to the arguments of a constructor, and the name of a type, respectively.

$$mkMapName\ (LApply\ s\ t) = parens\ (mkMapName\ s$$
$$<+>\ hsep\ (map\ mkMapName\ t)$$
$$)$$

mkMapName (*Var s*)	= *text* ('f' : *s*)
mkMapName (*Con s*)	= *text* ("map" ++ *s*)
mkMapName (*List t*)	= *text* "map" <+> *mkMapName t*
mkMapName _	= *error* "mkMapName"
getName (*LApply s t*)	= *getName s*
getName (*Var s*)	= *s*
getName (*Con s*)	= *s*
getName (*List t*)	= *getName t*
getName _	= *error* "getName"

Template Haskell

Template Haskell is a language extension that allows meta-programming within the Haskell language. Template Haskell consists of multiple components.

A library (exported by *Language.Haskell.TH*) provides access the the abstract syntax of the Haskell language. This makes it possible to analyze and construct Haskell programs within Haskell. A monad Q is provided to generate fresh names on demand.

Haskell expressions can be *quoted* to easily construct terms in the abstract syntax. For example,

⟦2 + 2⟧ :: Q Exp.

Template Haskell supports reflection (*reification*), so that it is possible to analyze the structure of an already defined value or data type:

reify :: Name → Q Info.

The Info data type has multiple constructors corresponding to different kinds of declarations, but in particular, there is a constructor for data types:

```
data Info = ...
          | TyConI Dec
data Dec = ...
         | DataD Cxt Name [Name] [Con] [Name]
data Con = NormalC Name [StrictType]
         | RecC Name [VarStrictType]
         | InfixC StrictType Name StrictType
         | ForallC [Name] Cxt Con.
```

Each data type comprises a context (possible class constraints), a name, a list of parameters, a list of constructors, and a list of classes it automatically derives. Constructors can either be normal constructors, records, infix constructors, or constructors with quantification. A StrictType is a type with a possible strictness annotation, a VarStrictType additionally contains a record label.

Finally, in Template Haskell we can *splice* values constructed in the abstract syntax into Haskell programs, making it possible to run programs that are generated by meta-programs. Splicing is dual to quoting, so that

$$\$([\![2 + 2]\!]) :: \mathsf{Int}$$

results in 4.

By its very nature, Template Haskell can be used to write programs that cannot be expressed, or are at least difficult to express, in the Haskell language, such as generic programs. With Template Haskell, we can analyze data-type definitions, and depending on their structure, generate specialized code.

It is important to realize that Template Haskell itself is not an approach to generic programming, but more like an implementation technique. Template Haskell gives the programmer a lot of power and freedom, but does not provide any guidance or even a framework for generic programming.

While DrIFT's main focus is to generate type-class instances, we can use Template Haskell much more flexibly:

- we can generate the structure-representation type (like in Generic Haskell) for a given data type, plus the embedding-projection pairs;
- for a generic function, we can construct a recipe that uses the abstract syntax of a data type to construct the abstract syntax of a specialized instance of the generic function;
- we can generate instances of a type class, both for a generic function directly (like in DrIFT, Derivable Type Classes, or Generics for the Masses), or for a powerful combinator like *gfold* in Scrap Your Boilerplate.

In principle, Template Haskell can be used to simulate or support any approach to generic programming in Haskell. However, we also run into many of the problems that we encountered in DrIFT:

- everything happens at the syntactic level, not the semantic level. While constructing generic functions, we have to pay attention to low-level concepts such as free and bound variables;
- the analysis of data types is also purely syntactic. We do not have access to kind information, or recursion on the type level, directly, but have to infer that from the definitions; writing generic functions for mutually recursive data types or higher-kinded data types is difficult, because we have to implement parts of a compiler;
- there is no guarantee that the meta-programs produce correct code under all circumstances. The generated code is type-checked, so we are safe from errors in the end, but this is a much weaker guarantee than we get from other approaches such as Generic Haskell, where we know that the type-correctness of a generic definition implies the type-correctness of all instances.

Because of the above-mentioned freedom, it is difficult to implement the canonical examples for generic programming using Template Haskell: there is no single idiomatic version of a generic function, but there are many different possibilities. We therefore don't include specific examples in this document.

We are aware of one attempt to provide a serious framework for generic programming within Template Haskell: Norell and Jansson [82] present a very sophisticated embedding of both PolyP and Generic Haskell into Template Haskell. Among other things, they describe how to define generic *map* in the two different encodings.

Evaluation

Structural dependencies. DrIFT and Template Haskell support the definition of functions that take the abstract syntax of a data type as an argument, and return executable Haskell code. In principle, both DrIFT and Template Haskell can generate any document, even type-indexed data types. Especially for DrIFT, generating anything other than class instances amounts to writing part of a compiler for generic programming. In Template Haskell, it is feasible to design at least a reusable framework for such advanced tasks. Both systems provide no way to access type or kind information of the analyzed code. In particular, the lack of kind inference for data types makes the creation of generic programs on complex data types tedious.

Full reflexivity. DrIFT is not fully reflexive with respect to the set of data types definable in Haskell 98: it cannot handle data types with higher-kinded type variables, such as GRose. Just like Generic Haskell, DrIFT cannot generate instances of functions on existential types or on GADTs.

We see, however, no reason in principle why DrIFT cannot be fully reflexive with respect to the data types definable in Haskell 98.

Template Haskell's abstract syntax handles all of Haskell 98 and beyond. It does not yet support GADTs, but there is no reason why it could not be extended in that way. Full reflexivity therefore depends on the generic programming approach one tries to simulate within Template Haskell.

Type universes. There is no support for type universes in DrIFT. Neither does Template Haskell have any direct support for this concept.

First-class generic functions. DrIFT rules are plain Haskell functions, they can take rules as arguments. First-class rules are inherited from Haskell. But it needs a lot of imagination to see rules as generic programs. And an instance of a class cannot be explicitly passed as an argument to a function or a class instance, so a rule that generates an instance of a class (the only supported kind of definition in DrIFT) cannot be passed as argument to a rule that generates a function or a class instance.

Similarly, we have all the abstraction possibilities of Haskell for generic programs within Template Haskell. We can write generic meta-programs that are parametrized over other generic meta-programs.

However, both DrIFT and Template Haskell are two-level approaches. DrIFT always needs to be invoked before compilation of a Haskell module to fill in the missing code. Template Haskell requires splicing of the generated code. Splicing is a syntactic construct which is foreign to the Haskell language and furthermore underlies certain restrictions (sometimes, code that contributes to Template Haskell programs must reside in several modules). Therefore, DrIFT and Template Haskell cannot provide generic functions that are truly first-class.

Multiple type arguments. Rules cannot take multiple type arguments in DrIFT. In Template Haskell, there are no theoretical limits.

Type system. Rules for generic functions all have the same type in DrIFT: Data → Doc. There is no separate type system for rules; rules are ordinary Haskell functions. In Template Haskell, the situation is similar. All Haskell expressions, for instance, are of type Exp in the abstract syntax of expressions, but no further type information about the actual constructed expression is maintained. In particular, it is possible to construct type-incorrect expressions, causing type errors only when spliced.

Note that in addition to type errors, it is easy to generate lexer and parser errors in DrIFT.

Type safety. A type-correct rule does not guarantee that the generated code is type correct, as well. It is easy to define a type-correct rule that generates code that does not type-check in Haskell. DrIFT is not type safe. The same holds for Template Haskell, where the type correctness of a meta-program does not imply that the use of that meta-program produces type-correct code.

The type of a generic function. In DrIFT, every rule has type Data → Doc. Thus it is impossible to distinguish generic functions by type. For Template Haskell, the type of generic functions depends completely on the approach that is simulated. Generally, however, not much of a generic function's type is reflected in the type of the meta-program: as in DrIFT, generic functions in Template Haskell typically map the abstract syntax of one or more data types to a number of Haskell declarations. Lynagh [74] shows how to give more informative types to Template Haskell programs.

Properties of generic functions. Since rules generate pretty-printed documents (syntax), it is virtually impossible to specify properties of rules. For Template Haskell, it is similarly impossible to specify properties. However, libraries for generic programming defined in Template Haskell may allow to state and prove properties.

Integration with the underlying programming language. If a user wants to implement and use a new rule, DrIFT has to be recompiled. If a user wants to use a rule, adding a directive to a Haskell file suffices. Template Haskell is superior here, because Template Haskell code can almost freely be mixed with normal Haskell code. Sometimes, code has to be divided in separate modules.

Specialization versus interpretation. DrIFT specializes rules on data types following directives. Template Haskell also generates the programs in advance, but a hybrid approach is conceivable: in the simulation of a lightweight approach, some code would be generated for each data type, but a generic function would be interpreted.

Code optimization. Code can be optimized by hand by specifying a more sophisticated rule or meta-program. There need not be a run-time efficiency penalty when using DrIFT or Template Haskell.

Separate compilation. It is easy to use rules on data types that appear in a new module. Rules are separately compiled in DrIFT, and can then be used in any module. Separate compilation in Template Haskell is possible because of its integration with Haskell.

Practical aspects. DrIFT is actively maintained. The last release is from April 2006. It runs on many platforms. The user guide explains how to use DrIFT. Template Haskell is actively maintained as part of GHC; the flag -fth must be passed to GHC to be able to use it. Template Haskell is, however, still in development, with new GHC releases regularly changing the interface in an incompatible way. Documentation for the current state of affairs is difficult to come by, but this situation is likely to improve when the speed of development slows down.

No error messages are given for data types for which DrIFT cannot generate code. Error messages provided by Template Haskell are often in terms of the generated code and difficult to interpret for the user of a generic programming library.

4.5   Lightweight Approaches to Generic Programming

Due to Haskell's advanced type language and type classes it is possible to write generic programs in Haskell itself, without extending the language. An approach in which generic programs are plain Haskell programs is called a lightweight approach. Lightweight approaches to generic programming in Haskell have become popular in the last couple of years. In this section we discuss three relatively lightweight approaches to generic programming: "A Lightweight Implementation of Generics and Dynamics", "Generics for the Masses", and "Derivable Type Classes". The last approach is actually a language extension, but since it shares many characteristics with the other two approaches, it is listed here.

We do not include a comparison of some very recent lightweight approaches to generic programming such as Replib [97], Smash your boiler-plate without class and Typeable [59], and TypeCase [83]. Neither do we discuss PolyP2 here: the subsection on PolyP discusses the main ideas behind PolyP.

Lightweight Implementation of Generics and Dynamics

Lightweight Implementation of Generics and Dynamics [15] (LIGD) is an approach to embedding generic functions and dynamic values into Haskell 98 augmented with existential types. For the purposes of these lecture notes we concentrate on the generics (which slightly simplifies the presentation). For the treatment of dynamics the interested reader is referred to the original paper [15] or to the companion lecture notes on Generic Programming, Now!, which elaborate on a closely related approach to generic programming.

A generic function in Generic Haskell is parametrized by types, essentially performing a dispatch on the type argument. The basic idea of the lightweight approach is to reflect the type argument onto the value level so that the type-case can be implemented by ordinary pattern matching. As a first try, we could, for instance, assign the generic *encode* function the type Rep → t → [Bit], where Rep is the type of type representations. A moment's reflection, however, reveals that this won't work. The parametricity theorem [92] implies that a function of this type necessarily ignores its second argument. The trick is to use a parametric type for type representations: *encode* :: Rep t → t → [Bit]. Here Rep t is the type representation of t. In this section we will show a number of ways in which such a type can be defined.

Using a recent extension to Haskell, so-called generalized algebraic data types, Rep can be defined directly in Haskell; see also Generic Programming, Now! (Section 3.1 in [42], where Rep is called Type).

> **data** Rep :: ⋆ → ⋆ **where**
> *Unit* :: Rep Unit
> *Int* :: Rep Int
> *Sum* :: Rep a → Rep b → Rep (a :+: b)
> *Pair* :: Rep a → Rep b → Rep (a :*: b)

A type t is represented by a term of type Rep t. Note that the above declaration cannot be introduced by a Haskell 98 data declaration since none of the data constructors has result type Rep a.

If one wants to stick to Haskell 98 (or modest extensions thereof), one has to encode the representation type somehow. We discuss a direct encoding in the sequel and a more elaborate one in Section 4.5. The idea is to assign, for instance, *Int*, the representation of Int, the type Rep t with the additional constraint that t = Int. The type equality is then encoded using the equivalence type a ↔ b introduced in Section 2.2. An element of t ↔ t′ can be seen as a 'proof' that the two types are equal. Of course, in Haskell, an equivalence pair only guarantees that t can be cast to t′ and vice versa. This, however, turns out to be enough for our purposes. Figure 3 displays the fully-fledged version of Rep that uses equivalence types. The constructors *Unit*, *Int*, *Char*, *Sum*, *Pair* and *Con* correspond to the type patterns Unit, Int, Char, :+:, :*: and Con in Generic Haskell. The constructor *Type* is used for representing user-defined data types; see below.

data Rep t =   *Unit*   (t ↔ Unit)
    | *Int*   (t ↔ Int)
    | *Char*   (t ↔ Char)
    | ∀a b. *Sum* (Rep a) (Rep b) (t ↔ (a :+: b))
    | ∀a b. *Pair* (Rep a) (Rep b) (t ↔ (a :*: b))
    | ∀a . *Type*   (Rep a) (t ↔ a)
    | *Con* String (Rep t)

Fig. 3. A type-representation type

In general, approaches to generics contain three components: code for generic
values, per data type code, and shared library code. In Generic Haskell and other
approaches the per data type code is not a burden upon the programmer but
is generated automatically. Here the programmer is responsible for supplying
the required definitions. (Of course, she or he may use tools such as DrIFT or
Template Haskell to generate the code automatically.) To see what is involved,
re-consider the List data type

    data List a = *Nil* | *Cons* a (List a),

and recall that the structure type of List a is Unit :+: (a :*: (List a)). To turn
List a into a *representable type*, a type on which a generic function can be used,
we define

    list   :: Rep a → Rep (List a)
    list a = *Type* ((*Con* "Nil" *unit*) + (*Con* "Cons" (a ∗ (*list* a))))
              (*EP fromList toList*),

where *unit*, + and ∗ are smart versions of the respective constructors (defined
in the LIGD library) and *fromList* and *toList* convert between the type List and
its structure type.

    fromList   :: List a → Unit :+: (a :*: (List a))
    fromList Nil   = *Inl Unit*
    fromList (*Cons* a as) = *Inr* (a :*: as)
    toList   :: Unit :+: (a :*: (List a)) → List a
    toList (*Inl Unit*)   = *Nil*
    toList (*Inr* (a :*: as)) = *Cons* a as

Note that the representation of the structure type records the name of the constructors.

So, whenever we define a new data type and we intend to use a generic function
on that type, we have to do a little bit of extra work. However, this has to be
done only once per data type.

Function encode. The definition of *encode* is very similar to the Generic Haskell
definition.

$$encode \qquad\qquad :: \mathsf{Rep}\; t \to t \to [\mathsf{Bit}]$$
$$encode\;(Unit \qquad ep)\; t = \mathbf{case}\; from\; ep\; t\; \mathbf{of}$$
$$Unit \to [\,]$$
$$encode\;(Char \qquad ep)\; t = encodeChar\;(from\; ep\; t)$$
$$encode\;(Int \qquad ep)\; t = encodeInt\;(from\; ep\; t)$$
$$encode\;(Sum\; a\; b\; ep)\; t = \mathbf{case}\; from\; ep\; t\; \mathbf{of}$$
$$Inl\; x \to O : encode\; a\; x$$
$$Inr\; y \to I : encode\; b\; y$$
$$encode\;(Pair\; a\; b\; ep)\; t = \mathbf{case}\; from\; ep\; t\; \mathbf{of}$$
$$x :*: y \to encode\; a\; x +\!\!+ encode\; b\; y$$
$$encode\;(Type\; a \quad ep)\; t = encode\; a\;(from\; ep\; t)$$
$$encode\;(Con\; s\; a) \qquad t = encode\; a\; t$$

The main difference is that we have to use an explicit cast, *from ep*, to turn the second argument of type t into a character, an integer, and so forth. In Generic Haskell this cast is automatically inserted by the compiler.

Function decode. For *decode* we have to cast an integer and values of other types into an element of the result type t using *to ep*.

$$decodes \qquad\qquad :: \mathsf{Rep}\; t \to \mathsf{Parser}\; t$$
$$decodes\;(Unit \qquad ep)\; bs = [(to\; ep\; Unit, bs)]$$
$$decodes\;(Char \qquad ep)\; bs = mapP\;(to\; ep)\; decodesChar\; bs$$
$$decodes\;(Int \qquad ep)\; bs = mapP\;(to\; ep)\; decodesInt\; bs$$
$$decodes\;(Sum\; a\; b\; ep)\; bs = bitCase\;(mapP\;(to\; ep\,.\,Inl)\;(decodes\; a))$$
$$(mapP\;(to\; ep\,.\,Inr)\;(decodes\; b))$$
$$bs$$
$$decodes\;(Pair\; a\; b\; ep)\; bs = [\,(to\; ep\;(x :*: y), ds)$$
$$|\;(x, cs) \leftarrow decodes\; a\; bs$$
$$,(y, ds) \leftarrow decodes\; b\; cs\,]$$
$$decodes\;(Type\; a \quad ep)\; bs = mapP\;(to\; ep)\;(decodes\; a)\; bs$$
$$decodes\;(Con\; s\; a) \qquad bs = decodes\; a\; bs$$

A big plus of the lightweight approach is that *encode* and *decode* are ordinary Haskell functions. We can, for instance, pass them to other functions or we can define other functions in terms of them.

$$decode :: \mathsf{Rep}\; a \to [\mathsf{Bit}] \to a$$
$$decode\; a\; bs = \mathbf{case}\; decodes\; a\; bs\; \mathbf{of}$$
$$[(x, [\,])] \to x$$
$$\_ \qquad \to error\; \texttt{"decode: no parse"}$$

Function eq. The equality function is again very similar to the version in Generic Haskell.

$$eq \qquad\qquad :: \mathsf{Rep}\; t \to t \to t \to \mathsf{Bool}$$
$$eq\;(Int \qquad ep)\; t_1\; t_2 = from\; ep\; t_1 == from\; ep\; t_2$$

$$eq \ (Char \quad ep) \ t_1 \ t_2 = from \ ep \ t_1 \ \text{==} \ from \ ep \ t_2$$
$$eq \ (Unit \quad ep) \ t_1 \ t_2 = \textbf{case} \ (from \ ep \ t_1, from \ ep \ t_2) \ \textbf{of}$$
$$(Unit, Unit) \rightarrow True$$
$$eq \ (Sum \ a \ b \ ep) \ t_1 \ t_2 = \textbf{case} \ (from \ ep \ t_1, from \ ep \ t_2) \ \textbf{of}$$
$$(Inl \ a_1, Inl \ a_2) \rightarrow eq \ a \ a_1 \ a_2$$
$$(Inr \ b_1, Inr \ b_2) \rightarrow eq \ b \ b_1 \ b_2$$
$$\_ \qquad\qquad \rightarrow False$$
$$eq \ (Pair \ a \ b \ ep) \ t_1 \ t_2 = \textbf{case} \ (from \ ep \ t_1, from \ ep \ t_2) \ \textbf{of}$$
$$(a_1 :*: b_1, a_2 :*: b_2) \rightarrow eq \ a \ a_1 \ a_2 \wedge eq \ b \ b_1 \ b_2$$
$$eq \ (Type \ a \quad ep) \ t_1 \ t_2 = eq \ a \ (from \ ep \ t_1) \ (from \ ep \ t_2)$$
$$eq \ (Con \ s \ a) \ t_1 \ t_2 \quad = eq \ a \ t_1 \ t_2$$

Function map. The function *map* abstracts over a type constructor of kind $\star \rightarrow \star$, or is indexed by kind as in Generic Haskell. Defining such a version of *map* requires a different type representation. A discussion of the design space can be found in the companion lecture notes on Generic Programming, Now!.

Function show. The implementation of *show* is again straightforward. The constructor names can be accessed using the *Con* pattern (an analogous approach can be used for record labels).

$$shows \qquad\qquad\qquad :: \ \textsf{Rep} \ t \rightarrow t \rightarrow \textsf{ShowS}$$
$$shows \ (Int \qquad ep) \ t \quad = showsInt \ (from \ ep \ t)$$
$$shows \ (Char \quad ep) \ t \quad = showsChar \ (from \ ep \ t)$$
$$shows \ (Unit \quad ep) \ t \quad = showString \ \text{""}$$
$$shows \ (Sum \ a \ b \ ep) \ t \quad = \textbf{case} \ from \ ep \ t \ \textbf{of}$$
$$Inl \ a_1 \rightarrow shows \ a \ a_1$$
$$Inr \ b_1 \rightarrow shows \ b \ b_1$$
$$shows \ (Pair \ a \ b \ ep) \ t \quad = \textbf{case} \ from \ ep \ t \ \textbf{of}$$
$$(a_1 :*: b_1) \rightarrow \ shows \ a \ a_1$$
$$\cdot \ showString \ \text{" "}$$
$$\cdot \ shows \ b \ b_1$$
$$shows \ (Type \ a \quad ep) \ t \quad = shows \ a \ (from \ ep \ t)$$
$$shows \ (Con \ s \ (Unit \ ep)) \ t = showString \ s$$
$$shows \ (Con \ s \ a) \ t \qquad = \quad showChar \ \text{'('}$$
$$\cdot \ showString \ s$$
$$\cdot \ showChar \ \text{' '}$$
$$\cdot \ shows \ a \ t$$
$$\cdot \ showChar \ \text{')'}$$

Since types are reflected onto the value level, we can use the full convenience of Haskell pattern matching. For instance, in the definition of *shows* we treat nullary constructors in a special way (omitting parentheses) through the use of the pattern *Con s (Unit ep)*.

Function update. An implementation of *update* requires an extension of the Rep data type, which means that one has to modify the source of the library.

Alternatively, one could turn Rep into a so-called *open data type* [72]. The code for *update* is then entirely straightforward and omitted for reasons of space.

Derivable Type Classes

Haskell's major innovation is its support for *overloading*, based on type classes. For example, the Haskell Prelude defines the class *Eq* (slightly simplified):

> **class** *Eq* a **where**
> *eq* :: a → a → Bool.

This *class declaration* defines an overloaded top-level function, called *method*, whose type is

> *eq* :: (*Eq* a) ⇒ a → a → Bool.

Before we can use *eq* on values of, say Int, we explain how to take equality over Int values:

> **instance** *Eq* Int **where**
> *eq* = *eqInt*.

This *instance declaration* makes Int an element of the type class *Eq* and says 'the *eq* function at type Int is implemented by *eqInt*'. As a second example consider equality of lists. Two lists are equal if they have the same length and corresponding elements are equal. Hence, we require equality over the element type:

> **instance** (*Eq* a) ⇒ *Eq* (List a) **where**
> $\quad eq\ Nil\ Nil \qquad\qquad\qquad = True$
> $\quad eq\ Nil\ (Cons\ a_2\ as_2) \qquad\ = False$
> $\quad eq\ (Cons\ a_1\ as_1)\ Nil \qquad = False$
> $\quad eq\ (Cons\ a_1\ as_1)\ (Cons\ a_2\ as_2) = eq\ a_1\ a_2 \wedge eq\ as_1\ as_2.$

This instance declaration says 'if a is an instance of *Eq*, then List a is an instance of *Eq*, as well'.

Though type classes bear a strong resemblance to generic definitions, they do not support generic programming. A type-class declaration corresponds roughly to the type signature of a generic definition – or rather, to a collection of type signatures. Instance declarations are related to the type cases of a generic definition. The crucial difference is that a generic definition works for all types, whereas instance declarations must be provided explicitly by the programmer for each newly defined data type. There is, however, one exception to this rule. For a handful of built-in classes Haskell provides special support, the so-called 'deriving' mechanism. For instance, if you define

> **data** List a = *Nil* | *Cons* a (List a) **deriving** (*Eq*),

then Haskell generates the 'obvious' code for equality. What 'obvious' means is specified informally in an Appendix of the language definition [86]. *Derivable type classes* (DTCs) [41] generalize this feature to arbitrary user-defined classes: generic definitions are used to specify *default methods* so that the programmer can define her own derivable classes.

Functions encode and decode. A type class usually gathers a couple of related methods. For that reason, we put *encode* and *decode* into a single class, called *Binary*.

> **class** *Binary* a **where**
>   *encode* :: a → [Bit]
>   *decodes* :: Parser a

Using two generic definitions we provide default methods for both *encode* and *decode*.

$$
\begin{aligned}
encode\{|\text{Unit}|\} \quad & Unit \quad &&= [\,] \\
encode\{|\text{b}\text{ :+: }\text{c}|\} \;& (Inl\ x) &&= O : encode\ x \\
encode\{|\text{b}\text{ :+: }\text{c}|\} \;& (Inr\ y) &&= I : encode\ y \\
encode\{|\text{b}\text{ :*: }\text{c}|\} \;& (x\ \text{:*:}\ y) &&= encode\ x +\!\!+ encode\ y \\[4pt]
decodes\{|\text{Unit}|\} \quad & bs &&= [(Unit, bs)] \\
decodes\{|\text{b}\text{ :+: }\text{c}|\} \;& bs &&= bitCase\ (mapP\ Inl\ decodes) \\
& && \qquad\qquad\; (mapP\ Inr\ decodes) \\
& && \qquad\qquad\; bs \\
decodes\{|\text{b}\text{ :*: }\text{c}|\} \;& bs &&= [(x\ \text{:*:}\ y, ds)\ |\ (x, cs) \leftarrow decodes\ bs \\
& && \qquad\qquad\;\;, (y, ds) \leftarrow decodes\ cs]
\end{aligned}
$$

Incidentally, DTCs use the same structure-representation types as Generic Haskell, so the corresponding definitions can be copied almost verbatim. There is one small difference though: explicit type arguments, written in curly braces, are only specified on the left-hand side of default method definitions. Elsewhere, Haskell's overloading resolution automatically determines the instance types, as for every other class method.

The function *decode* is defined in terms of *decodes*. We decided to turn the latter function into an overloaded function rather than a class method since its code is the same for all instances.

> *decode* :: (*Binary* a) ⇒ [Bit] → a
> *decode bs* = **case** *decodes bs* **of**
> $[(x, [\,])] \rightarrow x$
>   _   → *error* "decode: no parse"

Now, if we intend to use *encode* or *decode* on a particular type, we must first provide an instance declaration. However, by virtue of the default methods the instance declaration may be empty.

instance *Binary* CharList
instance *Binary* Tree
instance (*Binary* a) ⇒ *Binary* [a]

The compiler then automatically fills in the missing method definitions. However, if we say

instance (*Binary* a) ⇒ *Binary* [a] **where**
   encode xs   = *encode* (*length xs*) ⧺ *concatMap encode xs*
   decodes bs   = [(*xs, ds*) | (*n, cs*) ← *decodes bs*
                     , (*xs, ds*) ← *times n decodes cs*]
   times :: Int → Parser a → Parser [a]
   times 0   *p bs* = [([], *bs*)]
   times (*n* + 1) *p bs* = [(*x* : *xs, ds*) | (*x, cs*) ← *p bs*, (*xs, ds*) ← *times n p cs*]

then this programmer-supplied code is used. Thus, the programmer can override the generic definition on a type-by-type basis. This ability is crucial to support *abstract types*. We can also — indeed, we must — use ordinary instance declarations to specify what a generic definition should do on primitive types such as Char or Int.

   instance *Binary* Char **where**
     encode = *encodeChar*
     decodes = *decodesChar*
   instance *Binary* Int **where**
     encode = *encodeInt*
     decodes = *decodesInt*

Function eq. The predefined *Eq* class can be thought of as a derivable type class.

   class *Eq* a **where**
     eq, neq   :: a → a → Bool
     eq{|Unit|}   *Unit*   *Unit*   = *True*
     eq{|b :+: c|} (*Inl x*)   (*Inl v*)   = *eq x v*
     eq{|b :+: c|} (*Inl x*)   (*Inr w*) = *False*
     eq{|b :+: c|} (*Inr y*)   (*Inl v*)   = *False*
     eq{|b :+: c|} (*Inr y*)   (*Inr w*) = *eq y w*
     eq{|b :*: c|} (*x* :*: *y*) (*v* :*: *w*) = *eq x v* ∧ *eq y w*
     neq x y   = *not* (*eq x y*)

The class definition contains an ordinary default definition for inequality and a generic one for equality. Equality on characters and integers is specified using ordinary instance declarations.

     instance *Eq* Char **where**
       eq = *eqChar*
     instance *Eq* Int **where**
       eq = *eqInt*

Function map. Generic definitions for default methods may only be given for type classes whose type parameter ranges over types of kind ⋆. For that reason, we cannot specify a generic mapping function, There is, however, no principle hindrance in adding this feature.

Function show. A missing feature of DTCs is a *c* of a construct, with which one can access the names of constructors and labels. So, currently, one cannot define a generic version of *show* or *read*.

Function update. We can define *update* as a variant of the generic identity, or copy function.

```
class Update a where
    update                    :: a → a
    update{|Unit|}    Unit    = Unit
    update{|b :+: c|} (Inl x)  = Inl (update x)
    update{|b :+: c|} (Inr y)  = Inr (update y)
    update{|b :*: c|} (x :*: y) = update x :*: update y
```

Again, we have to provide instance declarations for all the types, on which we wish to use *update*.

```
instance Update Char where
    update = id
instance (Update a) ⇒ Update [a]

instance Update Company
instance Update Dept
instance Update SubUnit
instance Update Employee
instance Update Person
instance Update Salary where
    update (S s) = S (s * (1 + 0.15))
```

All the instance declarations are trivial except the one for salary which specifies the salary increase.

Generics for the Masses

Generics for the Masses [35,36] (GM) is similar in spirit to LIGD. The approach shows that one can program generically within Haskell 98 obviating to some extent the need for fancy type systems or separate tools. Like LIGD, Generics for the Masses builds upon an encoding of the type-representation type *Rep*, this time a class-based one. The details of the encoding are not relevant here; the interested reader is referred to the journal paper [36].

Function encode. To define a generic function the generic programmer has to provide a signature and an implementation. Rather unusually, the type of a generic function is specified using a **newtype** declaration.

> **newtype** Encode a = *Encode*{ *applyEncode* :: a → [Bit]}

We already know that the generic function *encode* cannot be a genuine polymorphic function of type a → [Bit]. Data compression does not work for arbitrary types, but only for types that are *representable*, that is, where the *type* can be represented by a certain *value*. Here a type representation is simply an overloaded value called *rep*. The first part of the generic compression function is then given by the following definition.

> $encode :: (Rep\ a) \Rightarrow a \rightarrow [Bit]$
> $encode = applyEncode\ rep$

Loosely speaking, we apply the generic function to the type representation *rep*. Of course, this is not the whole story. The code above defines only a convenient shortcut. The actual definition of *encode* is provided by an instance declaration, but one should read it instead as just a generic definition.

> **instance** *Generic* Encode **where**
> $unit = Encode\ (\lambda x \rightarrow [\,])$
> $plus = Encode\ (\lambda x \rightarrow$ **case** x **of** $Inl\ l \rightarrow O : encode\ l$
> $\qquad\qquad\qquad\qquad\qquad\qquad\qquad Inr\ r \rightarrow I\ : encode\ r)$
> $pair = Encode\ (\lambda x \rightarrow encode\ (outl\ x) +\!\!+ encode\ (outr\ x))$
> $datatype\ descr\ iso$
> $\qquad = Encode\ (\lambda x \rightarrow encode\ (from\ iso\ x))$
> $char = Encode\ (\lambda x \rightarrow encodeChar\ x)$
> $int\ \ = Encode\ (\lambda x \rightarrow encodeInt\ \ \ x)$

Most of the cases are familiar – just read the method definitions as type cases. To encode an element of an arbitrary data type, we first convert the element into a sum of products, which is then encoded. That said it becomes clear that GM uses the same structure types as Generic Haskell. The function *from* is the record selector *from* of the data type $\cdot \leftrightarrow \cdot$ introduced in Section 2.2.

That's it, at least, as far as the generic function is concerned. Before we can actually compress data to strings of bits, we first have to turn the types of the to-be-compressed values into representable types. Consider as an example the type of binary leaf trees.

> **data** BinTree a = *BTLeaf* a | *BTBin* (BinTree a) (BinTree a)

We have to show that this type is representable. To this end we exhibit an isomorphic type built from representable type constructors. This is the familiar *structure type* of BinTree, denoted BinTree°.

> **type** BinTree° a = (Constr a) :+: (Constr ((BinTree a) :*: (BinTree a)))

The main work goes into defining two mappings, *fromBinTree* and *toBinTree*, which certify that BinTree a and its structure type BinTree° a are indeed isomorphic.

$$
\begin{array}{ll}
fromBinTree & :: \text{BinTree a} \rightarrow \text{BinTree° a} \\
fromBinTree\ (BTLeaf\ x) & = Inl\ (Con\ x) \\
fromBinTree\ (BTBin\ l\ r) & = Inr\ (Con\ (l :*: r)) \\
\\
toBinTree & :: \text{BinTree° a} \rightarrow \text{BinTree a} \\
toBinTree\ (Inl\ (Con\ x)) & = BTLeaf\ x \\
toBinTree\ (Inr\ (Con\ (l :*: r))) & = BTBin\ l\ r
\end{array}
$$

The *Con* constructor just marks the position of the original data constructors *BTLeaf* and *BTBin*. The isomorphism is then used to turn BinTree into a representable type.

instance $(Rep\ a) \Rightarrow Rep$ (BinTree a) **where**
$\quad rep = datatype\ ("BTLeaf"\ ./\ 1\ .|\ "BTBin"\ ./\ 2)$ -- syntax
$\qquad\qquad\quad (EP\ fromBinTree\ toBinTree)$ -- semantics

The operator ./ turns a constructor name and an arity into a constructor description, and the operator .| combines two alternatives into a data description, see Figure 4. The declaration *rep* specifies the syntax – name and arity of the constructors – and the semantics – the structure – of the tree data type. Such a declaration has to be provided once per data type and is used for all instances of generic functions on that data type.

For reference, Figure 4 lists the definition of the class *Generic* (g is the type of a generic function).

Function decode. The definition of *decodes* follows exactly the same scheme.

newtype Decodes a $= Decodes\{ applyDecodes :: \text{Parser a} \}$

$decodes :: (Rep\ a) \Rightarrow \text{Parser a}$
$decodes = applyDecodes\ rep$

instance *Generic* Decodes **where**
$\quad unit\ = Decodes\ (\lambda bs \rightarrow [(\,Unit, bs)])$
$\quad plus\ = Decodes\ (\lambda bs \rightarrow bitCase\ (mapP\ Inl\ decodes)$
$\qquad\qquad\qquad\qquad\qquad\quad (mapP\ Inr\ decodes)$
$\qquad\qquad\qquad\qquad\qquad\quad bs)$
$\quad pair\ = Decodes\ (\lambda bs \rightarrow [(x :*: y, ds) \mid (x, cs) \leftarrow decodes\ bs$
$\qquad\qquad\qquad\qquad\qquad\qquad\qquad , (y, ds) \leftarrow decodes\ cs])$
$\quad datatype\ descr\ iso$
$\qquad = Decodes\ (\lambda bs \rightarrow mapP\ (to\ iso)\ decodes\ bs)$
$\quad char = Decodes\ (\lambda bs \rightarrow decodesChar\ bs)$
$\quad int\ \ = Decodes\ (\lambda bs \rightarrow decodesInt\ \ bs)$

It is worth noting that Haskell's overloading resolution automatically determines the instance types: we just call *decodes* rather than *decodes*{|t|}.

```
class Generic g where
  unit     ::                          g Unit
  plus     :: (Rep a, Rep b) ⇒         g (a :+: b)
  pair     :: (Rep a, Rep b) ⇒         g (a :*: b)
  datatype :: (Rep a) ⇒ DataDescr → a ↔ b → g b
  char     ::                          g Char
  int      ::                          g Int
  list     :: (Rep a) ⇒                g [a]
  constr   :: (Rep a) ⇒                g (Constr a)
  list   = datatype ("[]" ./ 0 .| ":" ./ 2) (EP fromList toList)
  constr = datatype ("Con" ./ 1)       (EP arg Con)
data DataDescr = NoData
             | ConDescr{ name :: String,      arity :: Int}
             | Alt       { getl   :: DataDescr, getr :: DataDescr}
infix  2 ./
infixr 1 .|
f ./ n  = ConDescr{ name = f,  arity = n}
d₁ .| d₂ = Alt        { getl   = d₁, getr  = d₂}
newtype Constr a = Con{ arg :: a}
```

Fig. 4. The class *Generic*

The function *decode* can easily be defined in terms of *decodes*.

```
decode :: (Rep a) ⇒ [Bit] → a
decode a bs = case decodes a bs of
                [(x, [])] → x
                _         → error "decode: no parse"
```

Note that the class context only records that *decode* depends on some generic function. This is in sharp contrast to DTC where the context precisely records, on which overloaded function(s) *decode* depends: $(Binary\ a) \Rightarrow [Bit] \rightarrow a$.

Function eq. The definition of *eq* is straightforward.

```
newtype Equal a = Equal{ applyEqual :: a → a → Bool}
eq :: (Rep a) ⇒ a → a → Bool
eq = applyEqual rep
instance Generic Equal where
  unit = Equal (λx₁ x₂ → True)
  plus = Equal (λx₁ x₂ → case (x₁, x₂) of
                            (Inl a₁, Inl a₂) → eq a₁ a₂
                            (Inr b₁, Inr b₂) → eq b₁ b₂
                            _                → False)
  pair = Equal (λx₁ x₂ → eq (outl x₁) (outl x₂) ∧ eq (outr x₁) (outr x₂))
  datatype descr iso
```

$$= Equal\ (\lambda x_1\ x_2 \rightarrow eq\ (from\ iso\ x_1)\ (from\ iso\ x_2))$$
$$char = Equal\ (\lambda x_1\ x_2 \rightarrow x_1 == x_2)$$
$$int\ = Equal\ (\lambda x_1\ x_2 \rightarrow x_1 == x_2)$$

Function map. The function *map* cannot be defined using the *Generic* class that we have employed for *encode* and *decode*. Rather, we need a new tailor-made class *Generic2* that allows us to define generic functions whose type is parametrized by two type arguments (see Section 2.5). The definition is then very similar to what we have seen before.

newtype Map a$_1$ a$_2$ = $Map\{\ applyMap :: $ a$_1 \rightarrow$ a$_2\ \}$

instance *Generic2* Map **where**
   $unit\ \ \ \ = Map\ (\lambda x \rightarrow x)$
   $plus\ a\ b = Map\ (\lambda x \rightarrow$ **case** x **of** $Inl\ l\ \rightarrow Inl\ (applyMap\ a\ l)$
                                      $Inr\ r\ \rightarrow Inr\ (applyMap\ b\ r))$
   $pair\ a\ b = Map\ (\lambda x \rightarrow applyMap\ a\ (outl\ x)\ \text{:*:}\ applyMap\ b\ (outr\ x))$
   $datatype\ iso_1\ iso_2\ a$
             $= Map\ (\lambda x \rightarrow to\ iso_2\ (applyMap\ a\ (from\ iso_1\ x)))$
   $char\ \ \ = Map\ (\lambda x \rightarrow x)$
   $int\ \ \ \ = Map\ (\lambda x \rightarrow x)$

Using *frep*, the representation of types of kind $\star \rightarrow \star$, we can define a generic version of Haskell's *fmap*.

$$fmap\ \ :: (FRep\ f) \Rightarrow (\text{a}_1 \rightarrow \text{a}_2) \rightarrow (\text{f a}_1 \rightarrow \text{f a}_2)$$
$$fmap\ f = applyMap\ (frep\ (Map\ f))$$

Function show. To implement *show* we have to access the syntax of data constructors. To this end, we extend *shows'* by an additional argument of type DataDescr that provides information about the syntax of the to-be-printed value. This argument is initialized to *NoData*, because initially we have no information.

$$shows :: (Rep\ \text{a}) \Rightarrow \text{a} \rightarrow \text{ShowS}$$
$$shows = shows'\ NoData$$

In the *datatype* case, which signals that the current argument is an element of some data type, we use the first argument of *datatype* as the new syntax description.

newtype Shows' a = $Shows'\{\ applyShows' :: $ DataDescr $\rightarrow$ a $\rightarrow$ ShowS $\}$

$$shows'\ \ :: (Rep\ \text{a}) \Rightarrow \text{DataDescr} \rightarrow \text{a} \rightarrow \text{ShowS}$$
$$shows'\ = applyShows'\ rep$$

instance *Generic* Shows' **where**
   $unit\ \ = Shows'\ (\lambda d\ x \rightarrow showString\ \text{""})$
   $plus\ \ = Shows'\ (\lambda d\ x \rightarrow$ **case** x **of** $Inl\ l\ \rightarrow shows'\ (getl\ d)\ l$

$$Inr\ r \rightarrow shows'\ (getr\ d)\ r)$$

$$
\begin{aligned}
pair\quad &= Shows'\ (\lambda d\ x \rightarrow shows\ (outl\ x)\\
&\qquad\qquad\qquad\cdot\ showChar\ '\ '\\
&\qquad\qquad\qquad\cdot\ shows\ (outr\ x))\\
char\quad &= Shows'\ (\lambda d\ x \rightarrow showsChar\ x)\\
int\quad &= Shows'\ (\lambda d\ x \rightarrow showsInt\quad x)\\
list\quad &= Shows'\ (\lambda d\ x \rightarrow showsl\ shows\ x)\\
datatype\ &descr\ iso\\
&= Shows'\ (\lambda d\ x \rightarrow shows'\ descr\ (from\ iso\ x))\\
constr &= Shows'\ (\lambda d\ x \rightarrow \textbf{if}\ arity\ d == 0\ \textbf{then}\\
&\qquad\qquad\qquad showString\ (name\ d)\\
&\qquad\qquad \textbf{else}\\
&\qquad\qquad\qquad showChar\ '('\cdot showString\ (name\ d)\\
&\qquad\qquad\qquad\cdot\ showChar\ '\ '\cdot shows\ (arg\ x)\\
&\qquad\qquad\qquad\cdot\ showChar\ ')')
\end{aligned}
$$

The implementation of *shows'* has a special case for lists which are converted to Haskell list syntax, with brackets and commas. The helper function *showsl* does the main work.

$$
\begin{aligned}
showsl &:: (a \rightarrow \mathsf{ShowS}) \rightarrow ([a] \rightarrow \mathsf{ShowS})\\
showsl\ &p\ []\qquad\qquad = showString\ "[]"\\
showsl\ &p\ (a:as)\qquad = showChar\ '['\cdot p\ a\cdot rest\ as\\
&\textbf{where}\ rest\ []\qquad = showChar\ ']'\\
&\qquad\quad\ rest\ (x:xs) = showChar\ ','\cdot p\ x\cdot rest\ xs
\end{aligned}
$$

Function update. An implementation of *update* requires an extension of the class *Generic*, which means that one has to modify the source of the library. An alternative approach based on subclasses is described in a recent paper [84].

Evaluation

Structural dependencies. All lightweight approaches support the definition of functions in the style of Generic Haskell. Type-indexed data types are out of reach.

Using a different representation type in LIGD we can also define generic functions that are indexed by first- or higher-order kinds (this is not detailed in the original paper).

GM supports the definition of generic functions on types and type constructors. For each brand of generic functions a tailor-made *Generic* class must be used. Because of the class-based encoding the code looks somewhat different to that of Generic Haskell. The difference is, however, only superficial.

Full reflexivity. LIGD is in principle fully reflexive. However, to support types of arbitrary ranks, rank-n types are required.

GM is not fully reflexive: for different kinds we need different type representations. But it is possible to construct a family of incompatible GM implementations. Rank-n types are required in order to support types of higher kinds. Furthermore, if one wants to use the convenience of the *Rep* class, one additionally needs higher-order contexts; see the evaluation of SYB.

DTCs also share the limitations of class-based systems: higher-order contexts are needed to apply generic functions to higher-kinded data types such as GRose.

Type universes. By changing the classes for type representations used in LIGD and GM other type universes can be introduced and used. Since type representations are given by the user, they are very flexible.

DTCs support default cases, but otherwise the type universe is fixed.

First-class generic functions. In LIGD, a generic function is an ordinary polymorphic Haskell function of type *Rep* t $\rightarrow$ *Poly* t. As such it is first-class, assuming that rank-n functions are supported.

Similarly, in GM a generic function is an ordinary polymorphic Haskell function of type (*Rep* t) $\Rightarrow$ *Poly* t. Again, in a language with rank-n types, generic functions are first-class citizens.

In DTCs, generic functions are tied to class methods. However, type classes are not first-class citizens. Consequently, generic functions are not first class either.

Multiple type arguments. In both LIGD and GM a generic function may have multiple type arguments. Derivable type classes may only abstract over a single type argument.

Type system. All approaches are fully integrated into Haskell's type system.

Type safety. All approaches are fully type-safe. A missing type-case in LIGD, however, only generates a warning at compile-time. Depending on the complexity of the 'type' patterns it may not be detected at all (in particular, if patterns are used in conjunction with guards). In this case, we get a pattern-matching failure at run-time. In GM a missing case branch issues a warning at compile-time (about a missing method). Since instance declaration must be explicitly provided, missing instances in DTCs are detected at compile-time.

The type of a generic function. The types are intuitive; we only have to prefix a '*Rep* t $\rightarrow$' argument or a '(*Rep* t) $\Rightarrow$' context for LIGD and GM, respectively. The types of member functions of DTCs are familiar to Haskell programmers.

Properties of generic functions. For all approaches, properties of a generic function can be stated and proven as in Generic Haskell.

Integration with the underlying programming language. All approaches are fully integrated into Haskell. For DTCs, only the module `Data.Generics` need be imported and the options `-fglasgow-exts` and `-fgenerics` must be passed to the GHC.

In LIGD and GM the user has to specify the structure representation type and the embedding-projection pair between the data type and the structure representation type for every data type on which generic functions are used.

In DTCs, a generic function g, implemented in the class G, can be used on a data type t by writing **instance** G t. No other data-type-specific code is needed.

Specialization versus interpretation. Representations of types are passed and analyzed at run-time in LIGD. A generic function can be seen as an interpreter. In GM, instances of generic functions are assembled at compile-time. In DTCs, generic code is specialized for each instance.

Code optimization. In LIGD, the run-time passing of type representations incurs a small overhead compared to Generic Haskell. For GM and DTCs the overhead is similar to that of Generic Haskell. The code quality possibly depends a bit more on GHC's optimizer.

Separate compilation. All approaches support separate compilation.

Practical aspects. The implementation of LIGD consists of a few dozen lines of code (see Appendix A of the original paper), so it can be easily integrated into one's programs and also be adapted to one's needs (for instance, if additional type cases are required).

GM comprises three major implementations of generics and a few variations. The approach is extremely light weight; each implementation consists of roughly two dozen lines of Haskell code. It is less suited as a library (unless one makes do with the predefined type cases), but it can easily be adapted to one's needs.

The original DTCs proposal is partially implemented in GHC, the most popular compiler for Haskell. Names of constructors and labels cannot be accessed in DTCs, so one cannot define a generic version of *show* or *read*. The documentation is integrated into GHC's user guide (Section 7.11, "Generic classes"). Error messages are usually good.

5   Conclusions and Future Work

In this section we draw conclusions from the evaluations in the previous section. Using these conclusions, we try to answer the question we posed in the introduction of these lecture notes: 'How do you choose between the different approaches to generic programming in Haskell?' This question is a bit similar to the question how you choose a programming language for solving a programming problem. Answers to this question usually contain 'religious' aspects. We try to avoid religion as much as possible, and answer the question in two ways. First, we summarize the evaluations of the previous section, and draw conclusions about the suitability of the different approaches for different generic programming concepts. Second, to end on a positive note, for each approach we try to give arguments why you would use it. Furthermore, we describe future work.

5.1   Suitability for Generic Programming Concepts

Figure 5 shows the results of our evaluations of the different approaches to generic programming in Haskell. Such a presentation does not offer the possibility to make subtle distinctions, but it does give an overview of the evaluation results. We use the following categories in this table:

++ :   satisfies (almost) all requirements.
+   :   satisfies the requirements except for some small details.
o   :   satisfies a number of requirements.
−   :   satisfies just a few of the requirements.
−− :   does not satisfy the requirements.

The results are obtained by an informal translation of our evaluations into points on this five-point scale.

	Structure	Completeness	Safe	Info	Integration	Tools
GH	++	+	++	++	++	+
Clean	o	+	++	++	++	+
PolyP	o	−	+	+	+	−
SYB	o	+	++	+	++	+
DrIFT	+	o	−−	−	+	+
TH	+	+	−	−	++	o
LIGD	o	+	++	++	++	+
GM	o	+	++	++	++	+
DTCs	o	o	++	++	++	+

Fig. 5. Evaluation results for approaches to generic programming

Structure in programming languages. Generic Haskell allows the definition of type-indexed functions with kind-indexed types, and type-indexed data type with kind-indexed kinds. Since DrIFT and Template Haskell can generate anything, they can also be used to generate type-indexed types. There is no support (library, predefined constructs) for doing so, however. The other approaches only allow the definition of type-indexed functions.

The type completeness principle. No approach truly satisfies the type completeness principle.

SYB, GM, and DTCs suffer from the fact that higher-order contexts (not implemented in Haskell) are needed to generate instances of generic functions on higher-kinded data types. On the other hand, both SYB and GM allow higher-order generic functions. Just as with classes, DTCs cannot represent higher-order generic functions. Furthermore, DTCs cannot access constructor names, which limits their usability a bit. LIGD allows higher-order generic functions and generic functions on almost all data types definable in Haskell. However, it is impossible to define the generic map function in LIGD and SYB. GM allows higher-order generic functions, and the definition of generic map, but needs different classes for different brands of generic functions.

Generic Haskell and Clean do not offer higher-order generic functions, but generic functions work on almost any data type definable in the underlying programming language, and defining the generic map function is no problem. Higher orders do not really play a rôle in DrIFT and Template Haskell, and DrIFT cannot handle higher-kinded data types. PolyP does not allow higher-order generic functions either and only works for regular data types of kind $\star \to \star$.

Generic views in Generic Haskell allow defining generic functions for different views on data types, which can be used to specify different type universes. LIGD and GM allow very flexible sets of types on which generic functions can be defined, and it is possible to define many type universes. Clean, PolyP, SYB, and DTCs have a fixed type universe. DrIFT and Template Haskell offer no support for type universes.

Well-typed expressions do not go wrong. Generic Haskell, Clean, SYB, LIGD, GM, and DTCs are type safe. PolyP does not complain about undefined arms, but otherwise type checks generic functions. DrIFT offers no safety at all: a generated document can represent a completely bogus program. Template Haskell offers very limited safety: splicing in code may lead to type errors.

Information in types. In Generic Haskell, Clean, PolyP, and LIGD types of generic functions generally correspond to intuition, and there exists a theory of generic functions by means of which properties for generic functions can be proved. Proving properties of generic functions in SYB is hard because they rely on properties of, possibly user-defined, instances of the classes *Data* and *Typeable*.

In DrIFT all rules have the same type, namely Data → Doc, and it is virtually impossible to prove anything about the functions represented by the documents. The same holds for Template Haskell, although libraries for generic programming defined in Template Haskell may allow to state and prove properties.

Integration with the underlying programming language. Generic Haskell, Clean, SYB, Template Haskell, LIGD, GM, and DTCs are fully integrated with the underlying programming language, where Clean, SYB, Template Haskell, LIGD, GM, and DTCs don't even need a separate compiler. PolyP can only deal with a subset of Haskell. DrIFT has to be recompiled if a new generic function is added to the rules.

To use a generic function on a new data type, almost no work is required in Generic Haskell, Clean, PolyP, SYB, DrIFT, Template Haskell, and DTCs. In the lightweight approaches LIGD and GM the structure representation type and the embedding-projection pair between the structure representation type and the original data type have to be supplied.

Tools. Generic Haskell, LIGD, GM, and DTCs do not do any optimization on the generic code, but otherwise provide good error messages. Clean does optimize the generated code, but provides no error messages. PolyP is not very actively maintained anymore. SYB is shipped as a library of GHC, and is fully supported. The latest versions of SYB have not been included yet in GHC, which means that the current version still suffers from some of the limitations of previous versions of SYB, in particular the limitation that generic functions cannot be extended. DrIFT is maintained, but also provides no error messages. Template Haskell is maintained, but the documentation is outdated, and error messages are not always very helpful.

5.2   Why Would I Use This Approach?

- Use Generic Haskell if you want to experiment with type-indexed functions with kind-indexed types and/or type-indexed data types, in particular if you want to play with higher-kinded and/or nested data types. Generic Haskell is probably the most expressive generic programming extension of Haskell. A disadvantage of using Generic Haskell is that the generated code contains quite a number of mappings from data types to structure types and back again, and hence not as efficient as hand-written code might be.
- Use Clean if you want to use an approach to generic programming that is similar to Generic Haskell, is fully integrated into its underlying programming language, and generates nearly optimal code for generic functions. Clean does not support the advanced features of Generic Haskell such as dependencies, type-indexed data types, and default cases.
- Use PolyP if you want to define generic functions that use the recursive structure of data types, such as a generalization of the *foldr* function on lists, the catamorphism. Remember that PolyP only generates code for data types of kind $\star \to \star$.
- Use Scrap Your Boilerplate if you want to manipulate a value of a large abstract syntax at a particular place in the abstract syntax, and if you want to have an approach to generic programming that is fully integrated in the underlying programming language.
- Use DrIFT if you want a lot of flexibility in the way you generate code, or if you want to format the code you generate in a particular way. Make sure you don't generate code on higher-kinded data types.
- Use Template Haskell if you want to experiment with different implementations of generic programming styles.
- Use the LIGD approach if you want to use a simple but expressive library for generic programming, and your generic functions don't have to work on many different data types.
- Use Generics for the Masses if you want a fully Haskell 98 compatible library that supports generic programming.
- Use Derivable Type Classes if you want (limited) Generic Haskell like generic programming functionality fully integrated into the underlying programming language. DTCs don't support type-indexed data types, or higher-kinded data types.

We distinguished three related groups between the nine approaches to generic programming in Haskell described in these lecture notes:

– Generic Haskell and Clean.
– DrIFT and TH.
– Lightweight approaches: Lightweight Generics and Dynamics, Generics for the Masses, and Derivable Type Classes.

PolyP and SYB form their own subcategories (but we might have placed PolyP2 in the lightweight approaches). The difference between Generic Haskell and Clean is that Generic Haskell is more expressive and provides more features, whereas Clean produces better code. The various lightweight approaches can be compared as follows. GM and DTCs use classes for defining generic functions, so higher-kinded data types are out of reach for these approaches. DTCs automatically generate the conversion functions for instances of generic functions, something that has to be done by hand for LIGD and GM. Also, DTCs allow to extend generic functions with new, type-specific cases without modifying already existing code.

5.3 Future Work

These lecture notes only compare approaches to generic programming in Haskell. The only approaches to generic programming in Haskell we have not addressed are Strafunski, Generic Programming, Now!, and several other new lightweight approaches which have appeared only very recently (after the first drafts of these lecture notes were written). Strafunski is rather similar to SYB, but has a more combinator-like, point-free flavor. Generic Programming, Now! is described at length, including a comparison to other approaches, in this volume.

We have yet to perform the same exercise for approaches to generic programming in different programming languages.

Acknowledgements. We thank the participants of the 61st IFIP WG 2.1 meeting for their comments on a presentation about this work. The participants of the Spring School on Datatype-Generic Programming, Nottingham, April 2006 also provided a number of useful suggestions. Jeremy Gibbons, Patrik Jansson, and Ralf Lämmel carefully read a previous version of this paper, and suggested many improvements.

References

1. Achten, P., van Eekelen, M., Plasmeijer, R.: Generic Graphical User Interfaces. In: Trinder, P., Michaelson, G.J., Peña, R. (eds.) IFL 2003. LNCS, vol. 3145, pp. 152–167. Springer, Heidelberg (2004)
2. Alimarine, A.: Generic Functional Programming - Conceptual Design, Implementation and Applications. PhD thesis, University of Nijmegen, The Netherlands (2005)

3. Alimarine, A., Plasmijer, R.: A generic programming extension for Clean. In: Arts, T., Mohnen, M. (eds.) IFL 2002. LNCS, vol. 2312, pp. 168–186. Springer, Heidelberg (2002)
4. Alimarine, A., Smetsers, S.: Optimizing generic functions. In: Kozen, D. (ed.) MPC 2004. LNCS, vol. 3125, pp. 16–31. Springer, Heidelberg (2004)
5. Alimarine, A., Smetsers, S.: Improved fusion for optimizing generics. In: Hermenegildo, M.V., Cabeza, D. (eds.) Practical Aspects of Declarative Languages. LNCS, vol. 3350, pp. 203–218. Springer, Heidelberg (2005)
6. Altenkirch, T., McBride, C.: Generic programming within dependently typed programming. In: Gibbons and Jeuring [27] , pp. 1–20
7. Atanassow, F., Clarke, D., Jeuring, J.: Scripting XML with Generic Haskell. In: Proceedings of the 7th Brazilian Symposium on Programming Languages, SBLP 2003, An extended version of this paper appears as ICS, Utrecht University, technical report UU-CS-2003-023 (2003)
8. Atanassow, F., Jeuring, J.: Customizing an XML-Haskell data binding with type isomorphism inference in Generic Haskell. Science of Computer Programming 65(2), 72–107 (2007)
9. Augustsson, L.: Cayenne – a language with dependent types. In: Proceedings of the ACM SIGPLAN International Conference on Functional Programming, ICFP 1998, pp. 239 250. ACM Press, New York (1998)
10. Backhouse, R., Gibbons, J.: The EPSRC project on Datatype-Generic Programming (2003-2006), http://web.comlab.ox.ac.uk/oucl/research/pdt/ap/dgp/
11. Benke, M., Dybjer, P., Jansson, P.: Universes for generic programs and proofs in dependent type theory. Nordic Journal of Computing 10(4), 265–289 (2003)
12. Bird, R., Meertens, L.: Nested datatypes. In: Jeuring, J. (ed.) MPC 1998. LNCS, vol. 1422, pp. 52–67. Springer, Heidelberg (1998)
13. Bird, R., Paterson, R.: Generalised folds for nested datatypes. Formal Aspects of Computing 11(2), 200–222 (1999)
14. Chen, J., Appel, A.W.: Dictionary passing for polytypic polymorphism. Technical Report TR-635-01, Princeton University (2001)
15. Cheney, J., Hinze, R.: A lightweight implementation of generics and dynamics. In: Chakravarty, M. (ed.) Haskell '02. Proceedings of the 2002 ACM SIGPLAN workshop on Haskell, pp. 90–104. ACM Press, New York (2002)
16. Clarke, D., Löh, A.: Generic Haskell, specifically. In: Gibbons and Jeuring [27], pp. 21–48
17. Clavel, M., Duran, F., Marti-Oliet, N.: Polytypic programming in Maude. In: Workshop on Rewriting Logic and its Applications 2000 (2000)
18. Cockett, R., Fukushima, T.: About Charity. Yellow Series Report No. 92/480/18, Dep. of Computer Science, Univ. of Calgary (1992)
19. Crary, K., Weirich, S., Morrisett, J.G.: Intensional polymorphism in type-erasure semantics. In: Proceedings of the ACM SIGPLAN International Conference on Functional Programming, ICFP 1998, pp. 301–312. ACM Press, New York (1998)
20. Demers, A., Donahue, J., Skinner, G.: Data types as values: polymorphism, type-checking, encapsulation. In: Conference Record of POPL '78: The 5th ACM SIGPLAN-SIGACT Symposium on Principles of Programming Languages, pp. 23–30. ACM Press, New York (1978)
21. Dubois, C., Rouaix, F., Weis, P.: Extensional polymorphism. In: Conference Record of POPL '95: The 22nd ACM SIGPLAN-SIGACT Symposium on Principles of Programming Languages, pp. 118–129 (1995)
22. Furuse, J.: Generic polymorphism in ML. In Journées Francophones des Langages Applicatifs (January 2001)

23. Garcia, R., Jarvi, J., Lumsdaine, A., Siek, J.G., Willcock, J.: A comparative study of language support for generic programming. In: OOPSLA '03: Proceedings of the 18th annual ACM SIGPLAN conference on Object-oriented programing, systems, languages, and applications, pp. 115–134. ACM Press, New York (2003)
24. Gibbons, J.: Patterns in datatype-generic programming. In: Striegnitz, J., Davis, K. (eds.) Multiparadigm Programming. John von Neumann Institute for Computing (NIC), First International Workshop on Declarative Programming in the Context of Object-Oriented Languages (DPCOOL), vol. 27, pp. 277–289 (2003)
25. Gibbons, J.: Datatype-generic programming. In: Backhouse, R., Gibbons, J., Hinze, R., Jeuring, J. (eds.) Generic Programming, Advanced Lectures. LNCS, vol. 4719, pp. 1–71. Springer, Heidelberg (2006)
26. Gibbons, J.: Metamorphisms: Streaming representation-changers. Science of Computer Programming 65(2), 108–139 (2007)
27. Gibbons, J., Jeuring, J.: Generic Programming. IFIP, vol. 243. Kluwer Academic Publishers, Dordrecht (2003)
28. Gibbons, J., Paterson, R.: Parametric datatype-genericity. Unpublished manuscript (2006)
29. Hagg, P.: A framework for developing generic XML Tools. Master's thesis, Department of Information and Computing Sciences, Utrecht University (2002)
30. Harper, R., Morrisett, G.: Compiling polymorphism using intensional type analysis. In: Conference Record of POPL '95: The 22nd ACM SIGPLAN-SIGACT Symposium on Principles of Programming Languages, pp. 130–141 (1995)
31. Hinze, R.: A generic programming extension for Haskell. In: Meijer, E. (ed.) Proceedings of the Third Haskell Workshop, Technical report of Utrecht University, UU-CS-1999-28 (1999)
32. Hinze, R.: Functional pearl: Perfect trees and bit-reversal permutations. Journal of Functional Programming 10(3), 305–317 (2000)
33. Hinze, R.: Generic Programs and Proofs. Habilitationsschrift, Bonn University (2000)
34. Hinze, R.: Polytypic values possess polykinded types. Science of Computer Programming 43(2-3), 129–159 (2002)
35. Hinze, R.: Generics for the masses. In: Proceedings of the ACM SIGPLAN International Conference on Functional Programming, ICFP 2004, pp. 236–243. ACM Press, New York (2004)
36. Hinze, R.: Generics for the masses. Journal of Functional Programming 16, 451–482 (2006)
37. Hinze, R., Jeuring, J.: Generic Haskell: applications. In: Backhouse, R., Gibbons, J. (eds.) Generic Programming. LNCS, vol. 2793, pp. 57–97. Springer, Heidelberg (2003)
38. Hinze, R., Jeuring, J.: Generic Haskell: practice and theory. In: Backhouse, R., Gibbons, J. (eds.) Generic Programming. LNCS, vol. 2793, pp. 1–56. Springer, Heidelberg (2003)
39. Hinze, R., Jeuring, J., Löh, A.: Type-indexed data types. Science of Computer Programming 51(1–2), 117–151 (2004)
40. Hinze, R., Jeuring, J., Löh, A.: Comparing Approaches to Generic Programming in Haskell. Technical Report UU-CS-2006-022, Utrecht University (2006)
41. Hinze, R., Jones, S.P.: Derivable type classes. In: Hutton, G. (ed.) Proceedings of the 4th Haskell Workshop (2000)
42. Hinze, R., Löh, A.: Generic programming, now! In: Backhouse, R., Gibbons, J., Hinze, R., Jeuring, J. (eds.) Datatype-Generic Programming, Advanced Lectures. LNCS, vol. 4719, Springer, Heidelberg (2006)

43. Hinze, R., Löh, A.: Scrap Your Boilerplate revolutions. In: Uustalu, T. (ed.) MPC 2006. LNCS, vol. 4014, pp. 180–208. Springer, Heidelberg (2006)
44. Hinze, R., Löh, A., Oliveira, B.C.d.S.: Scrap Your Boilerplate reloaded. In: Wadler, P., Hagiya, M. (eds.) FLOPS 2006. LNCS, vol. 3945, Springer, Heidelberg (2006)
45. Holdermans, S., Jeuring, J., Löh, A., Rodriguez, A.: Generic views on data types. In: Uustalu, T. (ed.) MPC 2006. LNCS, vol. 4014, pp. 209–234. Springer, Heidelberg (2006)
46. Huet, G.: The zipper. Journal of Functional Programming 7(5), 549–554 (1997)
47. Hughes, J.: The design of a pretty-printing library. In: Jeuring, J., Meijer, E. (eds.) Advanced Functional Programming. LNCS, vol. 925, pp. 53–96. Springer, Heidelberg (1995)
48. Jansson, P., Jeuring, J.: PolyP – a polytypic programming language extension. In: Conference Record of POPL '97: The 24th ACM SIGPLAN-SIGACT Symposium on Principles of Programming Languages, pp. 470–482. ACM Press, New York (1997)
49. Jansson, P., Jeuring, J.: PolyLib - a polytypic function library. In: Workshop on Generic Programming, Marstrand (June 1998)
50. Jansson, P., Jeuring, J.: Polytypic data conversion programs. Science of Computer Programming 43(1), 35–75 (2002)
51. Jansson, P., Jeuring, J.: students of the Utrecht University Generic Programming class. In: Horváth, Z. (ed.) Testing properties of generic functions. Proceedings 18th International Symposium on Implementation and Application of Functional Languages, IFL'06. LNCS, vol. 4449, Springer, Heidelberg (2007)
52. Barry Jay, C.: Programming in FISh. International Journal on Software Tools for Technology Transfer 2, 307–315 (1999)
53. Barry Jay, C.: Distinguishing data structures and functions: the constructor calculus and functorial types. In: Abramsky, S. (ed.) TLCA 2001. LNCS, vol. 2044, pp. 217–239. Springer, Heidelberg (2001)
54. Barry Jay, C.: The pattern calculus. ACM Trans. Program. Lang. Syst. 26(6), 911–937 (2004)
55. Barry Jay, C., Kesner, D.: Pure pattern calculus. In: Sestoft, P. (ed.) ESOP 2006 and ETAPS 2006. LNCS, vol. 3924, Springer, Heidelberg (2006)
56. Barry Jay, C., Bellé, G., Moggi, E.: Functorial ML. Journal of Functional Programming 8(6), 573–619 (1998)
57. Jeuring, J., Jansson, P.: Polytypic programming. In: Launchbury, J., Meijer, E., Sheard, T. (eds.) Advanced Functional Programming. LNCS, vol. 1129, pp. 68–114. Springer, Heidelberg (1996)
58. Jeuring, J., Plasmeijer, R.: Generic programming for software evolution. In: Informal proceedings of the ERCIM workshop on Software Evolution (2006)
59. Kiselyov, O.: Smash your boiler-plate without class and Typeable, Published on the Haskell mailing list (2006)
60. Koopman, P., Alimarine, A., Tretmans, J., Plasmeijer, R.: Gast: Generic Automated Software Testing. In: Peña, R., Arts, T. (eds.) IFL 2002. LNCS, vol. 2670, Springer, Heidelberg (2003)
61. Lämmel, R., Peyton Jones, S.: Scrap your boilerplate: a practical approach to generic programming. ACM SIGPLAN Notices 38(3), 26–37 (2003)
62. Lämmel, R., Peyton Jones, S.: Scrap your boilerplate with class: extensible generic functions. In: Proceedings of the ACM SIGPLAN International Conference on Functional Programming, ICFP 2005, pp. 204–215. ACM Press, New York (2005)

63. Lämmel, R., Meijer, E.: Revealing the X/O impedance mismatch. In: Backhouse, R., Gibbons, J., Hinze, R., Jeuring, J. (eds.) Datatype-Generic Programming, Advanced Lectures. LNCS, vol. 4719, Springer, Heidelberg (2006)
64. Lämmel, R., Peyton Jones, S.: Scrap more boilerplate: reflection, zips, and generalised casts. In: Proceedings of the ACM SIGPLAN International Conference on Functional Programming, ICFP 2004, pp. 244–255. ACM Press, New York (2004)
65. Lämmel, R., Visser, J.: Typed Combinators for Generic Traversal. In: Krishnamurthi, S., Ramakrishnan, C.R. (eds.) PADL 2002. LNCS, vol. 2257, pp. 137–154. Springer, Heidelberg (2002)
66. Lang, B.: Threshold evaluation and the semantics of call by value, assignment and generic procedures. In: Conference Record of POPL '77: The 4th ACM SIGPLAN-SIGACT Symposium on Principles of Programming Languages, pp. 227–237. ACM Press, New York (1977)
67. Lehman, M.M.: Programs, life cycles and the laws of software evolution. Proc. IEEE 68(9), 1060–1078 (1980)
68. Lehman, M.M., Belady, L.A.: Program Evolution: Processes of Software Change. Academic Press, London (1985)
69. Lieberherr, K.J.: Adaptive Object-Oriented Software: The Demeter Method with Propagation Patterns. PWS Publishing Company, Boston (1996)
70. Löh, A.: Exploring Generic Haskell. PhD thesis, Utrecht University (2004)
71. Löh, A., Clarke, D., Jeuring, J.: Dependency-style Generic Haskell. In: Shivers, O. (ed.) Proceedings of the ACM SIGPLAN International Conference on Functional Programming, ICFP 2003, pp. 141–152. ACM Press, New York (2003)
72. Löh, A., Hinze, R.: Open data types. In: Maher, M. (ed.) Proceedings of the 8th ACM-SIGPLAN International Symposium on Principles and Practice of Declarative Programming, PPDP'06 (2006)
73. Löh, A., Jeuring, J.(eds.). The Generic Haskell user's guide, Version 1.42 - Coral release. Technical Report UU-CS-2005-004, Utrecht University (2005)
74. Lynagh, I.: Typing Template Haskell: Soft Type (August 2004), http://web.comlab.ox.ac.uk/oucl/work/ian.lynagh/papers/ Typing_Template_Haskell:_Soft_Types.ps
75. Malcolm, G.: Data structures and program transformation. Science of Computer Programming 14, 255–279 (1990)
76. McBride, C.: Epigram: practical programming with dependent types. In: Vene, V., Uustalu, T. (eds.) AFP 2004. LNCS, vol. 3622, pp. 130–170. Springer, Heidelberg (2005)
77. Milner, R.: A theory of type polymorphism in programming. Journal of Computer and Systems Sciences 17, 348–375 (1978)
78. Moggi, E., Bellè, Barry Jay, C.: Monads, shapely functors and traversals. In: Hoffman, M., Pavlovič, Rosolini, P. (eds.) Proceedings of the 8th Conference on Category Theory and Computer Science, CTCS'99. Electronic Lecture Notes in Computer Science, vol. 24, pp. 265–286. Elsevier, Amsterdam (1999)
79. Musser, D.R., Derge, G.J., Saini, A.: STL Tutorial and Reference Guide, Second Edition: C++ Programming with the Standard Template Library, 2nd edn. Addison-Wesley, Reading (2001)
80. Nogueira, P.: Context-parametric polykinded types. In: Hinze, R. (ed.) Proceedings of the of the ACM SIGPLAN Workshop on Generic Programming 2006, pp. 45–54. ACM Press, New York (2006)
81. Norell, U., Jansson, P.: Polytypic programming in Haskell. In: Trinder, P., Michaelson, G.J., Peña, R. (eds.) IFL 2003. LNCS, vol. 3145, pp. 168–184. Springer, Heidelberg (2004)

82. Norell, U., Jansson, P.: Prototyping generic programming in Template Haskell. In: Kozen, D. (ed.) MPC 2004. LNCS, vol. 3125, pp. 314–333. Springer, Heidelberg (2004)

83. Oliveira, B.C.d.S., Gibbons, J.: TypeCase: A design pattern for type-indexed functions. In: Löh, A. (ed.) Proceedings Haskell Workshop, ACM Press, New York (2005)

84. Oliveira, B.C.d.S., Hinze, R., Löh, A.: Generics as a library. In: Nilsson, H. (ed.) Proceedings of the 7th Symposium on Trends in Functional Programming, Nottingham, UK, April 19-21, 2006 (2006)

85. OMG.Corba, http://www.omg.org/corba/

86. Peyton Jones, S., et al.: Haskell 98, Language and Libraries. The Revised Report. A special issue of the Journal of Functional Programming (2003)

87. Powell, A.L.: A literature review on the quantification of software change. Technical Report YCS 305, Computer Science, University of York (1998)

88. Reig, F.: Generic proofs for combinator-based generic programs. In: Loidl, H.-W. (ed.) Trends in Functional Programming, vol. 5, Intellect (2006)

89. Schuman, S.A.: On generic functions. In: Schuman, S.A. (ed.) First IFIP WG 2.1 Working Conference on New Directions in Algorithmic Languages 1975, pp. 169–192 IRIA (1975)

90. Sheard, T.: Generic programming in Ωmega. In: Backhouse, R., Gibbons, J., Hinze, R., Jeuring, J. (eds.) Datatype-Generic Programming, Advanced Lectures, LNCS, vol. 4719, Springer, Heidelberg (2006)

91. de Vries, M.: Specializing type-indexed values by partial evaluation. Master's thesis, Rijksuniversiteit Groningen (2004)

92. Wadler, P.: Theorems for free! In: Functional Programming Languages and Computer Architecture, FPCA '89, pp. 347–359. ACM Press, New York (1989)

93. Wadler, P.: How to replace failure by a list of successes. In: Jouannaud, J.-P. (ed.) Functional Programming Languages and Computer Architecture. LNCS, vol. 201, pp. 113–128. Springer, New York (1985)

94. Wallace, M., Runciman, C.: Heap compression and binary I/O in Haskell. In: 2nd ACM Haskell Workshop (1997)

95. Watt, D.A.: Programming Language Design Concepts. John Wiley & Sons, Chichester (2004)

96. Weirich, S.: Higher-order intensional type analysis. In: Le Métayer, D. (ed.) ESOP 2002 and ETAPS 2002. LNCS, vol. 2305, pp. 98–114. Springer, Heidelberg (2002)

97. Weirich, S.: Replib: a library for derivable type classes. In: Haskell '06: Proceedings of the 2006 ACM SIGPLAN workshop on Haskell, pp. 1–12. ACM Press, New York (2006)

98. Weirich, S., Huang, L.: A design for type-directed programming in Java. In: Workshop on Object-Oriented Developments, WOOD 2004 (2004)

99. Winstanley, N., Meacham, J.: The DrIFT manual (1997-2005), http://repetae.net/~john/computer/haskell/DrIFT/

100. Xi, H.: Dependent types in practical programming. PhD thesis, Carnegie Mellon University (1998)

Generic Programming, Now!

Ralf Hinze and Andres Löh

Institut für Informatik III, Universität Bonn
Römerstraße 164, 53117 Bonn, Germany
{ralf,loeh}@informatik.uni-bonn.de

Abstract. Tired of writing boilerplate code? Tired of repeating essentially the same function definition for lots of different datatypes? Datatype-generic programming promises to end these coding nightmares. In these lecture notes, we present the key abstractions of datatype-generic programming, give several applications, and provide an elegant embedding of generic programming into Haskell. The embedding builds on recent advances in type theory: generalised algebraic datatypes and open datatypes. We hope to convince you that generic programming is useful and that you can use generic programming techniques today!

1 Introduction

A type system is like a suit of armour: it shields against the modern dangers of illegal instructions and memory violations, but it also restricts flexibility. The lack of flexibility is particularly vexing when it comes to implementing fundamental operations such as showing a value or comparing two values. In a statically typed language such as Haskell 98 [38] it is simply not possible, for instance, to define an equality test that works for all types. As a rule of thumb, the more expressive a type system, the more fine-grained the type information and the more difficult it becomes to write general-purpose functions.

This problem has been the focus of intensive research for more than a decade. In Haskell 1.0 and in subsequent versions of the language, the problem was only partially addressed: by attaching a so-called *deriving form* to a datatype declaration the programmer can instruct the compiler to generate an instance of equality for the new type. In fact, the deriving mechanism is not restricted to equality: parsers, pretty-printers and several other functions are derivable, as well. These functions have become known as *datatype-generic* or *polytypic* functions, functions that work for a whole family of types. Unfortunately, Haskell's deriving mechanism is closed: the programmer cannot introduce new generic functions.

A multitude of proposals have been put forward that support exactly this, the *definition* of generic functions. Some of the proposals define new languages, some define extensions to existing languages, and some define libraries within existing languages. The early proposals had a strong background in category theory; the recent years have seen a gentle shift towards type-theoretic approaches. In these lecture notes, we present a particularly pragmatic approach: we show how to *embed* generic programming into Haskell. The embedding builds upon recent

R. Backhouse et al. (Eds.): Datatype-Generic Programming 2006, LNCS 4719, pp. 150–208, 2007.

advances in type theory: generalised algebraic datatypes and open datatypes. Or to put it the other way round, we propose and employ language features that are useful for generic programming. Along the way, we will identify the basic building blocks of generic programming and we will provide an overview of the overall design space.

To cut a long story short, we hope to convince you that generic programming is useful and that you can use generic programming techniques today!

To get the most out of the lecture notes you require a basic knowledge of Haskell. To this end, Section 2 provides a short overview of the language and its various extensions. (The section is, however, too dense to serve as a beginner's guide to Haskell.) Section 3 then provides a gentle introduction to the main topic of these lecture notes: we show how to define generic functions and dynamic values, and give several applications. The remaining sections are overviewed at the end of Section 3.

2   Preliminaries

2.1   Values, Types and Kinds

Haskell has the three level structure depicted on the right. The lowest level, that is, the level where computations take place, consists of *values*. The second level, which imposes structure on the value level, is inhabited by *types*. Finally, on the third level, which imposes structure on the type level, we have so-called *kinds*. Why is there a third level? Haskell allows the programmer to define parametric types such as the popular datatype of lists. The list type constructor can be seen as a function on types and the kind system allows us to specify this in a precise way. Thus, a kind is simply the 'type' of a type constructor.

kinds
———
types
———
values

Types and their kinds   In Haskell, new datatypes are declared using the **data** construct. Here are three examples: the type of booleans, the type of pairs and the type of lists:

$$
\begin{array}{ll}
\textbf{data } \mathsf{Bool} & = \mathit{False} \mid \mathit{True} \\
\textbf{data } \mathsf{Pair}\ \alpha\ \beta & = (\alpha, \beta) \\
\textbf{data } [\alpha] & = \mathit{Nil} \mid \mathit{Cons}\ \alpha\ [\alpha]
\end{array}
$$

In general, a datatype comprises one or more *constructors*, and each constructor can have multiple fields. A datatype declaration of the schematic form

$$\textbf{data } \mathsf{T}\ \alpha_1\ \ldots\ \alpha_s = C_1\ \tau_{1,1}\ \ldots\ \tau_{1,m_1} \mid \cdots \mid C_n\ \tau_{n,1}\ \ldots\ \tau_{n,m_n}$$

introduces data constructors $C_1, \ldots, C_n$ with signatures

$$C_i :: \forall \alpha_1\ \ldots\ \alpha_s\ .\ \tau_{i,1} \to \cdots \to \tau_{i,m_i} \to \mathsf{T}\ \alpha_1\ \ldots\ \alpha_s$$

The constructors *False* and *True* of Bool have no arguments. The list constructors *Nil* and *Cons* are written [] and ':' in Haskell. For the purposes of these lecture notes, we stick to the explicit names, as we will use the colon for something else.

The following alternative definition of the pair datatype

data Pair α β = $Pair\{fst :: \alpha, snd :: \beta\}$

makes use of Haskell's *record syntax*: the declaration introduces the data constructor *Pair* and two accessor functions

fst :: $\forall\alpha$ β . Pair α $\beta \rightarrow \alpha$
snd :: $\forall\alpha$ β . Pair α $\beta \rightarrow \beta$

Pairs and lists are examples of parametrised datatypes or *type constructors*. The kind of types such as Bool is $*$, whereas the kind of a type constructor is a function of the kind of its parameters to $*$. The kind of Pair is $* \rightarrow * \rightarrow *$; the kind of [] is $* \rightarrow *$.

In general, the order of a kind is given by

$order$ $(*)$ $= 0$
$order$ $(\iota \rightarrow \kappa) = max\{1 + order\ (\iota), order\ (\kappa)\}.$

Haskell supports kinds of arbitrary order.

Values and their types Functions in Haskell are usually defined using pattern matching. Here is the function *length* that computes the number of elements in a list:

$length$ :: $\forall\alpha$. $[\alpha] \rightarrow$ Int
$length\ Nil$ $= 0$
$length\ (Cons\ x\ xs) = 1 + length\ xs$

The *patterns* on the left hand side are matched against the actual arguments from left to right. The first equation, from top to bottom, where the match succeeds is applied. The first line of the definition is the *type signature* of *length*. Haskell can infer types of functions, but we generally provide type signatures of all top-level functions. The function *length* is *parametrically polymorphic*: the type of list elements is irrelevant; the function applies to arbitrary lists.

In general, the rank of a type is given by

$rank$ (T) $= 0$
$rank$ $(\forall\alpha\ .\ \tau) = max\{1, rank\ (\tau)\}$
$rank$ $(\sigma \rightarrow \tau) = max\{inc\ (rank\ (\sigma)), rank\ (\tau)\},$

where *inc* $0 = 0$ and *inc* $(n + 1) = n + 2$. Most implementations of Haskell support rank-2 types, although the Haskell 98 standard [38] does not. Recent versions of the Glasgow Haskell Compiler (GHC) [40] support types of arbitrary rank. In Haskell, type variables that appear free in a type signature are implicitly universally quantified on the outside. For example, the type signature of *length* could have been defined as *length* :: $[\alpha] \to$ Int.

Sometimes, we use *pattern definitions* as a form of syntactic sugar. (Pattern definitions are not currently supported by any Haskell implementation.) A definition such as

$$Single\ x = Cons\ x\ Nil$$

defines *Single x* to be a transparent abbreviation of *Cons x Nil*. We can use *Single* on the right-hand side of a function definition to construct a value, but also as a derived pattern on the left-hand side of a function definition to destruct a function argument.

2.2   Generalised Algebraic Datatypes

Using a recent version of GHC, there is an alternative way of defining datatypes: by listing the signatures of the constructors explicitly. For example, the definition of lists becomes

data $[\,]$ :: $* \to *$ **where**
   Nil   :: $\forall \alpha\,.\,[\alpha]$
   Cons :: $\forall \alpha\,.\,\alpha \to [\alpha] \to [\alpha]$

The first line declares the kind of the new datatype: $[\,]$ is a type constructor that takes types of kind $*$ to types of kind $*$. The type is then inhabited by listing the signatures of the data constructors. The original datatype syntax hides the fact that the result type of all constructors is $[\alpha]$; this is made explicit here. We can now also define datatypes where this is not the case, so-called *generalised algebraic datatypes* (GADTs):

data Expr :: $* \to *$ **where**
   Num :: Int $\to$ Expr Int
   Plus :: Expr Int $\to$ Expr Int $\to$ Expr Int
   Eq   :: Expr Int $\to$ Expr Int $\to$ Expr Bool
   If   :: $\forall \alpha\,.$ Expr Bool $\to$ Expr $\alpha \to$ Expr $\alpha \to$ Expr α

The datatype Expr represents *typed expressions*: the data constructor *Plus*, for instance, can only be applied to arithmetic expressions of type Expr Int; applying *Plus* to a Boolean expression results in a type error. It is important to note that the type Expr cannot be introduced by a standard Haskell 98 **data** declaration since the constructors have different result types.

For functions on GADTs, type signatures are mandatory. Here is an evaluator for the Expr datatype:

eval :: $\forall \alpha\,.$ Expr $\alpha \to \alpha$
eval (*Num i*)   = i
eval (*Plus* e_1 e_2) = *eval* e_1 + *eval* e_2

$$eval\ (Eq\ e_1\ e_2)\quad = eval\ e_1 \mathbin{==} eval\ e_2$$
$$eval\ (If\ e_1\ e_2\ e_3) = \textbf{if}\ eval\ e_1\ \textbf{then}\ eval\ e_2\ \textbf{else}\ eval\ e_3$$

Even though *eval* is assigned the type $\forall \alpha$. Expr $\alpha \to \alpha$, each equation – with the notable exception of the last one – has a more specific type as dictated by the type constraints. As an example, the first equation has type Expr Int $\to$ Int as *Num* constrains α to Int. The interpreter is quite notable in that it is *tag free* — that is, no explicit type information is carried at run-time. If it receives a Boolean expression, then it returns a Boolean.

In the following, we often omit universal quantifiers in type signatures: type variables that occur free in a type signature are implicitly universally quantified at the outermost level.

2.3   Open Datatypes and Open Functions

Consider the datatype of expressions that we introduced in the previous section. The expression language supports integers, addition, equality and conditionals, but nothing else. If we want to add additional constructs to the expression language, then we have to extend the datatype.

In these lecture notes, we assume that we can extend datatypes that have been flagged as "open": new constructors can be freely added without modifying the code that already has been written. In order to mark Expr as an open datatype, we declare it as follows:

open data Expr :: $* \to *$

Constructors can then be introduced just by providing their type signatures. Here, we add three new constructors for strings, for turning numbers into strings and for concatenating strings:

$$Str\quad :: \text{String} \to \text{Expr String}$$
$$Show :: \text{Expr Int} \to \text{Expr String}$$
$$Cat\quad :: \text{Expr String} \to \text{Expr String} \to \text{Expr String}$$

In order to extend a function, we first have to declare it as open. This is accomplished by providing a type signature flagged with the **open** keyword:

open *eval* :: Expr $\alpha \to \alpha$

The definition of an open function need not be contiguous; the defining equations may be scattered around the program. We can thus extend the evaluator to cover the three new constructors of the Expr datatype:

$$eval\ (Str\ s)\qquad = s$$
$$eval\ (Show\ e)\qquad = show_{\text{Int}}\ (eval\ e)$$
$$eval\ (Cat\ e_1\ e_2) = eval\ e_1 \mathbin{+\!\!+} eval\ e_2$$

The semantics of open datatypes and open functions is the same as if they had been defined closed, in a single place. Openness is therefore mainly a matter of convenience and modularity; it does not increase the expressive power of the language. We use open datatypes and open functions throughout these lecture notes, but the code remains executable in current Haskell implementations that do not support these constructs: one can apply a preprocessor that collects into one place all the constructors for open datatypes and all the defining equations for open functions.

Using open datatypes and open functions gives us both directions of extensibility mentioned in the famous *expression problem* [42]: we can add additional sorts of data, by providing new constructors, and we can add additional operations, by defining new functions. Here is another function on expressions, which turns a given expression into its string representation:

open *string* :: Expr $\alpha \rightarrow$ String
$string\ (Num\ i)$ $=$ "(Num" $\mathbin{+\!\!\!+\!\!\!+}$ $show_{\mathsf{Int}}\ i \mathbin{+\!\!+}$ ")"
$string\ (Plus\ e_1\ e_2)$ $=$ "(Plus" $\mathbin{+\!\!\!+\!\!\!+}$ $string\ e_1 \mathbin{+\!\!\!+\!\!\!+} string\ e_2 \mathbin{+\!\!+}$ ")"
$string\ (Eq\ e_1\ e_2)$ $=$ "(Eq" $\mathbin{+\!\!\!+\!\!\!+}$ $string\ e_1 \mathbin{+\!\!\!+\!\!\!+} string\ e_2 \mathbin{+\!\!+}$ ")"
$string\ (If\ e_1\ e_2\ e_3)$ $=$ "(If" $\mathbin{+\!\!\!+\!\!\!+}$ $string\ e_1 \mathbin{+\!\!\!+\!\!\!+} string\ e_2 \mathbin{+\!\!\!+\!\!\!+} string\ e_3 \mathbin{+\!\!+}$ ")"
$string\ (Str\ s)$ $=$ "(Str" $\mathbin{+\!\!\!+\!\!\!+}$ $show_{\mathsf{String}}\ s \mathbin{+\!\!+}$ ")"
$string\ (Show\ e)$ $=$ "(Show" $\mathbin{+\!\!\!+\!\!\!+}$ $string\ e \mathbin{+\!\!+}$ ")"
$string\ (Cat\ e_1\ e_2)$ $=$ "(Cat" $\mathbin{+\!\!\!+\!\!\!+}$ $string\ e_1 \mathbin{+\!\!\!+\!\!\!+} string\ e_2 \mathbin{+\!\!+}$ ")"

The auxiliary operator '$\mathbin{+\!\!\!+\!\!\!+}$' concatenates two strings with an intermediate blank:

$$s_1 \mathbin{+\!\!\!+\!\!\!+} s_2 = s_1 \mathbin{+\!\!+} "\ " \mathbin{+\!\!+} s_2$$

As an aside, we note that $\forall \alpha$. Expr $\alpha \rightarrow$ String, the type of *string*, is isomorphic to the *existential type* $(\exists \alpha$. Expr $\alpha) \rightarrow$ String, as α does not occur in the result type.

For open functions, first-fit pattern matching is not suitable. To see why, suppose that we want to provide a default definition for *string* in order to prevent pattern matching failures, stating that everything without a specific definition is ignored in the string representation:

$$string\ \_ = ""$$

Using first-fit pattern matching, this equation effectively closes the definition of *string*. Later equations cannot be reached at all. Furthermore, if equations of the function definition are scattered across multiple modules, it is unclear (or at least hard to track) in which order they will be matched with first-fit pattern matching.

We therefore adopt a different scheme for open functions, called *best-fit left-to-right* pattern matching. The idea is that the most specific match rather than the first match wins. This makes the order in which equations of the open function appear irrelevant. In the example above, it ensures that the default case for *string* will be chosen only if no other equation matches. If open functions are implemented via a preprocessor, the defining equations have to be reordered in such a way that the more specific equations come first. The details of open datatypes and functions are described in a recent paper [33].

3   A Guided Tour

3.1   Type-Indexed Functions

In Haskell, showing values of a datatype is particularly easy: one simply attaches a **deriving** (*Show*) clause to the declaration of the datatype.

> **data** Tree α = *Empty* | *Node* (Tree α) α (Tree α)
>   **deriving** (*Show*)

The compiler then automatically generates a suitable *show* function. This function is used, for instance, in interactive sessions to print the result of a submitted expression (the string '*Now*⟩ ' is the prompt of the interpreter).

> *Now*⟩ *tree* [0 .. 3]
> *Node* (*Node* (*Node Empty* 0 *Empty*) 1 *Empty*) 2 (*Node Empty* 3 *Empty*)

Here *tree* :: [α] → Tree α transforms a list into a balanced tree (see Appendix A.1). The function *show* can be seen as a *pretty-printer*. The display of larger structures, however, is not especially pretty, due to lack of indentation.

> *Now*⟩ *tree* [0 .. 9]
> *Node* (*Node* (*Node* (*Node Empty* 0 *Empty*) 1 *Empty*) 2 (*Node* (*Node Em*
> *pty* 3 *Empty*) 4 *Empty*)) 5 (*Node* (*Node* (*Node Empty* 6 *Empty*) 7 *Empt*
> *y*) 8 (*Node Empty* 9 *Empty*))

In the sequel, we develop a replacement for *show*, a generic prettier-printer. There are several pretty-printing libraries around; since these lecture notes focus on generic programming techniques rather than pretty-printing we pick a very basic one (see Appendix A.2), which just offers basic support for indentation.

> **data** Text
> *text*   :: String → Text
> *nl*   :: Text
> *indent* :: Int → Text → Text
> (◊)   :: Text → Text → Text

The function *text* converts a string to a text, where Text is type of documents with indentation. By convention, the string passed to *text* must not contain newline characters. The constant *nl* has to be used for that purpose. The function *indent* adds a given number of spaces after each newline. Finally, '◊' concatenates two pieces of text.

Given this library it is a simple exercise to write a prettier-printer for trees of integers.

> *pretty*$_{\text{Int}}$ :: Int → Text
> *pretty*$_{\text{Int}}$ n = *text* (*show*$_{\text{Int}}$ n)
> *pretty*$_{\text{TreeInt}}$ :: Tree Int → Text

$$pretty_{\mathsf{TreeInt}}\ Empty \qquad = text\ \texttt{"Empty"}$$
$$pretty_{\mathsf{TreeInt}}\ (Node\ l\ x\ r) = align\ \texttt{"(Node\ "}\ (pretty_{\mathsf{TreeInt}}\ l\ \diamondsuit\ nl\ \diamondsuit$$
$$pretty_{\mathsf{Int}}\qquad x\ \diamondsuit\ nl\ \diamondsuit$$
$$pretty_{\mathsf{TreeInt}}\ r\ \diamondsuit\ text\ \texttt{")"})$$

$$align :: \mathsf{String} \to \mathsf{Text} \to \mathsf{Text}$$
$$align\ s\ d = indent\ (length\ s)\ (text\ s\ \diamondsuit\ d)$$

While the program does the job, it is not very general: we can print trees of integers, but not, say, trees of characters. Of course, it is easy to add another two ad-hoc definitions.

$$pretty_{\mathsf{Char}} :: \mathsf{Char} \to \mathsf{Text}$$
$$pretty_{\mathsf{Char}}\ c = text\ (show_{\mathsf{Char}}\ c)$$

$$pretty_{\mathsf{TreeChar}} :: \mathsf{Tree\ Char} \to \mathsf{Text}$$
$$pretty_{\mathsf{TreeChar}}\ Empty \qquad = text\ \texttt{"Empty"}$$
$$pretty_{\mathsf{TreeChar}}\ (Node\ l\ x\ r) = align\ \texttt{"(Node\ "}\ (pretty_{\mathsf{TreeChar}}\ l\ \diamondsuit\ nl\ \diamondsuit$$
$$pretty_{\mathsf{Char}}\qquad x\ \diamondsuit\ nl\ \diamondsuit$$
$$pretty_{\mathsf{TreeChar}}\ r\ \diamondsuit\ text\ \texttt{")"})$$

The code of $pretty_{\mathsf{TreeChar}}$ is almost identical to that of $pretty_{\mathsf{TreeInt}}$. It seems that we actually need a *family* of pretty printers: Tree is a parametrised datatype and quite naturally one would like the elements contained in a tree to be pretty-printed, as well. For concreteness, let us assume that the types of interest are given by the following grammar.

$$\tau ::= \mathsf{Char}\ |\ \mathsf{Int}\ |\ (\tau, \tau)\ |\ [\tau]\ |\ \mathsf{Tree}\ \tau$$

Implementing a type-indexed family of functions sounds like a typical case for Haskell's type classes, in particular, since the deriving mechanism itself relies on the class system: **deriving** (*Show*) generates an instance of Haskell's predefined *Show* class. However, this is only one of several options. In the sequel we explore a different route that does not depend on Haskell's most beloved feature. Sections 4 and 5 will then put this approach in perspective, providing an overview of the overall design space.

type-indexed functions. A simple approach to generic programming defines a family of functions indexed by type.

$$poly_\tau :: \mathsf{Poly}\ \tau$$

The family contains a definition of $poly_\tau$ for each type τ of interest; the type of $poly_\tau$ is parametrised by the type index τ. For brevity, we call *poly* a *type-indexed function* (omitting the 'family of').

Now, instead of implementing a type-indexed family of pretty-printers, we define a single function that receives the type as an additional argument and suitably dispatches on this type argument. However, Haskell doesn't permit the explicit passing of types. An alternative is to pass the pretty-printer an additional argument that *represents* the type of the value we wish to convert to text. As a first try, we could assign the pretty-printer the type Type $\rightarrow \alpha \rightarrow$ Text where Type is the type of type representations. Unfortunately, this is too simple-minded: the parametricity theorem [43] implies that a function of this type must necessarily ignore its second parameter. This argument breaks down, however, if we additionally parameterise Type by the type it represents. The signature of the pretty-printer then becomes Type $\alpha \rightarrow \alpha \rightarrow$ Text. The idea is that an element of type Type τ is a representation of the type τ. Using a *generalised algebraic datatype* (see Section 2.2), we can define Type directly in Haskell.

> **open data** Type :: $* \rightarrow *$ **where**
>   *Char* :: Type Char
>   *Int*   :: Type Int
>   *Pair* :: Type $\alpha \rightarrow$ Type $\beta \rightarrow$ Type (α, β)
>   *List* :: Type $\alpha \rightarrow$ Type $[\alpha]$
>   *Tree* :: Type $\alpha \rightarrow$ Type (Tree α)
> *String* :: Type String
> *String* = *List Char*

We declare Type to be *open* (Section 2.3) so that we can add a new type representation whenever we define a new datatype. The derived constructor *String*, defined by a *pattern definition* (Section 2.1), is equal to *List Char* in all contexts. Recall that we allow *String* to be used on the left-hand side of equations. Each type has a unique representation: the type Int is represented by the constructor *Int*, the type (String, Int) is represented by *Pair String Int* and so forth. For any given τ in our family of types, Type τ comprises exactly one element (ignoring $\bot$); Type τ is a so-called *singleton type*.

In the sequel, we often need to annotate an expression with its type representation. We introduce a special type for this purpose.[1]

> **infixl** 1 :
> **data** Typed $\alpha = (:)\{ val :: \alpha, type :: $ Type $\alpha \}$

The definition, which makes use of Haskell's record syntax, introduces the colon ':' as an infix data constructor. Thus, 4711 : *Int* is an element of Typed Int and (47, "hello") : *Pair Int String* is an element of Typed (Int, String). It is important to note the difference between $x : t$ and $x :: \tau$. The former expression constructs a pair consisting of a value x and a representation t of its type. The latter expression is Haskell syntax for 'x has type τ'.

---

[1] The operator ':' is predefined in Haskell for constructing lists. However, since we use type annotations much more frequently than lists, we use ':' for the former and *Nil* and *Cons* for the latter purpose. Furthermore, we agree upon the convention that the pattern $x : t$ is matched from *right to left*: first the type representation t is matched, then the associated value x. In other words: in proper Haskell source code, $x : t$ has to be written in reverse order, as t :> x.

Given these prerequisites, we can finally define the desired pretty-printer:

open *pretty* :: Typed $\alpha \to$ Text
pretty $(c : Char)$ $= pretty_{\mathsf{Char}}\ c$
pretty $(n : Int)$ $= pretty_{\mathsf{Int}}\ n$
pretty $((x, y) : Pair\ a\ b) = align$ "(" $(pretty\ (x : a))\ \Diamond\ nl\ \Diamond$
                                $align$ ", " $(pretty\ (y : b))\ \Diamond\ text$ ")"
pretty $(xs : List\ a)$ $= bracketed\ [\,pretty\ (x : a)\ |\ x \leftarrow xs\,]$
pretty $(Empty : Tree\ a)\ = text$ "Empty"
pretty $(Node\ l\ x\ r : Tree\ a)$
    $= align$ "(Node " $(pretty\ (l : Tree\ a)\ \Diamond\ nl\ \Diamond$
                      $pretty\ (x : a)\ \Diamond\ nl\ \Diamond$
                      $pretty\ (r : Tree\ a)\ \Diamond\ text$ ")")

We declare *pretty* to be open so that we can later extend it by additional equations. The function *pretty* makes heavy use of type annotations; its type Typed $\alpha \to$ Text is essentially an uncurried version of Type $\alpha \to \alpha \to$ Text. Even though *pretty* has a polymorphic type, each equation implements a more specific case as dictated by the type annotations. For example, the first equation has type Typed Int $\to$ Text.

Let us consider each equation in turn. The first two equations take care of integers and characters, respectively. Pairs are enclosed in parentheses, the two elements being separated by a linebreak and a comma. Lists are shown using *bracketed*, defined in Appendix A.2, which produces a comma-separated sequence of elements between square brackets. Finally, trees are displayed using prefix notation.

The function *pretty* is defined by explicit case analysis on the type representation. This is typical of a type-dependent function, but not compulsory: the wrapper function *show*, defined below, is given by a simple abstraction.

show   :: Typed $\alpha \to$ String
show $x = render\ (pretty\ x)$

The pretty-printer produces output in the following style.

Now⟩ *pretty* $(tree : Tree\ Int\ [0\,.\,.\,3])$
$(Node\ (Node\ (Node\ Empty$
                 0
                 $Empty)$
         1
         $Empty)$
  2
  $(Node\ Empty$
         3
         $Empty))$
Now⟩ *pretty* $([(47, \texttt{"hello"}), (11, \texttt{"world"})] : List\ (Pair\ Int\ String))$
$[\,(47$

```
  , [ 'h'
  , 'e'
  , 'l'
  , 'l'
  , 'o'])
 ,(11
  , [ 'w'
  , 'o'
  , 'r'
  , 'l'
  , 'd'])]
```

While the layout nicely emphasises the structure of the tree, the pretty-printed strings look slightly odd: a string is formatted as a list of characters. Fortunately, this problem is easy to remedy: we add a special case for strings.

$$pretty\ (s : String) = text\ (show_{String}\ s)$$

This case is more specific than the one for lists; best-fit pattern matching ensures that the right instance is chosen. Now, we get

$Now\rangle$ $pretty\ ([(47, \texttt{"hello"}), (11, \texttt{"world"})] : List\ (Pair\ Int\ String))$
```
[(47
 ,"hello")
,(11
 ,"world")]
```

The type of type representations is, of course, by no means specific to pretty-printing. Using type representations, we can define arbitrary type-dependent functions. Here is a second example: collecting strings.

open $strings :: \mathsf{Typed}\ \alpha \to [\mathsf{String}]$
$strings\ (i : Int)\qquad\quad = Nil$
$strings\ (c : Char)\qquad\ = Nil$
$strings\ (s : String)\qquad = [s]$
$strings\ ((x, y) : Pair\ a\ b) = strings\ (x : a) \mathbin{+\!\!+} strings\ (y : b)$
$strings\ (xs : List\ a)\qquad = concat\ [strings\ (x : a) \mid x \leftarrow xs]$
$strings\ (t : Tree\ a)\qquad = strings\ (inorder\ t : List\ a)$

The function $strings$ returns the list of all strings contained in the argument structure. The example shows that we need not program every case from scratch: the $Tree$ case falls back on the list case. Nonetheless, most of the cases have a rather ad-hoc flavour. Surely, there must be a more systematic approach to collecting strings.

type-polymorphic functions. A function of type

$$poly :: \forall\alpha \,.\, \text{Type } \alpha \rightarrow \text{Poly } \alpha$$

is called *type-polymorphic* or *intensionally polymorphic*. By contrast, a function of type $\forall\alpha$. Poly α is called *parametrically polymorphic*.

A note on style: if Poly α is of the form $\alpha \rightarrow \sigma$ where α does not occur in σ (*poly* is a so-called consumer), we will usually prefer the uncurried variant $poly :: \forall\alpha$. Typed $\alpha \rightarrow \sigma$ over the curried version.

3.2   Introducing New Datatypes

We have declared Type to be open so that we can freely add new constructors to the Type datatype and so that we can freely add new equations to existing open functions on Type. To illustrate the extension of Type, consider the type of perfect binary trees [13].

data Perfect $\alpha = Zero\ \alpha\ |\ Succ\ (\text{Perfect } (\alpha, \alpha))$

As an aside, note that Perfect is a so-called *nested data type* [3]. To be able to pretty-print perfect trees, we add a constructor to the type Type of type representations and extend *pretty* by suitable equations.

$Perfect ::$ Type $\alpha \rightarrow$ Type (Perfect α)

$pretty\ (Zero\ x : Perfect\ a) = align$ "(Zero " $(pretty\ (x : a) \Diamond text$ ")")
$pretty\ (Succ\ x : Perfect\ a)$
   $= align$ "(Succ " $(pretty\ (x : Perfect\ (Pair\ a\ a)) \Diamond text$ ")")

Here is a short interactive session that illustrates the extended version of *pretty*.

$Now\rangle\ pretty\ (perfect\ 4\ 1 : Perfect\ Int)$
$(Succ\ (Succ\ (Succ\ (Succ\ (Zero\ (((((1$
$\qquad\qquad\qquad\qquad\qquad\qquad ,1)$
$\qquad\qquad\qquad\qquad\qquad ,(1$
$\qquad\qquad\qquad\qquad\qquad\qquad ,1))$
$\qquad\qquad\qquad\qquad ,((1$
$\qquad\qquad\qquad\qquad\qquad ,1)$
$\qquad\qquad\qquad\qquad ,(1$
$\qquad\qquad\qquad\qquad\qquad ,1)))$
$\qquad\qquad\qquad ,(((1$
$\qquad\qquad\qquad\qquad ,1)$
$\qquad\qquad\qquad ,(1$
$\qquad\qquad\qquad\qquad ,1))$
$\qquad\qquad\qquad ,((1$
$\qquad\qquad\qquad\qquad ,1)$
$\qquad\qquad\qquad ,(1$
$\qquad\qquad\qquad\qquad ,1)))))))))$

The function *perfect d a* generates a perfect tree of depth *d* whose leaves are labelled with *a*s; its definition is given in Appendix A.1.

3.3   Generic Functions

Using type representations, we can program functions that work uniformly for all types of a given family, so-called *overloaded functions*. Let us now broaden the scope of *pretty* and *strings* so that they work for *all* datatypes, including types that the programmer has yet to define. For emphasis, we call these functions *generic functions*.

> **overloaded and generic functions.** An *overloaded function* works for a fixed family of types. By contrast, a *generic function* works for all types, including types that the programmer has yet to define.

We have seen in the previous section that whenever we define a new datatype, we add a constructor of the same name to the type of type representations and we add corresponding equations to *all* generic functions. While the extension of Type is cheap and easy (a compiler could do this for us), the extension of all type-indexed functions is laborious and difficult (can you imagine a compiler doing that?). In this section we develop a scheme so that it suffices to extend Type by a new constructor and to extend *one or two* particular overloaded functions. The remaining functions adapt themselves.

To achieve this goal we need to find a way to treat elements of a data type in a general, uniform way. Consider an arbitrary element of some datatype. It is always of the form $C\ e_1\ \cdots\ e_n$, a constructor applied to some values. For instance, an element of Tree Int is either *Empty* or of the form *Node l a r*. The idea is to make this applicative structure visible and accessible: to this end we mark the constructor using *Con* and each function application using '◊'. Additionally, we annotate the constructor arguments with their types and the constructor itself with information on its syntax. Consequently, the constructor *Empty* becomes *Con empty* and the expression *Node l a r* becomes *Con node* ◊ (*l* : *Tree Int*) ◊ (*a* : *Int*) ◊ (*r* : *Tree Int*) where *empty* and *node* are the tree constructors augmented with additional information. The functions *Con* and '◊' are themselves constructors of a datatype called Spine.

infixl 0 ◊
data Spine :: $* \rightarrow *$ **where**
    Con :: Constr $\alpha \rightarrow$ Spine α
    (◊)   :: Spine $(\alpha \rightarrow \beta) \rightarrow$ Typed $\alpha \rightarrow$ Spine β

The type is called Spine because its elements represent the possibly partial spine of a constructor application (a constructor application can be seen as the internal node of a binary tree; the path to the leftmost leaf in a binary tree is called its *left spine*). The following table illustrates the stepwise construction of a spine.

    node :: Constr (Tree Int $\rightarrow$ Int $\rightarrow$ Tree Int $\rightarrow$ Tree Int)
    Con node :: Spine (Tree Int $\rightarrow$ Int $\rightarrow$ Tree Int $\rightarrow$ Tree Int)

Con node ◊ (*l* : *Tree Int*) :: Spine (Int → Tree Int → Tree Int)
Con node ◊ (*l* : *Tree Int*) ◊ (*a* : *Int*) :: Spine (Tree Int → Tree Int)
Con node ◊ (*l* : *Tree Int*) ◊ (*a* : *Int*) ◊ (*r* : *Tree Int*) :: Spine (Tree Int)

If we ignore the type constructors Constr, Spine and Typed, then *Con* has the type of the identity function, $\alpha \to \alpha$, and '◊' has the type of function application, $(\alpha \to \beta) \to \alpha \to \beta$. Note that the type variable α does not appear in the result type of '◊': it is existentially quantified.[2] This is the reason why we annotate the second argument with its type. Otherwise, we wouldn't be able to use it as an argument of an overloaded function (see below).

An element of type Constr α comprises an element of type α, namely the original data constructor, plus some additional information about its syntax: its name, its arity, its fixity and its order. The order is a pair (i, n) with $1 \leqslant i \leqslant n$, which specifies that the constructor is the ith of a total of n constructors.

data Constr α = *Descr*{ *constr* :: α,
                name :: String,
                arity :: Int,
                fixity :: Fixity,
                order :: (Integer, Integer)}
data Fixity = *Prefix* Int | *Infix* Int | *Infixl* Int | *Infixr* Int | *Postfix* Int

Given a value of type Spine α, we can easily recover the original value of type α by undoing the conversion step.

fromSpine :: Spine $\alpha \to \alpha$
fromSpine (*Con c*) = *constr c*
fromSpine (*f* ◊ *x*) = (*fromSpine f*) (*val x*)

The function *fromSpine* is parametrically polymorphic; it works independently of the type in question, as it simply replaces *Con* with the original constructor and '◊' with function application.

The inverse of *fromSpine* is not polymorphic; rather, it is an overloaded function of type Typed $\alpha \to$ Spine α. Its definition, however, follows a trivial pattern (so trivial that the definition could be easily generated by a compiler): if the datatype comprises a constructor C with signature

$$C :: \tau_1 \to \cdots \to \tau_n \to \tau_0$$

then the equation for *toSpine* takes the form

$$toSpine \ (C \ x_1 \ \ldots \ x_n : t_0) = Con \ c \ ◊ \ (x_1 : t_1) \ ◊ \cdots ◊ \ (x_n : t_n)$$

where c is the annotated version of C and t_i is the type representation of τ_i. As an example, here is the definition of *toSpine* for binary trees.

---

[2] All type variables in Haskell are universally quantified. However, $\forall \alpha \ . \ (\sigma \to \tau)$ is isomorphic to $(\exists \alpha \ . \ \sigma) \to \tau$ provided α does not appear free in τ; this is where the term 'existential type' comes from.

open *toSpine* :: Typed $\alpha \to$ Spine α
toSpine (*Empty* : *Tree a*)   = *Con empty*
toSpine (*Node l x r* : *Tree a*) = *Con node* ◊ (*l* : *Tree a*) ◊ (*x* : *a*) ◊ (*r* : *Tree a*)
empty :: Constr (Tree α)
empty = *Descr*{ *constr* = *Empty*,
              name   = "Empty",
              arity = 0,
              fixity = *Prefix* 10,
              order = (0, 2) }
node :: Constr (Tree $\alpha \to \alpha \to$ Tree $\alpha \to$ Tree α)
node = *Descr*{ *constr* = *Node*,
              name   = "Node",
              arity = 3,
              fixity = *Prefix* 10,
              order = (1, 2) }

Note that this scheme works for arbitrary datatypes including generalised algebraic datatypes!

With all the machinery in place we can now turn *pretty* and *strings* into truly generic functions. The idea is to add a catch-all case to each function that takes care of all the remaining type cases in a uniform manner. Let's tackle *strings* first.

strings x = *strings*_ (*toSpine* x)

*strings*_ :: Spine $\alpha \to$ [String]
*strings*_ (*Con c*) = []
*strings*_ (*f* ◊ *x*) = *strings*_ *f* ++ *strings* x

The helper function *strings*_ traverses the spine calling *strings* for each argument of the spine.

Actually, we can drastically simplify the definition of *strings*: every case except the one for *String* is subsumed by the catch-all case. Hence, the definition boils down to:

strings :: Typed $\alpha \to$ [String]
strings (*s* : *String*) = [*s*]
strings x = *strings*_ (*toSpine* x)

The revised definition makes clear that *strings* has only one type-specific case, namely the one for *String*. This case must be separated out, because we want to do something specific for strings, something that does not follow the general pattern.

The catch-all case for *pretty* is almost as easy. We only have to take care that we do not parenthesize nullary constructors.

pretty x = *pretty*_ (*toSpine* x)
*pretty*_ :: Spine $\alpha \to$ Text

$$pretty_- (Con\ c) = text\ (name\ c)$$
$$pretty_- (f \diamond x)\ = pretty1_- f\ (pretty\ x)$$
$$pretty1_- :: \mathsf{Spine}\ \alpha \to \mathsf{Text} \to \mathsf{Text}$$
$$pretty1_- (Con\ c)\ d = align\ (\texttt{"("} + name\ c + \texttt{" "})\ (d \diamond text\ \texttt{")"})$$
$$pretty1_- (f \diamond x)\quad d = pretty1_- f\ (pretty\ x \diamond nl \diamond d)$$

Now, why are we in a better situation than before? When we introduce a new datatype such as, say, XML, we still have to extend the representation type with a constructor $XML :: \mathsf{Type}\ \mathsf{XML}$ and provide cases for the data constructors of XML in the $toSpine$ function. However, this has to be done only once per datatype, and it is so simple that it could easily be done automatically. The code for the generic functions (of which there can be many) is completely unaffected by the addition of a new datatype. As a further plus, the generic functions are unaffected by changes to a given datatype (unless they include code that is specific to the datatype). Only the function $toSpine$ must be adapted to the new definition, and possibly the type representation if the kind of the datatype changes.

3.4   Dynamic Values

Haskell is a statically typed language. Unfortunately, one cannot guarantee the absence of run-time errors using static checks only. For instance, when we communicate with the environment, we have to check dynamically whether the imported values have the expected types. In this section we show how to embed dynamic checking in a statically typed language.

To this end we introduce a *universal datatype*, the type Dynamic, which encompasses all static values. To inject a static value into the universal type we bundle the value with a representation of its type, re-using the Typed datatype.

data Dynamic :: * **where**
    $Dyn :: \mathsf{Typed}\ \alpha \to \mathsf{Dynamic}$

Note that the type variable α does not appear in the result type: it is effectively existentially quantified. In other words, Dynamic is the union of all typed values. As an example, $misc$ is a list of a dynamic values.

$$misc :: [\mathsf{Dynamic}]$$
$$misc = [Dyn\ (4711 : Int), Dyn\ (\texttt{"hello world"} : String)]$$

Since we have introduced a new type, we must extend the type of type representations.

$$Dynamic :: \mathsf{Type}\ \mathsf{Dynamic}$$

Now, we can also turn $misc$ itself into a dynamic value: $Dyn\ (misc : List\ Dynamic)$.

Dynamic values and generic functions go well together. In a sense, they are dual concepts.[3] We can quite easily extend the generic function *strings* so that it additionally works for dynamic values.

$$strings\ (Dyn\ x : Dynamic) = strings\ x$$

An element of type Dynamic just contains the necessary information required by *strings*. In fact, the situation is similar to the Spine datatype where the second argument of '$\diamond$' also has an existentially quantified type (this is why we had to add type information).

Can we also extend *toSpine* by a case for *Dynamic* so that *strings* works without any changes? Of course! As a first step we add Type and Typed to the type of representable types.

$$Type \quad :: \text{Type } \alpha \rightarrow \text{Type (Type } \alpha)$$
$$Typed :: \text{Type } \alpha \rightarrow \text{Type (Typed } \alpha)$$

The first line looks a bit intimidating with four occurrences of the same identifier, but it exactly follows the scheme for unary type constructors: the representation of T :: $* \rightarrow *$ is T :: Type $\alpha \rightarrow$ Type (T α).

As a second step, we provide suitable instances of *toSpine* pedantically following the general scheme given in Section 3.3 (*oftype* is the infix operator ':' augmented by additional information).

$$toSpine\ (Char : Type\ Char) \quad = Con\ char$$
$$toSpine\ (List\ t : Type\ (List\ a)) = Con\ list \diamond (t : Type\ a) \quad \text{-- } t = a$$
$$\ldots$$
$$toSpine\ ((x : t) : Typed\ a) \quad = Con\ oftype \diamond (x : t) \diamond (t : Type\ t) \quad \text{-- } t = a$$

Note that t and a must be the same type representation since the type representation of $x : t$ is *Typed t*. It remains to extend *toSpine* by a Dynamic case.

$$toSpine\ (Dyn\ x : Dynamic) = Con\ dyn \diamond (x : Typed\ (type\ x))$$

It is important to note that this instance does *not* follow the general pattern for *toSpine*. The reason is that *Dyn*'s argument is existentially quantified and in general, we do not have any type information about existentially quantified types at runtime (see also Section 5.1). But the whole purpose of *Dyn* is to pack a value and its type together, and we therefore can use this type information to define *toSpine*.

To summarise, for every (closed) type with n constructors we have to add $n + 1$ equations for *toSpine*, one for the type representation itself and one for each of the n constructors.

---

[3] The type Dynamic corresponds to the infinite union $\exists \alpha$. Typed α; a generic function of type Typed $\alpha \rightarrow \sigma$ corresponds to the infinite intersection $\forall \alpha$. (Typed $\alpha \rightarrow \sigma$) which equals $(\exists \alpha$. Typed $\alpha) \rightarrow \sigma$ if α does not occur in σ. Hence, a generic function of this type can be seen as taking a dynamic value as an argument.

Given these prerequisites *strings* now works without any changes. There is, however, a slight difference to the previous version: the generic case for *Dynamic* traverses *both* the static value *and* its type, as ':' is treated just like every other data constructor. This may or this may not be what is wanted.

For *pretty* we decide to give an ad-hoc type case for typed values (we want to use infix rather than prefix notation for ':') and to fall back on the generic case for dynamic values.

$$pretty\ ((x:t): Typed\ a) = align\ "(\ "\ (pretty\ (x:t))\ \Diamond\ nl\ \Diamond \quad -- t = a$$
$$align\ ":\ "\ (pretty\ (t: Type\ t))\ \Diamond\ text\ ")"$$

Here is a short interactive session that illustrates pretty-printing dynamic values.

```
Now⟩ pretty (misc : List Dynamic)
[(Dyn (4711
        : Int))
,(Dyn ("hello world"
        : (List Char)))]
```

The constructor *Dyn* turns a static into a dynamic value. The other way round involves a dynamic type check. This operation, usually termed *cast*, takes a dynamic value and a type representation and checks whether the type representation of the dynamic value and the one supplied are identical. The type-equality check itself is given by an *overloaded function* that takes two type representations and possibly returns a *proof* of their equality (a simple truth value is not enough). The proof states that one type may be substituted for the other. We define

$$\textbf{data}\ (:=:) :: * \to * \to *\ \textbf{where}\ Refl :: \alpha :=: \alpha$$

This generalised algebraic datatype has the intriguing property that it is non-empty if and only if its argument types are equal.[4] Given an equality proof of α and β, we can turn any value of type α into a value of type β by pattern matching on the proof and thus making the type-equality constraint available to the type checker:

$$apply :: (\alpha :=: \beta) \to (\alpha \to \beta)$$
$$apply\ p\ x = \textbf{case}\ p\ \textbf{of}\ \{\ Refl \to x\ \}$$

---

[4] We ignore the fact here, that in Haskell every type contains the bottom element. Alternatively, we can adapt Leibniz's principle of substituting equals for equals to types and define

$$\textbf{newtype}\ \alpha :=: \beta = Proof\{\ apply :: \forall \varphi\ .\ \varphi\ \alpha \to \varphi\ \beta\}$$

An element of $\alpha :=: \beta$ is then a function that converts an element of type $\varphi\ \alpha$ into an element of $\varphi\ \beta$ for *any* type constructor φ. Operationally, this function is always the identity.

The type-equality type has all the properties of a *congruence relation*. The constructor *Refl* itself serves as the proof of reflexivity. The equality type is furthermore symmetric, transitive, and congruent. Here are programs that implement the proofs of congruence for type constructors of kind $* \to *$ and $* \to * \to *$.

$$ctx_1 \quad :: \quad (\alpha :=: \beta) \to (\psi\ \alpha :=: \psi\ \beta)$$
$$ctx_1\ p = \ \mathbf{case}\ p\ \mathbf{of}\ \{\ Refl \to Refl\ \}$$
$$ctx_2 \quad\quad :: (\alpha_1 :=: \beta_1) \to (\alpha_2 :=: \beta_2) \to (\psi\ \alpha_1\ \alpha_2 :=: \psi\ \beta_1\ \beta_2)$$
$$ctx_2\ p_1\ p_2 = \mathbf{case}\ p_1\ \mathbf{of}\ \{\ Refl \to \mathbf{case}\ p_2\ \mathbf{of}\ \{\ Refl \to Refl\ \}\ \}$$

The type-equality check is now given by

```
equal :: Type α → Type β → Maybe (α :=: β)
equal Int         Int          = return Refl
equal Char        Char         = return Refl
equal (Pair a₁ a₂) (Pair b₁ b₂) = liftM2 ctx₂ (equal a₁ b₁) (equal a₂ b₂)
equal (List a)    (List b)     = liftM ctx₁ (equal a b)
equal _           _            = fail "types are not unifiable"
```

Since the equality check may fail, we must lift the congruence proofs into the Maybe monad using *return*, *liftM*, and *liftM2*. Note that the running time of the cast function that *equal* returns is *linear* in the size of the type (it is independent of the size of its argument structure).

The *cast* operation simply calls *equal* and then applies the conversion function to the dynamic value.

```
cast                    :: Dynamic → Type α → Maybe α
cast (Dyn (x : a)) t = fmap (λp → apply p x) (equal a t)
```

Again, we have to introduce an auxiliary datatype to direct Haskell's type-checker. Here is a short session that illustrates the use of *cast*.

```
Now⟩ let d = Dyn (4711 : Int)
Now⟩ pretty (d : Dynamic)
(Dyn (4711
      : Int))
Now⟩ d ʻcastʻ Int
Just 4711
Now⟩ fromJust (d ʻcastʻ Int) + 289
5000
Now⟩ d ʻcastʻ Char
Nothing
```

In a sense, *cast* can be seen as the dynamic counterpart of the colon operator: x ʻ*cast*ʻ T yields a static value of type τ if T is the representation of τ.

generic functions and dynamic values. Generics and dynamics are dual concepts:

$$\text{generic function: } \forall \alpha \text{ . Type } \alpha \to \sigma$$
$$\text{dynamic value: } \exists \alpha \text{ . Type } \alpha \times \sigma$$

This is analogous to first-order predicate logic where $\forall x{:}T$. $P(x)$ is shorthand for $\forall x$. $T(x) \Rightarrow P(x)$ and $\exists x{:}T$. $P(x)$ abbreviates $\exists x$. $T(x) \wedge P(x)$.

3.5 Stocktaking

Before we proceed, let us step back to see what we have achieved so far.

Broadly speaking, generic programming is about defining functions that work for all types but that also exhibit type-specific behaviour. Using a GADT we have reflected types onto the value level. For each type constructor we have introduced a data constructor: types of kind $*$ are represented by constants; parametrised types are represented by functions that take type representations to type representations. Using reflected types we can program *overloaded functions*, functions that work for a fixed class of types and that exhibit type-specific behaviour. Finally, we have defined the Spine datatype that allows us to treat data in a uniform manner. Using this uniform view on data we can generalise overloaded functions to *generic* ones.

In general, support for generic programming consists of three essential ingredients:

- a type reflection mechanism,
- a type representation, and
- a generic view on data.

Let us consider each ingredient in turn.

Type reflection. Using the type of type representations we can program functions that depend on or dispatch on types. Alternative techniques include Haskell's type classes and a type-safe cast. We stick to the GADT technique in these lecture notes.

Type representation.. Ideally, a representation type is a faithful mirror of the language's type system. To be able to define such a representation type or some representation type at all, the type system must be sufficiently expressive. We have seen that GADTs allow for a very direct representation; in a less expressive type system we may have to encode types less directly or in a less type-safe manner. However, the more expressive a type system, the more difficult it is to reflect the full system onto the value level. We shall see in Section 4 that there are several ways to model the Haskell type system and that the one we have used in this section is *not* the most natural or the most direct one. Briefly, the type Type models the type system of Haskell 1.0; it is difficult to extend to the more expressive system of Haskell 98 (or to one of its manifold extensions).

Generic view. The generic view has the largest impact on the expressivity of a generic programming system: it affects the set of datatypes we can cover, the class of functions we can write and potentially the efficiency of these functions. In this section we have used the spine view to represent data in a uniform way. We shall see that this view is applicable to a large class of datatypes, including GADTs. The reason for the wide applicability is simple: a datatype definition describes how to construct data, the spine view captures just this. Its main weakness is also rooted in the 'value-orientation': one can only define generic functions that consume data (*show*) but not ones that produce data (*read*). Again, the reason for the limitation is simple: a uniform view on individual constructor applications is useful if you have data in your hands, but it is of no help if you want to construct data. Section 5 shows how to overcome this limitation and furthermore introduces alternative views.

4 Type Representations

4.1 Representation Types for Types of a Fixed Kind

Representation Type for Types of Kind ∗. The type Type of Section 3.1 represents types of kind ∗. A type constructor T is represented by a data constructor T of the same name. A type of kind ∗ is either a basic type such as Char or Int, or a compound type such as List Char or Pair Int (List Char). The components of a compound type are possibly type constructors of higher kinds such as List or Pair. These type constructors must also be represented using the type Type of type representations. Since type constructors are reflected onto the value level, the type of the data constructor T depends on the kind of the type constructor T. To see the precise relationship between the type of T and the kind of T, re-consider the declaration of Type, this time making polymorphic types explicit.

> **open data** Type :: ∗ → ∗ **where**
>   *Char* :: Type Char
>   *Int*   :: Type Int
>   *Pair* :: ∀α . Type α → (∀β . Type β → Type (α, β))
>   *List* :: ∀α . Type α → Type [α]
>   *Tree* :: ∀α . Type α → Type (Tree α)

A type constructor T of higher kind is represented by a *polymorphic* function that takes a type representation for α to a type representation for T α, for all types α. In general, T_κ has the signature

> T_κ :: Type_κ T_κ

where Type_κ is defined

> **type** Type_* α = Type α
> **type** $\mathsf{Type}_{\iota \to \kappa}$ φ = ∀α . Type_ι α → Type_κ (φ α)

Thus, application on the type level corresponds to application of polymorphic functions on the value level.

So far we have only encountered first-order type constructors. Here is an example of a second-order one:

newtype Fix $\varphi = In\{\ out :: \varphi\ (\text{Fix } \varphi)\}$

The declaration introduces a fixed point operator, Fix, on the type level, whose kind is $(* \to *) \to *$. Consequently, the value counterpart of Fix has a rank-2 type: it takes a polymorphic function as an argument.

$Fix :: \forall \varphi\ .\ (\forall \alpha\ .\ \text{Type } \alpha \to \text{Type } (\varphi\ \alpha)) \to \text{Type } (\text{Fix } \varphi)$

Using *Fix*, the representation of type fixed points, we can now extend, for instance, *strings* by an appropriate case.

$strings\ (In\ x : Fix\ f) = strings\ (x : f\ (Fix\ f))$

Of course, this case is not really necessary: if we add a *Fix* equation to *toSpine*, then the specific case above is subsumed by the generic one of Section 3.3.

$toSpine\ (In\ x : Fix\ f) = Con\ in \diamond (x : f\ (Fix\ f))$

Here *in* is the annotated variant of *In*. Again, the definition of *toSpine* pedantically follows the general scheme.

Unfortunately, we cannot extend the definition of *equal* to cover the Fix case: *equal* cannot recursively check the arguments of *Fix* for equality, as they are polymorphic functions. In general, we face the problem that we cannot pattern match on polymorphic functions: *Fix List*, for instance, is not a legal pattern (List is not saturated). In Section 4.2 we introduce an alternative type representation that does not suffer from this problem.

Representation Type for Types of Kind $* \to *$. The generic functions of Section 3 abstract over a type of kind $*$. For instance, *pretty* generalises functions of type

Char $\to$ Text,   String $\to$ Text, $[[\text{Int}]] \to$ Text

to a single generic function of type

Type $\alpha \to \alpha \to$ Text   or equivalently   Typed $\alpha \to$ Text

A generic function may also abstract over a type constructor of higher kind. Take, as an example, the function *size* that counts the number of elements contained in some data structure. This function generalises functions of type

$[\alpha] \to$ Int,   Tree $\alpha \to$ Int, $[\text{Tree } \alpha] \to$ Int

to a single generic function of type

Type$'$ $\varphi \to \varphi\,\alpha \to$ Int   or equivalently   Typed$'$ $\varphi\,\alpha \to$ Int

where Type$'$ is a representation type for types of kind $* \to *$ and Typed$'$ is a suitable type, to be defined shortly, for annotating values with these representations.

How can we represent type constructors of kind $* \to *$? Clearly, the type Type$_{*\to*}$ is not suitable, as we intend to define *size* and other generic functions by case analysis on the type constructor. Again, the elements of Type$_{*\to*}$ are polymorphic functions and pattern-matching on functions would break referential transparency. Therefore, we define a new tailor-made representation type.

> **open data** Type$'$ :: $(* \to *) \to *$ **where**
>   *List* :: Type$'$ [ ]
>   *Tree* :: Type$'$ Tree

Think of the prime as shorthand for the kind index $* \to *$. Additionally, we introduce a primed variant of Typed.

> **infixl** 1 :$'$
> **data** Typed$'$ $\varphi\,\alpha = (:')\{\,val' :: \varphi\,\alpha, type' :: \text{Type}'\,\varphi\,\}$

The type Type$'$ is only inhabited by two constructors since the other datatypes have kinds different from $* \to *$.

An overloaded version of *size* is now straightforward to define.

> *size* :: Typed$'$ $\varphi\,\alpha \to$ Int
> *size* (Nil :$'$ $List$) $= 0$
> *size* ($Cons\ x\ xs$:$'$ $List$) $= 1 + size\ (xs$:$'$ $List$)
> *size* ($Empty$:$'$ $Tree$) $= 0$
> *size* ($Node\ l\ x\ r$:$'$ $Tree$) $= size\ (l$:$'$ $Tree$) $+ 1 + size\ (r$:$'$ $Tree$)

Unfortunately, *size* is not as flexible as *pretty*. If we have some compound data structure x, say, a list of trees of integers, then we can simply call *pretty* (x : *List* (*Tree Int*)). We cannot, however, use *size* to count the total number of integers, simply because the new versions of *List* and *Tree* take no arguments!

There is one further problem, which is more fundamental. Computing the size of a compound data structure is inherently ambiguous: in the example above, do we count the number of integers, the number of trees or the number of lists? Formally, we have to solve the type equation $\varphi\,\tau = $ List (Tree Int). The equation has, in fact, not three but four principal solutions: $\varphi = \Lambda\alpha \to \alpha$ and $\tau = $ List (Tree Int), $\varphi = \Lambda\alpha \to$ List α and $\tau = $ Tree Int, $\varphi = \Lambda\alpha \to$ List (Tree α) and $\tau = $ Int, and $\varphi = \Lambda\alpha \to$ List (Tree Int) and τ arbitrary. How can we represent these different container types? They can be easily expressed using functions: $\lambda a \to a$, $\lambda a \to$ *List a*, $\lambda a \to$ *List* (*Tree a*), and $\lambda a \to$ *List* (*Tree Int*). Alas, we are just trying to get rid of the functional representation. There are several ways out of this dilemma. One possibility is to *lift* the type constructors [15] so that they become members of Type$'$ and to include Id, defined as

> **newtype** Id $\alpha = In_{\text{Id}}\{\,out_{\text{Id}} :: \alpha\,\}$

as a representation of the type variable α:

$$
\begin{array}{ll}
Id & :: \mathsf{Type'}\ \mathsf{Id} \\
Char' & :: \mathsf{Type'}\ \mathsf{Char'} \\
Int' & :: \mathsf{Type'}\ \mathsf{Int'} \\
List' & :: \mathsf{Type'}\ \varphi \to \mathsf{Type'}\ (\mathsf{List'}\ \varphi) \\
Tree' & :: \mathsf{Type'}\ \varphi \to \mathsf{Type'}\ (\mathsf{Tree'}\ \varphi)
\end{array}
$$

The type List', for instance, is the lifted variant of List: it takes a type constructor of kind $* \to *$ to a type constructor of kind $* \to *$. Using the lifted types we can specify the four different container types as follows: Id, List' Id, List' (Tree' Id) and List' (Tree' Int'). Essentially, we replace the types by their lifted counterparts and the type variable α by Id. Note that the above constructors of Type' are *exactly identical* to those of Type except for the kinds.

It remains to define the lifted versions of the type constructors.

newtype Char' $\chi = In_{\mathsf{Char'}}\{\,out_{\mathsf{Char'}} :: \mathsf{Char}\,\}$
newtype Int' $\chi = In_{\mathsf{Int'}}\{\,out_{\mathsf{Int'}} :: \mathsf{Int}\,\}$
data List' α' $\chi = Nil' \mid Cons'\ (\alpha'\ \chi)\ (\mathsf{List'}\ \alpha'\ \chi)$
data Pair' $\alpha'\ \beta'\ \chi = Pair'\ (\alpha'\ \chi)\ (\beta'\ \chi)$
data Tree' α' $\chi = Empty' \mid Node'\ (\mathsf{Tree'}\ \alpha'\ \chi)\ (\alpha'\ \chi)\ (\mathsf{Tree'}\ \alpha'\ \chi)$

The lifted variants of the nullary type constructors Char and Int simply ignore the additional argument χ. The **data** definitions follow a simple scheme: each data constructor C with signature

$$ C :: \tau_1 \to \cdots \to \tau_n \to \tau $$

is replaced by a polymorphic data constructor C' with signature

$$ C' :: \forall \chi\ .\ \tau_1'\ \chi \to \cdots \to \tau_n'\ \chi \to \tau_0'\ \chi $$

where τ_i' is the lifted variant of τ_i.

The function *size* can be easily extended to Id and to the lifted types.

$$
\begin{array}{ll}
size\ (x :'\ Id) & = 1 \\
size\ (c :'\ Char') & = 0 \\
size\ (i :'\ Int') & = 0 \\
size\ (Nil' :'\ List'\ a') & = 0 \\
size\ (Cons'\ x\ xs :'\ List'\ a') & = size\ (x :'\ a') + size\ (xs :'\ List'\ a') \\
size\ (Empty' :'\ Tree'\ a') & = 0 \\
size\ (Node'\ l\ x\ r :'\ Tree'\ a') & \\
\quad = size\ (l :'\ Tree'\ a') + size\ (x :'\ a') + size\ (r :'\ Tree'\ a') &
\end{array}
$$

The instances are similar to the ones for the unlifted types, except that *size* is now also called recursively for list elements and tree labels, that is, for components of type α'.

Unfortunately, in Haskell *size* no longer works on the original data types: we cannot call, for instance, $size\ (x :'\ List'\ (Tree'\ Id))$ where x is a list of trees of integers, since List' (Tree' Id) Int is different from [Tree Int]. However, the two types are isomorphic: $\tau \cong \tau'$ Id where τ' is the lifted variant of τ [15]. We leave it at that for the moment and return to the problem later in Section 5.

We have already noted that Type' is similar to Type except for the kinds. This becomes even more evident when we consider the signature of a lifted type representation: the lifted version of T_κ has signature

$$T'_\kappa :: \mathsf{Type}'_\kappa \; T'_\kappa$$

where Type'_κ is defined

type Type'_* $\alpha = \mathsf{Type}' \; \alpha$
type $\mathsf{Type}'_{\iota \to \kappa} \; \varphi = \forall \alpha \, . \, \mathsf{Type}'_\iota \; \alpha \to \mathsf{Type}'_\kappa \; (\varphi \; \alpha)$

Defining an overloaded function that abstracts over a type of kind $* \to *$ is similar to defining a $*$-indexed function, except that one has to consider one additional case, namely Id, which defines the action of the overloaded function on the type parameter. It is worth noting that it is not necessary to define instances for the unlifted type constructors ([] and Tree in our running example), as we have done, because these instances can be automatically derived from the lifted ones by virtue of the isomorphism $\tau \cong \tau'$ Id (see Section 5.3).

Representation Type for Types of Kind ω. Up to now we have confined ourselves to generic functions that abstract over types of kind $*$ or $* \to *$. An obvious question is whether the approach can be generalised to *kind indices* of arbitrary kinds. This is indeed possible. However, functions that are indexed by higher kinds, for instance, by $(* \to *) \to * \to * \to *$ are rare. For that reason, we only sketch the main points. For a formal treatment see Hinze's earlier work [15]. Assume that $\omega = \kappa_1 \to \cdots \to \kappa_n \to *$ is the kind of the type index. We first introduce a suitable type representation and lift the datatypes to kind ω by adding n type arguments of kinds $\kappa_1, \ldots, \kappa_n$.

open data $\mathsf{Type}^\omega :: \omega \to *$ **where**
    $T^\omega_\kappa :: \mathsf{Type}^\omega_\kappa \; T^\omega_\kappa$

where T^ω_κ is the lifted version of T_κ and $\mathsf{Type}^\omega_\kappa$ is defined

type Type^ω_* $\alpha = \mathsf{Type}^\omega \; \alpha$
type $\mathsf{Type}^\omega_{\iota \to \kappa} \; \varphi = \forall \alpha \, . \, \mathsf{Type}^\omega_\iota \; \alpha \to \mathsf{Type}^\omega_\kappa \; (\varphi \; \alpha)$

The lifted variant T^ω_κ of the type T_κ has kind κ^ω where $(-)^\omega$ is defined inductively on the structure of kinds

$$*^\omega   = \omega$$
$$(\iota \to \kappa)^\omega = \iota^\omega \to \kappa^\omega$$

Types and lifted types are related as follows: τ is isomorphic to τ' $Out_1 \ldots Out_n$ where Out_i is the *projection type* that corresponds to the i-th argument of ω. The generic programmer has to consider the cases for the lifted type constructors plus n additional cases, one for each of the n projection types $Out_1, \ldots, Out_n$.

4.2   Kind-Indexed Families of Representation Types

We have seen that type-indexed functions may abstract over arbitrary type constructors: *pretty* abstracts over types of kind $*$, size abstracts over types of kind $* \to *$. Sometimes a type-indexed function even makes sense for types of *different* kinds. A paradigmatic example is the *mapping function*: the mapping function of a type φ of kind $* \to *$ lifts a function of type $\alpha_1 \to \alpha_2$ to a function of type $\varphi \, \alpha_1 \to \varphi \, \alpha_2$; the mapping function of a type ψ of kind $* \to * \to *$ takes two functions of type $\alpha_1 \to \alpha_2$ and $\beta_1 \to \beta_2$ respectively and returns a function of type $\psi \, \alpha_1 \, \beta_1 \to \psi \, \alpha_2 \, \beta_2$. As an extreme case, the mapping function of a type σ of kind $*$ is the identity of type $\sigma \to \sigma$.

Dictionary-Passing Style. The above discussion suggests turning *map* into a *family* of overloaded functions. Since the type of the mapping functions depends on the kind of the type argument, we have, in fact, a *kind-indexed family* of overloaded functions. To make this work we have to represent types differently: we require a kind-indexed family of representation types.

> **open data** $\mathsf{Type}_\kappa :: \kappa \to *$ **where**
> $\quad T_\kappa :: \mathsf{Type}_\kappa \, T_\kappa$

In this scheme $\mathsf{Int} :: *$ is represented by a data constructor of type Type_*; the type constructor $\mathsf{Tree} :: * \to *$ is represented by a data constructor of type $\mathsf{Type}_{* \to *}$ and so forth. There is, however, a snag in it. If the representation of Tree is not a function, how can we represent the application of Tree to some type? The solution is simple: we also represent type application syntactically using a family of kind-indexed constructors.

$$App_{\iota,\kappa} :: \mathsf{Type}_{\iota \to \kappa} \, \varphi \to \mathsf{Type}_\iota \, \alpha \to \mathsf{Type}_\kappa \, (\varphi \, \alpha)$$

The result type dictates that $App_{\iota,\kappa}$ is an element of Type_κ. Theoretically, we need an infinite number of $App_{\iota,\kappa}$ constructors, one for each combination of ι and κ. Practically, only a few are likely to be used, since types with a large number of type arguments are rare. For our purposes the following declarations suffice.

> **open data** $\mathsf{Type}_* :: * \to *$ **where**
> $\quad Char_* \qquad :: \mathsf{Type}_* \, \mathsf{Char}$
> $\quad Int_* \qquad\;\; :: \mathsf{Type}_* \, \mathsf{Int}$
> $\quad App_{*,*} \qquad :: \mathsf{Type}_{* \to *} \, \varphi \to \mathsf{Type}_* \, \alpha \to \mathsf{Type}_* \, (\varphi \, \alpha)$
> **open data** $\mathsf{Type}_{* \to *} :: (* \to *) \to *$ **where**
> $\quad List_{* \to *} \quad\; :: \mathsf{Type}_{* \to *} \, []$
> $\quad Tree_{* \to *} \quad :: \mathsf{Type}_{* \to *} \, \mathsf{Tree}$
> $\quad App_{*,* \to *} \quad :: \mathsf{Type}_{* \to * \to *} \, \varphi \to \mathsf{Type}_* \, \alpha \to \mathsf{Type}_{* \to *} \, (\varphi \, \alpha)$
> **open data** $\mathsf{Type}_{* \to * \to *} :: (* \to * \to *) \to *$ **where**
> $\quad Pair_{* \to * \to *} :: \mathsf{Type}_{* \to * \to *} \, (,)$

For example, $\mathsf{Tree} \, \mathsf{Int}$ is now represented by $Tree_{* \to *} \; `App_{*,*}` \; Int_*$. We have $(Pair_{* \to * \to *} \; `App_{*,* \to *}` \; Int_*) \; `App_{*,*}` \; Int_* :: \mathsf{Type}_* \, (\mathsf{Int}, \mathsf{Int})$. Since $App_{*,*}$ is a data constructor, we can pattern match both on $Tree_{*\to*}$ '$App_{*,*}$' a and on $Tree_{*\to*}$ alone. Since Haskell allows type constructors to be partially applied, the family Type_κ is indeed a faithful representation of Haskell's type system.

It is straightforward to adapt the type-indexed functions of Section 3 to the new representation. In fact, using a handful of *pattern definitions* we can re-use the code *without* any changes.

$$
\begin{aligned}
&Int &&:: \mathsf{Type}_* \ \mathsf{Int} \\
&Int &&= Int_* \\
&Char &&:: \mathsf{Type}_* \ \mathsf{Char} \\
&Char &&= Char_* \\
&Pair &&:: \mathsf{Type}_* \ \alpha \to \mathsf{Type}_* \ \beta \to \mathsf{Type}_* \ (\alpha, \beta) \\
&Pair \ a \ b &&= Pair_{*\to*\to*} \ `App_{*,*\to*}` \ a \ `App_{*,*}` \ b \\
&List &&:: \mathsf{Type}_* \ \alpha \to \mathsf{Type}_* \ [\alpha] \\
&List \ a &&= List_{*\to*} \ `App_{*,*}` \ a \\
&Tree &&:: \mathsf{Type}_* \ \alpha \to \mathsf{Type}_* \ (\mathsf{Tree} \ \alpha) \\
&Tree \ a &&= Tree_{*\to*} \ `App_{*,*}` \ a
\end{aligned}
$$

The definitions show that the old representation can be defined in terms of the new representation. The reverse, however, is not true: we cannot turn a polymorphic function into a data constructor.

Now, let's tackle an example of a type-indexed function that works for types of different kinds. We postpone the implementation of the mapping function until the end of the section and first re-implement the function *size* that counts the number of elements contained in a data structure (see Section 4.1).

$$size :: \mathsf{Type}_{*\to*} \ \varphi \to \varphi \ \alpha \to \mathsf{Int}$$

How can we generalise *size* so that it works for types of arbitrary kinds? The essential step is to abstract away from *size*'s action on values of type α, turning the action of type $\alpha \to \mathsf{Int}$ into an additional argument:

$$count_{*\to*} :: \mathsf{Type}_{*\to*} \ \varphi \to (\alpha \to \mathsf{Int}) \to (\varphi \ \alpha \to \mathsf{Int})$$

We call *size*'s kind-indexed generalisation *count*. If we instantiate the second argument of $count_{*\to*}$ to *const* 1, we obtain the original function back. But there is also an alternative choice: if we instantiate the second argument to *id*, we obtain a generalisation of Haskell's *sum* function, which sums the elements of a container.

$$
\begin{aligned}
&size &&:: \mathsf{Type}_{*\to*} \ \varphi \to \varphi \ \alpha \to \mathsf{Int} \\
&size \ f &&= count_{*\to*} \ f \ (const \ 1) \\
&sum &&:: \mathsf{Type}_{*\to*} \ \varphi \to \varphi \ \mathsf{Int} \to \mathsf{Int} \\
&sum \ f &&= count_{*\to*} \ f \ id
\end{aligned}
$$

Two generic functions for the price of one!

Let us now turn to the definition of $count_\kappa$. Since $count_\kappa$ is indexed by kind, it also has a kind-indexed type.

$$count_\kappa :: \mathsf{Type}_\kappa\ \alpha \to \mathsf{Count}_\kappa\ \alpha$$

where Count_κ is defined

type Count_* $\alpha = \alpha \to \mathsf{Int}$
type $\mathsf{Count}_{\iota\to\kappa}\ \varphi = \forall\alpha\ .\ \mathsf{Count}_\iota\ \alpha \to \mathsf{Count}_\kappa\ (\varphi\ \alpha)$

The definition looks familiar: it follows the scheme we have already encountered in Section 4.1 (Type_κ is defined analogously). The first line specifies that a 'counting function' maps an element to an integer. The second line expresses that $count_{\iota\to\kappa}\ f$ takes a counting function for α to a counting function for $\varphi\ \alpha$, for all α. This means that the kind-indexed function $count_\kappa$ maps type application to application of generic functions.

$$count_\kappa\ (App_{\iota,\kappa}\ f\ a) = (count_{\iota\to\kappa}\ f)\ (count_\iota\ a)$$

This case for $App_{\iota,\kappa}$ is truly generic: it is the same for all kind-indexed generic functions (in dictionary-passing style; see below) and for all combinations of ι and κ. The type-specific behaviour of a generic function is solely determined by the cases for the different type constructors. As an example, here are the definitions for $count_\kappa$:

open $count_*$ :: $\mathsf{Type}_*\ \alpha \to \mathsf{Count}_*\ \alpha$
$count_*\ (f\ `App_{*,*}`\ a) = (count_{*\to*}\ f)\ (count_*\ a)$
$count_*\ t$ $= const\ 0$

open $count_{*\to*}$ :: $\mathsf{Type}_{*\to*}\ \alpha \to \mathsf{Count}_{*\to*}\ \alpha$
$count_{*\to*}\ List_{*\to*}$ $c = sum_{[]}\ .\ map_{[]}\ c$
$count_{*\to*}\ Tree_{*\to*}$ $c = count_{*\to*}\ List_{*\to*}\ c\ .\ inorder$
$count_{*\to*}\ (f\ `App_{*,*\to*}`\ a)\ c = (count_{*\to*\to*}\ f)\ (count_*\ a)\ c$

open $count_{*\to*\to*}$ :: $\mathsf{Type}_{*\to*\to*}\ \alpha \to \mathsf{Count}_{*\to*\to*}\ \alpha$
$count_{*\to*\to*}\ (Pair_{*\to*\to*})\ c_1\ c_2 = \lambda(x_1, x_2) \to c_1\ x_1 + c_2\ x_2$

Note that we have to repeat the generic $App_{\iota,\kappa}$ case for every instance of ι and κ. The catch-all case for types of kind $*$ determines that elements of types of kind $*$ such as Int or Char are mapped to 0.

Taking the size of a compound data structure such as a list of trees of integers is now much easier than before: the count function for $\Lambda\alpha \to \mathsf{List}\ (\mathsf{Tree}\ \alpha)$ is the unique function that maps c to $count_{*\to*}\ (List_{*\to*})\ (count_{*\to*}\ (Tree_{*\to*})\ c)$. Here is a short interactive session that illustrates the use of $count$ and $size$.

$Now\rangle$ **let** $ts = [\,tree\ [0 \mathinner{.\,.} i]\ |\ i \leftarrow [0 \mathinner{.\,.} 9]\,]$
$Now\rangle$ $size\ (List_{*\to*})\ ts$
10
$Now\rangle$ $count_{*\to*}\ (List_{*\to*})\ (size\ (Tree_{*\to*}))\ ts$
55

The fact that $count_{*\to*}$ is parametrised by the action on α allows us to mimic type abstraction by abstraction on the value level. Since $count_{*\to*}$ receives the $*$-instance of the count function as an argument, we say that $count$ is defined in *dictionary-passing* style. There is also an alternative, type-passing style, which we discuss in a moment, where the type representation itself is passed as an argument.

The definition of the mapping function is analogous to the definition of *size* except for the type. Recall that the mapping function of a type φ of kind $* \to *$ lifts a function of type $\alpha_1 \to \alpha_2$ to a function of type $\varphi\, \alpha_1 \to \varphi\, \alpha_2$. The instance is doubly polymorphic: both the argument and the result type of the argument function may vary. Consequently, we assign map a kind-indexed type that has two type arguments:

$$map_\kappa :: \mathsf{Type}_\kappa\ \alpha \to \mathsf{Map}_\kappa\ \alpha\ \alpha$$

where Map_κ is defined

type Map_* $\alpha_1\ \alpha_2 = \alpha_1 \to \alpha_2$
type $\mathsf{Map}_{\iota\to\kappa}\ \varphi_1\ \varphi_2 = \forall \alpha_1\ \alpha_2\ .\ \mathsf{Map}_\iota\ \alpha_1\ \alpha_2 \to \mathsf{Map}_\kappa\ (\varphi_1\ \alpha_1)\ (\varphi_2\ \alpha_2)$

The definition of map itself is straightforward:

open map_* :: $\mathsf{Type}_*\ \alpha \to \mathsf{Map}_*\ \alpha\ \alpha$
$map_*\ Int_*$ $= id$
$map_*\ Char_*$ $= id$
$map_*\ (App_{*,*}\ f\ a) = (map_{*\to*}\ f)\ (map_*\ a)$
open $map_{*\to*}$ :: $\mathsf{Type}_{*\to*}\ \varphi \to \mathsf{Map}_{*\to*}\ \varphi\ \varphi$
$map_{*\to*}\ List_{*\to*}$ $= map_{[]}$
$map_{*\to*}\ Tree_{*\to*}$ $= map_\mathsf{Tree}$
$map_{*\to*}\ (App_{*,*\to*}\ f\ a) = (map_{*\to*\to*}\ f)\ (map_*\ a)$
open $map_{*\to*\to*}$ :: $\mathsf{Type}_{*\to*\to*}\ \varphi \to \mathsf{Map}_{*\to*\to*}\ \varphi\ \varphi$
$map_{*\to*\to*}\ Pair_{*\to*\to*}\ f\ g\ (a,b) = (f\ a, g\ b)$

Each instance simply defines the mapping function for the respective type.

kind-indexed functions. A kind-indexed family of type-polymorphic functions

$$poly_\kappa :: \forall \alpha\ .\ \mathsf{Type}_\kappa\ \alpha \to \mathsf{Poly}_\kappa\ \alpha$$

contains a definition of $poly_\kappa$ for each kind κ of interest. The type representation Type_κ and the type Poly_κ are indexed by kind, as well. For brevity, we call $poly_\kappa$ a *kind-indexed function* (omitting the 'family of type-polymorphic').

Type-Passing Style. The functions above are defined in dictionary-passing style, as instances of overloaded functions are passed around. An alternative scheme passes the type representation instead. We can use it, for instance, to define $*$-indexed functions in a less verbose way. To illustrate, let us re-define the overloaded function *pretty* in type-passing style. Its kind-indexed type is given by

type Pretty_* $\alpha = \alpha \to \mathsf{Text}$
type $\mathsf{Pretty}_{\iota \to \kappa}\ \varphi = \forall \alpha\ .\ \mathsf{Type}_\iota\ \alpha \to \mathsf{Pretty}_\kappa\ (\varphi\ \alpha)$

The equations for $pretty_\kappa$ are similar to those of *pretty* of Section 3.1, except for the 'type patterns': the left-hand side *pretty* $(T\ a_1\ \ldots\ a_n)$ becomes $pretty_\kappa\ T_\kappa\ a_1\ \ldots\ a_n$, where κ is the kind of T.

open $pretty_*\ ::\ \mathsf{Type}_*\ \alpha \to \mathsf{Pretty}_*\ \alpha$
$pretty_*\ Char_*\ c$ $= pretty_{\mathsf{Char}}\ c$
$pretty_*\ Int_*\ \ \ n$ $= pretty_{\mathsf{Int}}\ \ n$
$pretty_*\ (f\ {}^\backprime App_{*,*}{}^\backprime\ a)\ x$ $= pretty_{*\to*}\ f\ a\ x$

open $pretty_{*\to*}\ ::\ \mathsf{Type}_{*\to*}\ \alpha \to \mathsf{Pretty}_{*\to*}\ \alpha$
$pretty_{*\to*}\ List_{*\to*}\ a\ xs$ $= bracketed\ [pretty_*\ a\ x\ |\ x \leftarrow xs]$
$pretty_{*\to*}\ Tree_{*\to*}\ a\ Empty$ $= text\ \texttt{"Empty"}$
$pretty_{*\to*}\ Tree_{*\to*}\ a\ (Node\ l\ x\ r)$
   $= align\ \texttt{"(Node\ "}\ (pretty_{*\to*}\ Tree_{*\to*}\ a\ l\quad \Diamond\ nl\ \Diamond$
$pretty_*\ a\ x\ \Diamond\ nl\ \Diamond$
$pretty_{*\to*}\ Tree_{*\to*}\ a\ r\quad \Diamond\ text\ \texttt{")"})$
$pretty_{*\to*}\ (f\ {}^\backprime App_{*,*\to*}{}^\backprime\ a)\ b\ x$ $= pretty_{*\to*\to*}\ f\ a\ b\ x$

open $pretty_{*\to*\to*}\ ::\ \mathsf{Type}_{*\to*\to*}\ \alpha \to \mathsf{Pretty}_{*\to*\to*}\ \alpha$
$pretty_{*\to*\to*}\ Pair_{*\to*\to*}\ a\ b\ (x,y) = align\ \texttt{"(\ "}\ (pretty_*\ a\ x)\ \Diamond\ nl\ \Diamond$
$align\ \texttt{",\ "}\ (pretty_*\ b\ y)\ \Diamond\ text\ \texttt{")"}$

The equations for type application have a particularly simple form.

$$poly_\kappa\ (App_{\iota,\kappa}\ f\ a) = poly_{\iota \to \kappa}\ f\ a$$

Type-passing style is preferable to dictionary-passing style for implementing *mutually recursive* generic functions. In dictionary-passing style we have to tuple the functions into a single dictionary (analogous to the usual implementation of Haskell's type classes). On the other hand, using dictionary-passing style we can define truly polymorphic generic functions such as, for example, *size* :: $\mathsf{Type}_{*\to*}\ \varphi \to \forall \alpha\ .\ \varphi\ \alpha \to \mathsf{Int}$, which is not possible in type-passing style where *size* has type $\mathsf{Type}_{*\to*}\ \varphi \to \forall \alpha\ .\ \mathsf{Type}_*\ \alpha \to \varphi\ \alpha \to \mathsf{Int}$.

dictionary- and type-passing style. A kind-indexed family of overloaded functions is said to be defined in *dictionary-passing style* if the instances for type functions receive as an argument the instance (the dictionary) for the type parameter. If instead the type representation itself is passed, then the family is defined in *type-passing style*.

4.3   Representations of Open Type Terms

Haskell's type system is somewhat peculiar, as it features type application but not type abstraction. If Haskell had type-level lambdas, we could determine the instances of $* \rightarrow *$-indexed functions using suitable type abstractions: for our running example we could use representations of $\varLambda\alpha \rightarrow$ List (Tree Int), $\varLambda\alpha \rightarrow \alpha$, $\varLambda\alpha \rightarrow$ List α, or $\varLambda\alpha \rightarrow$ List (Tree α). Interestingly, there is an alternative. We can represent an anonymous type function by an *open type term*: $\varLambda\alpha \rightarrow$ List (Tree α), for instance, is represented by *List (Tree a)* where a is a suitable representation of α.

Representation Types for Types of a Fixed Kind. To motivate the representation of *free* type variables, let us work through a concrete example. Consider the following version of *count* that is defined on Type, the original type of type representations.

$$
\begin{aligned}
&count :: \text{Type } \alpha \rightarrow (\alpha \rightarrow \text{Int}) \\
&count\ (Char) \quad = const\ 0 \\
&count\ (Int) \quad\quad = const\ 0 \\
&count\ (Pair\ a\ b) = \lambda(x, y) \rightarrow count\ a\ x + count\ b\ y \\
&count\ (List\ a) \quad = sum_{[]}\ .\ map_{[]}\ (count\ a) \\
&count\ (Tree\ a) \quad = sum_{[]}\ .\ map_{[]}\ (count\ a)\ .\ inorder
\end{aligned}
$$

As it stands, *count* is point-free, but also pointless, as it always returns the constant 0 (unless the argument is not fully defined, in which case *count* is undefined, as well). We shall see in a moment that we can make *count* more useful by adding a representation of unbound type variables to Type. The million-dollar question is, of course, what constitutes a suitable representation of an unbound type variable? Now, if we extend *count* by a case for the unbound type variable, its meaning must be provided from somewhere. An intriguing choice is therefore to identify the type variable with its meaning. Thus, the representation of an open type variable is a constructor that embeds a *count* instance, a function of type $\alpha \rightarrow$ Int, into the type of type representations.

$$Count :: (\alpha \rightarrow \text{Int}) \rightarrow \text{Type } \alpha$$

Since the 'type variable' carries its own meaning, the *count* instance is particularly simple.

$$count\ (Count\ c) = c$$

A moment's reflection reveals that this approach is an instance of the 'embedding trick' [9] for higher-order abstract syntax: *Count* is the pre-inverse or right inverse of *count*. Using *Count* we can specify the action on the free type variable when we call *count*:

$$
\begin{aligned}
&Now\rangle\ \textbf{let}\ ts = [\,tree\ [0 .. i]\ |\ i \leftarrow [0 .. 9 :: \text{Int}]\,] \\
&Now\rangle\ \textbf{let}\ a = Count\ (const\ 1)
\end{aligned}
$$

$Now\rangle$ $count$ $(List$ $(Tree$ $Int))$ ts
0
$Now\rangle$ $count$ a ts
1
$Now\rangle$ $count$ $(List$ $a)$ ts
10
$Now\rangle$ $count$ $(List$ $(Tree$ $a))$ ts
55

Using a different instance we can also sum the elements of a data structure:

$Now\rangle$ **let** $a = Count$ id
$Now\rangle$ $count$ $(Pair$ Int $Int)$ $(47, 11)$
0
$Now\rangle$ $count$ $(Pair$ a $Int)$ $(47, 11)$
47
$Now\rangle$ $count$ $(Pair$ Int a $)$ $(47, 11)$
11
$Now\rangle$ $count$ $(Pair$ a a $)$ $(47, 11)$
58

The approach would work perfectly well if *count* were the only generic function. But it is not:

$Now\rangle$ $pretty$ $(4711 : a)$
*** Exception: Non-exhaustive patterns in function *pretty*

If we pass *Count* to a different generic function, we get a run-time error. Unfortunately, the problem is not easy to remedy, as it is impossible to define a suitable *Count* instance for *pretty*. We simply have not enough information to hand. There are at least two ways out of this dilemma: we can augment the representation of unbound type variables by the required information, or we can use a different representation type that additionally abstracts over the type of a generic function. Let us consider each alternative in turn.

To define a suitable equation for *pretty* or other generic functions, we basically need the representation of the instance type. Therefore we define:

infixl ' Use '
Use :: Type $\alpha \rightarrow$ Instance $\alpha \rightarrow$ Type α

where Instance gathers instances of generic functions:

open data Instance :: $* \rightarrow *$ **where**
  $Pretty$ :: $(\alpha \rightarrow$ Text$) \rightarrow$ Instance α
  $Count$ :: $(\alpha \rightarrow$ Int$)$ $\rightarrow$ Instance α

Using the new representation, Count c becomes a ' Use ' Count c, where a is the representation of c's instance type. Since Use couples each instance with a representation of the instance type, we can easily extend *count* and *pretty*:

$count\ (Use\ a\ d) = \mathbf{case}\ d\ \mathbf{of}\ \{\ Count\ c \to c;\ otherwise \to count\ a\}$
$pretty\ (Use\ a\ d) = \mathbf{case}\ d\ \mathbf{of}\ \{\ Pretty\ p \to p;\ otherwise \to pretty\ a\}$

The definitional scheme is the same for each generic function: we first check whether the instance matches the generic function at hand, otherwise we recurse on the type representation. It is important to note that the scheme is independent of the number of generic functions, in fact, the separate Instance type was introduced to make the pattern matching more robust. A type representation that involves Use such as $Int\ `Use`\ Count\ c\ `Use`\ Pretty\ p :: \mathsf{Type\ Int}$ can be seen as a mini-environment that determines the action of the listed generic functions at this point. The above instances of $count$ and $pretty$ effectively perform an environment look-up at runtime.

Let us now turn to the second alternative. The basic idea is to parameterise Type by the type of generic functions.

open data $\mathsf{PType} :: (* \to *) \to * \to *$ **where**
$\quad PChar\ :: \mathsf{PType\ poly\ Char}$
$\quad PInt\quad :: \mathsf{PType\ poly\ Int}$
$\quad PPair\ :: \mathsf{PType\ poly}\ \alpha \to \mathsf{PType\ poly}\ \beta \to \mathsf{PType\ poly}\ (\alpha, \beta)$
$\quad PList\ :: \mathsf{PType\ poly}\ \alpha \to \mathsf{PType\ poly}\ [\alpha]$
$\quad PTree\ :: \mathsf{PType\ poly}\ \alpha \to \mathsf{PType\ poly}\ (\mathsf{Tree}\ \alpha)$

A generic function then has type $\mathsf{PType\ Poly}\ \alpha \to \mathsf{Poly}\ \alpha$ for some suitable type Poly. As before, the representation of an unbound type variable is a constructor of the inverse type, except that now we additionally abstract away from Poly.

$\quad PVar :: \mathsf{poly}\ \alpha \to \mathsf{PType\ poly}\ \alpha$

Since we abstract over Poly, we make do with a single constructor: $PVar$ can be used to embed instances of arbitrary generic functions.

The definition of $count$ can be easily adapted to the new representation (for technical reasons, we have to introduce a **newtype** for $count$'s type).

newtype $\mathsf{Count}\ \alpha = In_{\mathsf{Count}}\{\ out_{\mathsf{Count}} :: \alpha \to \mathsf{Int}\}$
$pcount :: \mathsf{PType\ Count}\ \alpha \to (\alpha \to \mathsf{Int})$
$pcount\ (PVar\ c)\quad = out_{\mathsf{Count}}\ c$
$pcount\ (PChar)\quad = const\ 0$
$pcount\ (PInt)\qquad = const\ 0$
$pcount\ (PPair\ a\ b) = \lambda(x, y) \to pcount\ a\ x + pcount\ b\ y$
$pcount\ (PList\ a)\quad = sum_{[]}\ .\ map_{[]}\ (pcount\ a)$
$pcount\ (PTree\ a)\quad = sum_{[]}\ .\ map_{[]}\ (pcount\ a)\ .\ inorder$

The code is almost identical to what we have seen before, except that the type signature is more precise.

Here is an interactive session that illustrates the use of $pcount$.

$Now\rangle\ \mathbf{let}\ ts = [\ tree\ [0..i]\ |\ i \leftarrow [0..9 :: \mathsf{Int}]]$
$Now\rangle\ \mathbf{let}\ a = PVar\ (In_{\mathsf{Count}}\ (const\ 1))$

```
Now⟩ :type a
a :: ∀α . PType Count α
Now⟩  pcount (PList (PTree PInt)) ts
0
Now⟩  pcount (a) ts
1
Now⟩  pcount (PList a) ts
10
Now⟩  pcount (PList (PTree a)) ts
55
Now⟩  let a = PVar (In_Count id)
Now⟩  :type a
PType Count Int
Now⟩  pcount (PList (PTree a)) ts
165
```

Note that the type of a now limits the applicability of the unbound type variable: passing it to *pretty* would result in a static type error.

We can also capture our standard idioms, counting elements and summing up integers, as abstractions.

```
psize f  = pcount (f a) where a = PVar (In_Count (const 1))
psum f  = pcount (f a) where a = PVar (In_Count id)
```

Given these definitions, we can represent type constructors of kind $* \to *$ by ordinary, value-level λ-terms.

```
Now⟩  let ts = [tree [0 .. i] | i ← [0 .. 9 :: Int]]
Now⟩  psize (λa → PList (PTree PInt)) ts
0
Now⟩  psize (λa → a) ts
1
Now⟩  psize (λa → PList a) ts
10
Now⟩  psize (λa → PList (PTree a)) ts
55
Now⟩  psum (λa → PPair PInt PInt) (47, 11)
0
Now⟩  psum (λa → PPair a      PInt) (47, 11)
47
Now⟩  psum (λa → PPair PInt a   ) (47, 11)
11
Now⟩  psum (λa → PPair a      a   ) (47, 11)
58
```

It is somewhat surprising that the expressions above type-check, in particular, as Haskell does not support anonymous type functions. The reason is that we can assign *psize* and *psum* Hindler-Milner types:

$psize$ :: (PType Count α $\rightarrow$ PType Count β) $\rightarrow$ (β $\rightarrow$ Int)
$psum$ :: (PType Count Int $\rightarrow$ PType Count β) $\rightarrow$ (β $\rightarrow$ Int)

The functions also possess $F\omega$ types [10], which are different from the types above:

$psize$ :: $\forall\varphi$. PType$_{*\rightarrow*}$ Count φ $\rightarrow$ ($\forall\alpha$. φ α $\rightarrow$ Int)
$psum$ :: $\forall\varphi$. PType$_{*\rightarrow*}$ Count φ $\rightarrow$ ($\forall\alpha$. φ Int $\rightarrow$ Int)

Using $F\omega$ types, however, the above calls do not type-check, since Haskell employs a kinded first-order unification of types.

Kind-Indexed Families of Representation Types The other representation types, Type$'$ and Type$_\kappa$, can be extended in an analogous manner to support open type terms. For instance, for Type$_\kappa$ we basically have to introduce kind-indexed versions of Use and Instance.

open data Instance$_\kappa$ :: $\kappa \rightarrow *$ **where**
 $Poly_\kappa$ :: Poly$_\kappa$ α $\rightarrow$ Instance$_\kappa$ α
Use_κ :: Type$_\kappa$ α $\rightarrow$ Instance$_\kappa$ α $\rightarrow$ Type$_\kappa$ α
$poly_\kappa$ (Use_κ a d) = **case** d **of** {Poly$_\kappa$ $p \rightarrow p$; $otherwise \rightarrow poly_\kappa$ a}

The reader may wish to fill in the gory details and to work through the implementation of the other combinations.

5   Views

In Section 4 we thoroughly investigated the design space of type representations. The examples in that section are without exception overloaded functions. In this section we explore various techniques to turn these overloaded functions into truly generic ones. Before we tackle this, let us first discuss the difference between *nominal* and *structural* type systems.

Haskell has a *nominal type system*: each **data** declaration introduces a new type that is incompatible with all the existing types. Two types are equal if and only if they have the same name (and hence the same structure). In contrast, in a *structural type system* two types are equal if they have the same structure, even if they have different names. In a language with a structural type system there is no need for a generic view; a generic function can be defined exhaustively by induction on the structure of types.

For nominal systems the key to genericity is a uniform view on data. In Section 3.3 we introduced the spine view, which views data as constructor applications. Of course, this is not the only generic view. PolyP [27], for instance, views data types as fixed points of regular functors; Generic Haskell [20] uses a sum-of-products view. We shall see that these two approaches can be characterised as *type-oriented*: they provide a uniform view on all elements of a datatype. By contrast, the spine view is *value-oriented*: it provides a uniform view on single elements.

View. For the following it is useful to make the concept of a view explicit.

> **infixr** 5 $\rightarrow$
> **infixl** 5 $\leftarrow$
> **type** $\alpha \leftarrow \beta = \beta \rightarrow \alpha$
> **data** View :: $* \rightarrow *$ **where**
> $\quad$ View :: Type $\beta \rightarrow (\alpha \rightarrow \beta) \rightarrow (\alpha \leftarrow \beta) \rightarrow$ View α

A view consists of three ingredients: a so-called *structure type* that constitutes the actual view on the original datatype, and two functions that convert to and fro. To define a view the generic programmer simply provides a view function

> *view* :: Type $\alpha \rightarrow$ View α

that maps a type to its structural representation. The view function can then be used in the catch-all case of a generic function. Take as an example the modified definition of *strings* (the original catch-all case is defined in Section 3.1).

> *strings* $(x : t) =$ **case** *view* t **of**
> $\qquad\qquad$ View u *fromData toData* $\rightarrow$ *strings* (*fromData* $x : u$)

Using one of the conversion functions, $x : t$ is converted to its structural representation *fromData* $x : u$, on which *strings* is called recursively. Because of the recursive call, the definition of *strings* must contain additional case(s) that deal with the structure type. For the spine view, a single equation suffices.

> *strings* $(x : Spine\ a) = strings_{-}\ x$

Lifted view. For the type Type' of lifted type representations, we can set up similar machinery.

> **infixr** 5 $\overset{\cdot}{\rightarrow}$
> **infixl** 5 $\overset{\cdot}{\leftarrow}$
> **type** $\varphi \overset{\cdot}{\rightarrow} \psi = \forall \alpha\ .\ \varphi\ \alpha \rightarrow \psi\ \alpha$
> **type** $\varphi \overset{\cdot}{\leftarrow} \psi = \forall \alpha\ .\ \psi\ \alpha \rightarrow \varphi\ \alpha$
> **data** View' :: $(* \rightarrow *) \rightarrow *$ **where**
> $\quad$ View' :: Type' $\psi \rightarrow (\varphi \overset{\cdot}{\rightarrow} \psi) \rightarrow (\varphi \overset{\cdot}{\leftarrow} \psi) \rightarrow$ View' φ

The view function is now of type

> *view'* :: Type' $\varphi \rightarrow$ View' φ

and is used as follows:

> *map* $f\ m\ x =$ **case** *view'* f **of**
> $\qquad\qquad$ View' g *fromData toData* $\rightarrow$ (*toData* . *map* $g\ m$. *fromData*) x

In this case, we require both the *fromData* and the *toData* function.

5.1   Spine View

The spine view of the type τ is simply $\mathsf{Spine}\ \tau$:

$spine \quad :: \mathsf{Type}\ \alpha \rightarrow \mathsf{View}\ \alpha$
$spine\ a = View\ (Spine\ a)\ (\lambda x \rightarrow toSpine\ (x : a))\ fromSpine$

Recall that *fromSpine* is parametrically polymorphic, while *toSpine* is an overloaded function. The definition of *toSpine* follows a simple pattern: if the datatype comprises a constructor C with signature

$$C :: \tau_1 \rightarrow \cdots \rightarrow \tau_n \rightarrow \tau_0$$

then the equation for *toSpine* takes the form

$$toSpine\ (C\ x_1\ \ldots\ x_n : t_0) = Con\ c \diamond (x_1 : t_1) \diamond \cdots \diamond (x_n : t_n)$$

where c is the annotated version of C and t_i is the type representation of τ_i. The equation is only valid if $vars\ (t_1) \cup \cdots \cup vars\ (t_n) \subseteq vars\ (t_0)$, that is, if C's type signature contains no existentially quantified type variables (see also below).

The spine view is particularly easy to use: the generic part of a generic function only has to consider two cases: *Con* and '$\diamond$'.

A further advantage of the spine view is its generality: it is applicable to a large class of datatypes. Nested datatypes, for instance, pose no problems: the type of perfect binary trees (see Section 3.2)

data $\mathsf{Perfect}\ \alpha = Zero\ \alpha \mid Succ\ (\mathsf{Perfect}\ (\alpha, \alpha))$

gives rise to the following two equations for *toSpine*:

$toSpine\ (Zero\ x : Perfect\ a) = Con\ zero \diamond (x : a)$
$toSpine\ (Succ\ x : Perfect\ a) = Con\ succ \diamond (x : Perfect\ (Pair\ a\ a))$

The equations follow exactly the general scheme above. We have also seen that the scheme is applicable to *generalised algebraic datatypes*. Consider as an example the typed representation of expressions (see Section 2.2).

data $\mathsf{Expr} :: * \rightarrow *$ **where**
    Num :: $\mathsf{Int} \rightarrow \mathsf{Expr}\ \mathsf{Int}$
    $Plus$ :: $\mathsf{Expr}\ \mathsf{Int} \rightarrow \mathsf{Expr}\ \mathsf{Int} \rightarrow \mathsf{Expr}\ \mathsf{Int}$
    Eq :: $\mathsf{Expr}\ \mathsf{Int} \rightarrow \mathsf{Expr}\ \mathsf{Int} \rightarrow \mathsf{Expr}\ \mathsf{Bool}$
    If :: $\mathsf{Expr}\ \mathsf{Bool} \rightarrow \mathsf{Expr}\ \alpha \rightarrow \mathsf{Expr}\ \alpha \rightarrow \mathsf{Expr}\ \alpha$

The relevant equations for *toSpine* are

$toSpine\ (Num\ i : Expr\ Int) \quad\quad = Con\ num \diamond (i : Int)$
$toSpine\ (Plus\ e_1\ e_2 : Expr\ Int) = Con\ plus \diamond (e_1 : Expr\ Int) \diamond (e_2 : Expr\ Int)$
$toSpine\ (Eq\ e_1\ e_2 : Expr\ Bool) = Con\ eq \diamond (e_1 : Expr\ Int) \diamond (e_2 : Expr\ Int)$

$toSpine\ (If\ e_1\ e_2\ e_3 : Expr\ a)$
$\quad = Con\ if \diamond (e_1 : Expr\ Bool) \diamond (e_2 : Expr\ a) \diamond (e_3 : Expr\ a)$

Given this definition we can apply *pretty* to values of type Expr without further ado. Note in this respect that the Glasgow Haskell Compiler (GHC) currently does not support **deriving** (*Show*) for GADTs. When we turned Dynamic into a representable type (Section 3.4), we discussed one limitation of the spine view: it cannot, in general, cope with existentially quantified types. Consider, as another example, the following extension of the expression datatype:

$Apply :: Expr\ (\alpha \to \beta) \to Expr\ \alpha \to Expr\ \beta$

The equation for *toSpine*

$toSpine\ (Apply\ f\ x : Expr\ b)$
$\quad = Con\ apply \diamond (f : Expr\ (a \to b)) \diamond (x : Expr\ a) \quad \text{-- not legal Haskell}$

is not legal Haskell, as a, the representation of α, appears free on the right-hand side. The only way out of this dilemma is to augment x by a representation of its type, as in Dynamic.[5]

To summarise: a **data** declaration describes how to construct data; the spine view captures just this. Consequently, it is applicable to almost every datatype declaration. The other views are more restricted: Generic Haskell's original sum-of-products view is only applicable to Haskell 98 types excluding GADTs and existential types (however, we will show in Section 5.4 how to extend the sum-of-products view to GADTs); PolyP is even restricted to fixed points of regular functors excluding nested datatypes and higher kinded types.

On the other hand, the classic views provide more information, as they represent the complete datatype, not just a single constructor application. The spine view effectively restricts the class of functions we can write: one can only define generic functions that consume or transform data (such as *show*) but not ones that produce data (such as *read*). The uniform view on individual constructor applications is useful if you have data in your hands, but it is of no help if you want to construct data. We make this more precise in the following section.

Furthermore, functions that abstract over type constructors (such as *size* or *map*) are out of reach for the spine view. In the following two sections we show how to overcome both limitations.

5.2   The Type-Spine View

A *generic consumer* is a function of type Type $\alpha \to \alpha \to \tau$ ($\cong$ Typed $\alpha \to \tau$), where the type we abstract over occurs in an argument position and possibly in the result type τ. We have seen in Section 3.3 that the generic part of a consumer follows the general pattern below.

---

[5] Type-theoretically, we have to turn the existential quantifier $\exists \alpha\ .\ \tau$ into an intensional quantifier $\exists \alpha\ .$ Type $\alpha \times \tau$. This is analogous to the difference between parametrically polymorphic functions of type $\forall \alpha\ .\ \tau$ and overloaded functions of type $\forall \alpha\ .$ Type $\alpha \to \tau$.

$consume$ :: Type $\alpha \rightarrow \alpha \rightarrow \tau$

$\ldots$

$consume\ a\ x\ = consume_-\ (toSpine\ (x : a))$

$consume_-$ :: Spine $\alpha \rightarrow \tau$

$consume_-\ \ldots = \ldots$

The element x is converted to the spine representation, over which the helper function $consume_-$ then recurses. By duality, we would expect that a generic producer of type Type $\alpha \rightarrow \tau \rightarrow \alpha$, where α appears in the result type *but not* in τ, takes on the following form.

$produce$ :: Type $\alpha \rightarrow \tau \rightarrow \alpha$

$\ldots$

$produce\ a\ t\ = fromSpine\ (produce_-\ t)$

$produce_-$ :: $\tau \rightarrow$ Spine α -- does not work

$produce_-\ \ldots = \ldots$

The helper function $produce_-$ generates an element in spine representation, which $fromSpine$ converts back. Unfortunately, this approach does not work. The formal reason is that $toSpine$ and $fromSpine$ are different beasts: $toSpine$ is an overloaded function, while $fromSpine$ is parametrically polymorphic. If it were possible to define $produce_-$ :: $\forall \alpha\ .\ \tau \rightarrow$ Spine α, then the composition $fromSpine$. $produce_-$ would yield a parametrically polymorphic function of type $\forall \alpha\ .\ \tau \rightarrow \alpha$, which is the type of an unsafe cast operation. And, indeed, a closer inspection of the catch-all case of $produce$ reveals that a, the type representation of α, does not appear on the right-hand side. However, as we already know, a truly polymorphic function cannot exhibit type-specific behaviour.

Of course, this does not mean that we cannot define a function of type Type $\alpha \rightarrow \tau \rightarrow \alpha$. We just require additional information about the datatype, information that the spine view does not provide. Consider in this respect the syntactic form of a GADT (eg Type itself or Expr in Section 2.2): a datatype is essentially a sequence of signatures. This motivates the following definitions.

type Datatype $\alpha = $ [Signature α]

infixl 0 $\square$

data Signature :: $* \rightarrow *$ **where**

$\quad Sig$ :: Constr $\alpha \rightarrow$ Signature α

$\quad (\square)$ :: Signature $(\alpha \rightarrow \beta) \rightarrow$ Type $\alpha \rightarrow$ Signature β

The type Signature is almost identical to the Spine type, except for the second argument of '$\square$', which is of type Type α rather than Typed α. Thus, an element of type Signature contains the types of the constructor arguments, but not the arguments themselves. For that reason, Datatype is called the *type-spine view*.

This view is similar to the sum-of-products view (see Section 5.4): the list encodes the sum, the constructor '$\square$' corresponds to a product and Sig is like the unit element. To be able to use the type spine view, we additionally require an overloaded function that maps a type representation to an element of type Datatype α.

$$
\begin{array}{ll}
\textbf{open } datatype :: \text{Type } \alpha \to \text{Datatype } \alpha \\
datatype \ (Bool) & = [Sig \ false, Sig \ true] \\
datatype \ (Char) & = [Sig \ (char \ c) \mid c \leftarrow [minBound \,..\, maxBound]] \\
datatype \ (Int) & = [Sig \ (int \ i) \mid i \leftarrow [minBound \,..\, maxBound]] \\
datatype \ (List \ a) & = [Sig \ nil, Sig \ cons \ \square \ a \ \square \ List \ a] \\
datatype \ (Pair \ a \ b) & = [Sig \ pair \ \square \ a \ \square \ b] \\
datatype \ (Tree \ a) & = [Sig \ empty, Sig \ node \ \square \ Tree \ a \ \square \ a \ \square \ Tree \ a]
\end{array}
$$

Here, *char* maps a character to its annotated variant and likewise *int*; *nil*, *cons* and *pair* are the annotated versions of *Nil*, *Cons* and '(,)'. As an aside, the second and the third equation produce rather long lists; they are only practical in a lazy setting. The function *datatype* plays the same role for producers as *toSpine* plays for *consumers*.

The first example of a generic producer is a simple test-data generator. The function *generate a d* yields all terms of the data type α up to a given finite depth d.

$$
\begin{array}{ll}
generate :: \text{Type } \alpha \to \text{Int} \to [\alpha] \\
generate \ a \ 0 & = [\,] \\
generate \ a \ (d+1) & = concat \ [generate_- \ s \ d \mid s \leftarrow datatype \ a] \\[4pt]
generate_- :: \text{Signature } \alpha \to \text{Int} \to [\alpha] \\
generate_- \ (Sig \ c) \ d & = [constr \ c] \\
generate_- \ (s \ \square \ a) \ d & = [f \ x \mid f \leftarrow generate_- \ s \ d, x \leftarrow generate \ a \ d]
\end{array}
$$

The helper function *generate_* constructs all terms that conform to a given signature. The right-hand side of the second equation essentially computes the cartesian product of *generate_ s d* and *generate a d*. Here is a short interactive session that illustrates the use of *generate*.

Now⟩ generate (List Bool) 3
[[], [False], [False, False], [False, True], [True], [True, False], [True, True]]
Now⟩ generate (List (List Bool)) 3
[[], [[]], [[]], [[]], [[False]], [[False], []], [[True]], [[True], []]]

As a second example, let us define a generic parser. For concreteness, we re-implement Haskell's *readsPrec* function of type $\text{Int} \to \text{ReadS } \alpha$. The Int argument specifies the operator precedence of the enclosing context; ReadS abbreviates $\text{String} \to [\text{Pair } \alpha \text{ String}]$, the type of backtracking parsers [26].

$$
\begin{array}{lll}
\textbf{open } readsPrec :: \text{Type } \alpha \to \text{Int} \to \text{ReadS } \alpha \\
readsPrec \ (Char) & d = readsPrec_{\mathsf{Char}} \ d \\
readsPrec \ (Int) & d = readsPrec_{\mathsf{Int}} \ d \\
readsPrec \ (String) & d = readsPrec_{\mathsf{String}} \ d \\
readsPrec \ (List \ a) & d = readsList \ (reads \ a)
\end{array}
$$

$readsPrec\ (Pair\ a\ b)\ d$
$\quad = readParen\ False\ (\lambda s_0 \rightarrow [((x,y),s_5)\ |\ ("(",s_1) \leftarrow lex \qquad s_0,$
$\qquad\qquad\qquad\qquad\qquad\qquad\quad (x,\quad s_2) \leftarrow reads\ a\ s_1,$
$\qquad\qquad\qquad\qquad\qquad\qquad\quad (",",s_3) \leftarrow lex \qquad s_2,$
$\qquad\qquad\qquad\qquad\qquad\qquad\quad (y,\quad s_4) \leftarrow reads\ b\ s_3,$
$\qquad\qquad\qquad\qquad\qquad\qquad\quad (")",s_5) \leftarrow lex \qquad s_4])$

$readsPrec\ a \qquad\qquad d$
$\quad = alt\ [readParen\ (arity'\ s > 0 \wedge d > 10)\ (reads\_\ s)\ |\ s \leftarrow datatype\ a]$

The overall structure is similar to that of *pretty*. The first three equations delegate the work to tailor-made parsers. Given a parser for elements, *readsList*, defined in Appendix A.3, parses a list of elements. Pairs are read using the usual mix-fix notation. The predefined function *readParen b* takes care of optional ($b = False$) or mandatory ($b = True$) parentheses. The catch-all case implements the generic part: constructors in prefix notation. Parentheses are mandatory if the constructor has at least one argument and the operator precedence of the enclosing context exceeds 10 (the precedence of function application is 11). The parser for α is the alternation of all parsers for the individual constructors of α (*alt* is defined in Appendix A.3). The auxiliary function *reads_* parses a single constructor application.

$reads\_ :: \mathsf{Signature}\ \alpha \rightarrow \mathsf{ReadS}\ \alpha$
$reads\_ (Sig\ c)\ s_0 = [(constr\ c,s_1)\ |\ (t,s_1) \leftarrow lex\ s_0, name\ c == t]$
$reads\_ (s \mathbin{\square} a)\ s_0 = [(f\ x,s_2)\ |\ (f,s_1) \leftarrow reads\_\ s\ s_0,$
$\qquad\qquad\qquad\qquad\qquad (x,s_2) \leftarrow readsPrec\ a\ 11\ s_1]$

Finally, *arity'* determines the arity of a constructor.

$arity' :: \mathsf{Signature}\ \alpha \rightarrow \mathsf{Int}$
$arity'\ (Sig\ c) = 0$
$arity'\ (s \mathbin{\square} a) = arity'\ s + 1$

As for *pretty*, we can define suitable wrapper functions that simplify the use of the generic parser.

$reads :: \mathsf{Type}\ \alpha \rightarrow \mathsf{ReadS}\ \alpha$
$reads\ a\ = readsPrec\ a\ 0$

$read\ :: \mathsf{Type}\ \alpha \rightarrow \mathsf{String} \rightarrow \alpha$
$read\ a\ s = \mathbf{case}\ [x\ |\ (x,t) \leftarrow reads\ a\ s, ("","") \leftarrow lex\ t]\ \mathbf{of}$
$\qquad\qquad [x] \rightarrow x$
$\qquad\qquad []\ \ \rightarrow error\ \texttt{"read: no parse"}$
$\qquad\qquad \_\ \ \rightarrow error\ \texttt{"read: ambiguous parse"}$

From the code of *generate* and *readsPrec* we can abstract a general definitional scheme for generic producers.

$produce :: \mathsf{Type}\ \alpha \rightarrow \tau \rightarrow \alpha$
$\quad \dots$

$produce\ a\ t\ \ =\ \dots[\dots produce_-\ s\ t\dots\mid s\leftarrow datatype\ a]$
$produce_-\ \ ::\ \textsf{Signature}\ \alpha\rightarrow\tau\rightarrow\alpha$
$produce_-\ \dots\ =\ \dots$

The generic case is a two-step procedure: the list comprehension processes the list of constructors; the helper function *produce_* takes care of a single constructor.

The type-spine view is complementary to the spine view, but independent of it. The latter is used for generic producers, the former for generic consumers or transformers. This is in contrast to Generic Haskell's sum-of-products view or PolyP's fixed point view where a single view serves both purposes.

The type-spine view shares the major advantage of the spine view: it is applicable to a large class of datatypes. Nested datatypes such as the type of perfect binary trees can be handled easily:

$$datatype\ (Perfect\ a) = [\,Sig\ zero\ \square\ a, Sig\ succ\ \square\ Perfect\ (Pair\ a\ a)\,]$$

The scheme can even be extended to generalised algebraic datatypes. Since Datatype α is a homogeneous list, we have to partition the constructors according to their result types. Consider the expression datatype of Section 2.2. We have three different result types, Expr Bool, Expr Int and Expr α, and consequently three equations for *datatype*.

$datatype\ (Expr\ Bool)$
$\ \ = [\,Sig\ eq\ \square\ Expr\ Int\ \square\ Expr\ Int,$
$\ \ \ \ \ \ Sig\ if\ \square\ Expr\ Bool\ \square\ Expr\ Bool\ \square\ Expr\ Bool\,]$
$datatype\ (Expr\ Int)$
$\ \ = [\,Sig\ num\ \square\ Int,$
$\ \ \ \ \ \ Sig\ plus\ \square\ Expr\ Int\ \square\ Expr\ Int,$
$\ \ \ \ \ \ Sig\ if\ \square\ Expr\ Bool\ \square\ Expr\ Int\ \square\ Expr\ Int\,]$
$datatype\ (Expr\ a)$
$\ \ = [\,Sig\ if\ \square\ Expr\ Bool\ \square\ Expr\ a\ \square\ Expr\ a\,]$

The equations are ordered from specific to general; each right-hand side lists all the constructors that have the given result type *or* a more general one. Consequently, the *If* constructor, which has a polymorphic result type, appears in every list. Given this declaration we can easily generate well-typed expressions (for reasons of space we have modified *generate Int* so that only 0 is produced):

Now⟩ **let** *gen a d* = *putStrLn* (*show* (*generate a d* : *List a*))
Now⟩ *gen* (*Expr Int*) 4
[(*Num* 0), (*Plus* (*Num* 0) (*Num* 0)), (*Plus* (*Num* 0) (*Plus* (*Num* 0) (*Num* 0))), (*Plus* (*Plus* (*Num* 0) (*Num* 0)) (*Num* 0)), (*Plus* (*Plus* (*Num* 0) (*Num* 0)) (*Plus* (*Num* 0) (*Num* 0))), (*If* (*Eq* (*Num* 0) (*Num* 0)) (*Num* 0) (*Num* 0)), (*If* (*Eq* (*Num* 0) (*Num* 0)) (*Num* 0) (*Plus* (*Num* 0) (*Num* 0))), (*If* (*Eq* (*Num* 0) (*Num* 0)) (*Plus* (*Num* 0) (*Num* 0)) (*Num* 0)), (*If* (*Eq* (*Num* 0) (*Num* 0)) (*Plus* (*Num* 0) (*Num* 0)) (*Plus* (*Num* 0) (*Num* 0)))]
Now⟩ *gen* (*Expr Bool*) 4

$[(Eq\ (Num\ 0)\ (Num\ 0)), (Eq\ (Num\ 0)\ (Plus\ (Num\ 0)\ (Num\ 0))), (Eq\ (Plus$
$(Num\ 0)\ (Num\ 0))\ (Num\ 0)), (Eq\ (Plus\ (Num\ 0)\ (Num\ 0))\ (Plus\ (Num\ 0)$
$(Num\ 0))), (If\ (Eq\ (Num\ 0)\ (Num\ 0))\ (Eq\ (Num\ 0)\ (Num\ 0))\ (Eq\ (Num\ 0)$
$(Num\ 0)))]$
Now⟩ gen (Expr Char) 4
[]

The last call shows that there are no character expressions of depth 4.

In general, for each constructor C with signature

$$C :: \tau_1 \to \cdots \to \tau_n \to \tau_0$$

we add an element of the form

$$Sig\ c \,\square\, t_1 \,\square\, \cdots \,\square\, t_n$$

to each right-hand side of *datatype t* provided τ_0 is more general than τ.

5.3   Lifted Spine View

We have already mentioned that the original spine view is not suitable for defining $* \to *$-indexed functions, as it cannot capture type abstractions. To illustrate, consider a variant of Tree whose inner nodes are annotated with an integer, say, a balance factor.

data BalTree $\alpha = Empty \mid Node$ Int (BalTree α) α (BalTree α)

If we call a generic function on a value of type BalTree Int, then the two integer components — the labels and the balance factors — are handled in a uniform way. This is fine for generic functions on types, but not acceptable for generic functions on type constructors. For instance, a generic version of *sum* must consider the label of type $\alpha = $ Int, but ignore the balance factor of type Int. In the sequel we introduce a suitable variant of Spine that can be used to define the latter brand of generic functions.

A constructor of a lifted type has the signature $\forall \chi . \tau_1' \chi \to \cdots \to \tau_n' \chi \to \tau_0' \chi$ where the type variable χ marks the parametric components. We can write the signature more perspicuously as $\forall \chi . (\tau_1' \to' \cdots \to' \tau_n' \to' \tau_0') \chi$, using the lifted function space:

infixr $\to'$
newtype $(\varphi \to' \psi)\ \chi = Fun\{\ app :: \varphi\ \chi \to \psi\ \chi\}$

For technical reasons, '$\to$'' must be defined by a **newtype** rather than a **type** declaration.[6] As an example, here are variants of *Nil'* and *Cons'*:

nil' $\quad :: \forall \chi . \forall \alpha' . ($List$'\ \alpha')\ \chi$
nil' $\quad = Nil'$

---

[6] In Haskell, types introduced by **type** declarations cannot be partially applied.

$cons' :: \forall\chi . \forall\alpha' . (\alpha' \to' \text{List}' \; \alpha' \to' \text{List}' \; \alpha') \; \chi$
$cons' = Fun \; (\lambda x \to Fun \; (\lambda xs \to Cons' \; x \; xs))$

An element of a lifted type can always be put into the applicative form $c' \; \text{'}app\text{'}$
$e_1 \; \text{'}app\text{'} \cdots \text{'}app\text{'} \; e_n$. As in the first-order case we can make this structure visible
and accessible by marking the constructor and the function applications.

data Spine$'$ :: $(* \to *) \to * \to *$ **where**
   $Con' :: (\forall\chi . \varphi \; \chi) \to \text{Spine}' \; \varphi \; \alpha$
   $(\diamond') \quad :: \text{Spine}' \; (\varphi \to' \psi) \; \alpha \to \text{Typed}' \; \varphi \; \alpha \to \text{Spine}' \; \psi \; \alpha$

The structure of Spine$'$ is very similar to that of Spine, except that we are now
working in a higher realm: Con' takes a *polymorphic function* of type $\forall\chi$.
$\varphi \; \chi$ to an element of Spine$'$ φ; the constructor '$\diamond'$' applies an element of type
Spine$'$ $(\varphi \to' \psi)$ to a Typed$'$ φ yielding an element of type Spine$'$ ψ.

   Turning to the conversion functions, *fromSpine$'$* is again *polymorphic*.

$fromSpine' :: \text{Spine}' \; \varphi \; \alpha \to \varphi \; \alpha$
$fromSpine' \; (Con' \; c) = c$
$fromSpine' \; (f \diamond' x) \quad = fromSpine' \; f \; \text{'}app\text{'} \; val' \; x$

Its inverse is an *overloaded* function that follows a pattern similar to *toSpine*:
each constructor C' with signature

$$C' :: \forall\chi . \tau'_1 \; \chi \to \cdots \to \tau'_n \; \chi \to \tau'_0 \; \chi$$

gives rise to an equation of the form

$$toSpine' \; (C' \; x_1 \; \ldots \; x_n \; :' \; t'_0) = Con \; c' \diamond (x_1 : t'_1) \diamond \cdots \diamond (x_n : t'_n)$$

where c' is the variant of C' that uses the lifted function space and t'_i is the type
representation of the lifted type τ'_i. As an example, here is the instance for lifted
lists.

$toSpine' :: \text{Typed}' \; \varphi \; \alpha \to \text{Spine}' \; \varphi \; \alpha$
$toSpine' \; (Nil' :' \text{List}' \; a') \qquad\quad = Con' \; nil'$
$toSpine' \; (Cons' \; x \; xs :' \text{List}' \; a') = Con' \; cons' \diamond' (x :' a') \diamond' (xs :' \text{List}' \; a')$

The equations are surprisingly close to those of *toSpine*; pretty much the only
difference is that *toSpine$'$* works on lifted types.

   Let us make the generic view explicit. In our case, the structure view of φ is
simply Spine$'$ φ.

$Spine' :: \text{Type}' \; \varphi \to \text{Type}' \; (\text{Spine}' \; \varphi)$
$spine' :: \text{Type}' \; \varphi \to \text{View}' \; \varphi$
$spine' \; a' = View' \; (Spine' \; a') \; (\lambda x \to toSpine' \; (x :' a')) \; fromSpine'$

Given these prerequisites we can turn *size* (see Section 4.1) into a generic
function.

$$size \ (x :' \ Spine' \ a') = size_- \ x$$
$$size \ (x :' \ a') \qquad = \textbf{case} \ spine' \ a' \ \textbf{of}$$
$$View' \ b' \ from \ to \rightarrow size \ (from \ x :' \ b')$$

The catch-all case applies the spine view: the argument x is converted to the structure type, on which $size$ is called recursively. Currently, the structure type is always of the form $\mathsf{Spine}' \ \varphi$ (this will change in a moment), so the first equation applies, which in turn delegates the work to the helper function $size_-$.

$$size_- :: \mathsf{Spine}' \ \varphi \ \alpha \rightarrow \mathsf{Int}$$
$$size_- \ (Con' \ c) = 0$$
$$size_- \ (f \ \diamond' \ x) \ = size_- \ f + size \ x$$

The implementation of $size_-$ is entirely straightforward: it traverses the spine, summing up the sizes of the constructor's arguments. It is worth noting that the catch-all case of $size$ subsumes all the previous instances except the one for Id, as we cannot provide a $toSpine'$ instance for the identity type. In other words, the generic programmer has to take care of essentially three cases: Id, Con' and '$\diamond$'.

As a second example, here is an implementation of the generic mapping function:

$$map :: \mathsf{Type}' \ \varphi \rightarrow (\alpha \rightarrow \beta) \rightarrow (\varphi \ \alpha \rightarrow \varphi \ \beta)$$
$$map \ Id \qquad\qquad m = In_{\mathsf{Id}} \ . \ m \ . \ out_{\mathsf{Id}}$$
$$map \ (Spine' \ a') \ m = map_- \ m$$
$$map \ a' \qquad\qquad m = \textbf{case} \ spine' \ a' \ \textbf{of}$$
$$View' \ b' \ from \ to \rightarrow to \ . \ map \ b' \ m \ . \ from$$
$$map_- :: (\alpha \rightarrow \beta) \rightarrow (\mathsf{Spine}' \ \varphi \ \alpha \rightarrow \mathsf{Spine}' \ \varphi \ \beta)$$
$$map_- \ m \ (Con' \ c) \qquad = Con' \ c$$
$$map_- \ m \ (f \ \diamond' \ (x :' \ a')) = map_- \ m \ f \ \diamond' \ (map \ a' \ m \ x :' \ a')$$

The definition is stunningly simple: the argument function m is applied in the Id case; the helper function map_- applies map to each argument of the constructor. Note that the mapping function is of type $\mathsf{Type}' \ \varphi \rightarrow (\alpha \rightarrow \beta) \rightarrow (\varphi \ \alpha \rightarrow \varphi \ \beta)$ rather than $(\alpha \rightarrow \beta) \rightarrow (\mathsf{Typed}' \ \varphi \ \alpha \rightarrow \varphi \ \beta)$. Both variants are interchangeable, so picking one is just a matter of personal taste.

Bridging the Gap. We have noted in Section 4.1 that the generic size function does not work on the original, unlifted types, as they are different from the lifted ones. However, both are closely related: if τ' is the lifted variant of τ, then $\tau' \ \mathsf{Id}$ is isomorphic to τ [15]. (This relation only holds for Haskell 98 types, not for GADTs; see also below.) Even more, $\tau' \ \mathsf{Id}$ and τ can share the same run-time representation, since Id is defined by a **newtype** declaration and since the lifted datatype τ' has exactly the same structure as the original datatype τ.

As an example, the functions $fromList \ In_{\mathsf{Id}}$ and $toList \ out_{\mathsf{Id}}$ exhibit the isomorphism between $[]$ and $\mathsf{List}' \ \mathsf{Id}$.

$$fromList :: (\alpha \rightarrow \alpha' \ \chi) \rightarrow ([\alpha] \rightarrow \mathsf{List}' \ \alpha' \ \chi)$$
$$fromList \ from \ Nil \qquad\qquad = Nil'$$
$$fromList \ from \ (Cons \ x \ xs) = Cons' \ (from \ x) \ (fromList \ from \ xs)$$

$$toList \quad :: (\alpha' \chi \to \alpha) \to (\mathsf{List}' \, \alpha' \, \chi \to [\alpha])$$
$$toList \; to \; Nil' \qquad\qquad = Nil$$
$$toList \; to \; (Cons' \; x \; xs) = Cons \; (to \; x) \; (toList \; to \; xs)$$

Operationally, if the types τ' Id and τ have the same run-time representation, then $fromList \; In_{\mathsf{Id}}$ and $toList \; out_{\mathsf{Id}}$ are identity functions (the Haskell Report [38] guarantees this for In_{Id} and out_{Id}).

We can use the isomorphism to broaden the scope of generic functions to unlifted types. To this end we simply re-use the view mechanism.

$$spine' \; List = View' \; (List' \; Id) \; (fromList \; In_{\mathsf{Id}}) \; (toList \; out_{\mathsf{Id}})$$

The following interactive session illustrates the use of *size*.

$Now\rangle$ **let** $ts = [\,tree \,[0 \mathbin{.\,.} i :: \mathsf{Int}] \mid i \leftarrow [0 \mathbin{.\,.} 9]\,]$
$Now\rangle$ *size* $(ts :' List)$
10
$Now\rangle$ *size* $(fromList \; (fromTree \; In_{\mathsf{Int}'}) \; ts :' List' \; (Tree' \; Int'))$
0
$Now\rangle$ *size* $(In_{\mathsf{Id}} \; ts :' Id)$
1
$Now\rangle$ *size* $(fromList \; In_{\mathsf{Id}} \; ts :' List' \; Id)$
10
$Now\rangle$ *size* $(fromList \; (fromTree \; In_{\mathsf{Id}}) \; ts :' List' \; (Tree' \; Id))$
55

With the help of the conversion functions we can implement each of the four different views on a list of trees of integers. Since Haskell employs a kinded first-order unification of types [28], the calls almost always additionally involve a change on the value level. The type equation $\varphi \, \tau = \mathsf{List} \, (\mathsf{Tree} \, \mathsf{Int})$ is solved by setting $\varphi = \mathsf{List}$ and $\tau = \mathsf{Tree} \, \mathsf{Int}$, that is, Haskell picks one of the four higher-order unifiers. Only in this particular case we need not change the representation of values: *size* $(ts :' List)$ implements the intended call. In the other cases, $\mathsf{List} \, (\mathsf{Tree} \, \mathsf{Int})$ must be rearranged so that the unification with $\varphi \, \tau$ yields the desired choice.

Discussion. The lifted spine view is almost as general as the original spine view: it is applicable to all datatypes that are definable in Haskell 98. In particular, nested datatypes can be handled with ease. As an example, for the datatype Perfect (see Section 3.2), we introduce a lifted variant

data $\mathsf{Perfect}' \; \alpha' \; \chi = Zero' \; (\alpha' \; \chi) \mid Succ' \; (\mathsf{Perfect}' \; (\mathsf{Pair}' \; \alpha' \; \alpha') \; \chi)$
$Perfect \; :: \mathsf{Type}' \; \mathsf{Perfect}$
$Perfect' :: \mathsf{Type}' \; \varphi \to \mathsf{Type}' \; (\mathsf{Perfect}' \; \varphi)$
$toSpine' \; (Zero' \; x :' Perfect' \; a') = Con' \; zero' \; \diamond' \; (x :' a')$
$toSpine' \; (Succ' \; x :' Perfect' \; a') = Con' \; succ' \; \diamond' \; (x :' Perfect' \; (Pair' \; a' \; a'))$

and functions that convert between the lifted and the unlifted variant.

spine′ (*Perfect*)
   = *View′* (*Perfect′ Id*) (*fromPerfect In*$_{\mathsf{Id}}$) (*toPerfect out*$_{\mathsf{Id}}$)
fromPerfect :: ($\alpha \to \alpha'\ \chi$) $\to$ (Perfect $\alpha \to$ Perfect′ $\alpha'\ \chi$)
fromPerfect from (*Zero x*) = *Zero′* (*from x*)
fromPerfect from (*Succ x*) = *Succ′* (*fromPerfect* (*fromPair from from*) *x*)
toPerfect   :: ($\alpha'\ \chi \to \alpha$) $\to$ (Perfect′ $\alpha'\ \chi \to$ Perfect α)
toPerfect to (*Zero′ x*) = *Zero* (*to x*)
toPerfect to (*Succ′ x*) = *Succ* (*toPerfect* (*toPair to to*) *x*)

The following interactive session shows some examples involving perfect trees.

Now⟩ *size* (*Succ* (*Zero* (1, 2)) :′ *Perfect*)
2
Now⟩ *map* (*Perfect*) (+1) (*Succ* (*Zero* (1, 2)))
Succ (*Zero* (2, 3))

We have seen that the spine view is also applicable to *generalised algebraic datatypes*. This does not hold for the lifted spine view, as it is not possible to generalise *size* or *map* to GADTs. Consider the expression datatype of Section 2.2. Though Expr is parametrised, it is not a container type: an element of Expr Int, for instance, is an expression that evaluates to an integer; it is not a data structure that contains integers. This means, in particular, that we cannot define a mapping function ($\alpha \to \beta$) $\to$ (Expr $\alpha \to$ Expr β): How could we possibly turn expressions of type Expr α into expressions of type Expr β? The type Expr β might not even be inhabited: there are, for instance, no terms of type Expr IO. Since the type argument of Expr is not related to any component, Expr is also called a *phantom type* [32,17].

It is instructive to see where the attempt to generalise *size* or *map* to GADTs fails technically. We can, in fact, define a lifted version of the Expr type (we confine ourselves to one constructor).

data Expr′ :: ($* \to *$) $\to * \to *$ **where**
   Num′ :: Int′ $\chi \to$ Expr′ Int′ χ

However, we cannot establish an isomorphism between Expr and Expr′ Id: the following code simply does not type-check.

fromExpr :: ($\alpha \to \alpha'\ \chi$) $\to$ (Expr $\alpha \to$ Expr′ $\alpha'\ \chi$)
fromExpr from (*Num i*) = *Num′* (*In*$_{\mathsf{Int}'}$ *i*)   -- wrong: does not type-check

The isomorphism between τ and τ' Id only holds for Haskell 98 types.

We have seen two examples of generic consumers or transformers. As in the first-order case, generic producers are out of reach, and for exactly the same reason: *fromSpine′* is a polymorphic function while *toSpine′* is overloaded. Of course, the solution to the problem suggests itself: we must also lift the type-spine view to type constructors of kind $* \to *$. In a sense, the spine view really comprises two views: one for consumers and transformers and one for pure producers.

The spine view can even be lifted to *kind indices* of arbitrary kinds. The generic programmer then has to consider two cases for the spine view and additionally n cases, one for each of the n projection types $Out_1, \ldots, Out_n$.

Introducing lifted types for each possible type index sounds like a lot of work. Note, however, that the declarations can be generated completely mechanically (a compiler could do this easily). Furthermore, we have already noted that generic functions that are indexed by higher kinds, for instance, by $(*\rightarrow*)\rightarrow*\rightarrow*$, are rare. In practice, most generic functions are indexed by a first-order kind such as $*$ or $* \rightarrow *$.

5.4 Sum of Products

Let us now turn to the 'classic' view of generic programming: the *sum-of-products view*, which is inspired by the semantics of datatypes. Consider the schematic form of a Haskell 98 **data** declaration.

$$\textbf{data } \mathsf{T}\ \alpha_1\ \ldots\ \alpha_s = C_1\ \tau_{1,1}\ \ldots\ \tau_{1,m_1}\ |\ \cdots\ |\ C_n\ \tau_{n,1}\ \ldots\ \tau_{n,m_n}$$

The **data** construct combines several features in a single coherent form: type abstraction, n-ary disjoint sums, n-ary cartesian products and type recursion. We have already the machinery in place to deal with type abstraction (type application) and type recursion: using type reflection, the type-level constructs are mapped onto value abstraction and value recursion. It remains to model n-ary sums and n-ary products. The basic idea is to reduce the n-ary constructs to binary sums and binary products.

> **infixr** 7 $\times$
> **infixr** 6 $+$
> **data** Zero
> **data** Unit $\quad= Unit$
> **data** $\alpha + \beta = Inl\ \alpha\ |\ Inr\ \beta$
> **data** $\alpha \times \beta = Pair\{\, outl :: \alpha, outr :: \beta\,\}$

The Zero datatype, the empty sum, is used for encoding datatypes with no constructors; the Unit datatype, the empty product, is used for encoding constructors with no arguments. If a datatype has more than two alternatives or a constructor more than two arguments, then the binary constructors '$+$' and '$\times$' are nested accordingly. With respect to the nesting there are several choices: we can use a right-deep or a left-deep nesting, a list-like nesting or a (balanced) tree-like nesting [34]. For the following examples, we choose – more or less arbitrarily – a tree-like encoding.

We first add suitable constructors to the type of type representations.

> **infixr** 7 $\times$
> **infixr** 6 $+$
> o $\quad$ :: Type Zero

1 $::$ Type Unit
$(+)$ :: Type $\alpha \rightarrow$ Type $\beta \rightarrow$ Type $(\alpha + \beta)$
$(\times)$ :: Type $\alpha \rightarrow$ Type $\beta \rightarrow$ Type $(\alpha \times \beta)$

The view function for the sum-of-products view is slightly more elaborate than the one for the spine view, as each datatype has a tailor-made structure type: Bool has the structure type Unit + Unit, $[\alpha]$ has Unit $+ \alpha \times [\alpha]$ and finally Tree α has Unit + Tree $\alpha \times \alpha \times$ Tree α.

structure :: Type $\alpha \rightarrow$ View α
structure Bool $= View (1 + 1) fromBool toBool$
  where
  fromBool :: Bool $\rightarrow$ Unit + Unit
  fromBool False $= Inl \ Unit$
  fromBool True $= Inr \ Unit$

  toBool   :: Unit + Unit $\rightarrow$ Bool
  toBool (Inl Unit) $= False$
  toBool (Inr Unit) $= True$
structure (List a) $= View (1 + a \times List \ a) fromList \ toList$
  where
  fromList :: $[\alpha] \rightarrow$ Unit $+ \alpha \times [\alpha]$
  fromList Nil $= Inl \ Unit$
  fromList (Cons x xs) $= Inr \ (Pair \ x \ xs)$
  toList   :: Unit $+ \alpha \times [\alpha] \rightarrow [\alpha]$
  toList (Inl Unit) $= Nil$
  toList (Inr (Pair x xs)) $= Cons \ x \ xs$
structure (Tree a) $= View (1 + Tree \ a \times a \times Tree \ a) fromTree \ toTree$
  where
  fromTree :: Tree $\alpha \rightarrow$ Unit + Tree $\alpha \times \alpha \times$ Tree α
  fromTree Empty $= Inl \ Unit$
  fromTree (Node l x r) $= Inr \ (Pair \ l \ (Pair \ x \ r))$
  toTree   :: Unit + Tree $\alpha \times \alpha \times$ Tree $\alpha \rightarrow$ Tree α
  toTree (Inl Unit) $= Empty$
  toTree (Inr (Pair l (Pair x r))) $= Node \ l \ x \ r$

Two points are worth noting. First, we only provide structure types for concrete types that are given by a **data** or a **newtype** declaration. Abstract types including primitive types such as Char or Int cannot be treated generically; for these types the generic programmer has to provide ad-hoc cases. Second, the structure types are not recursive: they express just the top 'layer' of a data element. The tail of the encoded list, for instance, is again of type $[\alpha]$, the original list datatype. We could have used explicit recursion operators but these are clumsy and hard to use in practice. Using an implicit approach to recursion has the advantage that there is no problem with mutually recursive datatypes, nor with datatypes with many parameters.

A distinct advantage of the sum-of-products view is that it provides more information than the spine view, as it represents the complete data type, not just a single constructor application. Consequently, the sum-of-products view can be used for defining both consumers and producers. The function *memo*, which memoises a given function, is an intriguing example of a function that both analyses and synthesises values of the generic type.

$$
\begin{array}{ll}
memo :: \mathsf{Type}\ \alpha \to (\alpha \to \nu) \to (\alpha \to \nu) \\
memo\ Char \quad f\ c & = f\ c \quad \text{-- no memoisation} \\
memo\ Int \quad f\ i & = f\ i \quad \text{-- no memoisation} \\
memo\ \mathbf{1} \quad\quad f\ Unit & = f_{Unit} \\
\quad \mathbf{where}\ f_{Unit} & = f\ Unit \\
memo\ (a + b)\ f\ (Inl\ x) & = f_{Inl}\ x \\
\quad \mathbf{where}\ f_{Inl} & = memo\ a\ (\lambda x \to f\ (Inl\ x)) \\
memo\ (a + b)\ f\ (Inr\ y) & = f_{Inr}\ y \\
\quad \mathbf{where}\ f_{Inr} & = memo\ b\ (\lambda y \to f\ (Inr\ y)) \\
memo\ (a \times b)\ f\ (Pair\ x\ y) & = (f_{Pair}\ x)\ y \\
\quad \mathbf{where}\ f_{Pair} & = memo\ a\ (\lambda x \to memo\ b\ (\lambda y \to f\ (Pair\ x\ y))) \\
memo\ a \quad\quad f\ x & = f_{View}\ x \\
\quad \mathbf{where}\ f_{View} & = \mathbf{case}\ structure\ a\ \mathbf{of} \\
& \quad View\ b\ from\ to \to memo\ b\ (f\ .\ to)\ .\ from
\end{array}
$$

To see how *memo* works, note that the helper definitions f_{Unit}, f_{Inl}, f_{Inr}, f_{Pair} and f_{View} do not depend on the actual argument of f. Thus, once f is given, they can be readily computed. Memoisation relies critically on the fact that they are computed only on demand and then at most once. This is guaranteed if the implementation is *fully lazy*. Usually, memoisation is defined as the composition of a function that constructs a memo table and a function that queries the table [14]. If we fuse the two functions, thereby eliminating the memo data structure, we obtain the *memo* function above. Despite appearances, the memo data structures did not vanish into thin air. Rather, they are now built into the closures. For instance, the memo table for a disjoint union is a pair of memo tables. The closure for *memo* $(a + b)$ f consequently contains a pair of memoised functions, namely f_{Inl} and f_{Inr}.

The sum-of-products view is also preferable when the generic function has to relate different elements of a datatype, the paradigmatic example being ordering.

$$
\begin{array}{lll}
compare :: \mathsf{Type}\ \alpha \to \alpha \to \alpha \to \mathsf{Ordering} \\
compare\ Char \quad c_1 & c_2 & = compare_{Char}\ c_1\ c_2 \\
compare\ Int \quad i_1 & i_2 & = compare_{Int}\ i_1\ i_2 \\
compare\ \mathbf{1} \quad\quad Unit & Unit & = EQ \\
compare\ (a + b)\ (Inl\ x_1) & (Inl\ x_2) & = compare\ a\ x_1\ x_2 \\
compare\ (a + b)\ (Inl\ x_1) & (Inr\ y_2) & = LT \\
compare\ (a + b)\ (Inr\ y_1) & (Inl\ x_2) & = GT \\
compare\ (a + b)\ (Inr\ y_1) & (Inr\ y_2) & = compare\ b\ y_1\ y_2 \\
compare\ (a \times b)\ (Pair\ x_1\ y_1)\ (Pair\ x_2\ y_2) \\
\quad = \mathbf{case}\ compare\ a\ x_1\ x_2\ \mathbf{of} \\
\quad\quad EQ \to compare\ b\ y_1\ y_2 \\
\quad\quad ord \to ord
\end{array}
$$

$$compare\ a \qquad x_1 \qquad\qquad x_2$$
$$= \textbf{case}\ structure\ a\ \textbf{of}$$
$$View\ b\ from\ to \rightarrow compare\ b\ (from\ x_1)\ (from\ x_2)$$

The central part of the definition is the case for sums: if the constructors are equal, then we recurse on the arguments, otherwise we immediately return the relative ordering (assuming $Inl < Inr$). The case for products implements the so-called *lexicographic ordering*: the ordering of two pairs is determined by the first elements, and only if they are equal do we recurse on the second elements.

Implementing *compare* using the spine view faces the problem that the elements of a spine possess existentially quantified types: even if we know that the constructors of two values are identical, we cannot conclude that the types of corresponding arguments are the same — and, indeed, this property fails, for instance, for the type Dynamic. Consequently, a spine-based implementation of *compare* must either involve a dynamic type-equality check, or the type of compare must be generalised to

$$compare :: \mathsf{Type}\ \alpha \rightarrow \alpha \rightarrow \mathsf{Type}\ \beta \rightarrow \beta \rightarrow \mathsf{Ordering}$$

The latter twist is not without problems, as we have to relate elements of different types.

The sum-of-products view in its original form is more restricted than the spine view: it is only applicable to Haskell 98 datatypes. However, using a similar technique to that in Section 5.2 we can to broaden the scope of the sum-of-products view to include generalised algebraic datatypes. A GADT introduces a family of Haskell 98 types indexed by the type argument of the GADT. If we partition the constructors according to their result types, we can provide an individual view for each instance. Consider the expression datatype of Section 2.2. We have three different result types, Expr Bool, Expr Int and Expr α, and consequently three equations for *structure*.

$$
\begin{aligned}
&structure\ (Expr\ Bool) = View\ expr\ fromExpr\ toExpr \\
&\quad\textbf{where} \\
&\quad expr \qquad\qquad\qquad = Expr\ Int \times Expr\ Int\ + \\
&\qquad\qquad\qquad\qquad\qquad\quad Expr\ Bool \times Expr\ Bool \times Expr\ Bool \\
&\quad fromExpr\ (Eq\ x_1\ x_2) \quad = Inl\ (Pair\ x_1\ x_2) \\
&\quad fromExpr\ (If\ x_1\ x_2\ x_3) \quad = Inr\ (Pair\ x_1\ (Pair\ x_2\ x_3)) \\
&\quad toExpr\ (Inl\ (Pair\ x_1\ x_2)) = Eq\ x_1\ x_2 \\
&\quad toExpr\ (Inr\ (Pair\ x_1\ (Pair\ x_2\ x_3))) \\
&\qquad\qquad\qquad\qquad\qquad = If\ x_1\ x_2\ x_3 \\
&structure\ (Expr\ Int) \quad = View\ expr\ fromExpr\ toExpr \\
&\quad\textbf{where} \\
&\quad expr \qquad\qquad\qquad = Int\ + \\
&\qquad\qquad\qquad\qquad\qquad\quad Expr\ Int \times Expr\ Int\ + \\
&\qquad\qquad\qquad\qquad\qquad\quad Expr\ Bool \times Expr\ Int \times Expr\ Int \\
&\quad fromExpr\ (Num\ i) \qquad = Inl\ i
\end{aligned}
$$

$$fromExpr\ (Plus\ x_1\ x_2) \quad = Inr\ (Inl\ (Pair\ x_1\ x_2))$$
$$fromExpr\ (If\ x_1\ x_2\ x_3) \quad = Inr\ (Inr\ (Pair\ x_1\ (Pair\ x_2\ x_3)))$$
$$toExpr\ (Inl\ i) \quad\quad\quad = Num\ i$$
$$toExpr\ (Inr\ (Inl\ (Pair\ x_1\ x_2)))$$
$$\quad\quad = Plus\ x_1\ x_2$$
$$toExpr\ (Inr\ (Inr\ (Pair\ x_1\ (Pair\ x_2\ x_3))))$$
$$\quad\quad = If\ x_1\ x_2\ x_3$$
$$structure\ (Expr\ a) \quad = View\ expr\ fromExpr\ toExpr$$

where

$$expr \quad\quad\quad\quad\quad\quad = Expr\ Bool \times Expr\ a \times Expr\ a$$
$$fromExpr\ (If\ x_1\ x_2\ x_3) \quad = Pair\ x_1\ (Pair\ x_2\ x_3)$$
$$toExpr\ (Pair\ x_1\ (Pair\ x_2\ x_3)) = If\ x_1\ x_2\ x_3$$

For the details we refer to the description of *datatype* in Section 5.2.

5.5   Lifted Sums of Products

The sum-of-products view can be quite easily adapted to the type Type′ of lifted type representations. We only have to lift the type constructors of the structure types.

infixr 7 ×′
infixr 6 +′
data Zero′ α
data Unit′ α $\quad = Unit'$
data $(\varphi +'\ \psi)\ \alpha = Inl'\ (\varphi\ \alpha)\ |\ Inr'\ (\psi\ \alpha)$
data $(\varphi \times'\ \psi)\ \alpha = Pair'\{\ outl' :: \varphi\ \alpha, outr' :: \psi\ \alpha\}$

The reader may wish to fill in the details.

6   Related Work

There is a wealth of material on the subject of generic programming. The tutorials of previous summer schools [2,20,19] provide an excellent overview of the field.

We have seen that support for generic programming consists of three essential ingredients:

– a type reflection mechanism,
– a type representation, and
– a generic view on data.

The first two items provide a way to write overloaded functions, and the third a way to access the structure of values in a uniform way. The different approaches to generic programming can be faithfully classified along these dimensions. Figure 1 provides an overview of the design space. Since the type representation is

view(s)	representation of overloaded functions			
	type reflection	type classes	type-safe cast	specialisation
none	ITA [12,8,7,41,44]	–	–	–
fixed point	Reloaded [23]	PolyP [36,37]	–	PolyP [27]
sum-of-products	LIGD [5,17]	DTC [25], GC [1], GM [18]	–	GH [16,20,34,35]
spine	Reloaded [23], Revolutions [22]	SYB [31], Reloaded [24]	SYB [39,30]	–

Fig. 1. Generic programming: the design space

closely coupled to the generic view, we have omitted the representation dimension. The two remaining dimensions are largely independent of each other and for each there are various choices. Overloaded functions can be expressed using

– *type reflection*: This is the approach we have used in these lecture notes. Its origins can be traced back to the work on intensional type analysis [12,8,7,41,44] (ITA). ITA is intensively used in typed intermediate languages, in particular, for optimising purely polymorphic functions. Type reflection avoids the duplication of features: a type case, for instance, boils down to an ordinary **case** expression. Cheney and Hinze [5] present a library for generics and dynamics (LIGD) that uses an *encoding* of type representations in Haskell 98 augmented by existential types.
– *type classes* [11]: Type classes are Haskell's major innovation for supporting ad-hoc polymorphism. A type class declaration corresponds to the type signature of an overloaded value — or rather, to a collection of type signatures. An instance declaration is related to a type case of an overloaded value. For a handful of built-in classes, Haskell provides support for genericity: by attaching a **deriving** clause to a **data** declaration the Haskell compiler automatically generates an appropriate instance of the class. *Derivable type classes* (DTC) [25] generalise this feature to arbitrary user-defined classes. A similar, but more expressive variant is implemented in Generic Clean [1] (GC). Clean's type classes are indexed by kind, so that a single generic function can be applied to type constructors of different kinds. A pure Haskell 98 implementation of generics (GM) is described by Hinze [18]. The implementation builds upon a class-based encoding of the type Type of type representations.
– *type-safe cast* [45]: A cast operation converts a value from one type to another, provided the two types are identical at run-time. A cast can be seen as a type-case with exactly one branch. The original SYB paper [39] is based on casts.

– *specialisation* [15]: This implementation technique transforms an overloaded function into a family of polymorphic functions (*dictionary translation*). While the other techniques can be used to write a library for generics, specialisation is mainly used for implementing full-fledged generic programming systems such as PolyP [27] or *Generic Haskell* [35], that are set up as preprocessors or compilers.

The approaches differ mostly in syntax and style, but less in expressiveness — except perhaps for specialisation, which cannot cope with higher-order generic functions. The second dimension, the generic view, has a much larger impact: we have seen that it affects the set of datatypes we can cover, the class of functions we can write and potentially the efficiency of these functions.

– *no view*: Haskell has a *nominal type system*: each **data** declaration introduces a new type that is incompatible with all the existing types. Two types are equal if and only if they have the same name. In contrast, in a *structural type system* two types are equal if they have the same structure. In a language with a structural type system, there is no need for a generic view; a generic function can be defined exhaustively by induction on the structure of types. The type systems that underlie ITA are structural.
– *fixed point view*: PolyP [27] views data types as fixed points of regular functors, which are in turn represented as lifted sums of products. This view is quite limited in applicability: only datatypes of kind $* \to *$ that are regular can be represented, excluding nested datatypes and higher kinded datatypes. Its particular strength is that recursion patterns such as cata- or anamorphisms can be expressed generically, because each datatype is viewed as a fixed point, and the points of recursion are visible. The original implementation of PolyP is set up as a preprocessor that translates PolyP code into Haskell. A later version [36] embeds PolyP programs into Haskell augmented by multiple parameter type classes with functional dependencies [29]. Oliveira and Gibbons [37] present a lightweight variant of PolyP that works within Haskell 98.
– *sum-of-products view*: Generic Haskell [20,34,35] (GH) builds upon this view. In its original form it is applicable to all datatypes that are definable in Haskell 98. We have seen in Section 5.4 that it can be generalised to GADTs. Generic Haskell is a full-fledged implementation of generics based on ideas by Hinze [16,21] that features generic functions, generic types and various extensions such as default cases and constructor cases [6]. Generic Haskell supports the definition of functions that work for all types of all kinds, such as, for example, a generalised mapping function.
– *spine views*: The spine view treats data uniformly as constructor applications. The SYB approach has been developed by Lämmel and Peyton Jones in a series of papers [39,30,31]. The original approach is *combinator-based*: the user writes generic functions by combining a few generic primitives. The first paper [39] introduces two main combinators: a type-safe cast for defining ad-hoc cases and a generic recursion operator, called *gfoldl*, for implementing the generic part. It turns out that *gfoldl* is essentially the catamorphism

of the Spine datatype [23]: *gfoldl* equals the catamorphism composed with *toSpine*. The second paper [30] adds a function called *gunfold* to the set of predefined combinators, which is required for defining generic producers. The name suggests that the new combinator is the anamorphism of the Spine type, but it is not: *gunfold* is actually the catamorphism of Signature, introduced in Section 5.2.

A   Library

This appendix presents some auxilliary functions used in the main part of the chapter, but relegated here so as not to disturb the flow.

A.1   Binary Trees

The function *inorder*, used in Section 3.1, yields the elements of a tree in symmetric order.

$$inorder :: \forall \alpha . \text{Tree } \alpha \rightarrow [\alpha]$$
$$inorder\ Empty \qquad = Nil$$
$$inorder\ (Node\ l\ a\ r) = inorder\ l \mathbin{+\!\!\!+} [a] \mathbin{+\!\!\!+} inorder\ r$$

The function *tree*, also used in Section 3.1, turns a list of elements into a balanced binary tree, a so-called *Braun tree* [4].

$$tree :: \forall \alpha . [\alpha] \rightarrow \text{Tree } \alpha$$
$$tree\ x$$
$$\quad | \ null\ x \qquad\qquad = Empty$$
$$\quad | \ otherwise \qquad\quad = Node\ (tree\ x_1)\ a\ (tree\ x_2)$$
$$\quad\quad \textbf{where}\ (x_1, Cons\ a\ x_2) = splitAt\ (length\ x\ `div`\ 2)\ x$$

The function *perfect d a*, used in Section 3.2, generates a perfect tree of depth d whose leaves are labelled with as.

$$perfect :: \forall \alpha . \text{Int} \rightarrow \alpha \rightarrow \text{Perfect } \alpha$$
$$perfect\ 0 \qquad\ a = Zero\ a$$
$$perfect\ (n + 1)\ a = Succ\ (perfect\ n\ (a, a))$$

A.2   Text with Indentation

The pretty-printing library, used in Section 3, is implemented as follows.

$$\textbf{data}\ \text{Text} = Text\ \text{String}$$
$$\qquad\qquad\ |\ NL$$
$$\qquad\qquad\ |\ Indent\ \text{Int Text}$$
$$\qquad\qquad\ |\ \text{Text} :\Diamond \text{Text}$$
$$text \quad = Text$$
$$nl \quad\ = NL$$

$$indent = Indent$$
$$(\Diamond) \quad = (:\Diamond)$$

Each Text-generating function is implemented by a corresponding data constructor. The main work is done by the function *render*, which can be seen as an interpreter for Text-documents.

$$render' :: \mathsf{Int} \to \mathsf{Text} \to \mathsf{String} \to \mathsf{String}$$
$$render'\ i\ (Text\ s) \quad x \quad = s +\!\!+ x$$
$$render'\ i\ NL \qquad x \quad = \texttt{"\textbackslash n"} +\!\!+ replicate\ i\ \texttt{'\ '} +\!\!+ x$$
$$render'\ i\ (Indent\ j\ d)\ x = render'\ (i + j)\ d\ x$$
$$render'\ i\ (d_1 :\Diamond\ d_2)\ x \quad = render'\ i\ d_1\ (render'\ i\ d_2\ x)$$
$$render :: \mathsf{Text} \to \mathsf{String}$$
$$render\ d \qquad\qquad\qquad = render'\ 0\ d\ \texttt{""}$$

The functions *append* and *bracketed* are derived combinators:

$$append :: [\mathsf{Text}] \to \mathsf{Text}$$
$$append = foldr\ (\Diamond)\ (text\ \texttt{""})$$
$$bracketed :: [\mathsf{Text}] \to \mathsf{Text}$$
$$bracketed\ Nil \qquad\quad = text\ \texttt{"[]"}$$
$$bracketed\ (Cons\ d\ ds) = align\ \texttt{"["}\ d$$
$$\Diamond\ append\ [nl\ \Diamond\ align\ \texttt{", "}\ d \mid d \leftarrow ds]\ \Diamond\ text\ \texttt{"]"}$$

The function *append* concatenates a list of documents; *bracketed* produces a comma-separated sequence of elements between square brackets.

Finally, we provide a *Show* instance for Text, which renders a text as a string (this instance is particularly useful for interactive sessions).

instance *Show* Text **where**
$$showsPrec\ p\ x = render'\ 0\ x$$

A.3   Parsing

The type ReadS is Haskell's parser type. The function *alt*, used in Section 5.2, implements the alternation of a list of parsers.

$$alt :: [\mathsf{ReadS}\ \alpha] \to \mathsf{ReadS}\ \alpha$$
$$alt\ rs = \lambda s \to concatMap\ (\lambda r \to r\ s)\ rs$$

Give a parser for elements, *readsList*, also used in Section 5.2, parses a list of elements written as a comma-separated sequence between square brackets.

$$readsList :: \mathsf{ReadS}\ \alpha \to \mathsf{ReadS}\ [\alpha]$$
$$readsList\ r = readParen\ False\ (\lambda s \to [x \mid (\texttt{"["}, s_1) \leftarrow lex\ s, x \leftarrow readl\ s_1])$$
$$\mathbf{where}\ readl\ \ s = [(Nil, \qquad\quad s_1) \mid (\texttt{"]"}, s_1) \leftarrow lex \qquad s]$$
$$+\!\!+ [(Cons\ x\ xs, s_2) \mid (x, \quad s_1) \leftarrow r \qquad s,$$

$$
\begin{aligned}
readl' \; s = [\,(Nil, & & s_1) \mid & ("]\,", s_1) & \leftarrow lex & s\,] \\
+\!\!+ \, [\,(Cons \; x \; xs, s_3) \mid & & & (",\,", s_1) & \leftarrow lex & s, \\
& & & (x, \quad s_2) & \leftarrow r & s_1, \\
& & & (xs, \quad s_3) & \leftarrow readl' & s_2\,]
\end{aligned}
$$

with the top lines:
$$
\begin{aligned}
& & (xs, \quad s_2) & \leftarrow readl' \; s_1\,]
\end{aligned}
$$

References

1. Alimarine, A., Plasmeijer, R.: A generic programming extension for Clean. In: Arts, T., Mohnen, M. (eds.) IFL 2002. LNCS, vol. 2312, Springer, Heidelberg (2002)
2. Backhouse, R., Jansson, P., Jeuring, J., Meertens, L.: Generic Programming: An Introduction. In: Swierstra, S.D., Henriques, P.R., Oliveira, J.N. (eds.) AFP 1998. LNCS, vol. 1608, pp. 28–115. Springer, Heidelberg (1999)
3. Bird, R., Meertens, L.: Nested datatypes. In: Jeuring, J. (ed.) MPC 1998. LNCS, vol. 1422, pp. 52–67. Springer, Heidelberg (1998)
4. Braun, W., Rem, M.: A logarithmic implementation of flexible arrays. Memorandum MR83/4, Eindhoven University of Technology (1983)
5. Cheney, J., Hinze, R.: A lightweight implementation of generics and dynamics. In: Chakravarty, M.M.T. (ed.) Proceedings of the 2002 ACM SIGPLAN Haskell Workshop, pp. 90–104. ACM Press, New York (2002)
6. Clarke, D., Löh, A.: Generic Haskell, specifically. In: Gibbons, J., Jeuring, J. (eds.) Proceedings of the IFIP TC2 Working Conference on Generic Programming, Schloss Dagstuhl, pp. 21–48. Kluwer Academic Publishers, Dordrecht (2002)
7. Crary, K., Weirich, S.: Flexible type analysis. ACM SIGPLAN Notices 34(9), 233–248 (1999) (Proceedings of the fourth ACM SIGPLAN International Conference on Functional Programming (ICFP '99), Paris, France)
8. Crary, K., Weirich, S., Morrisett, G.: Intensional polymorphism in type-erasure semantics. In: Proceedings of the ACM SIGPLAN International Conference on Functional Programming (ICFP '98), Baltimore, MD, vol. (34)1 of ACM SIGPLAN Notices, pp. 301–312. ACM Press, New York (1999)
9. Fegaras, L., Sheard, T.: Revisiting catamorphisms over datatypes with embedded functions (or, programs from outer space). In: Proceedings of the 23rd ACM SIGPLAN-SIGACT symposium on Principles of programming languages, St. Petersburg Beach, Florida, United States, pp. 284–294 (1996)
10. Girard, J.-Y.: Interprétation foncionnelle et élimination des coupures de l'arithmétique d'order supérieur. PhD thesis, Université de Paris VII (1972)
11. Hall, C.V., Hammond, K., Peyton Jones, S.L., Wadler, P.L.: Type classes in Haskell. ACM Transactions on Programming Languages and Systems 18(2), 109–138 (1996)
12. Harper, R., Morrisett, G.: Compiling polymorphism using intensional type analysis. In: 22nd Symposium on Principles of Programming Languages, POPL '95, pp. 130–141 (1995)
13. Hinze, R.: Functional Pearl: Perfect trees and bit-reversal permutations. Journal of Functional Programming 10(3), 305–317 (2000)
14. Hinze, R.: Memo functions, polytypically! In: Jeuring, J. (ed.) Proceedings of the 2nd Workshop on Generic Programming, Ponte de Lima, Portugal. The proceedings appeared as a technical report of Universiteit Utrecht, UU-CS-2000-19, pp. 17–32 (2000)

15. Hinze, R.: A new approach to generic functional programming. In: Reps, T.W. (ed.) Proceedings of the 27th Annual ACM SIGPLAN-SIGACT Symposium on Principles of Programming Languages (POPL'00), Boston, Massachusetts, January 19-21, pp. 119–132 (2000)
16. Hinze, R.: Polytypic values possess polykinded types. Science of Computer Programming 43, 129–159 (2002)
17. Hinze, R.: Fun with phantom types. In: Gibbons, J., de Moor, O. (eds.) The Fun of Programming, pp. 245–262 Palgrave Macmillan (2003) ISBN 1-4039-0772-2 hardback, ISBN 0-333-99285-7 paperback
18. Hinze, R.: Generics for the masses. J. Functional Programming 16(4&5), 451–483 (2006)
19. Hinze, R., Jeuring, J.: Generic Haskell: Applications. In: Backhouse, R., Gibbons, J. (eds.) Generic Programming. LNCS, vol. 2793, pp. 57–97. Springer, Heidelberg (2003)
20. Hinze, R., Jeuring, J.: Generic Haskell: Practice and theory. In: Backhouse, R., Gibbons, J. (eds.) Generic Programming. LNCS, vol. 2793, pp. 1–56. Springer, Heidelberg (2003)
21. Hinze, R., Jeuring, J., Löh, A.: Type-indexed data types. Science of Computer Programming 51, 117–151 (2004)
22. Hinze, R., Löh, A.: Scrap Your Boilerplate revolutions. In: Uustalu, T. (ed.) MPC 2006. LNCS, vol. 4014, pp. 180–208. Springer, Heidelberg (2006)
23. Hinze, R., Löh, A., Oliveira, B.C.d.S.: Scrap Your Boilerplate reloaded. In: Hagiya, M., Wadler, P. (eds.) FLOPS 2006. LNCS, vol. 3945, pp. 13–29. Springer, Heidelberg (2006)
24. Hinze, R., Löh, A., Oliveira, B.C.d.S.: Scrap Your Boilerplate reloaded. Technical Report IAI-TR-2006-2, Institut für Informatik III, Universität Bonn. (2006)
25. Hinze, R., Peyton Jones, S.L.: Derivable type classes. In: Hutton, G. (ed.) Proceedings of the 2000 ACM SIGPLAN Haskell Workshop. Electronic Notes in Theoretical Computer Science, vol. 41.1, Elsevier, Amsterdam (2001) The preliminary proceedings appeared as a University of Nottingham technical report
26. Hutton, G.: Higher-order functions for parsing. Journal of Functional Programming 2(3), 323–343 (1992)
27. Jansson, P., Jeuring, J.: PolyP-a polytypic programming language extension. In: Conference Record 24th ACM SIGPLAN-SIGACT Symposium on Principles of Programming Languages (POPL'97), Paris, France, pp. 470–482. ACM Press, New York (1997)
28. Jones, M.P.: A system of constructor classes: overloading and implicit higher-order polymorphism. Journal of Functional Programming 5(1), 1–35 (1995)
29. Jones, M.P.: Type classes with functional dependencies. In: Smolka, G. (ed.) ESOP 2000 and ETAPS 2000. LNCS, vol. 1782, pp. 230–244. Springer, Heidelberg (2000)
30. Lämmel, R., Peyton Jones, S.L.: Scrap more boilerplate: reflection, zips, and generalised casts. In: Fisher, K. (ed.) Proceedings of the 2004 International Conference on Functional Programming, Snowbird, Utah, September 19-22, 2004, pp. 244–255 (2004)
31. Lämmel, R., Peyton Jones, S.L.: Scrap your boilerplate with class: extensible generic functions. In: Pierce, B. (ed.) Proceedings of the 2005 International Conference on Functional Programming, Tallinn, Estonia, September 26-28, 2005 (2005)
32. Leijen, D., Meijer, E.: Domain-specific embedded compilers. In: Proceedings of the 2nd Conference on Domain-Specific Languages, Berkeley, CA, USENIX Association, pp. 109–122 (1999)

33. Löh, A., Hinze, R.: Open data types and open functions. In: Proceedings of the 8th ACM SIGPLAN Symposium on Principles and Practice of Declarative Programming, Venice, Italy, pp. 133–144. ACM Press, New York (2006)
34. Löh, A.: Exploring Generic Haskell. PhD thesis, Utrecht University (2004)
35. Löh, A., Jeuring, J.: The Generic Haskell user's guide, version 1.42 - Coral release. Technical Report UU-CS-2005-004, Universiteit Utrecht (January 2005)
36. Norell, U., Jansson, P.: Polytypic programming in Haskell. In: Trinder, P., Michaelson, G.J., Peña, R. (eds.) IFL 2003. LNCS, vol. 3145, pp. 168–184. Springer, Heidelberg (2004)
37. Oliveira, B.C.d.S., Gibbons, J.: TypeCase: A design pattern for type-indexed functions. In: Leijen, D. (ed.) Proceedings of the 2005 ACM SIGPLAN workshop on Haskell, Tallinn, Estonia, pp. 98–109 (2005)
38. Peyton Jones, S.L.: Haskell 98 Language and Libraries. Cambridge University Press, Cambridge (2003)
39. Peyton Jones, S.L., Lämmel, R.: Scrap your boilerplate: a practical approach to generic programming. In: Proceedings of the ACM SIGPLAN Workshop on Types in Language Design and Implementation (TLDI 2003), New Orleans, pp. 26–37 (2003)
40. The GHC Team. The Glorious Glasgow Haskell Compilation System User's Guide, Version 6.4.1 (2005), Available from http://www.haskell.org/ghc/
41. Trifonov, V., Saha, B., Shao, Z.: Fully reflexive intensional type analysis. In: Proceedings ICFP 2000: International Conference on Functional Programming, pp. 82–93. ACM Press, New York (2000)
42. Wadler, P.: The expression problem. Note to Java Genericity mailing list (November 12, 1998)
43. Wadler, P.: Theorems for free! In: The Fourth International Conference on Functional Programming Languages and Computer Architecture (FPCA'89), London, UK, pp. 347–359. Addison-Wesley, Reading (1989)
44. Weirich, S.: Encoding intensional type analysis. In: Sands, D. (ed.) ESOP 2001 and ETAPS 2001. LNCS, vol. 2028, pp. 92–106. Springer, Heidelberg (2001)
45. Weirich, S.: Type-safe cast. Journal of Functional Programming 14(6), 681–695 (2004)

Generic Programming with Dependent Types

Thorsten Altenkirch, Conor McBride, and Peter Morris

School of Computer Science and Information Technology
University of Nottingham

1   Introduction

In these lecture notes we give an overview of recent research on the relationship
and interaction between two novel ideas in (functional) programming:

Generic programming. Generic programming [15,22] allows programmers to
explain how a single algorithm can be instantiated for a variety of datatypes,
by computation over each datatype's structure.

Dependent types. Dependent types [29,38] are types containing data which
enable the programmer to express properties of data concisely, covering the
whole spectrum from conventional uses of types to types-as-specifications
and programs-as-proofs.

Our central thesis can be summarized by saying that dependent types provide
a convenient basis for generic programming by using *universes*. A universe is
basically a type $U : \star$ which contains names for types and a dependent type, or
family, $El : U \to \star$ which assigns to every name $a : U$ the type of its elements
$El\ a : \star$—we call this the *extension* of the name a. Historically, universes have
been already used by Type Theory to capture the predicative hierarchy of types,
first introduced by Russell to prevent set-theoretic paradoxes:

$$\star_0 : \star_1 : \star_2 : \ldots \star_i : \star_{i+1} : \ldots$$

If we want to avoid chains of : we can represent this hierarchy as:

$$U_i : \star$$
$$El_i : U_i \to \star$$
$$u_i : U_{i+1}$$

Here $\star$ plays the role of a superuniverse in which all universes can be embedded,
while U_i is the type of (names of) types at level i. The operation El_i assigns
to any name of a type at level i the type of its elements. In particular u_i is the
name of the previous universe at level $i + 1$ and hence $El_{i+1}\ u_i = U_i$.

The predicative hierarchy of universes is necessary to have types of types
without running into paradoxes (e.g. by having a type of all types). Here we
are interested in the application of universes to programming, which leads us
to consider a wider variety of smaller universes, less general but more usefully
structured than the ones above.

R. Backhouse et al. (Eds.): Datatype-Generic Programming 2006, LNCS 4719, pp. 209–257, 2007.

Related Work
The idea to use dependent types for generic programming isn't new: starting with the pioneering work by Pfeifer and Rueß [37] who used the LEGO system as a vehicle for generic programming, the authors of [16] actually introduced a universe containing codes for dependent types. The latter is based on the work by Dybjer and Setzer on Induction-Recursion [20,21] which can also be understood as universe constructions for non-dependent and dependent types. The first two authors of the present notes presented a universe construction for the first order fragment of Haskell datatypes including nested datatypes in [9] which was motivated by the work on generic Haskell [14,26].

Structure of the Paper
We start our discourse with a quick introduction to dependently typed programming (section 2) using the language Epigram as a vehicle. Epigram is described in more detail elsewhere, see [33] for a definition of the language with many applications, [11] for a short and more recent overview and [32] for an introductory tutorial. Epigram is not just a language but also an interactive program development system, which is, together with further documentation, available from the Epigram homepage [31].

As a warm up we start with a very small, yet useful universe, the universe of finite types (section 3). The names for types in this universe are particularly simple, they are just the natural numbers.

We soon move to bigger universes which include infinite types in section 4, where we introduce a general technique how to represent universes which contain fixpoints of types — this section is based on [36]. We also discuss the tradeoff between the size of a universe and the number of generic operations it supports.

While the universes above are defined syntactically, we also present a semantic approach based on *Container Types* (section 5), see [1,2,3,4]. However, here we will not study the categorical details of containers in detail but restrict ourselves to using them to represent datatypes and generic operations in Epigram.

As an example of a library of generic operations we consider the generic zipper [25] (section 6), which is a useful generic tool when implementing functional programs which use the notion of a position in a data structure. As observed by McBride [30], the zipper is closely related to the notion of the derivative of a datatype, which has many structural similarities to derivatives in calculus. This topic has been explored from a more categorical perspective in [5,7]; the presentation here is again based on [36].

Finally, we present our conclusions and possible directions for further work (section 7). All the code contained with these notes is available to download from the Epigram website [12].

2   Programming with Dependent Types in Epigram

Epigram is an experimental dependently typed functional language and an interactive program development system. It is based on previous experiences with systems based on Type Theory whose emphasis has been on the representations of proofs like LEGO [27]. The design of the interactive program and proof development environment is heavily influenced by the ALF system [28].

Epigram uses a two-dimensional syntax to represent the types of operators in a natural deduction style. This is particularly useful for presenting programs with dependent types—however, we start with some familiar constructions, e.g. we define the Booleans and the Peano-style natural numbers as follows:

```
data (----------!  where (-------------! ;   (--------------!
      ! Bool : * )         ! true : Bool )    ! false : Bool )


                                        (   n : Nat   !
data (---------!  where (------------! ;  !-------------!
      ! Nat : * )        ! zero : Nat )   ! suc n : Nat )
```

We first give the *formation rules*, Bool and Nat are types (⋆ is the type of types) without any assumptions. We then introduce the *constructors*: true and false are Booleans; zero is a natural number and suc n is a natural number, if n is one. These declarations correspond to the Haskell datatypes:

```
data Bool = True | False
data Nat = Zero | Succ Nat
```

The natural deduction notation may appear quite verbose for simple definitions, but you don't have to manage the layout for yourself—the editor does it for you. On paper, we prefer LaTeX to ASCII-art, and we take the liberty of typesetting declarations without the bracket delimiters and semicolon separators.

$$\underline{\text{data}} \ \frac{}{\text{Nat} : \star} \quad \underline{\text{where}} \ \frac{}{\text{zero} : \text{Nat}} \quad \frac{n : \text{Nat}}{\text{suc}\, n : \text{Nat}}$$

The formation rule may contain assumptions as well, declaring the arguments to type constructors, e.g. in the case of lists:

```
     (   A : *   !                        ( a : A ; as : List A !
data !------------! where (--------------! ;  !----------------------!
     ! List A : * )        ! nil : List A )   ! cons a as : List A  )
```

In LaTeX this becomes:

$$\underline{\text{data}} \ \frac{A : \star}{\text{List}\, A : \star} \quad \underline{\text{where}} \ \frac{}{\text{nil} : \text{List}\, A} \quad \frac{a : A \quad as : \text{List}\, A}{\text{cons}\, a\, as : \text{List}\, a}$$

Here the type-valued arguments to the constructors are left implicit. However, as we shall see, the use of implicit arguments becomes more subtle with dependent types. Hence, Epigram offers an explicit notation to indicate where implicit arguments should be expected. The definition above can be spelt out in full:

```
         ( A : * !                          ( a : A ;  as : List A !
data !---------! where (----------! ;    !-----------------------!
     ! List A !         ! nil _A : !     !      cons _A a as      !
     !   : *   )        !   List A )     !        : List A        )
```

Here, the underscore overrides the implicit quantifier to allow the user to specify its value explicitly. In LaTeX we denote this by subscripting the argument itself, as you can see in the typeset version of the above:

$$\underline{\text{data}} \ \frac{A : \star}{\text{List } A : \star} \quad \underline{\text{where}} \ \frac{A : \star}{\text{nil}_A : \text{List } A} \quad \frac{A : \star \quad a : A \quad as : \text{List } A}{\text{cons}_A \ a \ as : \text{List } a}$$

Under normal circumstances, Epigram's *elaborator* will be able to infer values for these arguments from the way these constructors are used, following a standard unification-based approach to type inference. Previously, we also omitted the declaration of $A : \star$ in the premise: again, this can be inferred by the elaborator as well, with the natural deduction rule acting like Hindley-Milner 'let', implicitly generalising local free variables.

Defining Functions
We define functions using <u>let</u> and generate patterns interactively. The text of a program records its construction. E.g. we define boolean not by <u>case</u> analysis on its first argument:

$$\underline{\text{let}} \ \frac{b : \text{Bool}}{\text{not } b : \text{Bool}} \qquad \begin{array}{l} \text{not } b \ \Leftarrow \ \underline{\text{case }} b \\ \quad \text{not true} \ \Rightarrow \ \text{false} \\ \quad \text{not false} \ \Rightarrow \ \text{true} \end{array}$$

Let-declarations use the two-dimensional rule syntax to declare a program's type: in Epigram, all top-level identifiers must be typed explicitly, but this type information is then propagated into their definitions, leaving them relatively free of annotation. Epigram programs are not sequences of prioritised equations as is traditional [34]. Rather, they are treelike: on the left-hand side, the *machine* presents a 'programming problem', e.g., to compute not b; on the right-hand side, we explain how to attack the problem in one of two ways:

$\Leftarrow$ **'by'** refinement into subproblems, using an *eliminator* like <u>case</u> b, above; the machine then generates a bunch of subproblems for us to solve;

$\Rightarrow$ **'return'** an answer directly, giving an expression of the appropriate return type, which may well be more specific than the type we started with, thanks to the analysis of the problem into cases.

In ASCII source, this tree structure is made explicit using $\{\dots\}$ markings: here, we drop these in favour of indentation.

Epigram programs thus explain the strategy by which they compute values: case analysis is one such strategy. By ensuring that the available strategies are total (e.g., <u>case</u> eliminators cover all constructors), we guarantee that all programs terminate.[1] To implement a recursive program, we can invoke a <u>rec</u> eliminator, capturing the strategy of structural recursion on the nominated argument: recursive calls have to be structurally smaller in this argument. As simple examples, consider addition and multiplication of Peano natural numbers:

$$\underline{\text{let}} \; \frac{x, y \; : \; \text{Nat}}{\text{plus} \; x \; y \; : \; \text{Nat}} \quad \begin{aligned} &\text{plus} \; x \; y \; \Leftarrow \; \underline{\text{rec}} \; x \\ &\text{plus} \; x \; y \; \Leftarrow \; \underline{\text{case}} \; x \\ &\text{plus} \; \text{zero} \; y \; \Rightarrow \; y \\ &\text{plus} \; (\text{suc} \; x) \; y \; \Rightarrow \; \text{suc} \; (\text{plus} \; x \; y) \end{aligned}$$

$$\underline{\text{let}} \; \frac{m, n \; : \; \text{Nat}}{\text{times} \; m \; n \; : \; \text{Nat}} \quad \begin{aligned} &\text{times} \; m \; n \; \Leftarrow \; \underline{\text{rec}} \; m \\ &\text{times} \; m \; n \; \Leftarrow \; \underline{\text{case}} \; m \\ &\text{times} \; \text{zero} \; n \; \Rightarrow \; \text{zero} \\ &\text{times} \; (\text{suc} \; m) \; n \; \Rightarrow \; \text{plus} \; n \; (\text{times} \; m \; n) \end{aligned}$$

It should be noted that these programs produce terms in Epigram's underlying type theory which use only standard elimination constants to perform recursion or case analysis. Programming with <u>rec</u> is much more flexible than 'primitive recursion': it is straightforward to implement programs with deeper structural recursion, like the Fibonacci function, or lexicographically combined structural recursions, like the Ackermann function.

Data-Type Families
So far we haven't used dependent types explicitly. Dependent types come in *families* [19], indexed by data. A standard example is the family of vectors *indexed by length*:

$$\underline{\text{data}} \; \frac{n \; : \; \text{Nat} \quad X \; : \; \star}{\text{Vec} \; n \; X} \quad \underline{\text{where}} \; \frac{}{\text{vnil} \; : \; \text{Vec} \; \text{zero} \; X} \quad \frac{a \; : \; A \quad as \; : \; \text{Vec} \; n \; X}{\text{vcons} \; a \; as \; : \; \text{Vec} \; (\text{suc} \; n) \; X}$$

Here Vec n X is the type of vectors, length n, of items of type X.

We can now implement a safe version of the head function, whose type makes it clear that the function can only be applied to non-empty lists:

$$\underline{\text{let}} \; \frac{ys \; : \; \text{Vec} \; (\text{suc} \; m) \; Y}{\text{vhead} \; ys \; : \; Y} \quad \begin{aligned} &\text{vhead} \; ys \; \Leftarrow \; \underline{\text{case}} \; ys \\ &\text{vhead} \; (\text{vcons} \; y \; ys) \; \Rightarrow \; y \end{aligned}$$

Note that Epigram does not ask for a vnil case—vnil's length, zero, does not unify with suc m, the length of ys, so the case cannot ever arise.

---

[1] The condition that the use of universes has to be stratified is present in the language definition but absent from the current implementation. As a consequence, the machine will accept a bogus non-terminating term based on Girard's paradox.

More generally, we can implement a function which safely accesses any element of a vector. To do this we first define the family of finite types, with the intention that Fin n represents the finite set $\{0, 1, \ldots, n-1\}$, i.e. exactly the positions in a vector of length n.

$$\underline{\text{data}} \ \frac{n \ : \ \text{Nat}}{\text{Fin} \ n \ : \ \star} \ \underline{\text{where}} \ \frac{}{\text{fz} \ : \ \text{Fin} \ (\text{suc} \ n)} \ \frac{i \ : \ \text{Fin} \ n}{\text{fs} \ i \ : \ \text{Fin} \ (\text{suc} \ n)}$$

Here fz represents 0 which is present in any non-empty finite set, and fs i : Fin (suc n) represents $i+1$, given that i : Fin n. Note that Fin zero is meant to be empty: case analysis on a hypothetical element of Fin zero leaves the empty set of patterns. The following table enumerates the elements up to Fin 4:

Fin 0	Fin 1	Fin 2	Fin 3	Fin 4	$\cdots$
	fz_0	fz_1	fz_2	fz_3	$\cdots$
		$\text{fs}_1 \ \text{fz}_0$	$\text{fs}_2 \ \text{fz}_1$	$\text{fs}_3 \ \text{fz}_2$	
			$\text{fs}_2 \ (\text{fs}_1 \ \text{fz}_0)$	$\text{fs}_3 \ (\text{fs}_2 \ \text{fz}_1)$	
				$\text{fs}_3 \ (\text{fs}_2 \ (\text{fs}_1 \ \text{fz}_0))$	

As you can see, each non-empty column contains a copy of the previous column, embedded by fs, together with a 'new' fz at the start.

We implement the function `proj` which safely accesses the ith element of a vector by structural recursion over the vector. We analyse the index given as an element of Fin n and since both constructors of Fin n produce elements in Fin (suc m) the subsequent analysis of the vector needs only a vcons case.

$$\underline{\text{let}} \ \frac{xs \ : \ \text{Vec} \ n \ X \quad i \ : \ \text{Fin} \ n}{\text{proj} \ xs \ i \ : \ X}$$

$$\text{proj} \ xs \ i \ \Leftarrow \ \underline{\text{rec}} \ xs$$
$$\quad \text{proj} \ xs \ i \ \Leftarrow \ \underline{\text{case}} \ i$$
$$\quad\quad \text{proj} \ xs \ \text{fz} \ \Leftarrow \ \underline{\text{case}} \ xs$$
$$\quad\quad\quad \text{proj} \ (\text{vcons} \ x \ xs) \ \text{fz} \ \Rightarrow \ x$$
$$\quad\quad \text{proj} \ xs \ (\text{fs} \ i) \ \Leftarrow \ \underline{\text{case}} \ xs$$
$$\quad\quad\quad \text{proj} \ (\text{vcons} \ x \ xs) \ (\text{fs} \ i) \ \Rightarrow \ \text{proj} \ xs \ i$$

Let's look more closely at what just happened. Here's `proj` again, but with the numeric indices shown as subscripts:

$$\underline{\text{let}} \ \frac{xs \ : \ \text{Vec} \ n \ X \quad i \ : \ \text{Fin} \ n}{\text{proj}_n \ xs \ i \ : \ X}$$

$$\text{proj}_n \ xs \ i \ \Leftarrow \ \underline{\text{rec}} \ xs$$
$$\quad \text{proj}_n \ xs \ i \ \Leftarrow \ \underline{\text{case}} \ i$$
$$\quad\quad \text{proj}_{(\text{suc} \ n)} \ xs \ (\text{fz}_n) \ \Leftarrow \ \underline{\text{case}} \ xs$$
$$\quad\quad\quad \text{proj}_{(\text{suc} \ n)} \ (\text{vcons}_n \ x \ xs) \ (\text{fz}_n) \ \Rightarrow \ x$$
$$\quad\quad \text{proj}_{(\text{suc} \ n)} \ xs \ (\text{fs}_n \ i) \ \Leftarrow \ \underline{\text{case}} \ xs$$
$$\quad\quad\quad \text{proj}_{(\text{suc} \ n)} \ (\text{vcons}_n \ x \ xs) \ (\text{fs}_n \ i) \ \Rightarrow \ \text{proj}_n \ xs \ i$$

When we analyse i, we get patterns for i, but we learn more about n at the same time. Case analysis specialises the whole programming problem, propagating the consequences of inspecting one value for others related to it by type dependency. The extra requirements imposed on the construction of dependently typed data become extra guarantees when we take it apart.

Exercise 1. Implement the function transpose which turns an $m \times n$ matrix represent as an m vector of n vectors into an $n \times m$ matrix represented as a n vector of m vectors:

$$\underline{\text{let}} \quad \frac{xys \;:\; \mathsf{Vec}\; n\; (\mathsf{Vec}\; m\; X)}{\text{transpose}\; xys \;:\; \mathsf{Vec}\; m\; (\mathsf{Vec}\; n\; X)}$$

Predefined Types in Epigram

Epigram provides very few predefined types: the empty type Zero, the unit type One and the equality type $a = b \;:\; \star$ for any a, b not necessarily of the same type. The only constructor for equality is refl $\;:\; a = a$ in the special case that both sides of the equation compute to the same value. For example,

$$\mathsf{refl} \;:\; \mathsf{plus}\; (\mathsf{suc}\; (\mathsf{suc}\; \mathsf{zero}))\; (\mathsf{suc}\; (\mathsf{suc}\; \mathsf{zero})) = \mathsf{suc}\; (\mathsf{suc}\; (\mathsf{suc}\; (\mathsf{suc}\; \mathsf{zero})))$$

Epigram has dependent function types $\forall a : A \Rightarrow B$, where firstly $A \;:\; \star$ and secondly $B \;:\; \star$ under the assumption $a \;:\; A$. We retain the conventional $A \to B$ notation for function types where the latter assumption is not used. Lambda abstraction is written $\lambda x : A \Rightarrow b$. The domain information can be omitted in λ and $\forall$, if it can be inferred from the context. Several abstractions of the same kind can be combined using ;, i.e. we write $\lambda x; y \Rightarrow c$ for $\lambda x \Rightarrow \lambda y \Rightarrow c$. The rule notation is just a convenient way to declare functions, e.g. the type of vhead can be written explicitly as $\forall \_m; \_Y \Rightarrow \mathsf{Vec}\; (\mathsf{suc}\; m)\; Y \to Y$.

Common Datatypes in This Paper

There are a few additional standard type constructors which we shall use in this paper: we define a type for disjoint union corresponding to Either in Haskell:

$$\underline{\text{data}} \;\; \frac{A, B \;:\; \star}{\mathsf{Plus}\; A\; B \;:\; \star} \quad \underline{\text{where}} \;\; \frac{a \;:\; A}{\mathsf{Inl}\; a \;:\; \mathsf{Plus}\; A\; B} \quad \frac{b \;:\; B}{\mathsf{Inr}\; b \;:\; \mathsf{Plus}\; A\; B}$$

Epigram hasn't currently a predefined product type, hence we define it:

$$\underline{\text{data}} \;\; \frac{A, B \;:\; \star}{\mathsf{Times}\; A\; B} \quad \underline{\text{where}} \;\; \frac{a \;:\; A \quad b \;:\; B}{\mathsf{Pair}\; a\; b \;:\; \mathsf{Times}\; A\; B}$$

We also introduce the Σ-type, giving us *dependent* tupling: [2]

$$\underline{\text{data}} \;\; \frac{A \;:\; \star \quad B \;:\; A \to \star}{\mathsf{Sigma}\; A\; B \;:\; \star} \quad \underline{\text{where}} \;\; \frac{a \;:\; A \quad b \;:\; B\, a}{\mathsf{Tup}\; a\; b \;:\; \mathsf{Sigma}\; A\; B}$$

---

[2] Some authors call this a 'dependent product', as it's the dependent version of Times. Other call it a 'dependent sum', as it's the infinitary analogue of Plus, and say 'dependent product' for functions, as these are the infinitary analogue of tuples. To avoid confusion, we prefer to talk of 'dependent function types' and 'dependent tuple types'.

Exercise 2. Define the first and second projection for Σ-types using pattern matching:

$$\text{let} \ \frac{p \ : \ \text{Sigma} \ A \ B}{\text{fst} \ p \ : \ A} \qquad \text{let} \ \frac{p \ : \ \text{Sigma} \ A \ B}{\text{snd} \ p \ : \ B \ (\text{fst} \ p)}$$

W-Types

Later in the paper, we shall also need a general-purpose inductive datatype, abstracting once and for all over *well-founded* tree-like data. Tree-like data is built from nodes. Each node carries some sort of data—its *shape*—usually, a tag indicating what sort of node it is, plus some appropriate labelling. In any case, the node shape determines what *positions* there might be for subtrees. This characterisation of well-founded data in terms of shapes and positions is presented via the W-type:

$$\text{data} \ \frac{S \ : \ \star \quad P \ : \ S \to \star}{\mathsf{W} \ S \ P \ : \ \star} \qquad \text{where} \ \frac{s \ : \ S \quad f \ : \ P \ s \to \mathsf{W} \ S \ P}{\text{Sup} \ s \ f \ : \ \mathsf{W} \ S \ P}$$

The constructor packs up a choice s of shape, together with a function f assigning subtrees to the positions appropriate to that shape. It is traditional to call the constructor Sup for 'supremum', as a node is the least thing bigger than its subtrees. We often illustrate this pattern—choice of shape, function from positions—as a *triangle* diagram. We write the shape s in the apex, and we think of the base as the corresponding set $P \ s$ of positions. The function f, part of the node hence inside the triangle, attaches subtrees w to positions p.

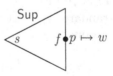

For example, the natural numbers have *two* node shapes, suc with one subtree and zero without. Correspondingly, we can use Bool for the shapes; the positions are given by the following type family which captures 'being true':

$$\text{data} \ \frac{b \ : \ \text{Bool}}{\text{So} \ b \ : \ \star} \qquad \text{where} \ \frac{}{\text{oh} \ : \ \text{So true}}$$

$$\text{let} \ \frac{p \ : \ \text{So false}}{\text{notSo} \ p \ : \ X} \qquad \text{notSo} \ p \ \Leftarrow \ \underline{\text{case}} \ p$$

We may now *define* the natural numbers as a W-type:

<u>let</u> $\overline{\text{wNat} : \star}$

wNat $\Rightarrow$ W Bool So

<u>let</u> $\overline{\text{wZero} : \text{wNat}}$

wZero $\Rightarrow$ Sup false notSo

<u>let</u> $\dfrac{n : \text{wNat}}{\text{wSuc } n : \text{wNat}}$

wSuc $n \Rightarrow$ Sup true $(\lambda p \Rightarrow n)$

The pictures show us the components we can plug together to make numbers. 'Two' looks like this:

Lots of our favourite inductive datatypes fit this pattern. Another key example is the type of *finitely branching trees*, W Nat Fin, where the shape of each node is its arity.

Exercise 3. Construct the W-type corresponding to Haskell's

```
data BTree l n = Leaf l | Node (BTree l n) n (BTree l n)
```

Later, we shall exploit the W-type analysis of data in terms of shapes and positions to characterise *containers*, more generally.

Views in Epigram

Once we have the idea of programming by stepwise refinement of problems, it becomes interesting to ask 'What refinements can we have? Are we restricted to <u>case</u> and <u>rec</u>?'. The *eliminators* which we use to refine programming problems are first-class Epigram values, so it is entirely possible to implement your own. This flexibility is central to the design of Epigram [33], and it gives rise to a novel and useful programming technique inspired by Wadler's notion of 'views' [40].

We can specify a new way to analyse data, just by indexing a datatype family with it. Consider pairs of Boolean values, for example: regardless of whether they are true or false, it is surely the case that either they coincide, or the second is the negation of the first. We can express this idea by defining a datatype family—the *view relation*—with one constructor for each case of our desired analysis:

<u>data</u> $\dfrac{b, a : \text{Bool}}{\text{EqOrNot } b\, a : \star}$ <u>where</u> $\overline{\text{same} : \text{EqOrNot } b\, b \quad \text{diff} : \text{EqOrNot } b\, (\text{not } b)}$

If we had an element p of EqOrNot $b\,a$, then case analysis for p as same or diff tells us *ipso facto* whether a is b or not b. Let us make sure that we can always have such a p by writing a *covering function* to show that the view relation always holds.

$$\underline{\text{let}} \ \frac{}{\text{eqOrNot } b \ a \ : \ \text{EqOrNot } b \ a}$$

$$
\begin{aligned}
\text{eqOrNot } b \ a &\Leftarrow \underline{\text{case}} \ b \\
\text{eqOrNot true } a &\Leftarrow \underline{\text{case}} \ a \\
\text{eqOrNot true true} &\Rightarrow \text{same} \\
\text{eqOrNot true false} &\Rightarrow \text{diff} \\
\text{eqOrNot false } a &\Leftarrow \underline{\text{case}} \ a \\
\text{eqOrNot false true} &\Rightarrow \text{diff} \\
\text{eqOrNot false false} &\Rightarrow \text{same}
\end{aligned}
$$

How do we use this information in practice? Epigram has syntactic support for case analysis derived in this style: if p is a proof that the view relation holds, $\underline{\text{view}} \ p$ is the eliminator which delivers the corresponding analysis of its indices. For example, we may now write

$$\underline{\text{let}} \ \frac{x, y \ : \ \text{Bool}}{\text{xor } x \ y \ : \ \text{Bool}}$$

$$
\begin{aligned}
\text{xor } x \ y &\Leftarrow \underline{\text{view}} \ (\text{eqOrNot } x \ y) \\
\text{xor } x \ x &\Rightarrow \text{false} \\
\text{xor } x \ (\text{not } x) &\Rightarrow \text{true}
\end{aligned}
$$

There is no need to be alarmed at the appearance of repeated pattern variables and even *defined* functions on the left-hand side. Operationally, this program computes an element of EqOrNot $x \ y$, then forks control accordingly as it is same or diff. What you see on the left comes from the specialisation of y which accompanies that constructor analysis.

Views are important tools for testing data on which types depend. Our EqOrNot construction may be more complex than the ordinary Boolean 'equivalence' test, but it is also more revealing. The view actually shows the typechecker what the equality test learns.

To see this in action, consider implementing an equality test for wNat. At each node, we shall need to compare shapes, and if they coincide, check equality at each position. How do we know that the position sets must be identical whenever the shapes coincide? Our view makes the connection.

$$\underline{\text{let}} \ \frac{x, y \ : \ \text{wNat}}{\text{wNatEq } x \ y \ : \ \text{Bool}}$$

$$
\begin{aligned}
\text{wNatEq } x \ y &\Leftarrow \underline{\text{rec}} \ x \\
\text{wNatEq } x \ y &\Leftarrow \underline{\text{case}} \ x \\
\text{wNatEq (Sup } b \ f) \ y &\Leftarrow \underline{\text{case}} \ y \\
\text{wNatEq (Sup } b \ f) \ (\text{Sup } a \ g) &\Leftarrow \underline{\text{view}} \ (\text{eqOrNot } b \ a) \\
\text{wNatEq (Sup } b \ f) \ (\text{Sup } b \ g) &\Leftarrow \underline{\text{case}} \ b \\
\text{wNatEq (Sup true } f) \ (\text{Sup true } g) &\Rightarrow \text{wNatEq } (f \ \text{oh}) \ (g \ \text{oh}) \\
\text{wNatEq (Sup false } f) \ (\text{Sup false } g) &\Rightarrow \text{true} \\
\text{wNatEq (Sup } b \ f) \ (\text{Sup (not } b) \ g)) &\Rightarrow \text{false}
\end{aligned}
$$

3   The Universe of Finite Types

We have already implicitly introduced our first example of a universe: the universe of finite types. The names of finite types are the natural numbers which tell us how many elements the type has and the extension of such a type name is given by the family Fin given in the previous section, which assigns to any n : Nat a type Fin n with exactly n elements. We will now identify basic operations on types within this universe, namely coproducts $(0, +)$, products $(1, \times)$ and leave exponentials $(\rightarrow)$ as an exercise. This reflects the well known fact that the category of finite types is bicartesian closed.

Coproducts

The coproduct of two finite types m, n : Nat is simply their arithmetical sum plus $m\, n$: Nat, which we have defined previously. Coproducts come with injections and an eliminator which gives us case analysis. We will use Epigram's views to implement a view on coproducts in the finite universe. As a consequence we can use Epigram's pattern matching to analyse elements of Fin $(\text{plus } m\, n)$ as if they were elements of an ordinary top-level coproduct (Plus).

We are going to parametrize the injections finl and finr explicitly with the type parameters m, n : Nat leading to the following signatures:

$$\underline{\text{let}} \quad \frac{m, n \,:\, \mathsf{Nat} \quad i \,:\, \mathsf{Fin}\ m}{\mathsf{finl}\ m\ n\ i \,:\, \mathsf{Fin}\ (\mathsf{plus}\ m\ n)} \qquad \underline{\text{let}} \quad \frac{m, n \,:\, \mathsf{Nat} \quad j \,:\, \mathsf{Fin}\ n}{\mathsf{finr}\ m\ n\ j \,:\, \mathsf{Fin}\ (\mathsf{plus}\ m\ n)}$$

finl will map the elements of Fin m to the first m elements of Fin $(\text{plus } m\, n)$ and finr will map the elements of Fin n to the subsequent n elements of Fin $(\text{plus } m\, n)$. These ideas can be turned into structural recursive programs over m: in the case of finl

$$
\begin{aligned}
&\mathsf{finl}\ m\ n\ i \ \Leftarrow\ \underline{\mathsf{rec}}\ m \\
&\mathsf{finl}\ m\ n\ i \ \Leftarrow\ \underline{\mathsf{case}}\ i \\
&\quad \mathsf{finl}\ (\mathsf{suc}\ m)\ n\ \mathsf{fz} \ \Rightarrow\ \mathsf{fz} \\
&\quad \mathsf{finl}\ (\mathsf{suc}\ m)\ n\ (\mathsf{fs}\ i) \ \Rightarrow\ \mathsf{fs}\,(\mathsf{finl}\ m\ n\ i)
\end{aligned}
$$

we analyse the element i : Fin m mapping the constructors fs, fz in Fin m to their counterparts in Fin $(\text{plus } m\, n)$. To implement finr we follow a different strategy:

$$
\begin{aligned}
&\mathsf{finr}\ m\ n\ j \ \Leftarrow\ \underline{\mathsf{rec}}\ m \\
&\mathsf{finr}\ m\ n\ j \ \Leftarrow\ \underline{\mathsf{case}}\ m \\
&\quad \mathsf{finr}\ \mathsf{zero}\ n\ j \ \Rightarrow\ j \\
&\quad \mathsf{finr}\ (\mathsf{suc}\ m)\ n\ j \ \Rightarrow\ \mathsf{fs}\,(\mathsf{finr}\ m\ n\ j)
\end{aligned}
$$

We analyse the type name m : Nat to apply m successor operations fs to lift Fin n into Fin $(\text{plus } m\, n)$. It is worthwhile to note that the above implementations of finl and finr only work for the given implementation of plus which recurs over the first argument. Had we chosen a different one, we would have to either have chosen a different implementation of finl and finr or would have to employ equational reasoning to justify our implementation. We tend to avoid the latter as much as possible by carefully choosing the way we implement our functions.

How can we compute with elements of Fin (plus $m\ n$)? One way to answer this question is to provide an eliminator in form of a case-function:

$$\text{let}\ \frac{s\ :\ \text{Fin (plus } m\ n)\quad l\ :\ \text{Fin } m \to X \quad r\ :\ \text{Fin } n \to X}{\text{fcase}_{m\,n}\ s\ l\ r\ :\ X}$$

However, Epigram offers a general mechanism which allows the user to extend the predefined pattern matching mechanism by providing a view, i.e. an alternative covering of a given type which is represented as a family:

$$\text{data}\ \frac{i\ :\ \text{Fin (plus } m\ n)}{\text{FinPlus } m\ n\ i}\ \text{where}$$

$$\frac{i\ :\ \text{Fin } m}{\text{isfinl } i\ :\ \text{FinPlus } m\ n\ (\text{finl } m\ n\ i)} \qquad \frac{j\ :\ \text{Fin } n}{\text{isfinr } j\ :\ \text{FinPlus } m\ n\ (\text{finr } m\ n\ j)}$$

To use the FinPlus view for pattern matching we have to implement a function which witnesses that the covering is exhaustive:

$$\text{let}\ \overline{\text{finPlus } m\ n\ i\ :\ \text{FinPlus } m\ n\ i}$$

$$
\begin{aligned}
&\text{finPlus } m\ n\ i\ \Leftarrow\ \underline{\text{rec}}\ m \\
&\text{finPlus } m\ n\ i\ \Leftarrow\ \underline{\text{case}}\ m \\
&\quad \text{finPlus zero } n\ i\ \Rightarrow\ \text{isfinr } i \\
&\quad \text{finPlus (suc } m)\ n\ i\ \Leftarrow\ \underline{\text{case}}\ i \\
&\quad\quad \text{finPlus (suc } m)\ n\ \text{fz}\ \Rightarrow\ \text{isfinl fz} \\
&\quad\quad \text{finPlus (suc } m)\ n\ (\text{fs } i)\ \Leftarrow\ \underline{\text{view}}\ \text{finPlus } m\ n\ i \\
&\quad\quad\quad \text{finPlus (suc } m)\ n\ (\text{fs (finl } m\ n\ i))\ \Rightarrow\ \text{isfinl (fs } i) \\
&\quad\quad\quad \text{finPlus (suc } m)\ n\ (\text{fs (finr } m\ n\ j))\ \Rightarrow\ \text{isfinr } j
\end{aligned}
$$

We can now use <u>view</u> to do pattern matching over Fin (plus $m\ n$), e.g. to implement fcase:

$$
\begin{aligned}
&\text{fcase}_{m\,n}\ s\ l\ r\ \Leftarrow\ \underline{\text{view}}\ \text{finPlus } m\ n\ s \\
&\quad \text{fcase}_{m\,n}\ (\text{finl } m\ n\ i)\ l\ r\ \Rightarrow\ l\ i \\
&\quad \text{fcase}_{m\,n}\ (\text{finr } m\ n\ j)\ l\ r\ \Rightarrow\ r\ j
\end{aligned}
$$

Products

Given type names m, n : Nat their cartesian product is denoted by the arithmetic product times $m\ n$. Elements of Fin (times $m\ n$) can be constructed using pairing:

$$\text{let}\ \frac{i\ :\ \text{Fin } m \quad j\ :\ \text{Fin } n}{\text{fpair } m\ n\ i\ j\ :\ \text{Fin (times } m\ n)}$$

The intuitive idea is to arrange the elements of Fin (times $m\ n$) as a rectangle and assign to pair $i\ j$ the jth column in the ith row. This is realised by the following primitive recursive function which uses the previously defined constructors for coproducts, since our products are merely iterated coproducts:

fpair $m\,n\,i\,j$ $\Leftarrow$ <u>rec</u> i
fpair $m\,n\,i\,j$ $\Leftarrow$ <u>case</u> i
  fpair (suc m) n fz j $\Rightarrow$ finl n (times $m\,n$) j
  fpair (suc m) n (fs i) j $\Rightarrow$ finr n (times $m\,n$) (fpair $m\,n\,i\,j$)

Indeed the pair $m\,n\,i\,j$ just computes $j + i * n$, however our implementation verifies that the result is less than $m * n$ simply by type checking.

As in the case for coproducts we extend pattern matching to cover our products by providing the appropriate view:

<u>data</u> $\dfrac{i\ :\ \text{Fin (times } m\,n)}{\text{FinTimes } m\,n\,i\ :\ \star}$

<u>where</u> $\dfrac{i\ :\ \text{Fin } m \qquad j\ :\ \text{Fin } n}{\text{isfpair } i\,j\ :\ \text{FinTimes } m\,n\,(\text{fpair } m\,n\,i\,j)}$

As before we show that this view is exhaustive:

<u>let</u> $\dfrac{}{\overline{\text{finTimes } m\,n\,i\ :\ \text{FinTimes } m\,n\,i}}$

finTimes $m\,n\,i$ $\Leftarrow$ <u>rec</u> m
finTimes $m\,n\,i$ $\Leftarrow$ <u>case</u> m
finTimes zero $n\,i$ $\Leftarrow$ <u>case</u> i
finTimes (suc m) $n\,i$ $\Leftarrow$ <u>view</u> finPlus n (times $m\,n$) i
finTimes (suc m) n (finl n (times $m\,n$) i) $\Rightarrow$ isfpair fz i
finTimes (suc m) n (finr n (times $m\,n$) j) $\Leftarrow$ <u>view</u> finTimes $m\,n\,j$
  finTimes (suc m) n (finr n (times $m\,n$) (fpair $m\ n\,i\,j$))
    $\Rightarrow$ isfpair (fs i) j

Note that we are using the previously defined **FinPlus** view to analyse the iterated coproducts. We can use both derived pattern matching principles to show that products distribute over coproducts

<u>let</u> $\dfrac{x\ :\ \text{Fin (times } m\,(\text{plus } n\,o))}{\text{dist } m\,n\,o\,x\ :\ \text{Fin (plus (times } m\,n)\,(\text{times } m\,o))}$

dist $m\,n\,o\,x$ $\Leftarrow$ <u>view</u> finTimes m (plus $n\,o$) x
dist $m\,n\,o$ (fpair m (plus $n\,o$) $i\,j$) $\Leftarrow$ <u>view</u> finPlus $n\,o\,j$
  dist $m\,n\,o$ (fpair m (plus $n\,o$) i (finl $n\,o\,j$))
    $\Rightarrow$ finl (times $m\,n$) (times $m\,o$) (fpair $m\,n\,i\,j$)
  dist $m\,n\,o$ (fpair m (plus $n\,o$) i (finr $n\,o\,j$))
    $\Rightarrow$ finr (times $m\,n$) (times $m\,o$) (fpair $m\,o\,i\,j$)

The categorically inclined may notice that this is not an automatic consequence of having products and coproducts, but usually established as a consequence of having exponentials. We leave it as an exercise to define exponentials.

Exercise 4. Define exponentials (i.e. function types) by implementing a function to represent the name of a function type:

$$\text{let} \;\; \frac{m, n \;:\; \mathsf{Nat}}{\exp m\, n \;:\; \mathsf{Nat}}$$

and a constructor corresponding to lambda abstraction:

$$\text{let} \;\; \frac{f \;:\; \mathsf{Fin}\, m \;\to\; \mathsf{Fin}\, n}{\text{flam}\; m\, n\, f \;:\; \mathsf{Fin}\, (\exp m\, n)}$$

Unlike in the previous cases we cannot implement a pattern matching principle due to the lack of extensionality in Epigram's type system.[3]

However, we can define an application operator:

$$\text{let} \;\; \frac{f \;:\; \mathsf{Fin}\, (\exp m\, n) \quad i \;:\; \mathsf{Fin}\, m}{\text{fapp}\; m\, n\, f\, i \;:\; \mathsf{Fin}\, n}$$

4   Universes for Generic Programming

The previously introduced universe of finite types is extensional, any two functions which are extensionally equal are given the same code. E.g. using the example from [13] we can see that the functions $\lambda f : \mathsf{Bool} \to \mathsf{Bool} \Rightarrow f$ and $\lambda f : \mathsf{Bool} \to \mathsf{Bool}; x : \mathsf{Bool} \Rightarrow f\, (f\, (f\, x))$ are extensionally equal by encoding them using the combinators defined in the previous section and observing that they compute the same element in $\mathsf{Fin}\, 256$.[4]

While extensionality is a desirable feature, it is not always as easy to achieve as in the case of finite types. Hence, when moving to larger universes which allow us to represent infinite datatypes we shall use a different approach. Instead of identifying our type constructors within a given type of names, we inductively define the type of type names and the family of inhabitants.

Finite Types, Revisited

To illustrate this let us revisit the universe of finite types, we can inductively define the type names generated from $0, +, 1, \times$:

$$\text{data} \; \frac{}{\mathsf{Ufin} \;:\; \star} \; \text{where} \quad \frac{}{\text{'0'} \;:\; \mathsf{Ufin}} \quad \frac{a, b \;:\; \mathsf{Ufin}}{\text{'plus'}\, a\, b \;:\; \mathsf{Ufin}}$$

$$\frac{}{\text{'1'} \;:\; \mathsf{Ufin}} \quad \frac{a, b \;:\; \mathsf{Ufin}}{\text{'times'}\, a\, b \;:\; \mathsf{Ufin}}$$

---

[3] We cannot show that two functions are equal if they are pointwise equal. As a consequence we cannot show for example that there are exactly 4 functions of type $\mathsf{Bool} \to \mathsf{Bool}$ which would be necessary if we want to establish a case analysis principle for finite types. Our ongoing work on *Observational Type Theory* [10] will address this issue.

[4] We don't recommend trying this with the current implementation of Epigram.

We could also have included function types, however, they will require special attention later when we introduce inductive types.

We define the family of elements Elfin inductively:

$$\underline{\text{data}} \quad \frac{a \ : \ \mathsf{Ufin}}{\mathsf{Elfin} \ a \ : \ \star}$$

$$\underline{\text{where}} \quad \frac{b, a \ : \ \mathsf{Ufin} \quad x \ : \ \mathsf{Elfin} \ a}{\mathsf{inl} \ x \ : \ \mathsf{Elfin} \ (\text{`plus'} \ a \ b)} \quad \frac{a, b \ : \ \mathsf{Ufin} \quad y \ : \ \mathsf{Elfin} \ b}{\mathsf{inr} \ y \ : \ \mathsf{Elfin} \ (\text{`plus'} \ a \ b)}$$

$$\frac{}{\mathsf{void} \ : \ \mathsf{Elfin} \ \text{`1'}} \quad \frac{x \ : \ \mathsf{Elfin} \ a \quad y \ : \ \mathsf{Elfin} \ b}{\mathsf{pair} \ x \ y \ : \ \mathsf{Elfin} \ (\text{`times'} \ a \ b)}$$

Indeed, we have seen inductively defined families already when we introduced Vec and Fin. We can reimplement the dist function for this universes without having to resort to views, the built in pattern matching will do the job:

$$\underline{\text{let}} \quad \frac{x \ : \ \mathsf{Elfin} \ (\text{`times'} \ a \ (\text{`plus'} \ b \ c))}{\mathsf{dist} \ x \ : \ \mathsf{Elfin} \ (\text{`plus'} \ (\text{`times'} \ a \ b) \ (\text{`times'} \ a \ c))}$$

$$\begin{aligned}
\mathsf{dist} \ x \ &\Leftarrow \ \underline{\text{case}} \ x \\
\mathsf{dist} \ (\mathsf{pair} \ x \ y) \ &\Leftarrow \ \underline{\text{case}} \ y \\
\mathsf{dist} \ (\mathsf{pair} \ x \ (\mathsf{inl} \ y)) \ &\Rightarrow \ \mathsf{inl} \ (\mathsf{pair} \ x \ y) \\
\mathsf{dist} \ (\mathsf{pair} \ x \ (\mathsf{inr} \ z)) \ &\Rightarrow \ \mathsf{inr} \ (\mathsf{pair} \ x \ z)
\end{aligned}$$

4.1   Enumerating Finite Types

So far we haven't defined any proper generic operations, i.e. an operation which works on all types of a universe by inspecting the name. A generic operation which is *typical* for finite types is the possibility to enumerate all elements of a given type. We shall use binary trees instead of lists to represent the results of an enumeration so that the path in the tree correspond to the choices we have to make to identify the element. Since our types may be empty we require a special constructor to represent an empty tree:

$$\underline{\text{data}} \quad \frac{A \ : \ \star}{\mathsf{ET} \ A \ : \ \star}$$

$$\underline{\text{where}} \quad \frac{a \ : \ A}{V \ a \ : \ \mathsf{ET} \ A} \quad \frac{l, r \ : \ \mathsf{ET} \ A}{C \ l \ r \ : \ \mathsf{ET} \ A} \quad \frac{}{E \ : \ \mathsf{ET} \ A}$$

Our generic enumeration function has the following type:

$$\underline{\text{let}} \quad \frac{a \ : \ \mathsf{Ufin}}{\mathsf{enum} \ a \ : \ \mathsf{ET} \ (\mathsf{Elfin} \ a)}$$

To implement enum it is helpful to observe that ET is a monad, with

$$\underline{\text{let}} \ \frac{a : A}{\text{returnET } a \ : \ \text{ET } A} \qquad \text{returnET } a \ \Rightarrow \ \mathsf{V} \, a$$

$$\underline{\text{let}} \ \frac{t : \text{ET } A \quad f : A \rightarrow \text{ET } B}{\text{bindET } t \, f \ : \ \text{ET } B}$$

$$\begin{aligned}
\text{bindET } t \, f \ &\Leftarrow \ \underline{\text{rec}} \ t \\
\text{bindET } t \, f \ &\Leftarrow \ \underline{\text{case}} \ t \\
\text{bindET } (\mathsf{V} \, a) \, f \ &\Rightarrow \ f \, a \\
\text{bindET } (\mathsf{C} \, l \, r) \, f \ &\Rightarrow \ \mathsf{C} \, (\text{bindET } l \, f) \, (\text{bindET } r \, f) \\
\text{bindET } \mathsf{E} \, f \ &\Rightarrow \ \mathsf{E}
\end{aligned}$$

Consequently, ET is also functorial:

$$\underline{\text{let}} \ \frac{f : A \rightarrow B \quad t : \text{ET } A}{\text{mapET } f \, t \ : \ \text{ET } B}$$

$$\text{mapET } f \, t \ \Rightarrow \ \text{bindET } t \, (\lambda x \Rightarrow \text{returnET } (f \, x))$$

We are now ready to implement enum by structural recursion over the type name:

$$\begin{aligned}
\text{enum } a \ &\Leftarrow \ \underline{\text{rec}} \ a \\
\text{enum } a \ &\Leftarrow \ \underline{\text{case}} \ a \\
\text{enum '0'} \ &\Rightarrow \ \mathsf{E} \\
\text{enum ('plus' } a \, b) \ &\Rightarrow \ \mathsf{C} \, (\text{mapET inl } (\text{enum } a)) \, (\text{mapET inr } (\text{enum } b)) \\
\text{enum '1'} \ &\Rightarrow \ \mathsf{V} \, \text{void} \\
\text{enum ('times' } a \, b) \ & \\
&\Rightarrow \ \text{bindET } (\text{enum } a) \, (\lambda x \Rightarrow \text{mapET } (\lambda y \Rightarrow \text{pair } x \, y) \, (\text{enum } b))
\end{aligned}$$

Exercise 5. Add function types to Ufin and extend Elfin. The naive definition of Elfin using functions would destroy positivity, but this problem can be overcome by using Vec instead.

Can you extend enum to cover function types?

Context-Free Types

By context-free types[5] we mean types which can be constructed by combining the polynomial operators from the previous section $(0, +, \times, 1)$ with an operator μ to construct inductive types, or in categorical terms initial algebras. We have already seen some examples of context-free types, for instance Nat can be expressed as $\text{Nat} = \mu X.1 + X$ and List which can be encoded: $\text{List } A = \mu X.1 + A \times X$. Other examples we will use include binary trees with data at the nodes which can be given by the expression $\text{Tree } A = \mu X.1 + (X \times A \times X)$. Finally, rose trees

---

[5] We previously used the term 'regular *tree* types' [36] in a vain attempt to avoid confusion with regular *expressions*.

which are given by the code $\mathsf{RT}A = \mu X.\mathsf{List}\,(A \times X) = \mu X.\mu Y.1 + (A \times X) \times Y.$[6]
We use the term context-free types because the types have the same structure as
context-free grammars, identifying parameters with terminal symbols, recursive
variables with non-terminal symbols, choice with + and sequence with ×.

The first technical issue we need to address is how to represent variables.
We use a deBruijn style representation of variables, this seems to be essential
since we are going to represent types as an inductive family, using names would
cause a considerable overhead and also would mean that we have to deal with
issues like alpha conversion. Moreover, we are free to implement a function which
translates a name carrying type into our internal deBruijn representation. This
choice is a variation on the approach taken by McBride [30] when he first gave
an inductive characterisation of these types. The names of context-free types
becomes a family indexed by the number of free variables:

$$\underline{\mathsf{data}}\ \ \frac{n\ :\ \mathsf{Nat}}{\mathsf{Ucf}\,n\ :\ \star}\ \ \underline{\mathsf{where}}$$

As constructors we retain the polynomial operators which leave the number of
free variables unchanged:

$$\frac{}{\text{'0'}\ :\ \mathsf{Ucf}\,n}\qquad \frac{a,b\ :\ \mathsf{Ucf}\,n}{\text{'plus'}\,a\,b\ :\ \mathsf{Ucf}\,n}$$

$$\frac{}{\text{'1'}\ :\ \mathsf{Ucf}\,n}\qquad \frac{a,b\ :\ \mathsf{Ucf}\,n}{\text{'times'}\,a\,b\ :\ \mathsf{Ucf}\,n}$$

To represent variables we introduce two constructors: vl which represents the
last variable in a non-empty context, and wk a which means that the type name
a is weakened, i.e. the last variable is not used and vl now refers to the variable
before the last:

$$\frac{}{\mathsf{vl}\ :\ \mathsf{Ucf}\,(\mathsf{suc}\,n)}\qquad \frac{a\ :\ \mathsf{Ucf}\,n}{\mathsf{wk}\,a\ :\ \mathsf{Ucf}\,(\mathsf{suc}\,n)}$$

An alternative is to use the previously defined family of finite types directly, i.e.
only to introduce one constructor:

$$\frac{x\ :\ \mathsf{Fin}\,n}{\mathsf{var}\,x\ :\ \mathsf{Ucf}\,n}$$

but it is slightly more convenient to use wk and vl because otherwise we have to
define operations on Fin and Ucf instead of just for Ucf.

Dual to weakening is an operator representing *local definitions*, which allows
us to replace the last variable by a given type name:

$$\frac{f\ :\ \mathsf{Ucf}\,(\mathsf{suc}\,n)\qquad a\ :\ \mathsf{Ucf}\,n}{\mathsf{def}\,f\,a\ :\ \mathsf{Ucf}\,n}$$

---

[6] Our definition of RT is isomorphic to leaf-labelled binary trees, while the trees in
[17], p.16, $\mu X.A \times (\mathsf{List}\,X)$ are isomorphic to node-labelled binary trees.

Alternatively, we could have defined substitution by recursion over the structure of type names. In the presence of a binding operator, here μ, this is not completely trivial. Later, we will see that another advantage of local definitions is that it allows us to define operations by structural recursion whose termination would have to be justified otherwise.

Finally, we introduce the constructor for inductive types, which binds the last variable and hence decreases the number of free variables by one:

$$\frac{f \ : \ \mathsf{Ucf}\,(\mathsf{suc}\,n)}{\text{`mu'}\,f \ : \ \mathsf{Ucf}\,n}$$

Our examples (natural numbers, lists, trees and rose trees) can be translated into type names in Ucf:

$$\underline{\mathsf{let}} \ \frac{}{\mathsf{nat} \ : \ \mathsf{Ucf}\,n} \quad \mathsf{nat} \ \Rightarrow \ \text{`mu'}\,(\text{`plus'}\,\text{`1'}\,\mathsf{vl})$$

$$\underline{\mathsf{let}} \ \frac{}{\mathsf{list} \ : \ \mathsf{Ucf}\,(\mathsf{suc}\,n)} \quad \mathsf{list} \ \Rightarrow \ \text{`mu'}\,(\text{`plus'}\,\text{`1'}\,(\text{`times'}\,(\mathsf{wk}\,\mathsf{vl})\,\mathsf{vl}))$$

$$\underline{\mathsf{let}} \ \frac{}{\mathsf{tree} \ : \ \mathsf{Ucf}\,(\mathsf{suc}\,n)}$$

$$\mathsf{tree} \ \Rightarrow \ \text{`mu'}\,(\text{`plus'}\,\text{`1'}\,(\text{`times'}\,\mathsf{vl}\,(\text{`times'}\,(\mathsf{wk}\,\mathsf{vl})\,\mathsf{vl})))$$

$$\underline{\mathsf{let}} \ \frac{}{\mathsf{rt} \ : \ \mathsf{Ucf}\,(\mathsf{suc}\,n)} \quad \mathsf{rt} \ \Rightarrow \ \text{`mu'}\,(\mathsf{def}\,\mathsf{list}\,(\text{`times'}\,(\mathsf{wk}\,\mathsf{vl})\,\mathsf{vl}))$$

While **nat** and **rt** are closed types and hence inhabit $\mathsf{Ucf}\,n$ for any $n \ : \ \mathsf{Nat}$, list is parametrized by the last type variable and hence inhabits $\mathsf{Ucf}\,(\mathsf{suc}\,n)$. We exploit this in the definition of rose trees where we construct rose trees as the initial algebra of list. Alternatively we can instantiate list to any type name using let, e.g. let list nat $: \ \mathsf{Ucf}\,n$ represents the type of lists of natural numbers.

4.2   Elements of Context-Free Types

How are we going to define the family of elements for Ucf? We have to take care of the free type variables. A first attempt would be to say that we have to interpret any type variable by a type, leading to the following signature[7] :

$$\frac{a \ : \ \mathsf{Ucf}\,n \quad Xs \ : \ \mathsf{Vec}\,n\,\star}{\mathsf{Elcf}\,a\,Xs \ : \ \star}$$

This approach works fine for the polynomial operators, which are interpreted as before, and the variables which correspond to projections; however, we run in difficulties for μ. Let's see why: A reasonable attempt is to say:

$$\frac{x \ : \ \mathsf{Elcf}\,f\,(\mathsf{vcons}\,(\mathsf{Elcf}\,(\text{`mu'}\,f)\,Xs)\,Xs)}{\mathsf{in}\,x \ : \ \mathsf{Elcf}\,(\text{`mu'}\,f)\,Xs}$$

---

[7] We are exploiting here $\star \ : \ \star$, however, this use can be stratified, i.e. if $Xs \ : \ \star_i$ then $\mathsf{Elcf}\,a\,Xs \ : \ \star_{i+1}$.

However, this definition is not accepted by Epigram's schema checker, since it is not able to verify that the nested occurrence of Elcf is only used in a strictly positive fashion. This check is necessary to keep Epigram's type system sound by avoiding potentially non-terminating programs.

However, if we restrict ourselves to interpreting only closed types, we can overcome this problem. We define the Elcf wrt to a *closing substitution* or telescope, which interprets any free type variable by a type name with fewer free variables. Hence we define the family of telescopes:

$$\text{data} \ \frac{n \ : \ \text{Nat}}{\text{Tel} \ n \ : \ \star} \ \text{where} \ \frac{}{\text{tnil} \ : \ \text{Tel zero}} \quad \frac{a \ : \ \text{Ucf} \ n \quad as \ : \ \text{Tel} \ n}{\text{tcons} \ a \ as \ : \ \text{Tel} \ (\text{suc} \ n)}$$

We can now define an interpretation for an open type together with a fitting telescope:

$$\text{data} \ \frac{a \ : \ \text{Ucf} \ n \quad as \ : \ \text{Tel} \ n}{\text{Elcf} \ a \ as \ : \ \star}$$

the constructors for the polynomial operators stay the same, only indexed with a telescope which is passed through:

$$\frac{b, a \ : \ \text{Ucf} \quad x \ : \ \text{Elcf} \ a \ as}{\text{inl} \ x \ : \ \text{Elcf} \ (\text{'plus'} \ a \ b) \ as} \quad \frac{a, b \ : \ \text{Ucf} \quad y \ : \ \text{Elcf} \ b \ as}{\text{inr} \ y \ : \ \text{Elcf} \ (\text{'plus'} \ a \ b) \ as}$$

$$\frac{}{\text{void} \ : \ \text{Elcf} \ \text{'1'} \ as} \quad \frac{x \ : \ \text{Elcf} \ a \quad y \ : \ \text{Elcf} \ b \ as}{\text{pair} \ x \ y \ : \ \text{Elcf} \ (\text{'times'} \ a \ b) \ as}$$

The interpretation of the last variable is simply the interpretation of the first type name in the telescope:

$$\frac{x \ : \ \text{Elcf} \ a \ as}{\text{top} \ x \ : \ \text{Elcf} \ \text{vl} \ (\text{tcons} \ a \ as)}$$

Meanwhile, the interpretation of a weakened type is given by popping off the first item of the telescope:

$$\frac{x \ : \ \text{Elcf} \ a \ as}{\text{pop} \ x \ : \ \text{Elcf} \ (\text{wk} \ a) \ (\text{tcons} \ b \ as)}$$

A local definition is explained by pushing the right hand side of the definition onto the telescope stack:

$$\frac{x \ : \ \text{Elcf} \ f \ (\text{tcons} \ a \ as)}{\text{push} \ x \ : \ \text{Elcf} \ (\text{def} \ f \ a) \ as}$$

We can finally reap the fruits of our syntactic approach by providing an interpretation of mu which doesn't require a nested use of Elcf:

$$\frac{x \ : \ \text{Elcf} \ f \ (\text{tcons} \ as \ (\text{'mu'} \ f))}{\text{in} \ x \ : \ \text{Elcf} \ (\text{'mu'} \ f) \ as}$$

We can now derive constructors for our encoded types and provide a derived case analysis using views. We show this in the case of nat and leave the other examples as an exercise.

We derive the constructors representing 0 and successor:

$$\underline{\text{let}} \quad \frac{}{\text{'zero'} : \text{Elcf nat } as} \quad \text{'zero'} \Rightarrow \text{in (inl void)}$$

$$\underline{\text{let}} \quad \frac{n : \text{Elcf nat } as}{\text{'suc' } n : \text{Elcf nat } as} \quad \text{'suc' } n \Rightarrow \text{in (inr (top } n))$$

Our view is that all elements of Elcf nat are constructed by one of the constructors, this is expressed by the family NatView:

$$\underline{\text{data}} \quad \frac{n : \text{Elcf nat } as}{\text{NatView } n : \star}$$

$$\underline{\text{where}} \quad \frac{}{\text{isZ} : \text{NatView 'zero'}} \quad \frac{n : \text{Elcf nat } as}{\text{isS } n : \text{NatView ('suc' } n)}$$

We show that NatView is exhaustive:

$$\underline{\text{let}} \quad \frac{n : \text{Elcf nat } as}{\text{natView } n : \text{NatView } n}$$

$$\begin{aligned}
\text{natView } n &\Leftarrow \underline{\text{case}} \, n \\
\text{natView (in } x) &\Leftarrow \underline{\text{case}} \, x \\
\text{natView (in (inl } x)) &\Leftarrow \underline{\text{case}} \, x \\
\text{natView (in (inl void))} &\Rightarrow \text{isZ} \\
\text{natView (in (inr } y)) &\Leftarrow \underline{\text{case}} \, y \\
\text{natView (in (inr (top } n'))) &\Rightarrow \text{isS } n'
\end{aligned}$$

We can now use the derived pattern matching principle to implement functions over the encoded natural numbers:

$$\underline{\text{let}} \quad \frac{m, n : \text{Elcf nat } as}{\text{'add' } m \, n : \text{Elcf nat } as}$$

$$\begin{aligned}
\text{'add' } m \, n &\Leftarrow \underline{\text{rec}} \, m \\
\text{'add' } m \, n &\Leftarrow \underline{\text{view}} \, \text{natView } m \\
\text{'add' (in (inl void)) } n &\Rightarrow n \\
\text{'add' (in (inr (top } m'))) \, n &\Rightarrow \text{in (inr (top ('add' } m' \, n)))
\end{aligned}$$

Unfortunately, Epigram always normalizes terms which appear in patterns, expanding 'zero' and 'suc', which makes the pattern not very readable.

Note that we don't need to derive a new recursion principle since structural recursion over the encoded natural numbers is the same as structural recursion over the natural numbers.

A natural question is whether we should have to distinguish between *encoded natural numbers* and *natural numbers* at all. The answer is clearly **no**, since they are isomorphic anyway. To exploit this fact and avoid unnecessary duplication of definitions we need to build in a reflection mechanism into Epigram which allows us to access the names of the top level universe as data.

Exercise 6. Define a pattern matching principle for lists, that is first define 'constructors'

$$\underline{\text{let}} \quad \frac{}{\text{`nil'} : \text{Elcf list } X}$$

$$\underline{\text{let}} \quad \frac{x : \text{Elcf } a \text{ } as \quad xs : \text{Elcf list } (\text{tcons } a \text{ } as)}{\text{`cons'} \text{ } x \text{ } xs : \text{Elcf list } (\text{tcons } a \text{ } as)}$$

and then create an appropriate view, following the nat example. Consider how to do this for rose trees.

The *typical* generic operation on context-free types is generic equality. We can implement generic equality ($\geq$) by structural recursion over the elements in Elcf.

The algorithm is completely data-driven — indeed we never inspect the type. However, using the type information, the choice of the first argument limits the possible cases for the 2nd. This is what dependently typed pattern matching buys us, that it records the consequences of choices we have already made.

$$\underline{\text{let}} \quad \frac{x, y : \text{Elcf } a \text{ } as}{\text{geq } x \text{ } y : \text{Bool}}$$

```
geq x y  ⇐  rec x
 geq x y  ⇐  case x
   geq (inl xa) y  ⇐  case y
     geq (inl xa) (inl ya)  ⇒  geq xa ya
     geq (inl xa) (inr yb)  ⇒  false
   geq (inr xb) y  ⇐  case y
     geq (inr xb) (inl ya)  ⇒  false
     geq (inr a) (inr yb)  ⇒  geq xb yb
   geq void y  ⇐  case y
     geq void void  ⇒  true
   geq (pair xa xb) y  ⇐  case y
     geq (pair xa xb) (pair ya yb)  ⇒  and (geq xa ya) (geq xb yb)
   geq (top x) y  ⇐  case y
     geq (top x) (top y)  ⇒  geq x y
   geq (pop x) y  ⇐  case y
     geq (pop x) (pop y)  ⇒  geq x y
   geq (push x) y  ⇐  case y
     geq (push x) (push y)  ⇒  geq x y
   geq (in x) y  ⇐  case y
     geq (in x) (in y)  ⇒  geq x y
```

Note that we don't have to assume that the equality of type parameters is decidable. This is due to the fact that we only derive generic operations for closed types here.

Exercise 7. Instead of just returning a boolean we can actually show that we can decide equality of elements of Elcf. We say that a type is **decided**, if it can be established whether it is empty or inhabited. This is reflected by the following definition:

$$\underline{\text{let}}\ \frac{A\ :\ \star}{\text{Not}\ A\ :\ \star}\qquad \text{Not}\ A\ \Rightarrow\ A\ \rightarrow\ \text{Zero}$$

$$\underline{\text{data}}\ \frac{A\ :\ \star}{\text{Dec}\ A\ :\ \star}\ \underline{\text{where}}\ \frac{a\ :\ A}{\text{yes}\ a\ :\ \text{Dec}\ A}\qquad \frac{f\ :\ \text{Not}\ A}{\text{no}\ f\ :\ \text{Dec}\ A}$$

Here Zero is Epigram's built in empty type, establishing a function of type $\text{Not}\,A$, i.e. $A \rightarrow \text{Zero}$ establishes that A is uninhabited.

To show that equality for context-free types is decidable we have to implement:

$$\underline{\text{let}}\ \frac{x, y\ :\ \text{Elcf}\ a\ as}{\text{geqdec}\ x\ y\ :\ \text{Dec}\ (x = y)}$$

geqdec is a non-trivial refinement of geq using Epigram's type system to show that the implementation of the program delivers what its name promises.

4.3 Strictly Positive Types

Context-free types capture most of the types which are useful in daily functional programming. However, in some situations we want to use trees which are infinitely branching. E.g. we may want to define a system of ordinal notations, which extends natural numbers by the possibility to form the limit, i.e. the least upper bound, of an infinite sequence of ordinals.

$$\underline{\text{data}}\ \frac{}{\text{Ord}\ :\ \star}\ \underline{\text{where}}\ \frac{}{\text{oz}\ :\ \text{Ord}}\qquad \frac{a\ :\ \text{Ord}}{\text{os}\ a\ :\ \text{Ord}}\qquad \frac{f\ :\ \text{Nat} \rightarrow \text{Ord}}{\text{olim}\ f\ :\ \text{Ord}}$$

We can embed the natural numbers into the ordinals:

$$\underline{\text{let}}\ \frac{n\ :\ \text{Nat}}{\text{o2n}\ n\ :\ \star}$$

$$
\begin{aligned}
&\text{n2o}\ n\ \Leftarrow\ \underline{\text{rec}}\ n\\
&\text{n2o}\ n\ \Leftarrow\ \underline{\text{case}}\ n\\
&\text{n2o}\ \text{zero}\ \Rightarrow\ \text{oz}\\
&\text{n2o}\ (\text{suc}\ n)\ \Rightarrow\ \text{os}\ (\text{n2o}\ n)
\end{aligned}
$$

and using this embedding we define the first infinite ordinal (ω) as the limit of the sequence of all natural numbers:

$$\underline{\text{let}}\ \frac{}{\text{omega}\ :\ \text{Ord}}\qquad \text{omega}\ \Rightarrow\ \text{olim}\ \text{n2o}$$

We can also do arithmetic on ordinals, using structural recursion we define addition[8] of ordinals:

$$\text{let } \frac{a, b \ : \ \mathsf{Ord}}{\mathbf{oplus} \ a \ b \ : \ \mathsf{Ord}}$$

$$\mathbf{oplus} \ a \ b \ \Leftarrow \ \underline{\mathrm{rec}} \ b$$
$$\mathbf{oplus} \ a \ b \ \Leftarrow \ \underline{\mathrm{case}} \ b$$
$$\mathbf{oplus} \ a \ \mathsf{oz} \ \Rightarrow \ a$$
$$\mathbf{oplus} \ a \ (\mathsf{os} \ b) \ \Rightarrow \ \mathsf{os} \ (\mathbf{oplus} \ a \ b)$$
$$\mathbf{oplus} \ a \ (\mathsf{olim} \ f) \ \Rightarrow \ \mathsf{olim} \ (\lambda n \ \Rightarrow \ \mathbf{oplus} \ a \ (f \ n))$$

Categorically, Ord is an initial algebra $\mu X.1 + X + \mathsf{Nat} \to X$, it is an instance of a *strictly positive type*. Strictly positive types may use function types, like in $\mathsf{Nat} \to X$ but we do not allow type variables to appear on the left-hand side of the arrow. I.e. $\mu X.X \to \mathsf{Bool}$ is not strictly positive because X appears negatively, but neither is $\mu X.(X \to \mathsf{Bool}) \to \mathsf{Bool}$ because X appears positively but not strictly positive.

We introduce the universe of strictly positive types by amending the universe of context-free types. That is we define

$$\mathbf{data} \ \frac{n \ : \ \mathsf{Nat}}{\mathsf{Usp} \ n \ : \ \star}$$

$$\mathbf{data} \ \frac{a \ : \ \mathsf{Usp} \ n \quad as \ : \ \mathsf{Tel} \ n}{\mathsf{Elsp} \ a \ as \ : \ \star}$$

with all the same constructors as Ucf and Elcf and additionally a constructor for constant exponentiation:

$$\frac{A \ : \ \star \quad b \ : \ \mathsf{Usp} \ n}{\text{'arr'} \ A \ b \ : \ \mathsf{Usp} \ n}$$

and a corresponding constructor for Elsp:

$$\frac{f \ : \ A \to \mathsf{Elsp} \ b \ as}{\mathbf{fun} \ f \ : \ \mathsf{Elsp} \ (\text{'arr'} \ A \ b) \ as}$$

It is now easy to represent ordinals in this universe:

$$\text{let } \frac{}{\mathsf{ord} \ : \ \mathsf{Usp} \ n} \quad \mathsf{ord} \ \Rightarrow \ \text{'mu'} \ (\text{'plus'} \ \text{'1'} \ (\text{'plus'} \ \mathsf{vl} \ (\text{'arr'} \ \mathsf{Nat} \ \mathsf{vl})))$$

We have been cheating a bit, because the constructor 'arr' refers to a type. Thus $\mathsf{Usp} \ n \ : \ \star_{i+1}$ if $A \ : \ \star_i$ in 'arr' $A \ b$. An alternative would be to insist that

---

[8] To reflect the standard definition of ordinal addition we **have** to recur on the 2nd argument. Ordinal addition is not commutative, $\omega + 1$ denotes the successor of ω, while $1 + \omega$ is order-isomorphic to ω.

the codomain of 'arr' is a closed strictly positive type, but this causes problems when introducing fun because of a negative occurrence of Elsp.

Exercise 8. Derive the constructors for ord : Usp n and a view which allows pattern matching over ord. Use this to define ordinal addition for the encoded ordinals.

4.4   Generic Map

We don't know many useful generic operations which apply to closed strictly positive types, but there is an important one for open ones: generic map. While we have given only an interpretation for closed types we are able to express generic map by introducing maps between telescopes.

We introduce a family representing maps between telescopes, which correspond to a sequence of maps between the components of the telescopes:

$$\underline{\text{data}} \ \frac{as, bs \ : \ \text{Tel} \ n}{\text{Map} \ as \ bs \ : \ \star}$$

and generic map simply lifts maps on telescope to a function between the element of a type instantiated with the telescopes:

$$\underline{\text{let}} \ \frac{fs \ : \ \text{Map} \ as \ bs \quad x \ : \ \text{Elsp} \ a \ as}{\text{gmap} \ fs \ x \ : \ \text{Elsp} \ a \ bs}$$

What are the constructors for Map? There are two obvious ones, which correspond to the idea that Map as bs is simply a sequence of maps between the components of as and bs:

$$\frac{}{\text{mnil} \ : \ \text{Map tnil tnil}} \qquad \frac{f \ : \ \text{Elsp} \ a \ as \rightarrow \text{Elsp} \ b \ bs \quad fs \ : \ \text{Map} \ as \ bs}{\text{mcons} \ f \ fs \ : \ \text{Map} \ (\text{tcons} \ a \ as) \ (\text{tcons} \ b \ bs)}$$

However, it is useful to introduce a 3rd constructor, which extends a given sequence of maps by the identity function:

$$\frac{fs \ : \ \text{Map} \ as \ bs}{\text{mext} \ fs \ : \ \text{Map} \ (\text{tcons} \ a \ as) \ (\text{tcons} \ a \ bs)}$$

Note that mext fs isn't just mcons $(\lambda x \Rightarrow x) \ fs$ because instead of the identity we need a function of the type Elsp a $as \rightarrow$ Elsp a bs. It would be possible to define mext mutually with gmap but it is much easier to introduce an additional constructor which also keeps the program structural recursive.

The definition of gmap is now rather straightforward by structural recursion on the argument:

$$
\begin{aligned}
&\text{gmap } fs\ x \ \Leftarrow\ \underline{\text{rec }} x \\
&\text{gmap } fs\ x \ \Leftarrow\ \underline{\text{case }} x \\
&\quad \text{gmap } fs\ (\text{inl } x) \ \Rightarrow\ \text{inl } (\text{gmap } fs\ x) \\
&\quad \text{gmap } fs\ (\text{inr } y) \ \Rightarrow\ \text{inr } (\text{gmap } fs\ y) \\
&\quad \text{gmap } fs\ \text{void} \ \Rightarrow\ \text{void} \\
&\quad \text{gmap } fs\ (\text{pair } x\ y) \ \Rightarrow\ \text{pair } (\text{gmap } fs\ x)\ (\text{gmap } fs\ y) \\
&\quad \text{gmap } fs\ (\text{fun } f) \ \Rightarrow\ \text{fun } (\lambda x \ \Rightarrow\ \text{gmap } fs\ (f\ x)) \\
&\quad \text{gmap } fs\ (\text{top } x) \ \Leftarrow\ \underline{\text{case }} fs \\
&\quad\quad \text{gmap } (\text{mcons } f\ fs)\ (\text{top } x) \ \Rightarrow\ \text{top } (f\ x) \\
&\quad\quad \text{gmap } (\text{mext } fs)\ (\text{top } x) \ \Rightarrow\ \text{top } (\text{gmap } fs\ x) \\
&\quad \text{gmap } fs\ (\text{pop } x) \ \Leftarrow\ \underline{\text{case }} fs \\
&\quad\quad \text{gmap } (\text{mcons } f\ fs)\ (\text{pop } x) \ \Rightarrow\ \text{pop } (\text{gmap } fs\ x) \\
&\quad\quad \text{gmap } (\text{mext } fs)\ (\text{pop } x) \ \Rightarrow\ \text{pop } (\text{gmap } fs\ x) \\
&\quad \text{gmap } fs\ (\text{push } x) \ \Rightarrow\ \text{push } (\text{gmap } (\text{mext } fs)\ x) \\
&\quad \text{gmap } fs\ (\text{in } x) \ \Rightarrow\ \text{in } (\text{gmap } (\text{mext } fs)\ x)
\end{aligned}
$$

The cases for the proper data constructors (inl, inr, void, pair, fun and in) are standard and just push gmap under the constructor. The other cases deal with the environment: top and pop have to analyse whether the environment has been constructed using mcons or mext while in the line for push we can reap the fruits by using mext instead having to use a non-structural recursive call to gmap.

As before in the case of geq the program is data-driven, i.e. we never have to inspect the type. However, the type-discipline helps us to find the right definition, which in many cases is the only possible one.

Exercise 9. Instantiate, gmap for list:

$$
\underline{\text{let }} \ \frac{}{\text{list : Usp (suc } n)} \quad \text{list} \ \Rightarrow\ \text{'mu' ('plus' '1' ('times' (wk vl) vl))}
$$

to obtain

$$
\underline{\text{let }} \ \frac{f \ : \ \text{Elsp } a\ as \rightarrow \text{Elsp } b\ as \quad xs \ : \ \text{Elsp list (tcons } a\ as)}{\text{map } f\ xs \ : \ \text{Elsp list (tcons } b\ as)}
$$

4.5 Relating Universes

In the previous section we have incrementally defined three universes, each one extending the previous one together with a *typical* generic operation:

	universe of	inhabited by	generic operation
Ufin	finite types	Booleans (bool)	Enumeration (enum)
Ucf	context-free types	Rose trees (rt)	Equality (geq)
Usp	strictly positive types	Ordinals (ord)	Map (gmap)

We could have factored out the common parts of the definitions and established that every universe can be embedded into the next one but for pedagogical reasons we chose the incremental style of presentation. We note that the generic operations are typical for a given universe because they do not extend to the next level, i.e. enumeration doesn't work for context-free types because they contain types with an infinite number of elements; equality doesn't work for strictly positive types because equality here is in general undecidable (e.g. for ordinals).

Are there any important universes we have left out? Between Ufin and Ucf we can find the universe of regular types, i.e. types which are represented as regular expressions, where the datatype of lists plays the role of Kleene's star. Another possibility is to also allow coinductive context-free types like streams by including codes for terminal coalgebras, e.g. $\text{Stream}\, X = \nu X.A \times X$. However, this doesn't fit very well with our way to define El inductively.

What about the universe of positive types extending the strictly positive types? It is unclear how to understand a type like $\mu X.(X \to \text{Bool}) \to \text{Bool}$[9] intuitively and there seem to be only very limited applications of positive inductive types. However, for gmap it is sensible to allow parameters in non-strict positive positions without closing under μ.

4.6   Universes and Representation Types

There is a very strong connection between the notion of universe in Type Theory and the more recent notion of *representation type* which has emerged from work on type analysis [18] to become a popular basis for generic programming in Haskell [24,23,41]. The two notions are both standard ways to give a data representation to a collection of things, in this case, types:

- Martin-Löf's universes (U, El) collect types as the *image of a function* $El :$ $U \to \star$. Elements of U may thus be treated as proxies for the types to which they map.
- Representation types characterise a collection of types as a *predicate*, Rep : $\star \to \star$. An element of Rep T is a *proof* that T is in the collection, and it is also a piece of data from which one may compute.

The former approach is not possible in Haskell, because $U \to \star$ is not expressible when U is a type rather than a 'kind'. However, the latter has become possible, thanks to the recent extension of (ghc) Haskell with a type-indexed variant of inductive families [19], the so-called 'Generalized Algebraic Data Types' [39]. For example, one might define a universe of regular expression types as follows

```
data Rep a where
  Char  :: Rep Char
  Unit  :: Rep ()
  Pair  :: Rep a -> Rep b -> Rep (a,b)
```

---

[9] Note that $(X \to \text{Bool}) \to \text{Bool}$ is covariant, unlike $X \to \text{Bool} \times \text{Bool}$ which is contravariant.

```
Either :: Rep a -> Reb b -> Rep (Either a b)
List   :: Rep a -> Rep [a]
```

and then write a function generic with respect to this universe by pattern-matching on Rep, always making sure to keep the type representative to the left of the data which indirectly depends on it:

```
string :: Rep a -> a -> String
string Char            c          = [c]
string Unit            ()         = ""
string (Pair a b)      (x, y)     = string a x ++ string b y
string (Either a b)    (Left x)   = string a x
string (Either a b)    (Right y)  = string b y
string (List a)        xs         = xs >>= string a
```

Of course, in Epigram, these two kinds of collection are readily interchangeable. Given U and El, we may readily construct the predicate for 'being in the image of El':

$$\text{Rep } X \;\Rightarrow\; \text{Sigma } U \;(\lambda u \Rightarrow El\ u = X)$$

In the other direction, given some Rep, we may 'name' a type as the dependent pair of the type itself and its representation: we interpret such a pair by projecting out the type!

$$\mathbf{U} \Rightarrow \text{Sigma} \star (\lambda X \Rightarrow Rep\ X)$$
$$\mathbf{El} \Rightarrow \text{fst}$$

One can simulate this to some extent in Haskell by means of *existential* types

```
data U = forall a. U (Rep a)
```

and thus provide a means to compute one type from another—some sort of auxiliary data structure, perhaps—by writing a function aux :: U -> U. For example, aux might compute the notion of 'one-hole context' appropriate to its argument, in an attempt to support generic structure editing. Unfortunately, U is not a Sigma type but a System F 'weak' existential: direct access to the type it packages is not possible. There is no way to express operations whose types explicitly invoke these functions, e.g., plugging a value into a one-hole context to recover an element of the original type.

System F's capacity for secrecy is rather useful in other circumstances, but it is a problem here. The nearest we can get to El is a rank-2 accessor which grants *temporary* access to the witness to facilitate a computation whose type does not depend on it.

```
for :: U -> (forall a. Rep a -> b) -> b
```

This problem is not the fault of representation types as opposed to universes (although the latter are a little neater for such tasks): it's just a shortfall in the expressivity of Haskell.

5   Containers

In section 3 we started with a semantic definition of the universe of finite types, while in the previous section we introduced universes syntactically, i.e. using inductive definitions. In the present section we will exploit our work on container types to give a semantic interpretation of the universe of context-free types which also works for strictly positive types. It is good to have both views of the universes available, we have seen that the inductive approach is very practical to define generic and non-generic operations on data. However, the semantic approach we introduce here often provides an alternative approach to defining generic functions semantically. We will demonstrate this in more detail in the next section using the example of derivatives of datatypes. Another advantage of the semantic view is that it allows us to interpret open datatypes directly as operations on types, e.g. we can apply list to types which don't have a name in our universe.

5.1   Unary Containers

Before embarking on the more general concept of n-ary containers, which as we will see can model exactly the universe of strictly positive types, we have a look at unary containers, which model type constructors with one parameter, i.e. inhabitants of $\star \to \star$, where the parameter represents a type of *payload* elements to be stored within some structure. A unary container is given by a type of shapes $S : \star$ and a family of positions $P : S \to \star$. I.e. we define:

$$\underline{\text{data}} \quad \overline{\text{UCont} : \star}$$

$$\underline{\text{where}} \quad \frac{S : \star \quad P : S \to \star}{\text{ucont}\, S\, P : \text{UCont}}$$

We illustrate containers with *triangle diagrams*, intended to resemble a node in a tree with its root at the left. As with W-types, we indicate a choice of shape in the apex, and the base then represents a *set* of points, dependent on the shape; the arrow at the top of the base indicates that the points in this set are positions for payload.

The *extension* of a container is the parametric datatype which it describes: its values consist of a choice of shape and an assignment of payload to positions, represented functionally.

$$\underline{\text{data}} \quad \frac{C : \text{UCont} \quad X : \star}{\text{UExt}\, C\, X : \star}$$

$$\underline{\text{where}} \quad \frac{s : S \quad f : P\, s \to X}{\text{uext}\, s\, f : \text{UExt}\, (\text{ucont}\, S\, P)\, X}$$

We can also illustrate inhabitants of such a type by a diagram, labelling the base with the function f which takes each position p to some payload value x.

An example of a unary container is this representation of List:

$$\text{let } \frac{}{\text{cList : UCont}} \quad \text{cList} \Rightarrow \text{ucont Nat Fin}$$

The shape of a list is its length, i.e. a natural number, and a list with shape n : Nat has Fin n positions. We can re-implement the constructors for lists to target the container representation

$$\text{let } \frac{i \,:\, \text{Fin zero}}{\text{noFin } i \,:\, X} \quad \text{noFin } i \Leftarrow \underline{\text{case}} \; i$$

$$\text{let } \frac{}{\text{cnil : UExt cList } X} \quad \text{cnil} \Rightarrow \text{uext zero noFin}$$

$$\text{let } \frac{x \,:\, X \quad f \,:\, \text{Fin } n \to X \quad i \,:\, \text{Fin (suc } n)}{\text{caseFin } x \, f \, i \,:\, X}$$

caseFin $x \, f \, i \Leftarrow \underline{\text{case}} \; i$
caseFin $x \, f \, \text{fz} \Rightarrow x$
caseFin $x \, f \, (\text{fs } i) \Rightarrow f \, i$

$$\text{let } \frac{x \,:\, X \quad xs \,:\, \text{UExt cList } X}{\text{ccons } x \, xs \,:\, \text{UExt cList } X}$$

ccons $x \, xs \Leftarrow \underline{\text{case}} \; xs$
ccons $x \, (\text{uext } n \, f) \Rightarrow \text{uext (suc } n) \, (\text{caseFin } x \, f)$

Exercise 10. We can also give a container representation for binary trees, here shapes are given by trees containing data, positions by paths through such a tree:

$$\text{data } \frac{}{\text{cTreeS : } \star} \quad \text{where} \quad \frac{}{\text{sleaf : cTreeS}} \quad \frac{l, r \,:\, \text{cTreeS}}{\text{snode } l \, r \,:\, \text{cTreeS}}$$

$$\text{data } \frac{s \,:\, \text{cTreeS}}{\text{cTreeP } s \,:\, \text{Type}} \quad \text{where} \quad \frac{}{\text{phere : cTreeP (node } l \, r)}$$

$$\frac{q \,:\, \text{cTreeP } l}{\text{pleft } q \,:\, \text{cTreeP (node } l \, r)} \quad \frac{p \,:\, \text{cTreeP } r}{\text{pright } p \,:\, \text{cTreeP (node } l \, r)}$$

$$\text{let } \frac{}{\text{cTree : UCont}} \quad \text{cTree} \Rightarrow \text{uext cTreeS cTreeP}$$

Implement leaf and node for cTree:

$$\text{let } \frac{}{\text{cleaf} : \text{UExt cTree } X}$$

$$\text{let } \frac{r : \text{UExt cTree } X \quad x : X \quad r : \text{UExt cTree } X}{\text{cnode } l \, x \, r : \text{UExt cTree } X}$$

Each container gives rise to a functor. We can implement map for unary containers by applying the function to be mapped directly to the payload:

$$\text{let } \frac{C : \text{UCont} \quad f : X \to Y \quad c : \text{UExt } C \, X}{\text{ucmap } C \, f \, c : \text{UExt } C \, Y}$$

$$\text{ucmap } C \, f \, c \; \Leftarrow \; \underline{\text{case}} \; c$$
$$\text{ucmap (ucont } S \, P) \, f \, (\text{uext } s \, g) \; \Rightarrow \; \text{uext } s \, (\lambda x \Rightarrow f \, (g \, x))$$

A morphism between functors is a natural transformation, e.g. *reverse* is a natural transformation from list to list. We can explicitly represent morphisms between containers: given unary containers ucont $S \, P$ and ucont $T \, Q$, a morphism is a function on shapes $f : S \to T$ and a family of functions on positions, which assigns to every position in the target a position in the source, i.e.

$$u : \forall s{:}S \Rightarrow Q \, (f \, s) \to P \, s$$

The contravariance of the function on positions may be surprising, however, it can be intuitively understood by the fact that we can always say where a piece of payload comes from but not where it goes to, since it may be copied or disappear. Hence we define:

$$\underline{\text{data}} \; \frac{C, D : \text{UCont}}{\text{UMor } C \, D : \star} \quad \underline{\text{where}} \quad \frac{f : S \to T \quad u : \forall s{:}S \Rightarrow Q \, (f \, s) \to P \, s}{\text{umor } f \, u : \text{UMor (ucont } S \, P) \, (\text{ucont } T \, Q)}$$

To every formal morphism between containers we assign a family of maps, parametric in the payload type:

$$\text{let } \frac{m : \text{UMor } C \, D \quad c : \text{UExt } C \, X}{\text{UMapp } m \, c : \text{UExt } D \, X}$$

$$\text{UMapp } m \, c \; \Leftarrow \; \underline{\text{case}} \; m$$
$$\text{UMapp (umor } f \, u) \, c \; \Leftarrow \; \underline{\text{case}} \; c$$
$$\text{UMapp (umor } f \, u) \, (\text{uext } s \, g) \; \Rightarrow$$
$$\text{uext } (f \, s) \, (\lambda q \Rightarrow g \, (u \, s \, q))$$

As an example we can define cHead for the container representation of lists, since we require totality we will define a morphism between cList and cMaybe, which relates to Haskell's `Maybe` type:

$$\text{let } \frac{}{\text{cMaybe} : \text{UCont}} \quad \text{cMaybe} \Rightarrow \text{ucont Bool So}$$

There are two possible layouts for cMaybe containers:

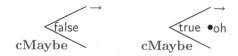

There are then two cases to consider when defining our morphism. For the zero shape of cList, we choose the false shape of cMaybe, leaving no positions to fill. For any other input shape, we choose true, leaving one position to fill: we fetch its payload from input position fz—the head.

$\underline{\text{let}}$ $\dfrac{n\ :\ \text{Nat}}{\text{isSuc}\ :\ \text{Bool}}$

isSuc n $\Leftarrow$ $\underline{\text{case}}$ n
isSuc zero $\Rightarrow$ false
isSuc (suc n) $\Rightarrow$ true

$\underline{\text{let}}$ $\dfrac{n\ :\ \text{Nat}\quad q\ :\ \text{So}\,(\text{isSuc}\ n)}{\text{least}\ n\ q\ :\ \text{Fin}\ n}$

least n q $\Leftarrow$ $\underline{\text{case}}$ n
least zero q $\Leftarrow$ $\underline{\text{case}}$ q
least (suc n) q $\Rightarrow$ fz

$\underline{\text{let}}$ $\dfrac{}{\text{cHead}\ :\ \text{UMor cList cMaybe}}$

cHead $\Rightarrow$ umor isSuc least

We illustrate these two cases as follows:

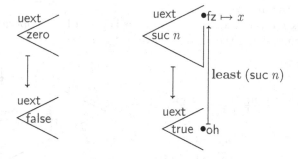

It is not hard to show that these families of maps are always natural transformations in the categorical sense, with respect to UExt's interpretation of unary containers as functors. Indeed, it turns out that all natural transformations between functors arising from containers can be given as container morphisms, see theorem 3.4. in [2].

Exercise 11. Give the representation of *reverse* as morphism between unary containers, i.e.

$\underline{\text{let}}$ $\dfrac{}{\text{cRev}\ :\ \text{UMor cList cList}}$

Exercise 12. While the interpretation of morphisms is full, i.e. every natural transformation comes from a container morphism, the same is not true for containers as representations of functors. Can you find a functor which is not representable as a unary container?

5.2 n-ary Containers

We are now going to interpret strictly positive types Usp as containers by implementing operations on containers which correspond to constructors of Usp. We reap the fruits by defining a simple evaluation function which evalC which interprets Usps as containers. First of all we have to generalize our previous definition to n-ary containers to reflect the presence of variables in Usp:

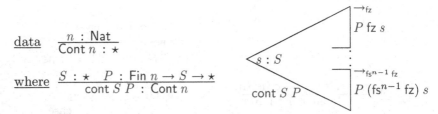

$$\underline{\text{data}} \quad \frac{n \ : \ \mathsf{Nat}}{\mathsf{Cont}\ n \ : \ \star}$$

$$\underline{\text{where}} \quad \frac{S \ : \ \star \quad P \ : \ \mathsf{Fin}\ n \to S \to \star}{\mathsf{cont}\ S\ P \ : \ \mathsf{Cont}\ n}$$

It is important to understand that we use only one shape but n sets of positions. E.g. consider the two-parameter container of leaf and node labelled trees, the shape of a tree is given by ignoring the data, but the positions for leaf-data and node-data are different. Accordingly, in our diagrams, we may segment the base of the triangle to separate the surfaces where each sort of payload attaches and we index the arrows accordingly.

The extension of an n-ary container is given by an operator on a sequence of types, generalizing the sketch above to the n-ary case:

$$\underline{\text{data}} \quad \frac{C \ : \ \mathsf{Cont}\ n \quad Xs \ : \ \mathsf{Fin}\ n \to \star}{\mathsf{Ext}\ C\ Xs \ : \ \star}$$

$$\underline{\text{where}} \quad \frac{P \ : \ \mathsf{Fin}\ n \to S \to \star \quad Xs \ : \ \mathsf{Fin}\ n \to \star}{s \ : \ S \quad f \ : \ \forall i{:}\mathsf{Fin}\ n \Rightarrow P\ i\ s \to Xs\ i}{\mathsf{ext}\ s\ f \ : \ \mathsf{Ext}\ (\mathsf{cont}\ S\ P)\ Xs}$$

Exercise 13. Show that n-ary containers give rise to n-ary functors, i.e. implement:

$$\underline{\text{let}} \quad \frac{C \ : \ \mathsf{Cont}\ n \quad Xs, Ys \ : \ \mathsf{Fin}\ n \to \star}{fs \ : \ \forall i{:}\mathsf{Fin}\ n \Rightarrow Xs\ i \to Ys\ i \quad x \ : \ \mathsf{Ext}\ C\ Xs}{\mathsf{map}\ C\ fs\ x \ : \ \mathsf{Ext}\ C\ Ys}$$

5.3   Coproducts and Products

A constant operator is represented by a container which has no positions, e.g. the following containers represent the empty and the unit type:

$\underline{\text{let}}$ $\dfrac{}{\text{cZero : Cont } n}$ $\text{cZero} \Rightarrow \text{cont Zero } (\lambda i; s \Rightarrow \text{Zero})$

$\underline{\text{let}}$ $\dfrac{}{\text{cOne : Cont } n}$ $\text{cOne} \Rightarrow \text{cont One } (\lambda i; s \Rightarrow \text{Zero})$

Given two containers $C = \text{cont} S\,P, D = \text{cont} T\,Q$ we construct their coproduct or sum, representing a choice between C and D. On the shapes this is just the type-theoretic coproduct $\text{Plus } S\ T$ as defined earlier. What is a position in $\text{Plus } S\ T$? If our shape is of the form $\text{Inl } s$ then it is given by $P\ s$, on the other hand if it is of the form $\text{Inr } t$ then it is given by $Q\ t$. Abstracting shapes and positions, we arrive at:

$\underline{\text{data}}$ $\dfrac{P\ :\ A \to \star \quad Q\ :\ B \to \star \quad ab\ :\ \text{Plus } A\ B}{\text{PPlus } P\ Q\ ab\ :\ \star}$

$\underline{\text{where}}$ $\dfrac{p\ :\ P\ a}{\text{pinl } p\ :\ \text{PPlus } P\ Q\ (\text{Inl } a)}$ $\quad$ $\dfrac{q\ :\ Q\ b}{\text{pinr } q\ :\ \text{PPlus } P\ Q\ (\text{Inr } b)}$

Putting everything together we define the containers as follows, with the two typical layouts shown in the diagrams:

$\underline{\text{let}}$ $\dfrac{C, D\ :\ \text{Cont } n}{\text{cPlus } C\ D\ :\ \text{Cont } n}$

$\text{cPlus } C\ D \Leftarrow \underline{\text{case}}\ C$
$\quad \text{cPlus } (\text{cont } S\ P)\ D \Leftarrow \underline{\text{case}}\ D$
$\quad \text{cPlus } (\text{cont } S\ P)\ (\text{cont } T\ Q)$
$\qquad \Rightarrow \text{cont } (\text{Plus } S\ T)$
$\qquad\quad (\lambda i \Rightarrow \text{PPlus } (P\ i)\ (Q\ i))$

pinl $(p : P\ i\ s)$

pinr $(q : Q\ i\ t)$

Let's turn our attention to products: on shapes again this is just the type-theoretic product, Times—each component has a shape. Given two containers $C = \text{cont } S\ P, D = \text{cont } T\ Q$, as above, what are the positions in a product shape $\text{Pair } s\ t\ :\ \text{Times } S\ T$? There are two possibilities: either the position is in the left component, then it is given by $P\ s$ or it is in the right component then it is given by $Q\ t$. Abstracting shapes and positions again we define abstractly:

$\underline{\text{data}}$ $\dfrac{P\ :\ A \to \star \quad Q\ :\ B \to \star \quad ab\ :\ \text{Times } A\ B}{\text{PTimes } P\ Q\ ab\ :\ \star}$ $\underline{\text{where}}$

$\dfrac{p\ :\ P\ a}{\text{pleft } p\ :\ \text{PTimes } P\ Q\ (\text{Pair } a\ b)}$ $\quad$ $\dfrac{q\ :\ Q\ b}{\text{pright } q\ :\ \text{PTimes } P\ Q\ (\text{Pair } a\ b)}$

and we define the product of containers as:

$$\underline{\text{let}} \ \frac{C, D \ : \ \mathsf{Cont} \ n}{\mathbf{cTimes} \ C \ D \ : \ \mathsf{Cont} \ n}$$

$$\mathbf{cTimes} \ C \ D \ \Leftarrow \ \underline{\text{case}} \ C$$
$$\mathbf{cTimes} \ (\mathsf{cont} \ S \ P) \ D \ \Leftarrow \ \underline{\text{case}} \ D$$
$$\mathbf{cTimes} \ (\mathsf{cont} \ S \ P) \ (\mathsf{cont} \ T \ Q)$$
$$\Rightarrow \ \mathsf{cont} \ (\mathsf{Times} \ S \ T)$$
$$(\lambda i \Rightarrow \mathsf{PTimes} \ (P \ i) \ (Q \ i))$$

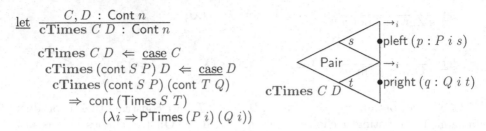

Exercise 14. Define an operation on containers which interprets constant exponentation as described in section 4.3, i.e. define

$$\underline{\text{let}} \ \frac{A \ : \ \star \quad C \ : \ \mathsf{Cont} \ n}{\mathbf{cArr} \ A \ C \ : \ \mathsf{Cont} \ n}$$

5.4   Structural Operations

If we want to interpret the universe of context-free or strictly positive types faithfully, we also have to find counterparts for the structural operation vl (last variable), wk (weakening) and def (local definition).

The interpretation of vl is straightforward: There is only one shape and in the family of positions $P \ : \ \mathsf{Fin} \ (\mathsf{suc} \ n)$ there is only one position at index fz:

$$\underline{\text{let}} \ \frac{}{\mathbf{cvl} \ : \ \mathsf{Cont} \ (\mathsf{suc} \ n)}$$
$$\mathbf{cvl} \ \Rightarrow \ \mathsf{cont} \ \mathsf{One} \ (\lambda i; s \Rightarrow i = \mathsf{fz})$$

Weakening isn't much harder: the shape stays the same but the position indices get shifted by one assigning no positions to index fz. We define first an auxiliary operator on positions:

$$\underline{\text{let}} \ \frac{P \ : \ \mathsf{Fin} \ n \to S \to \star \quad i \ : \ \mathsf{Fin} \ (\mathsf{suc} \ n) \quad s \ : \ S}{\mathbf{Pwk} \ P \ i \ s \ : \ \star}$$

$$\mathbf{Pwk} \ P \ i \ s \ \Leftarrow \ \underline{\text{case}} \ i$$
$$\mathbf{Pwk} \ P \ \mathsf{fz} \ s \ \Rightarrow \ \mathsf{Zero}$$
$$\mathbf{Pwk} \ P \ (\mathsf{fs} \ i) \ s \ \Rightarrow \ P \ i \ s$$

and use this to define:

$$\underline{\text{let}} \ \frac{C \ : \ \mathsf{Cont} \ n}{\mathbf{cwk} \ C \ : \ \mathsf{Cont} \ (\mathsf{suc} \ n)}$$

$$\mathbf{cwk} \ C \ \Leftarrow \ \underline{\text{case}} \ C$$
$$\mathbf{cwk} \ (\mathsf{cont} \ S \ P) \ \Rightarrow \ \mathsf{cont} \ S \ (\mathbf{Pwk} \ P)$$

The case of local definition is more interesting. We assume as given two containers: $C = \mathsf{cont} \ S \ P \ : \ \mathsf{Cont} \ (\mathsf{suc} \ n), D = \mathsf{cont} \ T \ Q \ : \ \mathsf{Cont} \ n$. We create a new

n-ary container by *binding* variable fz of C to D, hence attaching D-structures to each fz-indexed position of a C-structure. The i-positions of the result correspond either to i-positions of some inner D, or the *free* (fs i)-positions of the outer C.

To record the shape of the whole thing, we need to store the outer C shape, some $s : S$, and the inner D shapes: there is one for each outer fz-position, hence we need a function $f : P$ fz $s \to T$. As before we abstract from the specific position types and define abstractly:

$$\underline{\text{data}} \ \frac{S : \star \quad P_0 : S \to \star \quad T : \star}{\text{Sdef } S \ P_0 \ T \ : \ \star} \ \underline{\text{where}} \ \frac{s : S \quad f : P_0 \ s \to T}{\text{sdef } s \ f \ : \ \text{Sdef } S \ P_0 \ T}$$

What is a position in the new container, for a given index i? It must either be a 'free' outer position, given by P (fs i), or the pair of a 'bound' outer position with an inner position given by Q i. Hence, we define a general operator for positions in Sdef, which we can instantiate suitably for each index:

$$\underline{\text{data}} \ \frac{P_0, P' : S \to \star \quad Q : T \to \star \quad x : \text{Sdef } S \ P_0 \ T}{\text{Pdef } P_0 \ P' \ Q \ x \ : \ \star}$$

$$\underline{\text{where}} \ \frac{p : P' \ s}{\text{ppos } p \ : \ \text{Pdef } P_0 \ P' \ Q \ (\text{sdef } s \ f)} \quad \frac{p : P_0 \ s \quad q : Q \ (f \ p)}{\text{qpos } p \ q \ : \ \text{Pdef } P_0 \ P' \ Q \ (\text{sdef } s \ f)}$$

Putting the components together, we can present the definition operator:

$$\underline{\text{let}} \ \frac{C : \text{Cont} \, (\text{suc} \, n) \quad D : \text{Cont} \, n}{\text{cdef } C \ D \ : \ \text{Cont} \, n}$$

cdef $C \ D \ \Leftarrow \ \underline{\text{case}} \ C$
  cdef (cont $S \ P$) $D \ \Leftarrow \ \underline{\text{case}} \ D$
    cdef (cont $S \ P$) (cont $T \ Q$)
      $\Rightarrow$ cont (Sdef $S \ (P \text{ fz}) \ T$) ($\lambda i \Rightarrow$ Pdef (P fz) (P (fs i)) ($Q \ i$))

5.5 Inductive Types (μ)

To interpret the mu constructor we take an $n + 1$-ary container $C = \text{cont } S \ P :$ Cont (suc n) and try to find a container which represents the initial algebra with respect to the 'bound' index fz. For each shape $s : S$, P fz s gives the positions of recursive subobjects. Meanwhile the positions for i-indexed payload at each node are given by P (fs i).

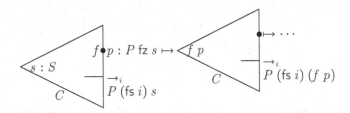

Clearly, to be able to construct a tree at all, there must be at least one 'base case' s for which P fz s is empty. Otherwise there are no leaves and the corresponding tree type is empty.

How can we describe the shapes of these trees? At each node, we must supply the top-level shape, together with a function which gives the shape f the subtrees. This is given exactly by W S (P fz). Given a shape in form of a W-tree, the positions at index i correspond to path leading to a P (fs i) somewhere in the tree. We can define the types of paths in a tree in general:

$$\underline{\text{data}} \quad \frac{S : \star \quad P_0, P' : S \to \star \quad x : \text{W } S \, P_0}{\text{PW } S \, P_0 \, P' \, x : \star}$$

$$\underline{\text{where}} \quad \frac{x : P' \, s}{\text{here } x : \text{PW } S \, P_0 \, P' \, (\text{Sup } s \, f)} \quad \frac{p : P_0 \, s \quad r : \text{PW } S \, P_0 \, P' \, (f \, p)}{\text{under } p \, r : \text{PW } S \, P_0 \, P' \, (\text{Sup } s \, f)}$$

The idea is that a path either exits at the top level node here at a position in P' s or continues into the subtree under a positions in P_0 s. Putting shapes and paths together we arrive at the following definition:

$$\underline{\text{let}} \quad \frac{C : \text{Cont (suc } n)}{\text{cMu } C : \text{Cont } n}$$

$$\text{cMu } C \Leftarrow \underline{\text{case}} \, C$$
$$\text{cMu (cont } S \, P) \Rightarrow \text{cont (W } S \, (P \text{ fz})) \, (\lambda i \Rightarrow \text{PW } S \, (P \text{ fz}) \, (P \, (\text{fs } i)))$$

5.6   Interpreting Universes

Since we have constructed semantic counterparts to every syntactic constructor in Ucf we can interpret any type name by a container with the corresponding arity:

$$\underline{\text{let}} \ \frac{a \ : \ \mathsf{Ucf} \ n}{\mathsf{evalC} \ a \ : \ \mathsf{Cont} \ n}$$

evalC a ⇐ <u>rec</u> a
  evalC a ⇐ <u>case</u> a
   evalC vl ⇒ cvl
   evalC (wk a) ⇒ cwk (evalC a)
   evalC '0' ⇒ cZero
   evalC ('plus' $a \ b$) ⇒ cPlus (evalC a) (evalC b)
   evalC '1' ⇒ cOne
   evalC ('times' $a \ b$) ⇒ cTimes (evalC a) (evalC b)
   evalC (def $f \ a$) ⇒ cdef (evalC f) (evalC a)
   evalC ('mu' f) ⇒ cMu (evalC f)

Combining **evalC** with **Ext** we can assign to any name in Ucf an operator on types:

$$\underline{\text{let}} \ \frac{a \ : \ \mathsf{Ucf} \ n \quad Xs \ : \ \mathsf{Fin} \ n \to \star}{\mathsf{eval} \ a \ Xs \ : \ \star} \quad \mathsf{eval} \ a \ Xs \ \Rightarrow \ \mathsf{Ext} \, (\mathsf{evalC} \ a) \ Xs$$

The advantage is that we can apply our operators to any types, not just those which have name. Using the solution to exercise 13 we also obtain a generic map function.

So far we have only interpreted the type names, i.e. the inhabitants of Ucf n, what about the elements, i.e. the inhabitants of Elcf $a \, as$? Using Ext we can define a semantic version of Elcf:

$$\underline{\text{data}} \ \frac{n \ : \ \mathsf{Nat}}{\mathsf{CTel} \ n \ : \ \star} \ \underline{\text{where}} \ \frac{}{\mathsf{ctnil} \ : \ \mathsf{Tel} \ \mathsf{zero}} \quad \frac{a \ : \ \mathsf{Cont} \ n \quad as \ : \ \mathsf{Tel} \ n}{\mathsf{ctcons} \ a \ as \ : \ \mathsf{Tel} \, (\mathsf{suc} \ n)}$$

$$\underline{\text{let}} \ \frac{Cs \ : \ \mathsf{Tel} \ n \quad i \ : \ \mathsf{Fin} \ n}{\mathsf{TelEl} \ Cs \ i \ : \ \star}$$

TelEl $Cs \ i$ ⇐ <u>rec</u> Cs
  TelEl $Cs \ i$ ⇐ <u>case</u> i
   TelEl Cs fz ⇐ <u>case</u> Cs
    TelEl (tcons $C \ Cs$) fz ⇒ Ext C (TelEl Cs)
   TelEl Cs (fs i) ⇐ <u>case</u> Cs
    TelEl (tcons $C \ Cs$) (fs i) ⇒ TelEl $Cs \ i$

$$\underline{\text{let}} \ \frac{C \ : \ \mathsf{Cont} \ n \quad Cs \ : \ \mathsf{Tel} \ n}{\mathsf{CEl} \ C \ Cs \ : \ \star} \quad \mathsf{CEl} \ C \ Cs \ \Rightarrow \ \mathsf{Ext} \ C \, (\mathsf{TelEl} \ Cs)$$

Exercise 15. Implement semantic counterparts of the constructor for Elcf giving rise to an interpretation of Elcf by CEl. Indeed, this interpretation is exhaustive and disjoint.

5.7   Small Containers

We have given a translation of the context-free types as containers, but as exercise 14 shows, these capture more than just the context-free types, in fact it corresponds to the strictly positive universe. As a result we cannot derive a semantic version of generic equality which is *typical* of the smaller universe.

We can, however, define a notion of container which captures precisely the context-free types and give a semantic version geq for these containers which we christen 'small containers'.

A container is small if there is a decidable equality on its shapes and if the positions at a given shape are finite, so:

$$\underline{\text{let}} \quad \frac{A \, : \, \star}{\text{DecEq } A \, : \, \star}$$

$$\text{DecEq } A \;\Rightarrow\; \forall a, a' : A \Rightarrow \text{Dec}\,(a = a')$$

$$\underline{\text{data}} \quad \frac{n \, : \, \text{Nat}}{\text{SCont } n \, : \, \star}$$

$$\underline{\text{where}} \quad \frac{S \, : \, \star \quad eqS \, : \, \text{DecEq } S \quad P \, : \, \text{Fin } n \to S \to \text{Nat}}{\text{scont } S \; eqS \; P \, : \, \text{SCont } n}$$

$$\underline{\text{data}} \quad \frac{C \, : \, \text{SCont } Xs \, : \, \text{Fin } n \to \star}{\text{SExt } C \; Xs \, : \, \star}$$

$$\underline{\text{where}} \quad \frac{s \, : \, S \quad f \, : \, \forall i : \text{Fin } n \Rightarrow \text{Fin}\,(P \; i \; s) \to Xs \; i}{\text{sext } s \, f \, : \, \text{SCont } S \; eq \; P}$$

We can redefine the variable case, disjoint union, products and the fix point operator for these containers, for instance:

$$\underline{\text{let}} \quad \frac{C, D \, : \, \text{SCont } n}{\text{SCTimes } C \; D \, : \, \text{Cont } n}$$

$$\text{SCTimes } C \; D \;\Leftarrow\; \underline{\text{case}} \; C$$
$$\text{SCTimes }(\text{scont } S \; eqS \; P)\, D \;\Leftarrow\; \underline{\text{case}} \; D$$
$$\text{SCTimes }(\text{scont } S \; eqS \; P)\,(\text{scont } T \; eqT \; Q)$$
$$\Rightarrow\; \text{scont }(\text{Times } S \; T)$$
$$(\text{TimesEq } eqS \; eqT)$$
$$(\lambda i; s \Rightarrow \text{plus}\,(P \; i \; s)\,(Q \; i \; s))$$

Where **TimesEq** is a proof that cartesian product preserves decidable equality by comparing pointwise:

$$\underline{\text{let}} \quad \frac{eqS \, : \, \text{DecEq } S \quad eqT \, : \, \text{DecEq } T}{\text{TimesEq } eqS \; eqT \, : \, \text{DecEq}\,(\text{Times } S \; T)}$$

Our generic equality for small containers is then a proof that SExt preserves equality:

$$\underline{\text{let}} \quad \frac{C \,:\, \mathsf{SCont}\, n \quad Xs \,:\, \mathsf{Fin}\, n \to \star \quad eqs \,:\, \forall i \!:\! \mathsf{Fin}\, n \Rightarrow \mathsf{DecEq}\,(Xs\, i)}{\mathsf{SContEq}\, C\, Xs\, eqs \,:\, \mathsf{DecEq}\,(\mathsf{SExt}\, C\, Xs)}$$

Exercise 16. Complete the construction of **SCTimes** and develop operators constructing disjoint union, local definition, fixed points, and variables for small containers. Finally construct the definition of **SContEq**.

To work with Epigram's built in equality you will need to use the fact that application preserves equality:

$$\underline{\text{let}} \quad \frac{f, g \,:\, S \to T \quad a, b \,:\, S \quad p \,:\, f = g \quad q \,:\, a = b}{\mathsf{applEq}\, p\, q \,:\, f\, a = g\, b}$$

$$\mathsf{applEq}\, p\, q \;\Leftarrow\; \underline{\text{case}}\; p$$
$$\mathsf{applEq}\, \mathsf{refl}\, q \;\Leftarrow\; \underline{\text{case}}\; q$$
$$\mathsf{applEq}\, \mathsf{refl}\, \mathsf{refl} \;\Rightarrow\; \mathsf{refl}$$

And that constructors are disjoint, so for example $\mathsf{Inl}\, a = \mathsf{Inr}\, b$ is a provably empty type:

$$\underline{\text{let}} \quad \frac{a \,:\, A \quad b \,:\, B \quad p \,:\, (\mathsf{Inl}\, a \,:\, \mathsf{Plus}\, A\, B) = (\mathsf{Inr}\, b \,:\, \mathsf{Plus}\, A\, B)}{\mathsf{InlneqInr}\, p \,:\, X}$$

$$\mathsf{InlneqInr}\, p \;\Leftarrow\; \underline{\text{case}}\; p$$

6   Derivatives

In [25] Huet introduced the *zipper* as a datatype to represent a position within a tree. The basic idea is that at every step on the path to the current position, we remember the context left over. E.g. in the example of unlabelled binary trees,

$$\underline{\text{data}} \quad \frac{}{\mathsf{BT} \,:\, \star} \quad \underline{\text{where}} \quad \frac{}{\mathsf{leaf} \,:\, \mathsf{BT}} \quad \frac{l, r \,:\, \mathsf{BT}}{\mathsf{node}\, l\, r \,:\, \mathsf{BT}}$$

the corresponding zipper type is:

$$\underline{\text{data}} \quad \frac{}{\mathsf{Zipper} \,:\, \star}$$

$$\underline{\text{where}} \quad \frac{l \,:\, \mathsf{Zipper} \quad r \,:\, \mathsf{BT}}{\mathsf{left}\, l\, r \,:\, \mathsf{Zipper}} \quad \frac{l \,:\, \mathsf{BT} \quad r \,:\, \mathsf{Zipper}}{\mathsf{right}\, l\, r \,:\, \mathsf{Zipper}} \quad \frac{}{\mathsf{here} \,:\, \mathsf{Zipper}}$$

We can think of a Zipper as a tree with one subtree chopped out at the place marked here. One of the operations on a zipper is to plug a binary tree into its hole, i.e. we define:[10]

$$\underline{\text{let}} \quad \frac{z : \text{Zipper} \quad t : \text{BT}}{\text{plug } z\, t : \text{BT}}$$

> plug $z\, t \ \Leftarrow \ \underline{\text{rec }} z$
> plug $z\, t \ \Leftarrow \ \underline{\text{case }} z$
> plug $(\text{left } l\, r)\, t \ \Rightarrow \ \text{node } (\text{plug } l\, t)\, r$
> plug $(\text{right } l\, r)\, t \ \Rightarrow \ \text{node } l\, (\text{plug } r\, t)$
> plug here $t \ \Rightarrow \ t$

Clearly, the zipper is a generic construction which should certainly work on any context-free type. When trying to express the general scheme of a zipper, Conor McBride realised that a zipper is always a sequence of basic steps which arise as the formal derivative of the functor defining the datatype. I.e. if our datatype is $\mu X.F\, X$, e.g. $\mu X.1 + X \times X$ in the example of binary trees, then the corresponding zipper is $\text{List}(\partial F\, (\mu X.F\, X))$. In the binary tree example $F\, X = 1 + X \times X$ and $\partial F\, X = 2 \times X$. Indeed Zipper is isomorphic to $\text{List}\,(2 \times \text{BT})$.

6.1   Derivatives of Context-Free Types

We will here concentrate on the notion of the partial derivative of an n-ary operator on types, which corresponds to the type of *one hole contexts* of the given type. This is an alternative explanation of the formal laws of derivatives and we shall define an operator on context-free types following this intuition:

$$\underline{\text{let}} \quad \frac{a : \text{Ucf } n \quad i : \text{Fin } n}{\text{partial } a\, i : \text{Ucf } n}$$

The parameter i denotes the argument on which we take the derivative, indeed the partial derivative really is a variable binding operation, this is obliterated by the usual notation $\frac{\partial F}{\partial X}$ which really binds X.

We define this operation by structural recursion on a, let's consider the polynomial cases: what is the derivative, i.e. the type of one hole contexts of 'plus' $a\, b$? We either have a hole in an element of a or a hole in an element of b, hence:

$$\text{partial } (\text{'plus' } a\, b)\, i \ \Rightarrow \ \text{'plus' } (\text{partial } a\, i)\, (\text{partial } b\, i)$$

Maybe slightly more interesting, what is the type of one-hole contexts of 'times' $a\, b$? A hole in a pair is either a hole in the first component, leaving the second intact or symmetrically, a hole in the second, leaving the first intact. Hence we arrive at

---

[10] Here we have chosen the root-to-hole representation of contexts. Huet's hole-to-root presentation uses the same datatype. Both are useful, with the choice depending on where you need the most rapid access.

$$\text{partial ('times' } a\ b)\ i\ \Rightarrow\ \text{'plus' ('times' (partial } a\ i)\ b)\ \text{('times' } a\ \text{(partial } b\ i))$$

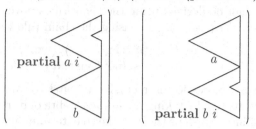

which indeed corresponds to the formal derivative of a product, although we arrived at it using a rather different explanation. Unsurprisingly, the derivative of a constant is '0', since there are no holes to plug:

$$\text{partial '0' } i\ \Rightarrow\ \text{'0'}$$
$$\text{partial '1' } i\ \Rightarrow\ \text{'0'}$$

Structural operations like variables and weakening are usually ignored in Calculus, an omission we will have to fill here to be able to implement partial for those cases. In both cases we have to inspect i: for vl we have exactly one choice if $i = \text{fz}$ and none otherwise, hence we have:

$$\text{partial vl fz } \Rightarrow\ \text{'1'}$$
$$\text{partial vl (fs } i)\ \Rightarrow\ \text{'0'}$$

In the case of wk a the situation is reversed, there is no choice if $i = \text{fz}$ and otherwise we recur structurally:

$$\text{partial (wk } a)\ \text{fz } \Rightarrow\ \text{'0'}$$
$$\text{partial (wk } a)\ \text{(fs } i)\ \Rightarrow\ \text{wk (partial } a\ i)$$

The case of local definitions def f a corresponds to the chain rule in Calculus. An i- hole in an element of def f a is either a (fs i) hole in the outer f, or it is a hole in f for the defined variable fz together with an i-hole in some a. More formally we have:

$$\text{partial (def } f\ a)\ i$$
$$\Rightarrow\ \text{'plus' (def (partial } f\ \text{(fs } i))\ a)\ \text{('times' (def (partial } f\ \text{fz)}\ a)\ \text{(partial } a\ i))$$

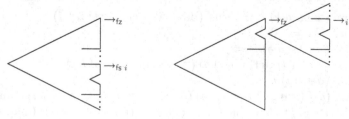

The case for initial algebras 'mu' f has no counterpart in calculus. However, it can be derived using the chain rule above: we know that 'mu' f is isomorphic to def f ('mu' f). Now using the chain rule we arrive at

'plus' (def (partial f (fs i)) ('mu' f))
         ('times' (def (partial f fz) ('mu' f)) (partial ('mu' f) i))

This expression is recursive in partial ('mu' f) i hence we obtain the formal derivative by taking the initial algebra of it, recording the contexts for a sequence of internal steps through the tree, terminated by the node with the external hole:

partial ('mu' f) i $\Rightarrow$ 'mu' ('plus' (wk (def (partial f (fs i)) ('mu' f)))
                     ('times' (wk (def (partial f fz) ('mu' f))) vl))

A closer analysis shows that the use of initial algebras here is justified by the fact that we are only interested in holes which appear at some finite depths.

As an example consider the derivative of lists partial list fz: after applying some simplification we obtain 'mu'('plus'(wklist)('times'vl(wkvl))) or reexpressed in a more standard notation $\mu X.(\text{list } A) + A \times X$, which can be easily seen to correspond to lists with a hole for A.

We summarize the definition of partial:

partial a i $\Leftarrow$ <u>rec</u> a
  partial a i $\Leftarrow$ <u>case</u> a
   partial vl i $\Leftarrow$ <u>case</u> i
    partial vl fz $\Rightarrow$ '1'
    partial vl (fs i) $\Rightarrow$ '0'
   partial (wk a) i $\Leftarrow$ <u>case</u> i
    partial (wk a) fz $\Rightarrow$ '0'
    partial (wk a) (fs i) $\Rightarrow$ wk (partial a i)
   partial '0' i $\Rightarrow$ '0'
   partial ('plus' a b) i $\Rightarrow$ 'plus' (partial a i) (partial b i)
   partial '1' i $\Rightarrow$ '0'
   partial ('times' a b) i $\Rightarrow$
    'plus' ('times' (partial a i) b) ('times' a (partial b i))
   partial (def f a) i $\Rightarrow$
    'plus' (def (partial f (fs i)) a) ('times' (def (partial f fz) a) (partial a i))
   partial ('mu' f) i $\Rightarrow$ 'mu' ('plus' (wk (def (partial f (fs i)) ('mu' f)))
                    ('times' (wk (def (partial f fz) ('mu' f))) vl))

Exercise 17. Calculate (by hand) the derivative of rose trees, i.e. the value of partial fz rt

6.2   Generic Plugging

To convince ourselves that the definition of derivatives as one hole contexts given above is correct we derive[11] a generic version of the generic plugging operation:

$$\text{let } \frac{a \quad i \quad x \; : \; \mathsf{Elcf}\,(\text{partial}\,a\,i)\,as \quad y \; : \; \mathsf{Elcf}\,(\text{var}\,i)\,as}{\text{gplug}\,a\,i\,x\,y \; : \; \mathsf{Elcf}\,a\,as}$$

That is given an element x of a partial derivative of a at i we can fill the hole with an element of the corresponding type of the telescope, obtaining an element of a.

We construct gplug by recursion over x, however, unlike in the previous examples, which were completely data driven we have to analyse the type directly, i.e. we have to invoke <u>case</u> a. We discuss the cases:

variable

$$\text{gplug vl fz void } y \; \Rightarrow \; y$$
$$\text{gplug vl (fs } i)\, x\, y \; \Leftarrow \; \underline{\text{case}}\, x$$

If the index is fz the argument y is the filler we are looking for, otherwise the derivative is the empty type and we eliminate it by a vacuous case analysis.

weakening

$$\text{gplug (wk } a)\, \text{fz }\, x\, y \; \Leftarrow \; \underline{\text{case}}\, x$$
$$\text{gplug (wk } a)\, (\text{fs } i)\, (\text{pop } x)\, (\text{pop } y) \; \Rightarrow \; \text{pop (gplug } a\, i\, x\, y)$$

This is in some way dual to the previous case: if the index is fz we have the empty derivative, otherwise we recur.

constant types

$$\text{gplug '0' } i\, x\, y \; \Leftarrow \; \underline{\text{case}}\, x$$
$$\text{gplug '1' } i\, x\, y \; \Leftarrow \; \underline{\text{case}}\, x$$

are easy because impossible, since the derivative is the empty type.

disjoint union

$$\text{gplug ('plus' } a\, b)\, i\, (\text{inl } xa)\, y \; \Rightarrow \; \text{inl (gplug } a\, i\, xa\, y)$$
$$\text{gplug ('plus' } a\, b)\, i\, (\text{inr } xb)\, y \; \Rightarrow \; \text{inr (gplug } b\, i\, xb\, y)$$

the injections are just carried through.

---

[11] We were unable to convince Epigram to check all of the definition below due to a space leak in the current implementation. We are hopeful that this will be fixed in the next release of Epigram.

Product

$$\text{gplug (`times' } a\ b)\ i\ (\text{inl (pair } xa\ xb)) \Rightarrow \text{pair (gplug } a\ i\ xa\ y)\ xb$$
$$\text{gplug (`times' } a\ b)\ i\ (\text{inr (pair } xa\ xb)) \Rightarrow \text{pair } xa\ (\text{gplug } b\ i\ xb\ y)$$

The derivative records the information in which component of the pair we can find the hole.

Local definition

$$\text{gplug (def } f\ a)\ i\ (\text{inl (push } x))\ y \Rightarrow \text{push (gplug } f\ (\text{fs } i)\ x\ (\text{pop } y))$$
$$\text{gplug (def } f\ a)\ i\ (\text{inr (pair (push } x)\ q))\ y \Rightarrow$$
$$\text{push (gplug } f\ \text{fz } x\ (\text{top (gplug } a\ i\ q\ y)))$$

In the first case the hole is in top-level (f) tree but not at the first variable, which is used in the definition. In the 2nd case the hole is in a subtree (a) which means we have to plug the hole there and then use the result to plug a hole in the top-level tree.

Exercise 18. Complete (using pen and paper) the definition of gplug by implementing the case for mu.

6.3   Derivatives of Containers

Previously, we have defined derivatives by induction over the syntax of types. Using containers we can give a more direct, semantic definition. The basic idea can be related to derivatives of polynomials, i.e. the derivative of $f\ x = x^n$ is $f'\ x = n \times x^{n-1}$. As a first step we need to find a type-theoretic counterpart to the predecessor of a type by removing one element of the type. We define:

$$\underline{\text{data}}\ \frac{A\ :\ \star \quad a\ :\ A}{\text{Minus } A\ a\ :\ \star}\ \underline{\text{where}}\ \frac{a'\ :\ A \quad na\ :\ \text{Not}\,(a = a')}{\text{minus } a\ na\ :\ \text{Minus } A\ a'}$$

We can embed Minus A a back into A:

$$\underline{\text{let}}\ \frac{m\ :\ \text{Minus } A\ a}{\text{emb } m\ :\ A}\quad \text{emb } m \Leftarrow \underline{\text{case}}\ m$$
$$\text{emb (minus } a'\ na) \Rightarrow a'$$

We can analyse A in terms of Minus A a by defining a view. An element of A is either a or it is in the range of emb:

$$\underline{\text{data}}\ \frac{a;\ a'\ :\ A}{\text{MinusV } a\ a'}$$

$$\underline{\text{where}}\ \frac{}{\text{same } a\ :\ \text{MinusV } a\ a}\quad \frac{m\ :\ \text{Minus } A\ a}{\text{other } m\ :\ \text{MinusV } a\ (\text{emb } m)}$$

This view is exhaustive, if A has a decidable equality:

$$\underline{\text{let}} \quad \frac{a, a' \,:\, A \quad eq \,:\, \text{Dec}\,(a = a')}{\text{minus}\text{V}' \, a \, a' \, eq \,:\, \text{MinusV} \, a \, a'}$$

$\text{minusV}' \, a \, a' \, eq \;\Leftarrow\; \underline{\text{case}} \; eq$
$\text{minusV}' \, a \, a \, (\text{yes refl}) \;\Rightarrow\; \text{same} \; a$
$\text{minusV}' \, a \, a' \, (\text{no}\, f) \;\Rightarrow\; \text{other}\,(\text{minus} \, a' \, f)$

$$\underline{\text{let}} \quad \frac{eqA \,:\, \text{DecEq} \, A \quad a, a' \,:\, A}{\text{minusV} \, eqA \, a \, a' \,:\, \text{MinusV} \, a \, a'}$$

$\text{minusV} \, eqA \, a \, a' \;\Rightarrow\; \text{minusV}' \, a \, a' \,(eqA \, a \, a')$

We are now ready to construct the derivative of containers and implement a variant plug for containers. To simplify the presentation we first restrict our attention to unary containers.

Given a unary container ucont $S \, P$ its derivative is given by shapes which are the original shapes together with a chosen position, i.e. Sigma $S \, P$. The new type of positions is obtained by subtracting this chosen element from P hence we define:

$$\underline{\text{let}} \quad \frac{P \,:\, S \to \star \quad sp \,:\, \text{Sigma} \, S \, P}{\text{derivP} \, P \, sp \,:\, \star}$$

$\text{derivP} \, P \, sp \;\Leftarrow\; \underline{\text{case}} \; sp$
$\text{derivP} \, P \,(\text{tup} \, s \, p) \;\Rightarrow\; \text{Minus}\,(P \, s) \, p$

and hence the derivative of a unary container is given by:

$$\underline{\text{let}} \quad \frac{C \,:\, \text{UCont}}{\text{derivC} \, C \,:\, \text{UCont}}$$

$\text{derivC} \, C \;\Leftarrow\; \underline{\text{case}} \; C$
$\text{derivC}\,(\text{ucont} \, S \, P) \;\Rightarrow\; \text{ucont}\,(\text{Sigma} \, S \, P)\,(\text{derivP} \, P)$

While the definition above works for any unary container, we need decidability of equality on positions to define the generic plugging operation. Intuitively, we have to be able to differentiate between position to identify the location of a hole. Hence, only containers with a decidable equality are differentiable. We define a predicate on containers:

$$\underline{\text{data}} \quad \frac{C \,:\, \text{UCont}}{\text{DecUCont} \, C \,:\, \star} \quad \underline{\text{where}} \quad \frac{decP \,:\, \forall s\!:\!S \Rightarrow \text{DecEq}\,(P \, s)}{\text{decUCont} \, decP \,:\, \text{DecUCont}\,(\text{ucont} \, S \, P)}$$

Given a decidable unary container we can define the function uplug which given an element of the extension of the derivative of a container $x \,:\, \text{UExt}(\text{derivC}\,C)X$ and an element $y \,:\, X$ we can plug the hole with y thus obtaining an element of $\text{UExt} \, C \, X$:

$$\text{let} \; \frac{\begin{array}{l} eq \; : \; \mathsf{DecEq} \; A \quad a \; : \; A \\ f \; : \; \mathsf{Minus} \; A \; a \to X \\ x \; : \; X \quad a' \; : \; A \end{array}}{\mathsf{mplug} \; eq \; a \; f \; x \; a' \; : \; X}$$

mplug $eq \; a \; f \; x \; a' \; \Leftarrow \; \underline{\text{view}} \; \mathsf{minusV} \; eq \; a \; a'$
  mplug $eq \; a \; f \; x \; a \; \Rightarrow \; x$
  mplug $eq \; a \; f \; x \; (\mathsf{emb} \; m) \; \Rightarrow \; f \; m$

$$\text{let} \; \frac{\begin{array}{l} C \; : \; \mathsf{UCont} \quad d \; : \; \mathsf{DecUCont} \; C \\ x \; : \; \mathsf{UExt} \, (\mathsf{derivC} \; C) \; X \quad y \; : \; X \end{array}}{\mathsf{uplug} \; C \; d \; x \; y \; : \; \mathsf{UExt} \; C \; X}$$

uplug $C \; d \; x \; y \; \Leftarrow \; \underline{\text{case}} \; C$
  uplug $(\mathsf{ucont} \; S \; P) \; d \; x \; y \; \Leftarrow \; \underline{\text{case}} \; d$
    uplug $(\mathsf{ucont} \; S \; P) \, (\mathsf{decUCont} \; decP) \; x \; y \; \Leftarrow \; \underline{\text{case}} \; x$
      uplug $(\mathsf{ucont} \; S \; P) \, (\mathsf{decUCont} \; decP) \, (\mathsf{uext} \; sp \; f) \; y \; \Leftarrow \; \underline{\text{case}} \; sp$
        uplug $(\mathsf{ucont} \; S \; P) \, (\mathsf{decUCont} \; decP) \, (\mathsf{uext} \, (\mathsf{tup} \; s \; p) \; f) \; y$
          $\Rightarrow \; \mathsf{uext} \; a \, (\mathsf{mplug} \, (decP \; a) \; b \; f \; y)$

Exercise 19. Extend the derivative operator for containers to n-ary containers, i.e. define

$$\text{let} \; \frac{C \; : \; \mathsf{Cont} \; n \quad i \; : \; \mathsf{Fin} \; n}{\mathsf{partialC} \; C \; i \; : \; \mathsf{Cont} \; n}$$

To extend the plug operator we have to define decidability for an n-ary container. We also need to exploit that equality for finite types is decidable.

7   Conclusions and Further Work

Using dependent types we were able to define different universes and generic operations on them. We have studied two fundamentally different approaches: a semantic approach, first using finite types and the container types and a syntactic approach where the elements are defined inductively. Further work needs to be done to relate the two more precisely, they are only two views of the same collection of types. We have already observed that there is a trade-off between the size of the universe, i.e. the collection of types definable within it, and the number of generic operations. The previous section suggests that there is a universe between the context-free types and the strictly positive types: the differentiable types, i.e. the types with a decidable equality on positions. Previous work in a more categorical framework [7] shows already that the types which are obtained by closing context-free types under a coinductive type former (ν) are still differentiable.

The size of a universe is not the only parameter we can very, the universes we have considered here are still very coarse. E.g. while we have a more refined type system on the meta-level, dependent types, this is not reflected in our universes. We have no names for the family of finite types, the vectors or the family of elements of a universe itself. Recent work shows that it is possible to extend both the syntactic and the semantic approach to capture families of types, see [35,8]. Another direction to pursue is to allow types where the positions are result of a quotient, like bags or multisets. We have already investigated this direction from a categorical point of view [6]; a typetheoretic approach requires a Type Theory which allows quotient types. Here our current work on *Observational Type Theory* [10] fits in very well.

Apart from the more theoretical questions regarding universes of datatypes there are more pragmatic issues. We don't want to work with isomorphic copies of our datatypes, but we want to be able to access the top-level types themselves. We are working on a new implementation of Epigram which will provide a quotation mechanism which makes the top-level universe accessible for the programmer. We also hope to be able to find a good pragmatic answer to vary the level of genericity, i.e. to be able to define generic operations for the appropriate universe without repeating definitions.

References

1. Abbott, M.: Categories of Containers. PhD thesis, University of Leicester (2003)
2. Abbott, M., Altenkirch, T., Ghani, N.: Categories of containers. In: Proceedings of Foundations of Software Science and Computation Structures (2003)
3. Abbott, M., Altenkirch, T., Ghani, N.: Representing nested inductive types using W-types. In: Díaz, J., Karhumäki, J., Lepistö, A., Sannella, D. (eds.) ICALP 2004. LNCS, vol. 3142, pp. 59–71. Springer, Heidelberg (2004)
4. Abbott, M., Altenkirch, T., Ghani, N.: Containers - constructing strictly positive types. Theoretical Computer Science 342, 3–27 (2005) (Applied Semantics: Selected Topics)
5. Abbott, M., Altenkirch, T., Ghani, N., McBride, C.: Derivatives of containers. In: Hofmann, M.O. (ed.) TLCA 2003. LNCS, vol. 2701, Springer, Heidelberg (2003)
6. Abbott, M., Altenkirch, T., Ghani, N., McBride, C.: Constructing polymorphic programs with quotient types. In: Kozen, D. (ed.) MPC 2004. LNCS, vol. 3125, Springer, Heidelberg (2004)
7. Abbott, M., Altenkirch, T., Ghani, N., McBride, C.: ∂ for data. Fundamentae Informatica 65(1,2), 1–28 (2005) (Special Issue on Typed Lambda Calculi and Applications 2003)
8. Altenkirch, T., Ghani, N., Hancock, P., McBride, C., Morris, P.: Indexed containers. Manuscript, available online (February 2006)
9. Altenkirch, T., McBride, C.: Generic programming within dependently typed programming. In: Generic Programming, 2003. Proceedings of the IFIP TC2 Working Conference on Generic Programming, Schloss Dagstuhl (July 2002)
10. Altenkirch, T., McBride, C.: Towards observational type theory. Manuscript, available online (February 2006)
11. Altenkirch, T., McBride, C., McKinna, J.: Why dependent types matter. Manuscript, available online (April 2005)
12. Altenkirch, T., McBride, C., Morris, P.: Code for generic programming with dependent types (2007), http://www.e-pig.org/downloads/GPwDT
13. Altenkirch, T., Uustalu, T.: Normalization by evaluation for $\lambda^{\to 2}$. In: Kameyama, Y., Stuckey, P.J. (eds.) FLOPS 2004. LNCS, vol. 2998, pp. 260–275. Springer, Heidelberg (2004)

14. Loeh, A., Jeuring, J., (ed.) Clarke, D., Hinze, R., Rodriguez, A., de Wit, J.: Generic Haskell User's Guide - Version 1.42 (Coral). Technical Report UU-CS-2005-004, Institute of Information and Computing Sciences, Utrecht University (2005)
15. Backhouse, R., Jansson, P., Jeuring, J., Meertens, L.: Generic Programming—An Introduction. In: Swierstra, S.D., Oliveira, J.N. (eds.) AFP 1998. LNCS, vol. 1608, pp. 28–115. Springer, Heidelberg (1999)
16. Benke, M., Dybjer, P., Jansson, P.: Universes for generic programs and proofs in dependent type theory. Nordic Journal of Computing 10(4), 265–289 (2003)
17. Bird, R., de Moor, O.: Algebra of Programming. Prentice Hall, Englewood Cliffs (1997)
18. Crary, K., Weirich, S., Morrisett, G.: Intensional polymorphism in type erasure semantics. Journal of Functional Programming 12(6), 567–600 (2002)
19. Dybjer, P.: Inductive Sets and Families in Martin-Löf's Type Theory. In: Huet, G., Plotkin, G. (eds.) Logical Frameworks. CUP (1991)
20. Dybjer, P., Setzer, A.: A finite axiomatization of inductive-recursive definitions. Typed Lambda Calculi and Applications 1581, 129–146 (1999)
21. Dybjer, P., Setzer, A.: Indexed induction-recursion. Journal of Logic and Algebraic Programming 66(1), 1–49 (2006)
22. Hinze, R.: Generic programs and proofs. Habilitationsschrift, Universität Bonn (2000)
23. Hinze, R., Löh, A.: Scrap Your Boilerplate Revolutions. In: Uustalu, T. (ed.) MPC 2006. LNCS, vol. 4014, pp. 180–208. Springer, Heidelberg (2006)
24. Hinze, R., Löh, A., Oliveira, B.C.D.S.: Scrap Your Boilerplate Reloaded. In: Hagiya, M., Wadler, P. (eds.) FLOPS 2006. LNCS, vol. 3945, pp. 13–29. Springer, Heidelberg (2006)
25. Huet, G.: The Zipper. Journal of Functional Programming 7(5), 549–554 (1997)
26. Löh, A.: Exploring Generic Haskell. PhD thesis, Utrecht University, Netherlands (September 2004)
27. Luo, Z., Pollack, R.: LEGO Proof Development System: User's Manual. Technical Report ECS-LFCS-92-211, Laboratory for Foundations of Computer Science, University of Edinburgh (1992)
28. Magnusson, L., Nordström, B.: The ALF proof editor and its proof engine. In: Barendregt, H., Nipkow, T. (eds.) TYPES 1993. LNCS, vol. 806, Springer, Heidelberg (1994)
29. Martin-Löf, P.: Intuitionistic Type Theory. Bibliopolis Napoli (1984)
30. McBride, C.: The Derivative of a Regular Type is its Type of One-Hole Contexts. Available online (2001)
31. McBride, C.: Epigram (2004), http://www.e-pig.org/
32. McBride, C.: Epigram: Practical programming with dependent types. In: Vene, V., Uustalu, T. (eds.) AFP 2004. LNCS, vol. 3622, Springer, Heidelberg (2005)
33. McBride, C., McKinna, J.: The view from the left. Journal of Functional Programming 14(1) (2004)
34. McBride, F.: Computer Aided Manipulation of Symbols. PhD thesis, Queen's University of Belfast (1970)
35. Morris, P., Altenkirch, T., Ghani, N.: Constructing strictly positive families. In: The Australasian Theory Symposium (CATS2007) (2007)
36. Morris, P., Altenkirch, T., McBride, C.: Exploring the regular tree types. In: Filliâtre, J.-C., Paulin-Mohring, C., Werner, B. (eds.) TYPES 2004. LNCS, vol. 3839, Springer, Heidelberg (2006)

37. Pfeifer, H., Rueß, H.: Polytypic abstraction in type theory. In: Backhouse, R., Sheard, T. (eds.) Workshop on Generic Programming (WGP'98). Dept. of Computing Science, Chalmers Univ. of Techn. and Göteborg Univ., (June 1998)
38. Nordström, B., Petersson, K., Smith, J.: Programming in Martin-Löf's type theory: an introduction. Oxford University Press, Oxford (1990)
39. Vytiniotis, D., Weirich, S., Jones, S.: Boxy type inference for higher-rank types and impredicativity. In: Proceedings of the International Conference on Functional Programming (ICFP 2006) (2006)
40. Wadler, P.: Views: A way for pattern matching to cohabit with data abstraction. In: Proceedings of POPL '87, ACM, New York (1987)
41. Weirich, S.: RepLib: A library for derivable type classes. In: Löh, A. (ed.) Proceedings of the ACM Haskell Workshop, 2006 (2006)

Generic Programming in Ωmega

Tim Sheard

Computer Science Department
Maseeh College of Engineering and Computer Science
Portland State University

1   Introduction

> "Generic programming is about making programs more adaptable by making them more general. Generic programs often embody non-traditional kinds of abstraction; ordinary programs are obtained from them by suitably instantiating their parameters. In contrast with normal programs, the parameters of a generic program are often quite rich in structure; for example they may be other programs, types or type constructors, class hierarchies, or even programming paradigms."

I wrote these words for the introduction of the first workshop on generic programming. They remain true today. But, in the intervening years, the languages in which we program have acquired ever richer abstraction mechanisms, and many non-traditional kinds of abstraction have become ordinary. This is certainly true of languages which support dependent types where "generic programs" often become ordinary programs. The language Ωmega supports a variant of dependent types (where types may depend upon type indexes, rather than values), and the purpose of these notes is to explain how we can exploit these types to build generic programs in Ωmega. The first point I wish to make, is that the richer the type system, the more generic the programs possible.

The second point I wish to make is that generic programs, while very general, tend to introduce a layer of interpretation, and may suffer from certain kinds of inefficiencies. The use of staging is a natural mechanism for removing these inefficiencies. I demonstrate that the use of index-dependent types is orthogonal to the use of staging[1], and in general the two techniques often complement each other.

1.1   Genericity and the Curry-Howard Isomorphism

Ωmega's type system makes it possible to realize the *Curry-Howard Isomorphism*. This states that programs are proofs, *and* types are properties. When we write $prog_1 :: type_1$, we are stating *both* that $prog_1$ has type $type_1$, *and* $prog_1$ is a proof of the property $type_1$. In Ωmega, this duality is the basis of generic programming. Ωmega's type system allows us to type many programs that are

---

[1] Fully dependent types are also orthogonal to staging, but that isn't illustrated in this paper.

R. Backhouse et al. (Eds.): Datatype-Generic Programming 2006, LNCS 4719, pp. 258–284, 2007.
© Springer-Verlag Berlin Heidelberg 2007

not typable in a language like Haskell. This allows Ωmega to support a number of new programming patterns including a large class of programs, which in other languages, are considered generic. Generic programming is all about abstraction. We show how to use the rich structures available in Ωmega to build unusual abstractions with all the properties of generic programs.

2   The Structure of Ωmega

We have adopted the following structure for the Ωmega language. Ωmega is a language with an infinite hierarchy of computational levels: value, type, kind, sort, etc. Computation at the value level is performed by reduction, and is largely unconstrained. Computation at all higher levels is constrained in several ways. First, all "data" at the type level and above is inductively defined data (no floats or primitive data for example). Second, functions at the type level and above must be inductively sequential (see Appendix A). This is a constraint on the form of the definition, not on the expressiveness of the language.

Terms at each level are classified by terms at the next level. Thus values are classified by types, types are classified by kinds, kinds are classified by sorts, etc. Programmers are allowed to introduce new terms and functions at every level, but any particular program will have terms at only a finite number of levels. We illustrate the level hierarchy for the many of the examples given in this paper in Figure 1.

We maintain a strict phase distinction — the classification of a term at level n cannot depend upon terms at lower levels. For example, no types can depend on values, and no kinds can depend on types. We formalize properties of programs by exploiting the Curry-Howard isomorphism. Terms at computational level n, are used as proofs about terms at level $n + 1$. We use indexed types to maintain a strict and formal connection between the two levels, and singleton types to maintain the strict separation between values and types.

3   A Simple Example

To illustrate the hierarchy of computational levels we give the following two-level example which uses natural numbers as a type index to lists that record their length in their type.

First, we introduce tree-like data (the natural numbers, Nat) at the *type level* by using the **data** introduction form. This form is a generalization over the **data** declaration in Haskell [15].

```
data Nat :: *1 where
  Z :: Nat
  S :: Nat ~> Nat
```

The line "data Nat :: *1 where" indicates that Nat is classified by *1 (rather than *0), which tells the programmer that Nat is a kind (rather than a type), and that Z and S are types (rather than values). The classifiers *0, *1, *2, etc. indicate the level of a term. All values are classified by types that are classified by *0. All types are classified by kinds that are classified by *1. All kinds are classified by sorts that are classified by *2, etc. This is illustrated with great detail in Figure 1.

Second, we write a function at the type level over this data (plus). At the type level and higher, we distinguish function application from constructor application by surrounding function application by braces ({ and }). For example, we write S x for constructor application, and {plus x y} for function application.

```
plus:: Nat ~> Nat ~> Nat
{plus Z m} = m
{plus (S n) m} = S {plus n m}
```

Third, using the data introduction form at the *value level*, we introduce the algebraic data structure (Seq). The types of such values are indexed by the natural numbers. These indexes describe an invariant about the constructed values — their length appears in their type — consider the type of 11.

```
data Seq:: *0 ~> Nat ~> *0 where
  Snil :: Seq a Z
  Scons:: a -> Seq a n -> Seq a (S n)
```

```
11 = (Scons 3 (Scons 5 Snil)) :: Seq Int (S(S Z))
```

Finally, we introduce a function at the value level over Seq values (app). The type of app describes one of its important properties — there is a functional relationship between the lengths of its two inputs, and the length of its output.

```
app:: Seq a n -> Seq a m -> Seq a {plus n m}
app Snil ys = ys
app (Scons x xs) ys = Scons x (app xs ys)
```

To see that the app is well typed, the type checker does the following. The expected type is the type given in the function prototype. We compute the type of both the left- and right-hand-side of the equation defining a clause. We compare the expected type with the computed type for both the left- and right-hand-sides. This comparison generates some necessary equalities (for each side) to make the expected and computed types equal. We assume the left-hand-side equalities to prove the right-hand-side equalities. To see this in action, consider the second clause of the definition of app.

expected type	Seq a n	$\to$ Seq a m $\to$ Seq a {plus n m}
equation	app (Scons x xs)	ys = Scons x (app xs ys)
computed type	Seq a (S b)	$\to$ Seq a m $\to$ Seq a (S {plus b m})
equalities		n = (S b) $\Rightarrow$ {plus n m}= S({plus b m})

The left-hand-side equalities let us assume n = S b. The right-hand-side equalities, require us to establish that {plus n m} = S{plus b m}. Using the assumption that n = S b, we are left with the requirement that {plus (S b) m} = S{plus b m}, which is easy to prove using the definition of plus.

← value name space | type name space →			
value	*type*	*kind*	*sort*
		Tree	:: *0 ~> *0	:: *1
Fork	:: Tree a -> Tree a -> Tree a	:: *0	:: *1
Node	:: a -> Tree a	:: *0	:: *1
Tip	:: Tree a	:: *0	:: *1
		Z	:: Nat	:: *1
		S	:: Nat ~> Nat	:: *1
		plus	:: Nat ~> Nat ~> Nat	:: *1
		{plus #1 #3 }	:: Nat	:: *1
		Seq	:: *0 ~> Nat ~> *0	:: *1
Snil	:: Seq a Z	:: *0	:: *1
Scons	:: a -> Seq a b -> Seq a (S b)	:: *0	:: *1
app	:: Seq a n -> Seq a m -> Seq a {plus n m}	:: *0	:: *1
		Fahrenheit	:: TempUnit	:: *1
		Celsius	:: TempUnit	:: *1
		Kelvin	:: TempUnit	:: *1
		Degree	:: TempUnit ~> *0	:: *1
F	:: Float -> Degree Fahrenheit	:: *0	:: *1
C	:: Float -> Degree Celsius	:: *0	:: *1
K	:: Float -> Degree Kelvin	:: *0	:: *1
plusK	:: Degree a -> Degree b -> Degree Kelvin	:: *0	:: *1
		T	:: Boolean	:: *1
		F	:: Boolean	:: *1
		le	:: Nat ~> Nat > Boolean	:: *1
		{le #0 #2}	:: Boolean	:: *1
		LE	:: Nat ~> Nat > *0	:: *1
LeZ	:: LE Z a	:: *0	:: *1
LeS	:: LE n m -> LE (S n) (S m)	:: *0	:: *1
		Even	:: Nat ~> *0	:: *1
EvenZ	:: Even Z	:: *0	:: *1
EvenSS	:: Even n -> Even (S(S n))	:: *0	:: *1

Fig. 1. The level hierarchy for some of the examples in the paper

The different levels of the objects introduced in this example (and elsewhere in the paper) are plotted in Figure 1. The reader may wish to consult the figure to help visualize the relationships involved.

3.1 Overview

The following sections tell a rather complex story that will culminate with some generic programs written as ordinary programs in Ωmega. To reach that end, we introduce a few tools. The tools include some backward compatible additions to Haskell, a number of interesting programming patterns that exploit the additions, and a set of illustrative examples. The new features we have added to Haskell that are discussed in this paper include:

– **Data Structures at All Levels.** Kinds are a type system for classifying types. Sorts are a type system for classifying kinds. There is no practical limit to this hierarchy. In Ωmega, programmers can introduce new tree-like structures at any level. In Haskell all introduced datatypes are classified by *0. I.e. the introduced types classify only values. In Figure 1, Haskell types are illustrated by `Tree`, which is a type constructor which classifies its constructor functions (`Fork`, `Node`, and `Tip`) which are values. In Ωmega, the `data` declaration is generalized to all levels.

- **GADTs.** Generalized Algebraic Datatypes allow constructor functions to have more general types than the types supported by the `data` declaration in Haskell. GADTs are important because the additional generality allows programmer to express properties of types as witness types, proof objects, or singleton types. GADTs are the machinery that support the Curry-Howard isomorphism in Ωmega. In Figure 1, the types `Seq`, `Degree`, `LE` and `Even` require the generality introduced by GADTs.
- **Functions at All Levels.** Ωmega supports functions over the tree-like structures at all levels. Such functions are written by pattern matching equations, in much the same manner one writes functions over data at the value level in Haskell. We restrict the form of such definitions to be inductively sequential (See Appendix A). This ensures a sound and complete strategy for answering certain type-checking time questions by the use of narrowing. The class of inductively sequential functions is a large one, in fact every Haskell function has an inductively sequential definition. The inductively sequential restriction affects the form of the equations, and not the functions that can be expressed. In Figure 1, `plus` and `le` are functions at the type level.
- **Code Constructing Quasi-Quotes.** Ωmega supports the run-time generation of code, along the lines of MetaML [18] and Template Haskell [19]. The meta-programming ability of code generation allows us to remove a layer of interpretation from our generic programs, that makes them efficient as well as general.

Some of the following sections are labeled with *Feature* if they are an addition to Haskell, *Pattern* if they are a paradigmatic use of the features to accomplish a particular end, or *Example* if they illustrate an important concept.

3.2   Relation to Other Systems

In order to make Ωmega accessible to as broad an audience as possible, it is built around a framework which appears to the user to be a pure but strict version of Haskell. Ωmega was designed, first and foremost, to be to be a programming language. Our goal was to design a language where program specifications, program properties, program analyses, proofs about programs, and programs themselves, are all represented using a single unifying notion of term. Thus programmers communicate many different things using the same language.

Our second goal was to make Ωmega a logic, in which our reasoning would be sound. This is the basis of our decision to make Ωmega strict. We made this design decision because the use of GADTs as proof objects requires that bottom not be an inhabitant of certain types. Strictness is part of our eventual strategy to accomplish that goal. This goal is not yet achieved.

There are many systems where soundness was the principal goal, and has been achieved. All of the examples, except for the staged examples, could be done in these languages as well. Such systems were principally designed to be logical frameworks or theorem provers. These include Inductive Families [7,9], theorem provers (Coq [23], Isabelle [14]), logical frameworks (Twelf [16], LEGO [11]), and proof assistants (ALF [13], Agda [6]). Recently, there has been much interest in systems that use dependent types to build "practical" systems that are part language, part reasoning system. These systems include Augustsson's Cayenne language [3,2], McBride's Epigram [12], Stump's Rogue-Sigma-Pi [21,24], Xi and Pfenning's Dependent ML [27,8], and Xi's Applied Type Systems [26,5]. In fact, we owe a large debt to all these systems for inspiration.

We realize that just *a little* loss in soundness makes all our reasoning claims vacuous, but we are working to fill these gaps. Our goal is to do this in a different manner than the system listed above, which require all functions to be total in order to ensure soundness. We wish to use types to separate terminating functions from non-terminating functions. And make logical claims only about the terminating fragment of the language. This seems almost a necessary condition for a system that claims to be a programming language. In any case, these issues have little effect on our use of Ωmega to program generic programs, since logical soundness is not an issue in this domain.

4   Introduction to Ωmega

Throughout this section we introduce the features of Ωmega by comparing and contrasting them with the features of Haskell. We assume a basic understanding of Haskell programs. In particular, we assume the reader understands about the introduction of algebraic data types with the **data** declaration (which introduces a type constructor and some constructor constants and functions), and the use of writing pattern matching equations to define functions.

Feature: Kinds. We can introduce new tree-like data at any level, including the type level and higher. The data declaration introduces both the constructors for tree-like data and the object that classifies these structures. We indicate the level where these objects reside using *0, *1, *2, etc. in the **data** declaration. Consider the kinds Nat (introduced earlier), Boolean, and TempUnit:

```
data Nat :: *1 where          data TempUnit:: *1 where
  Z :: Nat                      Fahrenheit:: TempUnit
  S :: Nat ~> Nat               Celsius:: TempUnit
                                Kelvin:: TempUnit
data Boolean:: *1 where
  T:: Boolean
  F:: Boolean
```

The new tree-like data at the type level are constructed by the type-constants (Z, T, F, Fahrenheit, Celsius, and Kelvin), and type constructors (S). The kinds Nat, Boolean, and TempUnit classify these structures, as shown explicitly in the declaration. For example `Celsius` is classified by `TempUnit`, and `S` is a constructor from `Nat` to `Nat`. Think of the operator `~>` as an function arrow at the type level. Note that while `Z`, `T`, `F`, `Fahrenheit`, `Celsius`, and `Kelvin` live at the type level, there are no values classified by them. Again, see Figure 1 to see where these objects reside in the larger picture.

Even though there are no values classified by these types, they are very useful. Instead of using them to classify values, we use them as indexes to value level data, i.e. types like `Degree Celsius` and `Seq a (S Z)`. The indexes like `Celsius` and `S z` indicate static (type-checking time) properties of values. For example, a value with type `Seq a (S Z)` is statically guaranteed to have length 1.

Feature: GADTs. Generalized Algebraic Datatypes allow constructor functions to have more general types than the types supported by `data` declaration in Haskell. GADTs are important because the additional generality allows programmer to express properties of types using type indexes and witnesses (or proof) objects. The `data` declaration in Ωmega defines generalized algebraic datatypes (GADT). These are characterized by explicitly classifying constructors in a `data` declaration with their full types. The additional generality arises because the range of a constructor in a GADT is not constrained to be the type constructor applied to only type variables. For example consider the value level types:

```
data Seq:: *0 ~> Nat ~> *0 where
  Snil :: Seq a Z
  Scons:: a -> Seq a n -> Seq a (S n)

data Degree:: TempUnit ~> *0 where
  F :: Float -> Degree Fahrenheit
  C :: Float -> Degree Celsius
  K :: Float -> Degree Kelvin
```

Note, that instead of ranges like `Degree a` and `Seq a b`, where only type variables like `a` and `b` can be used as parameters, the ranges contain sophisticated instantiations such as `Degree Celsius` and `Seq a (S n)`. Note that the second index to `Seq` (the one of kind `Nat`) is used to describe an invariant about the length of the sequence. The constructors of `Degree` each lift a scalar `Float` to a `Degree` with a different unit. Operations on `Degree` are easy to define. Note that in Ωmega, `(#+)` is the infix operator for addition on `Float`s.

```
add :: Degree a -> Degree a -> Degree a
add (F n) (F m) = F(n #+ n)
add (C n) (C m) = C(n #+ n)
add (K n) (K m) = K(n #+ n)
```

An interesting observation is that while the definition for `add` contains only three of the possible nine combinations of the constructors for `Degree`, it is total function. That is because any of the missing six patterns representing pairs of arguments, cannot both have the same `TempUnit` index: a, as declared by the prototype declaration.

Using kinds in this fashion is more expressive than just using phantom types. For example one might be tempted to use phantom types and write:

```
data Degree unit  = T Float
fah  :: Float -> Degree Fahrenheit
fah  = T
cel  :: Float -> Degree Celsius
cel  = T
kel  :: Float -> Degree Kelvin
kel  = T


add              :: Degree a -> Degree a -> Degree a
add (T x) (T y) = T (x #+ y) -- no need for 3 cases
```

This is strictly less general. First it admits nonsense types like (`Degree Bool`). Using new kinds, only `Fahrenheit`, `Celsius`, and `Kelvin` are classified by `TempUnit`, so types like `Degree Bool` are rejected. The kind system plays the role of a *type system* for types.

Second, with the GADT approach, one can write functions that do different things depending on the type of their inputs. For example we can write coercing operators that take inputs of any units, but always return outputs of a standard unit (say `Kelvin`).

```
plusK :: Degree a -> Degree b -> Degree Kelvin
plusK (K x) (K y) = K(x #+ y)
plusK (C x) (K y) = K(273.0 #+ x #+ y)
```

For brevity, we have shown here only two of the nine possible cases.

Feature: Type Functions. Kind declarations allow us to introduce new tree-like structures at the type level. We can use these structures to parameterize data at the value level as we did with `Nat` or `TempUnit`, or we can compute over these tree-like structures. Such functions are written by pattern matching equations, in much the same manner one writes functions over data at the value level. Several useful functions over types defined earlier are:

```
even :: Nat ~> Boolean              plus:: Nat ~> Nat ~> Nat
{even Z} = T                        {plus Z m} = m
{even (S Z)} = F                    {plus (S n) m} = S {plus n m}
{even (S (S n))} = {even n}
                                    and:: Boolean ~> Boolean ~> Boolean
le:: Nat ~> Nat ~> Boolean          {and T x} = x
{le Z n} = T                        {and F x} = F
{le (S n) Z} = F
{le (S n) (S m)} = {le n m}
```

Like functions at the value level, the type functions `plus`, `and`, `even`, and `le` are expressed using equations. The function `and` is a binary function that combines two `Boolean`s. The property `even` is a unary predicate that distinguishes odd from even numbers, and the property `le` is a binary less-than-or-equal-to predicate. All the type functions are strict total (terminating) functions.

Pattern: Witnesses. GADTs can be used to witness relational properties between types. This is because the parameters to types introduced using the GADT mechanism can play different roles. The natural number argument of the type constructor Seq (from Section 3) plays a qualitatively different role than type arguments in ordinary ADTs. Consider the declaration for a binary tree datatype in Haskell:

```
data Tree a = Fork (Tree a) (Tree a) | Node a | Tip
```

In this declaration the type parameter a is used to indicate that there are subcomponents of Trees that are of type a. In fact, Trees are parametric. Any type of value can be placed in the "sub component" of type a. The type of the value placed there is reflected in the Tree's type. Contrast this with the n in (Seq a n). Instead, the parameter n is used to stand for an abstract property (the length of the list represented). When we use a type parameters in this way we call it a type index [25,28] rather than a type parameter.

We can use indexes to GADTs to define value level data that we can think of as proofs, or witnesses to type level properties. This is a powerful idea. Consider the introduction of two new parameterized types Even and LE. Note that these are ordinary data structures that exist at the value level, but describe properties at the type level.

```
data Even:: Nat ~> *0 where          data Plus:: Nat ~> Nat ~> Nat ~> *0 where
  EvenZ:: Even Z                       PlusZ:: Plus Z m m
  EvenSS:: Even n -> Even (S (S n))    PlusS:: Plus n m z -> Plus (S n) m (S z)

data LE:: Nat ~> Nat ~> *0 where
  LeZ:: LE Z n
  LeS:: LE n m -> LE (S n) (S m)
```

These declarations introduce value-level constants (EvenZ, PlusZ, and LeZ) and constructor functions (EvenSS, PlusS, and LeS). Let's examine the types of several values constructed with these constructors. To make it easier to handle types of kind Nat, in Ωmega, we have special syntactic sugar for entering and displaying them. Z = #0, S Z = #1, S(S Z) = #2, etc. We may also write #(1+x) for S x, and #(2+x) for S(S x), etc.

```
EvenZ:: Even #0                      LeZ:: LE #0 a
(EvenSS EvenZ):: Even #2             (LeS LeZ):: LE #1 #(1+a)
(EvenSS (EvenSS EvenZ)):: Even #4    (LeS (LeS LeZ)):: LE #2 #(2+a)

p1 ::Plus #2 #3 #5
p1 = PlusS (PlusS PlusZ)
```

We write #0 for Z, and #1 for S Z, etc. to emphasize that we should view LE, Plus and Even as a relationships between natural numbers. The important thing to notice is that we may view ordinary values with types LE n m and Even n as proofs, since the types of all legally constructed values witness only true statements about n and m. For example we cannot build a term of type

Even #1. This is the essence of the Curry-Howard isomorphism. We can view
(EvenSS Even):: Even #2 as either the statement that EvenSS EvenZ has type
Even #2, or that EvenSS EvenZ is a proof of the property Even #2. All this follows directly from the introduction of new types with tree-like structure, and
the ability to *compute* over them.

Pattern: Witness vs. Type Function. The reader may have noticed that
even and Even are two different ways to express the same notion. Either we
write a (Boolean) function at the type level (even), or introduce a witness type
(Even) at the value level. For every n-ary function at the type level, we can
build an $(n + 1)$-ary witness type. The witness type turns the n-ary function
into an $(n + 1)$-ary type constructor. Each clause in the function definition is
named by a constructor function in the witness. If the right-hand-side of a clause
has m recursive calls, the constructor function becomes an m-ary constructor.
The right-hand-side of each clause becomes the $(n + 1)^{th}$ argument of the range,
where every recursive call to the function in the right-hand-side, is replaced with
a variable. Each recursive call becomes one of the m arguments. The $(n + 1)^{st}$
argument to these calls is the new variable replacing the corresponding recursive
call in the $(n + 1)^{st}$ argument of the range. For example: The clause of the
binary function {plus (S n) m} = S {plus n m}, becomes a ternary predicate
Plus (S n) m (S {plus n m}). By replacing the recursive call with z, and making
z be the $(n + 1)^{st}$ parameter to the first argument, we get the type of the unary
constructor PlusS:: Plus n m z -> Plus (S n) m (S z).

Witnesses and type functions express the same ideas, but can be used in very
different ways. Type functions are only useful at compile-time (they're static) and
their structure cannot be observed (they can only be applied, so we say they are
extensional). Witnesses, on the other hand, are actual data that is manipulated
at run time (they're dynamic). Their structure can also be observed and taken
apart (we say they're intensional). They are true data. A big difference between
the two ways of representing properties is the computational mechanisms used
to ensure that programs adhere to such properties.

Pattern: Singleton Types. Sometimes it is useful to direct computation at the
type level, by writing functions at the value level. Even though types cannot depend on values directly, this can be simulated by the use of singleton types. The
idea is to build a completely separate isomorphic copy of the type in the value
world, but still retain a connection between the two isomorphic structures. This
connection is maintained by indexing the value-world type with the corresponding type-world kind. This is best understood by example. Consider reflecting
the kind Nat into the value-world by defining the type constructor SNat using a
data declaration.

```
data SNat:: Nat ~> *0 where
  Zero:: SNat Z
  Succ:: SNat n -> SNat (S n)

three = (Succ (Succ (Succ Zero))):: SNat(S(S(S Z)))
```

Here, the value constructors of the **data** declaration for SNat mirror the type constructors in the **kind** declaration of Nat. We maintain the connection between the two isomorphic structures by the use of SNat's natural number index. This type index is in one-to-one correspondence with the shape of the value. Thus, the type index of SNat exactly mirrors its shape. For example, consider the example **three** above, and pay particular attention to the structure of the type index, and the structure of the value with that type.

This kind of relationship between values and types is called a *singleton type* because there is only one element of any singleton type. For example only Succ (Succ Zero) inhabits the type SNat(S (S Z)). It is possible to define a singleton type for any first order type (of any kind). All Singleton types always have kinds of the form I ~> *0 where I is the index we are reflecting into the value world. We sometimes call singleton types *representation types*. We cannot over emphasize the importance of the singleton property. Every singleton type completely characterizes the structure of its single inhabitant, and the structure of a value in a singleton type completely characterizes its type. Thus we can compute over a value of a singleton type, and the computation at the value level can express a property at the type level. By using singleton types we completely avoid the use of dependent types where types depend on values [20,17]. The cost associated with this avoidance is the possible duplication of data structures and functions at several levels.

Pattern: A pun: Nat'. We now define the type Nat', which is in all ways isomorphic to the type SNat. The type Nat' is also a singleton type representing the natural numbers, but it relies on an feature of the Ωmega type system. In Ωmega (as in Haskell) the name space for values is separate from the name space for types. Thus it is possible to have the same name stand for two things. One in the value space, and the other in the type space. The pun is because we use the names S and Z in both the value and type name spaces. We exploit this ability by writing:

```
data Nat':: Nat ~> *0 where
  Z:: Nat' Z
  S:: Nat' n -> Nat' (S n)
```

The value constructors Z:: Nat' Z and S:: Nat' n -> Nat' (S n) are ordinary values whose types mention the type constructors they pun. The name space partition, and the relationship between Nat and Nat' is illustrated below.

← *value name space*	*type name space* →		
value	*type*	*kind*	*sort*
	Z	:: Nat	:: *1
	S	:: Nat ~> Nat	:: *1
Z	:: Nat' Z	:: *0	:: *1
S	:: Nat' m -> Nat' (S m)	:: *0	:: *1

In Nat', the singleton relationship between a Nat' value and its type is emphasized even more strongly, as witnessed by the example **three'**.

```
three' = (S(S(S Z))):: Nat'(S(S(S Z)))
```

Here the shape of the value, and the type index appear isomorphic. We further exploit this pun, by extending the syntactic sugar for writing natural numbers at the type level (#0, #1, etc.) to their singleton types at the value level. Thus we may write (#2:: Nat' #2).

Pattern: Computing Programs and Properties Simultaneously. We can write programs that compute an indexed value along with a witness that the value has some additional property. For example, when we add two static length lists, the resulting list has a length that is related to the lengths of the two input lists, and we can simultaneously produce a witness to this relationship.

```
data Plus:: Nat ~> Nat ~> Nat ~> *0 where
  PlusZ:: Plus Z m m
  PlusS:: Plus n m z -> Plus (S n) m (S z)

app1:: Seq a n -> Seq a m -> exists p . (Seq a p,Plus n m p)
app1 Snil ys = Ex(ys,PlusZ)
app1 (Scons x xs) ys = case (app1 xs ys) of { Ex(zs,p) -> Ex(Scons x zs,PlusS p) }
```

The keyword **Ex** is the "pack" operator of Cardelli and Wegner [4]. Its use turns a normal type (Seq a p,Plus n m p) into an existential type exists p.(Seq a p,Plus n m p). The Ωmega compiler uses a bidirectional type checking algorithm to propagate the existential type in the signature inwards to the **Ex** tagged expressions. This allows it to abstract over the correct existentially quantified variables.

Pattern: Staging. Ωmega supports the staging annotations: brackets: ([| _ |]), escape ($(_)), and the two staging functions: lift::(forall a . a -> Code a) and run::(forall a . (Code a) -> a) for building and manipulating code. Ωmega uses the Template Haskell [19] conventions for creating code. Brackets ([| _ |]) are a quasi-quotation mechanism, and escape ($(_)) escapes from the effects of quasi-quotation. For example.

```
inc x = x + 1
c1a = [| 4 + 3 |]
c2a = [| \ x -> x + $c1a |]
c3 = [| let f x = y - 1 where y = 3 * x in f 4 + 3 |]
c4 = [| inc 3 |]
c5 = [| [| 3 |] |]
c6 = [| \ x -> x |]
```

In the examples above, inc is a normal function. The variable c1a names a piece of code with type Code Int. The variable c2a names a piece of code with type Code(Int -> Int). It is constructed by splicing the code c1a into the body of the lambda abstraction. The variable c3 names a piece of code with type Code Int. It illustrates the ability to define rich pieces of code with embedded let and where clauses. The variable c4 names a piece of code with type Code Int. It illustrates that functions defined in earlier stages (inc) can be lifted (or embedded) in code. The variable c5 names a piece of code with type Code (Code Int). It illustrates that code can be nested.

The purpose of the staging mechanism is to have finer control over evaluation order, which is exactly what we want to do when removing the interpretive overhead of generic programming. Ωmega supports many of the features of MetaML [18,22].

5   Generic Programming

We now know enough about Ωmega to write some generic functions. Generic programming is nothing more than abstracting over objects rich in structure. Usually this structure is some internal compiler structure not accessible to the programmer. Without some sort of reflection mechanism, the language cannot access this structure. Even with a reflection mechanism, the reflected structure is usually too complex to capture in a well-typed way. Instead an untyped abstraction of the internal structure is used. This often has no precise formal connection to real internal structure. In Ωmega, with its rich types, including the use of type indexes, we can often remedy these objections.

5.1   Datatype Generic Programs

The classic generic programming example is datatype generic programming, where a single program suffices to define a function over many different datatypes. When a function is defined over a fixed set of types we call it overloaded, when it is defined over all types, we call it generic.

The key to overloaded programs, is defining the overloaded functions over the structure of types. In order to do this effectively, the values representing the structure of types should be intimately connected to the actual type structure. In Ωmega we can use GADTs to build such a connection.

We will build a representation of types using GADTs and then generate several program families by abstracting over the type representation. Our example is extremely simple, but depends only on the use of GADTs. It makes no use of Ωmega's other features. In the companion paper in this collection, *Generic Programming, Now!*, by Ralf Hinze and Andres Löh, there are many richer examples that follow exactly this paradigm, which could also be programmed in Ωmega.

To build the connection between types, and their structure we use GADTs to define an indexed structure that represents Ωmega types. This GADT will have a type index. This index is the type that being represented.

Our example will represent base types, products, and sum types, but we could easily extend it to other types. In Ωmega the type a+b is like Either a b in Haskell. Vaules of sum types are created with the constructor functions L:: a -> (a+b) and R:: b -> (a+b). Note also, that the type Rep is a singleton type.

```
data Rep:: *0 ~> *0 where
  Rint:: Rep Int
  Rchar:: Rep Char
  Runit:: Rep ()
  Rpair:: Rep a -> Rep b -> Rep (a,b)
  Rsum::  Rep a -> Rep b -> Rep (a+b)

t1 :: Rep ((Int,Char)+((),Int))
t1 = Rsum(Rpair Rint Rchar) (Rpair Runit Rint)
```

Note, in example t1, that the index ((Int,Char)+((),Int)) is isomorphic to
the shape of its value Rsum (Rpair Rint Rchar) (Rpair Runit Rint). Next,
we define an overloaded function to sum up all the integer components of a rich
structure with type: Rep a -> a -> Int.

```
sumR :: Rep a -> a -> Int
sumR Rint n = n
sumR (Rpair r s) (x,y) = sumR r x + sumR s y
sumR (Rsum r s) (L x) = sumR r x
sumR (Rsum r s) (R x) = sumR s x
sumR _ x = 0
```

As we interpret the shape of the Rep, we recursively descend over sums and
pairs (summing the two components from each part of the pair), components
of type Int are returned, and other base types contribute zero. The overhead
of interpreting the type representation adds considerable cost to computing the
result. Staging the sum function can remove this overhead, and is simply a matter
of placing the staging annotations in the correct places.

```
sum2 :: Rep a -> Code a -> Code Int
sum2 Rint x = x
sum2 (Rpair x y) z =
  [| let (a,b) = $z in $(sum2 x [| a |]) + $(sum2 y [| b |]) |]
sum2 (Rsum r s) x =
  [| case $x of
       L m -> $(sum2 r [| m |])
       R m -> $(sum2 s [| m |]) |]
sum2 _ x = [| 0 |]

sumG:: Rep a -> Code (a -> Int)
sumG x = [| \ w -> $(sum2 x [| w |]) |]

ans3 = sumG t1
```

Note the use of the generated pattern match in the Rpair case to avoid the
duplication of the code z.

The strategy we use in the example above is a common one when staging
a function. Rather than define a function with type Rep a -> Code (a -> Int)
in one go, we do it in two steps. First defining a function (sum2) with type

`Rep a -> Code a -> Code Int`, and then using this function to build the function (sumG) with the type we really want. We do this because it is easier to manipulate code with first-order types. If we built `sumG` directly we would generate code with unnecessary explicit beta-redices and eta-expansions. The example `ans3` illustrates the residual code.

```
[| \ bbf ->
     case bbf of
       (L ebf) ->
          let (hbf, ibf) = ebf
          in hbf + 0
       (R jbf) ->
          let (mbf, nbf) = jbf
          in 0 + nbf |] : Code (((Int,Char)+((),Int)) -> Int)
```

Many richer examples of datatype generic polymorphism are illustrated in the companion paper *Generic Programming, Now!*. Such examples depend only upon the GADT mechanism and are programmed in the GHC extensions to Haskell. These examples could benefit additionally from staging. We now move to some examples that rely on the richer type mechanisms of Ωmega.

5.2   The n-Sum Example

We will build a well-typed generic program that captures the family of programs:

```
1.   \ x -> x
2.   \ x -> \ y -> x+y
3.   \ x -> \ y -> \ z -> x+y+z
4.   \ x -> \ y -> \ z -> \ w -> x+y+z+w
```

First, we define a function at the type level that maps a natural number i to the type of the ith function in this family.

```
sumTy :: Nat ~> *0
{sumTy Z} = Int
{sumTy (S n)} = Int -> {sumTy n}
```

For example, the type `{sumTy #3}` normalizes to the type `Int -> Int -> Int -> Int`. With this type function we can now capture the type of the generic sum over n integers: `nsum:: Nat' n -> {sumTy n}`. Which behaves as:

```
(nsum #1) =  \ x -> x
(nsum #2) =  \ x -> \ y -> x+y
(nsum #3) =  \ x -> \ y -> \ z -> x+y+z
```

We define the n-way sum function in two stages. We write a helper function `nsumAcc`, and then write a program `nsum` which captures the family of functions:

```
nsumAcc :: Nat' n -> Int -> {sumTy n}
nsumAcc Z x = x
nsumAcc (S n) x = \ y -> (nsumAcc n (x+y))

nsum :: Nat' n -> {sumTy n}
nsum n = nsumAcc n 0

testsum = (nsum #3 1 3 5) == (nsum #2 0 9)
```

Note how the number of integers `nsum` can consume depends upon its `Nat'` argument. It is truly generic in the sense that it abstracts over objects not in the vocabulary of most languages. Note also, that type checking this function must solve a narrowing problem.

expected type	Nat' n	→ Int → {sumTy n}
equation	nsumAcc (S n)	x = λ y → (nsumAcc n (x+y))
computed type	Nat' (S a) → Int → Int → {sumTy a}	
equalities	n = (S a) ⇒ Int → {sumTy a} = {sumTy n}	

We must show that under the assumption n = (S a), the type `Int -> {sumTy a}` is equal to the type `{sumTy n}`. Substituting for `n`, we must solve `Int -> {sumTy a} = {sumTy (S a)}`. Using the definition of `sumTy` we get `Int -> {sumTy a} = Int -> {sumTy a}`.

This program interprets the structure of its `Nat'` argument. It would be well to stage the function so that this interpretive over head is removed. This is easy to do using Ωmega's staging annotations. To stage the `nsum` program we write the nsum generator `nsumG`.

```
nsumG :: Nat' n -> Code Int -> Code {sumTy n}
nsumG Z x = x
nsumG (S n) x = [| \ y -> $(nsumG n [| $x + y |]) |]

sumGen:: Nat' n -> Code {sumTy n}
sumGen n = nsumG n (lift 0)
```

This is essentially the `nsumAcc` program with a few brackets and escapes judicially sprinkled over the program, to force the interpretation to happen in the first stage, and to produce the residual code. By executing `sumGen` we obtain the residual code when the size is #3.

```
sumGen (S(S(S Z)))

[| \ y1 -> \ y3 -> \ y5 -> 0 + y1 + y3 + y5 |]
:: Code (Int -> Int -> Int -> Int)
```

Analysis of the Generic Examples. The process followed in this and the previous example is common to many generic programming exercises. We review it here.

– First, develop some indexed data structure to capture the details of the problem. The index captures a semantic property of the generic program. In the nsum example the indexed data structure is the singleton natural numbers, and the index is related to the number of arguments. In the datatype generic example, the index relates the structure (Rep) to the type it represents.

– Second, write a type function(s) that computes the type of the generic result as a function of the specification structure. In the nsum example, sumTy plays this role. In the datatype generic sum function the type function was the identity and was not needed.

– Third, write a function that interprets the specification to produce the result (nsum and sum2).

– Fourth, stage the generic function to produce a generic generator (nsumG and sumG).

5.3   Generic n-Way Zip

In this example we illustrate the use of a type relation (or witness type) to specify a generic function. Sometimes such a witness type is more useful than a type function.

Consider the zip function that maps a ternary function over the elements of three lists. One way to approach this problem was suggested by Fridlender and Indrika in their paper *Do We Need Dependent Types* [10]. They develop an n-way zip that uses only polymorphism rather than indexed or dependent types. Their approach depends upon the following observation, that n-way zip is nothing more than repeated list-based application(apply), where a list of functions is applied to a list of arguments. We illustrate for $n = 3$.

```
zip3 f [1,2,3] [True,False] ['a','b','c','d']                                  -->
[f,f,f,f, ...] 'apply' [1,2,3] 'apply' [True,False] 'apply' ['a','b','c','d']  -->
[f 1, f 2, f 3] 'apply' [True,False] 'apply' ['a','b','c','d']                 -->
[f 1 True, f 2 False] 'apply' ['a','b','c','d']                               -->
[f 1 True 'a', f 2 False 'b']

apply (f:fs) (x:xs) = (f x) : (apply fs xs)
apply _ _ = []
```

The function zip3 first creates an infinite list of the function f, and then iterates the list-based application function over the three lists. Note how the length of the shortest of the three lists determines the length of the result. An infinite list of fs is necessary since the function zip3 cannot know how long its inputs are without testing them. The approach is to build the iterator as higher-order ordinals, i.e. functions that behave like zero and successor functions that build the natural numbers.

```
zero:: a -> a
zero x = x

succ:: ([a] -> b) -> [c -> a] -> [c] -> b
succ n fs xs = n(fs 'apply' xs)
```

```
zero:: a -> a
(succ zero):: [a -> b] -> [a] -> [b]
(succ(succ zero))::: [a -> b -> c] -> [a] -> [b] -> [c]
```

Note how successive application of **succ** to previous ordinals construct functions that use the list-based application strategy. The definition of **zip** is trivial, first building the infinite list of functions, and then applying the ordinal to do the work.

```
zip:: ([a] -> b) -> a -> b
zip n f = n (repeat f)
```

There are three problems with this approach. First, the ordinals are functions and not data structures. Because of this, their structure cannot be observed. This precludes building a staged implementation, which means there will always be a layer of interpretation that cannot be removed. Second, this strategy depends in a crucial way on the use of laziness. The infinite list of functions can only be built in a lazy language. In a strict language (like ML), the strategy must be severely modified to test for the maximum length of the n lists. This also adds some unnecessary overhead. Third, the approach builds n intermediate lists, none of which are absolutely necessary.

We will attack these problems one at a time. First, we can use GADTs to construct the ordinals. Using this approach the ordinals become data structures that can be observed. Consider the GADT **Zip** and the types of the first three ordinals:

```
data Zip:: *0 ~> *0 ~> *0 where
  Zero :: Zip [a] [a]
  Succ :: Zip [x] y -> Zip [a -> x] ([a] -> y)

zero :: Zip [a] [a]
zero = Zero

one :: Zip [a -> b] ([a] -> [b])
oned = Succ Zero

two:: Zip [a -> b -> c] ([a] -> [b] -> [c])
two = Succ(Succ Zero)
```

In general the type of the n way map has the type a -> b where the nth ordinal has type **Zip [a] b**. We can write these functions following the pattern of Fridlender and Indrika.

```
zip :: Zip [x] y -> x -> y
zip n f = zip' n (repeat f)
  where zip' :: Zip x y -> x -> y
        zip' Zero xs = xs
        zip' (Succ n) fs = \ xs -> zip' n (apply fs xs)
```

```
zip:: (a -> b -> c -> d) -> [a] -> [b] -> [c] -> [d]
zip f = \ list1 -> case list1 of
            (x : xs) ->
               \ list2 -> case list2 of
                  (y : ys) ->
                     \ list3 -> case list3 of
                        (z : zs) -> f x y z : zip f xs ys zs
                        [] -> []
                     [] -> \ _ -> []
                  [] -> \ _ -> \ _ -> []
```

Fig. 2. An example n-way zip, for $n=3$

First, create the infinite list of fs, and then repeatedly apply this list of functions to the next list of elements. Because the ordinal is a data structure we can easily stage this function.

```
zipGen :: Zip [x] y -> Code(x -> y)
zipGen n = [| \ f -> $(zip' n [| repeat f |]) |]
   where zip' :: Zip x y -> Code x -> Code y
         zip' Zero xs = xs
         zip' (Succ n) fs = [| \ xs -> $(zip' n [| apply $fs xs |] ) |]
```

Here the iteration over n becomes plain. For each n the function zip' unfolds generating a lambda expression over one of the n lists. For example: zipGen (Succ (Succ Zero)) generates the following Ωmega code:

```
[| \ f -> \ xs -> \ ys -> %apply (%apply (%repeat f) xs) ys |]
```

Unfortunately, this code still suffers from the use of laziness, and the creation of intermediate lists. An alternate approach is illustrated in Figure 2. The 3-ary zip illustrated is an instance of a generic n-way zip. It should be clear that there are two iterations going on. The first iteration is over n. For $n=3$, we see that the function unfolds into 3 lambdas and 3 case expressions. The second iteration is over the length of the shortest of the n lists. Note that this iteration begins only after the n way iteration. Note how this strategy neither depends upon laziness, nor builds unnecessary intermediate lists.

To type the general n-way zip (rather than the specific 3-way zip) consider the sequence of terms that appear in the definition of the 3-way zip.

```
f           :: (a -> b -> c -> d)
(f x)       :: (b -> c -> d)
(f x y)     :: (c -> d)
(f x y z)   :: d

(zip f)          :: ([a] -> [b] -> [c] -> [d])
(zip f xs)       :: ([b] -> [c] -> [d])
(zip f xs ys)    :: ([c] -> [d])
(zip f xs ys zs) :: [d]
```

There is a relationship between the types of the two sequences of terms. Note that the types of the second sequence can be obtained from the first by applying the list type constructor to each of the type variables in the types of the first sequence. This motivates the following witness type, that relates the number n, and the types of these two sequences.

```
data Zip' :: *0 ~> *0 ~> *0 where
  Zero':: Zip' a [a]
  Succ':: Zip' b c -> Zip' (a -> b) ([a] -> c)
```

Like the GADT Zip, the new values of the new GADT Zip' are isomorphic to the natural numbers, and Zip' is a relation between the two sequences of types given above. By observing the type of several successive values we can visualize this relationship.

```
zero' = Zero'                  :: Zip' a [a]
one'  = Succ' Zero'            :: Zip' (a -> b) ([a] -> [b])
two'  = Succ' (Succ' Zero') :: Zip' (a -> b -> c) ([a] -> [b] -> [c])
```

It should be clear, that the type of the n-way zip can be captured by using either Zip or Zip'

```
zip:: Zip [a] b -> a -> b.      and
zip:: Zip' a b -> a -> b.
```

To define zip using Zip', we write helper function, help :: Zip' a b -> a -> b -> b. The basic idea is captured by the table below.

2	f:: (a -> b -> c)	zip f:: [a] -> [b] -> [c]	help two' f (zip f):: [a] -> [b] -> [c]
1	f x:: (b -> c)	zip f xs:: [b] -> [c]	help one' (f x) (zip f xs):: [b] -> [c]
0	f x y:: c	zip f xs ys:: [c]	help zero' (f x y) (zip f xs ys):: [c]

As n decreases, the two arguments to help become more saturated, by applying them to the heads and tails of the n lists. We put this all together below:

```
zip n = let zip f =  help n f (\ x -> zip f x) in zip
  where default:: Zip' a b -> b
        default Zero' = []
        default (Succ' n) = \ ys -> default n

        help :: Zip' a b -> a -> b -> b
        help Zero' x xs = (x : xs)
        help (Succ' n) f rcall =
          (\ ys -> case ys of
             (z:zs) -> help n (f z) (rcall zs)
             _ -> default n)
```

There are two subtleties. The function default builds a lambda of n-arguments, that ignores all of them and returns the empty list. This is necessary since the early termination of the mth-list, means we must skip over the $(m+1)$st-list through nth-list, before we return the empty list. The second subtlety is the eta-expansion of map f as the third argument to help. Without this eta-expansion the definition of map would loop since Ωmega is a strict language. It is easy to stage this function.

```
zipGen:: Zip' a b -> Code (a -> b)
zipGen n = [| let zip f = $(zip' n [|f|] [|zip f|]) in map |]
 where default:: Zip' a b -> Code b
       default Zero' = [| [] |]
       default (Succ' n) = [| \ ys -> $(default n) |]

       zip' :: Zip' a b -> Code a -> Code b -> Code b
       zip' Zero' x xs = [| $x : $xs |]
       zip' (Succ' n) f rcall =
         [| \ ys -> case ys of
               (z:zs) -> $(zip' n [| $f z |] [| $rcall zs |])
               _ -> $(default n) |]
```

Because of the staging we no-longer need the eta-expansion of map f. We apply mapGen to a few ordinals to visualize the results. In the code below we have alpha-renamed some of the variables in the code that was actually generated to make the structure more obvious.

```
zipGen Zero'    ---->
[| let zip0 x = x : zip0 x in zip0 |] : forall a.Code (a -> [a])

zipGen  one'    ---->
[| let zip1 f =
        \ xs ->
            case xs of
              (y : ys) -> f y : zip1 f ys
              _ -> []
   in zip1 |] : forall a b.Code ((a -> b) -> [a] -> [b])


zipGen two'  ---->
[| let zip2 f =
        \ xs ->
            case xs of
              (e28 : f28) ->
                \ ys ->
                    case ys of
                      (k28 : l28) -> f e28 k28 : zip2 z27 f28 l28
                      _ -> []
              _ -> \ n28 -> []
   in zip2 |] : forall a b c.Code ((a -> b -> c) -> [a] -> [b] -> [c])
```

For $n=3$, this is exactly the same function which we used as our starting point in Figure 2. Moreover, we have fixed all three of the problems associated with the list-based application approach, with code that is only marginally longer.

Analysis of the Witness Based Examples. The witness based approach to generic programming is common. We review it here.

- First, develop some indexed data structure to witness the relationships between the input and output types of the generic function. The GADTs Zip and Zip' played this role.
- Second, write a function that interprets the witness type to produce the result (the two versions of zip).
- Third, stage the generic function to produce a generic generator (the two versions of zipGen).

5.4   Using Ωmega's Hierarchy of Levels

Our last example illustrates the utility of abstracting over kinds and other higher level entities in addition to the normal ability of abstracting over types. In the companion paper *Generic Programming, Now!*, kind-indexed families of generic functions are illustrated. To enable this, separate representations of types for each kind must be defined. For example, a representation for types with kind: *0 (TypeS), a representation for types with kind: *0 ~> *0 (TypeS_S), and a representation for types with kind: *0 ~> *0 ~> *0 (TypeS_S_S).

```
data TypeS:: *0 ~> *0  where
  Char:: TypeS Char
  Int:: TypeS Int
  AppS_S:: TypeS_S phi -> TypeS a -> TypeS (phi a)

data TypeS_S:: (*0 ~> *0) ~> *0  where
  List:: TypeS_S []
  Tree:: TypeS_S Tree
  AppSS_S:: TypeS_S_S phi -> TypeS a -> TypeS_S (phi a)

data TypeS_S_S:: (*0 ~> *0 ~> *0) ~> *0  where
  Pair:: TypeS_S_S (,)
```

An approach with a different representation for types, for types at every different kind, is a work-around at best. It requires multiple new datatypes, where logically only one is needed, and it requires duplicating the application type representation at every kind. While sufficient for the examples in the paper the three representation types are not complete. Type constructors with kind (*0 ~> *0) ~> *0 and *0 ~> *0 ~> *0 ~> *0, are rare, but not unheard of, and each would require an additional representation type. In Ωmega, only a single kind-indexed datatype is required.

```
data Type:: forall (k:: *2) (t::k) . k ~> t ~> *0  where
  Char:: Type *0 Char
  Int:: Type *0 Int
  App:: forall (i:: *1) (j:: *1) (f:: i~>j) (x:: i) .
        Type (i ~> j) f -> Type i x -> Type j (f x)
  List:: Type (*0 ~> *0) []
  Tree:: Type (*0 ~> *0) Tree
  Pair:: Type (*0 ~> *0 ~> *0) (,)
```

The representation type `Type k t` represents a type t classified by kind k. The type constructor `Type` is polymorphic-recursively kinded. It is applied at different kinds in its own definition.

To write a kind-indexed function, we define a type function that computes over kinds. For example to compute a generic `count` function we proceed as follows.

```
countTy:: forall (k:: *2) (t::k) . k ~> t ~> *0
{countTy *0 a} = a -> Int
{countTy (i ~> k) phi} = {countTy i a} -> {countTy k (phi a)}

count::  forall (k:: *1) (t::k) . Type k t -> {countTy k t}
```

Note that the range of `count` is a function of the kind that classifies t. This requires a single function, with one clause for each of the constructors of `Type`.

```
count::  forall (k:: *1) (t::k) . Type k t -> {countTy k t}
count Char = const 0
count Int = const 0
count (App f a) = (count f) (count a)     where theorem countTyInjective1
count List = \ c -> sumList . mapList c
count Tree = \ c -> sumTree . mapTree c
count Pair = \ c1 c2 (x,y) -> c1 x + c2 y
```

Typing this function requires a little bit of specialized knowledge. In order to type the `(App f a)` clause, we must prove that `{countTy _a e} -> {countTy _c (_d e)}` is equal to `{countTy _a _b} -> {countTy _c (_d _b)}`. I.e. we must find bindings for the existentially quantified variable e that make it true.

This can be proven by assigning the value _b to e, if we realize that `countTy` is injective in its first argument. I.e. `{countTy a x}={countTy a y}` if and only if x=y. This is the purpose of the theorem `countTyInjective1` in the where clause for the `(App f a)` case.

The theorem declaration is an important way of directing the type checker. It uses ordinary terms, with types that can be read logically, as specifcations for new type checking strategies. In Ωmega, there are currently three types of theorems. Each is used to direct the type checker to do things it might not ordinarily do. In the case of `countTyInjective1` the type is:

```
countTyInjective1:: Kind' a -> Equal {countTy a x} {countTy a y} -> Equal x y
```

Logically, this can be read as, *If* a *is a well formed kind, and* `{countTy a x}` *is equal to* `{countTy a y}`, *then* x *is equal to* y. The theorem clause directs the type checker to try proving x=y as one step in a strategy for proving `{countTy a x}={countTy a y}`.

Such a theorem is proved by induction over the structure of the kind k. In Ωmega, this manifests itself as recursive term, representing a proof by induction.

```
prop Kind':: *1 ~> *0 where
  Star :: Kind' *0
  Karr :: Kind' a -> Kind' b -> Kind' (a ~> b)

countTyInjective1:: Kind' a -> Equal {countTy a x} {countTy a y} -> Equal x y
countTyInjective1 Star Eq = Eq
countTyInjective1 (Karr x y) Eq = Eq
  where theorem ih1 = countTyInjective1 x,
                ih2 = countTyInjective1 y
```

Note, that the proof (i.e. the term that defines `countTyInjective1`), uses induction hypotheses, which manifest themselves as calls to `countTyInjective1` on smaller sub terms.

Finally we can define two generic functions `size` and `sum` for all types with kind `*0 ~> *0`.

```
size:: Type (*0 ~> *0) f -> f a -> Int
size f = count f (const 1)

sum:: Type (*0 ~> *0) f -> f Int -> Int
sum f = count f id
```

6 Ωmega's Approach to Dependent Types

In a dependently typed program, the type of some terms are dependent on the values of other terms. In the design of Ωmega, we separate values from types, so in Ωmega we use indexed types instead. For example, reconsider the `nsum` family of functions that sums 1, 2, 3, ... n inputs from Section 5. We could write such function with a dependent type: `f :: Pi (n:Natural). Int -> {sumTy n}`

In our hypothetical dependently-typed language:

```
f :: Pi (n::Natural). Int -> {sumTy n}
f 0  x = x
f n x = \ y -> f (n-1) (x+y)
```

Note how the type of `f` depends on the value of `f`'s first parameter. This violates our design decision separating values and types. But by using singleton types in Ωmega, we defined the `nsum` function from Section 5 with type `nsum :: Nat' n -> Int -> {sumTy n}`

Note how the range of `nsum` is not a function of the value of its first parameter. Instead it is a function of `nsum`'s first parameters' type index, `n`, which is still a type. This example illustrates our strategy for writing dependently typed functions. *Write functions whose types depend on the type-indexes of their arguments rather than the values of their arguments.*

6.1 Conclusion

Ωmega is a language which supports a limited kind of dependent typing, and supports the types-as-properties paradigm. We separate values from types to maintain a familiar functional programming style. Singleton types and other indexed types bridge the gap created by the phase distinction.

The generic programs we have written are ordinary Ωmega programs which abstract over rich values (like Rep, Nat', Zip, Zip', and Type). In addition, the overhead of interpretation of the generic specifications can be completely removed by staging.

References

1. Antoy, S.: Definitional trees. In: Kirchner, H., Levi, G. (eds.) Algebraic and Logic Programming. LNCS, vol. 632, pp. 143–157. Springer, Heidelberg (1992)
2. Augustsson, L.: Cayenne – a language with dependent types. ACM SIGPLAN Notices 34(1), 239–250 (1999)
3. Augustsson, L.: Equality proofs in Cayenne (July 11, 2000), http://www.cs.chalmers.se/~augustss/cayenne/eqproof.ps
4. Cardelli, L., Wegner, P.: On understanding types, data abstraction and polymorphism. ACM Computing Surveys 17(4), 471–522 (1985)
5. Chen, C., Xi, H.: Combining programming with theorem proving. In: ICFP 2005 (2005), http://www.cs.bu.edu/~hwxi/
6. Coquand, C.: Agda is a system for incrementally developing proofs and programs. Web page describing AGDA: http://www.cs.chalmers.se/~catarina/agda/
7. Coquand, T., Dybjer, P.: Inductive definitions and type theory: an introduction (preliminary version). In: Thiagarajan, P.S. (ed.) Foundations of Software Technology and Theoretical Computer Science. LNCS, vol. 880, pp. 60–76. Springer, Heidelberg (1994)
8. Davies, R.: A refinement-type checker for Standard ML. In: Johnson, M. (ed.) AMAST 1997. LNCS, vol. 1349, Springer, Heidelberg (1997)
9. Dybjer, P., Setzer, A.: A finite axiomatization of inductive-recursive definitions. In: Girard, J.-Y. (ed.) TLCA 1999. LNCS, vol. 1581, pp. 129–146. Springer, Heidelberg (1999)
10. Fridlender, D., Indrika, M.: Do we need dependent types? J. Funct. Program 10(4), 409–415 (2000)
11. Luo, Z., Pollack, R.: LEGO proof development system: User's manual. Technical Report ECS-LFCS-92-211, LFCS, Computer Science Dept., University of Edinburgh, The King's Buildings, Edinburgh EH9 3JZ, Updated version (May 1992)
12. McBride, C.: Epigram: Practical programming with dependent types. In: Notes from the 5th International Summer School on Advanced Functional Programming (August 2004)Available at: http://www.dur.ac.uk/CARG/epigram/epigram-afpnotes.pdf
13. Nordstrom, B.: The ALF proof editor (March 20, 1996), ftp://ftp.cs.chalmers.se/pub/users/ilya/FMC/alfintro.ps.gz
14. Paulson, L.C.: Isabelle: The next 700 theorem provers. In: Odifreddi, P. (ed.) Logic and Computer Science. Logic and Computer Science, pp. 361–386. Academic Press, London (1990)

15. Jones, S.P.: Special issue: Haskell 98 language and libraries. Journal of Functional Programming 13 (January 2003)
16. Pfenning, F., Schürmann, C.: System description: Twelf — A meta-logical framework for deductive systems. In: Ganzinger, H. (ed.) Automated Deduction - CADE-16. LNCS (LNAI), vol. 1632, pp. 202–206. Springer, Heidelberg (1999)
17. Shao, Z., Saha, B., Trifonov, V., Papaspyrou, N.: A type system for certified binaries. ACM SIGPLAN Notices 37(1), 217–232 (2002)
18. Sheard, T.: Using MetaML: A staged programming language. In: Swierstra, S.D., Oliveira, J.N. (eds.) AFP 1998. LNCS, vol. 1608, pp. 207–239. Springer, Heidelberg (1999)
19. Sheard, T., Peyton-Jones, S.: Template meta-programming for Haskell. In: Proc. of the workshop on Haskell, pp. 1–16. ACM Press, New York (2002)
20. Stone, C.A., Harper, R.: Deciding type equivalence in a language with singleton kinds. In: Conference Record of POPL'00: The 27th ACM SIGPLAN-SIGACT Symposium on Principles of Programming Languages, Boston, Massachusetts, pp. 214–227 (2000)
21. Stump, A.: Imperative LF meta-programming. In: Logical Frameworks and Meta-Languages workshop (July 2004), Available at: http://cs-www.cs.yale.edu/homes/carsten/lfm04/
22. Taha, W., Sheard, T.: MetaML: Multi-stage programming with explicit annotations. Theoretical Computer Science 248(1-2) (2000)
23. The Coq Development Team. The Coq Proof Assistant Reference Manual, Version 7.4. INRIA (2003), http://pauillac.inria.fr/coq/doc/main.html
24. Westbrook, E., Stump, A., Wehrman, I.: A language-based approach to functionally correct inperative programming. Technical report, Washington University in St. Louis, (2005), Available at: http://cl.cse.wustl.edu/
25. Xi, H.: Dependent Types in Practical Programming. PhD thesis, Carnegie Mellon University (1997)
26. Xi, H.: Applied type systems. In: Berardi, S., Coppo, M., Damiani, F. (eds.) TYPES 2003. LNCS, vol. 3085, pp. 394–408. Springer, Heidelberg (2004)
27. Xi, H., Pfenning, F.: Eliminating array bound checking through dependent types. ACM SIGPLAN Notices 33(5), 249–257 (1998)
28. Xi, H., Pfenning, F.: Dependent types in practical programming. In: ACM (ed.) POPL '99. Proceedings of the 26th ACM SIGPLAN-SIGACT on Principles of programming languages, ACM SIGPLAN Notices, New York, NY, USA, January 20-22, 1999, pp. 214–227. ACM Press, New York (1999)

A   Inductively Sequential Functions

We restrict the form of function definitions at the type level to be inductively sequential [1]. This ensures a sound and complete narrowing strategy for answering type- checking time questions. The class of inductively sequential functions is a large one, in fact every Haskell function has an inductively sequential definition. The inductively sequential restriction affects the form of the equations, and not the functions that can be expressed. Informally, a function definition is inductively sequential if all its clauses are non-overlapping. For example the definition of zip1 is not-inductively sequential, but the equivalent program zip2 is.

```
zip1 (x:xs) (y:ys) = (x,y): (zip1 xs ys)
zip1 xs ys = []

zip2 (x:xs) (y:ys) = (x,y): (zip2 xs ys)
zip2 (x:xs) []     = []
zip2 []      ys     = []
```

The definition for zip1 is not inductively sequential, since its two clauses overlap. In general any non-inductively sequential definition can be turned into an inductively sequential definition by duplicating some of its clauses, instantiating variable patterns with constructor based patterns. This will make the new clauses non-overlapping. We do not think this burden is too much of a burden to pay, since it is applied only to functions at the type level, and it supports sound and complete narrowing strategies. In addition to the inductively sequential form required for type functions, Ωmega assumes that each type function is a total terminating function. This assumption is not currently enforced, and it is up to the programmer to ensure that this is the case.

Revealing the X/O Impedance Mismatch
(Changing Lead into Gold)

Ralf Lämmel and Erik Meijer

Microsoft Corp., Data Programmability Team, Redmond, USA

Abstract. We take the term X/O impedance mismatch to describe the difficulty of the OO paradigm to accommodate XML processing by means of recasting it to typed OO programming. In particular, given XML types (say, XML schemas), it is notoriously difficult to map them automatically to object types (say, object models) that (i) reasonably compare to native object types typically devised by OO developers; (ii) fully preserve the intent of the original XML types; (iii) fully support round-tripping of arbitrary, valid XML data; and (iv) provide a general and convenient programming model for XML data hosted by objects.

We reveal the X/O impedance mismatch in particular detail. That is, we survey the relevant differences between XML and objects in terms of their data models and their type systems. In this process, we systematically record and assess X-to-O mapping options. Our illustrations employ XSD (1.0) as the XML-schema language of choice and C# (1.0–3.0) as the bound of OO language expressiveness.

1 Introduction

XML is ubiquitous in today's application development, which is otherwise biased towards the OO paradigm. XML data needs to be regularly produced or consumed by (OO) applications. Such need arises for the request/response tiers of WebServices, and the data storage tiers of many applications, as well as the import/export tiers of applications in 'standardized' industries. A very OO-biased developer (as opposed to an XML aficionado) expects to be able to exercise all these scenarios on the grounds of the familiar OO paradigm while taking advantage of a domain-specific object model tailored to the XML data at hand — without the need to deal with XML intimately. The so-called X/O Impedance Mismatch challenges this expectation.

1.1 What Is the X/O Impedance Mismatch Anyway?

Quoting Wikipedia[1], "*'Impedance mismatch' is derived from the usage of impedance as a measurement of the ability of one system to efficiently accommodate the output (energy, information, etc.) of another. [...] Although the term originated in the field of electrical engineering, it has been generalized and used as a term of art in systems analysis, electronics, computer science, informatics,*

---

[1] `http://en.wikipedia.org/wiki/Impedance_mismatch`, captured on 9 January, 2007.

R. Backhouse et al. (Eds.): Datatype-Generic Programming 2006, LNCS 4719, pp. 285–367, 2007.

and physics." In particular, the term is also used "*to refer to the difficulties encountered when attempting to connect two systems which have very different conceptual bases*".

In the case of the X/O Impedance Mismatch, we are talking about the "systems" of XML and objects with their data models, programming models and type systems as conceptual bases. "Connecting" XML and objects is best called X/O mapping, also known as *XML-data binding* [10,38,31,51,11]. In particular, the X/O Impedance Mismatch appears to be associated with *canonical XML-to-object type-based mappings* (abbreviated as X-to-O mappings from here on). Such a mapping is meant to automatically derive object types (say, object models) from given XML types (say, XML schemas) in a canonical manner. The qualifier 'canonical' emphasizes that the mapping is 'generic' as opposed to 'problem-specific', (or 'programmatic', or 'user-defined').

We take the term X/O Impedance Mismatch to refer to the difficulty of devising a (canonical) X-to-O mapping such that the resulting, schema-derived object types (i) reasonably compare to native object types typically devised by OO developers; (ii) fully preserve the intent of the original XML types; (iii) fully support round-tripping of arbitrary, valid XML data; and (iv) provide a general and convenient programming model for XML data hosted by objects. We contend that our 'definition' essentially subsumes the characterizations that have been suggested elsewhere [42,58,37,62,61,17] — except that we focus on the *X-to-O* direction of mapping; we also focus on *canonical* mappings. Our hypothesis is here that the mastery of canonical X-to-O mappings is the key foundation for any other form of mechanical X/O mappings. (We will elaborate on this hypothesis.) Admittedly, ontological aspects are not covered by our definition.

1.2   An Illustrative X-to-O Mapping Sample

Let us model simple arithmetic expressions. In XSD, we designate an element declaration Exp to expressions. Its content is of a complex type. We consider two expression forms (hence the <choice>): an int constant and a binary add expression. Thus:

```
<xs:element name="Exp">
  <xs:complexType>
    <xs:choice>
      <xs:element name="Const" type="xs:int"/>
      <xs:element name="Add">
        <xs:complexType>
          <xs:sequence>
            <xs:element ref="Exp"/>
            <xs:element ref="Exp"/>
          </xs:sequence>
        </xs:complexType>
      </xs:element>
    </xs:choice>
  </xs:complexType>
</xs:element>
```

For comparison, in BNF notation:

$$Exp ::= Int \mid Exp \text{ "+" } Exp$$

For another comparison, in the notation of the Haskell programming language:

$$\textbf{data } Exp = \text{Const } Int \mid \text{Add } Exp\ Exp$$

X-to-O mappings may largely differ with regard to the assumed mapping rules. In this paper, we often use the `xsd.exe` tool of the .NET platform as a means to gather data points for 'mainstream' X-to-O mappings. For the given XML schema, we get the following C# classes:[2]

```
// Generated by the xsd.exe tool

public class Exp
{
  public object Item;
}

public class ExpAdd
{
  public Exp Exp;
  public Exp Exp1;
}
```

We do not attempt to explain this result here, but it is clear that these schema-derived classes do *not* compare very well to the object model that an OO developer would typically come up with. For comparison, *one* reasonable design for expression forms would be to organize the forms in an inheritance hierarchy and to label fields for subexpressions suggestively. Thus:

```
// Devised by an OO developer

public abstract  class Exp          { }
public           class Const  : Exp { public int Value; }
public           class Add    : Exp { public Exp Left, Right; }
```

Looking back at the automatic mapping result, one should note that we are not necessarily facing a particular defect of a specific mapping tool. (For instance, the tool can hardly come up with reasonable labels, like Left and Right, without

---

[2] A note on the `xsd.exe` tool: whenever we show classes generated by the tool, we omit all generated custom attributes ('annotations' in Java terminology) that are meant to guide the de-/serialization framework. We also hide the 'partial class status' that makes the generated classes amenable to compile-time extensions. Finally, for conciseness, we use an option that prefers plain, public fields over properties (i.e., getter/setter methods) with private fields.

help.) The reader is invited to try out this example with any other mapping tool, be it an implementation of the JAXB 2.0 architecture for X/O mappings (say, XML-data binding) in the Java platform [54]. Some tools may perform better than others for any specific pattern — based on subjective judgment, while also trading off simplicity, programming convenience, performance, and other factors. We contend that the impedance between the conceptual bases of XML and objects suggests that *any* mapping needs to improvise (unless AI gets involved or humans intervene).

1.3   Dimensions of the X/O Impedance Mismatch

There is the *conceptual* impedance between XML and objects:

- The data models of XML and objects differ considerably, e.g.:
  - XML is based on *parented trees*; OO is based on *non-parented graphs* instead.
  - XML (but not OO) covers the concept of *mixed content* (interim text).
  - OO (but not XML) relies on *unambiguous* selectors for subcomponents.
  - XML assumes a rich *query language*; no such language is 'native' in OO.
- The type systems of XML and objects differ considerably, e.g.:
  - Classes aggregate members; XML leverages regular expression types instead.
  - OO-based data models use 'flat' classes; XML types use nested scopes.
  - XML relies on several forms of type abstractions; OO focuses on classes.
  - XML validation does not fully align with static typing for object models.

One may want to emphasize that XML and objects also differ considerably with regard to their programming models. Most notably, OO programming assumes the use of abstract data types and encapsulation. In contrast, XML processing uses 'concrete' XML languages (concrete data types without attached behavior) on which to devise 'functions' for queries and transformations. However, OO programming can also switch to the view of 'objects as public data containers'. So we contend that the dimension of programming models is less distressing than the ones of data models and type systems. (In fact, OO programming capabilities may add value to 'classic' XML processing.)

X-to-O mapping is also challenged by some subordinated dimensions:

- XML is idiosyncratic, e.g.:
  - How to map XML's element/attribute distinction to objects?
  - How to maintain XML's processing instructions in objects?
  - How to map XML's complicated namespaces to objects?
- The prominent XML type system, XSD, is idiosyncratic, e.g.:[3]
  - XSD's counterpart for regular expression operators is non-compositional.
  - Element substitutability requires extra, auxiliary type definitions.
  - There is no general way of hiding global schema components.

---

[3] An illustration of XSD's idiosyncrasies: http://www.w3.org/2002/ws/databinding/issues/37/

– Mainstream OO languages lack desirable expressiveness, e.g.:
  • Object construction over nested types is inconvenient.
  • Non-nullable types are not yet generally available.
  • Choices (type-indexed sums) are not supported.
– XSD's verbosity may imply that one cannot see the tree for the forest.[4]

Finally, a noteworthy dimension of the X/O Impedance Mismatch is the relative obscurity of the 'X/O mapping problem' itself. One can often find the expectation that an X/O mapping is supposed to relate an XML schema and an object model where both are *given*. When this general problem statement is chosen, then additional challenges are implied such as the potential need for a declarative mapping formalism, or the definite need for an ontological level of the mapping. For simplicity, we restrict ourselves to canonical mappings, thereby suggesting an obvious direction for future work on the X/O Impedance Mismatch.

1.4   The Ambition: Survey X/O Differences

There exist many views on the X/O Impedance Mismatch and X-to-O mapping: Is the mismatch perhaps overrated? Should we just be fine with DOM-like XML programming? Should we add some extras to DOM? Which extras? Should we disband the so-called 'schema first' model, thereby making X-to-O object mapping irrelevant? And so on. We do not stake any of these views (in this paper). Instead, we dive deep into the (contrived or overrated or real) X/O Impedance Mismatch. *The paper's goal is to provide the most comprehensive discussion (to date) of the differences between the data models and type systems of XML and objects. The idea is that such a survey can be used by practitioners and researchers who want to understand the mismatch and contribute to its further reconciliation in whatever way they see fit (up to the point to abandon XML entirely).* The X/O Impedance Mismatch has been discussed elsewhere [42,58,37,62,61,17], but the present paper is the first to systematically collect and assess the most obvious (and some of the less obvious) X-to-O mapping options.

1.5   The Setup: Map XSD to C#

We expect the reader to be versed in the OO paradigm and to be fluent in a statically typed OO language such as Java, Eiffel or C#. All illustrative mapping results are presented as C# fragments, but a very similar development would be possible for Java 1.5. We will mostly suffice with C# 2.0, but use the emerging C# 3.0 language [45,46] in a few places. We will explain C# specialties as we encounter them. XSD (XML Schema 1.0 [67]) is our schema language of choice. As of writing, XSD is by far the most widely used schema language, and it is very expressive (compared to DTD [68] or RELAX NG [49]). Our discussion of differences in the dimension of data models is largely independent of the choice of XSD — except that we need *some* schema notation for our samples. Our

---

[4] An illustration of XSD's verbosity: http://www.charlespetzold.com/etc/CSAML.html

discussion of differences in the dimension of type systems focuses on issues that are likely to hold for any 'comprehensive' schema language.[5] In so far that we touch upon some idiosyncrasies of XSD, the paper is somewhat specific to XSD. We do not expect the reader to be familiar with XSD, but we do expect some prior exposition to grammar-like formalisms and to XML processing of some kind (DOM, XSLT, XQuery). We will explain XSD specialties as we encounter them.

2   Background

Before we dive into the X-to-O mapping topic, let us establish additional context. In particular, let us organize possible mitigation strategies for the X/O Impedance Mismatch. Also, let us devise a simple programming problem that we can use for a discussion of different kinds of OO/XML programming cocktails. Ultimately, we identify desirable properties of X-to-O mappings.

2.1   Reconciliation of the X/O Impedance Mismatch

The mitigation strategies are listed in no particular order.

1. *Give up on the idea of X-to-O mapping, operate on untyped, DOM-like XML trees and reserve the role of XML schemas for validation.* There are indeed proponents for this position [37]. We have argued elsewhere [33] that this position may potentially 'throw out the baby with the bath water'. If one gives up on the idea of X-to-O mapping, as proposed, then schemas are not leveraged, in any way, to improve developer productivity by means of static typing. Also, the developer deals with XML intimately, which is not appreciated by OO-biased developers.

2. *Improve the aforementioned option by leveraging XML schemas for the design experience*: The development of VB9.0 [40] adopts this strategy. That is, schema-based IntelliSense (say, IDE support for tool tips) is under way such that it helps the programmer to guide queries over XML trees based on designated XML-member syntax and the construction of XML literals. No X-to-O mapping is performed. The developer still deals with XML intimately (just as in the case of DOM), but 'intelliSensial' XML types provide a design experience that compares to schema-derived object types (and the associated, conservative IntelliSense).

3. *Require an expressive OO language*: One may attempt to identify general language expressiveness (without committing to the idiosyncrasies of XML or XSD) that would simplify the X/O mapping effort. (Such expressiveness

---

[5] In particular, we have checked that most issues would also apply to RELAX NG, even though RELAX NG is sometimes considered a simpler schema language than XSD. For instance, the mere absence of substitution constructs in RELAX NG does not imply that mapping is simplified; instead it implies that substitution relationships must be discovered on the grounds of the assumed use of 'design patterns' [60].

may also imply corresponding extensions of the underlying virtual machine.) For instance, the combination of generics, functional OO programming and language-integrated queries may alleviate the impedance [33]. Regular expression types (and potentially pattern matching on such types) [22] may improve static typing for schema-derived object models. For instance, the C#-like research language Cω [42,41,6] comprises an extended type system to cover essentially the EBNF-part of XSD.

4. *Create a language cocktail such that typed XML is deeply embedded into (amalgamated with) an OO language*: The development of XJ [26,25,9,28] adopts this strategy. That is, XJ amalgamates the Java and XSD type systems; XML and XPath are embedded into Java and its type system; XML trees are represented as DOM trees at runtime. Other work on embedding includes XACT [30], Xtatic [21,20] and Cω. The Cω language does not opt for a full deep embedding of typed XML, but it covers the type-checked construction of XML trees on the grounds of a syntactical translation from XML literals to object construction.

5. *Devise a best-effort mapping*: one can take the position that the mismatch is overrated [61], and devise an informed and matured mapping, while accepting that some problems remain. For instance, the dreaded problem of preserving XML comments and mixed content goes away once we are willing to use DOM-like objects for the state part of the schema-derived object model [55,5,33].

6. *Profile the use of XML schemas; assuming that the profiled subset can be mapped in a satisfactory manner*: as of writing, there is a W3C Working Group for 'XML Schema Patterns for Databinding', which classifies XSD constructs in a way that *could* be interpreted as a profile [17] — even though the work is primarily meant to capture the degree of XSD support by actual X-to-O mapping technologies.

7. *Assume that X-to-O mapping cannot be automated in a satisfactory manner and engage in programmatic mappings*: hence an object model with de-/serialization functionality (to act as bridge between XML and objects) would be hand-crafted. The programmatic mapping may also be defined with the help of an (interactive) mapping tool. A less extreme instance of this strategy is the provision of a canonical X-to-O mapping technology with rich customization capabilities.

8. *Disband the 'schema first' model; proclaim the 'code first' model*: suitable object models would define the de-/serializable data structures for interoperable applications. XML schemas *may* be still used in describing the data interchange format, such as in the case of WCF's data contracts for .NET types [47]. In an extreme case, XML, as such, may be disbanded for the on-wire data interchange format, such as in the case of JSON [29].

9. *Surrender and stay with a more XML-centric language*: Typically, this would imply the use of languages such as XSLT and XQuery. One may still hope to interoperate with OO applications on the grounds of an appropriate foreign-language interface or simple exchange formats.

```
<orders>
  <order id="47" zip="98052">
   <item id="23">
    <price>42</price>
    <quantity>2</quantity>
   </item>
   <item id="32">
    <price>33</price>
    <quantity>3</quantity>
   </item>
  </order>
  <!-- ... more orders elided ... -->
</orders>
```

Fig. 1. An XML document with a batch of purchase orders

10. *Use functional instead of OO programming*: The type systems of languages
    like F#, Haskell or SML with their support for algebraic data types, make
    it relatively easy to represent content models. Also, functional programming
    is generally convenient for modeling XML-like queries and transformations.
    For instance, these capabilities are demonstrated by existing X/O mapping
    technologies for Haskell [71,2]. One may still hope to interoperate with OO
    applications.

2.2   OO Programming on XML Data with DOM and Co.

X-to-O mappings deliver 'domain-specific' object models (for purchase orders,
health-care workflows, configuration files) for OO programming on XML data.
Most obviously, the domain-specific object model is meant to enable static typing, but, generally, the use of a domain-specific object model implies that the various, known capabilities of OO programming can be leveraged for XML processing. For instance, XML processing functionality can be expressed by means of
(potentially virtual) methods to be attached to the schema-derived object model.
Also, XML-processing code can be debugged in a type-aware manner.

Before we engage in typed XML processing based on schema-derived object
models, we will illustrate 'untyped' XML processing, using generic, DOM-like objects. This makes it easy to pronounce the potential benefits of X-to-O mapping.

A Running Example
Consider the following problem:

> *Total price times quantity for all items of a batch of purchase orders.*

```
DOM/XPath style using the System.Xml namespace

  static double GetTotalByZip(XmlDocument d, int zip)
  {
    var total = 0.0;
    var query = string.Format("orders/order[@zip={0}]/item", zip);
    foreach (XmlElement x in d.SelectNodes(query)) {
      var price = Double.Parse(x.SelectSingleNode("price").InnerText);
      var quantity = Int32.Parse(x.SelectSingleNode("quantity").InnerText);
      total += price * quantity;
    }
    return total;
  }
```

```
System.Xml.Linq combined in imperative mode

  public static double GetTotalByZip(XElement os, int zip)
  {
    var total = 0.0;
    foreach (var o in os.Elements("order"))
      if ((int)o.Attribute("zip") == zip)
        foreach (var i in o.Elements("item"))
          total += (double)i.Element("price") * (int)i.Element("quantity");
    return total;
  }
```

```
System.Xml.Linq combined with LINQ syntax

  public static double GetTotalByZip(XElement os, int zip)
  {
    return ( from o in os.Elements("order")
             from i in o.Elements("item")
             where (int)o.Attribute("zip") == zip
             select ((double)i.Element("price") * (int)i.Element("quantity"))
           ).Sum();
  }
```

Fig. 2. Compute the total for orders with a given zip code

Fig. 1 shows illustrative XML data. For the sake of a slightly more interesting
example, let us assume that the total should only comprise orders with a specific
zip code. Fig. 2 implements the functionality. We exercise different programming
styles for the reader's convenience.[6]

---

[6] A note on C#: throughout the paper, we tend to use var style variable declarations,
as in var total = ..., as opposed to double total = ..., thereby relying on type inference
of C# 3.0.

- *DOM/XPath style using the System.Xml namespace* — The relevant orders are characterized by an XPath expression that is represented as a string value and interpreted by SelectNodes. In particular, the XPath expression comprises a predicate to filter out the relevant orders on the basis of the zip attribute. The resulting node set of orders is processed in a for-each loop. Price and quantity are (laboriously) extracted from the relevant children of each order.
- *System.Xml.Linq in imperative mode* — We use LINQ to XML — a simplified XML programming API [44,39]. The child axis of XPath is replaced by the API member Elements (...). The test for the zip code becomes a normal conditional in the scope of a for-each loop. The LINQ to XML API provides convenient casts to access an element's or an attribute's content (say, value).
- *System.Xml.Linq combined with LINQ syntax* — We switch to functional programming style based on LINQ's [46] language-integrated syntax for FLWOR/SQL-like queries. That is, we aggregate the total by a query *expression*; the clauses of a LINQ expression are reminiscent of list processing in higher-order functional programming (using map, filter and reduce).[7]

DOM-like programming suffers from two shortcomings. First, the XML-processing code is not type-checked with regard to the content model for purchase orders — assuming that such a content model exists. Second, the XML-processing code deals with XML intimately; it does not resemble OO programming style — even though the problem at hand is conceptually not tied to XML. These are the main issues that X/O mapping is supposed to address.

2.3   OO Programming on XML Data with 'Schema First'

We want to encode the functionality for totaling purchase orders at the level of a designated object model. Let us assume that a 'standardization body' has readily published an XML schema that describes the structure of purchase orders; cf. Fig. 3. Hence, the XML schema serves as the primary data model from which to derive an object model, if needed. Thus, we face a 'schema first' scenario as opposed to a 'code first' scenario.

The simple schema at hand can be mapped to an object model as follows:

- Root element declarations are mapped to classes.
- Root element names are mapped to class names.
- Local element declarations in an XSD <sequence> are mapped to fields.
- Local element names are mapped to field names.
- Local element types are mapped to field types.[8]

---

[7] A note on LINQ syntax: the expression form from x in l select y denotes the computation of a new list l' from the given list l such that each element x of l is mapped to an element y of l' (where x is a variable and y is an expression that may refer to x). One can add where clauses so as to filter the list l. There are also means for grouping and ordering. One can cascade from clauses and nest LINQ queries.

[8] A note on XSD: We use the term *element type* to refer to the type attribute of an element declaration, if present, or to the anonymous type of an element declaration, otherwise.

```
<xs:schema xmlns:xs="http://www.w3.org/2001/XMLSchema">

  <xs:element name="orders">
    <xs:complexType>
      <xs:sequence>
        <xs:element ref="order" minOccurs="0" maxOccurs="unbounded"/>
      </xs:sequence>
    </xs:complexType>
  </xs:element>

  <xs:element name="order">
    <xs:complexType>
      <xs:sequence>
        <xs:element ref="item" maxOccurs="unbounded"/>
      </xs:sequence>
      <xs:attribute name="id" type="xs:string" use="required"/>
      <xs:attribute name="zip" type="xs:int" use="required"/>
    </xs:complexType>
  </xs:element>

  <xs:element name="item">
    <xs:complexType>
      <xs:sequence>
        <xs:element name="price" type="xs:double" />
        <xs:element name="quantity" type="xs:int" />
      </xs:sequence>
      <xs:attribute name="id" type="xs:string" use="required"/>
    </xs:complexType>
  </xs:element>

</xs:schema>
```

Fig. 3. An XML schema for batches of purchase orders

(The explored simple types xs:string, xs:int and xs:double have straightforward counterparts in the .NET/C# type system.) Fig. 4 shows the mapping result, when
the xsd.exe tool is used. Fig. 5 shows the typed encoding for totaling purchase
orders; see Fig. 2 again for the untyped encoding. Clearly, the typed encoding is
type-checked and liberated from XML idiosyncrasies. In addition, the typed version is also considerably more concise because invocations of generic DOM-like API
members are replaced by direct OO member access to objects for purchase orders.
   The untyped approach of the previous subsection assumes that the XML data
is held in memory based on a generic object type for XML trees. In contrast, the
typed approach in the present subsection assumes that instances of schema-derived

```
public class orders {
    public order [] order;
} public class order {
    public item [] item;
    public string id;
    public int zip;
} public class item {
    public double price;
    public int quantity;
    public string id;
}
```

Fig. 4. A schema-derived object model for purchase orders

```
public static double GetTotalByZip(orders os, int zip) {
    return ( from o in os.order
             from i in o.item
             where o.zip == zip
             select i.price * i.quantity
           ).Sum();
}
```

Fig. 5. OO programming on XML data with 'schema first'

object types are somehow populated with XML data. Typically, population is based on de-serialization. (In the other direction, we say that objects are serialized to XML. Elsewhere, the terms unmarshalling and marshalling are used.) As an illustration, the following code demonstrates de-serialization based on .NET's System.Xml.Serialization namespace; the code reads XML data into a new object of type orders before it invokes the computation of GetTotalByZip:

```
var serializer  = new XmlSerializer(typeof( orders ));
var reader      = XmlReader.Create(xmlFile);
var ords        = (orders) serializer . Deserialize ( reader );
Console.WriteLine(GetTotalByZip(ords,98052));
```

2.4 Plain Objects vs. XML Objects

The most tempting way of thinking of schema-derived object models is indeed to anticipate 'plain objects' based on classes with just 'plain fields', as exemplified by the object model in Fig. 4. However, there is another option: the schema-derived object model may serve as an *abstract data type* for typed XML access, while hiding the particular XML-data representation. We also use the term 'XML

```
public class orders : XElement
{
    public orders() : base("orders") { }
    public IEnumerable<order> order { get { return Elements("order").OfType<order>(); } }
}
public class order : XElement
{
    public order() : base("order") { }
    public IEnumerable<item> item   { get { return Elements("item").OfType<item>(); } }
    public string id                { get { return (string) Attribute ("id"); } }
    public int zip                  { get { return (int) Attribute ("zip"); } }
}
public class item : XElement
{
    public item() : base("item") { }
    public double price     { get { return (double)Element("price"); } }
    public int quantity     { get { return (int)Element("quantity"); } }
    public string id        { get { return (string) Attribute ("id"); } }
}
```

Fig. 6. XML objects for purchase orders (read only)

objects' [33] in this case. *The XML data may be stored in a database or in an object for an untyped XML tree, while the XML objects merely define a typed view on the XML data.*

The term 'view' is used in a similar manner in the database domain [4,24], XPath and XSLT processing [50] or functional programming [70,12,48]. In our case, the internal state of an object is meant to account for a precise (high-fidelity) representation, whereas the interface is tailored to observations (and updates) prescribed by the schema. Throughout the paper, we will mention trade-offs regarding the options 'plain objects vs. XML objects'; we refer to [33] for a related discussion.

Fig. 6 illustrates an instance of the notion of XML objects for our running example. That is, we use the LINQ to XML API as an 'XML store' while we define an object model to provide typed access properties, which are implemented in terms of untyped API idioms.[9] The XML object types are defined as subclasses of XElement — LINQ to XML's generic type for XML trees.[10] (Clearly, there are

---

[9] A note on C#: We use the language concept of a property, i.e., data access through getters and setters. (In the figure, we only define getters.) That is, properties are OO members that facilitate abstraction and information hiding for the state part of objects. Properties may comprise a getter for read access and a setter for write access. Intuitively, properties can be used like fields. In particular, setters may appear in the position of 'left values', and getters in the position of 'right values'. In a language without properties, one encodes getters and setters as methods using a name convention such as getPrice and setPrice.

[10] The getter implementations invoke the generic members of the LINQ to XML API (i.e., Element, Elements and Attribute) and perform casts for simple-typed content in the same way as the untyped XML processing code. In the case of the compound (and repeating) subtrees, LINQ's type-based filter method OfType<...> is put to work so as to 'downcast' LINQ to XML's tree type XElement to the schema-derived object types order and item.

```
[DataContract]
public class orders
{
  [DataMember] public order [] order;
}

[DataContract]
public class order
{
  [DataMember] public string id;
  [DataMember] public int zip;
  [DataMember] public item [] item;
}

[DataContract]
public class item
{
  [DataMember] public string id;
  [DataMember] public double price;
  [DataMember] public int quantity;
}
```

Fig. 7. An object model with declarations for a canonical XML representation

implementation options other than making XElement the base class of schema-derived object types.) The 'typed' interface provided by the XML objects is essentially the same as the one provided by the earlier plain objects — as far as typed read access is concerned. (Read access is based on 'getters' and the generic type IEnumerable for read-only lists. We omit typed setters for brevity; they are more complicated and not needed for the query in the running example.)

2.5   Object Serialization Based on 'Code First'

The X-to-O direction of mapping is associated with 'schema first'. Hence, the O-to-X direction of mapping is associated with 'code first'. In a 'code first' scenario, the OO developer devises an object model as the primary data model. A corresponding XML schema may be again derived in a canonical or in a problem-specific manner. The canonical option is prevalent because the routine purpose of O-to-X mappings is actually 'object serialization'. In such a case, the derived schema serves as 'contract' for the 'objects on the wire', i.e., the serialized objects.

For the record, we should note that, in principle, object serialization, by itself, does not necessitate O-to-X mapping since an untyped XML format could suffice. In fact, object serialization does not even require the use of XML since representation formats other than XML may be used [29].

Let us illustrate 'code first' and a typical, canonical O-to-X mapping. We use WCF's 'data contracts' [47] (which is now part of the .NET platform) as the 'code first' technology of choice. Several X/O mapping technologies, including xsd.exe, actually serve both X-to-O and O-to-X mappings, but we prefer a pure 'code first' technology for clarity. Fig. 7 shows an object model (for purchase orders) that is prepared for 'data contracts'. That is, there are custom attributes (annotations in the Java terminology) to 'mark' the classes and the members that are meant to participate in object de-/serialization; cf. DataContract and DataMember. As it happens, the object model in the figure is identical to the earlier schema-derived object model (the 'plain objects' version) — except for the additional custom attributes.

The data-contracts technology indeed leverages XML for 'objects on the wire' including an O-to-X mapping to derive an XML schema from a given object model. The customization of the XML format is deliberately very limited: one can just customize names and order (using additional custom attributes not exercised in the example). In addition, there are some controls that serve semantical aspects: one can take precautions so as to achieve round-tripping for unknown data; one can also deal with sharing in object graphs. Fig. 8 shows the O-to-X mapping result for our running example. The derived schema differs substantially from the 'schema first' version.[11] Clearly, the derived XML schema is more complex than the handcrafted one, but this is of no real concern — *if* we assume that the XML schema is not to be used directly by any developers. In particular, the XML representation of 'objects on the wire' is not to be the target of any 'native' XML processing code. In the case of data contracts, the serialization technology is indeed the only authority that needs to deal with XML directly.

In general, it may be that the derived XML schema does not just serve as a 'contract' and that XML does not just serve as a representation format. Instead, the XML format may be subject to 'native' XML processing, in which case the derived schema should be of help for the typed XML programmer. For instance, it is not uncommon to encounter the expectation that data modeling with XSD can be circumvented by means of object modeling (and O-to-X mapping). In such a case, O-to-X mappings would be expected to deliver schemas that reasonably compare to native schemas typically devised by an XML & XSD expert. We contend that the biggest challenge, in this case, is the conceptual clash between object *graphs* vs. XML *trees*; cf. Sec. 3.1. We either need to restrict the use of the object model to trees or serialize arbitrary object graphs as trees with the

---

[11] For completeness' sake, here is a list of differences:

- All content is mapped to elements; attributes are not used.
- A designated XML namespace for data contracts is used.
- At a given level, particles are sorted alphabetically.
- Arrays are mapped to wrapper elements with repeating elements inside.
- Most particles are said to be nillable, i.e., their content may be omitted.
- Named complex types are used (as opposed to anonymous ones).

```
<xs:schema xmlns:tns="http://schemas.datacontract.org/2004/07/"
           elementFormDefault="qualified"
           targetNamespace="http://schemas.datacontract.org/2004/07/"
           xmlns:xs="http://www.w3.org/2001/XMLSchema">

<xs:complexType name="orders">
 <xs:sequence>
  <xs:element minOccurs="0" name="order" nillable="true"
              type="tns:ArrayOforder" />
 </xs:sequence>
</xs:complexType>

<xs:element name="orders" nillable="true" type="tns:orders" />

<xs:complexType name="ArrayOforder">
 <xs:sequence>
  <xs:element  minOccurs="0" maxOccurs="unbounded"
               name="order" nillable="true" type="tns:order" />
 </xs:sequence>
</xs:complexType>

<xs:element  name="ArrayOforder" nillable="true" type="tns:ArrayOforder" />

<xs:complexType name="order">
 <xs:sequence>
  <xs:element minOccurs="0" name="id" nillable="true" type="xs:string" />
  <xs:element minOccurs="0" name="item" nillable="true" type="tns:ArrayOfitem" />
  <xs:element minOccurs="0" name="zip" type="xs:int" />
 </xs:sequence>
</xs:complexType>

<xs:element name="order" nillable="true" type="tns:order" />

<xs:complexType name="ArrayOfitem">
 <xs:sequence>
  <xs:element  minOccurs="0" maxOccurs="unbounded"
               name="item" nillable="true" type="tns:item" />
 </xs:sequence>
</xs:complexType>

<xs:element  name="ArrayOfitem" nillable="true" type="tns:ArrayOfitem" />

<xs:complexType name="item">
 <xs:sequence>
  <xs:element minOccurs="0" name="id" nillable="true" type="xs:string" />
  <xs:element minOccurs="0" name="price" type="xs:double" />
  <xs:element minOccurs="0" name="quantity" type="xs:int" />
 </xs:sequence>
</xs:complexType>

<xs:element name="item" nillable="true" type="tns:item" />

</xs:schema>
```

Fig. 8. A derived XML schema for purchase orders

encoding of object identities or ownerships, which implies complications for the
XML programmer. The 'trees vs. graphs' problem also shows up in the X-to-O
direction. In the sequel, we focus on X-to-O mappings, indeed.

2.6   Properties of X-to-O Mappings

Before we start to list X-to-O mapping options, let us identify important properties of X-to-O mappings, such as their completeness with regard to the supported schema constructs or the palatability of the derived object models. While all the properties to come are easily explained and intuitively desirable, the full set is hard (or impossible) to deliver consistently by X-to-O mappings (because of the X/O Impedance Mismatch).

Acceptor Completeness

A mapping should accept any valid XML schema. Also, the resulting object model should accept any XML document that is valid with regard to its associated schema. (That is, de-serialization must not throw.) Giving up on mapping completeness may be acceptable, if the supported 'schema profile' is well defined. In contrast, we definitely face a correctness issue in the case of an object model that 'rejects' a valid XML instance (during de-serialization).

Schema-Constraint Preservation

Ideally, every schema constraint would have a counterpart in the derived object model. We need to be prepared for two forms of counterparts. First, some constraints may be mapped to object-modeling concepts whose *static typing* faithfully corresponds to schema validation. Second, other constraints may be mapped to object-modeling concepts whose *dynamic semantics* faithfully corresponds to schema validation or constraint enforcement.

While acceptor completeness is 'state of the art' (modulo bugs), this is not the case for schema-constraint preservation. Admittedly, full preservation of schema constraints is very challenging. For instance, the xsd.exe tool does not preserve any of the following schema constraints:

- The element types of the branches in a choice; cf. Sec. 4.2.
- Mandatoriness (as opposed to optionality); cf. Sec. 4.1.
- Simple- and complex-content restrictions; cf. Sec. 4.8.
- The various identity constraints.

Palatability

This term has been coined in [17] and it makes nicely clear that we are entering an informal dimension here. Ideally, when mapping a given schema to an object model, the result should reasonably compare to a 'native object model', i.e., an object model that an OO developer would typically devise. This requirement is hard to measure, but our introductory example illustrated violations of palatability. For instance, a content model with recurrent element names led to name mangling (recall the field names Exp and Exp1). We will encounter many cases of unpalatability in the subsequent sections.

Programmability
Related to palatability is the concept of programmability. That is, we expect the schema-derived object model to be convenient in programming on XML data, when compared to native forms of XML processing such as XSLT or XQuery, while assuming equal familiarity with OO and XML programming. In particular, we expect to carry out queries, updates and construction in a convenient manner.

Programmability is a property that sets X-to-O mappings apart from the neighboring field of *schema-aware XML-to-relational mappings* [8,7,1,52]. An X-to-R mapping mainly focuses on the definition of a storage representation for XML data in a database such that the XML data can be efficiently retrieved and updated. It is not necessary to accommodate a rich XML programming model *directly* on the shredded XML data. In contrast, an X-to-O mapping should deliver object models whose interface is readily convenient for devising data processing functionality on the XML data.

XML Fidelity
We use the term 'XML fidelity' to refer to the capability of a schema-derived object model to grant access to all facets of XML data by observations (O), to maintain them along transformations (T), and to construct them (C). Here is a list of facets and an illustrative compliance matrix for `xsd.exe`:

Facet of XML data	O	T/C
Structured content (flat composites)	+	+
Structured content (nested composites)	+	?
Mixed content (interim text)	?	?
Whitespace	−	−
XML comments	−	−
Processing instructions (PIs)	−	−
Order of attributes	−	−
Namespace prefixes	−	−
Embedded DTDs	−	−
Encoding (Lämmel vs. Lämmel)	−	−

Legend:

- "+" — Fidelity definitely holds.
- "−" — Fidelity does not hold.
- "?" — Sloppy fidelity.
- The bars in the table separate groups of aspects that can be best labeled as follows:
  - Structured content.
  - Important infoset-like data [66].
  - Lower-level representation facets of XML data.

Round-Tripping
The property of maintaining facets of XML data along transformations can be formalized as a more specific round-tripping property. That is, a de-serialization

```
public static  T InOutSequence<T>(string filein, string  fileout ) {
  var reader  = new StreamReader(filein);
  var serial  = new XmlSerializer(typeof(T));
  var t       = (T)serial . Deserialize ( reader );
  reader . Close ();
  var writer  = new StreamWriter(fileout);
  serial . Serialize ( writer , t );
  return t ;
}
```

Fig. 9. Serialization + de-serialization sequence

An element declaration with a nested composite

```
<xs:element name="nest">
  <xs:complexType>
    <xs:sequence>
      <xs:element name="a" type="x"/>
      <xs:sequence maxOccurs="unbounded">
        <xs:element name="b" type="y"/>
        <xs:element name="c" type="z"/>
      </xs:sequence>
    </xs:sequence>
  </xs:complexType>
</xs:element>
```

A possible mapping result

```
public class nest {
  public x a;
  public y[]  b;
  public z[]  c;
}
```

A trace of a round-tripping attempt

```
            <nest>                         <nest>
              <a/>                           <a/>
              <b/>                           <b/>
INPUT:        <c/>          OUTPUT:          <b/>
              <b/>                           <c/>
              <c/>                           <c/>
            </nest>                        </nest>
```

Fig. 10. Illustration of a round-tripping violation

phase (or a 'load' operation) followed by an immediate serialization phase (or a 'save' operation) is supposed to preserve all (or some) facets of XML data.

As a clarification, Fig. 9 shows a C# function that would be helpful in establishing round-tripping compliance or revealing violations thereof. The function exercises de-serialization, followed by serialization for a given type, input file and output file based on the System.Xml.Serialization namespace that goes with the xsd.exe tool. We can then use (external) 'diffing' functionality to compare the original input and the result of the de-serialization/serialization sequence.

Fig. 10 runs an XML schema by xsd.exe; it turns out that the order of structured content is not preserved by the plain de-serialization+serialization sequence. The particular example exercises nested composites, and round-tripping fails because the schema-derived object type does not maintain nesting (neither at the level of static type structure, nor by means of extra 'housekeeping state').

Extensibility and Customizability

It is not uncommon to hear of a requirement that the mapping result must be (in some sense) extensible or customizable. In fact, the borderline between mapping customization and 'programmatic mapping' remains blurred until we find a reasonable definition of both terms. For instance, extra methods or state may need to be accommodated by the resulting object model, e.g., for the purpose of event handling. Compile-time class extension (such as with partial classes of .NET) or post-compile-time class extension (such as with extension methods of the C# 3.0 language [45,46]) are specific linguistic means of tackling such extensibility and customizability. Also, the mapping itself may be subjected to a requirement for customization. For instance, it may be desirable to turn XML-data binding off for some parts of the schema so that the corresponding XML data is exposed through a generic, DOM-like API as opposed to schema-derived object types. For the record, XML objects (cf. Sec. 2.4) make this particular kind of mapping customization unnecessary since both typed and untyped access would be provided anyhow.

3   The X/O Data Models

The crux of the X/O Impedance Mismatch lies in the difference between the data models of X and O, say their 'semantic domains' with the *essential operations on XML data and objects*.[12] In the present section, we characterize these domains and point out differences that may contribute to the X/O Impedance Mismatch. To give a simple example, XML distinguishes element vs. attributes, whereas objects are composed from sub-objects in a uniform manner, and hence

---

[12] For the record, the official definition of the semantic domain for XML is the XML information set ('infoset' [66]), which covers *observation operations* on XML trees. (Observations may be rendered as queries in a language like XPath [65]). XML support for imperative OO languages also provides *update operations*, such as those defined by DOM [64]. Ultimately, *validation* is a further assumed operation (a predicate, in fact) on XML trees.

An object model that admits cycles

```
public class Foo
{
    public Foo bar;
}
```

A derived schema for the above object model

```
<xs:element name="Foo" nillable="true" type="Foo" />
<xs:complexType name="Foo">
 <xs:sequence>
  <xs:element minOccurs="0" name="bar" type="Foo" />
 </xs:sequence>
</xs:complexType>
```

An illustrative use of the object model

```
// Create cyclic object
var x = new Foo();
x.bar = x;
// Serialize to XML
var myWriter = new StreamWriter("foo.xml");
XmlSerializer serializer = new XmlSerializer(typeof(Foo));
serializer . Serialize (myWriter,x); // THROWS!
```

Fig. 11. Illustration of a serialization problem for object graphs

XML's distinction may be hard to represent by objects. The following subsections contrast 'X vs. O' in the following respects:

1. Trees vs. graphs
2. Accessible vs. unavailable parents
3. Ambiguous vs. unique nominal selectors
4. Queriable trees vs. dottable objects
5. Node labels vs. edge labels
6. Ordered vs. unordered edges
7. Qualified vs. local selectors
8. Semi-structured vs. structured content
9. Tree literals vs. object initialization

3.1 Trees vs. Graphs

The semantic domain for objects is essentially a certain class of (constructable, navigable, updatable) graphs. In contrast, the semantic domain for XML is essentially a certain class of (constructable, navigable, queriable, and potentially updatable) trees. When object graphs are used to represent XML trees, then the object semantics may give *too much freedom* to the programmer who is operating on XML data in objects. That is, one can freely create object graphs with sharing or cycles.

When a violation of the intended tree invariant of XML data goes unnoticed, then this may lead to problematic serialization behavior. Different things may happen: serialization may loop, run out of resources, or throw due to cycle detection — depending on the technology in question. Fig. 11 illustrates this issue. The object model at the top admits the construction of cyclic object graphs. The shown XML schema in the middle of the figure was derived from the object model (using the xsd.exe tool in the O-to-X direction). Of course, the element declaration is recursive, but without the admitted semantics of data-level recursion. When we execute the test code, given at the bottom of the figure, serialization throws due to cycle detection.

Hence, the use of object types imposes an obligation on the programmer: 'Do not create cycles!' For sharing (without cycles), the situation is perhaps less severe; depending on the technology in question, sharing may be admitted modulo the potentially too *implicit* effect of losing sharing along serialization. (As a result, object graphs with sharing do not round-trip.) The typical OO type system is not helpful in enforcing the tree invariant. One can imagine idiomatically implemented object types (on the grounds of 'XML objects'; cf. Sec. 2.4) that enforce the tree invariant at runtime, through dynamic checks based on extra 'housekeeping state', potentially complemented by a cloning semantics. Such a tree-like semantics for objects is not straightforward and may be considered unpalatable.

In principle, one can serialize object graphs as XML trees (by using generated ids in the serialized XML). However, such an approach is not helpful in the X-to-O direction of mapping, i.e., for the 'schema first' model, unless the given XML schemas readily used ids/idrefs or other means of representing graph shape.

3.2   Accessible vs. Unavailable Parents

XML's semantic domain does not just assume the tree invariant for XML data, it actually assumes that *tree shape is observable* in the sense that one can navigate from a subtree to its parent. The semantic domain of objects does not provide any counterpart. As a result, certain idioms of XML processing are no longer expressible when XML data resides in 'plain objects'. One can imagine idiomatically implemented object types (on the grounds of 'XML objects'; cf. Sec. 2.4) that provide parent access.

Consider the following illustrative assignment:

> *Suppose we want to process a list of order items (as opposed to a batch of orders). The idea is that this list may be pre-selected by a different program component. For instance, this list may comprise all those items (from a batch of orders) that require a backing purchase before sale can be confirmed. Further suppose that the processing functionality must*

```
public static XElement ItemsPerZip(IEnumerable<XElement> items)
{
  return
    new XElement("groups",
          from i in items
          group i by i.Parent.Attribute("zip").Value into g
          select
            new XElement("group",
                    new XAttribute("zip", g.Key),
                    g.Elements())));
}
```

Fig. 12. Untyped LINQ to XML code for grouping items by zip code

```
public static bool EditAddress(XElement addr)
{
  XElement edit = new XElement(addr);   // Clone for editing
  bool change   = ModalXmlEdit(edit);   // GUI data binding
  if (change) addr.ReplaceWith(edit);   // Replace if necessary
  return change;
}
```

Fig. 13. In-place data manipulation for GUI data binding of XML tree (an address)

determine the zip code per item, be it to group the items per zip code so that the transport for the backing purchases can be organized per zip code.

In this case, we need access to the parent axis so that we can retrieve the zip code for each item. Fig. 12 shows a corresponding function that groups the incoming list of items by zip code.[13]

The expressiveness of the parent axis is not limited to queries, but it also applies to updates. For instance, due to the parent axis, a reference to an XML (sub)tree is sufficient to replace the tree. (Clearly, a plain object reference cannot facilitate such in-place updates.)

Fig. 13 shows a function EditAddress with an argument for an address (an XML tree) to be edited. The actual editing phase operates on a cloned XML tree, thereby enabling a simple means of an UNDO capability. Per convention, the call of the function ModalXmlEdit returns true, if the editorial changes are to be

---

[13] A note on LINQ constructs: we use the LINQ notation for grouping items in a collection by a grouping key; cf. "group ... by ... into ...". The grouping operation returns a nested collection where each outer item (a group) is paired with a grouping key.

committed back to the caller of EditAddress. Hence, if true is returned, then the original XML tree is replaced by the changed clone. To this end, we use the ReplaceWith operation, which is one of the update operations of the LINQ to XML API. Clearly, this update operation must navigate to the parent and update its child list.

3.3   Ambiguous vs. Unique Nominal Selectors

Given an object, its sub-objects are uniquely addressable by means of 'edge labels', i.e., field or property names. No such unique, *nominal* selectors are generally available for XML trees. There are unique *positions* for each subtree, but name-based selection would be based on 'node labels', i.e., element names, and these can be ambiguous.

An element declaration may carry a non-default maxOccurs constraint, in which case contiguous subsequences of subtrees in a tree may carry the same label. More severely, a content model may involve multiple element declarations with the same name. As a result, an otherwise tempting 1:1 mapping from element particles (of a given content model) to field or property declarations (of a corresponding object type) is problematic. For instance, how do we map the following content model?

```
<xs:element name="line">
  <xs:complexType>
    <xs:sequence>
     <xs:element name="point" type="pointType"/>
     <xs:element name="point" type="pointType"/>
    </xs:sequence>
  </xs:complexType>
</xs:element>
```

(We saw a similar example in the introduction of the paper.) In mainstream OO languages, we cannot have multiple fields with the same name, point. A typical workaround, chosen by X-to-O mapping tools, is to engage in 'name mangling'. For instance, the two different occurrences of the element name point would result in two field or property names point and point2.

Instead of name mangling we may (or perhaps we should) adopt a different view on the problem. That is, we could give up on the 1:1 mapping from element particles to OO members. Instead, the mapping would be 1:1 from element *names* to OO members. An OO member may be of a collection type so as to reflect that multiple element declarations are covered (in addition to the trivial case of a single declaration for a repeating element). In the example, the resulting object type provides a single field point of a list type; cf. Fig. 14. Read access (say, 'query mode') for such OO members may be seen as an XPath-like child axis. Write access (say, 'update mode') is potentially challenging for content models with nested composites; cf. Sec. 4.3.

This (uncommon) approach is the required basis for a correct mapping such that XPath queries (using the child axis) can be mapped to object queries in

---

An XML schema that exercises recurrent element names

```
<xs:element name="line">
  <xs:complexType>
    <xs:sequence>
      <xs:element ref="point"/>
      <xs:element ref="point"/>
    </xs:sequence>
  </xs:complexType>
</xs:element>

<xs:element name="point">
  <xs:complexType>
    <xs:sequence>
      <xs:element name="x" type="xs:int"/>
      <xs:element name="y" type="xs:int"/>
    </xs:sequence>
  </xs:complexType>
</xs:element>
```

A possible mapping result

```
public class line
{
  public List<point> point;
}

public class point
{
  public int x;
  public int y;
}
```

Fig. 14. Illustration of a mapping rule for recurrent element names

a semantics-preserving manner. That is, for a given XML tree t and an XPath query q, we should be able to obtain the same objects in the following two ways: (i) evaluate q on t and map the result to objects; (ii) map q to an object query q', map t to an object on which to evaluate q'.

Instead of using a more involved mapping rule, we may also require a slightly more powerful OO language. The C#-like research language Cω [42,41,6] provides a type language that admits recurrent field names. Cω generalizes normal member access (".") so that the multiple occurrences can be referred to by the recurrent name. The update direction for generalized member access is a subject for future work.

Adaptive coding style for totaling purchase orders

```
public static double GetTotalByZip(XElement os, int zip)
{
  return (from i in os.Descendants("item")
          where (int)i.Parent.Attribute("zip") == zip
          select ((double)i.Element("price") * (int)i.Element("quantity"))
          ).Sum();
}
```

For comparison: the original encoding

```
public static double GetTotalByZip(XElement os, int zip)
{
  return (from o in os.Elements("order")
          from i in o.Elements("item")
          where (int)o.Attribute("zip") == zip
          select ((double)i.Element("price") * (int)i.Element("quantity"))
          ).Sum();
}
```

Fig. 15. Illustration of the use of the descendant and parent axes

3.4   Queriable Trees vs. Dottable Objects

We have already mentioned the additional parent axis for XML trees. Also, we
have explained that an XPath-like child axis is different from the mainstream
member access ("."). for objects. There are further axes for XML queries that
do not come with any obvious counterpart in mainstream OO languages. This
is another kind of expressiveness aspect of the X/O Impedance Mismatch. An
XML programmer (used to say XQuery) would be 'disappointed' when moving
to Java or C# (assuming a classic X-to-O mapping). Here is a comprehensive
list of XML axes that are missing in OO:

 − Attribute axis
 − Parent axis
 − Descendant/Descendant-or-self axes
 − Ancestor/Ancestor-or-self axes
 − Following-/Preceding-sibling axes
 − Following/Preceding axes (i.e., nodes following/preceding in document order)

Also, XPath provides a general idiom for expressing *filters* on axes.

Fig. 15 shows another (somewhat contrived) encoding for totaling orders;
it leverages both the descendant and parent axis. One could argue that this
example is more 'adaptive' in that the use of the descendant axis helps us to

detach ourselves from the precise shape of the XML tree; we only commit to the fact that there are items and that zip codes are found at the parents of items — no matter how many levels we need to descend to find items; no matter what the element name may be for the parent of items.

There are several OO programming techniques and language extensions that make a related contribution. Adaptive programming [35], which has been embedded into various OO languages, provides an efficiently executable selector language with coverage of an idiom that is reminiscent of the descendant axis. Similarly, there are advanced visitor techniques and OO embeddings of term-traversal strategies [63,34]. The C#-like research language Cω [42,41,6] provides a primitive ("...") that mimics the descendant axis. When faced with general (potentially cyclic) object graphs, it is actually not obvious what the behavior of such an axis would be.

3.5   Node Labels vs. Edge Labels

Elements names are essentially node labels whereas property names are essentially edge labels. An element name is semantically part of the element itself, whereas an OO member name (of a field or a property) is a selector for a sub-component. In fact, objects are also labeled — by means of a type tag. While these type tags seem to be similar to element names, they do not serve any established purpose for member selection. Mainstream technologies for X-to-O mappings tend to 'neglect' this difference. A common XSD mapping rule (used by various X-to-O mapping tools) reads as follows.

> *When mapping a content model, given a local element declaration with element name n and element type t, the corresponding field declaration leverages n as name and t as type.*

In Fig. 16, we illustrate the intuition that goes with the above mapping rule. The first schema style really 'makes one think' that element particles are like field declarations. However, semantically, the local element declarations define local types of elements with the local element names as intrinsic parts. The second schema style is perhaps less misleading: the types of elements are 'prefabricated' in global declarations and then merely referenced in content models. The two formulations define the same XML language (modulo some fine details).

It should be clear by now that the choice of the (mapped) element type (cf. "type="..."" in an element declaration) as the type of the associated field or property implies imprecision. Consider the XPath expression item/price which selects all price *trees* as opposed to price *values*. Hence, mapping the element particle price to a field of type double is sloppy. One could say that this sort of mapping rule *composes node selection and value access*. In any case, there are some potentially harmful implications:

- We effectively lose information: the element name. If we later inspect a price in the form of a value of type double, it is impossible to observe that it is actually a price.

Use of local element declarations

```
<xs:element name="item">
 <xs:complexType>
  <xs:sequence>
   <xs:element name="price" type="xs:double" />
   <xs:element name="quantity" type="xs:int" />
  </xs:sequence>
  <xs:attribute name="id" type="xs:string" use="required"/>
 </xs:complexType>
</xs:element>
```

Use of references to global element declarations

```
<xs:element name="item">
 <xs:complexType>
  <xs:sequence>
   <xs:element ref="price"/>
   <xs:element ref="quantity"/>
  </xs:sequence>
  <xs:attribute name="id" type="xs:string" use="required"/>
 </xs:complexType>
</xs:element>

<xs:element name="price" type="xs:double"/>
<xs:element name="quantity" type="xs:int"/>
```

Fig. 16. Different styles of schema organization

- It follows that type equivalence for elements (such as prices) is relaxed to type equivalence for element types (such as doubles).

- We also lose the parent axis — at least for simple element types because we cannot possibly attach any parent pointer to values of primitive types.

With some effort, we can preserve XML's node labels in the object world. To this end, we need to designate distinct object types to all global and local element declarations. (For the sake of a homogeneous situation, we may also designate object types to attribute declarations.) Despite the use of element names as type names, the element names may continue to serve as property names (modulo qualification problems for element names, as discussed later).

When we apply the new rule to the schema for purchase orders, we end up with the following additional object types: id, zip, price, quantity; cf. Fig 17. The new types are defined as 'wrapper types'; they wrap content of the appropriate types, i.e., double, int or string. The wrapping idiom is factored out to a generic class

Node-labeled object types of a complex types

```
public class orders
{
   public  order []   order ;
}
public class order
{
   public  item []   item ;
   public  id        id ;
   public  zip       zip ;
}
public class item
{
   public  price     price ;
   public  quantity  quantity ;
   public  id        id ;
}
```

Node-labeled object types of a simple types

```
public class id        :  Wrapper<string> { }
public class zip       :  Wrapper<int> { }
public class price     :  Wrapper<double> { }
public class quantity  :  Wrapper<int> { }
```

Generic helper class

```
public class Wrapper<T>
{
   public T Value;
   public static implicit operator T(Wrapper<T> it) { return it.Value; }
}
```

Fig. 17. Illustration of a node-label-preserving mapping

Wrapper. This class also provides an implicit cast operation for wrappee access.[14] The implicitness of the cast implies that the original query code for computing

---

[14] A note on C#: User-defined cast operators are very much like static methods except that they mediate between two types. There is the explicit operator form which can be seen as a user-defined down-cast as in (double)aPriceObject. There is also the implicit operator form; implicit operators are automatically applied, just as up-casts, whenever the context of an expression requires the target type. In both cases, the two involved types must not engage in subtyping relationships so that the extra casts do not introduce any ambiguities.

the total does not need to be changed in a single detail. Hence, the increased precision of the new object model does not negatively affect query convenience.

This development triggers a question:

> *Why is such a node-label-preserving mapping not commonly used?*
> *It appears to be the only sensible option from a conceptual point of view!*

Here is an attempt of an explanation:

– The mapping is not too obvious in the first place.
– Field declarations of the form "`public price price;`" are arguably unpalatable.
– Programmers expect the systematic use of familiar value types (such as `double`).
– The weaknesses of a more sloppy mapping have not been discussed thoroughly.
– The mapping of local element declarations may lead to heavily nested object types.
– The additional 'object types' may be overwhelming and imply overhead.
– Object construction may require construction of many 'mini objects'.

We will regularly return to the tension between node-label omission and preservation. We will further substantiate that the (common) node-label-omitting mapping is indeed inferior in a conceptual sense, but the (uncommon) node-label-preserving mapping is challenged by palatability considerations and technical problems.

3.6   Ordered vs. Unordered Edges

The edges of an XML tree are *positionally* labeled, thereby expressing significance of order among the immediate subtrees of an XML tree. This order is programmatically relevant in various ways (in the context of XPath-like XML processing). For instance, there are sibling axes. Most importantly, there is the notion of *document order* that defines the order of nodes in query results.

In contrast, the edges in an object graph are *nominally* labeled while the order of these labels (such as the textual order in the program text) does not matter, as far as the idealized, mathematical semantics is concerned. (It may matter with regard to performance due to object layout. It may also be observable by reflection.) In fact, XML *attributes* are nominally labeled, too.

When performing canonical X-to-O (and O-to-X) mappings, it is common to identify textual order of OO member declarations with XSD's <sequence> composites. When XML data is de-serialized into objects, then it is common to be flexible with regard to order. That is, an object is populated with subtrees even if they appear in an order that is different from the schema-prescribed <sequence> composite. One argument in favor of such behavior is that the added flexibility increases interoperability.

A class with three fields

```
public class abc
{
  public int a;
  public int b;
  public int c;
}
```

The XML schema derived from the above object model

```
<xs:element name="abc" nillable="true" type="abc" />
<xs:complexType name="abc">
 <xs:sequence>
  <xs:element name="a" type="xs:int" />
  <xs:element name="b" type="xs:int" />
  <xs:element name="c" type="xs:int" />
 </xs:sequence>
</xs:complexType>
```

Input — incomplete and disordered	Output — complete and ordered

`<abc>`
`  <c>1</c>`
`  <a>2</a>`
 	
`</abc>`
	`<abc>`
	`  <a>2</a>`
	`  <b>0</b>`
	`  <c>1</c>`
	`</abc>`

Fig. 18. A test case for ordering and presence

`<all>` composites[15] are typically mapped just as if they were `<sequence>` composites (while de-serialization would be more relaxed, if it was order-aware for `<sequence>` composites). However, one could argue that the order of children in the input should be maintained by populated objects (for the purpose of round-tripping; also order may matter). Likewise, an object type for an `<all>` composite should admit different orders of populating the composite. Such a behavior cannot be expected from plain objects.

Fig 18 demonstrates a typical form of treating *order along de-serialization and serialization*. The class at the top is the 'native' object type from which we start. The schema in the middle of the figure has been derived by **xsd.exe** (used

---

[15] A note on XSD: there is the `<all>` compositor used for the construction of content models. The compositor expresses that the components may occur in any order as opposed to the sequential order of the `<sequence>` compositor. (`<all>` groups are reminiscent of 'permutation phrases' for string grammars [13].) One may think that such grouping expresses deviation from ordered edges, but it rather expresses *insignificance of order during validation*.

in the O-to-X direction). We see that a <sequence> composite is set up. Here it is assumed that the textual order of member declarations in a serializable class may indeed be a hint at the preferred serialization order. Also, XSD's <all> cannot be generally used anyhow because of XSD 1.0 expressiveness limitations. Despite the commitment to <sequence>, de-serialization may still be more liberal with regard to order (and therefore effectively handle the <sequence> like an <all>).

The input/output pair in the figure shows the behavior for de-serialization followed by immediate serialization. Hence, disordered content is accepted, and defaults are inferred for absent subtrees. One may argue that these are actually two independent issues: *flexible handling of order* vs. *default values for missing subtrees or attributes*. One may also argue that the violations should be subjected to a relaxed validation scheme to be demanded explicitly by user code.

3.7   Qualified vs. Local Selectors

At the value level, the element names (labels) in XML may be unqualified or qualified, but there are also rules for a sort of implicit qualification. At the type level, element names may be unqualified or qualified. The potential of qualification stresses the mapping of selectors in the XML sense (i.e., element names) to selectors in the OO sense (i.e., OO member names) because OO member names are always local — relative to an object type. Here are typical options for dealing with potentially qualified element names; all of them leave a bad aftertaste:

1. Ignore qualifiers; adopt name mangling for disambiguation, if necessary.
2. Append namespace prefixes to member names for disambiguation, if necessary.
3. Drop into an untyped, DOM-like representation.

Fig. 19 shows a 'test case' for qualified element names. We define a content model with three different bar's. The first bar comes from the target namespace of the schema at hand; cf. prefix tns. The second bar is contributed by a local element declaration. The third bar is imported from the namespace with prefix ins. The options 'ignore qualifiers' and 'append namespace prefixes to member names' are illustrated in Fig. 19. (The option 'ignore qualifiers' is adopted by the xsd.exe tool where name mangling appends an index "1", "2", etc. to a field name, if disambiguation is required. JAXB [54] adopts the option to 'drop into the DOM' for content models of certain shapes, including the one used in the test case.)

So we should reconsider the idea of leveraging element names as OO member names. We may use a different protocol for member access: *type-driven OO member access*. Conceptually, element references are indeed similar to type references as one is used to in OO programming languages — including the possibility of qualification for such type references. However, a type-driven access protocol results in an 'unusual' programming model . The type-driven protocol is sketched in App. A.1; it turns out to require cumbersome encoding efforts.

An XML schema with an import

```
<xs:schema targetNamespace="http://tempuri.org/foo"
           xmlns:tns="http://tempuri.org/foo"
           xmlns:ins="http://tempuri.org/bar"
           xmlns:xs="http://www.w3.org/2001/XMLSchema">

  <xs:import namespace="http://tempuri.org/bar"/>

  <xs:element name="foo">
    <xs:complexType>
      <xs:sequence>
        <!-- Three different bar's -->
        <xs:element ref="tns:bar" />
        <xs:element name="bar" type="xs:int"/>
        <xs:element ref="ins:bar"/>
      </xs:sequence>
    </xs:complexType>
  </xs:element>

  <xs:element name="bar" type="xs:string"/>

</xs:schema>
```

An imported XML schema

```
<xs:schema targetNamespace="http://tempuri.org/bar"
           xmlns:tns="http://tempuri.org/bar"
           xmlns:xs="http://www.w3.org/2001/XMLSchema">

  <xs:element name="bar" type="xs:double"/>

</xs:schema>
```

Mapping option: names without hints at qualifiers

```
public class foo
{
  public   string   bar;
  public   int      bar1;
  public   double   bar2;
}
```

Mapping option: names with namespace prefixes appended to them

```
public class foo
{
  public   string   barTns;
  public   int      bar;
  public   double   barIns;
}
```

Fig. 19. Mapping qualified element names

3.8   Semi-structured vs. Structured Content

A 'plain object' for data representation can be viewed as a dictionary that maps field names to values. As we have discussed, node-labeled XML trees do not fully align with this view (due to the lack of unambiguous, nominal selectors). Even more seriously, there is no straightforward OO counterpart for semi-structured content, i.e., content that intersperses elements and text. XML also admits additional components such as *XML comments and PIs*. Hence, we face a representation challenge: what sort of X-to-O mapping do we devise so that the additional XML-isms do not get lost. In addition, we would also want a reasonable programming model such that the XML-isms can be accessed in queries and updates.

Let us focus on interim text in the sense of mixed content. (XML comments and PIs require similar efforts.) Fig. 20 shows an XML document with a letter that involves mixed content; the figure also shows a corresponding schema fragment; cf. mixed="true", as well as the mapping result obtained with the xsd.exe tool. The schema-derived class devises a field, Text, that stores interim text in a string array. At the bottom of the figure, we also show the letter as it looks like after a de-serialization + serialization sequence. As we can see, the XML data does not round-trip; all interim text is appended to the child elements.

In general, there are the following options for handling mixed content:

1. Drop into a DOM-like representation.
2. Store text separately from the fields for child elements.
3. Provide a collection of interim text and typed objects.

X/O mapping technologies exercise all these options. As we have illustrated, the second option is chosen by xsd.exe; cf. Fig. 20. JAXB (ever since version 1) favors the third option, where the access to the heterogeneous collection (say, list) is provided by a so-called 'general content property'. This approach, when compared to 'dropping into the DOM', is more typed because the items in the list (besides text nodes) are still of schema-derived object types as opposed to a generic element type. A general content property provides less static typing than regular OO members for child elements. In particular, a general content property makes it easy to construct a node list that violates the relative order constraints defined by a <sequence> composite.

Ultimately, one may want to combine the strengths of a 'general content property' (which is convenient for observing and constructing mixed content) and OO members for the child elements. We attempt such a combination for the letter example in Fig. 21. The design can be summarized as follows. We store all content in a plain list, nodes, thereby maintaining the order of element and text nodes. The properties for the child elements operate on the nodes list in a type-driven manner. (We only show getters in the figure; setters are more complicated because of order constraints.) Without loss of generality, we assume a node-label-preserving mapping. (A node-label-omitting mapping would require extra 'housekeeping state' to maintain labels aside.) 'XML objects', as discussed in Sec. 2.4, would naturally provide both, a general content property and OO members for the

A semi-structured letter

```
<letter>
  Dear Mr.<name>Foo Smith</name>.
  Your order <id>8837</id>
  will be shipped on <shipdate>2008-04-01</shipdate>.
</letter>
```

A schema for semi-structured letters

```
<xs:schema xmlns:xs="http://www.w3.org/2001/XMLSchema">
  <xs:element name="letter">
    <xs:complexType mixed="true">
      <xs:sequence>
        <xs:element name="name" type="xs:string"/>
        <xs:element name="id" type="xs:unsignedInt"/>
        <xs:element name="shipdate" type="xs:date"/>
      </xs:sequence>
    </xs:complexType>
  </xs:element>
</xs:schema>
```

A possible mapping result

```
public class letter
{
    // Fields for element nodes
    public string name;
    public uint id;
    public System.DateTime shipdate;
    // Interim text
    public string [] Text;
}
```

Serialization result

```
<letter>
  <name>Foo Smith</name>
  <id>8837</id>
  <shipdate>2008-04-01</shipdate>
  Dear Mr..
  Your order
  will be shipped on .
</letter>
```

Fig. 20. Illustration of mixed content models

```
public class letter
{
    // State as a plain list of nodes
    public List<object> nodes = new List<object>();
    // Getters as type−driven filters
    public name name       { get { return nodes.OfType<name>().FirstOrDefault(); } }
    public id id           { get { return nodes.OfType<id>().FirstOrDefault(); } }
    public shipdate shipdate { get { return nodes.OfType<shipdate>().FirstOrDefault(); } }
}

// Node−label−preserving object types for simple−typed elements
public class name       : Wrapper<string>   { }
public class id         : Wrapper<uint>     { }
public class shipdate   : Wrapper<DateTime> { }

// Generic helper class
public class Wrapper<T>
{
    public T Value;
    public static implicit operator T(Wrapper<T> it) { return it.Value; }
}
```

Fig. 21. Mixed content preservation along round-tripping

child element. However, the present discussion alludes to the relative complexity of such an implementation — also taking into account arbitrary XSD patterns and assuming full-fledged getter/setter functionality.

3.9   Tree literals vs. Object Initialization

XML trees (say, XML literals) are constructed by essentially listing subtrees (and other nodes) at each level. An XML literal is the complete and direct representation of data as opposed to any form of private state in OO programming. In contrast, objects are constructed by designated (implicitly or explicitly defined) constructor members that initialize the state of a new object in a programmer-defined manner, potentially taking into account constructor arguments. Also the state space of an object type is typically exercised by calling methods. Despite this fundamental difference, one would hope that 'nested object construction' is capable of simulating the construction of XML literals. Unfortunately, the means for static type checking of object construction are too weak to rule out the construction of invalid XML content. (Arguably, our discussion starts to shift from 'data models' to 'type systems'.)

Fig. 22 illustrates programmatic XML-tree construction in different styles. As a baseline, at the top, we construct an untyped XML tree using the functional element constructor of the LINQ to XML API; cf. new XElement(...). This form follows closely the shape of the original XML data. That is, the various attributes and child elements of orders or items are passed as arguments to the constructors.

The middle and the bottom parts in the figure illustrate typed construction assuming two different mappings and different idioms for construction. The code in the middle relies on a node-label-omitting mapping. Also, we employ the

---

Construct an untyped, nested XML tree

```
new XElement("order",
  new XAttribute("id", "47"),
  new XAttribute("zip", "98052"),
    new XElement("item",
      new XAttribute("id", "23"),
      new XElement("price", "42"),
      new XElement("quantity", "2")),
    new XElement("item",
      new XAttribute("id", "32"),
      new XElement("price", "33"),
      new XElement("quantity", "3")));
```

Object initialization for a node-label-omitting mapping

```
new order {
  id   = "47",
  zip  = 98052,
  item = new item[] {
    new item { id = "23", price = 42, quantity = 2 },
    new item { id = "32", price = 33, quantity = 3 }}};
```

Functional construction for a node-label-preserving mapping

```
new order(
  new id("47"),
  new zip(98052),
  new item[] {
    new item(new id("23"), new price(42), new quantity(2)),
    new item(new id("32"), new price(33), new quantity(3)) } );
```

Relevant functional constructors

```
public order(id id, zip zip, item[] item)
{
  this.id = id;
  this.zip = zip;
  this.item = item;
}

public item(id id, price price, quantity quantity)
{
  this.id = id;
  this.price = price;
  this.quantity = quantity;
}
```

Fig. 22. Different construction styles

expression-oriented syntax for object initialization of C# 3.0. To clarify this construct, let us expand the expression-oriented syntax for one item of a purchase order:

```
// Object– initialization syntax
var i = new item { id = "23", price = 42, quantity = 2 };
```

```
// Expanded form
var i        = new item();
i . id       = "23";
i . price    = 42;
i . quantity = 2;
```

The code at the bottom of the figure relies on a node-label-preserving mapping. Also, we use 'functional constructors' to obtain an expression-oriented style of nested tree construction. We did not show these constructors before, but they are trivially defined, given the simplicity of the schema for purchase orders, as shown in the figure.

At first sight, both of the methods for typed construction seem to be quite reasonable. However, there are several issues that should be called out:

– OO constructors are more 'type-oriented' than 'instance-oriented'. That is, the objects that correspond to the repeating item element must be grouped as a collection. (In contrast, the item elements would be part of a flat list of children of the order element — when forming an XML literal.) We want to argue that an OO programmer may actually appreciate this deviation from XML style.

– Type checking for the object-initialization syntax does not account for occurrence constraints and the constraints implied by the different compositors. For instance, type checking does not establish that all 'required' sub-objects are determined.

– Functional constructors are convenient for sequences of mandatory sub-objects. As soon as we have to deal with choices or even nested composites, we would need multiple constructors. The approach does not scale for optional particles, <all> composites, and attributes.

– The use of functional constructors requires the (uncommon) node-label-preserving mapping for the benefit of program comprehension. That is, XML literals systematically identify element labels for all subtrees whereas the node-label-omitting mapping would not provide any counterparts for the element labels.

– Object initializers cannot be used for content models with recurrent element names (unless we assume an object initializer to make multiple contributions to a given sub-object of a collection type). Functional constructors naturally deal with this problem since multiple argument positions can be of the same type.

– Both techniques equally fail on mixed content and XML comments.

App. A.2 engages in a heavy encoding showing that, in principle, one can provide a construction protocol solving most of the above problems. We use a technique that encodes content models as finite-state machines *at the type level*. Arguably, the encoding is too convoluted for practical X-to-O mappings.

One may argue that language support for regular expression types [27,22] would allow us to better type-check object construction. Such type-system extensions are not available in mainstream languages such as C# and Java. It is important to note that plain, regular expression types are insufficient to cover a comprehensive XML-type system like XSD. Think of subtyping; think of the dichotomy elements vs. attributes. Also, <all> composites and attribute collections are not compatible with basic regular expression types (because these constructs abstract from order). Furthermore, mixed content would require extra expressiveness. Finally, the effective use of regular expression types would generally require the (uncommon) node-label-preserving mapping because all type distinctions from the content models would need to be observed by the regular expression types.

4   The X/O Type Systems

We will now look into aspects of the X/O Impedance Mismatch that involve XML types and object types in a more intimate manner, even though many of the aspects are grounded in the differences between the data models of XML and objects. The following subsections discuss a number of challenges offered by XML schemas:

1. Occurrence constraints
2. Choice types
3. Nested composites
4. Local elements
5. Element templates
6. Type extension
7. Element substitution
8. Type restriction
9. Simple types

A small part of the discussion is specific to (idiosyncrasies of) XSD.

4.1   Occurrence Constraints

We will focus here on optionality and mandatoriness. The discussion generalizes in a unsurprising manner for arbitrary minOccurs/maxOccurs constraints — in particular for possibly empty, non-empty and bounded repetitions of elements.

XSD offers regular expression-like optionality; cf. minOccurs="0" (and maxOccurs="1" per default). Mainstream programming languages like C# and Java provide optionality for reference types *by default* since these types are nullable, i.e., their value domains comprise the null reference. This implies that optionality is covered 'automatically' by an X-to-O mapping, except for fields or properties of

Optional elements both of simple and complex types

```
<xs:element name="opts">
 <xs:complexType>
  <xs:sequence>
   <xs:element name="a" type="xs:int"/>
   <xs:element name="b" type="xs:int" minOccurs="0"/>
   <xs:element name="c" type="foo"/>
   <xs:element name="d" type="foo" minOccurs="0"/>
  </xs:sequence>
 </xs:complexType>
</xs:element>

<xs:complexType name="foo"> ... details elided  ...  </xs:complexType>
```

A node-label-omitting mapping

```
public class opts
{
  public int a;    // Required field
  public int? b;   // Uses a .NET nullable type
  public foo c;    // Required field
  public foo d;    // Rely on null reference
}
public class foo { ... }
```

A node-label-preserving mapping

```
public class opts
{
  public a a;
  public b b;
  public c c;
  public d d;
}

public class a : Wrapper<int> { }
public class b : Wrapper<int> { }
public class c : Wrapper<foo> { }
public class d : Wrapper<foo> { }

public class foo { ... }
```

Fig. 23. Mapping of optionality

value types. We can explicitly express optionality for value types by using an appropriate type constructor; in fact, .NET readily provides nullable (value) types.[16]

Fig. 23 shows an XML schema that exercises optionality for simple and complex element types, while required elements are also declared for comparison. Both a node-label-omitting and a node-label-preserving mapping are exercised. (Again, we use the Wrapper class from Sec. 3.5.) The first option illustrates the asymmetry of implicit nullability for reference types and explicit nullability for value types. The second option only uses reference types, and hence the asymmetry vanishes — at the cost of losing all discoverability of optionality. That is, optional and mandatory particles both end up as implicitly nullable members. (The schema constrains may still be enforced through run-time checks of properties.) The lack of discoverability is worrying. For instance, during object access, members of implicitly nullable types do not tell the programmer which parts of an object may be perfectly missing and hence require a programmatic case discrimination for optionality. Tool tips and other IDE techniques may help to mitigate this problem.

In principle, one could adopt a discipline such that optionality is generally made explicit (not just for value types). We defer such an experimental treatment of nullability to App. A.3. Such a degree of explicitness may be potentially considered as unpalatable.

An Idiosyncrasy: Nillability

XSD complements optionality with nillability — a way of saying that 'an element is there and not there'. That is, by setting xsi:nil to true on an instance element, the content of the element can (in fact, must) be omitted. However, the empty element can carry attributes as prescribed by its schema type. An X-to-O mapping can deal with nillability in these ways:

- Infer xsi:nil from absence of content.
- Provide a property to set xsi:nil.

Unfortunately, feature interaction complicates the matter. That is, there are potentially hybrids: 'niloptables', i.e., nillable, optional particles:

```
<xs:element name="niloptable">
 <xs:complexType>
  <xs:sequence>
   <xs:element name="foo" type="xs:int" minOccurs="0" nillable="true"/>
  </xs:sequence>
 </xs:complexType>
</xs:element>
```

---

[16] A note on .NET nullable types: The type constructor Nullable (also denotable as "?" in C#) can only be applied to a value type, as opposed to a reference type. It provides observations HasValue to check for a non-null value and Value to extract a non-null value.

So we may need to distinguish 'omitted in the sense of optional' vs. 'present but nil'. Fortunately, nillability, even without optionality, is used relatively seldom according to a study [32] — at least in the case of hand-crafted schemas. However, we have seen components for schema generation (or export) that systematically use nillability.

Enforced Mandatoriness

Since optionality is the default for reference types, we may want to enforce mandatoriness; cf. minOccurs="1". In particular, we may check at run-time that no nulls are passed to setters for mandatory particles, and no nulls are returned by the getters. For instance, the mandatory element particle c would be implemented as a property as follows:

```
public foo c {
  get { if (_c==null) throw ...; return _c; }
  set { if (value==null) throw ...; _c = value; }
}
private foo _c;
```

As long as we admit default constructors, there is no guarantee that objects are fully defined with regard to mandatory particles; hence the getters should indeed perform checks. The elimination of default constructors would be a radical step; OO programmers are used to the idea of initializing instances and defining sub-objects incrementally. More importantly, a general scheme of non-default constructors is not in sight, as we discussed in Sec. 3.9.

This also leads us to review non-nullable types [18], as they are becoming available through extensions of C# and Java. As demonstrated by Cω [42,41,6], non-nullable types can also be seamlessly integrated with regular expression types. In the following experiment, we make mandatoriness for reference types explicit:

```
public class opts
{
  public int a;      // required element of simple type
  public int? b;     // optional element of simple type
  public foo! c;     // required element of complex type
  public foo d;      // optional element of complex type
}
```

We assume the type constructor "!" for non-nullable types. In the context of X-to-O mapping, we need a form of non-nullable types that admits 'transient nulls' (as part of a stepwise object initialization protocol) or nulls due to 'slightly invalid' content. Active assignment of nulls should be prohibited by the type system, but fields of non-nullable types should be allowed to hold null, as long as they are not accessed (say, read). Hence, such non-nullable types would still involve some degree of dynamic checking.

```
┌─────────────────────────────────────────────────────────────────────┐
│ Different element types                                              │
│                                                                      │
│   <xs:element name="AorB">          ┌─────────────────────────────┐ │
│    <xs:complexType>                 │ Coinciding element types    │ │
│     <xs:choice>                     │                             │ │
│      <xs:element name="a" type="A"/>│  <xs:element name="CorD">   │ │
│      <xs:element name="b" type="B"/>│   <xs:complexType>          │ │
│     </xs:choice>                    │    <xs:choice>              │ │
│    </xs:complexType>                │     <xs:element name="c" type="X"/> │
│   </xs:element>                     │     <xs:element name="d" type="X"/> │
│                                     │    </xs:choice>             │ │
│   <xs:complexType name="A">         │   </xs:complexType>         │ │
│   ... details elided ...            │  </xs:element>              │ │
│   </xs:complexType>                 │                             │ │
│                                     │  <xs:complexType name="X">  │ │
│   <xs:complexType name="B">         │  ... details elided ...     │ │
│   ... details elided ...            │  </xs:complexType>          │ │
│   </xs:complexType>                 └─────────────────────────────┘ │
└─────────────────────────────────────────────────────────────────────┘
```

Fig. 24. Different kinds of choices

4.2   Choice Types

Choice types (such as XSD's `<choice>` composites or DTD's form "$a|b$") provide a special kind of discriminated union, in fact, *type-discriminated* unions, also known as *type-indexed co-products* (TICs; [53]).[17] Choice types or TICs are not natively available in OO mainstream languages. Type-system extensions for regular-expression types cover some form of choices. The research language $C\omega$ [42,41,6] integrates choice types into an otherwise C#-like type system (without updates though). For OO languages like Java and C#, the goal must be to devise a mapping for choice types by encoding them in some way.

For simplicity, we focus here on choices over plain element particles, deferring the discussion of nested composites until Sec. 4.3. Fig. 24 exercises two principled patterns for choices. On the left-hand side, we see a choice where the element types (A vs. B) are different. On the right-hand side, the element types coincide; only the element names are different. The latter pattern is more problematic in the context of the (common) node-label-omitting mapping, as we will demonstrate shortly.

The simplest kind of mapping for choices may look as follows:

```
public class AorB
{
  public object Item;
}
```

That is, a single Item field stores the value of the choice. The type of Item is the least upper bound of the participants in the choice; this bound tends to be object. Case discrimination must be based on instance-of tests. Neither the type system

---

[17] For the record, TICs [53] are more general than XSD choices in so far that they require pairwise distinct branch types but not the stricter UPA condition of XSD [67].

nor 'IntelliSense' can be expected to be helpful in picking reasonable types for these tests.

The mapping for the second sample must devise an extra tag field since the mapped element types by themselves do not admit discrimination. (The shown mapping results for AorB and CorD were obtained with the **xsd.exe** tool.)

```
public class CorD
{
  public X Item;
  public ItemChoiceType ItemElementName;
}
public enum ItemChoiceType { c,d }
```

There are obvious problems with the options discussed so far:

- We can store objects of inappropriate types in the slot for the choice.
- The tagged union is unsafe because the tag and the item are set independently.
- Object construction does not enforce population of either branch of the choice.
- Code for case discriminations may (accidentally) omit cases.

We can definitely improve on all these concerns, but the resulting mapping will become increasingly more complex. Also, several improved mapping options for choice types (that one can think of) rely on extra preconditions on the XSD patterns that involve <choice>. Ultimately, we seek a simple and general treatment of choices.

As an experiment, Fig. 25 shows a conceptually appealing mapping:

- The actual representation of the choice's value is opaque.
- The branch can be queried based on a read-only tag.
- Injection is facilitated by implicit cast and construction.
- Projection is facilitated by explicit cast.

This scheme suffers from several limitations: (i) while the first sample can be mapped in this manner, the second sample would require the (uncommon) node-label-preserving mapping so that sufficient type distinctions can be used by the casts; (ii) nested composites cannot be mapped in this manner, unless we somehow introduce (named) classes for the inner composites; (iii) the resulting programming model does not align with XML programming practice because there is no XPath-like child axis.

We could fix the last problem by adding query members as follows:[18]

```
public A a { get { return any as A; } } // set omitted
public B b { get { return any as B; } } // set omitted
```

---

[18] A note on C#: the "*e* **as** *T*" construct essentially behaves as follows: given the value of *e*, its type is checked to be a subtype of *T*, and if so, the value is casted to *T*; otherwise the expression form evaluates to **null**.

```
public class AorB
{
    // Injections (by construction)
    public AorB(A v) { any = v; _typeCode = TypeCode.a; }
    public AorB(B v) { any = v; _typeCode = TypeCode.b; }

    // Injections ("up-cast")
    public static implicit operator AorB(A v) { return new AorB(v); }
    public static implicit operator AorB(B v) { return new AorB(v); }

    // Projections ("down-cast")
    public static explicit operator A(AorB anOr) { return (A)anOr.any; }
    public static explicit operator B(AorB anOr) { return (B)anOr.any; }

    // Tag + inspection
    public enum TypeCode { a,b };
    public TypeCode typeCode { get { return _typeCode; } }

    // Private state
    private object any;
    private TypeCode _typeCode;
}
```

Fig. 25. Choices based on casts

```
public class CorD
{
    // Getters and setters
    public X c {
        get { return (_typeCode==1)?any:null; }
        set { any=value; _typeCode=1; }
    }
    public X d {
        get { return (_typeCode==2)?any:null; }
        set { any=value; _typeCode=2; }
    }

    // Private state
    private X any;
    private int _typeCode;
}
```

Fig. 26. Choices as sequences

We may also add setters that 'alter' the choice. We may further add a default constructor that sets up an uncommitted choice. Hence, the getters may return null. Incidentally, the getters and setters are expressive enough to operate on the choice, and hence we can eliminate the original injection/projection protocol; cf. Fig. 26 for the end result. In fact, we have obtained a general and relatively convenient mapping rule for choices. Admittedly, choices and sequences cannot be distinguished anymore in terms of the interface of a schema-derived class. (Only the behavior of the properties is different; the setters for a choice implement a mutual exclusion protocol.) Tool tips and other IDE techniques may restore some degree of discoverability for choices.

4.3   Nested Composites

'Flat' composites can be modeled by object types that plainly aggregate members. (Recurrent element names require more effort; cf. Sec. 3.3.) Nested composites cannot be modeled by nested object types (classes), unless we invent names for the inner composites. Here is a representative list of nesting patterns as they can be used in XSD (and other XML-schema languages); we use regular expression notation for conciseness:

element	choiceInSequence	$= a\ (b \mid c)$
element	sequenceInChoice	$= a \mid (b\ c)$
element	plusOnSequence	$= (a\ b)^+$
element	plusOnNestedSequence	$= a\ (b\ c)^+$
element	plusInAndOut	$= a\ (b^+\ c)^+$

In the terminology of grammars, the above patterns exercise expressiveness of EBNF. Mainstream X-to-O mapping technologies tend to be challenged by these patterns. In some cases, the schema-derived object models drop into untyped representations (DOM and friends); in other cases, the round-tripping requirement is violated. We can identify the following overall options for mapping nested composites:

1. Reject nested content models.
2. Model compositors as OO generics.
3. Introduce auxiliary classes for anonymous composites.
4. Relax nested content models so that they become flat.
5. View nested content models in a flat manner.

We discuss the details of these options in the sequel.

Reject Nested Content Models

This option is too limiting. Nested content models are frequently used in real-world schemas [32] according to a study. One may think that the XML programmer should be responsible to refactor the schema until all content models are flat. However, the benefits of *typed* XML processing and X-to-O mapping should be attainable without putting such a burden on the XML programmer.

```
plusOnNestedSequence = a (b c)+

<xs:element name="plusOnNestedSequence">
 <xs:complexType>
  <xs:sequence>
   <xs:element ref="a"/>
   <xs:sequence maxOccurs="unbounded">
    <xs:element ref="b"/>
    <xs:element ref="c"/>
   </xs:sequence>
  </xs:sequence>
 </xs:complexType>
</xs:element>
```

The mapping result

```
public class plusOnNestedSequence
    : Sequence<a,List<Sequence<b,c>>> // Content model as base type
{
  // Inherit functional constructor for outer sequence
  public plusOnNestedSequence(a first, List<Sequence<b,c>> second)
    : base( first , second) { }
}
```

Fig. 27. Map a nested content model using generics for composites

Model Compositors as OO Generics

Based on suitable generics, we can enable the structural composition of OO types in a way that parallels the composition of XSD composites. That is, we need generics for <sequence> and <choice> (perhaps also for <all>, which we ignore here because it is hardly used [32], according to a study, and hard to support faithfully). The discussion of choice types has alluded to a suitable model for the compositor <choice>. The compositor <sequence> is conceptually trivial; it corresponds to a product-type constructor in the sense of universal algebra. For completeness' sake, we include suitable generics in App. A.4. Fig. 27 illustrates the use of generics (including the List<...> class) for a non-trivial nesting pattern. The schema-derived object type simply inherits from the composed structural type. This approach suffers from a number of problems:

- The 'algebra of regular expressions' is not observed by compound generics expressions. For instance, in the algebra of regular expressions, we have $(x^*)^* = x^*$ while in the typical object-type system, we have List<List<x>> $\neq$ List<x>.

- If choices with type-driven injections and projections are favored, then the (uncommon) node-label-preserving mapping is needed. We may consider position indexes instead, at the cost of making the programming model less convenient.
- We need generic classes Sequence<...> and Choice<...> for all arities 2, 3, 4, ... The available polymorphism in mainstream OO languages does not allow us to parameterize over arity. As a remedy, we may switch to the nested use of the binary generic classes, again, at the cost of making the programming model less convenient.
- Using the structural type as the superclass of a schema-derived class rules out the use of class inheritance for schema-defined substitutability, if we assume single class inheritance. As a remedy, we may restrict the use of generic classes to inner (i.e., truly anonymous) composites, which however implies a naming challenge for top-level members that grant access to inner composites.
- Manipulation of nested generics is known to be inconvenient in mainstream OO languages [23] — due to limitations of type inference and other issues. Also, as a matter of palatability, OO developers are used to object navigation based on named members as opposed to positions or types.

Introduce Auxiliary Classes for Anonymous Composites
We may attempt to systematically name all anonymous composites. As a result, we could use (nested) object types to model the nested composites. As a result, familiar member-based access can be used (as opposed to the positions or types in the case of the previous option). As an experiment, we suggest some nomination rules:

- Use the following local type names for nested composites:
  - Sequence, Sequence2, ... for <sequence>.
  - Choice, Choice2, ... for <choice>.
- Use the following member names for accessing composites:
  - AsSequence for non-repeating <sequence>.
  - AsChoice for non-repeating <choice>.
  - AsList for a repeating <sequence> or <choice>.
    * Return type:
      - List<Sequence>, ... for repeating <sequence>.
      - List<Choice>, ... for repeating <choice>.

We illustrate these rules in Fig. 28. Additional refinements may be attractive. For instance, XSD's model-group definitions should be leveraged for providing more specific names instead of the generic nominations above.

There is an obvious problem with the nomination-based approach. The programmer must be intimately familiar with the (nesting) structure of the content model because it is resembled by local OO types and it therefore needs to be observed by member-based access. The resulting style of queries does not deliver on the expectation of an XPath-like child axis.

---

plusOnSequence = (a b)+

```
<xs:element name="plusOnSequence">
  <xs:complexType>
    <xs:sequence maxOccurs="unbounded">
      <xs:element name="a" type="x"/>
      <xs:element name="b" type="y"/>
    </xs:sequence>
  </xs:complexType>
</xs:element>
```

Informal summary of nomination

Before: plusOnSequence = (a b)$^+$
After: plusOnSequence = Sequence$^+$ **where** Sequence = a b

Resulting object model

```
public class plusOnSequence {
  public List<Sequence> AsList;
  public struct Sequence
  {
    public x a;
    public y b;
  }
}
```

Fig. 28. 'AsList' access to repeating, nested sequence

Relax Nested Content Models So That They Become Flat

So far we tried to derive object types whose nesting resembled the nesting of the content model. Instead, we may trade precision for simplicity. One option is to relax the content models, in the formal sense of subset order on tree languages, so that the resulting content model is flat (and queries can be simpler).

For instance, we can relax a nested choice to a nested sequence over optional items; cf. the upper part of Fig. 29. This is essentially another interpretation of the mapping rule that we already discussed for choices; cf. Sec. 4.2. This relaxation would result in a representation type that is too rich, if we were using plain objects over fields, but a property-based API with appropriate setter implementations may still enforce 'mutual exclusion' for the branches of the choice.

We face a more aggressive example of relaxation when nested, repeating composites are reduced to a repeating, element wildcard, say 'any'. In the lower part of Fig. 29, we carry out such a relaxation for two examples. The drawbacks of these relaxations are obvious. First, there is a naming issue: How do we name the property that provides access to the relaxed collection? The 'name concatenation' approach

```
Treat choices like sequences

Before: choiceInSequence = a (b | c)
  After:                      ↝ a b? c?

public class choiceInSequence
{
  public x a { get { ... } set { ... } }
  public y b { get { ... } set { ... } }
  public y c { get { ... } set { ... } }
}
```

```
Reduce repeating composites to untyped lists

Before: plusOnSequence = (a b)⁺
  After:                   ↝ any⁺

public class plusOnSequence
{
  public object[] aAndB;
}

Before: plusOnNestedSequence = a (b c)⁺
  After:                        ↝ a any⁺

public class plusOnNestedSequence
{
  public x a;
  public object[] bAndc;
}
```

Fig. 29. Relax nested content models to become flat

used in the figure (cf. aAndB) is strikingly pragmatic, and does not scale for more complex composites. Second, we lose some degree of static typing for such relaxed composites.

Some extra static typing is obtainable, if we use a repeating choice over all elements in the content model. (This form of relaxation can be compared with the notion of prime-type conversion in the XQuery semantics [69].) When mapping such an 'artificial', repeating choice to an object model, we can use the different element names (say, types of elements) for specialized access to an otherwise untyped list.

View Nested Content Models in a Flat Manner

For the sake of programming convenience, the schema-derived object types may 'view' the XML data as if it was of a very simple shape. Such views are particularly convenient for queries, but we need to be prepared to encounter update challenges. Views generally do not *relax* in the formal sense of subset order on

```
plusInAndOut = a (b⁺ c)⁺

  <xs:element name="plusInAndOut">
    <xs:complexType>
      <xs:sequence>
        <xs:element name="a" type="x"/>
        <xs:sequence maxOccurs="unbounded">
          <xs:element name="b" type="y" maxOccurs="unbounded"/>
          <xs:element name="c" type="z"/>
        </xs:sequence>
      </xs:sequence>
    </xs:complexType>
  </xs:element>
```

Mapping option: no support for round-tripping

```
public class plusInAndOut
{
  public x a;
  public y [] b;
  public z [] c;
}
```

Mapping option: untyped container + typed getters

```
public class plusInAndOut
{
  private enum label {a,b,c};
  private List<Pair<label,object>> content;
  public x a                { get { ... } set { ... } }
  public IEnumerable<y> b   { get { ... } set { ... } }
  public IEnumerable<z> c   { get { ... } set { ... } }
}
```

Fig. 30. Views on content models

tree languages. Here is a simple strategy for devising views on nested composites: relax choices as sequences, propagate quantifiers $(?, +, *)$ over sequences to the components, and apply simplifications.

- Relax choices
    - $e_1 \mid \cdots \mid e_n \rightsquigarrow e_1^? \cdots e_n^?$
- Propagate quantifiers
    - $(e_1 \cdots e_n)^q \rightsquigarrow e_1^q \cdots e_n^q$
- Simplification rules
    - $e^{qq} \rightsquigarrow e^q$

- $e^{?*} \leadsto e^*$
- $e^{?+} \leadsto e^*$
- etc.

The propagation rule clearly goes beyond relaxation. (Once we take recurrent element names into account, the rules become slightly more complicated.) Let us apply these rules to the most complex pattern in our suite — plusInAndOut:

$$\text{Content model: } \mathsf{plusInAndOut} = \mathsf{a}\ (\mathsf{b}^+\ \mathsf{c})^+$$
$$\text{Derived view:} \qquad\qquad \leadsto \mathsf{a}\ \mathsf{b}^+\ \mathsf{c}^+$$

Fig. 30 shows two mapping options for the content model plusInAndOut. The class at the top is the result of simply mapping the derived view to a plain object type with read/write-enabled fields. (The `xsd.exe` tool derives this class.) The grouping of b's and c's is not maintained in any way, thereby sacrificing round-tripping.

The class at the bottom of Fig. 30 devises an untyped (private) list to store all subtrees. For each element name, there is a getter and a setter, whose implementations actually leverage the fact that element names are stored. There are several challenges related to this approach. First, the mere definition of the correct semantics for the insertion mode of setters is non-trivial. Second, the programming model for constructing and updating nested composites is not straightforward, given that the original grouping for the nested composites is no longer discoverable. Third, normal type checking is insufficient to guarantee valid content at all times; hence, some scheme of dynamic checking may be necessary. Fourth, property access to a heterogeneous list is less efficient than field access for 'plain (sub)objects'.

4.4   Local Elements

A number of OO languages support 'nested classes' of different kinds. However, nesting is hardly seen as a data-modeling idiom. Nested classes are instead used for advanced forms of encapsulation and programming with closures. The use of nested classes is typically discouraged if it only serves for a namespace-like purpose such as qualification. In contrast, the use of local element declarations is established at least for XSD.

Fig. 31 shows an XML schema for libraries (say, collections of books) and corresponding C# classes that were obtained by a nesting-preserving mapping. Unfortunately, nested classes are inconvenient when used for the construction of 'data objects' because the scoping rules of OO languages do not provide any shorthand for accessing nested classes. This weakness is illustrated in Fig. 31; the sample code constructs a single book instance and adds it to a given library lib; notice the qualified names library .bookType and library .bookType.authorType.

Hence, it may seem that XML schemas should generally be flattened prior to the actual X-to-O mapping. There are several problems with this approach. Most obviously, flattening bears the potential of causing clashes in the global

---

A nested element declaration

```
<xs:element name="library">
  <xs:complexType>
    <xs:sequence>
      <xs:element name="book" minOccurs="0" maxOccurs="unbounded">
        <xs:complexType>
          <xs:sequence>
            <xs:element name="title" type="xs:string"/>
            <xs:element name="author" maxOccurs="unbounded">
              <xs:complexType>
                <xs:sequence>
                  <xs:element name="title" type="xs:string"/>
                  <xs:element name="name" type="xs:string"/>
                </xs:sequence>
              </xs:complexType>
            </xs:element>
            <xs:element name="publisher" type="xs:string"/>
            <xs:element name="year" type="xs:gYear"/>
          </xs:sequence>
        </xs:complexType>
      </xs:element>
    </xs:sequence>
  </xs:complexType>
</xs:element>
```

A mapping option that preserves nesting

```
public class library
{
    public List<bookType> book;
    public class bookType
    {
        public string  title ;
        public List<authorType> author;
        public string  publisher ;
        public System.DateTime year;
        public class authorType
        {
            public string  title ;
            public string  name;
        }
    }
}
```

Illustration of object construction

```
lib .book.Add(
  new library .bookType {
    title      = "COBOL Unleashed",
    author     = new List<library .bookType.authorType> {
      new library .bookType.authorType { name = "Jon Wessler" }
    },
    publisher  = "Macmillan Computer Publishing",
    year       = new System.DateTime(1998,9,1) } );
```

Fig. 31. Illustration of mapping for nested element declarations

---

Typed-oriented flattening ('Venetian blind')

```xml
<xs:element name="library">
  <xs:complexType>
    <xs:sequence>
      <xs:element name="book" type="book" minOccurs="0" maxOccurs="unbounded"/>
    </xs:sequence>
  </xs:complexType>
</xs:element>
<xs:complexType name="book">
  <xs:sequence>
    <xs:element name="title" type="xs:string"/>
    <xs:element name="author" type="author" maxOccurs="unbounded"/>
    <xs:element name="publisher" type="xs:string"/>
    <xs:element name="year" type="xs:gYear"/>
  </xs:sequence>
</xs:complexType>
<xs:complexType name="author">
  <xs:sequence>
    <xs:element name="title" type="xs:string"/>
    <xs:element name="name" type="xs:string"/>
  </xs:sequence>
</xs:complexType>
```

Element-oriented flattening ('Salami slice')

```xml
<xs:element name="library">
  <xs:complexType>
    <xs:sequence>
      <xs:element ref="book" minOccurs="0" maxOccurs="unbounded"/>
    </xs:sequence>
  </xs:complexType>
</xs:element>
<xs:element name="book">
  <xs:complexType>
    <xs:sequence>
      <xs:element name="title" type="xs:string"/>
      <xs:element ref="author" maxOccurs="unbounded"/>
      <xs:element name="publisher" type="xs:string"/>
      <xs:element name="year" type="xs:gYear"/>
    </xs:sequence>
  </xs:complexType>
</xs:element>
<xs:element name="author">
  <xs:complexType>
    <xs:sequence>
      <xs:element name="title" type="xs:string"/>
      <xs:element name="name" type="xs:string"/>
    </xs:sequence>
  </xs:complexType>
</xs:element>
```

Fig. 32. Flattened schemas for Fig. 31 in two different styles

scope. Also, the promotion of many locals to the global scope may make it more difficult to comprehend the data model. Furthermore, there is some element of arbitrariness in so far that there is more than just one flattening method, e.g.:

```
<xs:element name="library">
  <xs:complexType>
    <xs:sequence>
      <xs:element ref="book" minOccurs="0" maxOccurs="unbounded"/>
    </xs:sequence>
  </xs:complexType>
</xs:element>
<xs:element name="book">
  <xs:complexType>
    <xs:sequence>
      <xs:element ref="title"/>
      <xs:element ref="author" maxOccurs="unbounded"/>
      <xs:element ref="publisher"/>
      <xs:element ref="year"/>
    </xs:sequence>
  </xs:complexType>
</xs:element>
<xs:element name="author">
  <xs:complexType>
    <xs:sequence>
      <xs:element ref="title"/>
      <xs:element ref="name"/>
    </xs:sequence>
  </xs:complexType>
</xs:element>
<xs:element name="title" type="xs:string"/>
<xs:element name="name" type="xs:string"/>
<xs:element name="publisher" type="xs:string"/>
<xs:element name="year" type="xs:gYear"/>
```

Fig. 33. Extremely flat style

- Extract anonymous complex types of local elements as global type definitions.
- Promote local element declarations of complex types to the global scope.
- Promote local element declarations of simple types, too, for uniformity.
- Potentially even promote local attribute declarations, for uniformity.

The first two options are illustrated in Fig. 32. The last two options are phrased as refinements of the second option, and ultimately suggest 'universal promotion', which may may appear as the most principled option; cf. Fig. 33. However, universal promotion, when applied to the library example, causes an 'ontological clash'. The original schema comprised two local element declarations with label name; they were unified in the result, which was possible because the declarations also agreed on the element type. Reflection reveals that both kinds of names are different (in an ontological sense);[19] hence, it it not acceptable to unify the declarations. To summarize, (universal) promotion cannot be performed, in general. This problem also vitally contributes to the overall difficulty to favor a node-label-preserving mapping because flattening may be needed in preparation of such a mapping, if we agree that nested object types are inconvenient, as discussed above. This analysis provides further evidence for the X/O Impedance Mismatch.

---

[19] We face the title of a book vs. the title of a person. This example is adopted from a related mailing list discussion: http://xsd.stylusstudio.com/2006Apr/post00002.htm

4.5   Element Templates

When using object models for data representation, we mainly use one form of type abstraction for data: *classes* with nominal type equality and explicitly declared inheritance (subtyping) relationships. The situation for data modeling with XSD is less homogeneous. There are different kinds of types. XSD's *element declarations* qualify as *types* in the common sense of programming-language theory. That is, element declarations (both global and local) denote sets of semantically *meaningful* values: certain sets of XML trees. XSD's (complex) *type definitions* are not exactly like types in programming language theory. They seem to be modeling 'unlabeled trees'; such values do not really exist. We may think of (complex) type definitions as incomplete element declarations, say element templates.

One may feel tempted to dismiss such templates as macros for structural types, but this would be an oversimplification. For instance, the semantically meaningful notion of element substitution ('inheritance') is tied to type substitution; cf. Sec. 4.6 and Sec. 4.7.

For the record, XSD also comprises attribute-group definitions and model-group definitions, which we neglect here. Even if we focus on just element declarations and complex-type definitions, one may wonder whether these different forms of type abstractions must be regarded as an XSD idiosyncrasy. Arguably, there is a fundamental need for element templates because they enable an important form of reuse. To provide another data point, RELAX NG offers so-called 'named patterns' that are akin to the complex-type definitions of XSD.

Fig. 34 shows a typical XSD sample that illustrates the reuse value of complex-type definitions. The address type is used in two positions: billing addresses and shipping addresses. The exclusive use of element declarations would certainly simplify the devision of X-to-O mappings, but the example suggests that an elimination of complex types is generally not feasible without prohibitive code duplication.

Fig. 34 also shows the 'most obvious' option for mapping the customer schema. Both, global element declarations and complex-type definitions are mapped to classes that look alike, which is troublesome for the following reason. One might create an Address instance and then expect to be able to serialize it. However, the class Address is not associated with any element tag. Should we disallow serialization? Should we instead serialize addresses in a special way, as a sort of XML 'fragment'? Should we instead use the type name as the element name? How does the OO programmer comprehend the technical difference between the different kinds of object types: Address vs. Customer?

Also, the mapping further illustrates the dubiety of the common, node-label-omitting mapping. To see this, consider the following code fragment that operates on the object model of Fig. 34:

```
var myAddr = new Address();
myAddr.name = "Fred Mueller";
myAddr.street = "88th NE CT. place";
var myCust = new customer();
myCust.id = "123456";
myCust.billingAddress = myAddr;
myCust.shippingAddress = myCust.billingAddress;    // What's this?
```

An XML schema that leverages complex types for reuse

```
<xs:element name="customer">
  <xs:complexType>
    <xs:sequence>
      <xs:element name="id" type="xs:string"/>
      <xs:element name="billingAddress" type="Address"/>
      <xs:element name="shippingAddress" type="Address"/>
    </xs:sequence>
  </xs:complexType>
</xs:element>
<xs:complexType name="Address">
  <xs:sequence>
    <xs:element name="name" type="xs:string"/>
    <xs:element name="street" type="xs:string"/>
  </xs:sequence>
</xs:complexType>
```

An illustrative XML instance

```
<customer>
  <id>123456</id>
  <billingAddress>
    <name>Fred Mueller</name>
    <street>88th NE CT. place</street>
  </billingAddress>
  <shippingAddress>
    <name>Fred Mueller</name>
    <street>88th NE CT. place</street>
  </shippingAddress>
</customer>
```

An obvious mapping option

```
public class customer {
  public string id;
  public Address billingAddress;
  public Address shippingAddress;
}
public class Address {
  public string name;
  public string street;
}
```

Fig. 34. Illustration of the reuse aspect for complex types

That is, we assign a billing address to a field for a shipping address. In the original value domains for the XML addresses, this assignment does not make sense because we are facing different element names — billingAddress VS. shippingAddress, i.e., we face different types in the sense of programming-language theory. Hence, the above code seems to require that the element name billingAddress is replaced by shippingAddress underneath. It is quite unusual to think of an assignment that involves a hidden type change.

There is perhaps one way to improve on the indistinguishable mapping of global element declarations and complex-type definitions. We may 'de-prioritize' complex types and map them to *interfaces* as opposed to classes. These interfaces may be instrumental in establishing useful type-level relationships (rather than plain assignability). Here is an interface for the complex type Address:

```
public interface Address
{
    string name    { get; set; }
    string street  { get; set; }
}
```

Let us illustrate the interface-based scheme. To this end, we assume a node-label-preserving mapping. There are classes billingAddress and shippingAddress, which implement the interface Address. Further, these classes provide a *copy constructor* using an Address-bounded argument. As a result, the earlier code fragment can be rewritten as follows:[20]

```
var myAddr = new billingAddress();
myAddr.name = "Fred Mueller";
myAddr.street = "88th NE CT. place";
var myCust = new customer();
myCust.id = "123456";
myCust. billingAddress = myAddr;
myCust.shippingAddress = new shippingAddress(myAddr);
```

Hence, we can reuse a given address (say a billing address) in creating another address (say a shipping address). The use of the copy constructor makes explicit the conceptual type change that was previously hidden. The approach is not general: (i) it requires the (uncommon) node-label-preserving mapping; (ii) it cannot be used in combination with type derivation, as we will discuss in the next subsection. This failure of an attempted conceptual clean-up provides further evidence for the X/O Impedance Mismatch.

---

[20] For the record, the shown code rests on the assumption that implicit casts are available for all element declarations with simple element types. Otherwise, extra 'element constructors' would be needed in the various assignments such as new name("Fred Mueller") instead of "Fred Mueller".

An XML schema that involves type derivation

```
<xs:element name="items">
  <xs:complexType>
    <xs:sequence>
      <xs:element ref="product" minOccurs="0" maxOccurs="unbounded"/>
    </xs:sequence>
  </xs:complexType>
</xs:element>
<xs:element name="product" type="ProductType"/>
<xs:complexType name="ProductType">
  <xs:sequence>
    <xs:element name="number" type="xs:int"/>
    <xs:element name="name" type="xs:string"/>
  </xs:sequence>
</xs:complexType>
<xs:complexType name="ShirtType">
  <xs:complexContent>
    <xs:extension base="ProductType">
      <xs:sequence>
        <xs:element name="size" type="ShirtSizeType"/> <!-- ShirtSizeType elided -->
        <xs:element name="color" type="ColorType"/> <!-- ColorType elided -->
      </xs:sequence>
    </xs:extension>
  </xs:complexContent>
</xs:complexType>
```

A sample instance exercising type substitution

```
<items>
  <product xsi:type="ShirtType">
    <number>557</number>
    <name>Short-Sleeved Linen Blouse</name>
    <size>10</size>
    <color value="blue"/>
  </product>
</items>
```

An obvious mapping option

```
public class items
{
  public List<ProductType> product;
}
public class ProductType
{
  public int number;
  public string name;
}
public class ShirtType : ProductType
{
  public ShirtSizeType size ;
  public ColorType color ;
}
```

Fig. 35. Illustration of mapping type derivation by extension

4.6   Type Extension

XSD's type derivation by extension is (intentionally) similar to OO subclassing. That is, one can define new types by essentially extending other types (referred to by name). Extended types are substitutable for base types; cf. Fig. 35 for an example.[21] To provide another data point, RELAX NG does not provide such linguistic support, but one can still use a combination of 'design patterns' and annotations to effectively model the same kind of relationship [59,60].

The interface-oriented mapping rule of the previous section falls short for types that engage in type derivation (except for a special case that we will identify in Sec. 4.7). Classes are needed for derived complex types and their base types because we must be able to construct objects of all the types corresponding to the different members in the derivation hierarchy. For instance, in the example, there is just one root element, product, which can be of two different types, ProductType and ShirtType.

Hence we must be prepared to designate classes both to element declarations and complex-type definitions. A sensible optimization comes to mind. We may attempt to omit classes for element declarations with a nominal element type, namely, when the nominal element type implies the element name and all derived types imply the same element name. Consider again the schema in Fig. 35: product elements are of type ProductType or ShirtType, and there are no other elements of these types. Hence no designated class is needed for the root product. (Indeed, the xsd.exe tool maps the schema in this manner.)

We cannot apply this optimization, when there are multiple (global) element declarations referring to the same element type (or to types related to each other by type derivation). Hence, we have to accept ultimately that both element declarations and complex-type definitions are mapped to classes — except for some special cases, *if* we are willing to cater for exceptions. As a last attempt of restoring some discipline (that helps avoiding confusions between element declarations and complex-type definitions), we may assume two different base types for schema-derived classes, thereby replacing the implicit base class object, used until now:

- XLabeled — Base class for element declarations.
- XUnlabeled — Base class for complex-type definitions.

This discipline provides a bit of discoverability. Also, we may assume that only subclasses of XLabeled implement the general de-/serialization protocol, thereby avoiding accidental uses of complex types for serialization.

Global element declarations with nominal element types are mapped according to a 'wrapper scheme' that reflects the fact that the wrapper only provides the element name while the wrappee provides all the actual 'structure', i.e., children and attributes; cf. Fig 36 for an illustration. The constructor of the

---

[21] A note on XSD: Notice the attribute xsi:type="ShirtType" in the sample instance. In this manner, validation is informed to expect the derived type in place of the base type.

```
public class product : XLabeled
{
  public product() { content=new ProductType(); }

  public product(ProductType Content) { content=Content; }

  public ProductType Content { get { return content; }}

  public int number {
    get { return Content.number; }
    set { Content.number = value; }
  }
  public string name {
    get { return Content.name; }
    set { Content.name = value; }
  }
  private ProductType content;
}
```

Fig. 36. Mapping roots with nominal element types

wrapper class takes a wrappee. The interface of the base type of the wrappee is re-implemented by the wrapper type (through forwarding).

Let us investigate the convenience and clarity of the resulting programming model. To this end, we revisit the example for populating two addresses (billing vs. shipping) based on elements of the same nominal type for addresses. In the following code fragment, we attempt to reuse an address object:

```
var myAddr = new Address();
myAddr.name = "Fred Mueller";
myAddr.street = "88th NE CT. place";
var myCust = new customer();
myCust.id = "123456";
myCust.billingAddress = new billingAddress(myAddr);
myCust.shippingAddress = new shippingAddress(myAddr);
```

Hence, we pass the 'unlabeled object' myAddr to the wrapping constructors for the labeled types of billing and shipping addresses. One may wonder what exactly the semantics of the wrapping constructors should be. We recall that the interface-based mapping of the previous subsection assumed a *copy constructor* taking a labeled object and creating a labeled object. A plain copy semantics does not seem to be appropriate for the wrapping constructors because this would imply that 'unlabeled objects' are never integrated into object graphs, as is. A 'no-op' semantics, i.e., wrapping 'unlabeled objects' any number of times, does not seem to be appropriate either because it could never meet the tree invariant for XML. An alternative semantics would then be to *'parent' unlabeled objects when they are used for the first time, and to copy (clone) them from there on.* This discussion leaves a bad aftertaste, and hence, provides further evidence for the X/O Impedance Mismatch.

4.7 Element Substitution

In XSD, element declarations can engage in so-called substitution groups, thereby providing a form of substitutability for elements. (RELAX NG would again leverage 'design patterns' to this end [59,60].) As a simple illustration of substitution groups, let us add an element declaration to the earlier schema for products in Fig. 35:

```
<xs:element name="shirt" type="ShirtType" substitutionGroup="product"/>
```

As a result, there are the following associations:

Element name	Nominal element type
product	ProductType
shirt	ShirtType

According to the rules of XSD, all members of a substitution group, except for leafs, must be of a nominal element type. In practice, this implies that every 'concept' (such as the concept of 'shirts') gives rise to *two* schema abstractions; cf. the element declaration shirt and the complex-type definition ShirtType. One may expect a form of element substitution that does not rely on nominal element types.

There are the following mapping options for substitution groups:

- *The wrapping option*: Based on the discussion in Sec. 4.6, we map the members of the substitution group (which are element declarations with a nominal element type) to wrapper types on the object types for the element types. Both the wrapper and the wrappee classes engage in class inheritance.
- *The choice option*: We inline each reference to the head of a substitution group as a choice over all of its members; cf. Fig. 37. Thereby, we effectively eliminate the use of substitution groups. The members of a substitution group are still to be mapped to wrapper classes, but subclassing is restricted to unlabeled object types.
- *The normalization option*: If the element types of substitution-group members are not used elsewhere in the schema, and if there is one member per possible type (in the type-derivation hierarchy), then we can potentially omit the object types for the type-derivation hierarchy and map the substitution groups to a plain class hierarchy; cf. Fig. 38 for an illustration.

With the first option, the OO programmer may 'get lost' in the two parallel class hierarchies. With the second option, the OO programmer may be overwhelmed by extra-large choices. Both options transport the 'doubled' number of schema

```
The XML schema with a substitution group

<xs:element name="items">
  <xs:complexType>
    <xs:sequence>
      <xs:element ref="product" minOccurs="0" maxOccurs="unbounded"/>
    </xs:sequence>
  </xs:complexType>
</xs:element>
<xs:element name="product" type="ProductType"/>
<xs:element name="shirt" type="ShirtType" substitutionGroup="product"/>
```

```
The substitution group inlined as choice

<xs:element name="items">
  <xs:complexType>
    <xs:sequence>
      <xs:choice minOccurs="0" maxOccurs="unbounded">
        <xs:element ref="product"/>
        <xs:element ref="shirt"/>
      </xs:choice>
    </xs:sequence>
  </xs:complexType>
</xs:element>
<xs:element name="product" type="ProductType"/>
<xs:element name="shirt" type="ShirtType"/>
```

Fig. 37. Map substitution groups as choices

abstractions to the object model, thereby becoming unpalatable. The third option would lead to a concise object model, but its applicability is subject to preconditions. Also it takes away (subtle) options for content construction, as illustrated by the following sample data:

```
<items>
  <product xsi:type="ShirtType">  ... content elided  ... </product>
  <shirt>                         ... content elided  ... </shirt>
</items>
```

That is, the collection comprises two shirts; the first one (`<product xsi:type="ShirtType">` ...) exploits type substitution; the second one (`<shirt>` ...) exploits element substitution. The normalized object model of Fig. 38 cannot easily differentiate these two kinds of shirts along construction and observation.

Further, the normalization option is challenged by a naming issue: should we prioritize element names over type names, or vice versa? We would like to adopt the element names as class names (because element declarations may count as the primary form of XML types). However, we must adopt the type names as class names, as soon as the type-derivation hierarchy makes more type distinctions than the associated substitution group for elements. Likewise, we must adopt the element names, as soon as the substitution group makes more type distinctions. Hence, a relatively small change (such as the addition of one

---

Mapping option: prefer element declarations over type definitions

```
public class product
{
  public int number;
  public string name;
}
public class shirt : product
{
  public ShirtSizeType size ;
  public ColorType color ;
}
```

Mapping option: prefer type definitions over element declarations

```
public class ProductType
{
  public int number;
  public string name;
}
public class ShirtType : ProductType
{
  public ShirtSizeType size ;
  public ColorType color ;
}
```

Fig. 38. Illustration of mapping for substitution groups

global schema component) may trigger a different naming scheme for the entire schema.

4.8   Type Restriction

XSD provides another form of type derivation — by restriction. We will focus here on restriction for complex types, and defer the coverage of simple types to the next subsection. Restricted types may be used in type substitution ('xsi:type') in the same manner as extended types. The typical OO language has no counterpart for type derivation by restriction. In an effort to at least preserve XSD's substitutability, we suggest to map restriction relationships again to class inheritance, just as we did for extension relationships. It remains to further justify this mapping rule.

Fig. 39 shows a contrived example that demonstrates principled forms of complex-type restriction by a derivation chain foo, bar and abc. In the derivation of bar from foo, *an optional particle is eliminated.* In the derivation of abc from bar, *the element type of a particle is restricted to a subtype.*

```
<xs:complexType name="foo">
  <xs:sequence>
    <xs:element name="x" type="foo" minOccurs="0"/>
    <xs:element name="y" type="foo"/>
  </xs:sequence>
</xs:complexType>
<xs:complexType name="bar">
  <xs:complexContent>
    <xs: restriction  base="foo">
      <xs:sequence>
        <!-- Optional "x" dropped out. -->
        <xs:element name="y" type="foo"/>
      </xs:sequence>
    </xs: restriction >
  </xs:complexContent>
</xs:complexType>
<xs:complexType name="abc">
  <xs:complexContent>
    <xs: restriction  base="bar">
      <xs:sequence>
        <!-- Require subtype for "y". -->
        <xs:element name="y" type="bar"/>
      </xs:sequence>
    </xs: restriction >
  </xs:complexContent>
</xs:complexType>
```

Fig. 39. Illustration of complex-type derivation by restriction

There is the following scale for mapping restricted types to classes:

1. Just inherit the base class without any change; neglect restrictions.
2. Enforce restrictions when validation is requested for an object.
3. Enforce some restrictions as invariants based on dynamic checks.
4. Enforce some restrictions by means of the static type system.

Fig. 40 shows a mapping option where the restrictions are enforced by dynamically checked setters. (Depending on mapping rules and schema patterns, dynamic checks may also be required for getters.) Suppose we would want to enforce the restrictions by means of the static type system. In the derivation of bar, we would need to *remove* a member. Member removal is unsupported by several mainstream OO languages (including C#), and it is a controversial capability anyhow. In the derivation of abc, we would need to *co-variantly modify* the argument type of a setter. Covariance for arguments is unsupported by most mainstream OO languages (including C#), and it is a controversial capability because of the difficulty to reconcile static type safety.

```
public class foo
{
  public virtual foo x {  get { return _x; }  set { _x = value; } }
  public virtual foo y {  get { return _y; }  set { _y = value; } }
  private foo _x;
  private foo _y;
}
public class bar : foo
{
  public override foo x { set { Trace.Assert(value==null); base.x = value; }}
}
public class abc : bar
{
  public override foo y { set { Trace.Assert(value is bar); base.y = value; }}
}
```

Fig. 40. A mapping option for complex-type derivation by restriction

The use of class inheritance for restriction relationships may be said to systematically violate the substitution principle [36]. The problem is that subclass setters are constrained by stronger preconditions than the base-class setters. This situation is reminiscent of 'cheating servers' [43], which are in conflict with behavior-preserving subtyping and design-by-contract (DBC). We may adopt a mitigation technique that is also offered in the DBC literature. That is, we may take the view that restriction conditions are instance parameters in a sense. To this end, the object model anticipates 'variable' restriction conditions in separate, virtual, Boolean methods — one per property. A restricted subclass may then override the restriction condition. Fig. 41 illustrates this 'trick' for the running example.

4.9   Simple Types

Up to now, we used built-in simple types, which we mapped to a fixed set of primitive programming-language types such as string and double for C#. XSD also provides list types and union types, which we neglect here for brevity. Further, XSD provides type derivation by restriction for simple types, which we will discuss now.

Fig. 42 illustrates several mapping options for simple types when type derivation by restriction is involved. The first option assumes that all simple types (including the derived ones) are mapped to primitive types of the programming language at hand. In fact, a restricted type is mapped to the same type as its base type. In the sample schema in the figure, there is the restricted type uint42 with xs:unsignedInt as its base type. Both are mapped to C#'s type uint.

As a first enhancement, we may transport restrictions as dynamic checks into the object model; cf. the second mapping option in Fig. 42. The use of dynamic checks is similar to the treatment of minOccurs/maxOccurs constraints

```
public class foo
{
    // Boolean conditions for virtual contracts
    protected virtual bool xValid(foo x) { return true; }
    protected virtual bool yValid(foo y) { return true; }

    // State access with dynamically checked properties
    public virtual foo x {
        get { Trace.Assert(xValid(_x)); return _x; }
        set { Trace.Assert(xValid(value)); _x = value; }
    }
    public virtual foo y {
        get { Trace.Assert(yValid(_y)); return _y; }
        set { Trace.Assert(yValid(value)); _y = value; }
    }
    private foo _x;
    private foo _y;
}

public class bar : foo
{
    protected override bool xValid(foo x) {
        return base.xValid(x) && x == null;
    }
}

public class abc : bar
{
    protected override bool yValid(foo y) {
        return base.yValid(y) && y is bar;
    }
}
```

Fig. 41. More DBC-compliant, restriction-ready object types

and complex-type restrictions, as discussed earlier. In particular, setters are constrained by preconditions that model the schema restrictions.

As a second enhancement, we may designate object types (or struct types) to nominally defined simple types. Such a mapping option is motivated by the insight that even simple types may serve an important role in program comprehension and software evolution [19]. Also, the use of designated types would enable static type checking to guarantee that a value of a given restricted type does indeed meet the restrictions, thereby making repeated dynamic checks unnecessary.

The use of struct types (as opposed to classes) may be particularly attractive because struct types are potentially exempt from charges (subject to compiler

An XML schema with a simple-type restriction

```
<xs:simpleType name="uint42">
  <xs: restriction  base="xs:unsignedInt">
    <xs:maxInclusive value="42"/>
  </xs: restriction >
</xs:simpleType>
<xs:element name="simples">
  <xs:complexType>
    <xs:sequence>
      <xs:element name="anUint" type="xs:unsignedInt"/>    <!-- unrestricted type -->
      <xs:element name="anUint42" type="uint42"/>        <!-- restricted type -->
    </xs:sequence>
  </xs:complexType>
</xs:element>
```

Mapping option: replace derived types by their base types

```
public class simples
{
    public uint anUint;
    public uint anUint42;
}
```

Mapping option: enforce restrictions by dynamic checks

```
public class simples
{
    public uint anUint {
        get { return _anUint; }
        set { _anUint = value; } }
    public uint anUint42 {
        get { return _anUint42; }
        set { Trace. Assert(value<=42); _anUint42 = value; } }
    private uint _anUint;
    private uint _anUint42;
}
```

Mapping option: structs designated to simple-type definitions

```
public struct uint42
{
    public static implicit operator uint42(uint it ) {
        Trace. Assert( it <=42); return new uint42 { value = it };
    }
    public static implicit operator uint(uint42 it ) {
        return it . value;
    }
    private uint value;
}
public class simples
{
    public uint anUint;
    public uint42 anUint42;
}
```

Fig. 42. Lossy mappings for simple types

Schema-derived classes

```
public class uint42 : XsUnsignedInt
{
    public static implicit operator uint42(uint it) {
        Trace.Assert(it <=42);
        return new uint42 { value = it };
    }
    public static implicit operator uint(uint42 it) {
        return (uint)it.value;
    }
}

public class simples
{
    public XsUnsignedInt anUint;
    public uint42 anUint42;
}
```

Predefined classes for XSD's built-in simple types

```
// Base class of all simple types
public abstract class XsAnySimpleType
{
    protected object value;
}

// The counterpart for xs:unsignedInt
public class XsUnsignedInt : XsUnsignedLong
{
    public static implicit operator XsUnsignedInt(uint it) {
        return new XsUnsignedInt { value = it };
    }
    public static implicit operator uint(XsUnsignedInt it) {
        return (uint)it.value;
    }
}

// Other simple types, likewise
public class XsUnsignedLong        : XsNonNegativeInteger  { ... }
public class XsNonNegativeInteger  : XsInteger            { ... }
public class XsInteger             : XsDecimal            { ... }
public class XsDecimal             : XsAnySimpleType      { ... }
```

Fig. 43. Mapping simple types to a designated class hierarchy

optimizations) — if they only wrap a single component. The structs-based mapping option is illustrated at the bottom of Fig. 42. We use implicit casts for both directions of mediating between the struct type for the simple type and the associated primitive type. The restriction is only checked when a value of the restricted type is constructed. Unfortunately, a structs-based mapping does not enable proper substitution for simple types (because there is no subtyping for struct types). Consider the following XML data, which exercises simple-type substitution for the first child element labeled anUint:

```
<simples xmlns:xsi="http://www.w3.org/2001/XMLSchema−instance">
   <anUint xsi:type="uint42">41</anUint>
   <anUint42>41</anUint42>
</simples>
```

The property for the anUint element is of type uint (or perhaps of a designated struct type for xs:unsignedInt, if we decide to designate struct types for all of XSD's built-in simple types). Hence, the getter (based on a structs-based mapping) would never report the status of the datum to be of the restricted type uint42.

Fig. 43 makes the next step by designating wrapper classes to simple types. There are also predefined classes for XSD's built-in simple types so that XSD's substitutability can be preserved completely. Clearly, this approach is quite costly because of 'boxing' (cf. the field of type object in XsAnySimpleType) and wrapping (due to the use of classes). Also, the programming convenience is arguably impaired because OO programmers may prefer object models that leverage the familiar primitive types of their OO language (as opposed to the XSD types). One may provide implicit casts so that the objects of a 'simple-type class' can be used whenever the associated primitive type is expected, but the resulting hybrid may be difficult to comprehend by the programmer. To summarize, there is no fully satisfactory simple-type mapping. This circumstance also provides further evidence for the X/O Impedance Mismatch.

5   Concluding Remarks

The X/O Impedance Mismatch has to be primarily attributed to fundamental differences in the data models for XML and objects. The data models are so much different that the expectation of using 'plain objects' for the typed representation of XML trees should be internationally condemned. It appears that the X/O Impedance Mismatch must also be attributed to differences in the type systems (the type languages) for XML and objects. However, it is important to note that the differences in type systems are largely implied by the underlying data models. Finally, the complexity of XSD and its freewheeling use in the wild add considerably to the severity of the X/O Impedance Mismatch.

The work reported in this paper clearly substantiates that a full resolution of the X/O Impedance Mismatch is fundamentally impossible. The optimistic (more pragmatic) interpretation of our work is that the understanding of (canonical) X-to-O mappings has matured, and hence, more ambitious X-to-O mappings are in reach such that XML semantics and schema constraints are better preserved by the resulting object models, while also hiding the complexities and idiosyncrasies of XML and XSD — to some extent. More ambitious X-to-O mappings buy us time until something simpler than the current standards (XML 1.0/1.1+XSD 1.0/1.1) emerges. The pessimistic (more intellectual) interpretation of our work is that (canonical) X-to-O mappings remain hacks (and XSD is by far too complicated), no matter what, and hence a famous comment by Dijsktra (originally advised for Cobol) comes to mind [16]: *"you can really do only one of two things: fight the disease or pretend that it does not exist"*.

Acknowledgments. The authors acknowledge interactions with Umut Alev, Brian Beckmann, Sergey Dubinets, Priya Lakshminarayanan, Chris Lovett, Sergey Melnik, Dave Remy, Dan Rogers, Mark Shields, Huseyin Ulger, and Eugene Veselov. More generally, the authors have benefited from countless discussions with members of the Data Programmability team and further individuals at Microsoft.

References

1. Amer-Yahia, S., Du, F., Freire, J.: A comprehensive solution to the XML-to-relational mapping problem. In: Laender, A.H.F., Lee, D., Ronthaler, M. (eds.) Proceedings of 6th ACM CIKM International Workshop on Web Information and Data Management (WIDM'04), pp. 31–38. ACM Press, New York (2004)
2. Atanassow, F., Clarke, D., Jeuring, J.: UUXML: A Type-Preserving XML Schema-Haskell Data Binding. In: Jayaraman, B. (ed.) PADL 2004. LNCS, vol. 3057, pp. 71–85. Springer, Heidelberg (2004)
3. Baars, A.I., Löh, A., Swierstra, S.D.: Parsing permutation phrases. Journal of Functional Programming 14(6), 635–646 (2004)
4. Bancilhon, F., Spyratos, N.: Update semantics of relational views. ACM Transactions on Database Systems 6(4), 557–575 (1981)
5. Bau, D.: The Design of XMLBeans (2003), Parts 1–3:
   http://davidbau.com/archives/2003/11/14/the_design_of_xmlbeans_part_1.html;
   http://davidbau.com/archives/2003/11/19/the_design_of_xmlbeans_part_2.html;
   http://davidbau.com/archives/2003/12/18/the_design_of_xmlbeans_part_3.html.
6. Bierman, G., Meijer, E., Schulte, W.: The Essence of Data Access in Cω. In: Black, A.P. (ed.) ECOOP 2005. LNCS, vol. 3586, pp. 287–311. Springer, Heidelberg (2005)
7. Bohannon, P., Freire, J., Haritsa, J.R., Ramanath, M., Roy, P., Siméon, J.: Bridging the XML Relational Divide with LegoDB. In: Dayal, U., Ramamritham, K., Vijayaraman, T.M. (eds.) Proceedings of 19th International Conference on Data Engineering (ICDE'03), pp. 759–760. IEEE Computer Society Press, Los Alamitos (2003)
8. Bohannon, P., Freire, J., Roy, P., Simeon, J.: From XML Schema to Relations: A Cost-Based Approach to XML Storage. In: Proceedings of 18th International Conference on Data Engineering (ICDE'02), p. 64. IEEE Computer Society Press, Los Alamitos (2002)
9. Bordawekar, R., Burke, M.G., Peshansky, I., Raghavachari, M.: XJ: Integration of XML Processing into Java. In: Castagna, Raghavachari

10. Bourret, R.: Mapping W3C Schemas to Object Schemas (March 2001), http://www.rpbourret.com/xml/SchemaMap.htm
11. Bourret, R.: XML Data Binding Resources (2007), http://www.rpbourret.com/xml/XMLDataBinding.htm
12. Burton, F., Cameron, R.: Pattern Matching with Abstract Data Types. Journal of Functional Programming 3(2), 171–190 (1993)
13. Cameron, R.D.: Extending context-free grammars with permutation phrases. ACM Letters on Programming Language Systems 2(1-4), 85–94 (1993)
14. Castagna, G., Raghavachari, M. (eds.) PLAN-X 2006 Informal Proceedings, Charleston, South Carolina, January 14, 2006. BRICS, Department of Computer Science, University of Aarhus (2006)
15. Crocker, R., Stele Jr., G.L.: Proceedings of the 2003 ACM SIGPLAN Conference on Object-Oriented Programming Systems, Languages and Applications, OOP-SLA'03. ACM Press, New York (2003)
16. Dijkstra, E.W.: EWD 498: How do we tell truths that might hurt? In: Selected Writings on Computing: A Personal Perspective, pp. 129–131. Springer, Heidelberg (1992)
17. Downey, P.: W3C XML Schema Patterns for Databinding. In: Conference Proceedings XML'06 (2006)
18. Fähndrich, M., Leino, K.R.M.: Declaring and checking non-null types in an object-oriented language. In: Crocker and Jr. [15], pp. 302–312
19. Fowler, M.: When to Make a Type. IEEE Software, 12–13 (2003)
20. Gapeyev, V., Garillot, F., Pierce, B.C.: Statically Typed Document Transformation: An Xtatic Experience. In: Castagna and Raghavachari [14], pp. 2–13
21. Gapeyev, V., Levin, M.Y., Pierce, B.C., Schmitt, A.: XML Goes Native: Run-Time Representations for Xtatic. In: Bodik, R. (ed.) CC 2005. LNCS, vol. 3443, pp. 43–58. Springer, Heidelberg (2005)
22. Gapeyev, V., Pierce, B.C.: Regular Object Types. In: Cardelli, L. (ed.) ECOOP 2003. LNCS, vol. 2743, pp. 151–175. Springer, Heidelberg (2003)
23. Garcia, R., Jarvi, J., Lumsdaine, A., Siek, J.G., Willcock, J.: A comparative study of language support for generic programming. In: Crocker and Jr. [15], pp. 115–134
24. Gottlob, G., Paolini, P., Zicari, R.: Properties and update semantics of consistent views. ACM Transactions on Database Systems 13(4), 486–524 (1988)
25. Harren, M., Raghavachari, M., Shmueli, O., Burke, M.G., Bordawekar, R., Pechtchanski, I., Sarkar, V.: XJ: facilitating XML processing in Java. In: Ellis, A., Hagino, T. (eds.) WWW'05, 14th International Conference on World Wide Web, Proceedings, pp. 278–287. ACM Press, New York (2005)
26. Harren, M., Raghavachari, M., Shmueli, O., Burke, M.G., Sarkar, V., Bordawekar, R.: XJ: integration of XML processing into java. In: Feldman, S.I., Uretsky, M., Najork, M., Wills, C.E. (eds.) WWW'04, 13th International Conference on World Wide Web, Proceedings, pp. 340–341. ACM Press, New York (2004)
27. Hosoya, H., Pierce, B.C.: XDuce: A statically typed XML processing language. ACM Transactions on Internet Technology (TOIT) 3(2), 117–148 (2003)
28. IBM Research. XJ (2005), http://www.research.ibm.com/xj/
29. jsonJSON.org. Introducing JSON, 2006. Web site, http://www.json.org/.
30. Kirkegaard, C., Møller, A.: Type Checking with XML Schema in XACT. In: Castagna and Raghavachari [14], pp. 14–23
31. Kostoulas, M.G., Matsa, M., Mendelsohn, N., Perkins, E., Heifets, A., Mercaldi, M.: XML screamer: an integrated approach to high performance XML parsing, validation and deserialization. In: WWW'06, 15th International Conference on World Wide Web, Proceedings, pp. 93–102. ACM Press, New York (2006)

32. Lämmel, R., Kitsis, S., Remy, D.: Analysis of XML schema usage. In: Conference Proceedings XML'05 (2005)
33. Lämmel, R., Remy, D.: Functional OO Programming with Triangular Circles. In: Conference Proceedings XML'06 (2006)
34. Lämmel, R., Visser, E., Visser, J.: Strategic Programming Meets Adaptive Programming. In: AOSD'03, 2nd International Conference on Aspect-Oriented Software Development, Proceedings, pp. 168–177. ACM Press, New York (2003)
35. Lieberherr, K.: Adaptive Object-Oriented Software: The Demeter Method with Propagation Patterns. PWS Publishing Company, Boston (1996)
36. Liskov, B.: Keynote address - data abstraction and hierarchy. In: OOPSLA'87, Addendum to the Proceedings on Object-Oriented Programming Systems, Languages and Applications, pp. 17–34. ACM Press, New York (1987)
37. Loughran, S., Smith, E.: Rethinking the Java SOAP Stack. Technical Report HPL-2005-83, 20050517, External, HP Labs (2005)
38. McLaughlin, B.: Java and XML data binding. Nutshell handbook. O'Reilly & Associates, Inc., (2002)
39. Meijer, E., Beckman, B.: XLINQ: XML Programming Refactored (The Return Of The Monoids). In: Conference Proceedings XML'05, See [46] for the LINQ portal. XLinq is now called LINQ to XML (November 2005)
40. Meijer, E., Beckman, B.: XML Support in Visual Basic 9. In: Castagna and Raghavachari [14], p. 86
41. Meijer, E., Schulte, W., Bierman, G.: Programming with Circles, Triangles and Rectangles. In: Conference Proceedings XML'03 (2003)
42. Meijer, E., Schulte, W., Bierman, G.: Unifying Tables, Objects and Documents. In: Proceedings of Declarative Programming in the Context of OO Languages (DP-COOL) (2003)
43. Meyer, B.: Object-Oriented Software Construction, 2nd edn. The Object-Oriented Series. Prentice-Hall, Englewood Cliffs (1997)
44. Microsoft Corp. LINQ to XML Overview, See [46], for the LINQ portal. LINQ to XML was formerly called XLinq (2005–2007)
45. Microsoft Corp. C# Version 3.0 Specification, See [46] for the LINQ portal (2006–2007)
46. Microsoft Corp. The LINQ Project, (2006–2007), http://msdn.microsoft.com/netframework/future/linq/
47. Microsoft Corp. Windows Communication Foundation (2006–2007), http://windowscommunication.net/
48. Novak Jr, G.S.: Creation of views for reuse of software with different data representations. IEEE Transactions on Software Engineering 21(12), 993–1005 (1995)
49. OASIS. RELAX NG Specification (December 2001), http://www.oasis-open.org/committees/relax-ng/spec-20011203.html
50. Onizuka, M., Chan, F.Y., Michigami, R., Honishi, T.: Incremental maintenance for materialized XPath/XSLT views. In: WWW '05: Proceedings of the 14th International Conference on World Wide Web, pp. 671–681. ACM Press, New York (2005)
51. Perkins, E., Matsa, M., Kostoulas, M.G., Heifets, A., Mendelsohn, N.: Generation of efficient parsers through direct compilation of XML Schema grammars. IBM Systems Journal 45(2), 225–244 (2006)
52. Pradhan, M.: Default mapping for annotated XML schema. IBM developerWorks (April 2006), http://www-128.ibm.com/developerworks/db2/library/techarticle/dm-0604pr%adhan2/

53. Shields, M., Meijer, E.: Type-indexed rows. In: POPL'01: 28th ACM SIGPLAN-SIGACT Symposium on Principles Of Programming Languages, Proceedings, pp. 261–275. ACM Press, New York (2001)
54. Sun Microsystems. The Java architecture for XML binding (JAXB) (2006), http://java.sun.com/webservices/jaxb/.
55. The Apache XML Project. XMLBeans (2006), http://xmlbeans.apache.org/
56. Thiemann, P.: Modeling HTML in haskell. In: Pontelli, E., Costa, V.S (eds.) PADL 2000. LNCS, vol. 1753, pp. 263–277. Springer, Heidelberg (2000)
57. Thiemann, P.: A typed representation for HTML and XML documents in Haskell. Journal of Functional Programming 12(4&5), 435–468 (2002)
58. Thomas, D.: The Impedance Imperative: Tuples + Objects + Infosets = Too Much Stuff! Journal of Object Technology 2(5), 7–12 (2003)
59. van der Vlist, E.: RELAX NG. O'Reilly (December 2004)
60. van der Vlist, E.: RELAX NG and W3C XML Schema compared (continued) (July 2006), http://eric.van-der-vlist.com/blog/2814_RELAX_NG_and_W3C_XML_Schema_com pared_(continued).item
61. van Engelen, R., Govindaraju, M., Zhang, W.: Exploring Remote Object Coherence in XML Web Services. In: ICWS'06, International Conference on WebServices, Proceedings, pp. 249–256. IEEE Computer Society, Los Alamitos (2006)
62. Vinoski, S.: RPC Under Fire. IEEE Internet Computing 9(5), 93–95 (2005)
63. Visser, J.: Visitor combination and traversal control. ACM SIGPLAN Notices 36(11), 270–282 (2001) (OPSLA 2001 Conference Proceedings)
64. W3C. Document Object Model (DOM) (1997-2003), http://www.w3.org/DOM/
65. W3C. XML Path Language (XPath), Version 1.0, W3C Recommendation (November 16, 1999) http://www.w3.org/TR/xpath
66. W3C. XML Information Set (2nd edn.) (1999–2004) http://www.w3.org/TR/xml-infoset/
67. W3C. XML Schema, (2000–2003), http://www.w3.org/XML/Schema
68. W3C. Extensible Markup Language (XML) 1.0 (3rd edn.,) W3C Recommendation, (February 2004), http://www.w3.org/TR/2004/REC-xml-20040204/
69. W3C. XQuery 1.0 and XPath 2.0 Formal Semantics, W3C Candidate Recommendation, (June 8, 2006), http://www.w3.org/TR/xquery-semantics/
70. Wadler, P.: Views: a way for pattern matching to cohabit with data abstraction. In: POPL'87, 14th ACM SIGACT-SIGPLAN Symposium on Principles Of Programming Languages, Proceedings, pp. 307–313. ACM Press, New York (1987)
71. Wallace, M., Runciman, C.: Haskell and XML: Generic combinators or type-based translation? ACM SIGPLAN Notices 34(9), 148–159 (1999) (Conference Proceedings of International Conference on Functional Programming (ICFP'99))

A   Extreme Mapping Options

This appendix illustrates some mapping options that work hard to convey schema constraints into the derived object models. Arguably, the options are too complicated for practical use.

A.1   Type-Driven Member Access

Sec. 3.7 clarified that element references do not faithfully correspond to OO member names, and concluded that a type-driven access protocol may be more appropriate. In fact, we may use the types of children as (ambiguous) selectors, thereby mimicking the XPath model. To get started, we assume a mapping as follows:

- Map XSD namespaces to .NET namespaces in a 1:1 manner.[22]
- Map element declarations to classes in a 1:1 manner.
- Use a node-label-preserving mapping; cf. Sec. 3.5.

The last item is important because it guarantees that the resulting object types preserve all type distinctions (read as 'element-label distinctions') that are prescribed by the original schema. That is, the object types are sufficient for type-driven access.

A type-driven replacement of "." requires access operations for 'getting' and 'setting'. We use overloaded methods to this end; the overloads cover all possible types of children. The setter part is straightforward. For instance, the illustrative model group from Sec. 3.7 (recalled below) requires the following overloads:

```
<!-- The relevant model group -->
<xs:sequence>
 <xs:element ref="tns:bar" />
 <xs:element name="bar" type="xs:int"/>
 <xs:element ref="ins:bar"/>
</xs:sequence>

// The overloaded setter method
public void Set(tns.bar x)   { _1=x; }  // <tns:bar>
public void Set(bar x)       { _2=x; }  // local <bar>
public void Set(ins.bar x)   { _3=x; }  // <ins:bar>

// The underlying state
private tns.bar _1;
private bar     _2;  // bar is a local type
private ins.bar _3;
```

(Repeating and optional particles require a special treatment, which we do not discuss here.) The getter part requires more work. We may attempt an overloaded getter method such that the overloads vary in the *result* type. However, mainstream languages like Java and C# do not support such overloading. We may also attempt to set up the getter method with a type parameter (in the sense of generics). However, (bounded) parametric polymorphism would make the getter method too polymorphic; essentially, type checking would be unable to separate legal types of children from arbitrary schema-derived object types. Hence, we need to parameterize the getter method such that an *argument type* can drive access. However, we can not (and do not want to) pass a value of the type for which the getter is supposed to return a value. Instead, we pass a *proxy* for the type. Here is a generic class of proxies:

---

[22] A note on .NET: a namespace is essentially a scope for declarations of classes, interfaces, and others. It is very similar to package or module scopes in other languages.

```
public class Proxy<X>
{
  protected Proxy() { }
  public static Proxy<X> proxy { get { return null; } }
}
```

The type parameter X of Proxy is a 'phantom', i.e., it is not used by the class; it is only needed for fabricating distinctive types — one for each type of children. We do not even need to populate any type Proxy<X>; the proxy types do not serve any run-time purpose. Instead, the are only needed for overloading resolution at compile time. Let us now assume that each schema-derived object type X implements a static member proxy of type Proxy<X> so that proxies can be conveniently picked up from the types of interest. In the running example, we can invoke the overloaded getter as follows (assuming an object myFoo of the schema-derived object type):

```
// myFoo is of type tns.foo
Console.WriteLine(myFoo.Get(tns.bar.proxy));        // <tns:bar>
Console.WriteLine(myFoo.Get(tns.foo.bar.proxy));    // local <bar>
Console.WriteLine(myFoo.Get(ins.bar.proxy));        // <ins:bar>
```

A.2   Compile-Time Validation for Construction

Sec. 3.9 clarified that the common model of object construction and initialization is limited with regard to the statically checked validity of the constructed XML trees. We will now engage in a sophisticated encoding scheme that allows us to recover some static typing. The scheme is inspired by work on XML processing in Haskell using its type-class system [56,57]. Fig. 44 shows a small (contrived) schema that explores regular expression types and mixed content. The figure also shows a sample instance whose construction we hope to validate.

Let us look at *run-time validation* for inspiration. Each content model can be mapped to a finite-state machine (FSM) that performs 'shallow validation', i.e., the FSM checks element names (by means of instance-of tests) without descending into subtrees. Fig. 45 implements shallow validation for the stress test from Fig. 44; we assume a node-label-preserving mapping. Shallow validation is performed by the 'untyped' constructor of a schema-derived object type; cf. the params keyword.[23] Shallow validation commences as follows. There is an enum type with the states of the FSM. The nodes are passed as input to the FSM. Text nodes are accepted regardless of state because of the mixed content model. Validation throws when FSM simulation gets stuck or the input ends in a non-final state.

We can *move FSM simulation from run-time to compile-time* as follows:

- The states of the FSM become designated, distinct types.
- Each state type is a wrapper type around the constructed type.

---

[23] A note on C#: the params keyword enables open-ended argument lists of the array's item type. For instance, params object [] nodes means that any number of arguments of type object is admitted and collected in a single array nodes.

Sample schema

```
<xs:element name="foo">
 <xs:complexType mixed="true">
  <xs:sequence>
   <xs:element name="a" type="..."/>
   <xs:element name="b" type="..." maxOccurs="unbounded"/>
   <xs:choice minOccurs="0">
    <xs:element name="a" type="..."/>
    <xs:element name="c" type="..."/>
   </xs:choice>
  </xs:sequence>
 </xs:complexType>
</xs:element>
```

Sample instance

```
<foo>
 "Text before 'a'.",
 <a/>
 "Text before 1st (mandatory) 'b'.",
 <b/>
 "We could stop anywhere from here on."
 <b/>
 <b/>
 <c/>
 "Let's stop here, indeed."
</foo>
```

Fig. 44. A stress test for XML-tree construction

- There is a static method, New, to initiate validating construction.
- There is an overloaded Add method modeling the state transitions.
- There are implicit casts from final-state types to the constructed type.

The key idea is that the overloaded Add method enables the type-checked construction of objects by method chaining. Fig. 46 illustrates shallow, compile-time validation for the running example. The shown method chain resembles the original XML literal.

A pure FSM approach suffers from obvious scalability problems. Occurrence constraints (such as maxOccurs="42") cannot be checked efficiently with a plain FSM because of the number of states that would be needed for counting. However, in practice non-trivial occurrence constraints (other than '?', '+', '*') hardly occur [32]. More seriously, whenever content models prescribe free order, then a pure FSM approach would explode due to the number of permutations to be

```
public class foo {
    // Content
    private object [] nodes;

    // States of FSM
    public enum State {BeforeA,BeforeB,SeenB,BeforeChoice};

    // Run-time validating constructor
    public foo(params object [] nodes)
    {
        this .nodes = nodes;
        State s = State.BeforeA;
        foreach (var o in nodes)
            if (!(o is string ))
                switch (s) {
                    case State.BeforeA :
                        if (o is a) { s++; break; }
                        goto default ;
                    case State.BeforeB :
                        if (o is b) { s++; break; }
                        goto default ;
                    case State.SeenB :
                        if (o is b) break;
                        if (o is a) { s++; break; }
                        if (o is c) { s++; break; }
                        goto default ;
                    case State.BeforeChoice :
                        goto default ;
                    default :
                        throw ...;
                }
        if ((s!=State.SeenB) && (s!=State.BeforeChoice))
            throw ...;
    }
}

// classes a, b, c omitted
```

Construction sample

```
var myFoo = new foo(
                "Text before 'a'.",
                new a(),
                "Text before 1st (mandatory) 'b'.",
                new b(),
                "We could stop anywhere from here on.",
                new b(),
                new b(),
                new c(),
                "Let's stop here, indeed.");
```

Fig. 45. Shallow, run-time validation for the content model in Fig. 44

considered. Free order applies to attribute sets and <all> composites. We would
need more advanced techniques and type-system support [3] to recover from this
problem.

```
public class foo : List <object> {
    // Default construction in begin state
    public static foo.BeforeA New { get { return new BeforeA(new foo()); } }

    // States with transitions
    public struct BeforeA
    {
        internal BeforeA(foo v)        { it = v; }
        public BeforeA Add(string v)   { it.Add(v); return this; }
        public BeforeB Add(a v)        { it.Add(v); return new BeforeB(it); }
        internal foo it;
    }
    public struct BeforeB
    {
        internal BeforeB(foo v)        { it = v; }
        public BeforeB Add(string v)   { it.Add(v); return this; }
        public SeenB Add(b v)          { it.Add(v); return new SeenB(it); }
        internal foo it;
    }
    public struct SeenB
    {
        internal SeenB(foo v)          { it = v; }
        public SeenB Add(string v)     { it.Add(v); return this; }
        public SeenB Add(b v)          { it.Add(v); return this; }
        public BeforeChoice Add(a v)   { it.Add(v); return new BeforeChoice(it); }
        public BeforeChoice Add(c v)   { it.Add(v); return new BeforeChoice(it); }
        public foo End                 { get { return it; } }
        internal foo it;
    }
    public struct BeforeChoice
    {
        internal BeforeChoice(foo v)       { it = v; }
        public BeforeChoice Add(string v)  { it.Add(v); return this; }
        public foo End                     { get { return it; } }
        internal foo it;
    }

    // End states deliver the completed object
    public static implicit operator foo(SeenB v) { return v.it; }
    public static implicit operator foo(BeforeChoice v) { return v.it; }
}
```

Construction sample

```
foo myFoo       = foo.New
                . Add("Text before 'a'.")
                . Add(new a())
                . Add("Text before 1st (mandatory) 'b'.")
                . Add(new b())
                . Add("We could stop anywhere from here on.")
                . Add(new b())
                . Add(new b())
                . Add(new c())
                . Add("Let's stop here, indeed.");
```

Fig. 46. Shallow, compile-time validation for the content model in Fig. 44

Library support for Maybies

```
public abstract class Maybe<T> {
  public abstract bool   HasValue   { get; }
  public abstract T      Value      { get; set; }
}
public class Nothing<T> : Maybe<T> {
  public override bool HasValue { get { return false ; } }
  public override T    Value    { get { throw ...; } set { throw ...; } }
}
public class Just<T> : Maybe<T> {
  public override bool HasValue { get { return true; } }
  public override T Value {
    get { return value; }
    set { this.value = value; }
  }
  private T value;
}
```

A sample of using Maybe

```
public class opts {
  public int a;
  public int? b;
  public foo c;
  public Maybe<foo> d;
}
public class foo { ... }
```

Fig. 47. A blend of Haskell's Maybe and .NET's Nullable

A.3   Haskell-Like Maybies

Sec. 4.1 clarified that optionality of reference types is not discoverable by default. We could explicitly express optionality by the use of a designated type constructor, very much like .NET's existing type constructor Nullable, but without its restriction to value types. Fig. 47 defines such a type constructor; we use the name Maybe in reference to Haskell's standard type constructor for optionality.

The figure also illustrates the use of Maybe for the running example of Sec. 4.1. In principle, we could use Maybe in place of "?", even for value types. However, .NET's nullable types are linguistically richer and more efficient. In particular, primitive operations on the value types are lifted to nullable types, and some forms of boxing are optimized away.

An interface for optionality

```
public interface IMaybe<T> {
  bool HasValue { get; }
  T    Value    { get; }
}
```

A generic Nothing

```
public class Nothing<T> : IMaybe<T> {
  public bool HasValue { get { return false ; } }
  public T    Value    { get { throw ...; } set { throw ...; } }
}
```

A generic Just

```
public class Just<T> : IMaybe<T> where T : Just<T> {
  public bool HasValue { get { return true; } }
  public T    Value    { get { return (T)this; } }
}
```

A sample of using Maybe

```
public class opts : Just<opts> {
  // Reusable singleton
  internal static IMaybe<opts> Nothing = new Nothing<opts>();

  public int a;
  public int? b;

  public foo c
  {
    get { if (_c==null) throw ...; return _c; }
    set { if (value==null) throw ...; _c = value; }
  }
  public IMaybe<foo> d
  {
    get { if (_d==null) _d = global::d.Nothing; return _d; }
    set { _d=value; }
  }

  private foo _c;
  private IMaybe<foo> _d;
}
```

Fig. 48. Interface-based optionality

One minor problem with the simple optionality technique is that the concept of 'null' has become ambiguous: the code may need to be prepared to find both the normal null and Maybe's Nothing. This problem can be mitigated by switching from a field-based model to a property-based model with getters that never return normal nulls. Thus:

```
public class Choice<X1,X2> {
  // Injection by functional construction
  public Choice(X1 v) { any=v; idx=1; }
  public Choice(X2 v) { any=v; idx=2; }

  // Perform action
  public void Do(Action<X1> a1, Action<X2> a2) {
    switch (idx) {
      case 1: a1((X1)any); break;
      case 2: a2((X2)any); break;
    }
  }

  // Apply function
  public R Apply<R>(Func<X1,R> f1, Func<X2,R> f2) {
    switch (idx) {
      case 1: return f1((X1)any);
      case 2: return f2((X2)any);
      default: throw ...;  // impossible exception
    }
  }

  // Private state
  private object any;
  private int idx;
}
```

Relevant delegate types

```
public delegate void Action<T> (T it) // Actions that effect
argument public delegate Y Func<X,Y>(X x);   // Single-argument
functions
```

Fig. 49. A generic class for binary choices

```
public Maybe<foo> d {
  get { if (_d==null) _d = new Nothing<foo>(); return _d; }
  set { _d = value; }
}
private Maybe<foo> _d;
```

Obviously, we should use the singleton design pattern to avoid creating many instances of Nothing<T> for any given type. A more challenging source of overhead concerns the use of wrapping with Just; one extra object per XML subtree in an optional position would be created. These costs may be substantial. This problem can be mitigated by the use of interface polymorphism, as shown below.

```
public class Sequence<X1,X2> {
  // Functional construction
  public Sequence(X1 x1, X2 x2) { _x1=x1; _x2=x2; }

  // Getters and setters
  public X1 First    { get { return _x1; } set { _x1 = value; } }
  public X2 Second   { get { return _x2; } set { _x2 = value; } }

  // Private state
  private X1 _x1;
  private X2 _x2;
}
```

Fig. 50. A generic class for binary sequences

In Fig. 48, we use an interface, IMaybe, instead of the earlier class Maybe. Wrapping with Just is unnecessary because each and every schema-derived class implements the Just-like behavior — either locally or, when possible, by subclassing the class Just. We also show again property implementations; one for a mandatory particle; another one for an optional particle. The property implementation for the mandatory particle refuses the normal null. The getter implementation for the optional particle translates the normal null to Nothing.

A.4   Generics for Compositors

Sec. 4.3 suggested that XSD compositors may be modeled as generic classes, thereby providing one mapping option for nested composites. Fig. 49 defines a generic class for binary choices, in fact, binary, type-indexed co-products [53]. The class covers the following idioms: (i) construction such that one must commit to either branch of the choice; (ii) updates on the grounds of 'actions' to be performed on the object of the choice; (iii) queries on the grounds of 'functions' to be applied to the object of the choice. Further operations may be added, e.g., for cloning. Conceptually, choices are commutative, but the generic class is somewhat restrictive in this respect. That is, the textual order of the type parameters in Choice<X1,X2> is also assumed for the argument lists of Do and Apply. (We could attempt to enable all possible argument orders, except that this idea does not scale for choices with more branches.)

For <all> composites, we could use the dual concept of type-indexed co-products, i.e., type-indexed products. We omit this variation. Fig. 50 defines a (trivial) generic class for binary sequences. The class essentially corresponds to the type constructor for pairs. There are getters and setters for both components of the sequence. Construction must enumerate the components of the sequence. Order of the particles is relevant for sequences, and hence, we provide a positional access protocol based on members First, Second, ... (as opposed to a type-driven protocol).

Author Index

Lecture Notes in Computer Science

Sublibrary 1: Theoretical Computer Science and General Issues

For information about Vols. 1– 4525
please contact your bookseller or Springer